REBELLION, RASCALS, AND REVENUE

Rebellion, Rascals, and Revenue

TAX FOLLIES AND WISDOM
THROUGH THE AGES

MICHAEL KEEN

JOEL SLEMROD

PRINCETON UNIVERSITY PRESS
PRINCETON & OXFORD

Published by Princeton University Press
41 William Street, Princeton, New Jersey 08540
6 Oxford Street, Woodstock, Oxfordshire OX20 1TR

press.princeton.edu

All Rights Reserved

Library of Congress Control Number: 2020948499
ISBN 9780691199542
ISBN e-book 9780691199986

British Library Cataloging-in-Publication Data is available

Editorial: Joe Jackson and Jacqueline Delaney
Jacket Design: Karl Spurzem
Production: Erin Suydam
Publicity: James Schneider and Kate Farquhar-Thomson

Jacket/Cover Credit: Shutterstock

This book has been composed in Arno.

Printed on acid-free paper. ∞

Printed in the United States of America

10 9 8 7 6 5 4 3 2 1

To my beloved Géraldine, *ma femme,* Pippa, Eddie and Célina, who have borne so graciously with my follies

—*M. K.*

To Ava, my life partner, and Annie and Jonathan—who at times resisted my tax wisdom but have always welcomed, and returned, my love

—*J. S.*

CONTENTS

Preface   xv

Acknowledgments   xix

PART I. PLUNDER AND POWER   1

1   Any Public Matter   3

Bengal to Boston   5

Never Such Disgrace   11

Why Bolivia Is Landlocked   15

Taxing the Light of Heaven   17

Not Everything Is About Tax. But . . .   22

2   The Way We Were   24

A Quick Gallop through the Long History of Taxation   25

How Much?   34

Warfare and Welfare   38

Babbage's Nightmare   41

Debt, Default, and Princes   43

Making Money   47

3   By Another Name   55

Elizabeth I to Spectrum Auctions   56

Selling Sovereignty   62

Cheap Labor 63

  Working for Nothing 63

  A Rich Man's War and a Poor Man's Fight 65

Doing Your Bit 68

Paying Your (Feudal) Dues 71

Crossing the Line 73

And There's More 75

  Jobs for the Boys 75

  A Tax on Stupidity 77

PART II. WINNERS AND LOSERS 81

4 Fair Enough 83

Heads on Pikes 84

  Poll Taxes and the English 85

  Noble Causes 91

Trying to Be Fair 93

  Pay for What You Get? 94

  Pay What You Can? 96

Show Me a Sign 97

  Taxing by Class 98

  Taxing by Community 99

  Taxing the Finer Things in Life 102

  Presumptions of Prosperity 105

5 This Colossal Engine of Finance 108

The Work of Giants: The Income Tax in Britain 109

The Dred Scott Decision of the Revenue 116

A Crime of Passion and the French Income Tax 123

Old Fears and New Directions 127

6 Some Are More Equal Than Others 131

Taxing Femininity 132

Peculiar Tax Institutions 136

Leaps of Faith 138

Outsiders 144

Strangers in a Strange Land 144

Taxes as Punishment 145

Hard Choices 146

7 Stick or Shift? 149

False Starts 150

Burgling Other People's Intellect 155

You Must Remember This 158

Buddy, Can You Spare 1/20th of a Dime? 160

Things Aren't Always What They Seem 162

Helping the Working Poor (or Their Employers) 162

Are Tax-Free Municipal Bonds a Giveaway
to the Savvy Rich? 163

The Murky Incidence of the Corporate Tax 164

The Big Picture 167

PART III. CHANGING OUR WAYS 171

8 Breaking Bad and Making Good 173

Do the Right Thing 174

Family Matters 174

Taxing Knowledge 177

Tax Bads, Not Goods 179

Saving the Planet 180

Wind-Breaking Cows, Scary Dogs, and Cute Cats 183

The Wages of Sin   184

  The Vile Custome   184

  The Curse of the Drinking Classes   189

  Sex, . . .   190

  . . . Drugs, . . .   192

  . . . But Not Much Rock and Roll   193

  Unhealthy Living   193

Just Say No?   195

9 Collateral Damage   199

Spurring Ingenuity   200

  Stranger Things   200

  Drawing a Line   207

Excess Burden   214

  No Fire without Smoke   215

  A Window on Excess Burden   222

10 How to Pluck a Goose   225

Searching for the Holy Grail   227

  War Profiteers and the Corporate Tax Revisited   228

  Give Me Land, Lots of Land   230

  Conscripting Wealth   235

Limiting the Damage   237

  The Cleverest Man in England   237

  Broaden the Base, Lower the Rate (Maybe)   240

Shaping a Tax System   243

How Many Feathers?   247

11 Citizens of the World   251

Squeezing a Rice Pudding   254

Havens from the Tax Storm   257

The Rich Are Different from Us   261

    They Don't Live Here Any More   262

    Don't Tell   263

False Profits   265

    If I Were You, I Wouldn't Start from Here   266

    A Farewell to Arms (Length Pricing)?   270

Tumbling Taxes   276

PART IV. TAXES DON'T COLLECT THEMSELVES   281

12   Vlad the Impaler and the Gentle Art of Tax Collection   283

   Mind the Gap   285

    A Gallery of Tax Rascals   285

    Known Unknowns   288

   Many Sticks—and a Carrot or Two   289

    Get to the Money First   290

    Big Businesses Are the Tax Administrator's Friend . . .   296

    . . . And Small Businesses Are Their Nightmare   298

    Information Rules   300

   Trust but Verify   306

   Taxpayers Are People Too   308

    Principled (and Singing) Evaders   308

    Making Honesty the Easiest Policy   309

13   Someone Has to Do It   313

   The Tax Collectors' Gallery   314

   Who Collects?   318

    The Rise and Demise of Tax Farming
(and Tax Farmers)   319

    Kickbacks—Legal and Otherwise   324

Tax Independence 328

Privatizing Tax Collection 329

How Big Should Tax Administrations Be? 331

Tax Tech 333

PART V. MAKING TAXES 339

14 Taxing and Pleasing 341

The Finance Minister's Dream 341

Starving the Beast 346

From Coventry to K Street 348

The Naked Truth about Lobbying 348

I Can't Believe It's Not (Taxed Like) Butter 351

The Taxes Chain Store Massacre 352

One Man's Exemption 354

You Just Don't Do That: Four Centuries of
Not Taxing Food in Britain 355

Games Governments Play 358

Vanishing Acts 359

What's in a Name? 361

Oops 363

Some Triumphs of Pretty Good Tax Policy 363

Lessons from Gucci Gulch, and Elsewhere 365

The Rise (and Rise) of the VAT 368

15 The Shape of Things to Come 372

Taxes in Naboo and Utopia 372

Pillars of Tax Wisdom 375

Tax Revolts Are Rarely Just about Tax 375

Be Careful with Words 376

You May Be the One Paying for Lunch   377

Fair Taxation, Whatever That Is, Is Hard to Achieve   379

Taxation Is About Finding Good Proxies   380

Tax Avoiders and Evaders Are Wonderfully Creative   382

The Biggest Costs of Taxation May Be the
Ones You Can't See   383

Taxes Are Not Just for Raising Money   385

People Pay Taxes Because They Are Scared   386

Tax Sovereignty Is Becoming a Thing of the Past   387

Beware of Mantras   388

The Future and Beyond   389

Hard Times   390

Brave New Worlds   393

What Will They Think of Us?   397

Notes   399

References   453

Illustration Credits   495

Index   497

PREFACE

Taxation . . . is eternally lively; it concerns nine-tenths of us more
directly than either smallpox or golf, and has just as much drama in it;
moreover, it has been mellowed and made gay by as many gaudy,
preposterous theories.

H. L. MENCKEN[1]

At best the subject of antiquated taxes and fiscal mechanisms is
crabbed and unlovely.

GEORGE TENNYSON MATTHEWS[2]

ON THIS, we side with Mr. Mencken—and our aim in this book is to
persuade you to agree. Even Professor Matthews seems to have been
unpersuaded by his own rhetoric, as he proceeded to write 292 pages
about arcane tax arrangements in ancien régime France.

Tax stories from the past, we hope to show, can be entertaining—
sometimes in a weird way, sometimes in a gruesome one, and sometimes simply because they are fascinating in themselves. They are also
helpful in thinking about the tax issues that run through today's headlines and politics. The stories we tell in this book span several millennia,
from Sumerian clay tablets, Herodotus, and the unusual tax ideas of the
Emperor Caligula through to the slippery practices revealed by the
Panama Papers, the tax possibilities unleashed by blockchain, and the
outlook for taxation in a world transformed by the COVID-19 pandemic. But this book is not a history of taxation. Nor is it a primer on
tax principles. It is a bit of both.

The principles help frame the history, in understanding, for example, how rulers of the past, lacking anything like an income tax, invented other ways of tilting the tax burden away from the poorest (if only to ensure their own survival). Sometimes, too, the popular understanding of the few episodes in tax history that are widely known (which, it is true, are not many) turns out to be plain wrong, but in intriguing and significant ways. The tax that provoked the Peasants Rebellion of 1381, for instance, was not really a poll tax; and it was a tax cut, not an increase, that provoked the Boston Tea Party.

The history also helps clarify the principles of taxation. Sometimes these are harder to see at work in taxes that are familiar to us than they are to see in the oddities and even the physical relics of the past. It is easy to be distracted by the frothy political rhetoric that often accompanies the tax debates of our times. Shorn of polemic, past tax episodes can shed a clear light on these underlying principles. The intellectual case for using carbon taxes to save the planet from climate risk, for example, is much the same as that for the tax on beards introduced in Russia by Peter the Great in order to save Russia from the boyars.

Many of the tax episodes we look at may at first seem far-fetched or ridiculous. Some are stories of disastrous missteps and cruelty. Some, we admit, teach no useful lesson that we can discern, but are just pleasingly gaudy and preposterous. But along with the follies there are also episodes of remarkable wisdom. For it is a theme of the book that, when it comes to designing and implementing taxes, our ancestors were addressing fundamentally the same problems that we struggle with today. And they were no less ingenious—not just in creating taxes, but also in avoiding and evading them—than we are. We should not feel too superior to our forebears, given the taxes we have nowadays. The idea of taxing chimneys may seem quaint to us. But we suspect our descendants will find some of the things that we do today more than a little peculiar, such as taxing multinationals by trying to figure out what some entirely different and hypothetical set of companies would have done in the unlikely (possibly inconceivable) event that they found themselves in the same circumstances. And they would be right.

The purpose of this book is not to convince you that taxation explains everything—though we do suspect it helps explain more than is often recognized. It is more fun to hear of Henry VIII's lust for Anne Boleyn than of how he could ease his fiscal problems by breaking with Rome and taking for himself the taxes being paid to the Pope. Nor does the book promote any pet tax system of our own, though we do not hesitate to draw implications from the tax episodes that we discuss for today's tax controversies. That, after all, is the point. Today's tax landscape is quite different from those of classical Greece, colonial Sierra Leone, Tokugawa Japan, or the Depression-era United States. But it continues to be shaped by decisions made long in the past. One legacy of the debates over slavery and taxation in the new-born United States, for instance, is now a real obstacle to the introduction there of a wealth tax. The most fundamental point, however, at the heart of this book, is that many of the principles of good and bad taxation run through history. They can help us understand our past and choose wisely for a future that is being transformed by technological change, and seeing them at work in history provides a pleasing dose of gaudiness.

To bring out the themes running through the story of taxation, the book is organized not by timelines but by issues, and so jumps around across the centuries and over the continents. It is in five parts. The first sets the scene by taking in the big picture: It opens with some episodes in tax history—from the lurid to the quaint—that encapsulate some of the unchanging tax truths with which the book deals and then takes a broad look at how, over the ages, governments have set about trying to make the likes of us all pay for whatever it is they wanted to do. The second part, on winners and losers, is about fairness in taxation. This is something even wicked rulers have to care about if they want to survive, and we look at the many mistakes and occasional brilliance that they have shown in trying to cope. Figuring out exactly who the winners and losers from taxation are, however, turns out to be far from easy. We will see that the question of who exactly bears the real burden of taxation has vexed policy makers since at least medieval England and has even helped shape our political institutions. The third part of the book showcases the extraordinary power of human ingenuity—from Pharaonic

Egypt to today's multinationals—in finding ways to avoid paying taxes. It also considers how governments have, have not, and ought to take account of such rascality. The fourth part turns to the painful (sometimes fatal) art of tax collection, which brings out both the best and the worst of human nature, and to the ways that governments have found— from gorgeous bronze devices in ancient China to drones over Buenos Aires—to threaten, cajole, and sweet-talk us into paying whatever their rules say we ought to. The final part looks at the messy realities of making tax policy, describes spectacular successes and failures, and distills a few lessons to help cope with a future in which taxation, we can be pretty sure, is not going away but may well start to take quite different forms from those we are accustomed to. The book ends by speculating about what tax follies future generations will find to chuckle over when they see how we do things today.

We are economists, not historians. So we hope real historians will forgive our blundering over their terrain. For those economists who would like to use this book to support and liven up a more traditional and formal (maybe even dull) introduction to tax principles, these five parts correspond closely to obvious slabs of public finance learning, addressing, after a general overview: equity concerns (vertical and horizontal), incidence analysis, issues of efficiency and optimal taxation, tax administration, practical policy making, and core tax challenges and possibilities for the future.

There is thus a logical progression within the book. But, with some willingness to skim over a sentence or two, the chapters can be dipped into at will. For all readers, our aim is to entertain, persuading the skeptical that tax is not just important but also interesting. In that way, while rebellions will always be with us, taxes will always invite rascality, and follies will always happen, we hope this book may bring a little more wisdom to the future of taxation.

ACKNOWLEDGMENTS

MANY PEOPLE deserve our thanks. There are the several students (and some nonstudents) who worked at the University of Michigan diligently tracking down numbers, checking references, and verifying (or, sadly, refuting) implausible-sounding claims: Garrett Anstreicher, Catherine Cox, Sophia Davis-Rodak, Ben Elkins, Adelaide Knights, Jennifer Mayo, Page O'Piela, Kendra Robbins, Ambika Sinha, Taylor Sloan, Michael Sternbach, and Lydia Wang. Claudia Capos provided editorial guidance at an early stage. Professors Reuven Avi-Yonah, James R. Hines Jr., and Jeffrey Hoopes supplied extensive comments on an early draft. Our thanks also go to the anonymous reviewers of Princeton University Press.

Unlikely though it may seem, there is a small community of peculiar people who share our fascination with tax stories. Among the many who shared their own favorite oddities, helped us track down ours, or were generally helpful are Annette Alstadsæter, Matt Benge, Simon Black, Jean-Paul Bodin, David Bradbury, Gérard Chambas, Sijbren Cnossen, Israel Fainboim, Vitor Gaspar, Christian Gillitzer, Peter Harris, Shafik Hebous, Cory Hiller, Graham Holland, Edmund Keen, Alexander Klemm, Li Liu, Mario Mansour, Shalini Mathur, Adnan Mazarei, Jorge Martinez, Kiyoshi Nakayama, John Norregaard, Kazuki Onji, Ian Parry, Victoria Perry, Patrick Petit, Satya Poddar, Federico Salazar, Géraldine Simonnet, Janet Stotsky, Ricardo Varsano, Christophe Waerzeggers, Xiaxin Wang, Xuan Wang, and Shih-ying Wu. We owe thanks, however, to more people than we can name.

Joel thanks the Center for Business Taxation at Oxford University, which hosted him in the latter part of 2014 when the book was in its infancy. Michael thanks Géraldine for sharing so lovingly the long journey of this book. He thinks too of all he has received from his much-missed Mum and Dad and from Kate. He thanks his colleagues at the International Monetary Fund for their daily lessons on the fun and importance of making tax systems better (while, of course, exonerating the staff, management, and executive directors of the IMF from any blame for the views expressed in this book). Our widest debts, to the many we have learned from and worked with over the years, will, we hope, be evident on every page of what follows.

The team at Princeton University Press have earned our great gratitude. Joe Jackson, our editor, encouraged the project from its infancy and provided wise counsel about the organization and tone of the book. Other key players were Lisa Black, Jacqueline Delaney, Kate Farquhar-Thomson, Kourtnay King, Angela Piliouras, James Schneider, and Cyd Westmoreland.

The real burden of writing any book falls on those around the authors, and this one is no exception. For their patience and encouragement, we can only offer our heartfelt thanks.

REBELLION, RASCALS, AND REVENUE

PART I

Plunder and Power

What at first was plunder assumed the softer name of revenue.

THOMAS PAINE[1]

The spirit of a people, its cultural level, its social structure, the deeds its policy may prepare—all this and more is written in its fiscal history, stripped of all phrases.

JOSEPH SCHUMPETER[2]

1

Any Public Matter

The revenue of the state is the state.

EDMUND BURKE[1]

UNCOVERED BY Napoleon's soldiers in 1799, the Rosetta Stone famously held the key to deciphering ancient Egypt's hieroglyphics. The trick, of course, is that it bears the same text in three different scripts: knowing the others, scholars could begin to understand the hieroglyphics. But what could be so important as to be worth carving out in three scripts? The answer, you will have guessed, is taxation. The Rosetta Stone describes a tax break given to the temple priests of ancient Egypt, reinstating tax privileges they had enjoyed in prior times. (So it also teaches us an early lesson: tax exemptions are as old as taxes.) But taxes themselves are far older than the Rosetta Stone. Indeed, early recorded human history is largely the history of tax. Sumerian clay tablets from 2500 BCE include receipts for tax payments.[2]

These relics are visible reminders that powerful rulers have always exercised their powers of compulsion to divert resources to their own preferred use. (A "tax," to get the definition out of the way, is "a compulsory, unrequited payment to general government.")[3] Indeed, as Edmund Burke saw, that is largely what defines them as rulers. Conflicts centered around this exercise of their coercive power to tax sometimes blaze across the pages of history, playing a profound role in shaping the

Tax paid in Sumer.   Tax exempt in Ptolemaic Egypt.

institutions that we all live with. More mundanely, but with almost inconceivably deep and direct impact, the exercise of taxing powers has impacted the daily lives and struggles of ordinary people for millennia, whether it is peasants handing over some of their rice crop to the local lord's retainer in Tokugawa Japan or shopkeepers in Lagos wondering how to complete their value-added tax (VAT) return. For the ordinary masses of humanity, taxation has long been the most direct way in which government impinges on their lives. Rulers, and systems of government, are largely characterized—and their survival and development largely determined—by how they choose to exercise their power to tax. As de Tocqueville wrote, "There is scarcely any public matter that does not arise from a tax or end in one."[4]

Over the millennia, the fundamental challenges faced by rulers aiming to extract resources to fund the state's activities, or their own fancies, have remained largely unaltered. What has changed, and is still changing, is how they address them. This book is about those problems of taxation and what past tax episodes—dramatic and humdrum, appalling and amusing, foolish and wise—teach us about how best to shape tax systems so as to avoid calamity and maybe even do some good.

We start with four stories that provide vivid illustrations of some of the key themes of this book. Not the least of these themes (though we suspect this is rarely the purpose policy makers had in mind) is that tales of taxation can actually be entertaining.

Bengal to Boston

Not many incidents in tax history could be called "well known." The exceptions are a few conflicts in which tax issues were at the heart of wider disputes over sovereignty. These, however, are so well known as to have become close to founding myths. So it is with the barons forcing King John (ruled 1199–1216)[5] to sign Magna Carta,[6] and John Hampden refusing to pay King Charles I's ship money. But national legends are rarely quite what they are cracked up to be. Sometimes they are misremembered: "Does Magna Carta mean nothing to you?" asked the British comedian Tony Hancock, "Did she die in vain?" And sometimes the legend ignores important parts of the truth.

So it is with our first story, which is that of the American Revolution, ushered in by the Patriots of Liberty dumping tea into Boston Harbor—prompted, we are told, by oppressive British taxation. This is probably history's best-known tax revolt. But things were not quite how they have often come to be seen, one general lesson from this book being that, when it comes to taxation, myth is often more pervasive than reality. The Boston Tea Party was actually prompted not by some tax increase, but by a tax cut—with the back story being a complex interplay between increasingly desperate policy makers and powerful interest groups, all adept at spinning their own self-interest as something noble. And the most appalling British tax oppression in the story did not occur in the American colonies. It took place in India.

The story begins in 1763, when the British emerged from the Seven Years' War with both their empire and their debt massively expanded. In America, the colonies had been freed from French pressure on their borders. In India, the privately owned but state-sponsored East India Company had established itself as the preeminent and rising colonial power. But all this, with gains in Canada and the Caribbean as well, had not come cheap. The British had financed the war largely by massive borrowing: The national debt had close to doubled, rising to an alarming 120 percent or so of gross domestic product (GDP),[7] and two-thirds of all government spending was on interest payments. It was time for Britain to set its fiscal house in order—and for the colonies to do their bit.

By 1765, things did not seem to be going too badly for the British. True, the colonists in America had not taken kindly to the sugar duties of 1764, but perhaps stamp duties, levied on legal documents and other printed materials, would work better—after all, they had worked at home for many years with no great difficulty. Prime Minister George Grenville expected them to prove "equal, extensive, not burdensome, likely to yield a considerable revenue, and collected without a great number of officers."[8] Moreover, the proceeds were earmarked for the defense of the colonies. It was surely only fair that the colonists, who came up with only 6d (six pence, or half a shilling) a year per person in tax, compared to 25 shillings annually for the average Englishman, should chip in more.[9] And the news from India was spectacular. In that year, the Mughal Emperor granted the East India Company the *diwani*— the right to collect tax revenues in Bengal, Bihar, and Orissa. This was a truly glittering prize. The *Gentleman's Magazine* thought that "the prodigious value of these new acquisitions . . . may open to this nation such a mine of wealth as . . . in a few years to . . . pay off the national debt, to take off the land tax, and ease the poor of the burdensome taxes."[10] In 1767, it seemed that a start on this had been made when the East India Company agreed to pay the government £400,000 a year for the enjoyment of its possessions in India.

Soon, however, things were going very badly wrong. In America, fierce opposition to the stamp duty had led quickly to its repeal. The government of Pitt the Elder (doubtless distracted by then being

1767: The British gain tax base and power in Bengal.

"seriously disabled by mental illness"[11]) responded in 1767 with the
Townshend Duties on tea and other products. This was expected to produce only about one-tenth of the revenue of the *diwani*. But the point
was in the preamble, declaring it to be "expedient that a revenue should
be raised in Your Majesty's Dominions in America."[12] More resistance
and boycotts followed, and in 1770 all the taxes other than the 3d per
pound tax on tea were removed; that remained because, as the king continued to insist, "[there] must always be one tax to keep up the right [to
tax]."[13] The protests and boycotts continued, and in March of 1770, panicked British troops killed seven locals on the streets of Boston.

But things were even worse in India. The *diwani* was already proving
less spectacular than predicted, as famine came to Bengal in 1769. The
Company's revenues there fell from £1.8 million in 1766/1767 to £1.3
million in 1770/1771.[14] This reduction was smaller than might have been
expected, given the depth of the famine: 20 percent of the population
of Bengal may have died. But what stopped it falling further was the
Company's ruthless collection. "Indians were tortured to disclose their

treasure," reported one official of the old regime, "cities, towns and villages ransacked; jaghires and provinces purloined."[15] But these extreme
measures could not prevent a massive shortfall in revenue, compounding other difficulties facing the East India Company: uncontrolled over-
borrowing by its excessively entrepreneurial employees in India, massively increased military spending—and an accumulation of huge stocks
of tea that it could not sell, partly because of the boycott in America. The
Company's sales to the colonies fell by nearly 90 percent between 1768
and 1770.[16] By early 1772, the Company was in serious trouble.[17] It held
about 18 million pounds of unsold tea in its London warehouses;[18] had
effectively defaulted on the custom duties due on importing tea into Britain; and, far from paying a tidy sum to the government, needed to borrow large amounts from it.[19] But, being at the heart of English finances
(and the wealth of many of the elite[20]), the East India Company had
become too big to fail. "The monopoly of the most lucrative trades, and
the possession of imperial revenues," Edmund Burke was later to tell Parliament, "had brought you to the verge of beggary and ruin."[21]

There were, Lord North had declared in 1768, "two great national
questions, the state of the East India Company and the affairs of America."[22] And they became increasingly intertwined, with the solution to
each perhaps lying in the solution of the other. To secure the financing
of the East India Company, the key was to increase its sales of tea, and
the American market was the main hope. The potential for its expansion
was clear, but so was the obstacle to realizing it: Something like three-
quarters of the tea consumed in the colonies was being smuggled in.[23]
To some, these commercial problems could give convenient cover for a
politic removal of Townshend's tax. But, by now prime minister, Lord
North insisted that the principle had to be maintained: This was, as
Edmund Burke cattily put it, not a real tax but a "preambulary" one.[24]

This was when the hard-pressed bureaucrats and politicians in London came up with a cunning plan. In short, they reduced the price of
tea in the colonies by eliminating a tax due on tea in England, while
maintaining the preambulary principle by leaving the tax charged in the
colonies unchanged. The East India Company, to be more precise, had
until now been required to bring tea destined for the colonies into

England first, at which point an import tariff of about 24 percent was charged, and to put the tea up for auction. From July 1773, however, this tax was entirely removed for tea exported to America. For the cheapest tea, this would allow the price charged in the colonies to be cut by about 6s per pound.[25] Smugglers would still have the advantage of not paying the Townshend Duty, but with the East India Company also now enabled to sell directly to the colonies, the smugglers were clearly in for some real competition. Surely the Americans would now be unable to resist buying taxed tea in large quantities. And in so doing, they would not only be sending the East India Company, and the powerful interests behind it, on the way to recovery but also implicitly accepting the British government's right to tax them. Clever.

But this ruse was, it turned out, a bit too clever. The agents chosen by the East India Company to sell in the colonies the now extremely cheap tea were clearly going to be loyalists. And thus the British—having infuriated lawyers, publicans,[26] newspaper publishers, writers, and other smart and influential people by the Stamp Act of 1765—were now directly attacking another powerful interest group: the savvy, powerful and respectably disreputable businessmen who had been making good money from smuggling tea, and who were increasingly aligning themselves with the patriot cause.

Men, that is, like John Hancock, "a respectable large-scale smuggler"[27] who was the richest merchant in Boston and now closely associated with the patriot agitator Sam Adams (as well as subsequently and proverbially supplying the first—and largest and most flamboyant—signature of the Declaration of Independence). Not only could the American merchants no longer hope to sell smuggled tea, they could not even hope to sell the legitimate British tea. The happy thought in London was that these measures would undermine not only the commercial interests but also the influence of these powerful men. But they misjudged. Hancock chaired, and Adams inflamed, the meeting at the Old South Meeting House on December 16, 1773, which ended with the Sons of Liberty throwing 35,000 pounds of cut-price tea into Boston Harbor. Tea shipments were refused in Philadelphia and Charleston, and tea parties erupted again in Boston and New York. From there,

1773: The British lose tax base and power in Boston.

under the banner of "no taxation without representation," riot proceeded to revolution.

There is irony in this. The modern American Tea Party, vociferously
opposed to all but minimal taxation, takes its name from what was in
effect a violent protest *against* a tax cut. There are also lessons. It might
be too much to conclude that "as it turned out, [the Sons of Liberty]
were not just against taxation without representation—they were
against taxation, period."[28] But the Boston Tea Party was evidently
about more than just tax rates.

The Boston Tea Party, and the Revolution, were ultimately about sovereignty. The overt exercise of authority for its own sake in the form of the
tax on tea simply evoked and crystallized resistance. But these events were
also about the power of interest groups, which, like the smugglers in the
American colonies, can be ingenious in amassing support even from
groups whose own interests—like those of the average Bostonian tea
drinker—would seem to point in quite the opposite direction. And, as
with other calamitous tax episodes, it was largely about the way in which
taxes were implemented. Or, perhaps more to the point in this case, about
their being implemented at all. Smuggling was a normal part of life for the
colonists (as it was for many of their English brethren), and Britain's

consistent attempts to stifle it were not taken well: When the smuggler-hunting Royal Navy vessel *Gaspee* ran aground in 1772, the locals simply set it on fire.[29] Discontent is also more likely when there is little support for the way in which tax receipts are spent. So it did not help that the proceeds of the Townshend Duties were earmarked for the extremely unpopular purpose of financing British political appointees in the colonies and establishing commissioners of customs, who acted without juries.

Freed of the British, the new American government, soon faced its own tax revolt.[30] In 1791, Treasury Secretary Alexander Hamilton imposed a tax on whiskey (considered a somewhat sinful luxury) after finding that tariffs did not meet the revenue needs of the fledging federation.[31] Not entirely by chance, the tax tended to favor larger distillers,[32] a powerful lobby group. But it enraged another interest: whiskey-distilling farmers in Western Appalachia. These small rural distillers refused to pay the tax; tarred and feathered tax collectors; and, finally, resorted to armed rebellion and bloodshed. The new American government reacted in much the same way as had the British—with force. But with a different outcome. In 1794, troops led by President George Washington easily quelled the rebellion.[33]

The British did learn some lessons from the American Revolution. In 1931, Mahatma Gandhi challenged the legitimacy of British rule in India by scooping a teaspoon of salty mud, boiling it in seawater, and thereby producing illegal untaxed salt. His actions clearly paralleled those of the Sons of Liberty at the Boston Tea Party. This time, however, there was no punishment from the British comparable to the "Intolerable Acts" of 1774 that were leveled at post–Tea Party Boston. Even Gandhi noted that the British showed great restraint.[34] In the next story, however, they showed almost none.

Never Such Disgrace

This is a story of taxation at its most appallingly oppressive: targeted at a vulnerable and oppressed group, offensive not just in its amount but in how it was collected—and also reflecting the use of taxation as a means of social engineering.

In 1896, the British established a protectorate over Sierra Leone, appointing district commissioners to oversee indirect rule by the local chiefs. To pay for this, and for a planned railway, Governor Frederick Cardew announced the introduction, on January 1, 1898, of a tax on all houses—a hut tax. Such taxes were widely used in colonial Africa, part of the motivation being to induce the native population to participate in the cash economy in order to be able to remit the tax: an example, and we will see plenty of others, of a tax deliberately intended not only to raise revenue but also to change behavior. The chiefs, while proclaiming their loyalty to Queen Victoria, politely protested. Cardew responded by reducing the tax and introducing some exemptions (including for Christian missionaries). But then he proceeded with the tax anyway.

Collection soon ran into trouble. Chiefs were imprisoned and put to work breaking stones for refusing their role in collection, to their great humiliation. "Since the time of our ancestors," said one, "there has never been such disgrace to one of our Chiefs as this prison dress which I wear."[35] Fighting broke out first in the north, as the British moved to arrest a chief and regional leader, Bai Bureh, who was viewed, perhaps wrongly,[36] as instigating resistance. But he was, in any case, a respected and hardened warrior, who had once fought for the British and knew their ways only too well. (When Cardew offered £100 for Bai Bureh's head, Bai offered £500 for Cardew's.)[37] Soon it became a guerilla war, with British columns ambushed on the jungle paths and fighting multiple engagements each day.[38] The British responded with the systematic torching of towns and villages[39]—thereby destroying the tax base itself. Rebellion broke out in the south, too, and there the conflict was even more brutal, marked by the massacres of several hundred Europeans and Africans in European dress.[40]

By November, however, the rebellion was flagging. Bai Bureh was betrayed, captured, and exiled to the Gold Coast (now Ghana). Ninety-six of his comrades were hanged.[41] With that, what was called by the Colonial Secretary Joseph Chamberlain (destined to reappear later in this book) "a general rising against white rule,"[42] fizzled out. The suffering had been immense. Even Cardew came to be haunted by "[t]he thought of . . . the gallant officers and men who have fallen, of the de-voted missionaries who have been sacrificed, of the Sierra Leoneans who have been massacred and"—an afterthought perhaps being better than nothing—"of the many natives who have been killed."[43]

This conflagration came to be known as the Hut Tax War. But there was more to it than the hut tax. Though the resistance did not aspire to remove the British, the fight was nonetheless largely about an affront to local customs and honor. Taxing huts was seen as directly undermining property rights: "Paying for a thing in our country," one chief explained, "means you had no original right to it."[44] And it came along with the usurpation by the district commissioners of judicial and other powers that had rested with the chiefs (including, perhaps not incidentally, the revenue they received from exacting fines).[45] "The king of a country however small, if he cannot settle small matters, is no longer king."[46] Not least, the aggressive implementation of the tax by the Frontier Police[47]—sometimes ex-slaves taking revenge on their former masters—created antagonism. As so often, this conflict, while directly associated with taxation, reflected other, deeper sources of tension. And ham-fisted implementation can be as provocative as the tax itself.

A royal commissioner, sent to find out what had gone wrong, recog-nized the powerful mix of causes behind the war. Resistance arose, he said, from the "sense of personal wrong and injustice from the illegal and degrading severities made use of in enforcing the Tax," which was in itself "obnoxious to the customs and feeling of the people."[48] He rec-ommended that the hut tax be abolished, the police force brought under control, and the authority of the chiefs increased. The hut tax, however, was not removed. It was simply reduced to 3s. Bai Bureh, meanwhile, became an enduring national hero in Sierra Leone: a hospital and foot-ball club are named in his honor, and in 2013 he was pictured on the 1,000-leone banknote.

This revolt was far from being the only one prompted by colonial hut taxes. In German East Africa, 2,000 people are said to have been exe-cuted for nonpayment. Possibly the most bizarre colonial tax conflict, however, centered around dogs—who will make a surprisingly frequent appearance in our stories of taxation. This was the armed resistance by

Tax warriors: Bai Bureh and Hone Toia.

the Maori of Hokianga County in New Zealand to a tax on every dog in the district (as well as a "wheel tax" based on a vehicle's tire width). This tax was also seen as infringing the autonomy of the indigenous people. Troops were mustered. But things ended, happily, without (human) bloodshed. Not, however, before the leader of the resistance, Hone Toia, made one of the more memorable utterances in tax history: "If dogs were to be taxed" he prophesied, "men would be next."[49]

Another dog-tax episode, however, ended far from peacefully. In 1922, the Bondelswarts, a nomadic group in German Southwest Africa (now Namibia), rose up against an increase in the dog tax that had been imposed in 1917.[50] This tax was no small matter, as dogs were central to their pastoral way of life, used for hunting and protecting their livestock from vermin. The South African government, exercising its postwar mandate in the area, used aircraft to bomb the group into submission— one of the first instances of the deliberate bombing of civilians—and ultimately, more than 100 Bondelswarts were killed. Eyebrows were raised at the League of Nations, but nothing was actually done.[51]

The Hut Tax and Dog Tax Wars of Sierra Leone and New Zealand show how tax revolts, and their lasting consequences, are sometimes as much about the way in which the government treats taxpayers, and the claim to sovereignty underlying their exercise of coercion, as they are about how much the taxes aim to extract. In less bloody times, the concern has often been with mere intrusiveness. This is a recurrent theme in the story of taxation. For instance, later in this chapter we will get a taste of the resentment felt under the later Stuarts of tax officials' rights to enter people's homes to count their fireplaces. This is echoed by today's concerns that, in the digital age, governments may come to know more about us, for tax and other purposes, than we would like.

Why Bolivia Is Landlocked

In December 2019, the Trump administration threatened to levy hefty tariffs on selected and quintessentially Gallic imports from France (champagne, cheese, handbags, etc.), in retaliation for the planned introduction there of a "digital services tax." For the United States, this tax was just an attempt to grab revenue from American companies like Google and Facebook. For France, it was an attempt to ensure that companies making good money there also faced a reasonable tax bill. Who should tax multinationals, and how, has become the stuff of headlines and street protests over the past few years. But the issue is not new (even as between the United States and France, it turns out, a similar spat having broken out between them in very pre-digital 1934).[52] And while the dispute between the United States and France (soon joined by many others planning similar taxes) threatened to blow up into a trade war, in nineteenth-century Latin America a dispute over taxing rights led to a real war, and one that shaped our world not just metaphorically but literally.

This was the "Ten Cents War"[53] of 1879 to 1884, which pitched Chile against an alliance of Bolivia and Peru. It emerged from a longstanding argument about where to draw the border between Bolivia, which had access to the Pacific coast through the province of Atacama, and Chile. No one much cared who owned Atacama, largely desert, until the 1840s, when it was discovered to be rich in guano and nitrates. Chileans then moved in large numbers into the disputed region, as well as farther north into the Peruvian province of Tarapacá, which contained most of the rest of the world's nitrates. Some resolution was reached in a boundary treaty of 1874, by which Chile renounced its territorial claim in return for Bolivia's concession that:

> The duties of exportation that may be levied on minerals exploited in the [ceded] zone . . . shall not exceed those now in force; and Chilean citizens, industry, and capital shall not be subjected to any other contributions whatever except those now existing. The stipulations in this article shall last for twenty-five years.[54]

This is what would now be called a "fiscal stability clause," guaranteeing that Bolivia would not raise the tax rate on Chilean companies operating within its borders. Companies naturally value assurances about their future tax treatment, especially when, as in mining, they incur heavy up-front costs that cannot be recovered if things turn out badly. But governments can regret forgoing sources of revenue they may have much need of later. So it proved, at any rate, in this case.

In February 1878, Bolivia decided to impose an export tax on minerals of 10 centavos per quintal.[55] Chile immediately saw this tax increase as violating the 1874 treaty. Bolivia stood firm and announced on February 14, 1879, that it would liquidate the assets of the Compañía del Salitres y Ferrocarril, the primary Chilean company affected, so as to meet its tax obligations. That same day, troops from two Chilean ironclads occupied the Bolivian port of Antofagasta in the Atacama, and the war began. Peru, which had signed a secret treaty of mutual assistance with Bolivia in the event of war with Chile, entered the conflict the next month.

The war did not go well for Bolivia or Peru.[56] At its end, the province of Atacama passed to Chile, and Bolivia became landlocked. Peru lost Tarapacá. Chile gained land and control of most of the world's nitrate

Fighting for fiscal stability.

deposits and some of its richest copper deposits. Although Chile guaranteed Bolivia free commercial access to its Pacific ports, Bolivia's claim for a corridor of access remains a source of diplomatic tension to this day. The ongoing dispute was still before the International Court of Justice in 2018, when it ruled against Bolivia,[57] whereupon the Bolivian president vowed that "Bolivia will never give up." The missing province is still represented in Bolivia's parliament, and in the contest to become Miss Bolivia.[58]

Taxing the Light of Heaven

There is no bloodshed in our last story, but it takes us to the heart of the tax-design problem. This is the tale of the window tax, imposed in Britain from 1697[59] to 1851. At first blush, taxing windows may seem anachronistic or just plain folly. But it was actually pretty clever.

The problem faced by the government of the time was to find a tax based on something that: increased with wealth (for fairness); was easily verified (to avoid disputes); and—being intended to replace a tax on hearths (that is, fireplaces), much hated for requiring inspectors to check inside the property, imposed by the recently deposed Stuarts—observable from afar. The answer: windows.

The number of windows in a house was a decent proxy for the grandeur and wealth of its occupants, so that on average, wealthier people would owe more window tax. And it could be assessed from outside by "window peepers."[60] In an age that lacked Zillow.com or any other way to estimate on a large scale and with reasonable accuracy the value of residential property, this tax was not such a bad idea. Indeed, a window tax is essentially a (very) simple version of the computer-assisted mass appraisal systems by which some developing countries now assess property tax, valuing each house by applying a mathematical formula to a range of relatively easily observed characteristics (location, size, and so on).[61]

Clever though the window tax idea was, it had limitations of a kind that pervade other taxes as well. It was not, for instance, a very precise proxy. That led to unfairness. Adam Smith was irked that:

> A house of ten pounds rent in a country town may sometimes have more windows than a house of five hundred pounds rent in London; and though the inhabitant of the former is likely to be a much poorer man than that of the latter, yet so far as his contribution is regulated by the window-tax, he must contribute more to the support of the state.[62]

And even though the tax only applied to properties with more than a certain number of windows, which went some way toward easing the burden on the poorest families, the tenement buildings into which the urban poor were crowding counted as single units for the purposes of the tax, and so were usually not exempt from tax.

The window tax also encountered the difficulty that it induced changes in behavior by which taxpayers reduced how much they owed, but only at the expense of suffering some new harm. The obvious incentive created by the tax was to have fewer windows, if need be by bricking up existing ones, as remains quaintly visible to this day on distinguished old properties (and some undistinguished ones). Light and air were lost. The French economist and businessman Jean-Baptiste Say (1767–1832) experienced this response first-hand when a bricklayer came to his house to brick up a window so as to reduce his tax liability. He said this led to *jouissance de moins* (enjoyment of less) while yielding nothing to the Treasury, which is a felicitous definition of "excess burden":[63] the idea—one of the most central and hardest to grasp in thinking about taxation—is that the loss which taxpayers suffer due to a tax is actually greater than the amount of tax itself. Excess burden is the collateral damage of taxation, and we will take a close look at it in chapter 9.

The harm done by vanished windows was not trivial. Poor ventilation spread disease; lack of light led to a deficiency of vitamin B that stunted growth—what the French came to call the "British sickness." Opponents reviled the tax as one on "the light of heaven"; the medical press protested that it was a "tax on health."[64] Philanthropic societies hired architects to design accommodation for the poor so as to reduce liability to the window tax,[65] and great minds of the time railed against it. Benjamin Franklin, when Minister to France, may have had it in mind when in 1784 he wrote to the editor of the *Journal of Paris* musing on the benefits of natural light. Among his recommendations (ironic, we presume) was ringing church bells and/or firing cannons at sunrise to wake everyone up. (For our narrative, though, more noteworthy was Franklin's proposal for what is effectively the precise opposite of the window tax: a tax "on every window that is provided with shutters to keep out the light of the sun.")[66] Charles Dickens was straight up irate:

> The adage "free as air" has become obsolete by Act of Parliament. Neither air nor light have been free since the imposition of the window-tax . . . and the poor who cannot afford the expense are stinted in two of the most urgent necessities of life.[67]

France followed the British example, adopting a tax on windows (adding an equally hated tax on doors) in 1798, leading the saintly Bishop of Digne of *Les Misérables* to pity "the poor families, old women and young children, living in those hovels, the fevers and other maladies! God gives air to mankind and the law sells it."[68]

Let there be (a bit less) light.

At the other end of the scale, the super-rich might revel in the ostentation of their windows. When, in Jane Austen's *Pride and Prejudice*, the unctuous Mr. Collins proudly displays the magnificent property of his patrons to Elizabeth Bennett, she "could not be in such raptures as Mr. Collins expected the scene to inspire, and was but slightly affected by his enumeration of the windows in front of the house, and his relation of what the glazing altogether had originally cost Sir Lewis de Bourgh."[69] Because people preferred to both keep their windows and pay less tax, the response to the window tax, as with most taxes, was largely a story of evasion and avoidance, disputes, and legislative change trying to clarify the tax rules about what was and was not subject to tax. When visitors today take a punting outing on the River Cam in Cambridge, the guide may point out a house on the bank with a window on the corner of the building, supposedly designed to let light into two adjacent rooms that counted as just one window for purposes of the tax. The government caught on to that trick, however, and in 1747 introduced legislation stipulating that windows lighting more than one room were to be charged per room.[70] A less subtle ploy was to hoodwink the window peepers by temporarily blocking windows "with loose Bricks or Boards, which may be removed at Pleasure or with Mud, Cow-dung, Moarter, and Reeds, on the Outside, which are soon washed off with Shower of Rain, or with paper and Plateboard on the Inside."[71] In response, the same 1747 law also required that no window that had been blocked up previously could be unblocked without informing the surveyor, with heavy fines for violation.

Disputes, favoritism, and upset abounded. What exactly, for instance, is a window? Questions with seemingly obvious answers can get murky when lots of (tax) money is involved. The wording of the act seemed to imply that any hole in an exterior wall, even from a missing brick, was a taxable window.[72] The rules did become clearer (or at least more complex) over time; the 1747 reform, for instance, clarified that when two or more panes were combined in one frame, they counted as distinct windows if the partition between them was more than 12 inches wide. In any case, the tax commissions, consisting of local gentlemen, tended to apply the tax much as they wanted. This practice created many opportunities for favoritism. John Wesley, founder of Methodism, complained about an acquaintance with 100 windows paying only for 20.[73]

The window tax was very imperfect. But it was not a folly. And it illustrates the key challenges that are at the heart of the tax-design problem: the quest for tolerable fairness, the wasteful behavioral responses that the tax induces, and the desire to administer a tax cost effectively and nonintrusively. These challenges are taken up in turn in later chapters of this book. Many governments, as we will see, have done far worse that the window-taxers did.

Not Everything Is About Tax. But . . .

De Tocqueville's point can be overstated. Not all rebellions, wars, or political battles are about tax (mainly, at least). Even those that have been stuck with a "tax" label are almost always about much more than that. And sometimes it can be convenient to cloak baser motives in the grand rhetoric of high tax principles. There is a flavor of this subterfuge not only in patriotic Boston but also in arguments sometimes heard that root the American Civil War not in slavery but in a dispute over tariff policy between North and South.[74]

At other times, however, the tax angle may be more central than it is convenient to reveal. It may be too much, for example, to suppose that Henry VIII's break with Rome was triggered not by his passion for Anne Boleyn and the Pope's refusal to allow him to indulge it by divorcing Catherine of Aragon, but by his lust for the revenues being extracted by the papacy from the Church in England.[75] The massive fiscal side-benefit of expropriating those revenues, however, can hardly have been lost on a king whose recent revenue-raising attempts had resulted in rebellion. In any case, Henry used the threat of usurping the taxes paid by clerics to Rome as a lever in his maneuvering with the Pope; moved quickly to do so when the break came;[76] and in time managed, as a result, to more than double his revenue[77] (then proceeding to waste it on some of the most expensive wars that England had ever fought).[78] Revolts, riots, and even reformations are inherently about the exercise of government's coercive powers, and tax issues are then rarely far away.

Tax does not explain everything. Unlike some observers, we do not believe that President Kennedy was assassinated because he was about to roll back a tax break for the oil and gas industry.[79] But just as tax mistakes can have horrendous consequences, so we believe that good tax design and administration can deliver enormous benefits—and that a close look at the tax follies and wisdom of our ancestors can set us on the right course for doing so.

For this purpose, we start with the big picture of how, over the millennia, the ways in which governments have exercised their coercive taxing powers have changed while many of the underlying problems they face in doing so have not.

2

The Way We Were

The fiscal history of a people is above all an essential part of its general history.

JOSEPH SCHUMPETER[1]

IN *SCOOP*, Evelyn Waugh drew on his experiences in 1930s Abyssinia to imagine tax collection in fictional Ishmaelia:

> It had been found expedient to merge the functions of national defense and inland revenue in an office then held in the capable hands of General Gollancz Jackson; his forces were in two main companies, the Ishmaelite Mule Tax-gathering Force and the Rifle Excisemen with a small Artillery Death Duties Corps for use against the heirs of powerful noblemen.... Towards the end of each financial year the General's flying columns would lumber out into the surrounding country on the heels of the fugitive population and return in time for budget day laden with the spoils of the less nimble; coffee and hides, silver coinage, slaves, livestock, and firearms.[2]

It was from simple plundering of much this kind that today's often mind-numbingly complicated tax systems evolved. There is a commonality of purpose—the extraction of resources by coercive rulers—which means that taxation may be one of the few things in our lives that our ancestors would recognize from theirs. The past is not simply the present in fancy dress,[3] but our rulers face the same fundamental tax problems as did theirs. This chapter starts by scanning the millennia to identify these recurrent challenges and to see the changing ways in which rulers have tried to address them. It then provides more context for the rest of the book by looking at how much tax revenue governments have, over the ages, actually managed to extract—the past, it turns out, was no golden era of low and unobtrusive taxes—and at how tax systems have been shaped by two powerful forces: war (always) and the extension of the franchise (more recently). Finally, we see that the two main alternative ways in which governments finance themselves, by borrowing and by creating money, are in effect taxation by another name.

A Quick Gallop through the Long History of Taxation

Something recognizable as taxation doubtless began as simple plunder in the mold of General Jackson, long before Ptolemaic Egypt or even ancient Sumer.[4] Elements of plunder continued over the centuries. In the Roman Empire, victories were sometimes spectacular enough to allow remission of all other taxes for that year.[5] In England, a primary function of the Domesday Book of 1087 was to provide the newly installed Norman conquerors with a record of exactly how much they had acquired. Plunder continued through the conquest of resource-rich South America, though the plunderers themselves were occasionally plundered: Francis Drake's capture of the Spanish treasure ships (and other piracy against the Spanish in 1577–1580) brought Queen Elizabeth I the equivalent of about 1 year of her ordinary income.[6] And it has continued into modern times through conflicts over the control of petroleum and mineral deposits in Africa and the Middle East.

The more sophisticated plunderers have, though, learned to be more subtle than General Jackson in *Scoop*. More like Eli Wallach's bandit in *The Magnificent Seven*,[7] they have recognized that leaving those plundered just enough of their capital (and human) resources to rebuild their productive capacity can provide a basis for further happy plundering in the future. Herodotus tells of King Alyattes of Lydia, who, when attacking the ancient Greek city of Miletus, "refrained from tearing down their houses so that the Milesians could set forth from them to sow and work the fields, and through their work he would have something to plunder."[8] From this it was a short step to seeing that the hard work of actual plundering itself might not be needed, the threat of plundering being enough. Tribute—such as the *danegeld* paid by the English and the Franks to keep the Vikings from raiding—became a more elegant way to achieve, by blackmail, the same effect.

Plundering and extracting tribute from foreigners—or, more generally, from those regarded for some reason as outsiders (perhaps for religious reasons, as we will see later)—has always been a popular form of taxation. Rulers prefer to extract their resources from people on whom their popular support does not depend. The Athenians levied a poll tax on foreign residents;[9] Elizabethan England simply charged them double.[10] Machiavelli advised his Prince that "of that which is neither yours nor your subjects' you can be a ready giver, as were Cyrus, Caesar, and Alexander; because it does not take away your reputation if you squander that of others, but adds to it,"[11] advice which many seeking to tax foreign multinationals continue to follow to this day. But, as Bolivia discovered in chapter 1, taxing foreigners can be risky. And it has rarely provided enough to satisfy rulers' needs. Even Imperial Spain, despite the riches brought by the annual treasure fleet, suffered acute fiscal crises. Taxation of the insiders—those whom rulers feel in some way to be part of their own community—is also needed.

As societies became more settled, so too taxation took more settled forms. In preindustrial times, it was focused on the only two things in reasonably abundant supply: agricultural land and labor.

In ancient China, for instance, during the Western Zhou dynasty (1046–771 BCE), there emerged a system of dividing land into equal-sized three-by-three parcels of nine square plots, with the produce of the collectively farmed central square serving as a tax;[12] this was much praised by the philosopher Mencius (372–289 BCE), though by his time, it had largely broken down. (Unchanged, however, is the composition of the pictographic character for "tax" in China, which has always been made up of "crop" and "exchange.")[13] Governments have put immense resources into the collection of land-related taxes.[14] Under the Roman Emperor Diocletian (284–305), "[f]ields were measured out clod by clod, vines and trees were counted, every kind of animal was registered."[15] In Japan, the primary source of revenue until the Meiji restoration was a tax specified as a proportion of (actual or potential) rice production, often paid in kind. And the Mughal emperors derived about 90 percent of their revenue from land taxes, with officials collecting field-by-field information on areas, yields, and prices. Under the British, the officials of the Raj were traveling the country doing much the same, "inspecting and checking . . . the state of the wells and the irrigation systems, the survey and entries in the field register, the health of the cattle, the accuracy of boundaries."[16] Many of these techniques—focusing on physical indicators to establish a reasonable basis for assessment—would be familiar in low-income countries today.

Labor might be taxed explicitly through a poll tax: an equal amount for all (known in China as the "mouth" tax).[17] Or it might be taxed implicitly, though forced work, often backbreaking and sometimes lethal. More glamorous was the labor required from the knights of the classic European feudal systems, obliged, in return for their share of plundered land, to provide their prince with their own military service and that of their retainers.

There were other types of tax in preindustrial societies. In classical Athens, the wealthy were effectively required to contribute to liturgies that initially paid for festivals and then for wider state functions:[18] Pericles presented Aeschylus' *The Persians* as a liturgy in 462 BCE. Recognizable taxes in ancient Rome included a sales tax, which by 444 had risen to 4 percent,[19] and taxes on inheritance and slaves (both sale and manumission). The emperor Vespasian (69–79) imposed a tax on urine, using it to teach his son the lesson that *pecunia non olet*: money has no smell. Classical Athens taxed imports and exports at 1 percent.[20] But it was land and labor that were the dominant sources of the resources extracted by premodern rulers.

The elements of a clearly modern tax system began to emerge in medieval Western Europe—along with an acceptance that some degree of consent from the governed was needed if rulers were to meet their burgeoning and permanent financial needs. Traditionally, rulers were expected to "live of their own":[21] to fund their expenses, not least of waging war, from their own resources. These comprised income from their lands, service from their lords, and other feudal dues, supplemented by an eclectic range of expedients, such as the dissolution of the monasteries under Henry VIII. Unusual needs (meaning war) that these could not cover were met by occasional levies, often labeled in ways—"subsidies," "grants," or "aids" in Britain, *servicios* in Spain—that suggested a mutually agreeable pretense that their payment was voluntary. But from around the late fifteenth century, war became more expensive (driven in part by an existential threat from the Ottomans),[22] requiring increasingly powerful artillery (and stronger fortifications to guard against it) along with large trained infantries. Revenue from the traditional feudal sources had clearly become inadequate in England, for instance, by the reign of James I (1603–1625), and ad hoc charges, such as the sale of monopolies, did not fill the gap. The occasional special charges to finance war became increasingly regular, even in peacetime. As the search for more reliable and sustainable revenue bases intensified, commercial and other nonagricultural activities, and urban centers, became ever-more tempting targets for revenue extraction.[23] But rulers would have to pay a price for establishing a wide and permanent source of revenue: a diminution of their political power.

One of the longest established and permanent sources of revenue—perhaps the only one that rulers were traditionally seen as having an uncontested right to impose—is the taxation of trade. Borders have long been a convenient point at which to levy taxes, and they still are, again no doubt partly in the hope of taxing foreigners rather than insiders (although here we touch on questions of incidence—who really bears the burden of a tax—which are taken up in chapter 7). Trade taxes were major revenue- raisers in medieval Europe. In England, King John (1199–1216) charged around 7 percent on a wide range of both imports and exports,[24] and much of the revenue of the medieval English kings came from a tax on wool exports. Continental Europe was cut up by a swath of tolls and charges: In 1567, traveling between Roanne and Nantes on the Loire meant crossing 120 toll points.[25] And taxes on trade underpinned the grandeur of Byzantine Constantinople, at the junction of two major trade routes. These days, trade taxes are used in advanced economies more to protect domestic businesses than to raise revenue, but in many developing countries they still collect 20 percent or more of all tax revenue.

One consequence of rulers' need to secure extensive and reliable revenue streams was the regularization and extension of excises (meaning taxes on the domestic production of particular products, as well as on imports), enabled by monetization and an increasing concentration of production and consumption among a manageable number of firms and cities. The *alcabala* in Spain, which applied to a wide range of products, dates back to at least 1342,[26] and in France the hated salt tax (*gabelle*) became permanent in the 1340s. In the Florentine Republic of the Medicis, sales taxes in 1427 averaged about 6 percent of consumer spending and more in Florence itself, [27] much of it from taxes on wine and on salt. Over the years, excises on a wider range of things began to take hold: in Spain, where the *milliones* of 1590 even taxed basic foods, in the United Provinces (the word "excise" itself may derive from the Middle Dutch word *excijs*[28]) and in Britain during the interregnum of 1649–1660 (driven by the parliamentary hero, John Pym[29]). These attempts to expand the tax base were not always successful. Spanish efforts to impose the "tenth penny," a 10 percent tax on all goods, further stoked the Dutch revolt of 1568–1648, and the experience of the Commonwealth bred a resistance to broad-based commodity taxation in Britain that is still a political taboo. But commodity taxation became firmly established as a significant source of revenue, facilitated by monetization and industrial development.

Nonetheless, much of the taxation of this period was intended to be differentiated according to individuals' circumstances. The pockets— actually the fields, mills, and mines—of the well-to-do were where the money was, and perhaps also where the money should come from. Rulers could not, however, easily determine just how well-off their subjects were, especially when those subjects had an incentive not to be forthcoming, given that the more they declared the more they would be taxed. This remains a—arguably, the—central problem of all tax systems.

The Greeks had hit on a neat approach to this problem long ago: The wealthy could be exempted from financing the liturgies, but only if they would exchange all their property for that of someone who would take the charge on.[30] This gave them an incentive not to egregiously understate their own wealth, for fear of ending up with less. As a way of eliciting truthful self-assessment, this trick has occasionally been tried since. But the much more common approach to targeting the better-off was (and remains) to base an individual's tax liability on some proxy for their standard of living, such as, in strongly hierarchical societies, their social standing, or (as we saw in chapter 1) how many windows their residences sported. Another was to effectively delegate the differentiation to the local elite, with better local knowledge and, in any case, people the ruler wanted to keep on good terms with. Sometimes this discretion operated in a context in which the amount to be paid was specified not by individual but by quotas set for each locality. Inevitably, favoritism and mendacity were pervasive: "Our estates that be £30 or £40 in the Queen's books," Sir Walter Raleigh told Queen Elizabeth, "are not the hundredth part of our wealth."[31] The commodity-based excises and tariffs, in contrast, had a much more readily observed and verifiable tax base: bales of wool could be counted. This made possible a quite different approach to implementation: One that relied less on the inside knowledge of (and relations among) the wealthy and was more open to administration by public officials or tax-farming commercial enterprises, paying some fee in return for the right to collect taxes.

By around the late sixteenth century, rulers' revenue needs were making taxation not just a matter of raising extraordinary finance in times of war but a permanent reality. Struggles intensified as those being extracted from sought more control over how much was to be taken and how. They proceeded from the endemic tax revolts of the early Middle Ages through the fights of Philip II (King of Spain, 1556–1598) with the *Cortes* (national assemblies), the English Civil War, the American War of Independence, and the French Revolution. Matters played out at different paces and with different outcomes, but it was the "long nineteenth century," from 1789 to 1914, that finally saw the emergence in the West of a stable, adequate, and broadly consensual tax structure.

It happened first in Britain, with the growth of political stability after the Glorious Revolution of 1688 and during the wars with France that followed. Underpinned by a quota-based tax on land, customs revenue, an extraordinary range of excise taxes, and (not least) an increasingly professional tax administration, this power to tax and hence to borrow was recognized at the time as key to Britain's growing power. It worried even George Washington: "In modern wars, the longest purse must chiefly determine the event," and he feared that "though the [British] government is deeply in debt . . . their system of public credit is such, that it is capable of greater exertions than that of any other nation."[32] And all this was based on a genuine degree of consensus, as Prime Minister Robert Walpole[33] learned when, in 1733, any thought he might have had of extending the excise was quickly quashed by public anger.

As commercial and other activities grew, land taxes steadily declined in importance.[34] But they remained substantial. Attractive though they were, the new sources of tax revenue proved hard to observe and verify. The British land tax of 1697, for instance, was initially levied not only on land rents but also on personal property (including financial) and income from (nonmilitary) offices and employment. By the 1730s, however, elements other than land rent had largely fallen away: "No man contributes the least share to this tax," Robert Walpole recognized, "but he that is possessed of a landed estate."[35]

Revenue needs were amplified by the wars of the eighteenth century. Seeing the link, Frederick William I of Prussia (1713–1740) established a super-ministry of war and finance.[36] Governments struggled, some (such as the British) more successfully than others (such as the French). But even the British needed more to meet the unprecedented costs of the French and Napoleonic wars, leading to Pitt the Younger's introduction in 1799 of the first genuine income tax,[37] aiming to relate liability more precisely to individuals' circumstances. The transition to distinctly modern tax structures in Europe and North America continued, fueled by the expansion of the market sector and declining importance of agriculture, the concentration of employment in larger establishments, and growing literacy. Bureaucracies capable of reasonably disinterested and efficient tax collection were constructed. All of these economic and social changes facilitated the collection of revenue. And, as taxes became easier to collect, more money was collected.

By the eve of the First World War, stable and good-enough tax structures, along with decent-enough bureaucratic tax administrations, had become established in most of the industrialized countries, though even by then, surprisingly few had followed the British lead of adopting a personal income tax. Some stresses on national tax systems were, however, becoming evident. Social tensions led to the first steps, in Germany and Great Britain, toward a welfare state, which would need to be funded, and to pressures toward more progressive taxation, with the adoption of income taxes by the German states between 1891 and 1912. These tensions also underlay the constitutional crisis in Britain sparked by Lloyd George's "People's Budget" of 1909 (of which more later).[38] In the United States, swelling popular support for an income tax, in part to replace tariffs that were widely believed to unfairly burden the poor, led first to a modest tax on corporations and then to a constitutional amendment in 1913 that allowed a federal income tax.

These pressures were as nothing, however, compared to the massive increase in taxation in the belligerents once the First World War began. This led to the introduction of the income tax where it had not existed—in France days after the outbreak, in Russia in 1916—and to higher rates and lower exemption thresholds where it did. The standard rate in Britain rose to an unprecedented 30 percent, and its coverage more than doubled. The top rate of the U.S. income tax rose from 7 percent when it was introduced in 1913 to 77 percent in 1918. One innovation, conceived as temporary at the time, long-forgotten but now being looked at again, was the introduction by all the major powers of a company-level tax intended to capture excess wartime profits.

The Second World War proved even more transformative, with the income tax becoming for the first time something that applied to most ordinary people: In the United States, for example, the number of income tax returns filed soared from 7.7 million in 1939 to 49.9 million in 1945. This expansion was made possible by a critical advance in tax administration: the massive use of withholding—getting the employer to remit tax rather than trying to obtain it directly from the employee.

In the decades since, there has been relatively little development in the broad types of tax instruments that governments levy, with two major exceptions. One is the emergence of a distinct tax on corporations. The other, and more fundamental, is the rise of the value-added tax (VAT).

First proposed by a German businessman, Wilhelm von Siemens, in the 1920s,[39] the VAT must then have seemed a completely wacky idea, the essence of the tax being that every business owes tax on all its sales, but at the same time reduces its payment by the amount of tax levied on its own purchases (and remitted by its suppliers)—even getting a refund if the latter is more than the former. The upshot is that, leaving aside evasion and some other complications, the VAT is a tax on sales to final consumers. This may all sound gaudy and preposterous: Why not simply tax those final (that is, retail) sales and avoid all this crediting and refunding (with 40 percent of the VAT collected in the United Kingdom, for instance, being given back to companies)?[40] The point is that the VAT places the responsibility of remitting the tax not only on retailers (who are notoriously difficult to collect from) but on all businesses. So it is that from the mid-1960s, the VAT has taken the world by storm. It is now central to tax systems around the world—with the glaring exception, which we will try to understand later in the book, being the United States.[41]

This brisk tour of tax history is tilted toward the experiences of Europe and North America. There are other traditions: Many of the countries that emerged from the Ottoman Empire, for instance, retain quite heavy reliance on complicated fees; and highly resource-rich countries continue to get by without either a VAT or much of an income tax. Although the focus on these parts of the world betrays our own experiences, it also reflects the current dominance—for better or worse—of the model of taxation that has emerged there. Freed of the colonial powers in the postwar era, many developing countries inherited (and kept) tax systems based on those of the colonial powers, and the advice they have received has often been heavily influenced by the practices of more advanced economies: "Experts," the founding father of tax work at the International Monetary Fund once reflected ruefully, "often uncritically recommend transplanting the systems of their home countries, perhaps with modifications they have unsuccessfully proposed at home."[42] This may have left many developing countries struggling, for instance, with complex income taxes intended for mass application before these countries had the capacity to effectively implement them. In much of the world—perhaps most of it—the journey continues toward good-enough systems with decent-enough administration.

How Much?

Every generation, in every country, tends to assume that it is paying unprecedentedly heavy taxes. It is hard, of course, to meaningfully compare tax takes in Pharaonic Egypt with those in, say, modern Denmark, and such evidence on tax burdens as we have for premodern times is very patchy at best. But we should not assume that our ancestors were always blessed, if not with long and fruitful lives, then at least with low taxes.

It seems likely, for example, that the nobles and clergy of England thought otherwise when, in 1193, they were called on to pay an unprecedentedly extortionate ransom for the return of their glamorous king, Richard the Lionheart (1189–1199). Shipwrecked on his return from the Third Crusade, and his disguise having failed him, Richard fell into the hands of one enemy who promptly passed him along (for a price) to an even more powerful one, the Holy Roman Emperor Henry VI. Ransoms for nobles were commonplace at the time, but this was an extraordinarily large one; Henry (shrugging off his excommunication for such treatment of a crusader) demanded an astronomical 100,000 silver marks for Richard's return: equivalent to 35 tons of pure silver[43] and well over 10 times the crown's normal annual revenue at the time. To meet this, the chronicler Ralph de Diceto reported that "Archbishops, bishops, abbots, priors, earls and barons [contributed] a quarter of their annual income," while "the greater churches came up with treasures hoarded from the distant past, and the parishes with their silver chalices. . . . [T]he Cistercian monks and Premonstratensian canons their whole year's wool crop."[44] This was clearly a painful business. Nonetheless (and despite the best efforts of Richard's ambitious and not-so-loving brother John, who offered Henry VI an equivalent amount to hold on to Richard), Richard's forceful mother, Eleanor of Aquitaine, secured enough of the ransom—with hostages providing assurance of the rest, and Richard embarrassingly having to concede his crown and receive it back as the Emperor's vassal—to secure Richard's safe return in early 1194.

This example is extreme, but there are other cases in premodern circumstances of tax takes that look distinctly like today's or are even higher. Perhaps one-tenth of national product went to the state in Periclean Athens;[45] possibly one-third in the early Abbasid caliphate;[46] and at least one-third in Ottoman Egypt at the end of the sixteenth century.[47] In Tokugawa Japan (1603–1867), 30 percent or more of rice output was taken in tax throughout the eighteenth and early nineteenth centuries;[48] about one-quarter of the national produce went to the Imperial government in early Mughal India;[49] and about the same amount was collected by the United Provinces of the Netherlands in 1688.[50] These figures are not far off today's average tax take in advanced economies of around one-third of GDP. At times, of course, the take has been much higher. About two-thirds of the grain harvest was taken in Russia as taxes in 1710, "a level of fiscal extraction not seen again until Stalin's time."[51] And some have cited excessive taxes as one cause of the decline of the Roman Empire (among plenty of others). Through the ages, people have bemoaned their unbearable tax burdens but, somehow, generally borne them.

England was generally lightly taxed as the modern era took hold: In 1688, only about 3 percent of the national product went to taxation.[52] It has not always been so. The *danegeld* was not small beer: More Anglo-Saxon coins have been found in tribute-receiving Denmark than in tax-paying England.[53] And, only 5 years before the ransoming of Richard I, the "Saladin tithe," levied by Henry II (1154–1189) to fund a crusade aimed at recapturing Jerusalem, which Saladin had taken in 1187, was levied at a rate of 10 percent on revenues and movable properties.

Its implementation came with a judicious mix of carrot and stick: Those not complying were to be excommunicated, and those joining the crusade were exempt.[54]

What we would now recognize as similar to today's taxes, moreover, were often far from being the only compulsory levies that our ancestors had to put up with. Feudal dues still accounted for more than half of the British monarch's receipts (other than from crown lands) in the early seventeenth century.[55] And, on top of payments to the secular government, compulsory payments often went to religious authorities—tithes in Christian countries, *zakat* in Islamic—that commonly took 10 percent of agricultural output (which is more than it might sound: No allowance was made for farmers' costs). These payments persist in differing forms. Several northern European countries still have church "taxes," collected by the government (but generally not treated as taxes in official revenue statistics).[56] Information on the current extent of *zakat* is harder to find. There were also often local taxes, hard to document but important in financing poor relief.

There have also long been "informal" payments to the powerful and corrupt. In the United States, for example, it was a long-accepted practice that those given appointments by politicians would make a contribution to them or their parties in return. In the Louisiana of Huey Long,[57] state employees were expected to hand over 5–10 percent of their salaries to his political machine.[58] Moreover, rulers have proved adept at raising revenue in ways that would not be called "taxes"—some of which we look at in chapter 3.

A clearer but still shaky picture of tax take starts to emerge only in modern times. In Britain, it seems to have risen markedly over the eighteenth century, to around 10 percent of GDP in 1788,[59] on the eve of the French Revolution. In France, in contrast, it was then only about 7 percent, and financial crisis loomed—one of the few cases in history in which it was generally recognized that taxes were too low. By the start of the nineteenth century, we are on somewhat firmer ground when assessing tax ratios (that is, tax revenue as a share of a country's GDP). Considering only taxes levied by the central government, the British tax ratio stayed below about 10 percent from the Napoleonic Wars into the

1900s. In the United States, apart from an upward blip during the Civil War, the tax ratio (looking just at federal taxes) remained under 5 percent.[60] But tax ratios jumped sharply with the First World War and stayed in the low 20s for the United Kingdom and between 5 and 10 percent in the United States until World War Two. Tax ratios in both countries then again skyrocketed, but this time hardly came down after the war. In 1947, the tax ratio in the United Kingdom was about 36 percent—a little higher than today.[61] For the United States, federal receipts are also much the same as they were in 1947, at around 16 percent of GDP; adding state and local taxes brings that to about 26 percent of GDP.[62]

Each country has its own story, of course. Other members of the Organisation for Economic Co-operation and Development (OECD) have seen large increases—by nearly 10 percent of GDP on average—since 1965.[63] And the tax take differs widely among them: Although averaging about one-third, tax ratios in the OECD vary from a low of 16 percent in Mexico to a high of about 46 percent in France.[64] Contrary to what many Americans seem to think, the tax ratio in the United States is, by OECD standards, decidedly on the low side.

Comparing tax ratios in a meaningful way is not entirely straightforward, however, because of budgeting conventions. The oxymoronic term "tax expenditure" refers to preferences and concessions in a tax that have the nature of expenditure programs.[65] Suppose, for instance, that one country provides tax deductions for dependent children, while another gives direct payments, of exactly the same value, to parents for having children. The two approaches are doing the same thing, but the latter will give a higher measured ratio of taxes to GDP. Or consider the tax treatment of charitable donations. Presently in the United Kingdom, there is no charitable deduction from taxable income, as there is in the United States; instead the government sends to registered charities a check for an amount proportional to the gifts they receive from taxpayers. In both cases—a tax expenditure in the form of a deduction and a direct subsidy—the charity receives more than the taxpayer gives up, and the government makes up the difference. But only in the United States does the policy reduce measured taxes collected.

One critical and even tragic regularity is that tax ratios are low in developing countries. In about half of all low-income countries, it is less than 15 percent. Policy makers in higher-income countries may agonize over whether to increase or decrease their tax take: in much of the world, however, there is no such doubt. Tax ratios in low-income countries almost certainly need to be increased, in many cases substantially, to meet their development needs. On one estimate, low-income developing countries need to spend an additional 15 percent of GDP to meet key elements of the Sustainable Development Goals—a set of development objectives for 2030 endorsed by world leaders, under the auspices of the United Nations, in 2015.[66] Achieving that will be a (very) tall order.

Warfare and Welfare

Even from the brief gallop above, it is clear that taxation, historically, has been both the product and the progenitor of violence. Plunder generates resources, and those resources enable more plundering.

That military power rests on the capacity to tax has long been a truism: Cicero said the sinews of war are infinite money. To fight the Peloponnesian War, the Athenians in 428 BCE introduced a property tax, and soldiers' wages were the largest single expenditure in second- and third-century Rome, at perhaps 6 percent of national income.[67] Ever since, the experience and prospect of war have provided a uniquely strong incentive to invest in the capacity to raise revenue, spurring and drawing on advances in tax technology: the advent of the income tax under Pitt the Younger, the excess profits taxes of the First World War, and employer withholding of the second, all episodes we look at in later chapters. This enhanced tax technology not only provided a direct source of finance, it also reassured investors that the machinery was in place to pay off the increased government debt that is the other common consequence of war. The classic example—recognized at the time by George Washington, as seen then and cited widely[68] since—is the development of tax and borrowing capacity in Britain during its rise to global power during the bellicose eighteenth century. And the expanded ability of governments to raise substantial amounts of tax revenue also enabled them to exercise more fully all the powers of control and direction that define government: "War made the state, and the state made war."[69]

The role of war leaps out when looking at broad trends over the past century or so. In both the United States and the United Kingdom, tax ratios peaked in the two world wars, with the revolutionary wars in Britain and the civil war in the United States also showing upward jumps. There was a ratchet effect from both world wars: taxes going up in wartime, but then not coming down much after. Those who see this as key to explaining increased tax ratios over this period[70] argue that during wartime, governments push up tax rates, broaden tax bases, and tighten enforcement to generate the funds needed for defense spending; after the war, the new tax rates and tax structures tend to remain the same, as people have become used to them and the bureaucracy needed to implement them is already in place. Such ratcheting is not a law of nature: The centerpiece of British fiscal policy in much of the nineteenth century was precisely an effort to scale back tax rates elevated during the Revolutionary and Napoleonic wars—symbolized by the repeal of the income tax just one year after Waterloo[71]—while paying off the massive debt burden that had been accumulated. And after the American Civil War, most of the institutional tax apparatus built up during the war was quickly dismantled, the income tax, for instance, being removed in 1872.

The clear ratcheting up of the size of government in the United Kingdom and the United States after the First and, especially, Second World Wars marks the transition from a warfare state, in which the main purposes of taxation were to fund defense spending and to deal with debt accumulated in past wars, to a welfare state, in which most revenue is raised to finance benefits to the poor, stricken, aged, or otherwise vulnerable. Governments came to be expected to pay for a lot more than wars, roads, and the like: They are now also expected to provide at least basic health, education, and social support. In the OECD, social spending now accounts for an average of 20 percent of GDP.[72] Even that can be cast as akin to war. Introducing his People's Budget of 1909, which raised taxes on the wealthy to fund new social welfare programs, Lloyd

George said: "This is a war Budget. It is for raising money to wage implacable warfare against poverty and squalidness."[73]

Once again, there was nothing wholly new in the idea of using taxes to finance spending that benefits the less well off: Something like 10 percent of public spending in Rome, for example, went on grain and sometimes olive oil freely distributed to the plebeians.[74] And, now often forgotten, support of the poor had long been a core function of local government in, for instance, Britain, and had also become so in Germany.[75] Trends toward the strengthening of this welfare-delivery function, with a leading role for central government, were apparent in a modest increase in tax ratios around the end of the nineteenth century.[76] Joseph Schumpeter saw at this time "an expansion of the sphere of social sympathy," which he presciently expected to develop still further, "not because but in spite of the war."[77] Education spending became an accepted responsibility of government. Compulsory insurance against sickness and accident was pioneered—as some mixture of Junker paternalism and purposive undermining of socialism—in Bismarck's Germany in the 1880s, culminating with the introduction of old age and disability insurance, for all workers, in 1889. This last, critically, supplemented contributions by employers and employees with state underwriting of the scheme. Pension rights without the necessity of contributing followed in Denmark (1891), New Zealand (1898), and the United Kingdom (1910).

The German economist Adolph Wagner was already hypothesizing in 1890 that as countries industrialize, the share of national income allocated to public expenditure rises as a result of urbanization and the "pressure for social progress," a phenomenon now known (predictably enough) as "Wagner's law." Plausible though this sounds, the evidence is not overwhelming;[78] it is hard to see clear signs of such an effect in nineteenth-century Britain, for instance. And certainly other things matter, too. Tax ratios tend to be higher, for instance, in smaller countries. Nonetheless, tax ratios jumped during and remained high after the two world wars; the question is why these increases were to a large degree sustained.

Mass mobilization may be a large part of the answer, creating and bringing together two blades of a pair of scissors. One was the vast increase in the state's capacity to extract resources, without which it could not maintain large armies in the field. The other blade was a strong political and social imperative that those who had done the fighting—the ones mobilized—should find some benefit in the peace. This was explicit in the 1942 Beveridge Report in the United Kingdom, which set out a vision of a proactive postwar state sufficiently attractive for Churchill to be voted out of office as soon as the war was won. Mass mobilization and the costs of financing the war and recovery were accompanied by steeply progressive tax structures: Top rates of income tax in 1920 were 60 percent in the United Kingdom and Germany (for the federal income tax introduced after the war), 73 percent in the United States (down from its peak of 77 percent in 1918).[79] On average, these top rates were about 34 points higher than in countries that had not undergone mass mobilization.[80] The world wars, and especially the second one, created both the machinery that made the welfare state possible and the political environment that ensured it would become reality.

Babbage's Nightmare

There is a surprising absentee from this account of the growth of taxation and government over the years: The expansion of voting rights. One might have expected—as many expected at the time—that, as the franchise was extended beyond the well-heeled, the numerous not-well-off would vote to use the tax system to divert resources to themselves from the not-so-numerous well-off: "representation without taxation."[81] (After all, the not-numerous well-off had shown little hesitation in levying indirect taxes, such as the *gabelle*, that had likely been borne largely by the numerous not-well-off.) Historically, this was the central argument against universal suffrage, and it had already worried the political theorists of Renaissance Italy:

> As far as methods of taxation are concerned. I can assure you that the people's will normally be much worse and more unjust, because by nature they like to overburden the better off; and since the less well-off are more numerous, it is not difficult for them to do this.[82]

This was a core issue in the Putney Debates of 1647, when, after its (first) victory over Charles I, Cromwell's New Model Army argued over the shape to give the new world it had created. If voting rights were given to "any man that hath a breath and being," Henry Ireton[83] fumed, "why those men may not vote against all property?"[84] Two centuries later, in 1852, Charles Babbage—taking time off from inventing the computer— was terrified by his calculation that 850,000 of the one million voters in Britain were below the income tax threshold: "Amidst the political er- rors of the present century, I know of none possessing so truly revolu- tionary a character . . . none which, although seemingly fatal only to the rich, is in reality more fatal to all industry."[85] William Gladstone,[86] the high priest of fiscal rectitude in British public finances, also thought that "it is desirable in a high degree . . . to connect the possession of the fran- chise with the payment in taxes,"[87] and the right to vote has indeed in many cases been limited to those liable to some form of taxation. No- where was this done more perfectly than in Prussia, where—while there was universal suffrage at the federal level—taxpayers were ordered by the amount of their direct tax payment, and the Landtag (parliament) then split into three equal-sized groups, each accounting for the same total amount of tax but representing, of course, very different numbers of people.[88]

In practice, however, the tax consequences of extending the franchise to lower-income people have been far less dramatic than Ireton, Bab- bage, and many others feared—or at least seem to have occurred with such a delay as to be hard to detect. In 1900, for instance, the average top rate of income tax was if anything actually slightly lower in democracies than elsewhere.[89] Certainly there are signs of an electoral effect to be seen. The return of the British income tax came suggestively soon after the franchise-expanding Reform Bill of 1832; and between 1867 (the second reform act) and 1913, the share of direct taxes in total revenue quadrupled. But these developments were hardly revolutionary. In Brit- ain, the top rate of income tax, which was 2.9 percent at its (re)introduc- tion in 1842, was still only 5 percent in 1908[90]—more than 20 years after the reform bill of 1884 that enfranchised about two-thirds of adult males. Even after the People's Budget of 1909, it was only 8.3 percent.[91]

Disraeli's trust in an inherent conservatism of the working classes—the "leap in the dark"[92] he took with the 1867 reform bill in Britain—arguably proved close to the mark.[93]

It may be, of course, that the numerous poor had the same insight as the restrained plunderer King Alyattes. Even if wholly selfish, they would not simply want to impose on the rich the highest possible tax rate but would aim instead to extract the greatest possible amount of revenue from them, to then share among themselves.[94] And that—if they heeded Babbage's warning on fatality to industry, the risk of blunting the incentives of the rich to earn and invest—may call for not especially high rates, nor for especially steep progressivity. It may not even call for especially heavy reliance on income taxes: The rich bear some burden from commodity taxes, too. Even though we might be puzzled, perhaps we should not be too surprised by the relatively undramatic effects of extending the franchise. People do seem to have proved remarkably able to vote against their own interests.

So far, we have been talking about what are recognizably "taxes," and in modern times, at least, called that. But governments through the ages have financed themselves in other ways, too. Some are taxes in all but the label attached to them—we look at these in chapter 3. But governments have also financed themselves by borrowing and by simply creating money. These deserve attention in a book on taxes because, despite appearances, these are ultimately also forms of taxation.

Debt, Default, and Princes

At a dark moment of the Peloponnesian War, the Athenians melted down and turned to coin the golden statues of Nike, goddess of war, on the Acropolis.[95] William Gladstone would have approved. In 1854, contemplating the fiscal costs of the Crimean War, he rejoiced that "the expenses of a war . . . are the moral check which it has pleased the Almighty to impose upon the ambition and the lust of conquest that are inherent in so many nations."[96]

That check, however, has not always proved a very powerful one. Ancient wars were financed mainly from tax or other immediate sources, but by the Middle Ages, the thirst of bellicose kings and princes for funds beyond those they could immediately get their hands on was driving the development of European banking networks. The development of effective tax systems, however, actually made it less essential to rely on immediate tax finance: They made it easier to borrow by making it easier for creditors to believe they would be repaid. By the end of the seventeenth century, the United Provinces, beset by lengthy, painful wars of independence, had already developed institutions for taxing and borrowing that allowed them to live with public debt in excess of 100 percent of their national income.[97] Higher taxes continued to be recognized as a—usually the—main way in which to pay for war. In Britain, it was simply taken for granted that the peacetime rate of land tax, 10 percent, would be raised to 20 percent in wartime. But public debt came to assume an important role, too, financing 40 percent of British spending during the American War of Independence (1776–1783) and close to 30 percent during the wars against Revolutionary and Napoleonic France (1793–1815).[98] And the years since 2001 have seen an extreme case in the United States: Spending between 9/11 and the end of 2013 on the wars in Afghanistan and Iraq, and on anti-terror operations, totaling around $1.6 trillion,[99] was paid for without any major or associated tax increase; these expenses correspond to about 10 percent of the national debt in 2013.[100]

The high levels of debt that the victors of major wars have been saddled with—Britain's peaked at 275 percent of GDP in 1822[101]—generated continuing controversies over the balance between tax and debt finance, and over how high public debt can safely be allowed to go. This debate was rekindled by the Global Financial Crisis that began in 2007 and the 2020 coronavirus episode, which elevated debt in many advanced economies to levels not previously seen outside wartime.

On one view, there is no real difference between taxing and borrowing. When the government borrows £100, it is in effect promising to raise enough taxes at some point in the future to pay an amount worth just as much as the £100 the lender is giving up today—so the government might as well just levy a £100 tax today. And (with some leap of faith here) sensible people will understand that, and so will react to £100 of government debt issued today in exactly the same way as they would to £100 of taxation today. The choice, that is, is not whether to tax or not, but whether to tax now or in the future. Elegant though it is, this idea (known as Ricardian equivalence, after David Ricardo—of whom more in chapter 7) is less than compelling, and was so even for Ricardo. To see one reason for this, simply suppose that the debt is to be repaid not from taxes levied on you or your loved ones, but on that irritating kid down the street. Another difficulty is that the story ignores the cost imposed by taxation over and above the amount of tax itself—the excess burden of the kind associated with the window tax of chapter 1, as a result of its interference with economic decision-making.

An important characteristic of this excess burden (which we will try to convince you of in chapter 9) has strong implications for how to finance temporary increases in public spending like those associated with war: it increases more than proportionately with the tax rate itself. That is, doubling the tax rate more than doubles excess burden. This creates a presumption against varying tax rates too much over time, because the additional excess burden when the tax is high is larger than the reduction in the excess burden when it is low.[102] These "tax-smoothing" considerations suggest that the best way to finance a war is to combine an increase in borrowing with an increase in tax rates to a level that, sustained over time, will be enough to rein in that increase in debt.

These arguments assume, however, that the government ultimately honors its debt. But the history of rulers' borrowing is largely a history of default—failure by the borrower to repay the debt on the terms agreed. And by defaulting, a government effectively turns a promise to pay off its debt by levying a tax on someone in the future into a tax today on those holding the debt.

Prominent serial defaulters include Phillip II of Spain, who reneged on his debt four times during his reign[103]—Spain's golden age. His difficulties came from waging war across a vast empire, and war, while sometimes spurring the development of fiscal capacity, has sometimes simply spurred defaults: There was a flood of them during the Napoleonic Wars, for example. Other defaults simply reflect a downturn when a sudden stop in capital flows and economic growth makes previously manageable debt burdens unsupportable. Argentina has defaulted eight times since independence in 1816 (most recently in 2014). But nearly all countries have at some point defaulted—even the United States, many believe, did so in 1933.[104] And defaults continue: there were 169 episodes of default, with a median length of 3 years, between 1946 and 2008.[105]

Sometimes governments default even before they borrow, through forced loans. The element of compulsion gives these an inherently tax-like feature, as it means that the lender would have preferred to put their resources to other uses. Even beyond that, however, it has often been clear that the government has no intention of repaying the loan on the terms specified. As so often, the early Stuarts, desperately seeking resources without the need for parliamentary approval, are leading examples of this fiscal barrel-scraping. Following their failure to subscribe to a forced loan in 1627, Charles I (1625–1649) simply had more than 70 men imprisoned.

Things can get very nasty, for both lender and borrower (and others), when a government defaults. The lender suffers directly (as can those who have lent to those lenders, and the lenders to those lenders, and so forth). And sometimes the default has been only part of the injury. In medieval Europe, pogrom, massacre, and/or expulsion often accompanied the reneging on debts to Jews. Kings could benefit from this even when they did not themselves borrow from the Jewish community. Edward I (1272–1307) did not owe money to the Jews when he sanctioned their expulsion from England in 1290. But the nobles who were beginning to flex their parliamentary muscles did, and they marked their gratitude to Edward by granting him £116,000,[106] the largest sum any medieval English king ever received.[107] Centuries later, the good news for private lenders is that they can now in principle insure themselves against default on government debt by purchasing credit default swaps. Quite what shape the insurers would be in to pay out in the event of default by, say, the United States, however, is not entirely clear.

For the borrower, too, default has often proved painful and humiliating. In December 1902, Venezuela, having refused to honor foreign debts or pay reparations for damages from civil disturbances, found itself blockaded by gunboats from Britain and Germany—surprised and somewhat horrified to find themselves as bedfellows—and Italy. Ulti-mately, Venezuela ceded 30 percent of its customs revenue to service its debts.

But the main punishment for default is a loss of trust among potential lenders and hence higher interest charges on any borrowing that the government can manage to do in the future. Entering the revolutionary wars at the end of the eighteenth century, the British government, which had not defaulted since at least the Civil War, had a track record over the previous 50 years of being able to borrow at about 2.5 percentage points less than its soon-to-be enemy, France, which had defaulted many times.[108] These days, for those defaulters that cannot borrow from private markets, recourse to borrowing from the International Mone-tary Fund (IMF) can bring its own political costs and tensions.

Given the risks that government borrowing creates, to what level should that debt be reined in? Before the Global Financial Crisis, it was something of a rule of thumb that advanced economies could live with public debt on the order of 60 percent of GDP (as enshrined in the EU's Maastricht Treaty) and emerging economies with debt of about 40 percent. Now, many countries have debt levels far higher, lead-ing some to wonder whether debt really matters at all, at least for coun-tries able to borrow in their own currency. Few, though, would stray very far from the orthodoxy that a government's ability to borrow ulti-mately rests on its ability to tax. Debt, that is, is really just a promise of deferred taxation.

Making Money

Among the unique powers of government is that of compelling the ac-ceptance as payment for goods and services of something that it, and it alone, can create: money.[109] This power, known as "seigniorage" (from an Old French word for the right of the lord (*seigneur*) to mint money), gives governments another way to extract resources from the private sector, as it can be used to acquire things worth much more than that money costs to produce. And governments have not been shy about using this power.

Before the advent of paper money, debasing the value of physical coinage—reducing its intrinsic value by cutting the content of precious metals in the hope that, for a while at least, no one will notice—was the most notorious method of seigniorage. In the mid-first century AD, Rome minted coins that were 97 percent silver. However, by the third century, coins contained only 40 percent silver and, over a 20-year period, the silver content plummeted to just 4 percent.[110] With the advent of paper (or "fiat") money—backed only by some kind of promise from the government, not its intrinsic value—creating money became even cheaper. Manufacturing a $100 bill costs about 15 cents.[111] And literally "printing money" is not the only way that money can be directly created, or even, these days, the main one: The central bank can simply create electronic credits in the accounts that commercial banks hold with it. To the extent that it pays interest on those accounts at a rate lower than that it receives on the assets it acquires, this also provides a source of finance for the government (being the owner of the central bank).

There is in principle no reason that seigniorage should not take a perfectly honorable place among all the other instruments by which governments raise revenue.[112] Like those other instruments, however, it can create problems that should temper its use. In particular, seigniorage is closely related to (but not quite the same thing as) the "inflation tax." When resources are otherwise fully used, the only way the government can squeeze out more resources for itself is if everyone else ends up with fewer goods and services; and the way the market makes that come about is by making those goods and services more expensive—that is, by raising the price level. Put differently, the more money there is chasing things to buy, the higher prices will become. Such increases in the price level act like a tax, and one that creates clear winners as well as losers. The losers are those who hold assets, or receive income, denominated in the debasing currency. "By a continuing process of inflation," wrote the British economist John Maynard Keynes, "governments can confiscate, secretly and unobserved, an important part of the wealth of their citizens."[113] But there are winners, too: those whose debts are denominated in fixed nominal terms. But because the government gains from the confiscation, the losses to private lenders and those on fixed nominal incomes must outweigh the gains to private debtors. And the government gains even more to the extent that it is itself a debtor, with its own borrowing not indexed for inflation.

Done in moderation, seigniorage is hardly noticed. But it can get so out of hand that inflation becomes highly damaging. History supplies plenty of warnings. In America, the monthly inflation rate reached 47 percent in November 1779. During the American Civil War, when the Union government printed greenbacks to finance the war effort, inflation reached a monthly level of 40 percent in March 1864.[114] The first recorded hyperinflation (inflation of more than 50 percent per month)[115] came during the French Revolution.

That revolution itself was, in large part, the product of the fiscal crisis of the ancien régime. But the revolutionaries quickly dug themselves into an even bigger fiscal hole. The first act of the National Assembly, on June 17, 1789 (after declaring that it was in fact a national assembly), was to declare all existing taxes illegal (though decreeing that their collection should nonetheless continue—not a recipe for good compliance).[116] Soon after, on July 13, it committed to honoring the substantial national debt. And then, on the tumultuous night of August 4, 1789, the Assembly simply abolished many of the most hated feudal remnants, including the privileges at the heart of the tax system and all venal offices (ones, that is, that had simply been sold by the state), but promised to provide full compensation. All these actions left a vast hole in the public finances, which a voluntary "patriotic tax" was not enough to fill. How were these massive commitments to be met? The answer was by using the assets—the *biens nationaux*—that the state acquired by expropriating the property of the church (and, later, of the royal family and of émigrés). And so, enter the assignat. This was initially much like a bond, issued in very high denominations, carrying interest and backed by the guarantee that it could be used to purchase the *biens nationaux* in public auction (at which point the assignats would be destroyed). So they were presented not as paper money but as backed by the real value of those assets. What could be more secure?

Soon, however, the temptation to fund more and more government operations by printing paper became irresistible: The assignats became available in ever-smaller denominations, not paying interest, and functioning as money. Inflation, initially, was moderate, and land sales were brisk (even being recommended as a good investment by Marie Antoinette).[117] With the outbreak of an existential war in April 1792, however, issuance of assignats skyrocketed.[118] Under the Terror that soon followed, price controls helped keep inflation in some check. But, after the fall of the Jacobins, France was soon in hyperinflation.[119] By October 1795, inflation was running at about 140 percent per month, and an assignat was worth, in coin, only 2 percent of its face value. After one last splurge of issuance in late 1795, and amid public celebration, the printing presses were ceremonially destroyed.[120] Soon the assignat was entirely worthless, its only future being as a collector's item.[121]

There are many wrinkles to the story of the assignat. Some people, for instance, despised and rejected it from the start as being based on unjust appropriation of church property: so much, they thought, for the revolutionaries' commitment to property rights. "They rob," said Edmund Burke of the revolutionaries, "only to enable them to cheat."[122] Priests told their congregations that using assignats was a sin. Others saw using the assignat as a patriotic duty. For Mirabeau, "to doubt the value of an assignat is to doubt the Revolution—it's a crime."[123] In David's famous painting, the *Death of Marat,* the great (and/or despicable) demagogue is holding an assignat.

The lesson, however, is straightforward: Trying to cover an unsustainably large excess of public spending over tax revenue by printing money (or today's digital equivalent) can lead to massive inflation. Some of the revolutionaries, including Danton and Marat,[124] realized this risk from the outset. The then-bishop and later devious diplomat Talleyrand predicted in 1789 that "you can never compel a man to give you a thousand francs in coin in return for an assignat. . . . It is for that reason that the whole system will fail."[125] (For the British, pursuing their war against France, the risk was an opportunity: They set up printing presses in London intended to flood France with false assignats—a trick that Napoleon later tried to turn on them.[126]) The real trouble is that countries sometimes have little alternative to printing money. In 1792, the revolutionaries found themselves

> confronted with an empty treasury, with taxes which remained for the most part unpaid, and with an administration not so organized as to be able to enforce collection, with the liquidation of the affairs of the old regime still unachieved, with a foreign war requiring the active service of five armies, and presently a civil war.[127]

What else could they do? The deeper truth is that without a strong capacity to raise tax revenue, countries develop deep macroeconomic and political vulnerabilities.

Perhaps the most famous episode of hyperinflation, however, remains that of Weimar Germany during the 1920s. Like the French assignat episode, it helped pave the way to dictatorship, as trust in the institutions of government eroded. The root of the problem lay in the onerous reparation demands that the victors imposed on Germany after the First World War. By 1920, Germany was struggling to meet these payments and, with severely limited borrowing possibilities, the printing of marks skyrocketed, and their value fell as prices soared. In 1923, in addition to the main government printing office, more than 130 other printers churned out paper money.[128] People brought baskets and then wheelbarrows full of marks to the bakery; children built play structures of rubber-banded wads of marks; street cleaners swept bills into drains; banknotes were used as wallpaper. On November 2, 1923, the Reichsbank issued a 100-trillion mark note. Two weeks later, on November 15, the mark was replaced with the *rentenmark*, the value of which was fixed at 1 trillion paper marks and—the key point—which was issued in strictly limited quantities. Inflation fell back to reasonable levels.

There have been plenty of other hyperinflations. Austria, Hungary, Russia, and Poland also all experienced it in the aftermath of the First World War. (In Vienna, it was said that a prudent drinker should order two beers at a time, because the price was expected to have gone up before they got to the second.)[129] After the Second World War, the monthly inflation rate in Poland reached 4.19×10^{16} percent (yes, 16 zeros), equivalent to a doubling of prices every 15 hours. In Zimbabwe, the annual inflation

Young Germans making their mark.

rate in November 2008 hit 89,700,000,000,000,000,000,000 percent.[130] At one point, a loaf of bread cost Z$550 million in the regular market. In recognition of the very practical challenges this poses for daily life, in 2009 the governor of Zimbabwe's central bank was awarded the Ig Nobel Prize (for "achievements that make people laugh, then make them think") for making it easier to cope with a wide range of numbers—from very small to very big—by having the bank print banknote denominations ranging from 1 cent (Z$.01) to 100 trillion dollars (Z$100,000,000,000,000).

Even in more normal times, governments acquire some resources by creating money—sometimes a lot. For a sample of 90 countries between 1971 and 1990, seigniorage was modest but noticeable in most advanced countries: 0.4 percent of GDP in the United States, 0.5 percent in the United Kingdom, and about 0.7 percent in Germany.[131] For the sample as a whole, however, it averaged a substantial 2.5 percent of GDP and 10.5 percent of government spending. Less is heard of seigniorage these days—but it has not gone away. For 2005–2015, it was down to 0.2 percent in the United Kingdom and was actually negative in Sweden. But it was still a handy 0.4 percent of GDP in the United States and 0.55 percent in the eurozone.[132] One reason to expect declining seigniorage revenues is reduced demand for cash as payment technologies evolve (though central banks may themselves come to issue digital currencies—electronic analogues to today's cash). Another is a widespread trend toward giving central banks greater independence from political control. A principal aim in doing so is to take control of the money supply away from governments that may be tempted to finance their spending by issuing debt which they then require the central bank to acquire by creating money. An independent central bank has statutory protection against such political interference, and is often explicitly mandated to pursue some moderate level of inflation. Where governments constrain themselves in this way, inflation does indeed seem generally to be lower. But seigniorage persists, not only in the form of literal printing of money or the acquisition of government debt, but in the wider profits that the central bank—owned by the government—earns from money creation.

Indeed, largely unnoticed, the past few years have seen something of a resurgence of a form of seigniorage, with the unconventional policy of "quantitative easing" undertaken in the United States, Japan, the United Kingdom, and the eurozone since the Global Financial Crisis. This policy takes the form of the acquisition of a wide range of financial assets financed by creating additional commercial bank reserves at the central banks. In 2014, the Federal Reserve paid a record $96.9 billion in profit to the U.S. Treasury:[133] three times the normal amount, and about one-third, for example, of total federal corporate income tax receipts. This action did not result in inflation—perhaps it prevented actual deflation—and has proved a handy source of finance.

Indeed, these days it is the risk of too little inflation, not of too much, that is the main concern in advanced economies. Stubbornly low inflation, and even falling prices, is a syndrome from which Japan has suffered since the early 1990s, signaling low demand and growth. Now some fear that other advanced economies may be headed in the same direction. The obvious but controversial remedy sometimes proposed is precisely to create money in the hope of stoking inflation. And these issues have been made still more prominent by the COVID-19 pandemic, with the unprecedented levels of public spending in the "whatever it takes" phase of the crisis raising questions as to how this spending will be financed. Some fear "fiscal dominance" of the kind that confronted the French revolutionaries in 1792: a shortfall of revenue below spending needs so massive that the gap can be filled only by printing money. Times have certainly changed, as the taboo on central banks holding significant amounts of public debt has been breached, at least in some advanced economies. When considering how to finance the massive Coronavirus Aid, Relief, and Economic Security Act in 2020, one proposal was to finance it by simply having the U.S. Treasury mint two $1 trillion coins and deposit them with the Federal Reserve— that may sound absurd, but is not so different from the less-transparent device of issuing bonds that the Federal Reserve then creates money to buy. Some worry that there could be severe tests of central banks' independence and commitment to price stability ahead. Most, however, alarmed by the low-inflation experience of Japan, see little risk of damage from monetary-induced inflation in the advanced economies ahead—but they do not rule it out.[134]

As we have seen in this chapter, governments use their coercive powers to extract resources not only in the form of what are recognizable today as taxes, but also through seigniorage and by borrowing. But they have found many other ways to finance themselves that are pretty much taxes in all but name. Their creativity in doing so is worth a chapter in itself.

3

By Another Name

If there is one thing about kings ... which we seem to learn from the
history books, it is that more often than not they were hard up.

JOHN HICKS[1]

HAVING MURDERED the Emperor Pertinax, in the year 193 the Praetorian Guard put the entire Roman Empire up for public auction. Unable to resist, the wealthy Didius Julianus outbid his competitors and
duly became emperor. But this "infamous offer, the most insolent excess of military licence,"[2] was not well received. Revolt followed. Sixty-
six days later, Julianus, deserted, with sad predictability, by the Praeto-
rians, was beheaded.

Though rarely sold wholesale in this way (not explicitly, at least),
governments through the ages have been more than willing to sell
some of their most valuable powers and rights. More generally, rulers
have found plenty of ways in which they can extract resources without
using the word "tax," ways that have often been not only particularly
burdensome but also downright nasty. Throughout much of history,
these revenue-raisers have often been at least as important as things
recognizable or labeled as taxes—and they remain surprisingly important now.

Elizabeth I to Spectrum Auctions

Among the unique powers of government is that of restricting to certain people the right to do certain things. Governments have been adept at turning that power into a revenue source by granting state monopolies: establishing some body, public or private, as the sole provider of a particular good or service. Competition is prohibited by law, and prices can then be set high enough relative to costs to generate a nice profit. When that agency is publicly owned, those profits accrue directly to the government and are indistinguishable in all but name from taxes. When it is privately owned, the company keeps the profits as they arise, but the government usually either takes (or taxes) a share of those profits or gets money up-front by selling the right to those future profits.

The first, longest-lasting and probably the historically most contentious example—some say due for a revival—is salt. Although so ubiquitous that it is now called "common," salt was once a precious commodity, valued both because a modicum is essential for health and for preserving food. Its importance was clear, for instance, to Roman soldiers, part of whose compensation was money for the purchase of salt. (The word "salary" comes from the Latin word *salarium*,[3] whose root means "salt," and the tradition lives on in the description of someone being "worth their salt.") Controlling salt supplies was thus an enormously powerful lever for extracting resources.

So it is that in China a salt monopoly has operated continuously (with only brief periods of nonenforcement) for more than two millennia, originating in 119 BCE during the reign of Emperor Wu of the Han Dynasty.[4] At first, Chinese governments garnered salt revenues by managing production and sales directly. Later, imperial bureaucracies reaped these revenues indirectly by selling salt rights to merchants, who in turn sold the salt in retail markets. In the last century of the Tang dynasty (circa 800–900), salt taxes constituted more than half of China's revenues and helped pay for additions to the Great Wall. Even now, it is illegal for anyone except the China National Salt Industry Corporation to sell salt for household use in mainland China.[5]

Tax evaders blaze a trail: Salt tax smuggling routes in Qing China.

Anything that is taxed, however, is liable to be smuggled. In Imperial China, a side benefit of the alarm this caused officials was the production in 1780 of a gorgeous map, sent to the Qing emperor by two governors of Yunnan to show how tax revenue there was being eroded by the smuggling of salt through mountain passes from neighboring Sichuan. In ancient régime France, massive variations in local taxes on salt, the hated *gabelle*, led to massive smuggling—and brutal punishment.

Looking beyond salt, the practice of rulers creating monopoly powers as a source of revenue goes back to at least medieval times in Western Europe. Peasants who brought their grain to the mill for grinding were sometimes assessed a fee by the lord of the manor and obliged to use his ovens to bake the bread, also for a fee.[6] But it was around the start of the seventeenth century that the practice really took off. This was the period in which the great trading companies—the world's first multinationals—were chartered.

Several of the most powerful companies the world has ever seen, and whose influence is still being felt, were founded in the seventeenth century. These included a string of East India Companies. The English version—which came to be *the* East India Company—was chartered in 1600, being granted a monopoly on trade with all countries east of the Cape of Good Hope and west of the Strait of Magellan. The Dutch company (the Verenigde Oost-Indische Compagnie, or VOC) was chartered in 1602, and the French version (Louis XIV's Compagnie des Indes Orientales) was formed in 1664. Arguably most successful of all—it still exists, with an unbroken history—was the Hudson's Bay Company, chartered by Charles II to have control over all territories whose waters flowed into Canada's Hudson's Bay, which went on to lord it over vast swaths of what is now Canada and parts of the United States. And there were many other such companies, less famous (or notorious), for Africa, the West Indies, and elsewhere.

Many of these companies acted more like governments than businesses, dominating huge amounts of territory, minting their own coins, and with clashes between them setting much of the course of colonial history. That, indeed, more than their fiscal contribution, turned out to be their main legacy. It was the victory of the East India Company in the 1757 Battle of Plassey over the nawab of Bengal and his French allies, for instance, which paved the way for Britain to become the dominant colonial power in India.

The fiscal terms of the charter of the Hudson's Bay Company were especially unusual. Charles II required only that the Company provide to him and his successors, should they stop by, two elks and two black beavers. They rarely did stop by, of course, but when Queen Elizabeth II did in 1970:

> as the Queen bent over to accept the symbolic rent, the beavers, not versed in court etiquette, relieved their tensions . . . by making love. "Whatever are they doing?" Her Majesty demanded of the HBC governor . . . "Ma'am, it's no good asking me . . . I am a bachelor." The Queen assumed her customary mid-distance gaze and murmured, "I quite understand.[7]

In Britain, the right of the Crown to sell "patents" in much the same sense as we understand it today—time-limited monopolies for new crafts and activities—was long established before the first Queen Elizabeth (1558–1603). In the later part of her reign, however, the sale of monopolies spread to humdrum items, including not only salt (familiar enough) but also vinegar, salting and drying fish, the transport of leather, sea coals, and smoked pilchards.[8] These monopolies did not themselves then raise huge sums for the monarch, but they were underpriced and so brought huge benefit to those favored enough to purchase them—like Sir Walter Raleigh, who held the patent to issue licenses for pubs—along with hardship to purchasers and infuriation (as well as discouragement of future activities) for those whose investments in these activities were effectively expropriated.

These monopolies became deeply unpopular—"bloodsuckers of the commonwealth," one member of parliament called them, bringing "general profit into a private hand."[9] But they proved hard to kill. Elizabeth foreswore their use (other than for new ideas) in 1601; the practice was revived, by her successor, James I; proscribed again in 1624; and brought back once more by his son, Charles I, who, in his search for money without recourse to parliament, made prodigious and much-resented use of them: In the late 1630s one-tenth or more of his income came from selling monopolies.[10] Only with the development of explicit excise taxes did the sale of monopolies over daily products decline.

Monopolization by the state itself of the production and sale of a few key items of daily life did quietly become routine. From 1890 to the eve of the First World War, 10 percent of the revenue of the British government came from the post office. Tobacco perhaps comes closest to salt in the longevity of state monopolization, and this, too, has occasionally caused trouble. In the turmoil of 1848, with Italian nationalists bristling at the overbearing influence of the Austrian Habsburg Empire, nearly 60 people were seriously injured or killed during the "tobacco riots" in Milan, when protestors demonstrated against the high taxes imposed by Lombardy's Austrian authorities, who maintained a state monopoly on tobacco sales. Tensions were inflamed by groups of Austrian soldiers ostentatiously smoking tobacco that the Milanese had pledged to deny to themselves.[11]

Through much of the twentieth century, activities were taken into the public sector not to raise revenue but precisely the opposite: because it was felt that efficiency and/or social considerations implied that these activities should be run at a loss. Take, for instance, the case of a bridge (as did another giant of our profession, Jules Dupuit).[12] A bridge is costly to build, but once built, the resource cost of one more person crossing it is usually zero. So it is undesirable to charge any toll for crossing the bridge: doing so can only lead to some people choosing not to cross the bridge even though they would like to, and their crossing it would cost society nothing. The problem then is that no private company will choose to build a bridge and then charge nothing for its use. The obvious solution is for the government to either build the bridge itself or hire a private company to do so. The same point applies more generally to other instances of "natural monopoly": activities for which average costs of production are lower at higher levels of output (the cost of the bridge per bridge-crosser is lower, the more crossers there are), which implies a benefit from concentrating production in a single firm and charging a price less than is needed to cover costs. Public ownership, it would seem, is the answer.

As experience with public ownership grew, however, so did doubts about its efficiency. In the United Kingdom, they came to a head with the election of Margaret Thatcher in 1979. Critics argued that the absence of competition led state-owned enterprises to incur unnecessarily high costs; another argument was that the cost of building the bridge (say) has to be covered somehow, and doing so from general taxation may be more harmful than allowing some private operator to charge for the service being provided. They also argued that, in any case, it is far from clear that many state-owned operations—the post office, for example—really did meet the conditions for a natural monopoly. The outcome in the United Kingdom was a substantial program of privatization: restoring publicly owned assets to private ownership.[13]

Nonetheless, state monopolies continue to play an important revenue-raising role in many parts of the world. Finland, Iceland, Norway, Sweden, Ontario and Quebec in Canada, and several U.S. states, for instance, have government-owned monopolies for the retail sale of alcoholic drinks. Perhaps most important in revenue terms, countries rich in oil and other natural resources often organize their extraction through state-owned companies, either wholly or through joint ventures.

One aspect of the renewed faith in private operation that has a back-to-the-future flavor is the revival of one of the more hated practices of the past: the sale by government of state-sanctioned monopolies. This has come to be the preferred method of allocating rights to resources that are in fixed supply and are owned publicly rather than privately—notably natural resources like oil or minerals (typically owned by the state) and telecoms (for transmitting signals over specific bands of the electromagnetic spectrum). The key difference is that these monopolies are now (preferably) allocated not as they were in Jacobean times (and in much of recent times, too) by "beauty contests"—the simple choice of those in power (and something Elizabeth I may have taken more literally)—but instead by auction schemes that, through competitive bidding, aim to extract from the buyer the full value that the activity is expected to generate.

The idea of auctioning is not new: The ancient Greeks auctioned mining concessions, Praetorian guards obviously knew all about it, and the United States has used auctions for some time for offshore oil, raising about $280 billion between 1954 and 1990.[14] But the use of auctions has spread in recent years, and the amounts raised have sometimes been spectacular: The mobile phone license auction in the United Kingdom raised about £375 for each person then living there.[15] James I and Louis XIV would have no trouble recognizing these practices. Nor, indeed would the ancient Babylonians, who reportedly auctioned wives, or Caligula, who auctioned the lives of the gladiators.[16]

Selling Sovereignty

That brings us, naturally, to Elvis Presley. And to why, more precisely, his face appears on postage stamps issued by Burkina Faso. Why, in a similar spirit, did the Isle of Man issue six stamps commemorating the 400th anniversary of the founding of Jamestown, the first permanent English colony in America? And why—irresistible examples abound— is Marilyn Monroe on postage stamps from Chad, Groucho Marx on stamps from Chechnya, and the Three Stooges and the X-Men on Mongolian stamps? And why are there Montserrat stamps depicting the Grateful Dead's late guitarist Jerry Garcia? Most of these stamps never even reach the issuing country's shores, being designed, produced, and marketed by a foreign agency to stamp collectors around the world that pay the issuing country for the right to do so.

These are examples of the "commercialization of state sovereignty."[17] Anyone could print and offer for sale postage stamps, drawing tastefully on Elvis themes or Disney characters, but (presumably) no one would buy them: They would lack the element of significance and legitimacy that comes from issuance by a national authority. This is just one manifestation of the insight that a "state's power is derived, at least in part, from its designation as a state"[18]—a power that can be used for revenue raising.

An important feature of this aspect of state power is that it is more or less independent of the wealth, tax base, size, or any other feature of the state itself. A small Caribbean island is no more or less a state than is any G20 member, and so has just as much power to issue stamps that will appeal to many foreign philatelists—or put in place a tax system that will appeal to foreign multinationals. But because such states may have fewer other resources, the commercialization of state sovereignty can be especially obvious and important for them.[19] They may have little else to sell. The tiny Pacific Ocean island of Tuvalu, for instance—remote and not richly endowed—struck on the happy idea of using its name to create the .tv domain and sold the rights to use it for $50 million, increasing its GDP by a whopping 50 percent.[20] Citizenship is another valuable and marketable attribute of statehood. As many as two dozen countries offer citizenship, or a path to citizenship, for a price. One estimate is that

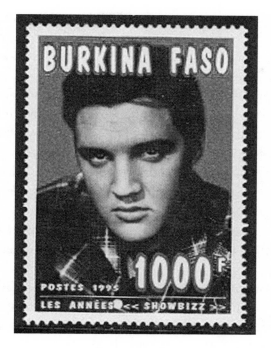

Return to sender.

St. Kitts and Nevis received in this way payments peaking at 14.2 percent of its GDP in 2014.[21] Some other Caribbean islands do much the same;[22] and larger and high-income countries also sometimes offer a perhaps more discrete path for large investors to buy citizenship.

Cheap Labor

Rulers have long found the hard work of others, and sometimes their lives, a handy resource.

Working for Nothing

Forced labor is as old as the hills. In fact, it made some of those hills. The world is dotted with tumuli—manmade mounds of earth or stone, often built over the graves of royalty—that required extraordinary amounts of labor. The construction of Silbury Hill in England, for instance—the largest tumulus in Europe (but mysteriously empty), dating back to around 2,400 BCE—is estimated to have taken about 18 million person-hours of hard slog.[23]

The great empires of antiquity also made heavy use of forced labor. The Egyptian Pharaoh Khufu (a.k.a. Cheops), who ruled in the 4th Dynasty (2551–2528 BCE), reportedly forced 100,000 workers to toil 3 months each year for 20 years to build the Great Pyramid of Giza.[24] Indeed in the ancient Egyptian language, the word "labor" was synonymous with the word "taxes." Forced labor was also heavily used in Imperial China. Qin Shi Huang (220 to 210 BCE), the country's first emperor, used forced labor for building ambitious public works, such as the Great Wall, the Grand Canal, and the system of national roads and highways.

Forced labor was also central to the feudal systems of medieval Europe. For the knight class, feudal service took the form of compulsory military service, along, typically, with providing for a retinue and equipment packing an appropriate degree of shock and awe: The greatest vassals of William the Conqueror were expected to provide 50 or so knights each.[25] For the peasants, it meant compulsory work in the field, fixing roads, and the like. Over time, these obligations were commuted into more explicit tax-like payments, though the timing and nature of the process varied widely. The transformation happened relatively early in England. In France, the nobility continued to claim exemption from explicit taxes largely on the grounds of the military service they were still in principle obliged to provide, while the levy on the peasants—the *corvée*—continued as a major grievance. In the Austrian lands, compulsory labor service, the *robot*, lasted until 1848.[26]

And it continues still. In Rwanda, the centuries-old tradition of *umuganda*, or community labor, persists:[27] unpaid work one Saturday a month. One recent study of ten developing countries found in-kind payments in the form of labor to be common in all of them.[28]

A Rich Man's War and a Poor Man's Fight

One form of forced labor sees these issues writ especially large, raises other issues, and has had a profound impact on the development of tax systems: conscription into the military.[29]

In modern times, the French introduced the *levée en masse* at the start of the revolutionary wars in 1793 and in 1798 established a permanent, regularized conscription system. Widespread insurance schemes quickly arose to cover the cost of a replacement conscriptee, in case a son was chosen in the draft lottery.[30] (The British, notably, did not then introduce conscription, but instead used their financial firepower to pay allies to do the bulk of the land-based fighting.) Conscription came to the United States in the Civil War: The Confederacy enacted it in May 1862, and the Union followed suit in March of the following year. It came to Britain in 1916, when too few volunteers stepped up to fill the rapidly depleting ranks of the regular army. In many Continental countries, meanwhile, conscription in peacetime—for just a few years, essentially as a form of training—had become the norm by the end of the nineteenth century. The draft could sometimes be avoided. The Confederacy initially allowed draftees to provide substitutes (hiring someone to take one's place), but this practice was later eliminated. The Union initially allowed both substitution and commutation at a price of $300—a tidy sum (something like $5,000 today), but one that a youthful John D. Rockefeller and future president Grover Cleveland[31] managed to come up with.

Some opponents of the draft asserted that only voluntary service would enlist the "best element" of society, implying that volunteers would be more patriotic and therefore better at soldiering. Conscription can also be critiqued from another angle: on the grounds that a volunteer armed force is a more efficient way of mobilizing resources, because people whose economic contribution to society (as indicated by the income they could otherwise earn) is relatively low will tend to find the armed forces more attractive. But there is a big problem with relying on voluntariness. The benefit from winning wars (or the costs of losing them) has many characteristics of a "public good," in the sense that it is hard to exclude from the benefits of victory those who made no contribution to it. The costs of fighting, however, are highly personal and potentially very high. Volunteer armies are thus likely to be systematically too small. This could in principle be addressed by paying sufficiently high wages, but that is a costly and potentially time-consuming route; one that the British in 1916, for example, on the brink of defeat and chaos, could not afford.

But efficiency is not everything. The ability to commute out of military service came to be seen as intrinsically unfair, violating the principle of "horizontal equity" (which we look at in chapter 6): the idea that people who are relevantly identical should be treated identically by the government. There is no difference, in this view, in the fitness for military service of young people simply because their parents differ in wealth. (Adolphe Thiers, first president [1871–1873] of the Third French Republic, took the contrary position, which has not proved a vote-winner: that the poor are better able to bear the conditions of the army camps, and sacrifice less in their work lives, than the well-off.) Commutation was not allowed in World War One or after in either the United States or the United Kingdom, or indeed in any major belligerent. There were exemptions, whether in terms of things like age or marital status (reflecting different dimensions of horizontal equity: married men were relevantly different from unmarried men) or for those in skilled occupations needed for the war effort—such as the "Bevan boys" (coal miners) in the United Kingdom during the Second World War. During the American Civil War, exemptions were widely available, and 41 percent of draft-eligible men received exemptions due to physical or mental impairment or being the only son of a widow, the son of infirm parents, or a widower with dependent children.[32]

Just as the rich often seem to find a way around high taxes, however, so many of them seem to find their way around conscription. In 1917, for instance, the American press grumbled over the widely publicized draft deferments obtained by the sons of Henry Ford[33] and newspaper magnate E. W. Scripps. It has not always been the case that, as one might suspect, the better off, if conscripted, find themselves in cushier jobs: In the First World War, 12 percent of the British army's ordinary soldiers were killed, but 17 percent of its officers.[34] Nonetheless, as we saw in chapter 2, the experience of mass mobilization in the twentieth century raised profound issues of fairness that underpinned support for the marked postwar increases in tax progressivity, generated new ideas on the taxation of income from capital and led to lasting changes in the size and role of government.[35]

When conscription is in place, problems of evasion and avoidance arise that any tax administrator would anticipate. There was outright (illegal) evasion. During the American Civil War, 19 percent of eligible Union army draftees failed to report for their medical examinations; and during the First World War, 12 percent of the men who were drafted in the United States became dodgers.[36] There was (legal) avoidance, too; marriage was no doubt encouraged where it conferred exemption. Some draftees showed up at the draft board with spurious wives or borrowed babies. Other issues arose from an excess of zeal that tax administrations rarely have to deal with, including wives occasionally bringing their husbands to the draft board for induction just to guarantee a regular income for the family (and sometimes, no doubt, for the sheer pleasure of sending them somewhere dangerous and far away).[37]

The tactics used to address draft noncompliance paralleled many of those used by modern tax administrations (the topic of chapter 13). Some avoidance devices were identified and closed down: During the American Civil War, exemption was available for "retracted testicles," but with the proviso that "voluntary retraction does not exempt."[38] Simple deterrence through risk of penalty was prominent, of course. But there were also measures intended to make it easy to comply. During the First World War, for example, the United States devised a draft system that made conscription look much like volunteering, or even voting, at least during the initial stage of the process. Local civilian volunteers registered eligible young men for the draft in a very similar way as persons registering to vote; for example, draft registration was held at each precinct's voting location.[39] And just as some countries now publish tax payments, partly in the hope of mobilizing public pressure for compliance, so the United States during World War One published the names of registrants, thereby implicitly outing nonregistrants. Social sanctions were also brought to bear, most notoriously through the "white feather" campaign in Britain, in which women castigated non-enlistees by sending or publicly handing them a white feather as a sign of cowardice.[40]

Doing Your Bit

When governments ask for gifts, you know they are in trouble. In the heady days of the revolution in 1789, the new National Assembly in France, having, as we have seen, enthusiastically amplified the fiscal crisis it inherited from the ancien régime, was soon appealing for patriotic gifts. This apparently worked for a while: Illustrious women appeared before the Assembly to donate jewelry, while even "the prostitutes of Paris and Versailles . . . offered a share of their earnings."[41] Nine years later, with the British by then deep into war with revolutionary France, Pitt the Younger sought a massive increase in revenue by his "Triple Assessment," which was actually a fivefold increase in tax liability for the better off. Nervous about the yield, he invited a voluntary top-up tax increase from those whose liability was still less than 10 percent of their income—which, with a mixture of disgust and relief, he found raised about the same amount of money as the widely evaded Triple Assessment.[42]

War has indeed been the main driver of gifts to government. Both sides in the English Civil War, from 1642 to 1651, were initially financed by gifts; the parliamentary force became known as the "thimble and bodkin army."[43] In Prussia, during the War of Liberation between 1813 and 1815, the royal family urged all citizens to contribute their gold and silver jewelry to fund the uprising against Napoleon. In return, the donors received iron jewelry, often with the inscriptions *Gold gab ich für Wehr* ("Gold I gave for defense") and *Für das Wohl des Vaterlands* ("For the welfare of the Fatherland"), or with a portrait of King Frederick William III on the back. The call was repeated during the First World War, when base-metal wedding rings, brooches, and jewelry picturing the Iron Cross were issued to patriotic citizens in return for their rather finer gold jewelry and ornaments. Mussolini followed suit in 1935, encouraging the public to donate gold jewelry in exchange for steel

Patriotic gift of illustrious French women.

wristbands bearing the words "Gold for the Fatherland"; his wife Rachele reportedly giving her wedding ring. Once the Second World War had broken out, in Britain the former prime minister Stanley Baldwin got into trouble not only for failing to prevent it but also for failing to donate his iron gateway to the war cause.[44]

It is not only in times of war, however, that gifts have been made to the state. In classical Athens, for some citizens the opportunity to provide liturgies was a welcome honor and an opportunity to display their wealth. For others—not so much. Even now, however, some people—at least in the United States—make voluntary contributions to government. In the late 1990s, financially strapped California saw contributions to local schools and school districts regularly exceed $100 per pupil and, in a handful of cases, $1,000 per pupil.[45] The explanation may be that, in the context of schools and school districts, a small community with close interactions among families has a group identity that leads to an informal, collective decision about how much to contribute. It also creates a social norm that, for some people, overcomes the incentive to free ride on the contributions of others. Consistent with this, the

"Gold I gave for defense, iron I took for honor."

level of contributions to schools was on average lower in larger communities, where it is more difficult to maintain such a social norm.

Less easily explained than contributions to local schools is that some Americans make gifts to the federal government. Since 1961, Congress has allowed people to contribute to reducing the national debt, and since 1982, the Internal Revenue Service (IRS) has included instructions in its income tax booklet on how to do so.[46] But this voluntary giving is unlikely to eliminate the U.S. federal deficit problem any time soon. In 2017, these contributions totaled $2.7 million, roughly 0.0001 percent of federal tax collections in that year. Occasionally, though, someone donates a substantial amount—in 2014, one anonymous donor contributed $2.2 million.

And sometimes, of course, gifts are not really so voluntary. Making a gift on the birth of a son to the Roman Emperor or to medieval kings may not have been compulsory but was certainly wise. "Benevolences"— gifts invited by the monarch—were a familiar resort of both the Tudors and the early Stuarts. Elizabeth I at least received these with good grace:

The Mayor of Coventry, handing her £100 in a handsome purse, elegantly told her that this came with a more precious gift for her, the hearts of her loyal subjects; "a great deal more, indeed," she responded.[47] Charles I could not muster the same charm: In 1622, he gave an 80-year-old cheese monger the choice between making him a large cash gift or serving cheese to the army in the field.[48]

Paying Your (Feudal) Dues

The period of high feudalism was marked by a bewildering array of compulsory payments to those higher up the feudal food chain. Among them was an obligation to pay ransom, explicitly listed in Magna Carta of 1215 as not requiring consent.[49] And, as it was for the subjects of Richard the Lionheart, ransoms could be big money. Things have not, though, always worked out as planned.

On September 19, 1356, at the Battle of Poitiers, Jean le Bon, the King of France, was defeated and captured by Edward, the Black Prince, son of the King of England. A rich prize, le Bon was taken to London, and a hefty ransom of 4 million *écus d'or* (plus payment for his upkeep) demanded. Le Bon's son, however, threw a spanner in the works by rejecting these demands. Negotiations followed, and le Bon was released in 1360, against the promise of a (cut-price) ransom of 3 million *écus d'or* and the holding hostage by the English of two of his sons and his brother. One of those sons, however, threw in another spanner by fleeing back to France. And then, in an extraordinarily chivalric gesture, le Bon took himself back to custody in London where, in 1364, he died.

In time, the feudal dues became central to the conflict over who exactly should exercise the coercive powers of taxation. In Britain, crisis came with the cash-strapped, Parliament-allergic Stuarts, who made heavy use of other feudal devices, often anachronistic even at the time. This was a period of "bastard revenues, neither medieval nor modern, neither legal nor illegal, unjustifiable in theory and indispensable in practice."[50] In 1631,[51] for example, Charles I, during his attempt to rule without parliament, rediscovered and applied the "distraint of knighthood" (based on a law of 1278),[52] which obliged all with land worth more than £40 to pay to assume the honor of a knighthood at his coronation in 1628—3 years earlier. During his reign, fining those who had failed to do so raised about £180,000.[53] The Crown also had the right to a fee on the assumption of property by heirs, recognizable as a form of inheritance or estate tax.

The king's right to levy these charges was not disputed. Nor was his right to levy "ship money": a charge on coastal towns and counties to provide, in times of emergency, a specified tonnage of ships and men to go with them.[54] Revived by Charles I in 1634, there was initially little opposition: This charge was fairly familiar (last used in 1619) and seemed reasonable enough when Barbary pirates were active near the English coast. The next year, however, the charge was extended inland. And in 1636, it was held that the king was the "sole judge" of whether there was indeed an emergency. Here then were the ingredients for permanent, substantial taxation without any need for parliamentary approval: Ship money was "the ultimate expression of the ingenuity of the king's advisers in the invention of means to enable him to rule without a parliament."[55] Things went downhill, slowly at first.[56] In 1638, judgment went against John Hampden for nonpayment (of £2 17s) by the narrowest of margins. Compliance fell as the ship writs went out each year. For the 1639 writ, only 20 percent of the amount sought was received in a reasonable time.[57] Faced with the need for more money to finance war with the Scots, the King recalled Parliament in 1640, and—in the short period before being dismissed once more—promptly forbade ship money and distraints of knighthood, and insisted on the curtailment of the king's tax and other powers set out in its 1628 Petition of Rights.[58] Civil war came in 1642.

The civil war put an end to feudal dues in Britain. But some quaint reminders remain. "By appointment to Her Majesty the Queen" is something that many British companies—such as Fortnum and Mason, and (formerly) Harrods—are proud to display on their products and store signs. This phrase is a reminder of the medieval right of "purveyance," by which British kings and—an ardent user—Elizabeth I were able to buy goods at below-market prices, a perk they made full use of. Monarchs have not always been such welcome customers as they are now.

Crossing the Line

The prospect of fines and other penalties on transgressors is one of the main ways in which governments try to make sure that taxes are actually paid. More generally, rulers through the ages have learned to turn law enforcement into a paying business.

The Babylonian king Hammurabi (1792 to 1750 BCE) decreed that stealing livestock be punished by a fine equal to up to 30 times the value of the stolen property.[59] In ancient Rome, anybody caught tampering with the water system had to pay a hefty fee of 100,000 sesterces.[60] And one of the few things that rulers tend to like about treachery is that the punishment has not only usually been gratifyingly grim but also remunerative, involving (until 1870 in the United Kingdom) the forfeiture of all property. The Emperor Tiberius (14–37) became notorious for using trumped-up treachery charges as a revenue source. During the French Revolution, the government confiscated the property of those condemned to the guillotine; a popular euphemism for saying that executions were under way was "they are coining money in the Place de la Révolution" (the location of the scaffold).[61] In similar spirit, and as another of his revenue-earners from breaking with Rome, in 1531, Henry VIII fined the English clergy a massive £118,000 for the offense of *praemunire*—asserting the jurisdiction of the Pope.[62] This was about 30 percent more than his annual recurrent revenue before the break with Rome.

The prospect of revenue from fines can spur impressive diligence in law enforcement, as those crossing city lines in parts of the American South and elsewhere have occasionally found. Doraville, Georgia, a 4-mile-square town with just over 10,000 residents, collected $2.2 million in fines in 2013, nearly one-fourth of its total revenues.[63] Many fine-happy towns line Highway I-75, a main route for Disney World–bound tourists, suggesting that this is another instance of the centuries-old taste for taxing "foreigners." In Ludowici (also in the state of Georgia), during the 1960s members of the local police constabulary, ensconced in a barbershop, allegedly manipulated the timing of the downtown traffic signal to catch unsuspecting out-of-town motorists running a

Speed trap or tax relief? Georgia, 1970.

suddenly changed red light. This abuse prompted the then-Governor of Georgia, Lester Maddox, to take the unusual step of erecting billboards warning motorists to stay away from Ludowici. Now the state of Georgia forbids speeding fines (except those for egregious moving violations) from exceeding 40 percent of a police department's budget.[64] But some extraordinarily pervasive reckless driving does seem to continue: in 2015, the Texas town of Palmer, population 2,023, wrote 1,080 speeding tickets in a month.[65]

Speeding tickets are irritating, but the amounts raised by fines and the like have sometimes been spectacular: $206 billion, for instance. This was the amount for which, in 1998, the four largest U.S. tobacco companies[66] settled with the attorneys general of 46 states,[67] who sought recovery of their tobacco-related health-care costs. Sweetening the pill, the companies gained exemption from private tort liability regarding harm caused by tobacco use. But this "Tobacco Master

Settlement Agreement" was not really a fine. Payments were not related, for instance, to past sales of cigarettes, and companies other than the four largest, along with new entrants into the industry, are effectively liable to payment under its terms. And it was obvious to all involved that the bulk of the real burden of the settlement would fall not on the tobacco companies or their shareholders or executives, as a penalty presumably would be intended to, but on future smokers. Indeed, the payments are effectively structured as a tax on future cigarette sales: Agreement was struck on specified money amounts for the next 25 years (adjusted for inflation and changes in sales), which are then spread across the companies in proportion to their market shares. So the more a company sells, the more it has to remit[68]—which is a tax. But it suited everyone not to call it that:

> The states had an incentive to frame their actions as a victory over "big tobacco" rather than a tax increase. . . . The contingency-fee lawyers could get fees as a percent of "damage payments" but maybe not as percentage of tax increases. And the companies wanted to describe their concessions as being painful rather than admit to having sold out their customers by agreeing to cigarette tax hikes in return for protection from lawsuits.[69]

And There's More

Here are two final examples of humankind's almost endless inventiveness in devising nontax taxes.

Jobs for the Boys

Venality—the sale of public positions, turning them into a form of personal property—has a long-enough history to have been condemned by both Plato and Aristotle.[70] It became widespread in Europe, nonetheless, from the early sixteenth century: modestly in Britain,[71] extensively in Spain, and pervasively in France. In the latter, it became a way of life: a "sprawling, tentacular state apparatus."[72] Already by 1522, a distinct government office, the *Parties Casuelles,* had been established to administer the increasingly complex system. In the 1630s, venality was bringing in a quarter or more of the king's revenue.[73] While it never returned to such importance in revenue terms,[74] venality was still going strong at the end of the ancien régime in 1789, by when perhaps 1 percent of all adult men held some venal position.[75]

There were offices to suit all pockets, from Parisian docker to the highest nobility. The grandest—accounting for perhaps three-quarters of the value of all offices in 1771, and about 18 percent of officeholders[76]— provided periodic payments to the officeholders (*gages*), and so were analogous to government borrowing in the form of annuities, with the *gages* generally set explicitly as a percentage of the price paid. Reinforcing the analogy, most venal positions also carried some fiscal privileges, exemption from the *gabelle,* for instance, or—most prized, not least as a sign of status—the *taille,* the most important direct tax.[77]

The system was, in effect, a massive, implicit borrowing operation: Jacques Necker—de facto minister of finance[78] from 1777 to 1781 and again from 1788 to early July 1790—put the amounts paid by the king at around 20 percent of his total debt service.[79]

There was rarely any pretense that venality served any purpose other than money raising: "The creation," one edict made clear in 1637, "has been made rather to draw help from the moneys it yields . . . than from any necessity to increase the number of officers."[80] The political costs, however, proved heavy. By introducing extensive venality into both the judiciary and the collection of direct taxes, it created a set of creditors powerfully placed to resist either restructuring of the implicit debt (by reducing their rights) or removing tax exemptions. Reforms had by custom to be registered by the *parlements,* composed largely of venal officers. The attempt to do so in 1648 led directly to the first of the *Fronde* (the French civil wars of the mid-seventeenth century), and it was the failure of the largely venal Paris *parlement* in November 1787 to approve Brienne's tax reform that ultimately prompted the summoning of the Estates General, which then ushered in the revolution. Tax reform in the ancien régime was stymied less by the reluctance of an absolute monarchy to attempt it than by the ability—short-sighted, as it proved—of its creditors to prevent it.

Venality in France came to an end in that tumultuous meeting of the National Assembly on the long night of August 4, 1789. Strikingly, and a sign of the disrepute the system had fallen into, about half of the deputies in the National Assembly that unhesitatingly decreed its abolition were themselves holders of venal office.[81] For this genuinely noble act, they were indeed to be compensated. Less pleasant to report is that by the end of the process, in 1794, the compensation was to be in assignats.[82]

Few have embraced venality as fully as ancien régime France. There is a similar flavor, however, to the use of honors in Britain.[83] These have been used as a form of payment-in-kind as, in the confident expectation of some title, generations of civil servants have hidden their contempt for their masters and worked for wages lower than they might otherwise have earned. But honors have also been sold for cash, and not always to the benefit of the state. Prime Ministers Lloyd George and Tony Blair both got into trouble on this score, the former selling honors for personal gain[84] and the latter nominating for life peerages men who had lent large amounts to the Labour Party. And, less remembered, some honors were created precisely to be sold. James I, having also sold knighthoods in unprecedented quantities, created the baronetcy in 1611 and priced it at £1,095. This came with a promise to sell only a fixed number, but (a temptation to which many monarchs succumb) he reneged: by 1622, a baronetcy could be bought for the knock-down price of £220.[85]

A Tax on Stupidity

Not our words, but, reportedly, Voltaire's. He had in mind lotteries, which appear as a source of government revenue as far back as the Chinese Han Dynasty (205 to 187 BCE). His point was that lottery organizers only make money if, on average, those making the bets lose—which they may happily do, because they overestimate their chances of winning, or perhaps because they simply enjoy the bet itself.[86] (Curiously, Voltaire himself once made a fortune by winning a lottery—by buying up all the tickets, which he and a mathematically inclined friend had worked out were underpriced.)[87] Stupidity or not, the widespread attraction to betting has tempted governments, for centuries, into the lottery business, with their profits akin to a tax—and a pretty regressive one, too.[88]

The 1607 establishment of Jamestown—the first British colony in America—was partly financed by a lottery introduced by James I. William III (1689–1702) and Anne (1702–1714) both also used lotteries to raise money. So did the French, where the first state-run lottery was run—presumably when he did not have better things to do—by Giacomo Casanova. The American colonies jumped on the bandwagon, using lottery proceeds to fund public-works projects such as bridges, libraries, roads and lighthouses. By the outbreak of the American Revolutionary War in 1775, about 160 colonial lotteries were pumping out tickets of chance.[89] Widespread abuses, including bribery of public officials, prompted a prohibition on lotteries in 1894 that lasted until New Hampshire broke ranks in 1964, following a state referendum. As of 2019, 44 U.S. states sponsor lotteries, with sales in 2015 amounting to $73.9 billion and profits of $20.9 billion.[90] Stupidity, if such it is, can be a lucrative source of revenue.

The list of nontax taxes could be continued. Indeed, many of the things that governments do that do not actually raise revenue are usefully best seen as forms of taxation. Take, for instance, the 1351 Statute of Laborers, which prohibited workers from seeking, and employers from paying, more than the nominal wage before the Black Death of 1348–1349. That was in effect a tax on laborers, equal to the difference between their market wage and its pre-plague level, the proceeds of which went to their employer. Conceptually, price regulation is much the same thing as taxation.

———

In this first part of the book, we have seen that governments over the millennia have been impressively adept and creative in financing themselves, and that while their precise methods have changed, the fundamental problems they faced in exercising their coercive tax power have not. These are to find ways to tax—and from here on we focus on what are taxes in name as well as substance—that not only raise the revenue needed but are also perceived to be at least fair enough for the regime to survive, that do not cause too much collateral damage to the wider economy (maybe even do some good), and that can actually be enforced. The next three parts of this book address these fundamental problems in turn. We start with the first and perhaps most critical of all: What have the past few millennia taught us about what makes a tax "fair"? And, a more subtle question to which that inevitably leads: Who, in any case, really bears the burden of taxation?

PART II

Winners and Losers

The obscure millions of a great empire have much less to dread from the cruelty than from the avarice of their masters; and their humble happiness is principally affected by the grievance of excessive taxes, which, gently pressing on the wealthy, descend with accelerated weight on the meaner and more indigent classes of society.

EDWARD GIBBON[1]

4

Fair Enough

Neither are men wont so much to grieve at the burthen itself,
as at the inequality.

THOMAS HOBBES[1]

IN THE YEAR 60, Queen Boudicca of the Iceni—spear in hand, "in
appearance most terrifying, . . . the glance of her eye most fierce"[2]—
harangued the army she had raised in revolt against the Roman occupi-
ers of Britain:

> Have we not been robbed . . . of most of our possessions . . . while for
> those that remain we pay taxes? . . . Do we not pay a yearly tribute for
> our very bodies? . . . How much better to have been slain and to have
> perished than to go about with a tax on our heads![3]

Those, at least, are the words put in her mouth a century later by the
historian Cassius Dio. In truth, he presumably had hardly the faintest
idea of what, if anything, she really said, and the speech he gives her had
more to do with rhetorical effect and his detestation of Nero, emperor
during the rebellion, than with historical accuracy. Better remembered
as a source of rebellion is the effective disinheritance and whipping of
Boudicca by the Romans, and the rape of her daughters, on the death
of her husband. Whatever imaginative liberties Cassius Dio may have
taken, however, oppression via tax-like means by a resented elite was

evidently among the causes that enraged the tribes gathered by Boudicca enough for them to burn Colchester and London to the ground, butchering any Romans or collaborators they could get hold of. Rome's control of Britain was saved only by a massively outnumbered but tactically astute and well-armed force of legionaries that, somewhere in the midlands of England, destroyed Boudicca's army. The Romans did, though, learn a lesson: After ruthlessly suppressing the revolt, they installed a new governor, who was expected to be more attuned to local sensitivities.

The wider truth illustrated by the revolt is that, even leaving aside any intrinsic concern with equity, no government that cares about its own survival, physical or electoral, can afford to ignore how oppressive or unfair it is perceived to be. That is, it needs to be fair enough. How a government goes about taxing is just one aspect of how fair it will be seen to be. But, given the direct impact that taxation can have on the everyday lives of ordinary people, it is perhaps the most powerful.

Fairness in taxation has many and overlapping aspects, which economists commonly divide into two. One is the relative treatment of rich and poor[4]—"vertical equity." The other is the treatment of people differing in some respect other than their material prosperity—"horizontal equity." This chapter and the next focus on vertical equity, leaving horizontal equity to chapter 6. We start with lessons from some episodes of what proved to be disastrously unfair taxation, before looking at what vertical equity might actually mean. We then see how, long before the modern income tax, governments have tried to make their tax systems at least fair enough for them to avoid the fate of the Roman settlers of Colchester.

Heads on Pikes

One of the most foolproof ways that governments (notably the English) have found to violate basic notions of vertical equity and jeopardize their own survival is to charge everyone the same amount of tax, taking no account of their differing material circumstances: a "poll tax." Some, it has to be said (notably the French), have managed to find an even more offensive approach by actually taxing the rich and privileged less than the poor.

Poll Taxes and the English

"Hegel remarks somewhere" remarks Karl Marx, somewhere, "that all great, world-historical events . . . occur . . . twice. He has forgotten to add: the first time as tragedy, the second time as farce."[5] As if for the sheer pleasure of doing so, the English have provided a magnificent illustration of this with their catastrophic tax choices of 1380 and 1990— the main difference being that while in the latter case the levy was called a "community charge" but was actually a poll tax, the former is known to history as a poll tax but was actually a community charge.

The tragic episode began with the meeting of a bad-tempered parliament in wintry Northampton late in 1380. It faced an appalling fiscal crisis: The new Lord Chancellor and Archbishop of Canterbury, Simon Sudbury, announced that they needed to find £160,000—an unprecedentedly large amount. Even the crown jewels had been pawned. And the country was in a foul mood. After initial successes, including the capture of the chivalrous French king Jean le Bon at the battle of Poitiers in 1356, the tide of the seemingly endless war with France had turned against the English, and fear of invasion was real. There was trouble on the Scottish border. And the lower orders were getting uppity. The Black Death of 1348–1349, which killed something like one-third of the population, had created massive pressures toward higher wages for the commoners and lower rents for the landholders—which the government was resisting, notably through the 1351 Statute of Laborers. That created its own strains: "Unless he [the landless laborer] be highly paid," says William Langland in *Piers Plowman*, "he curses the king and all the king's justices for making such laws that grieve the labourer."[6] The villeins— unfree serfs holding land in return for the payment of feudal dues[7]— were deeply resentful of the myriad of charges they faced. Added to all that, a revolt in the cloth manufacturing centers of Flanders had hammered the wool trade (and the considerable revenue it yielded). Parliament was meeting in Northampton because London had become too dangerous. About the only the source of optimism was that the country had a new boy king: Richard II.

The usual way of meeting the extraordinary revenue needs that war often led to was the "fifteenth and tenth." This was a tax on the value of movable goods—seed corn, agricultural tools, farm animals, and the like[8]—charged at the rate of one tenth for urban areas and royal demesne (land held by the Crown) and one fifteenth for rural areas.[9] After 1334, this tax was levied not at the individual level but as a fixed amount to be raised by each community, in line with its 1334 payment, in whatever way they wished.[10] The problem with this approach was that communities had been very differently affected by the Black Death, so that their relative prosperities in 1380 differed greatly from those in 1334.[11]

Caught between this antiquated instrument and spiraling revenue needs, the governments of the later 1370s tried more novel methods. One, in 1379, was a tax related to social class, of which more later. Before that, in 1377, they tried what the chronicler Walsingham called "a tax hitherto unheard of":[12] the splendidly named "tallage of groats" or, as it has come to be more prosaically known, the first poll tax. It was a charge of one groat—four pennies—on all adults over 14.[13] This had not gone too badly. It reached a massive number of taxpayers: 1,355,201[14] (in a population of 2–3 million)—coverage likely not reached again until the twentieth century—and ran into little opposition (except from the clergy, brought into tax for the first time). So the Northampton parliament decided to go down this route one more time—but at a massively increased rate: one shilling for every adult over 15, excepting "very beggars." This was a threefold increase over the 1377 rate, equivalent to several days work for an average agricultural worker, and was being levied at a time of year when people went hungry before harvest. It is this poll tax that has gone down as a proximate cause of the 1381 Peasants' Revolt.

Except that it was not really a poll tax. It was conceived not as literal payment of 1s by all, but as an average payment of 1s per head in every community. The law explicitly envisaged that "the strong might aid the weak."[15] The poorest were to pay at least 4d for a married couple[16]—an amount that had proved tolerable in 1379—but the richer were expected to aid the poorer up to a maximum payment of £1 for a married couple. Odd though it seems to us, the idea that the rich would help out the poor was not unfamiliar: Some such sharing of the communal obligation was an established part of the usual post-1334 fifteenth and tenth. Nor was it meaningless. In Brockley, a village in Suffolk, for instance, the willingness of an esquire and wealthy landowners to pay more meant that the poorest escaped with paying only the minimum 4d.[17] The 1381 poll tax would be better described by the term Mrs. Thatcher would later use: a "community charge."

It was soon clear, in any case, that the tax was in big trouble. The early returns suggested that much of the population of England had vanished. New and sterner commissioners were sent out to find them, but their behavior simply stoked animosity. Asking tax inspectors to verify whether young women are under or over the age of 15, it turns out, is not a good idea. Soon the countryside was in arms, with the rebels marching on London, beheading and destroying records along the way. The mysterious Wat Tyler—perhaps an experienced veteran of the French war[18]—emerged as a leader of the revolt, enraged, according to a legend, by the treatment of his daughter: "The daughter screamed, the mother screamed. Wat the Tiler . . . struck the collector dead at a blow."[19] By sundown on June 13, 1381, the rebels controlled London. Next day, the young King Richard—then 14 years old—meeting them at Mile End, conceded all their demands, which boiled down to granting them freedom. Clerks were set busy on the paperwork. Lord Chancellor Sudbury, meanwhile, was dragged from his prayers to be beheaded— requiring (or at any rate receiving) eight blows. His head was soon on a pike on London Bridge. It was the next day, however, that saw one of the great set pieces of English history.

For some reason—perhaps because Wat Tyler had not been present at Mile End—the rebels sought another meeting. This brought the boy king and Tyler, with their forces behind them, face to face at Smithfield. Tyler, it seems, showed disrespect to the king, maybe fingering a dagger, or swigging beer. A scuffle breaks out, Tyler is stabbed by the Lord Mayor of London, hacked by others, and falls dead from his horse as he makes his way back to his lines. The rebels ready their bows. But at that

A spectacular tax revolt fail: The death of Wat Tyler.

point the young king rides over to the rebels: "Sirs, will you shoot your King? I will be your chief and captain, you shall have from me that which you seek. Only follow me into the fields without."[20] And, having always proclaimed loyalty to the Crown, they did so. By nightfall, the revolt was effectively over.[21]

Reneging and retribution, however, followed swiftly. Wat Tyler's head replaced Sudbury's on London Bridge, the writs of freedom were canceled, and the king was soon telling a deputation foolish enough to reiterate some of the rebels' demands: "Villeins ye are still, and villeins ye shall remain."[22]

Parliament knew, however, that this had been a very close call. It quietly repealed the poll tax and went back to the fifteenth and tenth. This time, however, the landowners undertook to pay it all themselves, explaining, in an early example of English understatement, that this was "for the support, aid, and relief of the poor commonalty, who appeared to be weaker and poorer than theretofore."[23]

The 1381 poll tax was not the deep cause of the revolt: it did not even figure among the demands at Mile End or Smithfield. That lay in the attempt to deny to the lower orders the opportunities created for them by the radical shift in economic realities following the Black Death. But this was, nonetheless, a perfect storm of tax missteps. The tax was seen as burdensome and unfair; its administration was appallingly intrusive and offensive; it amplified severe pre-existing economic hardships and social tension; and the government imposing it had lost credibility and respect.

Failure to learn from history is a potent source of folly. Exhibit A: the poll tax levied by Margaret Thatcher's Conservative government in 1990.

Mirroring the tragedy of 1381, this also had its origin in the imperfections of a traditional tax that had come to be based on outdated valuations. The culprit this time, playing the role of the fifteenth and tenth, was the system of "rates": taxes applied to the rental values of both residential and business properties. This had been the main source of finance for local governments in the United Kingdom for generations. Revaluations, however, were rare. Mrs. Thatcher's Conservatives also believed that the residential rates system created a disconnect between the landlords who, on the surface, financed local government spending, and the tenants who benefited from (and voted on) it. As a consequence, they argued, local governments tended to bloat uncontrollably. There are, of course, issues here as to who really bore that tax: One would expect, for instance, that landlords would to some degree pass on the burden of the rates by charging higher rents, so that tenants bore some of the real burden even though they were not liable for remitting any tax.[24] But for those who did not have to hand over the money, the salience of the rates—that is, the extent to which they directly perceived the burden they were bearing—was evidently low. That, in any case, is what Mrs. Thatcher's government believed.

By the late 1970s, the need to reform local government taxation was widely accepted. The solution hit on by the Conservative Party was the "community charge." This was an annual tax of a fixed amount, irrespective of people's income or other circumstances[25] (though varying across local authorities according to their spending and how much they received in grants from the central government). Consistent with Mrs. Thatcher's core principle that "everyone should contribute something and therefore have something to lose from electing a spendthrift council,"[26] only prisoners were wholly exempt. And there was no 1380-style provision for the strong to help the weak. This was a real poll tax.

These reforms were "unusual in UK taxation history, in that . . . the entire package was informed by a unifying and coherent principle, namely accountability."[27] Financing local services through visible local taxes is generally seen as a good idea, enabling the political process to balance local desires for beneficial spending with local reluctance to levy taxes. And some recent scholarship on the fiscal sociology of taxation emphasizes the importance of having large numbers of people remit tax in order to increase citizens' engagement in holding their government accountable.[28] Intellectually, this was not the stupidest tax reform that any British government has ever attempted. But it was one of the most disastrous.

In England and Wales, where the charges went into effect in April 1990,[29] the average amount payable was around £360 per adult, almost 30 percent more than the government had projected.[30] The variation of the level of the poll tax across local authorities bore little obvious relation with local income levels: The charge was £499 in Hackney, one of the poorest boroughs of London, and £375 in the Royal Borough of Kensington and Chelsea, one of the richest.[31] The inequity of an evident shift of the burden from rich to the poor was keenly felt: "the Earl of Harewood . . . it's going to cost him something like £700 per year for his 4,000 acres of big mansion, and there are people living down here in this two-bedroomed house who are going to have to pay twice as much."[32]

A full-blown riot erupted in Trafalgar Square. Noncompliance was rampant and was equipped with a catchy slogan: "Can't pay, won't pay." Collections in the first year fell short of expectations by up to two-thirds, and in several London boroughs, one in every five taxpayers needed a summons before they paid anything.[33] Noncompliance spiked, unsurprisingly, where the level of the tax, and unemployment, were highest.[34] There was even another echo of 1381 in the impact on women:

usually secondary earners but subject to the same fixed amount, they felt the perceived unfairness especially keenly and were prominent in opposition to the community charge.[35] And just as the roots of the murderous rampage unleashed by the 1380 poll tax lay in decades of perceived oppression, so the 1990 poll tax was a culmination of what many saw as a decade of policies—a sharp shift in the balance of taxation toward the VAT and away from the income tax, confrontation with the trade unions, privatization—that were seen as systematically and deliberately harmful for the less well-off. In each case, the ammunition that the tax sparked had been long prepared.

By November 1990, the community charge was clearly doomed, and Mrs. Thatcher with it. In 1993, it was replaced by a new "council tax"— which looked (and still looks) much like the old system of rates.[36] There was, however, an electoral silver lining for the Conservatives. Noncompliers removed themselves from the electoral register,[37] which, as they tended to be the less well-off, benefited the Tories. Mrs. Thatcher was reported to believe that the poll tax "prevented many Labour supporters from registering on the electoral roll, . . . thus depriving Mr. Kinnock [the Labour Party leader] of a large number of votes. She puts the figure at one million."[38] And she may not have been far wrong. One estimate is that, without the poll-tax-induced failure to register, the Conservatives would still have won the April 1992 election but by a margin so small that they would have lost their majority with the first by-election defeat.[39]

Noble Causes

Much less well-remembered than the poll tax experiences, one of the most decisive transitions in English fiscal history—and its political and constitutional development—took place in the twelfth century. This was the replacement of the obligation of nobles to provide military service to the king (and likewise down the feudal food chain) by a system of cash payments known as "scutage." This development suited both sides: The nobles were spared from having to leave their lands to fight battles in France that were beginning to have little direct benefit to them, and the king was enabled to hire more of those scary foreign mercenaries. The change was gradual,[40] but scutage was well established by 1159 (another foray against the French, around Toulouse). The implications were profound. By accepting the practice of scutage, the nobility recognized some obligation to provide direct financial support to the king. And that, in turn, set the stage for nobles to insist on a measure of consent as to the amount to be raised. One of the most ringing provisions of Magna Carta, in 1215, was precisely that "scutage and aids shall only be levied in our kingdom by common counsel of our kingdom."[41] And so the principle was conceded that the nobles were willing to finance the king but expected to be consulted in the process.

Things played out differently, however, in much of continental Europe, where an increasingly meaningless feudal obligation was transformed into a tax exemption for the nobility. Such exemptions lasted into the eighteenth century in Prussia[42] and Habsburg Austria, and even longer in Hungary.[43] It was in France, however, that noble tax privileges did the most calamitous harm.[44]

At their core was a devil's bargain struck by Louis XIV, who secured the political emasculation of the nobility and clergy in exchange for their continued exemption from the *taille*—the closest France had to a tax related to wealth. Others were also exempted from the *taille*, including whole towns, large (Paris, not least) and small.[45] But it was the treatment of the nobility that most irked both the growing bourgeoisie and reform-minded ministers. Periodic attempts were made to overcome these tax (and other) privileges—even during the reign of Louis XIV[46]— but the nobility and the *parlements* (regional courts that had the power to confirm laws) that they dominated resisted or undermined these attempts at every turn. As late as the mid-1770s, nobles were still defending their tax exemption as a return for military service, driving the reforming Turgot, Controller-General of Finances (and former tax collector), to distraction with this "antiquated pretension abandoned by all intelligent men."[47]

Their exemption from the *taille* did not mean that the privileged were exempt from all direct taxes: the *capitation* (of which more soon), *dixième* and later the *vingtième*[48] were intended to apply to everyone, and the clergy made voluntary(-ish) payments in lieu of explicit tax obligations. These charges were whittled down over time, but nonetheless were in some cases a substantial levy on nobles. But these same taxes also applied to the nonprivileged, and so did not ease the inequality of tax payments. The tax burden in ancien régime France was not especially high, compared for example to that in England at the same time; it does though seem to have been shared extraordinarily unequally. When Pierre Samuel du Pont de Nemours—who played a prominent role in the Revolution and went on to found the du Pont dynasty in the United States—remarked that "there is only one way to escape tax, and that is to be rich,"[49] it was as much a description of ancien régime reality as it was a joke.

Just how important these tax inequities loomed is clear from the *Cahiers de doléances*: lists of grievances drawn up by each of the three Estates in the tumultuous spring of 1789. The Third Estate—broadly, propertied non-aristocrats—railed mostly about the financial privileges held by the nobles and clergy. Those of Dourdon, for instance, wanted all personal taxes abolished except for a tax on land and other property, to be borne "without distinction, by all classes of citizens and by all kinds of property, even feudal and contingent rights."[50] Parisians made their feelings clear on the night of July 12/13, 1789, when they ransacked customs posts around Paris, burning records and tearing down the wall that the tax collectors had built around the city to collect taxes on goods entering into it.[51] It was only after venting on taxation that, the next day, they went on to storm the Bastille. The nobility did, in the end, pay for its tax privileges.

Trying to Be Fair

These stories give us a sense of when taxes can be seen as egregiously unfair—and that this depends not just on their design, but on their implementation and the wider spirit of the times. But they do not give much idea of what would generally be regarded as "fair" taxation. One view is that fairness in taxation means you pay for what you get. Another is that it means you pay what you can.

Pay for What You Get?

"Who is it," asked the populist American politician William Jennings Bryan,[52] "most needs a navy? Is it the farmer who plods along behind the plow . . . ? [Or] is it the man whose property is situated in some great seaport where it could be reached by an enemy's guns?"[53] The implied question was: Why should the farmer pay for the navy? That was indeed the original logic, for example, of ship money in Stuart England discussed in chapter 3, which worked reasonably well when it was levied only on maritime towns and counties, presumably because it seemed an acceptable price to pay for a navy that would reduce the danger to them from pirates and privateers. It was an example of a tax levied according to the "benefit principle": that everyone's tax burden ought to be in line with the benefits they receive from the government.

But this reasoning does not get us very far. A payment for which commensurate benefit is received hardly qualifies as tax at all, since that, by definition, requires payment to be unrequited. And, as a practical matter, much of what governments do is not the provision of goods and services whose enjoyment is limited to identifiable individuals, but things that inescapably affect us all, like ensuring law and order, and providing for the common defense.

Taxation may be, as Oliver Wendell Holmes remarked, "what we pay for civilized society"[54]—the phrase that now adorns the headquarters of the Internal Revenue Service. But, if so, applying the benefit principle would require knowing how the benefits of civilization are shared out among us. Views differ. William Gates, Sr. (father of Microsoft co-founder Bill Gates) launched a campaign to defend progressive taxation in the United States on the grounds that the rich could not have become rich without strong legal and other institutions, physical infrastructure, and scientific research provided by government. In contrast, Charles Babbage, seen earlier worrying about the extension of the franchise, argued that it costs more to protect small capitalists than large ones: An apple seller on the street corner needed the police to prevent theft of the stock, whereas a great merchant house like Barings was able to avoid risk by shifting its capital around the world.[55] These days, the wealthy middle classes, secure in their gated communities and sending their children to private schools, may feel much the same. The implication is that the rich should pay less tax than do the poor. To many, that likely seems an unpalatable implication. Even short of that, however, the fundamental point is that the benefit principle is inherently hard to square, without some moral contortions, with the raising of revenue from one person for the purpose of benefiting another. Strictly applied, it points to very limited government.

In what might look like a form of benefit taxation, governments do sometimes earmark[56] the revenue from particular taxes to particular uses. In eighteenth-century England, for instance, receipts from certain taxes were committed to the repayment of specific loans.[57] And earmarking continues. Most prominently, social security contributions are so often linked to benefit entitlements that they are sometimes not thought of as taxes at all. But there is more to it than that. For instance, the United States still earmarks receipts from the federal excise tax on gasoline to expenditure on highways. And when Ghana raised the rate of VAT from 10 to 15 percent, the government promised that the additional revenue would be dedicated to improving health services. In some jurisdictions, earmarking is pervasive. In South Korea, about 17 percent of all government tax revenue was earmarked in 2005,[58] as, on average, was nearly one-quarter of all state revenues in the United States.[59]

Earmarking may make a tax increase more politically palatable by linking it to some popular spending project—or at least provide some assurance that the money will not just be absorbed in some mysterious morass of government spending. But the practice has several downsides. One is that there is no reason why the appropriate level of spending on something should be related to the revenue collected from any particular levy. Winston Churchill (who served as Chancellor of the Exchequer in the 1920s) put the argument best, speaking of vehicle levies:

> Who ever said that, whatever the yield of these taxes and whatever the poverty of the country, we were to build roads and nothing but roads, from this yield? We might have to cripple our trade by increased taxation of income. We might have to mutilate our Education for the sake

of economy. We might even be unable to pay for the upkeep of our fleet. But never mind, whatever happens, the whole yield of the taxes on motors must be spent on roads! . . . Such contentions are absurd and constitute at once an outrage upon the sovereignty of parliament and upon commonsense.[60]

Put more prosaically: "strong" earmarking (that is, tightly tying public spending on some item to some revenue source) can make it harder for government to spend what it receives in the most appropriate way. It may be, however, that earmarking is "weak," in the sense of not really constraining public spending. Money, after all, is fungible. Even though Ghana dedicated all those additional VAT proceeds to health spending— just by way of example—it might reduce its spending on health from other revenues, leaving total health spending increased by less than those VAT proceeds, or even, conceivably, reduced. So, if it bites, earmarking means inflexible budgeting. If it does not, it is "an exercise in . . . misleading taxpayers rather than expanding democracy."[61] For this reason, proposals to earmark tax revenue make public finance people very nervous.

Pay What You Can?

A second principle of tax fairness takes us a bit further toward the essence of current practice and thinking. This is the "ability-to-pay principle": the idea that the tax burden any individual bears ought to be related to their level of economic well-being. This idea runs through tax history. The first tax law in the American colonies—Virginia in 1634—spoke of assessing each man "[A]ccording to his estate and with consideration of all other his abilityes whatsoever."[62] That is, each person's tax burden should be related to their ability to bear the sacrifice of material well-being it implies. And the wealthier are likelier to have a higher ability to pay than the poorer: Handing over a dollar in tax is a lot less painful for a billionaire than for a single parent struggling to make ends meet. Few, we suspect—even the Northampton parliament that settled on the poll tax—would dispute that ability to pay matters for the fairness of any tax system. But two tricky steps are required to put the idea into practice.

The first is determining exactly what someone's ability to pay is. It being impossible to assess directly the happiness that their material circumstances give people, the natural approach is to judge the appropriate level of taxation using some external indicator of their material well-being: how much land they have, how many windows their home has, how much they earn. One problem with this is that any such external indicators are likely to reflect individuals' differing tastes and decisions, including their response to whatever taxes they face. And that leads to the idea that some inherent and immutable potential ability to pay should matter in shaping tax burdens. But a potential ability to pay is even harder to observe than a realized one.

The second tricky step, supposing we are able to identify everyone's ability to pay (observed or potential), is deciding precisely how the tax burden should vary across those differing abilities to pay. That is closely related to the question of what distribution of well-being after taxes are imposed would be most socially just.[63] Answering this question is a job for philosophers, not economists. One position, for instance, is the classical utilitarian view (associated with Jeremy Bentham) that the object of government should be to maximize the sum of such well-beings. Another (from the work of John Rawls)[64] is that the object of policy should be to maximize the well-being of the least well-off person (even if that reduces total well-being). And there are positions in between, attaching most weight to the welfare of the poorer among us but not entirely ignoring the richer. Economists, in any case, have no special wisdom for deciding precisely how policy ought to take into account differences in ability to pay. Ultimately, the ability-to-pay principle is just a grandiose expression of the intuitively appealing idea that an individual's tax liability should be linked to some measure of his or her material well-being, with reasonable people reasonably disagreeing as to what exactly that link should be.

Show Me a Sign

Long before the term was invented, wise rulers—through self-interest if not in pursuit of social justice—were looking for outward signs of ability to pay to which they could link tax obligations. Today's income tax is simply the point that this continuing process happens to have now reached.

Taxing by Class

In 1513, the youthful Henry VIII—not yet corpulent or multiply-wived, but, for the Venetian ambassador, "the handsomest potentate I ever set eyes on"[65]—set off on the traditional route to glory for English kings: across the Channel, to fight the French. And for once it ended well, in the "Battle of the Spurs"—so named for the rewarding sight of the French fleeing the field. But war was always expensive. To help pay for it, Henry levied a tax of £6 13s 4d on dukes, £4 on earls, £2 on barons, and so on, down to 4d on men older than 15 who had wages of less than 40s.[66]

This class-based tax was not a new idea. It was one of the innovations that the English tried, in 1379, before the catastrophic poll tax.[67] Nor was this its last outing. Between 1689 and 1698, Britain levied a variety of other taxes that varied according to social rank and condition.[68] In France, one of the attempts to circumvent the tax exemptions of the nobles was the *capitation* mentioned above, a class-based tax introduced in 1695 (and surviving until the Revolution) that divided society into 22 categories, with the highest charge, on the Dauphin, being 2,000 times that of the lowest, on day workers. In Prussia, a class-based tax (the *Klassensteuer*) was introduced (outside the towns) in 1821, with rural society divided into four social classes and some differentiation of tax payable, according to individuals' circumstances, within each.[69] That survived until 1873.[70]

Quaint though such taxes now seem, they have an obvious merit. In societies that were highly and explicitly stratified, social rank was a reasonable proxy for potential ability to pay. It was also easily observed and self-enforced by the massive powers of self-importance and pomposity— no duke, surely, would wish to be taken for a mere earl (and no peasant would want, let alone be able, to impersonate a highly taxed duke). In these circumstances, the tax would not lead to any form of avoidance. It would be (leaving aside outright evasion), in the jargon, a form of "lump-sum" taxation—meaning that tax liability does not depend on any action of the taxpayer—about which we will have more to say later. A poll tax is one form of lump-sum tax, but with the critical and distinguishing feature that (unlike, for example, taxes that vary by social class) everyone is charged the same amount.

Class-based taxes did, however, have more problems than this idealized characterization suggests. Doubtless some earls were better off than some dukes, but they would nonethless be charged less tax. Nor were pride and vanity enough to have made these taxes as self-enforcing as one might expect. On December 10, 1660, the diarist Samuel Pepys, having set aside £10 for his payment—the charge for an esquire—but finding himself assessed for just 10s, convinced himself, somewhat faint-heartedly, that "I think I am not bound to discover myself."[71] It seems too that "the Prussian subject, when it came to the question of taxation, did not seem to aspire to a high social position."[72] So these taxes fell short, in practice, of being truly lump-sum. And over time, of course, societies became more complex, and explicit social status ceased to be a good enough proxy for ability to pay.[73]

Taxing by Community

Herodotus tells how Darius the Great (522–486 BCE) divided the Achaemenid Empire into 20 satrapies, each with its required payment of gold or silver.[74] Kings (and kings of kings) had little concern about how exactly such tribute was raised. Something recognizably similar survived into modern times. As with the fifteenth and tenth of medieval England, taxes have often been set in the form of a quota, with the central ruler fixing an amount to be raised in some locality or region and then leaving it, in effect, to the regional or local elite to decide precisely how to come up with the money, subject to varying degrees of guidance for doing so.

In Britain, quota arrangements dominated direct taxation for centuries. Like the fifteenth and tenth, the later Tudor addition, the "subsidy," had its roots in notions of assessing individuals according to their specific circumstances; but it came to be a matter of fixed amounts raised in each locality according to custom. Assessing how much a particular

individual should contribute was in the hands of prominent local figures, often the leading landowners, using some underlying assessment
rules as a starting point but exercising considerable discretion. This approach "came to be regarded by the people almost as of constitutional
right."[75] With the introduction of the land tax[76] in 1693, an attempt was
again made to assess at the individual level—fixing a rate and taking
whatever revenue that produced. But revenue plummeted,[77] and from
1698, the government reverted to assessment by quota.[78] Pitt the Younger's income tax of 1799, the story of which is told in chapter 5, was remarkable not just for being a tax on income but also for marking a decisive step away from levying direct taxes by quota (specifying some
fixed amount to be raised) and towards defining liability in terms of
each individual's circumstances (specifying the tax rules and letting revenue then be whatever it turns out to be).

Quota arrangements were far from unique to England. In Renaissance Piedmont, the amount due from a community was assessed in
terms of land rents there, but the community could raise the money
however it wanted.[79] In Tokugawa Japan[80] and Imperial Russia,[81] tax
was imposed as a collective responsibility at the village level. So, too, in
the Abbasid caliphate, with the community responsible even for those
who had left the village.[82] In parts of ancien régime France, the *taille* was
levied by quota. And in colonial Vietnam, tax was levied on communities according to their presumed population—not unlike the 1380 poll
tax in England. If the sum was not remitted, the central tax authority
would hold an auction of whatever they could seize until they had collected the required sum. This system motivated the village notables,
who owned most of the goods worth seizing, to ensure that the taxes
were remitted.[83]

Quota arrangements have obvious attractions for the ruler, similar to
those of cruder tribute systems. They raised revenue and asserted authority without the need to maintain and monitor a large bureaucracy.
By delegating assessment and collection to local elites, they contributed
to stability by respecting established local power relationships. Seen
from a less self-interested perspective, they also provided a way in which
local knowledge could be used to make tax arrangements fairer and

more efficient than the blind application of common rules might be. So it was that such arrangements tended to persist for taxes related to people, while the more impersonal and less discretionary methods of tax farming, discussed in chapter 13, were more often used for the collection of taxes on transactions, as with customs and excises.

But that discretion, when seen as little short of favoritism, could also undermine stability. For instance, application of the land tax was a major political battleground in early eighteenth-century England, with bruising court cases and the naming of Land Commissioners a vexatious enough matter for the House of Commons to commonly vote on it: "Party spirit and the land tax made bad bedfellows."[84] Collection by quota also proved increasingly inflexible at a time when communities' relative prosperities began to change quickly. If one area within an assessed region came up short, the only possibility was to charge another one more. Short of the painful process of reassessment, the system could not accommodate the changing fortunes of assessed regions. No doubt, too, expanding horizons and the strengthening of a sense of national identity increased sensitivity to disparities of treatment across individuals in different regions, and the growing dominance of the center eased the need to placate and rely on traditional local and regional elites. Attention shifted, often very slowly, toward collection by rate rather than by quota, and—often an even later development—by bureaucrats answerable solely to the center.

The underlying attractions of quota arrangements—respect for local institutions, practices, and knowledge combined with a reluctance to create more new bureaucracy—still make it an attractive way to finance overarching supranational bodies. The European Union, for instance, rests on national contributions calculated according to each country's national income and VAT base, with each country free to come up with the money however it wishes. This is not so very different from how the United Provinces financed themselves in the late seventeenth century, with each province allotted a share of total revenue needed, to be financed however it chose.[85] One could even argue that the original article in the U.S. Constitution (which takes center stage in the next chapter) requiring direct taxes to be allocated across states according to their population was a way to ensure that whatever total tax the feds came up with, the implicit regional quotas would be "fair" relative to the population.

Taxing the Finer Things in Life

For the tax policymakers of eighteenth-century England, there were two good things about hats. One was that a rich person customarily owned a large number of expensive cocked hats and tricornes, whereas a poor one often claimed ownership of at most one cheap hat. The other was that it was easy to see whether someone was wearing one. And so, in 1784, the British government imposed the requirement that each hat have a revenue stamp pasted in its lining, with the cost of the stamp depending on the cost of the hat. Heavy fines befell those who failed to remit the tax; forgers of hat-tax revenue stamps could be executed. As, in 1798, the unfortunate John Collins was.[86] To avoid the levy, hatmakers stopped calling their creations "hats," prompting the government in 1804 to expand the duty to cover all materials used to make any kind of headgear.[87] Wigs, being similarly hard to hide (except beneath a taxable hat) and associated with a degree of prosperity, also attracted the attention of tax officials (as well as assorted pests). In 1795, the British government introduced an annual tax of one guinea on the right to apply the aromatic powders that men and women put on their wigs to mask odor. Pigtails then still being common, those who paid the tax were known as "guinea-pigs."[88]

Eighteenth- and nineteenth-century Britain produced many other taxes aimed at consumption items favored by the well-to-do, reflecting a principle laid down by Lord North in 1769: "Luxuries ought to be taxed . . . because the first weight ought to fall on the rich and opulent."[89] The consumption or ownership of particular items, that is, signaled some ability to pay tax. There was also, no doubt, an element of sumptuary taxation, keeping the lower orders in their station: The distinguished American economist Henry Simons referred disdainfully to textbooks implicitly defining luxuries as "commodities which poor people ought to do without and won't."[90] Clocks and watches, carriages, race horses, and the right to a coat of arms all had their special taxes.

Candle making at home was nearly snuffed out from 1709 to 1831, when people were forbidden to make their own candles unless they held a license and remitted tax. Many of these levies were structured to bear particularly on the better off. Wax candles, for instance, were taxed more heavily than tallow, and the very poorest were able to use untaxed rush lighting.[91] And a tax on male servants, to be remitted by the employer (1777–1882), was graduated according to the number of servants: 25 shillings per year for each of the first 10, but £3 each if 11 or more.[92]

The taxation of items associated with the rich was certainly not unique to Georgian Britain, and it continues still, often in the form of high import duties on goods deemed to be luxuries. As more or less random examples: In 2016, China imposed a 10 percent import tax on "super-luxury vehicles," defined as those priced above 1.3 million yuan (about $190,000); and in Nigeria, imports of yachts and luxury automobiles have been taxed at 70 percent. It is, nonetheless, Georgian Britain that takes the prize for the proliferation of selective excise taxes, especially though not only on luxuries. On the plus side, this cornucopia of excises at least became a ready source of good copy for generations of writers. By 1743, droll observers were complaining that "the Excise man is our constant companion from the crown of our head to the sole of our foot. If we clean our hair, he examines the powder. . . . He walks abroad in our shoes, at our tables he seasons our meats. . . . Is it daylight? He peeps in at our windows. Is it night? He shines in our candles."[93] In 1820, the wit (and clergyman, critic and philosopher) Sydney Smith could still complain that

> the dying Englishman pouring his medicine, which has paid 7 percent, into a spoon that has paid 15 percent, flings himself back upon his chintz bed, which has paid 22 percent, and expires in the arms of an apothecary who has paid a license of a hundred pounds for the privilege of putting him to death. His whole property is then immediately taxed from 2 to 10 percent . . . and he is then gathered to his fathers, to be taxed no more.[94]

This may all sound very silly. The proliferation of taxes on items that signaled some degree of affluence was evidently irritating, but the intention—to at least appear to be taxing more those with greater ability to pay—was clear. However, more fundamental difficulties result from the idea of targeting luxuries as a way to meaningfully tax the rich.

There is, as with any tax, the risk of unintended consequences. At least one attempt to target taxation on the rich failed, so it is said, due to pride. Until 1934, a toll was charged for crossing the lovely Queen Emma bridge in Curaçao. Hoping to alleviate the burden on the poor, the toll was levied only on those wearing shoes at the time of crossing. Curaçaoan lore holds that this scheme backfired, as many of the poor, too proud to admit their poverty, often borrowed shoes to cross the bridge, while many of the rich residents, too mean to pay, crossed barefoot.[95] Less quaint, but more systematic, is the point that just because a tax is attached to some luxury item does not mean that the real burden falls on those doing the luxuriating. Take, for instance, the British tax on maids and female servants introduced by Pitt in 1785 (and leave aside *The Time's* assertion that these were not a luxury at all, but a "staple commodity").[96] This tax proved especially controversial, the fear being that it pushed some women into prostitution. That could happen only if, at least in part, the tax was reflected not in an increased price paid by rich employers but in reduced wages of servants. The wider question that this issue raises—who really bears the burden of taxation?—is the topic of chapter 7.

Even if the burden of a tax on some luxury is sure to fall on those doing the luxuriating, however, targeting the rich by taxing luxuries faces two more limitations. One is that there is simply not enough spending on such items for taxes on them to raise very much revenue. Lord North, while recognizing that the first call should be on the better off, also saw the sad mathematical reality that "where great sums were to be borrowed the burden must lie upon the bulk of the people"[97] ("borrowing" here being something of a euphemism for "collected"). And so it was that, as seen in chapter 2, several necessities were indeed taxed in Georgian Britain.[98] The other problem is that consumption patterns reflect tastes as well as affluence. Not all rich Georgian gentlemen kept racehorses, for instance, and nor, we suspect, do all the very wealthy in Nigeria buy expensive yachts. There may even have been

Pitt, penury and prostitutes.

relatively poor people in Georgian England who had a thing about hats and wigs.

Presumptions of Prosperity

The approaches to making taxation reasonably fair that we have just looked at all use something reasonably observable—social rank, a region's prosperity, the consumption of particular things—that could be presumed to give some rough but reasonable indication of ability to pay. Governments have for centuries proved creative and energetic in looking for new and better proxies of this kind. At the same time as taxing a bewildering array of items consumed by the better off, the British—in similar presumptive spirit but sometimes with a larger revenue yield—were taxing land and windows, with the latter a successor to a tax on fireplaces. The list of presumptive approaches that governments have tried—taxing things related to ability to pay, though with no great pretense at exactness—is almost endless.

Taxes specified as fixed amounts for particular occupations have been a fairly common form of presumptive tax. The American colonies imposed "faculty" taxes on the presumed earnings of classified occupations.[99] Even today, Pennsylvania law enables counties, cities, boroughs, first-class townships, municipalities, and school districts to impose such a tax, levied at the highest level on physicians and at the lowest level on factory workers. Uruguay levied an occupation tax on "liberal professionals," such as architects, engineers, and lawyers, until 2007—presumably because it was proving simply too difficult to establish their true incomes. And one of the four taxes introduced in revolutionary France that were to last long enough to become known as *les quatre vieilles* (the four old women) was the *patente*,[100] a core element of which was a fixed fee that varied by profession. This practice, with various transformations, survived there until 1976. In parts of Francophone Africa, it lives on.

These days, consciously presumptive methods of this kind are most often found in relation to small businesses, which may find it hard to keep accurate records (or whose accurate records might be hard for the tax inspector to find). Some, like the Israeli *tachshiv*, which was in use officially from 1954 to 1975 and unofficially for a while afterward, looked at a battery of activity-specific indicators: A restaurant might be assessed, for instance, by some formula related to its location, square footage, number of tables, and perhaps the average price of items on the menu. This could become inordinately complex for relatively little revenue. More common now is to tax smaller businesses by reference to their turnover, perhaps at rates intended to reflect differing sector-specific markups.[101]

These modern and explicitly presumptive taxes are designed to approximate liability under an income tax that is now the central tool for pursuing vertical equity. And it is natural, looking back, to think of the taxes on social class, or on windows and the like, as strange landmarks along the way as our ancestors stumbled toward the modern income tax. The development of the income tax was indeed a culmination of the kind of efforts looked at in this chapter. Some, like Thomas Paine, saw it coming: "the real luxury" he wrote, critiquing the excises of eighteenth-century Britain, "does not consist in the article, but in the means of procuring it."[102] Income is indeed likely to be a better indicator of affluence than how many clocks or racehorses one has. But the income tax also has an element of presumption: Someone's income over a period of 1 year, for instance—reflecting the decisions and opportunities they happened to take and face over those months, and the stage of life they are in—may say very little about their level of affluence and their potential ability to pay. The advent of the income tax was not the end of tax history. It did, however, bring its own lessons—and stories of war and murder.

5

This Colossal Engine of Finance

Economic conditions have everywhere engendered a shifting of the basis of taxable faculty, and democracy has declared that the best criterion, on the whole, is to be found in income. Whether we like it or not, the development is irresistible, and the income tax will come to stay until some new criterion of ability approves itself to the democracy of the future.

EDWIN SELIGMAN[1]

IRKSOME THOUGH IT MAY BE, the income tax is nowadays generally accepted as a central part of any half-decent tax system, with a—usually, *the*—key role in shaping its vertical equity: how, that is, the tax burden is shared between the more and the less affluent. Politicians may and do talk of abolishing the VAT, or of eliminating estate taxes. But while they may promise to slash the rates at which it is applied, they rarely talk (outside the United States, at least) of abolishing the income tax altogether. And developing countries aspire, and are encouraged, to make their income taxes more effective, not to replace them with something else.

But it was not always so. This chapter tells the stories of the painful emergence of the modern income tax in three countries: Britain, the United States, and France. We choose these three not because they are representative of experiences elsewhere. On the contrary, every income tax has its own (usually contested) history, and, in important respects, these three experiences were very different. Apart from being good stories, the significance of the three episodes is rather that—these countries being great political and intellectual powers of their time—these experiences largely shaped developments elsewhere, and were themselves shaped by forces with which other countries also came to struggle. They also raised fundamental questions about the proper role and best design of the income tax that are with us still. But even though the questions are largely the same, and the income tax remains recognizably the handiwork of long-dead policymakers, the answers continue to change as both analytical tools and social values evolve. The last part of this chapter looks at how.

The Work of Giants: The Income Tax in Britain

By the late eighteenth century, the idea of taxing income was not new. The British themselves had tried it in 1689, in what degenerated into a tax only on landed income; and the French *capitation* of 1710 mentioned in the previous chapter has been seen as the first true income tax, although it degenerated as exemptions multiplied. Building on the quiet development of reasonably trusted and moderately effective institutions of government in Britain over the preceding century, an effective income tax finally emerged there as the last resort of a desperate government.

In late 1797, Britain was preparing to enter the fifth year of war with France. Things were not going well. The Low Countries—jumping-off points for invasion—were in the hands of the French; the fleet had mutinied during the summer; and in a series of stunning victories, the young Bonaparte had taken northern Italy and forced Austria, Britain's principal remaining ally, out of the war. This was going to be a long and expensive war, and an increasing interest rate on government debt signaled falling confidence that the British could raise enough money to pay for victory. The government of Pitt the Younger—then chancellor of the exchequer as well as prime minister—had, since the start of the war, introduced or increased a series of taxes of the kind discussed in chapter 4, but the additional revenue was being outpaced by spending that had more than doubled since peacetime.[2] Something more radical was needed.

Pitt's first attempt was his Triple Assessment of 1798.[3] This was a threefold increase (more, for some of the better off) of an eclectic mix of what were known as the "assessed taxes": those on housing[4] and windows, carriages, servants, horses, clocks, dogs, and the like. (These taxes were not excises, payable on the purchase of these commodities, but annual charges on their possession.)[5] Tellingly, the Triple Assessment set an upper bound on liability in terms of the taxpayer's income: Those with incomes below £60 per year were exempt, for instance, while the liability of those with incomes over £200 could not exceed 10 percent of their income. The Triple Assessment was thus "a half-way house between taxes on expenditure and a direct tax on income."[6] It was also a failure, raising less than half of the revenue expected: A surprisingly large number of people turned out to have incomes of just below £60, and the whole episode was marked by what Pitt called "shameful evasion, or rather . . . scandalous frauds."[7]

Half measures having failed, a full-blown income tax was introduced in 1799. This was a levy on all British subjects, and on all residents of Britain, on their total income from all sources and all countries, and on all income from British property even if received by foreigners: a large net. People were simply to declare their total income and be taxed on it. Incomes below £60 were exempt, with a top rate of 10 percent on incomes of £200 or more.[8]

The new income tax was successful enough to be highly unpopular, one relatively new complaint—destined to become very familiar—being its complexity: The Act was 152 pages long, and the rate applied increased in 28 tiny steps from 0.8 percent to the top 10 percent.[9] Taxpayers took some comfort, perhaps, in the tax being, as the title of the Act made clear, temporary: it was "an aid and contribution for the prosecution of the war." So when peace came in 1802, the tax went—with much celebratory burning of records.

The Peace of Amiens was short-lived, however, and the income tax was soon back, reintroduced, with Pitt briefly out of office, by Prime

John Bull is baffled by Pitt's income tax.

Minister Henry Addington. The 1803 variant differed from its predecessor in two important ways. First, it was "schedular": that is, tax was applied not to the sum of income of all types, but separately to five different categories of income (from land under Schedule A, for instance, and from employment under Schedule E).[10] This was done not to tax those different types differently—a source of controversy in itself, as will be seen—but rather to preserve an element of privacy: It meant that no revenue officer needed to know a gentleman's total income. The second innovation, even more significant, was an attempt to make widespread use of withholding ("stoppage at source," as it was then called). That is, the government was taking its cut before the income reached the income recipient, by requiring tenants, employers, companies and others to deduct tax when making a range of payments and remit the money to the government. Again, this feature was not in itself entirely new, but now the effort was more systematic.

This time the tax was an even greater success: It more than tripled the number of taxpayers[11] and raised only a little less than its predecessor with a much lower top rate of only 5 percent. Even though it was explicitly a wartime measure, the redesigned income tax proved so effective—raising by the end of the war 20 percent of all tax revenue[12]—that, with the defeat of Napoleon in 1815, many in government, faced now with the need to cope with the debt that had been built up during the war, were inclined to keep it. But, go it did.[13]

Only in 1842 did the income tax reappear, when Robert Peel "called forth from repose this giant, who had once shielded us in war, to come and assist our industrious toils in peace."[14] Just as he changed his mind on other key issues of the day—Catholic emancipation and (a topic for chapter 7) the Corn Laws—so Peel changed from an opponent of income taxation[15] to an adherent, seeing it as the only realistic way to pay for the tariff reductions that were his fiscal priority. Reintroduced at a modest rate of 2.9 percent, the tax was again "for a time to be limited." In his first budget, in 1853, Gladstone, a protégé of Peel, while eulogizing the income tax as a "colossal engine of finance," was "decidedly against the perpetuity of the tax as a permanent ordinary portion of our finances."[16] He planned to eliminate it in 7 years.[17] But the Crimean War of 1853–1856 put paid to his hopes, and the permanence of the income tax gradually, quietly, became accepted. In a last gasp, both sides during the 1874 election campaign promised its abolition.[18] But nothing happened, and the suggestion was not heard again. The income tax was here to stay.[19]

Throughout, the nature and design of the income tax was the subject of intense and sometimes extraordinarily sophisticated debate; this was the time, not coincidentally, in which public finance emerged as a substantive area of study in itself. Much of this debate focused on ideas of fairness, with two aspects center stage.

One was the question of "graduation," or, in more modern terms, progressivity: the extent to which—if at all—those with higher incomes should owe a higher proportion of that income in tax. Even before its introduction, Thomas Paine, in his *Rights of Man*, had argued for an income tax not just to raise revenue but also to achieve a more equal distribution of after-tax incomes, taking from the richer to give to (or at least take less from) the poorer. This radical tradition survived, but the idea that the income tax should be used for redistribution was staunchly resisted. The issue was not whether those with the lowest incomes should owe a smaller proportion of their income in tax—face, that is, a lower average tax rate—but whether those on the highest incomes should pay a larger proportion. Mathematically, these are much the same thing, which can make it hard to see what all the fuss was about. But the two things were viewed very differently. That the poorest should pay less tax had been accepted for centuries (even at the time of the 1380 poll tax), and this principle was reflected in the exemption from tax of a certain amount of income (which also served an administrative purpose of limiting the number of taxpayers to deal with) and "abatements" that limited the liabilities on taxpayers with the lowest incomes (though these actually made matters more complex). The issue was whether some additional rate should be imposed on the highest incomes.

Much ink was spilled on this in Victorian Britain, formalizing more precisely notions of the sacrifice taxpayers suffered as a consequence of taxation and of their ability to pay. This culminated in the shockingly socialistic conclusion reached by the "strange, shy,"[20] and curiously brilliant Oxford professor Francis Ysidro Edgeworth, published in 1897: In a world in which all individuals are imagined to derive the same happiness from any given income and (more plausibly) derive less additional happiness from another pound (or dollar) of income the higher their income is to begin with, the utilitarian objective of maximizing total happiness requires a tax system under which all end up with exactly the same after-tax income. This means a marginal tax rate—the tax rate, that is, on an additional dollar (pound, yen, whatever) of income—of 100 percent at all levels of income, and explicit transfers of income from the richer to the poorer. And that is as redistributive as you can get. What Edgeworth's math left out was that in such a world no one would have any self-interested incentive to earn anything, their after-tax income being the same regardless of how much they earned—a consideration fully recognized at the time, but not fully grappled with by economists for nearly another century.

The politics, however, got ahead of Edgeworth's math. In his 1894 budget, Chancellor William Harcourt[21] introduced graduated rates in death duties, and made clear that the Liberal Party supported graduation of the income tax too. In a sure sign they were losing the debate, opponents now stressed administrative difficulties.[22] One Royal Commission later,[23] graduation finally came as part of Lloyd George's landmark People's Budget of 1909, which introduced a "super-tax" of 2.5 percent on the highest incomes.[24] That prompted a constitutional crisis, as the budget was seen as breaching the principle that the tax system should not be used for redistribution.

Many of the measures in the People's Budget[25] strike us now as modest: an increase in the top rate of income tax to 8.3 percent, some increase in death duties, and a few other measures. More striking was the proposal of a tax on unearned increases in land value and on undeveloped land (much in the spirit of Henry George, discussed in chapter 10). But what really made this budget so incendiary was Lloyd George's rhetoric, both in the budget speech itself and in his magnificent Limehouse speech ("a fully equipped duke costs as much to keep up as two Dreadnoughts—and they are just as great a terror—and they last longer").[26] His aim, it was clear, was redistribution. For the first time in 200 years, the House of Lords rejected a budget. In the end, the Lords were subdued: The super-tax survived (but the land tax proposals did not). During the 1909 budget debate, Lloyd George also neatly and scornfully put to final rest any idea that the income tax should be temporary: "Why should taxes on the necessaries of life be regarded as permanent, and the taxes on high incomes as purely temporary?"[27] No one had much of an answer to that.

The other longstanding issue in the design of the income tax was that of differentiation: whether different types of income should be taxed at different rates. Whether, in particular, "spontaneous" or "permanent" income (such as income from land and interest on government debt—corresponding very roughly, in modern terms, to income from capital) should be taxed more heavily than "precarious" income (labor earnings, income from trade and professions, and the like), on the grounds that the greater stability of the former implied a lesser sacrifice from bearing a given amount of tax. Advocates of a lower rate on labor income also cited the lack of any tax deduction[28] for the depreciation of human capital (skills, knowledge, and experience) of the kind provided for physical capital. The point was made crisply by then-Chancellor Herbert Asquith, comparing two hypothetical individuals, one "who derives . . . £1000 a year from a perfectly safe investment in [government bonds], perhaps accumulated and left to him by his father," and another "making the same nominal sum by personal labour in the pursuit of some arduous and perhaps precarious profession. . . . To say that those two people are . . . to be taxed in the same way is, to my mind, flying in the face of justice and common sense."[29]

The debate had rumbled on through much of the nineteenth century,[30] and administrative difficulties came to be relied on more than objections of principle. For instance, how, for a small business, could one distinguish permanent and precarious components of income (which became known, tellingly, as "unearned" and "earned" incomes, respectively)? Differentiation finally came, however, in the Liberal budget of 1907, defended by Asquith in the words above, by reducing the rate on lower levels of "earned" income to 3.75 percent while maintaining that on "unearned" income at 5 percent.[31]

The presumption that unearned income should be taxed more heavily than earned income became entrenched. As late as 1979, an additional tax of 15 percent on unearned income brought the total tax rate on the highest incomes in the United Kingdom up to 98 percent: "There's one for you, nineteen for me," as The Beatles put it (with more despair than mathematical accuracy) in their song *Taxman*. Since then, however, the debate on differential taxation of income from labor and from capital has taken a very different turn—as will be seen later.

The Dred Scott Decision of the Revenue

The United States firmly embraced an income tax much later than Britain: just in time (like the French and several others) to help pay for the First World War. This late adoption was largely an unforeseen consequence of the "capitation clause" (Article I, Section 9) of the U.S. Constitution, which proved much less dull than it sounds—and is making a modern reappearance.

The idea of a federal income tax was first floated in 1815, but the war with the British ended before it came to anything.[32] It was another war, the Civil War—and the enormous cost of waging it—that triggered its first incarnation. The North (but not the South[33]) attempted an income tax in the first year of the conflict, 1861, championed in Congress by the appropriately named William Pitt Fessenden.[34] Before it went into effect, Congress met again and drafted a new income tax law, in which the single rate was just 5 percent, raised in 1864 to 10 percent.

While the war lasted, the tax was by all accounts reasonably popular: "The people," said the first Commissioner of Internal Revenue (admittedly not a disinterested observer), "have accepted it with cheerfulness, to meet a temporary exigency, and it has excited no serious complaint."[35] It was never a mass tax: In 1866, tax was due from only about 450,000 people.[36] Nonetheless, after a slow start, it produced considerable amounts, coming to account for about a quarter of all government revenue.[37] With the war's end, however—revenues from other sources being buoyant, and the national debt falling—there was no appetite for its continuation, and the tax expired in 1872.

The income tax was back on the political agenda soon enough, the revival stemming from dissatisfaction with a revenue-raising regime based on tariffs and internal taxes.[38] Discontent was particularly keen in rural areas, facing a steady decline in the prices of farm products from 1870 to 1897. State and local taxes, moreover, were viewed as discriminating against farmers.[39] Tariffs were seen as favoring the increasingly powerful and increasingly rich industrial interests of the Northeast; the *New York Times* editorialized that they "artificially and cruelly increase the cost of clothing, of bedding, of shelter, of tools, and of a thousand necessities of daily life."[40] Growing anger at the power of trusts, bankers, and railroads simmered and ultimately coalesced in the populist movement of the 1870s and 1880s. This movement gravitated toward the idea of an income tax to replace some or all of the apparently regressive tariffs and excise taxes in place. In 1893, with the election of Democrat Grover Cleveland as President, an income tax surfaced as a hot-button issue in Congress. Cleveland had run on a campaign platform that called for eliminating protectionist tariffs. That would need to be paid for, and so the tariff bill of 1894 included an income tax of 2 percent on individuals and corporations, with a $4,000 personal exemption for the former. Much was expected by some of the advocates, one seeing the income tax—without irony (though whether without drink, history does not record)—"more of sunshine, more of the songs of birds."[41]

How gaily the birds would have sung, however, we shall never know, because the 1894 income tax never took effect. This is where the capitation clause for the Constitution comes in. It states: "No Capitation, or other direct, Tax shall be laid, unless in Proportion to the Census or Enumeration herein before directed to be taken."[42]

By a "capitation tax" was clearly meant a poll tax: a uniform, fixed amount per taxpayer.[43] What was meant by a "direct" tax, however, had never been spelled out. Delegate Rufus King of Massachusetts had raised the question during the 1787 Constitutional Convention; but, James Madison comments in his notes, no one answered.[44] Alexander Hamilton spotted the problem: "It is a matter of regret," he said, "that terms so uncertain and vague in so important a point are to be found in the Constitution."[45] There was, however, some sense that the term "direct" referred to taxes on land and slaves, as well as a poll tax. So the Civil War income tax was widely seen[46] as an indirect tax and was often referred to—including in the legislation—as the "income duty."[47] This is a very weird interpretation given how the term is used today: a "direct" tax is now usually taken to be one that varies with taxpayers' attributes, so that an income tax is clearly in that sense direct.[48] The implication of the capitation clause, in any case, is that if something was found to be a "direct tax," then the per capita amount collected had to be the same in all states.

This odd provision—close to a folly in modern eyes—has unhappy roots: in slavery. Another provision in the Constitution required that

> Representatives and direct Taxes shall be apportioned among the several States . . . according to their respective Numbers, which shall be determined by adding to the whole Number of free Persons . . . and excluding Indians not taxed, three-fifths of all other Persons.[49]

Here was a grand bargain between North and South. The South wanted a full count of slaves when it came to representation; the North wanted the opposite. With direct taxes tied to representation, treating slaves as three-fifths of a person allowed a workable (if Faustian) compromise: The South got less representation than it wanted but could hope to be spared some taxes in recompense; the North had to accept more representation of slaveholders than it wanted but could hope to shift some taxes toward them. The qualification that this provision applied only to "direct" taxes seems to have been little more than convenient wordsmithing to recognize that such an arrangement would not be workable for import tariffs, taxes on consumption, and the other things that mattered for federal finances.

The capitation clause had long been generating mutterings as to the potential unconstitutionality of an income tax, but the general spirit had been, as one Congressman put it during the Civil War debates: "Why should we stickle about terms?"[50] By 1894, however—the year federal troops were sent to put down the nationwide Pullman railroad strike— class conflict was very much in the air. And opponents of the income tax, ready for a fight, picked the capitation clause as the battleground.

Charles Pollock, a shareholder in the Farmers' Loan & Trust Company, sued the company to prevent it from paying the income tax on the grounds that it was unconstitutional. He lost in the lower courts but appealed all the way to the Supreme Court, which in 1895, by a 5–4 vote, agreed with him. This meant that a federal income tax could not be levied unless the revenue raised from states was proportional to their respective populations. And achieving that equality of per capita revenue would not only be hard in practice but also highly objectionable, as it would require higher tax rates in less wealthy states.

The Supreme Court's decision in *Pollock v. Farmers' Loan & Trust Company* was a shining example of what we would now call "judicial activism." Justices who supported the decision did not hide their approval of the argument of the principal lawyer for the plaintiff that if this "communistic march" were not summarily halted, nothing would prevent future action by Congress to increase "the tax from two percent to ten percent, or to twenty percent."[51] True enough, it turned out, but hardly the legal point at issue. The political nature of the decision was clear to everyone. In his dissenting opinion, Justice Howell Edmunds Jackson railed that the decision "involves nothing less than a surrender of the taxing power to the moneyed class" and called the decision "the most disastrous blow ever struck at the constitutional power of Congress."[52]

Feelings ran high. Supporters of the income tax were apoplectic. Comparisons were made with the Dred Scott decision of 1857.[53] But the fight was not over. In May 1895, the *New York World* wrote that "the tax is dead, but the principle upon which it is based is alive and will yet in some form prevail."[54] Signs of this were clear enough. William Jennings Bryan included support for the tax in his 1896 "Cross of Gold" speech.

For the next decade or so, however, the populist movement was drawn away from tax to issues of antitrust, silver, and war with Spain. But the cause did not die and was taken up by progressive Republicans. Things started to move again in 1906, when Republican President Theodore Roosevelt spoke favorably in his message to Congress of introducing a graduated income tax and an inheritance tax to limit the growth of great fortunes. But, acknowledging the difficulty of overcoming the constitutional problem, and referring to the need for "long and careful study,"[55] he did nothing to make it happen.

But momentum kept on building. Even the early prohibitionists had a dog in this fight. One might think they would oppose an income tax if it led to a reduction of demand-inhibiting taxes on alcohol.[56] But many prohibitionists believed that taxes on alcohol legitimized the

The taxman's best friend.

alcohol business, and that the revenues it produced—about 30 percent of all federal receipts in 1910[57]—made the government an invisible partner in the immoral business, unwilling to see it founder.

In 1908, the Democratic Party adopted a pro-income-tax platform, arguing specifically for a constitutional amendment,[58] while the

Republican platform was silent on the issue: not quite the same thing as opposing it. Indeed, by then the political battle line on the income tax was less a matter of Democrats versus Republicans than of the sectional Northeast interest within the Republican Party versus everyone else. What scared the industrialists was not just the income tax (although they certainly remembered that New York alone had contributed about one-third of the revenue from the Civil War income tax, and Pennsylvania slightly more than 11 percent),[59] but that its success would make it harder for them to cling to high tariff protection. In the end, the Democrats, led by presidential nominee William Jennings Bryan, lost the 1908 election. With the election of William Howard Taft, the industrialists breathed a sigh of relief. But it was Taft—now, undeservedly, remembered mainly for his girth[60]—who was to pave the way for final adoption of an income tax.

The critical year was 1909, when the Taft administration did two things. One was to propose a 2 percent "excise" tax on the income of most corporations: Calling it an excise tax (on the privilege of doing business in a corporate capacity) avoided the constitutional pitfalls that likely would have derailed a tax labeled as one on income. In the event, in August, Congress passed a bill at half that rate, imposing a 1 percent tax on the net income of any corporation in excess of $5,000.[61] The other was to recommend, on June 16, 1909, that Congress propose a constitutional amendment empowering the federal government to levy an income tax without apportionment of the revenue among the states in proportion to population.

During the debate that followed, the Republican chairman of the House Ways and Means Committee, Sereno Payne, contended that an income tax would make "a nation of liars" and be "a tax on the income of the honest men and an exemption, to a greater or less extent, on the income of rascals."[62] Strong words. But they actually came from a supporter of the tax, which Payne saw as essential for the country to raise money in the event of war. In a similar vein, Congressman Cordell Hull argued that America would be "helpless to prosecute . . . any . . . war of great magnitude" without taxing "the wealth of the country in the form of incomes."[63] Both sides, it seemed, had absorbed the lesson of Pitt the

Younger, having war finance in mind years before any specter of major conflict.

The 16th amendment that finally emerged is clear-cut: "The Congress shall have the power to lay and collect taxes on incomes, from whatever source derived, without apportionment among the several states, and without regard to any census or enumeration." Ratification was not a foregone conclusion, given strong opposition in the Northeast. But with the Democrats sweeping the 1912 elections, any doubts were removed. And on February 3, 1913, with ratification by Delaware, the 16th amendment passed into the Constitution. Less than a fortnight later, Woodrow Wilson took office, with both houses also under Democratic control. And only 8 months after the final ratification, on October 3, 1913, he signed an income tax into law.

It was modest enough, with a tax of 1 percent on net income and surtax rates of 1 to 6 percent, the last kicking in at $500,000 of income (so the top rate was 7 percent). Each taxpayer having an exemption of $3,000, only a little over 350,000 returns were filed in 1913 and 1914,[64] from a population of just under 100 million. During the debate, Republican Congressman Ira C. Copley proposed—as a warning—graduating the rates to a maximum of 68 percent on income over $1,000,000, predicting that "within 10 years some such law will be written on the statute books of this country by the American Congress."[65] (Copley, it turned out, was too timid—it took 4 years, not 10.) For corporations, the tax rate was a flat 1 percent, with no exemption. The new income tax form, with its shockingly long 4-page return (including instructions), was simply given the next number in the system of sequential numbering of forms developed by the Bureau of Internal Revenue, the predecessor of today's IRS: the 1040 that will be familiar to American readers.

All this came just in time for the First World War. President Wilson signed the War Revenue Act of 1917 on October 3, exactly 4 years after he had signed the first income tax law. The exemption level was halved, adding 3 million people to the tax rolls, an eightfold increase.[66] The time had come to make serious use of the income tax. One telling argument for doing so, raised by prominent academics (including the redoubtable Irving Fisher of Yale University), made explicit the link with the implicit taxation of the military draft. As the draft was in effect a tax that deprived the draftees' families of their incomes, it made economic sense to tax the incomes of Americans who were not drafted. By 1918, the top rate had risen to that whopping 77 percent. And, by 1920, income taxes made up two-thirds of federal receipts. It was still not a mass tax: In 1920, only about 13 percent of the workforce was filing income tax returns. But the income tax was clearly not going away any time soon.

The United States did not follow the by-then established British practice of taxing "unearned" income at a higher rate than earned income. Secretary of the Treasury Andrew Mellon suggested it in the early 1920s, using language very similar to that which carried the day in the United Kingdom, but it did not become law.[67] It did, though, make it into the tax code, at least for a while, much later. The U.S. Tax Reform Act of 1969 introduced a provision designed to limit the tax rate on earned income (wages, salaries, and other employee compensation) to 50 percent for tax years 1972 and after, at a time when the top tax rate was 70 percent. This was later repealed for tax years after 1981. And things today are actually the other way around, with dividends and capital gains subject to lower rates than labor income[68]—a remarkable turnaround that we look at later.

One thing that has not changed, however, is the capitation clause, which is still in effect. So too is the ambiguity within it of what is meant by a "direct tax," which the 16th amendment simply skirted around. So if a tax were found that was deemed both "direct" and not a tax on income (explicitly allowed by the 16th amendment), it arguably would have to be apportioned: that is, the per capita amount paid would have to be the same in each state. And that has again become a real issue, with arguably strong grounds to suppose that an annual wealth tax— proposed by prominent aspirants to the 2020 Democratic presidential nomination—would be unconstitutional. Or at least that it could be tied up in the courts for many years.

A Crime of Passion and the French Income Tax

Late in the afternoon of March 16, 1914, Madame Henriette Caillaux, wife of the minister of finance, arrived at the offices of Le Figaro, the leading French newspaper of the time.[69] Asking for the editor, Gaston

Le Petit Journal

ADMINISTRATION   5 CENT.   SUPPLÉMENT ILLUSTRÉ   5 CENT.   ABONNEMENTS
61, RUE LAFAYETTE, 61
Les manuscrits ne sont pas rendus   25ᵐᵉ Année   —♦♦—   Numéro 1.219   SEINE et SEINE-ET-OISE   2 fr.   2 fr. 50
                                                                                          DÉPARTEMENTS.   2 fr.   4 fr.
                          DIMANCHE 29 MARS 1914   ÉTRANGER . . . . . . 2 50   8 fr. »

Tragique épilogue d'une querelle politique
Mᵐᵉ CAILLAUX, FEMME DU MINISTRE DES FINANCES, TUE A COUPS DE REVOLVER
M. GASTON CALMETTE DIRECTEUR DU " FIGARO "

Madame Caillaux gets even.

Calmette, she was told he was out but would be back in an hour or so.
She sat and waited calmly. Surprised and discomfited to find her there
when he returned, Calmette politely invited Madame Caillaux into his
office. At which point, she pulled out a small revolver and shot him four
times. Within a few hours, he was dead, and Henriette Caillaux was in
police headquarters, driven there by the chauffeur she had asked to wait
outside.

What had brought Henriette Caillaux to murder was the fear that *Le
Figaro* was about to publish amorous letters her husband Joseph had

written to her some years back, the inconvenient aspect being that he had written them while married to someone else. This exposé was to be the culmination of a very personal campaign that *Le Figaro* and others had been waging against Caillaux for weeks. Two things had aroused this fury. One was his support for a rapprochement with Germany. The other was that he was the leading advocate for introducing a modern income tax.

The possibility of introducing an income tax had been alive and contentious in France since the revolution of 1848.[70] Many hated the whole idea: The statesman and historian Adolphe Thiers called it "immorality written in law."[71] "What a frightful inquisition" this is, one observer commented, "which . . . compel[s] a rich man to reveal a fortune which it perhaps pleases him to surround with mystery."[72] The mystery came from the reliance at the time on those *quatre vieilles* that had emerged from the French Revolution, which were in effect an increasingly complex set of presumptive taxes. What was needed, thought Caillaux and others, was precisely to move away from this approach:

> You may rack your mind as much as you like. You may invent all the possible external signs in the world; you may combine them and intertwine them as much as you please—the day after you have worked out a law of two or three hundred paragraphs . . . the only result will be the discovery that you have committed the maximum of injustice.[73]

In moving away from such an overtly presumptive system, the battle line was drawn between those favoring a British-style schedular form of taxation, with flat-rate taxes on different types of income, and those preferring a progressive tax on total income, which came to be seen as the Prussian model. Advocates of the British version saw it as the best protection against an inquisitorial, dominating bureaucracy; those favoring the Prussian were more focused on achieving a stronger distributional effect. Caillaux himself came up with a combination of the two—a series of schedular taxes combined with a progressive "complementary" tax on the total after-tax income that then remained—that came to be known as *le projet Caillaux*.

These debates, and dozens of legislative proposals, had in any event, led nowhere. Caillaux himself resigned immediately after the murder. But while Madame Caillaux, and much of Paris, awaited her trial (curtains thoughtfully placed over the bars of her cell), the archduke Ferdinand was assassinated in Sarajevo. War started to look likely, as did the need to finance it. And so, on July 15, 1914, the Senate finally adopted an income tax.

Five days later, the trial of Henriette Caillaux began. The scandalous mixture of murder, sex, high political intrigue, and factious relations with Germany, involving the highest of French society—the president himself gave evidence—had the country spellbound for weeks. On July 28, Madame Caillaux, sensationally, was acquitted.[74] This, the jury decided, had been a crime of passion. The verdict competed for headlines with the news, the same day, that Austro-Hungary declared war on Serbia, starting the falling of dominos that led to the First World War.

In the event, the French income tax did not make a great contribution to war finance. It was not applied until 1916, and by 1918, the top rate had risen to only 20 percent. By then the income tax accounted for nearly 40 percent of all government revenue in the United States, and around 60 percent in the United Kingdom—but only 6.5 percent in France. Indeed, except for a spell in the 1920s, the personal income tax has never been such a money spinner in France as elsewhere. Even now, the share of total taxation in France that comes from the personal income tax is much lower than in the rest of the OECD.[75] This has been partly due to the erosion of its base through family and other allowances, but also because—in contrast to nearly all other countries—the income tax in France did not (until 2019) involve withholding by employers. That is, tax was not remitted by employers, but instead by employees. This, unsurprisingly, makes collection problematic. Largely to circumvent these limitations, France adopted in 1991 a distinct tax, the *Contribution Sociale Généralisée*, levied on a broad base, at flat rates, and subject to withholding. This has effectively functioned as a surrogate personal income tax.[76]

There is another strand to the story of the French income tax. It is a classic example of the way in which the great powers exported to their colonies tax instruments whose suitability in poorer countries was far from obvious, creating difficulties that lasted well into the era of independence. In France itself, the unique structure of the income tax under *le projet Caillaux* survived until 1959, when it was converted into a single, progressive tax.[77] In much of Francophone Africa, however, the system lingered for decades, with such revenue as it raised coming from withholding under the schedular taxes and almost nothing from the complementary tax.[78] In Cameroon, for instance, the Caillaux system was reformed only in 2004, and in Senegal only in 2012.

Old Fears and New Directions

What would the founding fathers of the income tax—Pitt, Addington, Taft,[79] Caillaux, and the others—make of their creation if they were to see it today? They would recognize a great deal of it—much more so than they would, for instance, if we tried to explain the value added tax to them. As the primary means by which the tax system explicitly adjusts to the notion of ability to pay, the income tax remains their work. Much more complex in its fine tuning, it is true, but complexity has been a criticism since 1799.

They would, however, be dumbfounded by the massive increase in the size of government to which the income tax has contributed: exactly the monster that many of them and their contemporaries had dreaded they were unleashing. And the progressive structures we now take for granted might seem to Gladstone, for one, as obvious validation of his fear that graduation would mean a "direct tendency to communism."[80] The high marginal tax rates—an average top statutory personal income tax rate of 43 percent in the OECD in 2019[81]—would leave them puzzled that industry and endeavor had not entirely dried up. Many of the founders would have more than a little sympathy with those countries that now impose "flat taxes": countries inspired by a Russian tax reform of 2001[82] that applies (above some exemption level) a single, low marginal tax rate of just 13 percent.

In one even more fundamental respect, the logic of graduation has been (and is increasingly being) taken further than the founding fathers are likely to have imagined, but which they would readily understand. From seeing income as a good indicator of ability to pay tax, it is a short step to seeing it as an indicator of possible need to receive payment. That indeed was an implication—to many, an awkward one—of Edgeworth's algebra. Income-related benefits emerged after the Second World War as key measures of social support, and—contrary to the hopes and expectation of, for instance, the Beveridge report published in the United Kingdom in 1942, which laid out a program of cradle-to-grave social insurance—became an increasingly central part of the welfare state. There is an obvious logic in integrating such tools into the income tax itself, reflected in Milton Friedman's idea of a "negative income tax" (meaning simply that at low levels of income, money is received from the government, not given to it) and the reality of the earned income tax credit pioneered in the United States and now spreading around the world. Increasingly, tax administrations are finding themselves not only collecting money from some but also giving it to others. Half the staff of the tax administration in New Zealand, for example, is involved in delivering benefits. This does not always please tax administrators themselves, who point to the quite different challenges that arise: Income tax is assessed over the fairly leisurely period of a year, for instance, while those in need of cash need it now. This is a trend, however, that seems set to continue.

Perhaps the major structural innovation the founding fathers would see is the introduction of an income tax on corporations, in tandem with the personal income tax. This was essentially an application of the logic of withholding. Through the nineteenth century, companies had been taxed on their earnings as in effect an advance payment of tax on the dividends they paid to shareholders; and that, because all dividends were taxed at the same rate, worked well enough. The advance payment idea did not work so well, however, when dividends, as an element of unearned income, came to be taxed at high and eventually progressive rates: Unless the company was itself charged at the highest of those rates, tax could be avoided by simply retaining profits in the company and not paying a dividend. A distinct corporate-level tax thus came into existence (a surprisingly recent development outside the United States, coming to the United Kingdom, for instance, only in 1965) not on the grounds (ludicrous, as we will see) that "corporations should pay their fair share of tax"[83] but to implement company-level taxation as a form of withholding.

Not least, the founding fathers would recognize the continuing dispute regarding the appropriate relative treatment of precarious and permanent incomes—the contrast now being phrased as that between capital and labor income. What would take them aback, however, is that whereas in their day the presumption was that, if anything, "unearned" (capital) income should be taxed *more* heavily than earned (labor) income, now the presumption—of most economists at least—tends to be that, if anything, it should be taxed *less* heavily. To the admiration of many, this principle has been made central to the tax design of several Nordic countries, which have adopted varieties of a dual income tax. As a result, labor income is taxed at progressive rates but capital income at a flat rate lower than the top marginal rate on labor income. The main difficulty with this approach—once again there is less new in the tax world than one might think—is the same as that raised by opponents of differentiation in the late nineteenth century: For smaller businesses, some way needs to be found to allocate income between capital and labor elements.

The proper treatment of capital income, and hence of the savings and investment that generate it, remains perhaps the main question overhanging the income tax. The view that savings should be excluded from taxation dates back to Thomas Hobbes, with John Stuart Mill arguing by the middle of the nineteenth century that "the portion of an income which was saved and converted into capital should be untaxed."[84] The idea boils down to taxing consumption, not income.

Taxing consumption does not necessarily mean relying on taxes like the VAT or retail sales tax that are levied at the same rate for all. It could mean taxing each individual's total consumption, added over all commodities, at progressive rates. More practicable, the same effect can be achieved by exempting from tax the capital income that is the return on savings. Or, alternatively, by allowing the amount saved as a deduction in calculating tax liability and then taxing all withdrawals of saving, both principal and return.[85]

Some see taxing consumption (what people take out of the economy) as fairer than taxing income (a measure of what they put in). But there are other considerations, relating to the excess burden reflected in effects on investment and growth, and of sheer practicality. A succession of eminent committees has argued in favor of moving toward some form of progressive consumption tax, and many of the profession's most gifted economists have plumbed theoretical depths to understand when entirely exempting the normal return on capital from tax best serves the collective interest. The answer, predictably, is that "it depends." But, with some notable exceptions,[86] few economists these days argue that capital income should be taxed at the same high rates as applied to the highest levels of labor income. And most governments provide one or other of these favorable treatments to many of the most important types of saving. Private pension contributions, for instance, are often deductible (up to some limit) and pension payouts are then fully taxable.

There is also a pragmatic case for relatively low rates on capital income: Attempts by any country to tax it at high rates will simply cause capital to flee abroad. By now it will be no surprise to learn that this issue is not new. It was a concern even for the founding fathers of the income tax. Addington's income tax exempted foreigners from taxation of the interest on government debt, presumably because they had a wider range of alternatives to invest in than did nationals;[87] and a 1920 Royal Commission agonized over the flight of foreign capital that graduation might cause.[88] Then, as now, these concerns have often proved overblown. Such taxes have survived, despite many learned articles since the early 1990s with titles along the lines of "Can capital/corporate taxes survive?"[89] But they are much lower than they were, and international considerations increasingly take center stage in thinking about the future of the income tax, and of taxation more generally. We look at these issues in chapter 11.

Views differ on how progressive the income tax should be, and on how different types of income should be taxed. In broad terms, however, taxing income is broadly accepted as fair, because income is seen as a reasonable proxy for ability to pay and because differences in people's ability to pay are seen as a legitimate basis on which to tax them differently. But people differ in many other ways than their income, and rulers through the ages have not shied away from using those differences for tax purposes—sometimes outrageously, sometimes with the best of intentions. This is our next topic: the "horizontal" dimension of fairness.

6

Some Are More Equal
Than Others

A tax is very much like a boil that a man had on his nose. He complained of its being there very much, and his friend asked him, "Where else would you like to have it?" He thought of the matter for a while, and then answered, "Well, . . . I believe I would rather have it on some other man's back."

LOGAN HOLT ROOTS[1]

IT WAS PROBABLY quite hard to live with, or under, the seventeenth-century King of Kongo, who was said to have collected a tax every time his beret fell off.[2] Few things irritate taxpayers so much as arbitrariness in setting taxes. Sometimes the capriciousness can be whimsical. There is the echo of a pleasant drunken evening or two in 1086 behind the account in the Rolls of the Exchequer that "the wife of Hugo de Nevill gives to the king 200 hens for permission to sleep with her husband," and "the Bishop of Winchester owes a tonell of good wine for not reminding the king about a girdle for the countess of Albemarle."[3] We have no idea what all that was about—which is what makes these examples of capricious taxation. Arbitrariness in taxation can threaten the legitimacy of government: "The genius of liberty," said Alexander Hamilton, "reprobates every thing arbitrary or discretionary in taxation."[4]

Beyond the merely capricious, however, taxes have long been used as an instrument of oppression or reward.

The history of taxation is largely the history of people trying to put the boil on someone else's back. One aspect of this is the relative tax burdens of rich and poor people. But fairness is also—sometimes even more—about the equal treatment of people who have more or less the same income and wealth, and seem to be pretty much the same in other ways, too. This is the principle of horizontal equity: people who are in relevant aspects identical should be treated the same for tax purposes. That is, some of the things that make people different should be off limits when determining tax liability.

That all sounds reasonable. But which characteristics are in practice treated as an inadmissible basis for differential tax treatment is shaped by the realities of political power. Much tax policy making is, if only implicitly, in the spirit of: "Don't tax you, don't tax me, tax the fellow behind that tree!"[5] But the person behind the tree is likely to be someone who is not like you and me: and maybe that's why they are there. Happily switching metaphors, we often want to place the boil on someone who is not like us. Reflecting and sometimes driving changes in power, views on what characteristics should be beyond the pale for tax purposes have changed considerably over time, and they still vary across and even within countries. Nor is it quite so obvious that characteristics which our hearts tell us should not matter for taxation really ought to be ignored—or that it is even possible to do so.

Taxing Femininity

In the early nineteenth century, kings of India ensured the subjugation of the lower castes by taxing them heavily. Peasants were taxed for the right to wear jewelry or grow a moustache. And in some regions, women of some low castes were subject to tax if they covered their breasts when they ventured outside their homes. This type of modesty being considered a privilege of upper-caste women, everything about this breast tax (the *mulakkaram*) suggests that it was designed to intentionally humiliate lower-caste women.

Nangeli's protest.

In 1840, the story goes, a woman named Nangeli, who lived in the town of Cherthala in the erstwhile kingdom of Travancore (now southern India), refused to pay the *mulakkaram*.[6] In protest, she cut off her breasts and presented them to the tax collectors in a plantain leaf. She died of blood loss later that night. During the cremation, her husband suicidally jumped onto the pyre. The government repealed the tax the next day. Cherthala became known later (although no longer) as Mulachiparambu, meaning "land of the breasted woman."

At much the same time, the modern movement for women's rights was beginning to notice the dissonance between the (lack of) suffrage and the (presence of) tax burden, and tax resistance was used as a tool in the fight for women's voting rights.[7] At the third National Woman's Rights Convention held in Syracuse, New York, in 1852, the prominent

No taxation without representation, suffragette version.

suffragette Susan B. Anthony read an address from the equally noted Elizabeth Cady Stanton, asserting the duty of property-holding women to refuse to pay taxes when not represented in legislative bodies. In the United Kingdom, the Women's Tax Resistance League took as its slogan "no vote, no tax." One committee member, Clemence Housman, went to inordinate lengths to give the authorities no choice but to imprison her for nonpayment, eventually managing to spend one week in Holloway Prison.[8] One odd twist to the situation in the United Kingdom was that married women were not required to remit tax on their incomes: their husbands were. And so it was that in 1910, Mark Wilks, husband of the treasurer of the Women's Tax Resistance League, Elizabeth Wilks, found himself in Brixton prison for not remitting the tax due on his wife's income, because she would not tell him what it was.[9]

These days, few tax systems explicitly differentiate by gender, though exceptions persist. In Morocco, for example, married men can take deductions for financially dependent spouses and up to six children, but married women can do so only if they can prove that husband and children are dependent on them.[10] But such examples are increasingly rare, and it is implicit rather than explicit gender discrimination that is now the issue.[11]

Clemence Housman: Gaol was her goal.

Tampons are the emblematic example. In 2016, Cristina Garcia introduced in the California State Assembly a bill to exempt tampons from the state sales tax base, calling it a "step in the right direction to fix . . . gender injustice." Chicago removed tampons and sanitary napkins from its city sales tax base in 2016, as did the states of Illinois and New York.[12] Several more states are considering similar legislation. Pressure to exempt tampons from commodity taxation has been felt around the world. Canada excluded feminine hygiene products from its VAT base in 2015, after 75,000 people signed a petition demanding its repeal, and France lowered the applicable VAT rate from 20 to 5.5 percent. In the United Kingdom, one of the first fruits of Brexit was that from 2021, no longer bound by EU rules on minimum rates, the government scrapped VAT on tampons.

Implicit gender discrimination pops up much more widely. Women are more likely to enter and exit the labor force, for instance, so tax features that make this behavior less attractive will affect them relatively more.[13] Some common tax features, however, disfavor men. Men smoke more[14] and go to more sporting events than do women, so excise taxes on these things burden them relatively more. Lower tax rates on medical services have the same effect, as men on average use them less than do women. In many developing countries, women are more likely to work in informal employment, so to the extent that income from such activity escapes taxation, this actually benefits women relatively more.

But there is more to the issue than toting up the total taxes levied on men and women. Other objectives also matter. One might argue, for instance, that there is a difference between tampons and sports tickets in that the former is more of a necessity than the latter, comprising a larger share of expenditure for lower-income people. So vertical equity is also coming into play. But then the question is why the concern should be handled by exempting tampons from sales taxation rather than through the income tax or social benefits. For instance, it is not clear why a rich woman should be more entitled to a break than a poor male Chelsea supporter. As a separate point, the fact that the demand for tampons is probably fairly insensitive to price actually makes it a good object for taxation, in the sense that the associated excess burden is likely to be low—for reasons we explain in chapter 10. It may be that horizontal equity, if taken to include implicit as well as explicit discrimination, is something that occasionally needs to be compromised in the pursuit of other desirable objectives of the tax system.

One other angle on the gender issue is the question of whether changing the formal tax liability of married men and women actually has any effects on their separate well-being and on the well-being of their children. The answer depends critically on whether tax affects the real control of household resources. Empirical studies suggest that the answer to this question is yes: Women spend a higher fraction of income under their control on goods such as food, education, and health care that improve the lot of their children, so it is possible that changing the gender aspects of taxation can matter a lot.[15]

Peculiar Tax Institutions

The mistreatment of people according to their race has always gone far beyond what tax discrimination alone could effect. But race and tax have sometimes become closely intertwined—and nowhere more so than in the United States.

The interaction goes back to the days of slavery. Considerable colonial revenue was raised from taxes on imported slaves as well as from poll taxes on them. After the Revolutionary War, a poll tax surfaced in some states as a substitute for property qualifications in establishing the right to vote. In the early nineteenth century, many states required a tax payment as a prerequisite for registration to vote. But it was after the Civil War had brought the "peculiar institution" of slavery to an end that the poll tax became a form of implicit—if wholly transparent—racial discrimination. Following the failures of Reconstruction, by 1890 Federal troops had withdrawn from the South. Carpetbaggers, scalawags, and some African-Americans had been replaced in power by white former Southern leaders or their descendants. It was then, mainly around 1890 to 1908, that most Southern states hit on the poll tax as a way to deny black voting rights. Few supporters of the tax bothered to camouflage their intent. In his closing remarks to the 1898 Louisiana constitutional convention, its president defended the poll tax by asking "Doesn't it let the white man vote, and doesn't it stop the negro from voting, and isn't that what we came here for?"[16]

Some states adopted a cumulative poll tax, requiring payment annually for a series of years. Until as late as 1953, Alabama stipulated that the poll tax could accumulate over 24 years, so that a potential voter might have to remit 24 years' worth of tax liability before being eligible to vote. In many states, the tax was due up to 9 months before an election. It was not only in former Confederate states that poll taxes cropped up: California, for instance, levied one until 1914, when it was struck down in a popular referendum.

The administration of the poll taxes often betrayed their intent. Statutory provisions commonly discouraged, rather than encouraged, their collection. Alabama had no penalties for delinquency: "No bills [are] sent out, and in most places, no effort is made by the tax collector to notify the taxpayers when the tax should be paid." The Mississippi constitution stipulated that no criminal proceedings were to be taken to enforce collection. Some states required the tax be paid in cash, at a time when many black southerners had low cash incomes, relying instead on barter and credit from merchants and landlords.[17]

The poll tax was implicit (although blatant) rather than explicit dis-crimination, of course, and it also effectively disenfranchised many poor whites. Some members of the southern elite saw this as an added plus, fearing the growing strength of the largely white-dominated populist parties. The populist Huey Long, however, wanted their votes and so simply paid the $1 poll tax for impoverished white farmers: "Paying the poll taxes," recalled one of his supporters, "kept all the politicians broke."[18] Many southern women activists came to view the poll tax as being a gender issue, too, asserting that it violated the 19th Amendment (adopted in 1920) that guaranteed all women the right to vote. They argued that, given the overall low incomes of white families and prevail-ing gender roles, if a choice had to be made between paying the poll tax to ensure the right to vote of a man or of a woman, the man would al-most always win out.[19]

The 24th Amendment, ratified in 1964, abolished the use of the poll tax (or any other tax) as a precondition for voting in federal elections.[20] But controversy continues in the United States. One current debate concerns whether requiring a citizen to purchase a state identification card in order to vote is tantamount to a poll tax, effectively barring poor people, disproportionately from minority communities, from voting. And "felony disenfranchisement" is widespread, amounting to 6 million Americans who are forbidden to vote because of laws restricting voting rights for those convicted of felony-level crimes: In Alabama in 2016, more than 285,000 felons were disenfranchised—more than half of them were black, even though African Americans comprise only around one-quarter of the state's population.[21] Scott Douglas, executive direc-tor of Greater Birmingham (Alabama) Ministries, has called the system "the poll tax in extreme."[22]

Leaps of Faith

Religion and taxation can be a combustible mixture. Rarely more so than in seventeenth-century Japan, where it produced the last major battle of the samurai era.[23]

The religious element was the persecution of Christians,[24] complete with hideous martyrdoms. This began late in the sixteenth century and intensified with the consolidation of the Tokugawa shogunate following the battle of Sekigahara in 1600. It was felt especially keenly in the area southeast of Nagasaki, including the Shimabara peninsula, where there were as many as 300,000 converts. These Christians were distrusted by a government that objected not so much to their ideas as to their potential role as agents of foreigners intent on seizing control for themselves— not without some reason.

The tax element came from the determination of the local daimyo (feudal lord), of the Matsukura clan, to build a spanking new castle in the city of Shimabara—at the expense, of course, of the peasantry. Tax liabilities were doubled, so that, in an area already devastated by bad weather, farmers were expected to hand over 60 percent of their crops:[25] "far more taxes," a Dutch merchant reported, "than they are able to do, in such manner that they languish from hunger." Tax enforcement was punitive at best, and murderous at worse: "Those who could not pay . . . were dressed in a rough straw coat . . . tied around the neck and body, the hands being tightly bound behind their backs with ropes, after which the straw coats were set on fire."

The abuse of women, among the triggers of the 1380 peasant revolt in England, proved critical in Shimabara, too. One story tells of a tax official placing a farmer's daughter-in-law in a "water jail"—a *Deer Hunter*-type partly submerged cage—until tax had been paid. After 6 days, she died. In December 1637, the rebellion began.

Led, at least nominally, by Jerome Amakusa,[26] little more than a boy but a charismatic Christian leader, the rebellion had real victories in its early days. The rebels included not just farmers, despised by the samurai class as barely worth fighting, but also *ronin*—samurai who had lost their leaders. The Shogun in Edo ordered more than 200,000 soldiers to Shimabara, and by spring, the rebels, numbering about 30,000, were besieged in Hara castle. When the castle's inevitable fall came, all but a few of those inside were either slaughtered or chose to hasten their path to heaven by throwing themselves into the flames. The heads of Jerome Amakusa and 17,000 others were displayed on pikes.

Lessons were learned. For his oppressive rule, Matsukura—having failed to take the hint and commit *seppuku*, the honorable thing to do— was beheaded, the only daimyo to be executed in the entire Tokugawa

The flames of tax revolt in Shimabara.

period. A decade after the rebellion, taxes in the region were halved.[27] For a wise ruler—and the Tokugawa regime was to last, more or less peacefully, for another two centuries—the loyalty of their subjects is something they cannot afford to lose, but the exact amount of tax they pay is negotiable.

Religions clearly often have trouble dealing with those of other faiths—to put it mildly. Mere discriminatory taxation does not rank in horror with 17,000 heads on spikes. But it, too, has played a prominent role in shaping tax systems.

Many of the most sordid instances of tax discrimination involve the treatment of Jews. After the destruction of the temple in Jerusalem in the year 70, the Emperor Vespasian imposed an extra poll tax on Jews throughout the empire, the *Fiscus Judaicus*, which was a fixed sum imposed on all Jews, including women, children, and the elderly.[28] During the Middle Ages, special taxes on Jews were common throughout Europe, in a nasty interplay between anti-Semitism and the attractions of taxing profits associated with Jews' ability to lend money (not being subject to the Christian prohibition on usury).[29] In England, from the late 1190s a dedicated Exchequer of the Jews recorded and regulated the taxation of the Jews. Some historians estimate that in the 1240s and 1250s, Henry II taxed away half the wealth of the Jewish community (helping to pay for, among other things, the rebuilding of Westminster Abbey)[30] and, as we have seen, in 1290 Edward I expelled them. The climate did eventually change. Jews began to resettle in England in the 1630s, and in 1689, Parliament voted against a special tax on Jews, for fear of driving them abroad.[31]

On the Continent, Louis XII, King of France, expelled the Jews from Provence in 1498, and to make up for the loss of revenue, in 1512 levied a tax—the "tax of the neophytes"[32]—on those who had nonetheless remained and now accepted baptism. In Hungary the tax on Jews, beginning in 1747, was called a "tolerance tax" (*Toleranzgebührer*), based on the German law that a Jew was obliged to remit tax in order to be "tolerated." Even some excise taxes had higher rates for Jews, who were, for example, subject to heavier bridge tolls (called *leibzoll*, or "body tax," in German) than were Christians.[33] They also faced a tax on kosher meat, a marriage tax, and a tax on their synagogues and cemeteries.[34]

But it is not only Jews that have been at the wrong end of this kind of discrimination. Christians have discriminated against Christians. In post-Reformation England, anyone missing church without good reason—and that would mean Catholics—was fined 12d each time.[35] That was a lot, but in practice, this provision[36] seems to have been used more for harassment than for wholesale oppression.[37] Robert Walpole introduced a special tax on Catholics, the "papists tax," in 1722,[38] and Catholics paid double land tax until 1794.[39]

Muslims, too—though historically relatively tolerant of other faiths—have levied discriminatory taxes on nonbelievers. The *jizya* tax targeted the *dhimmi* ("People of the Book"), a category that came to include not only Jews and Christians but also Hindus, Buddhists, Sikhs, and Jains in Moghul India. The precise charge varied over time and place, but generally it was levied on free-born, able-bodied men of military age and bore some rough relation to wealth. Poor people were exempt, as were slaves, women, children, the old, the sick, monks, and hermits (who were presumably pretty hard to collect from anyway).

The *jizya* was, perhaps, not quite as bad as it may sound. The Christians and Jews living in Jerusalem when it was taken from the Byzantines by Muslims in 637, for instance, may have found that their tax bills went down.[40] The tax was often viewed as a payment in return for protecting non-Muslims (who could not serve as soldiers), and there are noble examples of the tax being returned when this responsibility was not fulfilled. The twelfth-century sultan of Egypt and Syria Saladin is said to have returned the *jizya* to the Christians of Syria when, in the face of the crusaders, he withdrew his army.[41] Moreover, non-Muslims were exempt from the *zakat*, a 2.5 percent tax initially on savings but increasingly income-related that, as one of the five pillars of Islam, continues to be raised in many Muslim countries.[42] In many cases, it seems, the price being charged for keeping one's faith was seen as a reasonable one (and better than the alternatives).

There does not, in any case, seem to have been great resistance to the *jizya*. In 1679, the Mughal Emperor Aurangzeb reimposed the tax, which had been removed a century earlier by the tolerant Akbar. (This was part of a wider anti-Hindu campaign, but noticeably coincided with a weak point in the emperor's finances.[43]) Anxious advisers warned him there would be serious trouble, and their worries increased when an earthquake struck soon after the decree was issued—surely a bad omen. Aurangzeb, however, staying impressively on-message, simply tweeted (well, not really) that "It is true that the earth trembled, but it is a result of the joy it felt at the course I am adopting."[44] There was some mosque-burning and fasting (removing exemptions is generally hard), but not enough for the tax to be removed.

The *jizya* lasted into modern times. Until 1834, pilgrims to Jerusalem continued to owe a tax that Charlemagne had remitted on behalf of all the city's Christians a thousand years earlier.[45] *Jizya* was abolished in the Ottoman Empire in 1856, although it was replaced by a tax on non-Muslims in lieu of military service.[46] By the early twentieth century, however, discriminatory taxes on non-Muslims had virtually disappeared.

The *jizya* has, though, recently returned to the news. In Egypt, the Muslim Brotherhood reportedly levied it on Coptic Christians in 2013.[47] And the Islamic State issued ultimatums to northern Iraq's dwindling Christian population, demanding they either convert to Islam, pay a

levy, or face death. "We offer [non-Muslims] three choices" said a statement issued in July 2014 in parts of Iraq and Syria, "Islam; the *dhimma*
contract—involving payment of *jizya*; if they refuse this they will have
nothing but the sword."[48]

Hateful though we now find both forms of discrimination, there is
one difference between the case of religion and those of gender and race
that we looked at earlier: The first can be changed, or be made to appear
to change, but the others (with rare exceptions) cannot. Discriminatory
taxes give an incentive to convert to the favored religion—and that
seems in some cases to have been at least one of the objectives (or at
least an added benefit), although in other instances, the tax also applied
to converts. Religion-based taxes do seem to occasionally have had
some such effect. In Egypt, monasteries were in 714 forbidden to accept
any newcomers—monks being exempt from taxation—to limit this
tax-avoiding leap of (reported) faith;[49] and districts in which the poll
tax on non-Muslims (applied from 641 to 1856) was more strictly enforced experienced more conversion to Islam among poor Copts.[50]

It can be hard to tell, of course, if conversions are sincere. This was a
recurrent problem with the tax exemptions often provided to Buddhists
in ancient China and Japan. In China, as early as the year 486, people
were assuming the title "entered into religion" as a form of tax evasion.
Having evidently run out of patience, the Emperor Taizong ordered in
629 that monks illegally ordained for tax evasion were to be executed.[51]
In 830, about 300,000 apparent monks and nuns were found to have false
ordination certificates, and many of the legitimate ones had been simply
purchased.[52] In 845, Emperor Wu-tsung returned 270,000 Buddhist "religious" to lay life. The Emperor Constantine I (306–337) had similar
trouble from his favoring of Christianity in the Roman Empire: When
many prominent citizens sought to become tax-exempt clerics, he forbade them, and wealthy plebeians, from entering holy orders for tax
reasons. But it is always hard to divine other people's motivations, so as
a way to get them to reveal this, it was later required that citizens entering
the priesthood surrender their property, in whole or in part.[53]

False ordination for tax purposes survives to this day. In the United
States, a contribution to a church, synagogue, or other religious organization is potentially tax deductible, and occasionally phony churches

are created as tax dodges. Maybe the best/worst example involves a brothel "church" in Phoenix, Arizona, where in 2011, sisterly love was offered to male parishioners in exchange for "donations."[54] Coming a close second on this unsavory list is the case of Hardenburgh, New York, where in the early 1980s, 200 of the 236 property owners in the town were granted religious tax exemptions because their properties were designated as branches of the mail-order Universal Life Church.[55]

As with gender and race, so with religion, discrimination in taxation can be implicit rather than explicit, even if its intent is absolutely clear. The tax on kosher meat mentioned above is just one example.[56] The Dutch East India Company in Malacca, Malaysia, imposed a tax on pig slaughtering that by its nature would only be levied on non-Muslims, primarily Chinese and Christian households.[57] Tax rules do not need to mention race or religion to benefit members of some religious groups rather than others. Income tax measures that provide tax benefits to large families, for example through personal exemptions, favor those following religions that encourage, or even demand, large families.

Outsiders

Wherever the categories of "us" and "them" exist, discriminatory taxation has often followed.

Strangers in a Strange Land

Foreigners in our midst are an obvious "them." Often more than tinged with racism and xenophobia, special taxes on foreigners living among us date back to long before Machiavelli advised princes to look beyond their own subjects for revenue.

In classical Athens, as we saw earlier, foreigners paid a special poll tax; in 1440, the English introduced an alien poll tax; in 1885, Canada imposed a levy on the entry of Chinese immigrants, largely railroad workers (replaced in 1923 by an outright ban). And in recent times, several countries have imposed special taxes on foreigners' purchases of real estate, amid concerns of their driving up prices beyond the pocketbooks of locals. Among them, in 2016, was the provincial government of British Columbia, which imposed a 15 percent tax on foreign homebuyers in the Vancouver region—in practice mostly from China, reviving century-old tensions about racism.[58]

But views as to what is acceptable discrimination—who are the foreigners?—evidently change over time. One of the most tangible indications of the development of a common sense of identity—also serving to reinforce it—is a conscious prohibition of taxes of this kind. The "Comity Clause" of the U.S. Constitution,[59] for instance, prevents states from discriminating against other states. Nondiscrimination against those from other member states is a central principle of the European Union (and one that in the past few years has been powerfully applied to tax issues). And a standard element of the treaties that countries sign to guide their mutual tax treatment is a commitment to treat foreign enterprises in the same way as domestic ones. Indeed, the pressures on many countries these days are often to tax foreigners more favorably than their own citizens, in order to attract tax base and activity from abroad while exploiting their own less-mobile domestic tax base: We look at this trend in chapter 11.

Taxes as Punishment

Treason, in the aphorism of John Harington,[60] never prospers: for if it does, none dare call it treason. It does, in any case, often come if not with execution at least with a hefty tax. We saw earlier the expropriation of the assets of those guillotined during the French Revolution, but there are plenty of other examples. In ancient Rome, for example, and from at least the time of Sulla (circa 90 BCE),[61] confiscation of the estates of the treacherous was a handy source of revenue—with sometimes no great need to be sure that the treachery part had actually happened.

Taxation as punishment for political failure also came to the fore in England during the interregnum between the Civil War and the Restoration, when the country came as close to military rule as it ever has. In 1655, Oliver Cromwell levied the "decimation tax,"[62] charged at 10 percent on the income of unreformed Royalists with an estate worth more than £100 per year.[63] The tax fell on those who had borne arms for the late king (beheaded in 1649) or for his son Charles Stuart, or who "adhered to, assisted or abetted" them. Conversion offered a way out. Cromwell assured Royalists who shifted their allegiance to him that "the government would much more esteem their reformation, than desire their prejudice or harm."[64]

Implementation, however, was problematic. For instance, exactly what behavior was to count as having assisted or abetted? Avoidance by the rich—including through devices still common today, such as the use of trusts—threatened to make the laws into "spider-webs, to take small flies, and let the great ones 'scape."[65] Another problem came from how the tax was structured: having (or revealing) 1 more pound of income, from 99 to 100, increased tax liability by £10. This had predictable effects: "Men do now begin to be very industrious to bring in their estates to be under £100 per annum."[66] This feature of a tax rate schedule, where a small change in the base can trigger a discontinuous and disproportionately large change in tax liability, is known as a "notch." More pervasive in tax history (and today) than you might think, notches are irritating for taxpayers, but for reasons we will see in chapter 9, are loved by academics.

The idea of taxation as punishment has not gone away. After the Global Financial Crisis of 2007, the widespread calls for heavier taxation of the financial sector in general—and bankers in particular—were more than tinged with the color of vengeance. Taxation, however, is generally not a good instrument of revenge, in part because the guilty may well have left the scene by the time taxes can be enacted. Just as many Royalists were dead or had fled by the time Cromwell's Commonwealth was established, so the financial institutions whose risk-taking was most culpable for the crisis were those most likely to have gone under. And even if they had not, their stockholders at the time may well have sold their shares.

Hard Choices

Some personal characteristics are conventionally taken as perfectly reasonable attributes by which to differentiate tax treatment across otherwise identical people. Smokers, for instance, are accustomed to nonsmokers taxing them as pariahs. In other cases, however, we accept what might seem to be horizontal inequities on the grounds of sheer practicality. A tax on heating oil falls more heavily on residents of New England, where oil is commonly used to heat homes, than on those in New Mexico, but it would be administratively more expensive (and may induce bootlegging) to tax oil differentially by the region of use. And sometimes there may be broad agreement that some differences—in people's needs, for instance—are a legitimate basis for differential tax treatment, but not about the appropriate extent: Perhaps those with children should pay less tax on a given level of income than those without—but exactly how much?

Still more problematic is that it is almost impossible to eliminate implicit tax biases. Even an income tax (or a general sales tax) has implicit elements of horizontal inequity. This is because people differ in what economists call their "preference for goods versus leisure," and what everyone else would label as "acquisitiveness versus laziness." Someone who likes the things money can buy, and is willing to work to acquire them, suffers more from a tax on the income they earn in order to do so (or on that consumption itself) than would someone else who could earn exactly the same market wage but prefers to watch daytime soap operas. To avoid this kind of horizontal inequity, some academics like the idea of taxing people on the basis of their potential wage rate rather than on their actual wage income (the latter reflecting how hard they choose to work); working any less or more would then have no impact on tax liability. The result would effectively be a lump-sum tax related to potential ability to pay, along the lines mentioned in chapter 4 (and whose attractions are taken up in chapter 10). The rather large fly in the ointment here is of course the difficulty of measuring—even conceptualizing— someone's potential earnings.

There is at least one important area of tax policy where achieving horizontal equity is well-nigh impossible: the relative tax treatment of individuals and couples. As the early income taxes began to emerge, most countries treated the married couple as the legal tax unit—that is, tax was charged on the sum of the partners' income. This, though, has gradually changed, and while the income tax unit in the United States is generally the couple ("joint filing"),[67] in most other countries the income tax unit is the individual, meaning that each income earner owes tax based on their own income, irrespective of what their partner's income is.

But, so long as we want the tax system to be progressive, neither approach can simultaneously satisfy two attractive horizontal equity principles—that whether a couple is treated as a unit or separately makes no difference to their tax bill (no "marriage penalties" or bonuses); and that how a couple's income is split between them should make no difference for their combined tax liability. The second criterion can be met only if a couple's tax bill depends only on their total income. But if the tax system is progressive, the total tax paid when people are taxed separately will always depend not just on their total income but how it is split between them—so we cannot also meet the first criterion. The upshot is that under a progressive income tax getting married can greatly affect total taxes due.

The difficulties (and perhaps impossibility) of avoiding implicit discrimination, the possibility that such discrimination may even serve the desirable end of reducing excess burden, and logical conundrums all mean that—even if we agree on what characteristics the tax system ought to be blind to—achieving horizontal equity is much less straightforward than it may at first seem.

The last three chapters have looked at how various taxes stack up in terms of ideas of fairness. But a link is missing, as in almost all public discussion of these issues. A tax may be designed to be fair—tied, for example, to some proxy of ability to pay. But that does not mean that is how things will truly work out. We have seen some hints of this problem, such as the tax on female servants in Georgian England that bore not just on their employers but also led some of them to find less salubrious employment. This is just one instance of a key insight: The real burden of taxation does not always fall where it appears, or is intended to. It is time to look at this issue more closely.

7

Stick or Shift?

> I had a research student who took up that subject. He began about 1908; he had not finished before the beginning of the War, and I have not heard of him since.
>
> EDWIN CANNAN[1]

THE TOPIC TAKEN UP by this unhappy (and poorly advised) student was that of tax incidence: the question of who really bears the burden of taxation. Governments often seem to intend that the impact of a tax fall on some particular group. But taxes do not necessarily stick where they are intended to: Market forces mean that the real burden may be shifted to someone else. Figuring out where the burden ends up, as Professor Cannan's student discovered, is far from easy, and there is plenty of scope for unintended consequences. Those consequences and the implications of understanding tax incidence more generally can be profound.

Take, for instance, the tax on exports of wool, which from 1275, English kings discovered could raise vast amounts of revenue.[2] The tax was remitted by wool merchants, but landowners like the wool-growing Abbot of Meaux quickly realized that they were the ones who really bore the burden of the tax: "It is those who own the wool who pay this tax to the king, and not the merchants . . . for wools are sold at a lesser price the greater the tax payable to the king for them."[3] Parliament, dominated by wool producers, objected loudly. It did not succeed in having the tax removed, but a slow-moving constitutional crisis had begun. And the outcome was a fundamental step toward the supremacy of parliament: In 1362, the principle was established that it was parliament, not the merchants, who had the right to grant such taxes to the king.[4]

Medieval English kings may not have cared much (initially at least) about who really bore the burden of the export tax on wool. Sometimes, however, the workings out of tax incidence can undermine what is presumably the object of policy. In 1990, the U.S. Congress enacted a 10 percent tax on several luxury items, including boats costing more than $100,000, as a compromise measure that would burden the rich without taxing their income at increased rates. But things did not work out like that. The *New York Times* described the tax as "a stake driven into the heart of [the pleasure boat] industry,"[5] and the *Sun-Sentinel* reported that "Nationally, yacht sales dipped from 7,500 in 1990 to 3,500 in 1992. There were 30,000 jobs lost nationwide, 8,000 in South Florida, where one in every four of America's boats is built" (and where the *Sun-Sentinel* is based).[6] "It was the hard-working stiff who sanded the teak decks of those yachts who eventually lost his job because yacht sales and ownership plummeted."[7] The tax on luxuries, that is, had not stuck on the rich as intended, but had at least in part been shifted to others—just as Pitt had presumably not intended his tax on female servants to drive them into prostitution.

The lesson is that it is hard to make sensible tax policy without giving some thought to where the final burden of taxation will fall. But it can be hard to figure out where exactly that is. Even worse, however—and not uncommon—is not even trying to. Incidence is not always easy to see, but there are some robust principles to guide the search. And some tempting errors to avoid.

False Starts

There are several traps for the unwary—and opportunities for the unscrupulous—when thinking about tax incidence.

One is to presume that the name of a tax has anything to do with where the burden it imposes ultimately falls. Just because a tax is labeled as being "on" something or someone does not settle its incidence. Most social security systems, for instance, distinguish between an employer's and an employee's contribution. But both are typically levied as taxes on wage income, so—whatever their incidence may actually be—it is hard to see why there should be any difference in their real effects, at least in the long run. Obvious and uncontentious enough, you might think. Yet the widely watched *Doing Business* reports of the World Bank put great weight on precisely that distinction, with the employer's—but not the employee's—contribution being counted against countries as business-unfriendly in the tax part of the assessment. Governments have not failed to notice that shifting from the employer's to the employee's contribution, while leaving the total unchanged, is an easy and essentially meaningless way to get a better business-friendliness score.

There is a more general point here: Tax systems that sound or look different but effectively give equivalent treatment will have the same incidence. For example, if both are perfectly enforced, an 8 percent retail sales tax should generate the same pattern of burden as an 8 percent VAT (whatever that burden happens to be). That seems straightforward enough, and most analyses get this right. But many stumble when addressing less obvious tax equivalences. For example, a flat-rate tax on wages is essentially equivalent to a flat-rate consumption tax (such as a VAT). To see this, suppose that your only source of income is salary, and you do not plan to leave a bequest. Which would you hate least: a 25 percent tax on everything you earn or a 25 percent tax on everything you spend? Presumably you wouldn't care, as either way your lifetime consumption possibilities are reduced by 25 percent.[8] These are equivalent taxes. But incidence analyses often employ separate (and even logically inconsistent) methods to assess the pattern of burden for taxes on the basis of arbitrary and—because of an element of equivalence—to some degree meaningless categorization, such as "indirect" taxes on consumption and "direct" taxes on income.

A second trap is to place too much importance on where the legal liability for remitting a tax lies, meaning who writes the check to the government. The Emperor Nero at one point ordered that the 4 percent sales tax on slaves be remitted by the seller instead of the buyer. The Roman historian Tacitus, however, realized that "the tax of one twenty-fifth part of the goods for sale was remitted, nominally rather than with any real effect, because although the seller was ordered to pay it, it accrued to the buyer as part of the price."[9] In effect, Tacitus noted that the identity of the remitter mattered not at all.

We are not all as smart as Tacitus, but his point is largely just common sense. When the VAT rate is increased, shoppers do not worry any less about an increased burden because they are not the ones legally obliged to remit the money to the tax authority (businesses are). More generally, and setting aside possibilities for avoiding or evading the tax, it should not matter for the final outcome on which side of the market a tax is imposed. This point, and failure to grasp it, often crops up. A typical example: In 2018, controversy raged in Spain over who should remit a mortgage stamp duty, the banks or the consumer-borrowers. The Supreme Court of Spain got involved, first ruling that lenders would be legally responsible to remit the tax but then changing its ruling. A sensible skeptic in the debate was the finance director of the real estate company Neinor Homes, recognizing that even if remitted by lenders the tax would "end up falling on the customer anyway,"[10] the key word for our point being "anyway" (who actually remitted the tax being immaterial). To avoid conflating the distinct issues of who remits tax payments and who bears the real burden, we tend in this book to avoid talking of people "paying" taxes (even though, we admit, the result sometimes sounds odd).

The caveat about avoidance and evasion, however, is important. If opportunities to escape a tax differ depending on who is responsible for remitting it then where that liability is placed can matter a good deal. From the mid-1980s to mid-2000s, for instance, many U.S. states changed the point in the supply chain legally responsible for remitting state diesel fuel taxes. And the evidence is that moving the point of tax collection from the retail station to higher in the supply chain, where it could be more easily monitored, substantially raised the pass-through of diesel taxes to the retail price, suggesting that evasion had diminished.[11]

The thud of someone falling into the third trap is to be heard when they say "business should bear its fair share of tax." Mitt Romney, when running for U.S. president in 2012, famously remarked that "Corporations are people."[12] In a legal sense, he was right: In most jurisdictions, corporations are legal persons. The idea of a company as an association of people separate from its human creators dates back to the Romans.[13] In terms of tax incidence, however, this is all nonsense. Businesses are not real, live people, and so in themselves cannot suffer any meaningful burden from taxation. Their owners, those who work for them, and those who buy their products—real people all—might bear a tax burden, but not the business itself. Of course, the presumption behind this mantra is often that taxes labeled as being on businesses or corporations will somehow be borne by their wealthy owners: but we have already learned to beware of labels. The incidence of the corporation tax, as will be seen shortly, is far from clear in principle and far from settled as a matter of fact. But wherever it ends up, the burden must be on actual people.

The final trap is to suppose that incidence is something that can easily be controlled by government edict. When retail sales taxes first took hold in the United States, in the 1930s, some states—at the insistence of retailers, worried about the impact on their bottom lines—stipulated that the taxes "must" be passed on to consumers.[14] As one prominent tax scholar remarked, "To the economist accustomed to think in terms of impersonal forces operating over long periods of time, such an attempt to control the incidence of the tax without involving price fixing seems at first sight naïve."[15] And, we would add, at second and third sight, too. As long as retailers (and sellers more generally) can freely set their prices, no such guarantee can be effective.

Retailers also did not want to bear the ire of their customers due to increased prices, preferring that the government take the blame. This played a role in the U.S. presidential race of 1936. Facing an uphill campaign against the incumbent Democrat Franklin Delano Roosevelt,

Republicans tried to cast blame on his administration for the high consumer prices caused by excise taxes. The campaign encouraged butcher shops to display blackboards with three columns listing the price of each cut of meat absent tax, the amount of tax, and the total price, alongside the phrase, "Don't blame your butcher—meat is low, taxes are high." In response, the attorney general threatened to prosecute butchers displaying such information, citing a rarely used federal statute that imposed a fine and/or a jail sentence on any person who falsely attributed part of the cost of a product to a tax.[16]

An alternative strategy to blaming it all on the government is for retailers to give the impression that they are the ones bearing the tax burden. Governments tend not to like this ploy either, probably because the language used often suggests that the tax liability has somehow been removed. The state of Washington allows retailers to advertise that they pay the sales tax only if the words "tax included" are uttered as loudly as the rest of the commercial, or shown in letters at least half the size of the other words in the ad, and if the tax is also itemized separately on receipts. Several other states[17] simply prohibit retailers from using phrases like "Tax-Free Sale" or "We'll Pay Your Sales Tax."[18]

Nor is the Cnut-like effort to roll back the waves of tax incidence some American peculiarity. The French tried something similar in 2009: A cut in the VAT rate to 5.5 percent from 19.6 percent on restaurant food in 2009 was accompanied by a pledge from restaurateurs, unenforceable other than in the very short run, to pass along much of their tax savings in the form of lower menu prices.[19]

The problem with legislating tax incidence is that it is tantamount to controlling prices. Without such control, when a tax is imposed, any business is free to adjust the pretax price, so that the change in the consumer price reflects both the tax and any such price adjustment. Thus, the ultimate incidence of a tax depends on market forces that constrain business pricing decisions, not on the wishes of the government. So, to understand the incidence of a tax, there is no alternative to thinking through how it is likely to change market outcomes. That may sound dull. But incidence issues have sparked real conflict, and not only in medieval England.

Burgling Other People's Intellect

The repeal in 1846 of the Corn Laws—a complex set of tariffs on wheat[20] and other grains—is a landmark in British political history. It marked the ascendancy of manufacturing and commercial interests over an agriculture-based elite, and became the emblem of a British commitment to something like free trade. It is also when many of the central ideas still used in thinking about tax incidence were first hammered out.

The issues at stake were of real importance to the daily lives of many, and they drew into the debate two giants of the profession (and close friends). One was David Ricardo (1772–1823). After making his fortune in the City (most spectacularly, a reported gain of £1 million from betting right on the outcome of the Battle of Waterloo), Ricardo became one of history's great economists—and arguably the most brilliant tax economist of all time (which you may think a pretty low bar). The other was Thomas Malthus (1766–1834),[21] whose views of population dynamics prompted Thomas Carlyle to label economics as the "dismal science," a moniker that has stuck.[22]

The analytical question at the heart of the debate was how the import tariffs of the Corn Laws[23] affected the interests of the members of three key social classes: landowners, workers and capitalists. Everyone agreed that landowners were winners. Spelling out the precise way in which they won led Ricardo and Malthus to develop the theory of "rents."[24] The central idea is that there is only so much good agricultural land: it is in fixed—"perfectly inelastic"—supply. So the higher demand for agricultural land implied by tariff-induced higher food prices increases the price of such land (while also bringing some less-good land into cultivation). And those who own the good land get a premium that does not reflect any additional investment or effort on their part.[25] This (and not the everyday sense of payment for the use of some property) is what economists mean by "rent": payment in excess of the minimum that those undertaking some activity (growing crops, in this case) require in order to do so. This concept turns out to be critical for tax analysis.

No one thought that industrial workers benefited. The Corn Laws' upward pressure on the price of food was, for them, a huge issue:

David Ricardo: An intellect worth burgling.

Factory workers were spending about three-fifths of their income on food.[26] The question was whether the tariffs actually harmed them. Ricardo and Malthus (later supported by another public finance star, John Stuart Mill)[27] thought not. In the view famously developed by Malthus, the number of workers would adjust—through, for example, starvation—to any reduction in their real incomes triggered by rising food prices in such a way that, ultimately, they would earn only the minimum needed to survive. The supply of their labor, in modern terms, was seen as "perfectly elastic" at the subsistence wage, at least in the long term. That is, whatever labor was required would eventually be forthcoming at a fixed real wage[28] equal to the minimum needed for survival. Higher food prices might, in the short term, reduce workers' real wage. But their consequent earlier deaths and reduced birth rates, together with lower survival rates of their children, would in time cut the supply of workers and lead to an increase in their money wages just sufficient to offset the higher food prices and raise their real wage back up to subsistence level. Malthus's "dismal" label was well-earned. This absence of any long-term harm is, of course, very cold comfort—giving another meaning to Keynes's later dictum: "In the long run we are all dead."[29]

The capitalists were clear-cut losers, most obviously through the higher money wages that partly or wholly restored workers' real incomes in the face of higher food prices. They were unable to pass on these wage costs to buyers of their products, the argument went, because their core business was exporting (predominantly cloth, at this point), and higher prices would prompt foreigners to take their business elsewhere.

All this became the stuff of fractious public dispute, notably through the agitation of the Anti-Corn Law League, one of whose leading activists was credited with having "flooded the whole land with his arguments in pamphlets, in broadsides, in speeches, in letters, in addresses ... whereby the truths of philosophy and of political economy are made accessible even to the artisan in his workshop."[30] Nor is it a coincidence that The Economist, to this day a staunch supporter of free trade, was founded at this time. It is hard not to be amazed at the quality of (and public interest in) the debate and wistful that nowadays taxation rarely seems to receive such considered and widespread attention. And it is hard not to be struck by the contrast with the situation in the United States, where, at much the same time, the issue and politics were the other way around (culminating in the Nullification crisis of 1832–1833): The agricultural South was objecting to tariffs that protected manufacturing in the North. There, threats of violence were exchanged, rather than snappily titled pamphlets.

The Corn Law issue was settled by Prime Minister Robert Peel. Not a man for one-page memos, Peel claimed to have "read all that has been written by the gravest authorities on political economy on the subject of rent, wages, taxes, tithes."[31] For him, the key point was that "[if] the condition of the labourer has been rendered worse by the operation of the Corn-law," then "the Corn-law is practically at an end."[32] Drawing on experience in the early 1840s, which saw both high and low wheat prices, Peel arrived at his answer: "You will say, as writers upon political economy have already said, that the ultimate tendency of wages is to accommodate itself to the price of food. I must say that I do not believe it."[33]

With this, and hurried along by the prospect of a second failure of the potato harvest in Ireland, Peel was ready to work with the opposition to repeal the Corn Laws. For this, he became a despised outcast from the Tory Party: a "burglar," sneered the ambitious Benjamin Disraeli, "of other's intellect."[34] Two hours after the Corn Laws were finally repealed, the landed elite, his old allies, took their revenge by defeating Peel on unrelated legislation. Resigning, he became a rare example of a prime minister rejected by the House of Commons but, spotted by the crowds when he left Parliament through a side door, cheered in the street.[35]

You Must Remember This

The theory of tax incidence has spurred a huge literature since Ricardo and Malthus. By 1899, the great public finance economist Edwin R. A. Seligman was referring to the views of no fewer than 146 people who wrote on the subject, plus "anonymous writers" and even "American writers."[36] And the pace has not slackened since. Even Peel would have trouble keeping up with the literature today. Much of modern incidence theory, however, is built around a single idea that emerged from the Corn Law debate.

The idea is that which group it is that ends up bearing the burden of a tax depends on the relative ease with which all those involved can find some alternative to the taxed activity. We may no longer think of wages as determined by a Malthusian iron law of subsistence, for instance, but we can still absorb the key lesson that if an unlimited supply of labor were available so long as workers received at least some minimal after-tax wage, then they would not bear the burden of any tax. In the Malthusian view, workers' alternative in the case of being offered a lower wage was that of eventually dying out—an unhappy alternative, but one that prevented the after-tax wage from going any lower.

At the opposite extreme of something fixed in supply, land stands out as the obvious example. And economists have long been fascinated with it. Pursuing the inelasticity of its supply to its logical conclusion, the physiocrats, a school of Enlightenment-era economists in ancien régime France, argued that all taxes are ultimately taxes on land and are borne by landowners. John Locke took a similar if slightly more guarded position: "Taxes, however contrived, and out of whose Hand soever immediately taken, do . . . for the most part terminate upon Land."[37] How come? Take, say, a tax on wig powder. Suppose this tax leads to buyers being charged a higher price. Then the proudly adorned wig wearers will have less money left over to pay for other things, including their housing; so rents (in the everyday sense of the term) will fall, and landowners will consequently bear the final burden. The bewigged may spend less on walking canes, too, but then the walking cane manufacturers have less to spend on their housing, and the same result follows. Much the same argument applies if the tax is passed back to the powder maker as a reduced price.

The analysis of land in Ricardo and Malthus is subtler and more general. For them, inelasticity of supply is a signal that providers of land might be paid more than the minimum they need to put the land to work: that they might, in this sense, earn rents. By driving up the price of wheat, the Corn Laws raised rents on land already put to use, while also drawing more (but lower quality) land into production. That made the Corn Law good news for landlords.

All that is on the supply side. But similar considerations come into play on the demand side. The easier buyers find it to substitute into alternatives to whatever is being taxed (that is, the more elastic their demand)—buying glamorous vacation homes, for example, rather than fancy taxed yachts—the less burden they will suffer. Any tendency for the tax-included price to rise will be weakened by a flight of consumers to the untaxed alternatives. It is harder to think of things that are in perfectly inelastic demand than it is to think of things in perfectly inelastic supply: After all, if the price of something goes high enough, no one can afford to buy it. But the general principle still applies: Where demand is relatively inelastic—think of perfumes, say—buyers are likely to bear much of the burden of a tax.

Where the ultimate burden of a tax falls depends on the balance between these demand and supply elasticities. In short, people who consume or produce taxed activities for which there are few good alternatives end up holding the tax bag. These alternatives include switching to substitutes in consumption (footmen rather than female servants) that are untaxed or lightly taxed, using different production methods (using more labor and fewer machines), or even migrating to another jurisdiction. It is the people with the fewest alternatives that tend to get stuck with most of the tax burden. How this plays out may well differ in the short and long runs, as the options realistically can change: It takes some time, for example, for Malthusian workers to die out or breed less. But the things to remember—that incidence depends on the relative responsiveness of demand and supply, and to keep an eye open for rents—take us a very long way. They can provide insight into policies whose effect is far from obvious until one gets out of the habit of taking taxes at face value and into the habit of wondering about their true incidence. We look next at some contemporary examples that show the power of these ideas—indeed the necessity of using them, if we are to be serious in thinking about practical issues of wide public concern. Before that, however, tax history, as usual, has its curiosities.

Buddy, Can You Spare 1/20th of a Dime?

In the early 1930s, 13 U.S. states, desperate for revenue during the Great Depression, introduced retail sales taxes, generally at a rate of 2 or 3 percent. At the time, however, many retail items, such as soap and candy, sold for 10 cents or less. This created an interesting dilemma. Think of a retailer who had been charging 10 cents for, say a box of bran flakes. A tax of 2 percent amounted to 0.2 cents on each box. But because the smallest coin was the penny, the retailer could not simply charge 10.2 cents per box. One solution came in the form of sales tax tokens,

A tenth of a penny for your thoughts.

introduced first by the state of Illinois in 1933 and followed by many other states and dozens of communities. Typically denominated in multiples of one mill (1/10 cent) or ¼ cent, these were purchased by retailers from the government. So consider again that box of bran flakes. Now the customer might hand the cashier 11 cents and in return get eight 1-mill tax tokens, worth 0.8 cents, that could be used to buy things later, whether at the same or a different store.

The federal government took notice, however, because this practice conflicted with its unique mandate to issue the nation's money. The Roosevelt Administration petitioned Congress to authorize the issuance of two new coin denominations, the half cent and the tenth cent, but the idea died in committee. Ultimately, 12 states issued some form of tax token or scrip to address the problem of fractional coinage, but as prices rose and fractions of a cent faded in relative importance, the practice gradually disappeared. The state of Missouri was the last holdout, officially ending their use only in 1961.

Things Aren't Always What They Seem

Without considering incidence, the true effect of major tax policies can be—and often is—misunderstood.

Helping the Working Poor (or Their Employers)

The Earned Income Tax Credit (EITC) is the main policy tool used in the United States to alleviate poverty while encouraging work, with several other countries now having their own variant. It works as a subsidy on low earnings by providing a credit against income tax due that turns into a cash payment to the earner if the credit exceeds the liability (and is then withdrawn at higher income levels). In 2020, for example, the EITC provided an annual credit for a household with three children of up to $6,660.

Does the EITC stick and, as intended, benefit low-income workers? Maybe not completely. By making work more attractive, the EITC induces an increase in labor supply among low-income workers. Unless the demand for their labor is perfectly inelastic (meaning, improbably, that employers will employ the same amount of labor no matter what wage they have to pay), this increase in labor supply drives wages down. To the extent that wages fall, the benefit of the EITC to the intended beneficiaries—low-income, often low-skill, workers—is reduced, and some of the intended transfer redounds to employers. Moreover, low-skill workers who do not receive the EITC are hurt even more, because—as they compete with the workers who do receive it—they receive the lower wages but do not get the credit.

It seems that such shifting does not completely dissipate the intended effect. But nor is it trivial. One estimate is that for every dollar that single mothers receive from the EITC, they ultimately lose $0.30 through lower wages. Employers of low-skill labor capture a whopping $0.73 per dollar: $0.30 of this decline coming from those EITC-eligible single workers and another $0.43 from workers who are not EITC-eligible but whose wages nevertheless fall.[38] The net transfer to all low-skill workers, considering both those who get the EITC and those who do not, is, according to this study, just 27 (that is, 100 minus 73) cents per dollar of the EITC.[39]

The risk that measures intended to improve the lot of the poor can end up benefiting, maybe even more, the better-off, is a recurrent one. A hypothetical but splendid example was given by, of all people, Winston Churchill, during his time (before the First World War) as a (somewhat unconvincing) radical liberal, and an unlikely guru on tax incidence.[40] A church, he imagines, gives free food to the neighborhood's poor families. The poor move into the area, causing rents to rise. The poor stop moving into the area when the increased rental costs just offset the value of the free food. And thus the poor ultimately gain nothing; the gain is to the landlords, from being able to charge higher rents.

Are Tax-Free Municipal Bonds a Giveaway to the Savvy Rich?

Sometimes tax shifting can offset what might appear to be horizontal inequity. In the United States, the interest paid on state and local government bonds (often issued to cover the cost of building municipal airports, schools, sewage systems, and the like) is exempt from federal income tax.[41] Some investors buy tax-free municipal bonds, and some buy taxable bonds. Comparing them, it might seem at first glance to be horizontally inequitable that people who hold different types of bonds should on that account be treated very differently—some owe tax, and others don't. Superficially, savvy investors who hold tax-exempt bonds seem to be big winners.

But take a look at the yields listed in the *Wall Street Journal*.[42] In late July 2019, the yield on (taxable) 10-year U.S. Treasury bonds was 2.02 percent, while that on (tax-exempt) AAA-rated 10-year municipal bonds was only 1.55 percent. So, if your marginal tax rate were 23.3 percent,[43] you would earn exactly the same return after tax from investing in Treasury bonds as you would by investing in municipal debt. So ultimately no inherent benefit accrues to such an investor from holding municipal bonds. The benefit of the tax exemption goes instead to the state and local governments (and from there, one hopes, to their residents), because by issuing tax-exempt securities, they can borrow at a lower rate of interest than can other borrowers—corporations, for example—who offer securities that are of comparable risk but are fully taxable. The story is more complicated when individual marginal tax rates differ, as happens with a graduated tax schedule. But the basic point still holds: Because the tax exemption reduces the yield on municipal bonds, it is largely a benefit not to savvy investors but to state and local governments and their constituents.

The Murky Incidence of the Corporate Tax

One of the most contentious issues in incidence analysis—and some of the most vicious debates—relate to the corporate income tax. Right from the start, which in the United States came with the 1909 corporate franchise tax, supporters embraced the idea that taxing corporations would put a tax burden on corporate interests, presumably the rich shareholders of Standard Oil and the much-hated trusts. And many still think of the corporate tax in that way: for Standard Oil now read, say, Facebook. But there have always been doubts about its ultimate incidence. The powerful Senator William Borah from Idaho argued in 1909 that "the great corporations, controlling the great industries in this country, are standing side by side . . . in support of this [proposed corporation tax] in preference to the [personal] income tax . . . [b]ecause they can transfer this tax."[44]

So, what do the principles laid out above tell us about the likely incidence of the corporate tax? To apply them, start with what a typical corporate tax does. It taxes profits that are calculated as revenues minus the costs of doing business, including among these costs depreciation allowances for investment purchases and interest paid. That gives a tax base made up of two things. One is a return to equity that is just enough to keep shareholders investing in the business. The other is rent: an amount in excess of the minimum return that those investors required.

We take up the rent part in chapter 10. For the tax on equity returns, what matters are the alternative investment opportunities available to investors: the greater these are, the more elastic will be the supply of capital to the taxed corporate sector and the less the burden will fall on those who supply it. To the extent the tax reduces the return they earn in the corporate sector below the minimum they need, it will lead them to invest elsewhere. It could be, for example—an increasingly important possibility that we look at more closely in chapter 11—that investors will instead put their money abroad. In this case, the capital stock in the country imposing the tax declines, reducing labor productivity and so leading to a lower wage rate. In either case, the burden of the corporate tax may fall not on the plutocrats, but (again) on the hardworking stiffs they employ.[45] Or it could be that they will invest instead in businesses not subject to the corporate tax, such as, these days, partnerships, or those in the large "S-corporation" sector in the United States. Where the burden falls then depends in part on whether it is corporate or noncorporate businesses that use labor more intensively. If it is the noncorporate sector, then the burden on workers is dissipated as the shift in production away from the corporate sector actually increases the demand for labor.

As with the Corn Law debate, the effects of corporate tax changes may differ in the short and long runs. Those movements of capital between sectors and countries are likely to take some time to work out. Almost instantaneously, however, an unanticipated increase in the corporate income tax will depress share prices, and to that extent will be borne by those then holding shares in the companies affected. Also in the shorter run (and mitigating the extent of the real burden), firms will look for ways to avoid the tax. They will tend, for instance, to rely more heavily on borrowing rather than on equity to finance themselves, as a higher tax rate increases even more the attractions of being able to deduct interest.[46]

The question of how much of the burden of the corporate tax ultimately falls on labor is not only a tough one intellectually. It also requires toughness from those venturing a public opinion. The debate in the United States became personal, and very nasty, in late 2017, when the question was posed of who would benefit from a proposed massive cut in the U.S. federal corporate tax rate from 35 to, ultimately, 21 percent. The then-chair of President Trump's Council of Economic Advisers (CEA), Kevin Hassett, argued that this would increase the annual paycheck of the average household by between $4,000 and $9,000.

Prominent Democrat economists could hardly contain their contempt. Jason Furman, the previous CEA chair under President Obama, called the analysis "more than a little far-fetched," and "absurd."[47] In return, Hassett characterized one of the critiques as "scientifically indefensible" and "fiction." Former Secretary of the Treasury Lawrence Summers shot back by calling the CEA claim "dishonest, incompetent and absurd" and asserting that if a PhD student submitted the analysis as a term paper, he would be "hard pressed to give it a passing grade."[48] All pretty entertaining for onlookers, but the ad hominem assaults did not do our profession any good. So, let's go to the videotape: What does the evidence show?

A raft of studies has looked at the evidence. One survey found the studies it looked at were "seriously flawed, produce unreasonable estimates, are not robust, . . . or are inconsistent with theory," but managed, nonetheless, to conclude that the evidence suggests that workers shoulder between 16 and 40 percent of the corporate tax burden.[49] In 2013, the U.S. Joint Committee on Taxation—responsible for estimating the distributional impact of federal tax proposals—allocated 75 percent of the burden of corporate income taxes to owners of capital in the long run, with the remainder mostly borne by labor. Using a similar method, the Congressional Budget Office as of 2010 similarly allocates 25 percent of corporate income taxes to labor in its long-run estimates, while the Department of the Treasury allocates 18 percent.[50]

Of course, just because the key U.S. tax shops broadly agree that around one-quarter of the burden of the U.S. corporate tax falls on labor does not make that view correct. Still less does it tell us what its incidence may be elsewhere in the world. The more open an economy is to capital movements, for example, the more the burden is likely to fall on labor (because capital then has the easy alternative of moving abroad). We would also expect quite a different effect when one country alone increases its corporate tax rate than when they all do (and so cut off one route by which capital might escape the increase). Moreover, the right answer depends on the design of the corporate tax. To the extent that it is structured so as to bear only on rents, in particular, the burden can confidently be expected to be only on shareholders. The incidence of any corporate tax reform depends on the design of the tax and the context in which it operates.

Regardless of the truth, defenders of cuts in the corporate tax, or taxes on capital and business income more generally, will no doubt maintain that the reductions will end up largely benefiting workers. Happily for them, "the murky incidence of corporate taxation means [General Electric's] lobbyists can push to preserve its tax breaks in good conscience."[51] At the same time, however, those concerned with workers' welfare who assume that a tax on corporations falls only on those who own the corporations risk doing their cause a disservice.

The Big Picture

So far, we have been looking at the incidence of particular taxes. But there is a bigger question: Who bears the burden of a tax system as a whole?

The question is not new. In the 1920s, the British government established a Royal Commission to advise, among other things,[52] on exactly that. This was the issue that not only defeated Edwin Cannan's student but so exasperated the eminent professor himself that, giving evidence to that Commission, he could barely conceal his irritation: "I think that inquiry is a will-o'-the-wisp myself; I cannot help it if the House of Commons has asked you to do it."[53] But the question is one that people naturally still try to answer. In the United Kingdom, for example, the Office for National Statistics produces a study of this kind every year.[54] Recently, in the United States, the subject has become the subject of a fierce debate among academics.[55]

The usual approach is to take a snapshot of detailed information on household incomes and consumption levels and then allocate taxes and, usually, monetary transfers,[56] across households according to some incidence assumptions. A century later, it is hard not to feel almost as grumpy as Cannan. All the uncertainties above apply: on how, for instance, benefits might affect wage rates. But for these wider studies the issues are even deeper. What, for instance, is the counterfactual relative to which the current tax system is to be assessed? It is hard to even imagine a world with no taxes at all—so no defense, no courts—and even harder to imagine that in such a world people would have the same incomes as they do now. Sometimes the coverage of these studies is seriously incomplete. As we have seen with the Corn Laws, tariffs can raise major incidence issues.[57] But tariffs are often simply left out of the analysis altogether—a serious omission for developing countries, which still raise much of their revenue, perhaps up to one-quarter, from this source. Corporate taxes are also sometimes simply omitted.[58] Moreover, the shifting assumptions made often rest on internal contradictions.[59] At the end of the day, the results are highly sensitive to largely untested assumptions. A classic analysis of the Canadian tax system—of which Cannan would be proud—still holds a salutary lesson. This showed that under alternative plausible assumptions (regarding, for example, the view taken of the incidence of the corporate income tax), the system could be made to look either broadly proportional to income or highly progressive.[60]

This is not to say that these studies are uninformative, just that they need to be taken with a pinch of salt, or at least read carefully. One can interpret the kind of exercise reported in the United Kingdom, for instance, as simply describing people's net contributions to the tax-benefit system, which may be of interest in itself but does not say anything about the burden they bear.[61] What is called for may be not so much Cannan-like grumpiness as modesty and clarity.

Empirical understanding of incidence issues thus remains in many ways limited—a professionally embarrassing confession, given its centrality to the discipline of public finance. This means that many of the claims about tax incidence you may come across (especially those that are implicit—as they often are) should be read with caution. This applies not just to grand incidence studies of the entire tax and benefit system but also to the studies that think tanks and others produce looking, more narrowly, at the impact of the latest income tax or VAT proposal. These, too, often rest on strong incidence assumptions. Progress is being made, as better ways are found to identify the impact of tax changes. But these refinements sometimes relate to fairly narrow episodes—things like an increase in the VAT rate on car repairs in France—and with little clue as to their wider applicability. There is still almost no evidence, for instance, to support the common presumption that changes in the standard rate of VAT are fully passed on to consumers.[62] Smarter researchers using richer data and better methods are filling gaps in our understanding of tax incidence. Even more important than a search for empirical answers, however, is the basic message of incidence analysis: When it comes to thinking about taxes, things are not always what they seem—or what some people would like you to think they are.

———

We have seen in this part of the book that fairness in taxation has many dimensions. Prevailing views change over time, and irreducible differences of judgment will remain. We have seen, too, that the fairness actually achieved, and the impact of taxation on people's well-being more generally, depends on how individuals and companies respond to the taxes that they face. In part III, we look more closely at these reactions and their implications. Most often, these responses are unintended, or at least unwelcome. Sometimes, however, the whole point of a tax is precisely to change how we behave.

PART III

Changing Our Ways

A dog whose fleas had become unbearable sought the advice of an accountant. "Can I claim these fleas as exemptions?" he asked. The accountant smiled and shook his head. "Under certain conditions," he explained, "ticks can be claimed as blood relatives. Fleas, on the other hand, are considered luxuries and, far from being deductible, are actually subject to tax." The following day, the dog had no more fleas; or he didn't declare them, which comes to the same thing.

J. B. HANDELSMAN[1]

8

Breaking Bad and Making Good

An unlimited power to tax involves, necessarily, a power to destroy.

DANIEL WEBSTER[1]

IN 1698, Peter the Great launched a series of reforms aimed at modernizing Russia along the European lines he had seen during the boisterous tours of his youth. The construction of St. Petersburg was the grandest of these. Less sublime, but also part of this wider campaign, was his introduction of an annual tax on beards.

Its target was the boyars, Russia's traditional and, to Peter, infuriatingly backward nobility. Their proud hirsuteness was an in-your-face contrast to Europe's clean-shaven aristocrats, and the tax was one way of trying to put an end to it.[2] To enforce compliance and stigmatize those who chose to pay rather than shave, boyars who kept their beards had to purchase and display a "beard token." The copper or silver token had a Russian eagle on one side and on the other, a nose and mouth adorned with whiskers and beard, attesting that "the money has been taken."

The beard tax shows that sometimes taxes are levied not so much to raise revenue as to change behavior, either to discourage the bad or encourage the good. This distinct role for taxation is the focus of this chapter. In the jargon, it is referred to as a "corrective" role, which makes it sound less value laden than what it really is: a form of social engineering.

The cutting edge of tax policy under Peter
the Great: A beard token.

Do the Right Thing

The use of taxes to induce people to behave as their rulers think they
ought to dates back at least to the sumptuary taxes of the ancient
world: taxes on luxuries motivated not so much by a desire to tilt the
tax burden toward the better off as by a desire to keep the lower
orders in their place. Not so different was the 1928 decision of the
Swiss canton of Uri in Switzerland to tax women's bobbed hair, then
the height of fashion. What is regarded as behavior to be discouraged
or encouraged varies over time, place, and even people, but the instinct to use the tax system to get people to do the right thing remains
the same.

Family Matters

Social engineering through the tax system has been rife in relation to
marriage and, its close accompaniment, childbirth. We saw in chapter 6
how hard it is to secure horizontal equity between married couples and
single individuals. But that is a very modern concern, and through much
of history, marriage has been seen as something to be positively encouraged, largely as an indirect way of encouraging childbirth.

Taxes on bachelors have been one way to do this. In ancient Greece and Rome, the *aes uxorium* was levied on unmarried men after the normal age of marriage.[3] The Ottomans also had an annual tax on bachelors, and so too, between 1695 and 1706, did the British.[4] In the United States, bachelor taxes surfaced in colonial times and continued into the twentieth century: Georgia, Maryland, Montana, and Texas all at one time had bachelor taxes. Proponents of bachelor taxes offered many justifications. "Rich bachelors should be heavily taxed," declared Oscar Wilde: "It is not fair that some men should be happier than others."[5] A more standard argument (though to much the same effect) was that bachelors of a given income and wealth had more resources than did married men, as they had no family to support, so had a greater ability to pay.

Encouraging childbirth is a recurrent objective. It has often reflected a militaristic desire to build up numbers relative to rivals: Fascist Italy and Nazi Germany both had bachelor taxes (and other generous support for marriage and childbearing).[6] Protecting the position of favored races by expanding their numbers has also sometimes been a motive:[7] In South Africa, the Transvaal had a levy of this kind from 1917 to 1920, allegedly to encourage white procreation to keep up with a burgeoning black population.[8]

Tender-hearted policymakers did sometimes worry about those who were unlucky in love. Were they to be doubly cursed, embraced by the taxman but spurned by womankind? So they sometimes exempted bachelors who could prove that they had asked a woman to marry them, only to be rejected.[9] It was a wise man who made his proposals with a ring in one pocket and a tax waiver form in the other. In Argentina circa 1900, such a provision gave rise to one of history's more bizarre forms of tax avoidance. For a small fee, "professional lady rejecters" agreed to swear to the authorities that a particular man had indeed proposed to them and that they had declined the offer.[10]

Taxing bachelors encourages marriage, but not necessarily childbirth. If childbirth is the objective, then it is best to reward it directly, the indirect route having the presumably unintended consequence of producing marriages that were unhappy, childless, or both. This line of reasoning is just one instance of a general principle of tax design: If the idea is to encourage (or discourage) something, it is best to use the tax (or subsidy) most directly focused on that end.

This application of the principle of targeting was implemented from the 1940s in Stalin's Soviet Union and other Communist countries, with the imposition of a tax on childlessness designed to boost the birth rate and recover from wartime population losses. In the Soviet Union, an additional 6 percent income tax applied to childless men from age 25 to 50 and to childless married women from 20 to 45.[11] The levy in Romania, called a "celibacy tax"—with the happy connotation that having sex was being encouraged—was imposed on anyone still childless by the age of 25.[12]

The same principle was applied in Mao's China, but the other way around. There, from the late 1970s and early 1980s (and until 2016), tax-like measures were used to actively discourage families from having more than one child.[13] Although well targeted as a fiscal measure, unintended consequences kicked in—a regular occurrence with almost all taxes. Given a traditional preference for male offspring, there emerged a massive imbalance between the sexes: by 2014, there were 32 million more boys than girls in China.

The use of fiscal incentives to encourage childbirth may sound archaic, a remnant of times when a country's military power depended in large part on its sheer population. But it is making a comeback, as many countries struggle with the aging of their populations and the consequent difficulty of financing state-provided pensions and health care for the elderly. Going beyond the usual tax breaks or cash payments for child support, Australia, Canada, the Czech Republic, Lithuania, and Singapore all provide a baby bonus. In 2019, Hungary introduced a lifetime income tax exemption for women with four or more children.[14] And some of these policies do seem to affect births—or at least their timing. In 2004, the Australian government announced that parents of children born on or after July 1 that year would receive a $3,000 one-time dependent exemption. Sure enough, the number of births dipped sharply before July 1, and then, on July 1 itself, more Australian children were born than on any other day in the previous 30 years. Changes in the timing of induction and cesarean section procedures accounted for most of the extra deliveries.[15]

The childbirth example also shows the similarity between taxing bad things (not having children, in Romania) and subsidizing, or giving a tax break, to the good thing that is its opposite (having children, in Australia). Peter the Great could have had much the same impact by instead handing money to beardless boyars, and giving tax breaks for marriage creates much the same incentives as does taxing bachelors. The key advantage of taxing bad things rather than subsidizing good ones is of course that it provides government with additional resources rather than using them up. Revenue concerns, even if they are not the main motive for these policies, can never be entirely ignored.

Taxing Knowledge

When enacted in 1712, the British tax on newspapers (and the paper they were printed on) was just one in a long list of revenue-raising excises. As the popularity of the press grew, it came to inspire some impressive avoidance responses. Newspapers could be rented by the hour, and were passed from post office to post office and circulated in alehouses and coffee houses.[16] But by the early nineteenth century, revenue was clearly not the only purpose of the tax. The government's suppression of some parts of the press was explicit, with the censors' language in 1819 referring to pamphlets and papers that "excite Hatred and Contempt of the Government."[17] The publisher of two local "respectable" newspapers argued that removing the newspaper tax would "effect a revolution in the character of the nation" due to the infiltration of men of lower standing into the publishing business. He also contended that repeal would open the floodgates for cheap journals of dubious quality, depriving the more respectable journals of advertising revenue.[18]

Social reformers saw things differently, arguing that the tax blocked working households' access to news and information. Showing an eye for a good (and enduring) slogan, they dubbed it the "tax on knowl-edge." Chancellor of the Exchequer William Gladstone agreed, and abolished the paper duty in 1861—over the objections of Prime Minister Lord Palmerston, who thought the idea of suppressing a mass press rather a good one. So did Queen Victoria, and the patrician House of Lords went so far (before being brought in line) as to violate the con-vention that it could not reject tax measures by voting it down.[19]

One historian identifies the freedom of the press from taxation as the most important driver of changes in newspaper production in the nine-teenth century.[20] But the press was not free from taxation everywhere. The Austrian government of the late nineteenth century still felt much the same as Lord Palmerston. A correspondent of the New York *Nation* reckoned in 1897 that the newspaper tax there was responsible for "the extreme ignorance of the lower classes as regards all political, social, and industrial questions of the day. Indeed, this is the sole object of the re-actionary party in imposing such taxation."[21]

The United States has usually refrained from taxing newspapers, or the press generally, perhaps as a lasting consequence of the hated Stamp Act of 1765 imposed by Britain on all legal documents and printed ma-terials, including newspapers. But it has been tried. In 1934, Louisiana, under the thumb of Huey Long, passed a tax on advertising sales for newspapers with a circulation exceeding 20,000 (and so applying to the urban newspapers that opposed him). Long called it a "tax on lying," presumably an archaic term for fake news.[22] In 1936, however, his tax was unanimously rejected by the U.S. Supreme Court as violating free-dom of the press.

These days, many countries bend over backward to tax favor, rather than penalize, the media (now including digital forms). All but two EU members provide preferential VAT treatment to printed books, with the United Kingdom and Ireland going furthest and applying a zero rate; from December, 2020, the U.K. government removed VAT on e-books and online newspapers, which opponents had labeled the "reading tax."[23] In 1983, the Supreme Court rejected a Minnesota law taxing paper and ink products used by newspapers. As in many other areas of tax policy, Gladstone has prevailed.

Tax Bads, Not Goods

Although most slogans about tax design are untrustworthy, this one is hard to argue with. It is much easier, however, to identify what is bad than to put numbers on just how bad it is and therefore exactly how heavily it should be taxed. But economists have at least come up with a clear way of thinking about these things.

At the heart of their approach is the idea of an "externality": a damage (or benefit) that a transaction or action confers on those who have no say in whether it takes place—and whose interests are therefore presumably ignored by those who do have a say. Taking for definiteness something that generates a harmful externality, like pollution, this means there will be too much of it, in the sense that the benefit to those generating the externality from the last bit of pollution (which might be, for example, the expense spared by not using a cleaner technology) is less than the cost imposed on those suffering from it. In principle, this difference leaves scope for mutually beneficial bargaining between polluter and pollutee: Both sides would gain if those polluted were to induce the polluter to pollute a little less by paying them an amount larger than the expense of cutting emissions a bit but less than the harm they would suffer from those emissions.[24] That is a happy outcome, because pollution then ends up at an "efficient" level, in that there is no way to change it without reducing the net benefit enjoyed by the two sides taken together. The externality is fully dealt with.

That is a neat solution,[25] but in practice, externalities commonly affect so many people that this kind of direct bargaining between polluters and pollutees is impossible. Taxes, however, can also do the trick, as first seen a century ago by the Cambridge (U.K.) economist Arthur Cecil Pigou.[26] All that is needed is to tax the damaging activity at a rate equal to the monetary value of the damage that the last burst of that activity, beyond the efficient level, causes to others. In this way, the damage caused to those others will turn up as a cost to be taken into account, however selfish they are, by the polluters. So compelling is the case that, ever since Pigou, the recommendation that taxes be deployed to correct for ("internalize") externalities has been a standard part of the economist's tool kit (the only disagreement being whether such taxes should be described as Pigouvian or Pigovian).[27]

Polluting activities are the classic example of a negative externality—a laundry, for instance, that dumps dirty water into a river causes damage downstream to other businesses or swimmers. A Pigovian tax would charge that laundry an amount per liter of dumped water equal to the monetary value of the harm those others suffer. (This general idea is sometimes referred to as the "polluter pays principle," which alas falls into the category of slogans not to be trusted: our discomfort, being heartfelt but nerdy, is in a footnote).[28] But externalities can also be positive. For example, basic scientific progress can generate positive externalities by enabling other researchers to develop further advances. These cases call for a Pigovian subsidy.

Over the years, generations of bored students have had to sit through cheesy examples of externalities, like our laundry one,[29] to illustrate the idea of Pigovian taxation. Now, however, we have a very big and bad real-life externality to which to apply the idea: climate change.

Saving the Planet

Scientists pretty much agree that the accumulation of greenhouse gases—about 65 percent of which comes from carbon dioxide (CO_2) released by burning fossil fuels (oil, gas, coal)—is increasing average global temperatures by trapping heat reradiated from the earth's surface. The consequent change in climate patterns implies substantial and generally bad economic effects: more, and more damaging, extreme weather events, much lower output in many low-income countries,[30] and increased risk of *Day After Tomorrow*–like catastrophic events, such as a reversal of the Gulf Stream or collapse of the West Antarctic ice sheet.

The Pigovian response to this "mother of all externalities"[31] is straightforward: Tax greenhouse gas emissions in general, and emissions from burning fossil fuels in particular, at a level that reflects the global damage they will cause. Because the amount of CO_2 released in burning any fossil fuel is proportional to its carbon content, which is well known,[32] such a carbon tax is, in principle, easy to implement. Just figure out how much damage an additional CO_2 emission causes and charge each unit of fossil fuel that amount for each unit of CO_2 that its burning produces. (And do so similarly for other greenhouse gases—including from the farting cows who will cross our path later in the chapter—though implementation for them may be less straight-forward.)[33] Some or all of this tax will be passed on to the consumers of goods whose production uses carbon-based fuels, reducing de-mand for those goods. The rest will be passed back to those selling fossil fuels, leading them to reduce supply.[34] In this way, individuals and businesses will be induced to cut emissions to reflect the harm they do—not necessarily to stop emitting entirely, but to balance that harm against the costs of reducing emissions. And research and devel-opment into, and investment in, low-carbon energy technologies that avoid the tax would be spurred.

Technically, the hard part is gauging the level at which the carbon tax should be set. In the Pigovian logic, it should be the social damage caused by the last CO_2 emission. Views differ on exactly how large that marginal damage is, and even advocates of carbon taxation acknowledge that "there's no magic formula or perfect number."[35] But a reasonable ballpark figure, as of today, might be a charge of $35 per (metric) ton of CO_2,[36] which comes to about 31 cents per gallon of oil. This may not sound like much, and indeed it would be swamped by the swings in gasoline prices that we have all become used to. However, the biggest issue is not gasoline, but coal, which is dirty (that is, CO_2-intensive in its production of en-ergy), widely used, and available in vast quantities. In this respect, a car-bon tax takes us back to the future: The first coal tax in England was in-troduced in 1368, and a charge on coal entering London continued until 1889 (funding, among other things, the rebuilding of St Paul's Cathedral after the Great Fire of 1666).[37] For coal, carbon taxation is a very big deal: That same carbon tax of $35 per ton of CO_2 could roughly double coal prices. And, to have the intended effect, the charge on burning carbon should rise steadily over time, faster than prices in general, with a tax of something like $75 per ton needed by 2030 if warming is to be contained within the limits aspired to in the 2015 Paris Agreement.[38]

Importantly, there is another way of achieving the same effect as a carbon tax, illustrating the occasionally thin line between tax and other policy instruments. To see this, suppose that with a tax of $50 per ton of CO_2, emissions would be 30 billion tons. Viewed the other way around, that means that the right to emit a total of 30 billion tons could be sold for a price of $50 per ton. Hence the alternative: Create rights to emit 30 billion ton of CO_2, sell them, and allow private markets to trade in them. The price would then settle at that same $50 per ton. Such an emissions trading system—also known as "cap and trade" (because there's an upper limit to emissions, and because rights can be bought and sold)—can in principle replicate the effects of a carbon tax and raise the same revenue for the government if the rights to emit are sold at auction.[39]

Most of the world has recognized the need to reduce carbon emissions, with nearly 190 states plus the EU having ratified the landmark Paris Agreement of 2015, almost all of them submitting quantified pledges for their own mitigation strategies.[40] And there is remarkable consensus among economists, of all political leanings, on the importance of carbon pricing as the most efficient and effective way in which to meet these commitments (and, before too long, go further). But the world remains far from fully embracing the idea. Although there are about 60 carbon taxes or emissions trading schemes in place—including, for example, a much-admired carbon tax in British Columbia and an EU-wide trading scheme—the average price on global emissions is only about $2 per ton. For the inconvenient truth is that establishing meaningful carbon pricing often encounters powerful resistance. Governments are reluctant to act unilaterally for fear of making their firms less competitive in world markets. Countries and companies sitting on large deposits of fossil fuels worry that their assets will be stranded, losing value as emissions are taxed. Consumers do not like higher energy prices. Low-income countries wonder why they should make it harder for themselves to ensure decent access to energy for their poor in order to solve a problem created by the rich countries.

There are ways to address these issues (most of them, at least). Transfer payments can be used to protect the poorest from higher fuel prices and fossil-fuel-producing communities subject to displacement. And there are ways to price the use of carbon as an input so as to have similar effects on emissions without having such a large impact on the prices of what it is used to produce.[41] Armed with the economics of Pigovian taxation, climate change is not the biggest intellectual puzzle mankind has been presented with. The problem is an unwillingness to embrace this key part of the answer.

Wind-Breaking Cows, Scary Dogs, and Cute Cats

Animals generate externalities, too. We can, for instance, assign to the burping and farting of cows a big chunk of the immediate blame for climate change. "Enteric fermentation" during their digestive process generates methane that accounts for something like 6 percent of all greenhouse gas emissions[42]—not an amount to be sniffed at, being more than aviation and shipping combined. Adding in the damage from the feed they need and the deforestation they bring, beef and cattle milk account for around 9 percent of all greenhouse gas emissions. And the likely growth in global beef demand means this is a real problem. Pigovian remedies have come to mind. In 2010, the United Nations proposed a global levy on livestock emissions. Farmers, unsurprisingly, have not been impressed. In 2003, they refused to remit a tax in New Zealand targeted at flatulent farm animals, emphasizing their dissatisfaction by sending parcels of manure to government ministers.[43] But the problem is not going away, and taxes on livestock (taking us back to the future, once again, as taxes on cattle have played a role in simple agricultural societies throughout the millenia) may well be on the policy menu in the coming years.

Dog ownership, of course, has often been taxed. Under the German *Hundesteuer*, liability depends on where the owner lives and is higher for dogs deemed "dangerous" (such as Doberman Pinschers and Rottweilers), presumably reflecting the greater damage they may inflict on others. But who would want to tax adorable cats? Well, that would be avian expert Peter Berthold of the Max Planck Institute for Ornithology, who calls for an "ecological compensation tax" to help control the damage to bird populations inflicted by cats. Lobbyists for rats and mice doubtless agree.[44]

The Wages of Sin

Asked in his penurious retirement years what he had done with all his money, the great footballer George Best confessed that "I spent a lot . . . on booze, birds and fast cars—the rest I just squandered."[45] Sin, it seems, is something many of us are willing to pay for. And while the wages of sin may not always be death, they are quite often heavy taxation.

The Vile Custome

The first smokers in Europe hardly had time to light up before the complaints began. In 1604, King James I of England published *A Counterblaste to Tobacco*,[46] in which all the issues that have become so prominent since appear: addiction ("[t]o take a custome in anything that cannot bee left againe, is most harmefull to the people of any land"); adverse health effects ("Smoke . . . makes a kitchin . . . in the inward parts of men, soiling and infecting them, with an unctuous and oily kind of Soote"); impact on the impressionable ("like Apes, counterfeiting the maners of others, to our owne destruction"), and passive smoking:

> the husband shall . . . bee ashamed, to reduce thereby his delicate, wholesome, and cleane complexioned wife, to that extremitie, that either shee must also corrupt her sweete breath therewith, or else resolve to live in a perpetuall stinking torment.

Less in line with modern sensibilities, this diatribe came with a strong dose of racism, presenting smoking as imitating "the barbarous and beastly maners of the wilde, godlesse, and slavish *Indians*"—a slur for which, as we will see, some measure of revenge was to follow. In any case, King James was not just anyone. He could put his detestation of this "vile and stinking" custom into policy. So he introduced a swinge-ing tariff on tobacco aimed at curbing smoking, which, in true Pigovian spirit, "We conceave might in great part be restrayned by some good Imposition to be laid uppon it."[47]

People still tend to think of high taxes on smoking as justified primar-ily by the externalities that smokers impose on others in the forms of ill health and simple nuisance. Not all the externalities associated with smoking, however, are negative.[48] By dying early, smokers forgo their pensions and so give a fillip to the financing of everyone else's public pensions and long-term health care. On the other side of the ledger, there is wide consensus that the negative health effects of maternal smoking on infants and children are significant.[49] Overall, which way the balance of externalities goes is not entirely clear and may well vary across countries.[50] What is clear, however, is that it is pretty hard to argue that externalities can justify cigarette taxes at the levels now seen in many parts of Europe and the United States.

Smokers may not be wholly surprised to learn that, while the realiza-tion was setting in that the externality argument for heavy taxes on smoking might be less than overwhelming, there emerged a different rationale. This is that smokers have a self-control problem. The trouble is that, although people can rationally decide to smoke now while also resolving to quit sometime in the future, when that future time comes they may find that they would like to continue after all. That is, they lack the self-control to do what they had really, truly intended to do. The problem is not addiction as such, but an instance of what has come to be called "time inconsistency": planning rationally today on future ac-tions that, when the time comes, it will be rational not to take. High taxes can help overcome this self-control problem (called an "internal-ity," because the harm is to the smoker herself) by inducing people not to start smoking in the first place. This internality argument also turns on its head the concern that, because smokers tend to be relatively poor,[51] cigarette taxes are regressive. If the poor suffer more from prob-lems of self-control, then they gain more from taxes that help them over-come it.[52] To some, this reasoning smacks of paternalism. But it is a logical corollary of what is probably the best argument for very high taxes on cigarettes.

One widely cited estimate, circa 2002, was that a per-pack tax of as high as $9.37 (or even higher) might be appropriate to address this internality.[53] At the time, that seemed a very high number. Now, not so much. In New York City, the average price of a pack of cigarettes hovers around $13, jacked up by a state tax of $4.35 per pack, a city tax of $1.50 per pack, and a federal tax of $1.01 per pack. And, although not an explicit tax, the Tobacco Settlement of 1998 (discussed in chapter 3) is also playing a part. Since 2000, 48 states and the District of Columbia have passed 145 state cigarette-tax increases.[54] Nor have massive increases in tobacco taxes been limited to the United States. In France, for example, the price of a pack of cigarettes more than doubled from 2000 to 2015, and it also doubled between 2005 and 2017 in the United Kingdom.[55]

The behavioral rationale for tobacco taxation is thus a mixture of reasoning based on externalities and internalities, with a less well-articulated dose of sin-fighting—what might be called a "sinternality"—thrown in. But it is not all about changing behavior. Revenue concerns clearly play a role. Taxes on tobacco raise over $30 billion per year in the United States, more than €70 billion in the EU countries, and over 2 trillion yen in Japan, each amounting to about 1 percent of total revenue.[56] Though on the decline in terms of the relative contribution to overall revenues, tobacco taxes, like many of the others we look at in the rest of this chapter, reflect in large part the Willie Sutton[57] principle of taxation: going where the money is.

There is an obvious trade-off here. Raising the tax on cigarettes reduces demand—that, after all, is the corrective rationale for such taxes—but that may reduce revenue. However, cigarettes have historically been, or have been thought to be, in relatively inelastic demand (which means, recall, that demand is not much dampened by a higher price). This is very convenient for governments: By raising tax rates they can then increase revenue while at the same time reducing the extent of some bad thing. But not too much faith should be placed in the idea that cigarettes, and other sinful products, are in especially inelastic demand. Smoking by the young seems quite responsive to its price, and the overall demand for tobacco products is in fact not so especially inelastic as often thought.[58] Thus, in many advanced economies at least, the trade-off between revenue and health objectives may increasingly become a real one.

Some governments have found the adverse impact of high taxes on the tax base so irritating that they have tried to legislate it away. So it was for the citizens of the Chinese province of Hubei, who in 2009 found themselves given an ultimatum to smoke cigarettes or pay a fine. To boost their revenues, Hubei province officials had decided to set quotas for cigarette sales. *The Telegraph* reports that local teachers were given a smoking quota, and "one village was ordered to purchase 400 cartons of cigarettes a year for its officials."[59] Incidentally, much the same happened in ancien régime France: In some parts of the country, everyone (except infants) was required to buy at least some specified amount of taxed salt. (Even in those days, policy makers had an appetite to spin their taxes: In some regions, this was called a voluntary tax, on the grounds that you could pay this compulsory amount whenever you liked.)[60]

The impact on revenue of high tax rates is amplified by the incentive they can create to buy cigarettes from some neighboring jurisdiction that has a lower tax rate, whether through legal cross-border shopping or illegal smuggling. This is where Native Americans, so maligned by King James, come back into the tobacco tax story.

In both Canada and the United States, land reserved to Native American tribes is sovereign territory: State taxes, including tobacco excises, do not apply to in-reservation sales to members of the tribe.[61] They do apply to sales to nonmembers, but that is hard to enforce,[62] not least given sensitivities regarding enforcement activities in these areas and, in some cases, legal impediments.[63] So such sales have a tendency to proliferate, with potentially substantial amounts at stake: In 2010–2011, more than a quarter of smokers in New Mexico reported having bought from tribal retailers.[64]

Problems have been most dramatic in the reservations spanning the Canada-U.S. border. In the early 1990s, the problem was of cigarettes being exported from Canada, legally free of all tax, but then re-entering as illegally untaxed imports—with, as it turned out, more than a little complicity from some large manufacturers. R. J. Reynolds Tobacco Company was fined C$325 million for aiding and abetting smuggling, some executives faced criminal charges, and one served a U.S. prison term.[65] By 1993, about one-third of all cigarettes smoked in Canada had not been subject to any tax.[66] This effectively forced a large reduction in the federal excise tax, from C$10.36 to C$5.36 per carton.[67] Control measures have intensified since, and tax rates have been increased. But problems along the Canada-U.S. border persist, now centered around the manufacture of cigarettes (including counterfeit) that had begun in the same tribal lands, and with the stakes large enough to have attracted organized crime.[68] By 2017, the proportion of cigarettes bought in Ontario that were contraband may have been back to more than one-third.[69]

But this is just one instance of a much more general problem. In the United Kingdom, HM Revenue & Customs (HMRC) estimates that, in 2016–2017, as much as 18 percent of the duties that should have been paid on tobacco products were not.[70] Globally, about 10 percent of all cigarettes are illegally traded or produced, for a collective annual revenue loss of $40–50 billion.[71]

But an even greater revenue challenge is now emerging: from e-cigarettes.[72] These devices deliver the nicotine fix not by burning tobacco but in the form of a vapor, and they are free from much of the gunk that actually kills smokers. Nor do they generate the same harm from passive smoking. There is widespread agreement this makes them substantially less harmful than standard cigarettes: So say, for instance, the Acting U.S. Surgeon General, the American Cancer Society, and Public Health England.[73] Many governments have nonetheless shown a strong and almost Pavlovian instinct to tax e-cigarettes.[74] A dozen or so U.S. states do so, with more in the offing,[75] along with more than 20 countries.[76] But the levels and form of taxation differ so much[77] as to suggest that governments are still figuring out how to deal with e-cigarettes. That e-cigarettes are less harmful than burning tobacco (perhaps by a factor of ten), and may provide a pathway to quitting altogether, means that they should be taxed less heavily than cigarettes.[78] Quite how much less heavily, however, is unclear. Some tax on e-cigarettes (beyond revenue-raising needs) will be warranted to the extent, in particular, that they provide a pathway to burning tobacco. But little is yet known about the relative strengths of the pathways out of and into burning tobacco, so where to strike the balance in setting a differentially low rate on e-cigarettes is unclear. It may not be too cynical to see a risk of over-taxing them coming from governments' own addiction—to revenue.[79]

The Curse of the Drinking Classes

Drink has long been a target for taxation. By the early nineteenth century, taxes on tea raised about 5 percent of all Britain's tax revenue.[80] Some even saw sin in tea-drinking: "The exorbitant practice of tea-drinking," lamented the English grocer Thomas Turner in 1759, has "corrupted the morals of people of almost all ranks."[81]

Now, of course, it is alcoholic drink—which Mr. Turner bracketed together with tea—that gives rise to such concerns. In excess, it gives rise to all kinds of horrendous things: "fetal damage and child abuse, marital harm, road traffic accidents, crime and violence, increased mortality and some 60 alcohol-related diseases and conditions."[82] Measuring these external costs with any precision is hard, but no doubt they are huge: in the EU, on average, perhaps 0.7 percent of GDP.[83]

Taxes on alcoholic drink are among the world's oldest. Cleopatra was reputedly the first to tax beer, to finance her and Mark Antony's doomed war with Octavian.[84] Not remembered best for her Pigovian tendencies, she set the tone for policy makers by citing the curbing of drunkenness as one rationale. Since then, alcohol taxes have often been seen as partly serving to discipline the working class, making sure that they turn up in the field or factories (this work being, as Oscar Wilde saw, the curse of the drinking classes).[85] And, more generally, to ensure that they do not drink themselves into rebellion or rascality.[86] Far from least, these taxes have also raised serious amounts of tax revenue. In Victorian Britain, they accounted for around one-third of the government's total tax revenue (and sometimes more).[87] In Czarist Russia, at the outbreak of the First World War, nearly 30 percent of the state's total receipts came from vodka.[88]

Many of the issues that arise in taxing alcohol mirror those in taxing smoking. The demand of the young is fairly responsive to price, for instance, that of heavy users less so. High tax rates encourage smuggling and cross-border shopping. Taxes on smoking and alcohol also share the feature that high levels can induce consumption to shift to illicit variants. In India, for example, the smoking market is dominated by *bidis*—shredded tobacco hand rolled in a *tendu* leaf—which until very recently were taxed much less heavily than regular cigarettes.[89] And when the Russian government substantially increased the excise on vodka in 2012, they soon found that more than half of the market was taken by illegal products. In this respect, however, there is an important difference between smoking and drinking. Illicit cigarettes generally don't kill you, or at least they don't kill you very much more quickly than legally produced ones. The methanol that is a staple of moonshine liquor, however, can kill and blind—and regularly does. In Mumbai, just one incident in 2015 led to more than 100 deaths.[90]

Taxes were front and center in the U.S. Prohibition era. Before Prohibition (from 1920 to 1933), many states relied heavily on excise taxes on liquor sales: in New York, they provided almost 75 percent of the state's revenue. Once alcohol sales became illegal, that revenue dried up. Just as we have seen that advocates of prohibition pressed for the income tax to reduce dependence on revenues from taxing alcohol, so, when Prohibition came, the would-be-drinkers—like those who put up a sign outside a Milwaukee brewery—advocated for an end to Prohibition in order to reduce the income tax.

Sex, . . .

So far as we know, no government has gone so far as the embarrassed civil servants in a Monty Python sketch who debated introducing a tax on "thingy."[91] They have not, however, entirely ignored the revenue potential of thingy and its derivatives.

From 390, Christian emperors outlawed homosexual sex in the Roman Empire (punishable by burning alive), while continuing to collect taxes on male prostitutes.[92] Prostitutes were singled out for a special tax in

A win-win proposal.

ancient Athens, the *pornikon telos*, and the Emperor Caligula imposed a tax on prostitutes at a rate equal to the fare for a single act of sexual intercourse per day. Maybe that was not too bad as a presumptive tax (given the difficulty of observing the act itself), although with customary lunacy (or ill-judged humor), Caligula also levied it on ex-prostitutes. A Caligulaish $5 per act tax was proposed in 2009 in Nevada (the only U.S. state in which prostitution is legal, in some counties)—a fiscal trick to improve the state's budget. However, this proposal was never consummated.[93]

Sex shows are an occasional target. In 2007, Texas lawmakers levied a $5 per-customer tax on establishments hosting live nude shows and allowing alcohol consumption on their premises; this became known as the "pole tax." In Utah, establishments where "nude or partially nude individuals perform any service" are subject to a 10 percent tax on admissions and sales of merchandise, food, beverages, and services.[94]

Pornography, one might think, has many of the features that have led other sex- and sin-related activities to be heavily taxed. There are some examples. Italy introduced a 25 percent tax on hard-core pornography in 2005 (in addition to VAT). And in France, only nonpornographic movies are subject to a preferentially low VAT rate of 5.5 percent. A colleague of one of this book's authors once had the job of enforcing a tax differentiation between pornographic and other shows, challenging to be sure, but probably more interesting than enforcing the distinction between cakes and biscuits discussed in chapter 9. In the United States, nine Democratic U.S. Senators proposed in 2005 a 25 percent tax on the revenue of most adult-themed websites. But it was not to be.[95]

... Drugs, ...

Taxes on opium figure prominently in the history of China. The British (the East India Company, again), anxious to secure entry into China of the opium produced under their monopoly in India, secured its legalization in 1858 after the second opium war—one of the "unequal treaties" whose impact on China is still being felt ("I am in dread," said Gladstone, "of the judgements of God upon England for our national iniquity towards China."[96]) The Qing dynasty, reluctant to accept the social disaster that opium was causing, then levied a tariff on opium of 8 percent[97] (which also came in handy for paying the hefty indemnity that the British and their French allies imposed after the war). During the calamitous 1930s, the governments of the Republic of China and its provinces, the Communist Party, and the British colonial government of Hong Kong all relied heavily on opium taxes, as did the Japanese occupation governments during the Second Sino-Japanese War. More recently, both the Taliban in Afghanistan and FARC (the Revolutionary Armed Forces of Colombia) have levied taxes on narcotics traffic to raise money, and then became more directly involved in production by protecting opium shipments and running heroin labs in controlled areas.[98]

Nowadays the discussion centers on the legalization and taxation of marijuana. The Dutch have permitted low-level possession since 1976, and by 2008 were collecting about €400 million every year in corporate tax revenue from the country's 700-plus "coffee shops."[99] For the United

States, this would be a return to a past in which even harder drugs were treated in this way. The 1914 Harrison Narcotics Tax Act regulated and taxed the production, importation, and distribution of opiates and coca products, requiring the producers and distributors of narcotics to register with the IRS, record their sales, and pay a federal tax. The tide in the United States does now seem to have turned toward legalizing marijuana—perhaps in part at least because of the realization that there is big tax money to be had. In 2014, Colorado became the first U.S. state to permit sale for recreational use. At the same time, it levied a 15 percent excise tax, a 10 percent special sales tax, and a 2.9 percent sales tax on recreational marijuana, in addition to imposing application and license fees on growers and sellers. As a result, Colorado raised nearly twice as much from sales of pot as it did from sales of alcohol.[100] California's 15 percent tax on recreational marijuana, legal as of January 1, 2018, had generated 1 billion dollars by March of 2020.[101] Marijuana business owners are less than chilled out, however, by its continued listing in the United States as a Schedule I drug, which means that normal business expenses cannot be deducted. That makes the income tax equivalent to a tax on sales.[102]

. . . But Not Much Rock and Roll

Alas, we have no examples of taxes targeted to rock or any other kind of music, but rock stars themselves are nonetheless notable for two contributions to the story of taxation. One, detectable even without playing the record backward, is for complaining about them: not just the Beatles' "Taxman" mentioned earlier, but The Who[103] ("six for the tax man, and one for the band") and The Kinks ("and I can't sail my yacht, [tax man's] taken everything I've got"). The other contribution is famously avoiding them: more on that in chapter 12.

Unhealthy Living

Fatty foods and sugar-laden beverages seem set to become the new tobacco. Given their contribution to the growing problems of obesity, heart disease, and stroke—problems of self-control more than sources of adverse externalities—policy makers are increasingly drawn to taxing products that contain artery-clogging fat and to excises on sugary soft drinks.

"Fat taxes" have met heavy resistance. The only adopter so far is Denmark, which in 2011, introduced a tax that raised the price of a small package of butter by about 30 percent, putting a serious crimp on delectable jam-filled Spandauers and pretzel-like kringles. But it lasted only 1 year. Among the reasons cited for the about-face was the familiar problem with high taxes on particular products: people buy abroad instead. Many Danes—perhaps nearly one-half[104]—drove across the border to Germany or Sweden to get an untaxed fix of their favorite fat-laden foods.

While fat taxes have floundered (so far), taxing sugary drinks is catching on. Again, this idea is not actually new. In 1914, Woodrow Wilson asked the House Ways and Means Committee (where all tax legislation must originate) to consider taxing soft drinks (as well as beer and patent medicine) to help meet the revenue needs of the First World War. This did not happen, but taxes on such drinks are fairly widespread in developing countries—not necessarily with health in mind, but as a reasonable source of revenue, given that prepared soft drinks are not much consumed by the very poorest. Now soda taxes—more exactly, taxes on sugar-sweetened beverages—are spreading more widely. In 2014, voters in Berkeley, California, approved the first in the U.S., and at least eight American localities now have one. So do several advanced countries, including, in Europe, France, Ireland, Norway, and the United Kingdom.[105]

Mexico, where consumption of soft drinks is extraordinarily high and obesity has skyrocketed, imposed a 10 percent tax on non-alcoholic drinks with added sugar in 2014.[106] And the tax seems to have had some success. Purchases of sugary drinks fell by 10 percent in the following year,[107] although other factors, such as slow economic growth and shifting consumer tastes, may also have played a role. In any event, less soft-drink consumption does not necessarily translate into weight loss or health improvement. Mexicans may be switching to other unhealthy but untaxed drinks: beer sales, for example, went up after the tax was enacted. That, more generally, is the big open question with such taxes: There is no hard evidence on whether—given these possible switching effects—they lead to better health outcomes. (You might also wonder: If people in richer countries are basically eating too much, would it not be simpler to stop setting preferentially low tax rates on food?)

Other taxes are also sometimes advocated as making us healthier: Taxes on red meat, for instance, also aimed at the climate problems that beef brings.[108] And on tanning salons: After the International Agency for Research on Cancer moved tanning beds to its highest cancer risk category, putting them alongside asbestos, arsenic, and cigarettes, a 10 percent excise tax on tanning salons followed, as part of the 2010 Affordable Care Act.

Most of these sin taxes seem to bear on the perhaps not-so-innocent pleasures of the poor. Are there really no sins favored by the rich? Presumably designer drugs are fairly prevalent in some upper-income households, but these are not (yet) effectively taxed. The addiction of choice for many rich people may be workaholism, with internality ideas suggesting that income tax rates be adjusted upward to help these sad folks overcome their craving.[109]

Just Say No?

Taxation is not the only way to discourage people from doing what they should not do. Providing them with good information on the consequences of their actions is another. And there is often a choice to be made between taxation and regulation, meaning by the latter not just outright bans but also less extreme forms of non-price control. Whereas Peter the Great used taxation to discourage beards, for example, the Qing dynasty took a different route to ensure desired hair styling in seventeenth-century China: Until the fall of the dynasty in 1912, failure to shave the forehead and braid back the remaining hair, as a sign of subjection to the Manchu regime, was punishable by death. In Russia, Nicholas II addressed his concern that vodka drinking would undermine the war effort by banning vodka in 1914—thereby turning off his single largest source of revenue.

Revenue aside, the key advantage of taxation over regulatory measures is that it harnesses the power of the price mechanism to help ensure that resources are allocated efficiently. Compared to an outright ban, a well-designed tax approach has the advantage that those who really enjoy the taxed activity can continue to enjoy it. Take, for example, climate change. One way to reduce overall emissions would be by setting limits for individual businesses and devising standards for cars, buildings, and the like. The trouble with such a regulatory approach—even leaving aside the practical costs of setting and enforcing such targets—is that it would not ensure that the overall reduction in emissions is achieved at the least possible cost to society.

Tax measures, however, do just that. The problem with regulation is that unless it is possible to observe how much it costs particular firms to reduce their emissions—which it is not—then setting limits on emissions gives no guarantee that the cost of reducing CO_2 emissions by one more ton is the same for, say, some steel producer as it is for some bus company. But if it is not, then the same reduction in total emissions could be achieved by having whichever of them has the lower cost of doing so cut emissions a bit more and allowing the other to cut them a bit less. In this way, society could achieve the same total emissions reduction—which is what matters for the effect on climate—at lower overall cost. The clever thing about putting a price on burning carbon is that it automatically ensures that all firms will indeed end up with the same cost of reducing emissions a bit more. This is because they will cut emissions until the cost to them of doing so just equals the price of not doing so—which is the carbon price. So long as that carbon price is the same for everyone, everyone will thus end up with the same cost of cutting emissions a bit more. Even without policy makers being able to observe what those costs are, emissions will be reduced in the way that costs society the least. Adam Smith's invisible hand, with a bit of nudging from government, gets it right.

A disadvantage of taxation, however, is that it leaves uncertainty as to how much of the harmful activity will remain.[110] We can never be entirely sure, for example, what level of emissions a given carbon tax will lead to. That can be a real problem when small differences in the level of the externality-generating activity have large social consequences. During the First World War, when Lloyd George wanted to make sure that munitions workers did not turn up to work so drunk or hung over that, by some tiny error, they might blow up the whole factory, he relied in part on limiting pub opening hours. And so it is that the world—for once coming together in an effective international agreement to address a global externality—simply phased out the production and use of ozone-depleting chlorofluorocarbons.

The limits of taxation are amply illustrated by the other great externality of our time: the COVID-19 pandemic. Here the externality was the passing of infection through contact of various kinds. In this case, imposing a Pigovian tax in order to discourage contact was clearly not technologically practical; but even if it had been, it would not have been the right response. The huge uncertainties as to the risk of infection in differing circumstances mean that tax rates would surely have been set incorrectly. And the harm from setting rates too low, and contact consequently being too high (or setting taxes too high, and economic pain unnecessarily pronounced) would have been irreversible and large. Regulation in the form of social distancing was the better approach in theory, as well as the only one available in practice. What makes things different in the climate context is that, because damages depend on the cumulative stock of emissions, which builds up slowly, the level of carbon taxation can be adjusted over time to affect the path of annual flows. Pandemics are not so forgiving.

There are also cases in which both tax and regulation have a clear role. Taxing the purchase of some commodity, after all, is not the same thing as taxing its use, and the circumstances in which it is used can make a big difference to the externalities at issue. This is a fundamental difficulty with trying to tackle drunkenness by taxing alcohol, for example: The effect of drinking seven pints of beer in an evening is very different from that of drinking a pint a day for a week, but it is hard (although maybe technology will someday change this) to vary the rate of tax on beer consumed over the course of an evening. And indeed, some moderate drinking, as well as reducing the risk of coronary heart disease, has effects in reducing stress and increasing sociability that confer beneficial externalities on others (entertaining drunks being preferable to sober bores). A tax charged at the same rate on all alcohol purchases is a very blunt Pigovian instrument. This points to a role for regulation, too, such as drunk driving rules and alcoholic interlocks for cars. In the context of cigarettes, restrictions on smoking in public places can play an important role in easing the damage caused to nonsmokers.

As with all public policies, such restrictions can also have unintended consequences. Efforts by U.S. states to curtail drunk driving by enacting a minimum legal drinking age, for instance, do seem to have reduced youth involvement in fatal driving accidents. Except, that is, for driving within 25 miles of a state with a lower age limit: Young people are driving to drink legally in a neighboring state, and for 18- and 19- year-old drivers, involvement in fatal accidents then actually increases.[111]

By the same token—that principle of targeting again—taxes are more effective in addressing externalities the more closely targeted they are to the generation of the damage. One rationale for taxes on fuel, for instance, is to discourage congestion, and so reduce the costs each driver imposes on others by making them waste more time sitting in a traffic jam. But as the technology improves, explicit congestion charging is becoming more common and sophisticated. Singapore, the world leader in this area, plans to introduce congestion pricing that not only varies with vehicle type and, in a rough way, with the time of day, but also adjusts in real time to predicted traffic speeds (raising the charge when they are low). And that information, along with parking updates, is immediately available to potential drivers.[112] These developments suggest at least the possibility of some good news for drivers: as congestion charges become more common, so the argument for taxes on fuel to address congestion issues goes away. Taxes on road fuels should then fall—at least in principle.[113]

But perhaps the most obvious difference between taxation and regulation (and one pretty important to governments) is that, compared to restrictions or bans, a tax has the attraction of raising revenue. And that can prove addictive in itself. As with John Pym's excises, there are few things so permanent in life as a temporary tax.

Unlike many of those looked at in this chapter, for most taxes the only real aim is to raise money. That leads to behavioral responses that are sometimes unintended, often undesirable, and occasionally decidedly odd.

9

Collateral Damage

The Inland Revenue is not slow—and quite rightly—to take every advantage which is open to it under the taxing statutes for the purpose of depleting the taxpayer's pocket. And the taxpayer is, in like manner, entitled to be astute to prevent, so far as he honestly can, the depletion of his means by the Revenue.

LORD CLYDE[1]

BRITANNIA MAY HAVE RULED the waves during the nineteenth century, but, for much of it, her merchant ships had a troublingly high chance of ending up underneath them. They were "the most unsightly and unmanageable ships in Europe."[2] The reason, of course, was taxation. For nearly a century after 1773, ships were charged port and lighthouse fees by a formula that increased with their length and breadth but did not depend on their depth.[3] The way to maximize cargo capacity while minimizing taxes was thus to build thin ships with deep holds: which is a recipe for instability. In the building of merchant ships, wrote the author of an 1830 *Marine Directory*, "more attention is paid to evade the tax on tonnage than to their sailing well with the wind in different directions."[4] British merchant ships were not wholly seaworthy, but they were at least tax efficient.

It is clear enough that taxing things generally leads us to consume and produce less of them: The window tax led to fewer windows. What the despised British ships show us is that taxes also change the nature of the things we consume and produce. Both types of responses to taxation—in how much, and on what—imply a damage to people beyond that associated with the simple transfer of resources as tax payments. This chapter looks more closely at the nature of this excess burden.

Spurring Ingenuity

John Maynard Keynes is reported to have said that "the avoidance of taxes is the only intellectual pursuit that still carries any reward."[5] We often think of avoidance in terms of outlandish schemes cooked up by well-heeled lawyers in fancy offices, and there is indeed plenty of that, as we see in spades when we turn to international taxation in chapter 11. But sometimes avoidance is a matter of twisting everyday products into manifestly weird forms. And that weirdness is itself a sign of excess burden, because we see that things are manifestly not as they naturally would be. The underlying source of the weirdness is the same whether produced by today's snazzy lawyers or by nineteenth-century shipbuilders: Once a government has decided to tax something, it has to define what that thing is—and is not. Taxpayers will then look for, or invent, things that are untaxed but are much like the thing that is taxed.[6] Therein much mischief lies.

Stranger Things

Being a form of necessity, taxation has proved a mother of invention. Tax avoidance has inspired much impressive creativity, but most of it— twisting things into unnatural form—is worse than pointless in social terms. The consequences are most powerful and often most visible for things that are heavily taxed. Prominent among these, over the centuries, are housing, tobacco, alcoholic drink, and cars.

Taxes on buildings—long an attractive tax base, because they are visible indicators of wealth and profitability that do not move around— have been especially prone to induce strange contortions. Like becoming very skinny. Four hundred years ago, the homeowners of Poland owed property tax based on the width of the street-facing façade of their houses (and the number of windows on that side), presumably in part because that was easily checked by walking along the street. What followed is easy to guess: a lot of very thin houses, for which the property tax was a lot less per square meter of floor space. In the sixteenth century, the Dutch also taxed based on the width of their houses. This practice carried over to Dutch possessions in the Caribbean, such as Curaçao, where the capital city of Willemstad still features very narrow (but remarkably colorful) buildings along the waterfront. And during the Tokugawa period in Japan the government calculated some taxes based on the width of a house or storefront. As a result, many ancient Japanese buildings tend to be narrow and long, and storefronts in many cases came to feature tiny facades designed to conceal the actual size of the overall buildings.[7] Shopkeepers even incorporated Lilliputian doors into such designs in the hope, it is said, of convincing the taxman that their buildings were small and should be taxed less. In Vietnam, residences and shops were constructed as "rocket" houses to reduce taxes based on the width of street-facing home and shop fronts.[8]

Other tax-avoidance-induced building anomalies abound. In Greece, there is a 60 percent tax reduction for unfinished buildings, the predictable result being a glut of half-done buildings. In the United States, movable office partitions became plentiful following the introduction of the U.S. investment tax credit in the Revenue Act of 1962: Structures were not eligible for the credit, but movable partitions were. But it is the picturesque southeastern Italian town of Alberobello that provides the most moving (literally) housing tax folly. Its traditionally built stone houses, called *trulli*, are constructed using only dry stones, without the use of mortar. Many tourist Internet sites[9] attribute this to taxes, as the houses could be quickly dismantled when the tax inspector was expected to appear.

Smokers, too, have faced a variety of misshapen products. In many countries of the European Union, cigars are taxed at a lower rate than cigarettes, generating pressure to manufacture a cigar-like (for tax purposes) cigarette. Say hello to the filtered cigarillo, which worked for a while until a minimum weight rule (for cigars) was introduced. In

Rocketing real estate.

response, companies produced long cigarettes that were readily cut into smaller (and thus less weighty) units, leading to further tightening of EU product definitions. In 1990, "tobacco rolls" were launched in Germany, consisting of rolls of fine-cut tobacco wrapped in permeable paper that were to be inserted into an "empty," a separately sold cigarette tube, in order to be smoked. These tobacco rolls did not fall under the EU definition of cigarettes, because they were not "capable of being smoked as they are," but instead into the much lower-taxed category of fine-cut tobacco. Finally, there was the "party cigar." Many countries in the European Union define the excise tax rate for cigars and cigarillos per unit of product rather than on a weight basis. Hence an incentive to produce in massive units. This happened, for example, in Poland, where party cigars 35 centimeters (almost 14 inches) long appeared on the market. These consisted of mixed tobacco leaves in an outer wrapper of tobacco leaf and met the cigar/cigarillo definition—except that they were not meant to be smoked as such, but instead used to make 20 cigarettes each.[10]

Drink, too, has seen tax-avoiding innovation. In 1786, Scotland switched to taxing distilled spirits by charging a license duty proportional to the

Spot the house.

cubic capacity of the still used, the thought being that this would be a good proxy for the amount of spirits it produced. With a bit of creativity, however, that turned out not to be the case. What the duty led to was the adoption of shallower, wider stills that could turn out distilled spirits much faster. In a cat-and-mouse game that is a constant of tax history, the government raised the duty rate in response, and the distillers became even more creative. By the time this tax scheme was scrapped, the duty had risen from

Trulli a tax dodge?

£1.50 to £54 per gallon—and the time taken to run off 40 gallons of spirit had increased by a factor of 2,880.[11] Similar ingenuity was shown during the Gin Craze in England, discussed in chapter 12: Tax was specified as a fixed amount per gallon, which prompted distillers to increase the alcoholic content of what they produced, and charge more for it. Dr. Johnson spoke of retailers giving "Spirits thrice the Degree of Strength required, by which Contrivance, though they pay only the Duty of one Pint, they sell their liquors at the Price of Three; because it may be increased to thrice the Quantity distilled, yet retain sufficient Strength to promote the Purposes of wickedness."[12]

Taxation has also produced strange motor vehicles. When Chile imposed much higher taxes on cars than on panel trucks, the market soon offered a redesigned panel truck, featuring glass windows in place of panels and upholstered seats in the back.[13] The preferential tax treatment of motorcycles in Indonesia bred a contraption with three wheels and long benches at the back seating up to eight passengers: car-like, but not so car-like as to be taxed as a car. And since 2009, imports of passenger vans into the United States have been subject to a tariff of 2.5 percent, while cargo vans faced a 25 percent tax. Ford responded by importing the five-passenger Transit Connect, subject to the lower tariff, and then ripping out the backseats, flooring, and rear windows, and adding a new floor; this conversion from passenger van to cargo van apparently took 11 minutes.[14]

Many other instances of tax-induced innovation merit an honorable mention. The creativity shown by the governments of Georgian England in introducing a myriad of commodity taxes was matched only by the inventiveness of taxpayers in finding ways around them. Builders avoided a 1712 tax on printed wallpaper[15] by putting up plain, unprinted, wallpaper and then painting patterns on it. In 1745[16] came a tax on glass based on the weight of the final product, which the medical journal *The Lancet* described as an "absurd impost on light."[17] This did, though, lead to a spate of smaller, fancy objects, sometimes with hollow stems, that became known as "excise glasses"[18]—which are now collector's items. A tax on bricks and tiles followed in 1784, set as an amount per brick. Builders quickly realized that they could cut their tax bills by using bigger (and thus fewer) bricks. Eventually, the government caught on and levied a higher tax rate on bigger bricks. Pictures allegedly show the bricks from different tax periods side by side.[19] Around much the same time, in 1795, the Denmark-Norway Union levied a tax on the import of mirrors that was progressive in the size of the mirror, so that doubling the size of the mirror more than doubled the tax due. The story is told that small mirrors were then imported and connected to make big ones.

Dogs, who are proving to be unexpectedly frequent visitors to the story of taxation, also have a tale to tell. Hundreds of years ago, some say, the English crown levied a tax on dogs but allowed an exemption for working dogs with docked (that is, amputated) tails; the point was to allow poor folks to have dogs that were capable of working but not of interfering with the hunting of the elite, the supposition being that a bobbed tail would disrupt the animal's balance and mobility and thus curtail its hunting ability. Cash-strapped commoners did indeed adopt the practice of docking tails to reduce their tax liability. By the time the

Tax avoidance at its most elegant.

dog tax was repealed, tail docking had become a tradition that lives on today long after its tax advantages had been cur-tailed. There is, though, one problem with this tale: serious scholars of dog taxes (there are some)[20] do not believe it.

The common feature of these examples is that taxation was based on some physical characteristic of the product: the length and breadth of a ship, the presence of a painted design on wallpaper, the breadth of a whisky still. As with presumptive taxation of the kind discussed in connection with the income tax, those taxed characteristics are seen as proxying the essence of the thing itself. But many commodities have a complex set of attributes, and basing tax liability on just one or a few of them that are easily observed encourages would-be avoiders to substitute away from the taxed attributes and toward the untaxed ones while maintaining the essence of the commodity.[21] These consequences of characteristics-based taxation are generally unintended, and the

Another (but different) brick in the wall.

government's response, as with those bricks, is then likely to be to re-specify the basis of the tax. Avoidance is often a race between the invention of schemes by taxpayers and efforts by governments to close them down.

The obvious solution to these problems of attribute-based taxation—innovation that may be impressively creative but, tax benefits aside, if anything makes the product itself somewhat worse—is to tax instead on the basis of price: this is "ad valorem" taxation. That is indeed now the norm, as with the VAT and retail sales taxes; the main exception is when it really is some attribute—the alcohol in drinks, for instance, that for corrective reasons is the object of the tax.[22]

Drawing a Line

Much the same kind of tax-induced creativity that is spurred by attribute-based taxation continues to arise with ad valorem taxation, however, if different rates of taxation are applied to different products,

A possibly tall tale of short-tailed tax avoidance.

because it is then again necessary to choose some attributes that determine the rate to be applied: A line must be drawn to distinguish the products. This has spawned some notoriously silly legal cases, as we will see soon. Even putting aside the incentive to invent new products, any form of differentiation in tax treatment creates incentives to ensure, whether by restructuring whatever is being taxed or by hiring smart lawyers, that your product or activity falls into the more favored category. Tax avoidance thus crops up whenever the government chooses to apply discretely different tax rates in different situations—which is pretty much always.

Sometimes the rationale for differentiation is hard to see. In the Netherlands, feed for guinea pigs is taxed at 21 percent, while rabbit feed is taxed at 9 percent. Sometimes one can at least discern some reason for the differentiation, however ill-advised. So it is in the United Kingdom with the exclusion of foods from VAT, intended to shield the poor from tax burden (although, for reasons we will see in chapter 14, it is a particularly ineffective way of doing so). However, identifying exactly what kinds of food merit this treatment can be a lawyer's dream. So it

Cake or biscuit? Call my lawyer.

was with that well-known engine of economic growth called "Jaffa Cakes," biscuit-like cakes (or cake-like biscuits) named after Jaffa oranges. If Jaffa Cakes were considered cakes, they would, in 1991, incur a zero rate of VAT. However, if they were deemed to be chocolate-covered biscuits, they would be subject to the standard VAT rate, which was then 17.5 percent. A U.K. tax tribunal weighed in on the issue, considering a multitude of factors: ingredients, size, texture, packaging, marketing, and physical properties, including what happens when a Jaffa Cake goes stale and whether consumers eat them as finger food or with a fork. Ultimately, the tribunal decided that Jaffa Cakes were sufficiently cake-like to be zero-rated for VAT purposes. (This does all beg the question of why, to begin with, cakes and biscuits should be taxed differently.)

Jaffa Cakes may be a distinctly British institution, but complex and bizarre tax differentiation is not. If you are trying to sell an ice cream cake (or slice thereof) in Wisconsin, the Department of Revenue will explain to you whether it is taxable or not in a handy 1,437-word memo, complete with 10 examples.[23]

Sometimes policy makers try to differentiate tax treatment according to the use that the buyer has in mind. That brings its own problems. Pumpkins, for example, are exempt from sales tax in Iowa, Pennsylvania, and New Jersey—but only if they are to be eaten and not carved. How, though, is a pumpkin seller responsible for remitting the right amount of tax supposed to know if their customers will eat it or carve it? A similar issue, with many more dollars involved, arises in the administration of U.S. federal taxes on diesel. These apply to fuel used in transportation systems but not to fuel used for farming purposes, off-highway business purposes, or in an aircraft. One attempted solution to the problem was to dye the tax-exempt fuel, so that a roadside check of a truck (lorry) could readily reveal tax evasion if dyed fuel is in the gas (petrol) tank (we explain the "attempted" in chapter 13). And in 2010, New York City authorities began enforcing a rule that levies sales tax on a bagel eaten at a bagel shop, but not on a carry-out bagel. Slicing the bagel at the shop makes it a taxable transaction. How else, at least inexpensively and unobtrusively, could one tell whether it is eaten in the shop? In Manitoba as of 2014, sweetened baked goods were exempt from value-added tax unless they were pre-packaged in quantities of less than six.[24] Presumably this has something to do with intended use, but, to be honest, we have no idea what that might be.

Some of the sharpest instances of product innovation and other types of response come when the tax system imposes "notches": discrete jumps in liability when some line is crossed, like that in the decimation tax of chapter 3. In Japan, for instance, the tax on alcoholic malt beverages varies by malt content. Before 1996, if that was between 25 percent and 67 percent, the tax was 152.7 yen per liter; it was more at higher malt content, and less at lower. Tax-driven product innovation ensued. In 1994, Suntory introduced *happoshu*, "sparking alcoholic beverage," which had malt content of 65 percent, just under the high-tax notch. By 2003, the share of *happoshu* in the combined market of beer and *happoshu* had reached 40 percent. Sure enough, perhaps concerned about the drain on revenue, the tax rate on *happoshu* was raised in 2003. And, again sure enough, in 2004, Sapporo and Suntory introduced a zero-malt brew that was subject to the lowest tax rate; by 2008, this new category sold as much as the in-between malt content *happoshu*.[25] In a similar spirit, when the United Kingdom announced its sugar tax in 2018, the maker of the popular Scottish soft drink, Irn-Bru, responded by announcing that it was reducing the sugar content of most of its drinks to just below the tax threshold. More than 50,000 people signed a petition objecting to this tax-induced product (dis-) innovation.[26]

Line drawing can be even more problematic—and the economic consequences more severe—when it comes to concepts rather than stuff. There is an important line, for instance, between workers who are company employees (for whom the employer must withhold and remit income tax liability) and those who are independent contractors (for whom withholding does not apply). The U.S. tax law contains a 20-factor test to determine on which side of the line a worker stands. And this is becoming an increasingly significant issue as the rise of peer-to-peer enterprises, like Uber or Lyft, blurs the distinction between employees and employers. In 2016, Uber agreed to pay up to $100 million to settle a class-action lawsuit, allowing the company to continue classifying its California and Massachusetts drivers as independent contractors. In August 2016, the settlement was rejected by a federal judge, who argued that the amount was insufficient. As of 2020, the issue was still being litigated, with California officials suing Uber and Lyft for allegedly misclassifying drivers as independent contractors instead of employees. But, in November, California voters overwhelmingly approved a binding referendum that allows these and other gig economy companies to continue treating drivers as independent contractors.

Another important line drawn in the tax code has to do with how businesses finance themselves. If a business raises money by borrowing—debt financing—the interest it pays to the lenders is generally deductible from its taxable income as a cost of business. In contrast, when a corporation raises money by issuing shares, the returns to shareholders—in the form of dividends and capital gains—are not deductible from the corporate tax base. So corporations face a stark difference between the tax treatment of the two basic ways to raise money, and the tax code favors debt finance. That then inspires the search for ways to raise capital that have equity-type features (such as the absence of any promise of repayment), but somehow look enough like debt (for instance, having periodic fixed payments) to qualify for an interest deduction.

Regulated financial institutions have often been at the forefront of the search for such "hybrid instruments," the trick for them being to find instruments that generate the interest deduction but can be counted as equity when it comes to meeting their capital requirements. This search acquired special urgency after the Global Financial Crisis, as banks sought to rebuild their capital buffers without forgoing the advantages, not least the tax ones, of leverage. The primary product innovation they came up with was the Contingent Convertible Security (CoCo): interest-paying debt that converts to loss-absorbing equity in the event that some specified trigger event occurs (such as the bank's capital falling below regulatory requirements). And with more than $350 billion of CoCos issued between 2009 and 2015,[27] this is not small beer. While tax has not been the only factor favoring this way of meeting capital requirements, it has clearly been a big one. In Germany, for instance, no CoCos were issued until, in May 2014, it was made clear that coupon payments would be tax deductible; the next month, Deutsche Bank issued $4.7 billion's worth.[28]

There can be notches in time, too. Changes in tax rules create them, because one set of tax rules applies up to the end of the tax year and another starts the next day. That creates an incentive to postpone receiving taxable income when the effective tax rate will go down and to bring taxable income forward when the tax rate will rise. One of the most striking examples of this came in 1986, when the U.S. Tax Reform Act, to take effect on January 1, 1987, meant that the tax on realized capital gains was about to jump up precipitously for many people. Holders of assets with accrued capital gains took notice. Long-term capital gains in December of 1986 were almost seven times higher than their 1985 level, and six times the average for the rest of 1986.[29] There is also substantial evidence of tax sensitivity not only of the year-end timing of births,[30] but even, as we shall see in chapter 12, of the date of death. Occasionally, tax changes are deliberately made temporary precisely in order to create notches in time and so alter the timing of economic activity. To stimulate consumption in the recovery phase of the COVID-19 pandemic, for example, in July 2020, Germany reduced the standard rate of VAT for 6 months, from 19 to 16 percent—deliberately creating an incentive to buy now (especially durable goods) rather than later. And in the wake of the Global Financial Crisis, in 2008, the United Kingdom temporarily reduced the standard VAT rate from 17.5 to 15 percent, while the United States adopted a temporary "bonus" depreciation provision intended to bring forward investment.[31]

While on the subject of tax years, there is one oddity that no scholar of tax oddities can ignore. In most countries, including the United States, the tax year for individuals is the calendar year and always has been. Not so in the United Kingdom, where the first day of the new tax year is . . . April 6. This peculiarity goes back to the four main Christian religious holidays (including Christmas Day) having long served in England and Ireland as the days on which all debts and accounts had to be settled and when rent payments were due. For example, the hearth tax of the Restoration era that we look at in a moment was due in two instalments, on Lady Day (March 25) and Michaelmas (September 29). March 25 was celebrated as New Year's Day and observed, if not celebrated, as the first day of the British tax year. But in 1752, the country moved to the Gregorian calendar, by which time the British calendar was 11 days off from the rest of Europe, which had already adopted it. So Wednesday, September 2, 1752, was followed by Thursday, September 14, 1752. To avoid losing revenue in the short run, the British Treasury decreed that the tax year that began on March 25, 1752, would have the usual 365 days length, and so would end on April 4, 1753, with the next tax year starting on April 5. This lasted until 1800, when the Treasury moved the start of the tax year to April 6.[32]

But, in any case, why is the tax accounting period 1 year and not, for example, 2? Moving to a biennial approach would undoubtedly reduce administrative and compliance costs, and the picture of someone's affairs would be more accurate if one looked beyond a single and perhaps very unusual year. One scholar who came down in favor of moving to a biennial tax cycle, on the grounds of the cost savings, signaled that the idea has not received widespread support by including as an epigraph to his article the view of a "friend" that "your paper topic represents the single worst idea I have ever heard in my entire life."[33] We wholeheartedly disagree. (And the ancient Egyptians, by the way, taxed on a two-year cycle).[34]

It is easy to make fun of the misshaped cars, ludicrous legal wrangling, and the like that come from attribute-based taxation and line drawing. And sometimes the ridicule is fully deserved. But this kind of differentiation is often driven by practical necessity in pursuit of some objective that is at least well intentioned. Under most VATs, for instance, as a way of saving scarce administrative resources for other uses and easing compliance costs for small traders, firms are only required to remit the tax once their turnover exceeds some threshold level: a well-meant notch that results, however, in some firms artificially constraining their (apparent, at least) scale and growth to keep below the threshold.[35] And if one wants to tax food and other products at a lower rate, the inevitable Jaffa Cake–like fiascos may be a price worth paying. The question is whether the side effects from creative tax avoidance are too costly for the aims being pursued, and whether they can be limited. And prominent among those side effects, along with sheer costs of implementation, is the damage suffered, over and above the tax actually handed over to the government, as a result of changes in behavior. That is the excess burden of taxation, to which we turn next.

Excess Burden

That taxes generally impose a loss on taxpayers that is greater than the tax actually remitted is made manifest in the examples of tax-induced innovation discussed above. Who would want to live in an unfinished house, or one with a tiny door, if it were not to save taxes? These are all what are called "distortions": things that are done only because of incentives created by the tax system. And their importance is that they create a loss from taxation over and above that which the private sector must inevitably suffer from transferring resources to the government. The idea of this *additional* loss from taxation—"excess burden"—is one of the most fundamental and powerful of all ideas that can be brought to bear in thinking about taxation, yet it is rarely picked up in public debate. Perhaps it seems nerdy. But it is not as mysterious as it may seem. And it matters.

No Fire without Smoke

Not long after his restoration to the throne in 1660, Charles II was, like his beheaded father before him, short of money. Parliament had made sure, however, that there were no longer any bizarre feudal dues for him to revive: all taxation required its approval. And so in May 1662, Parliament gave England[36] a tax on hearths (that is, fireplaces, then often used for cooking as well as heating). Charged at 2 shillings (2s) per hearth per year (with exemptions for the poor), this was the first tax other than customs and excise to be levied routinely even in times of peace. Official records of the hearth tax have largely survived and become a treasured source for genealogists. They can also, with a bit of imagination, teach us a good deal about the effects of taxation.

The idea of taxing hearths made some sense, with the number of fireplaces in a house seeming to be a reasonable proxy for ability to pay, and a practicable one, too, as it was "easie to tell the number of Harths, which remove not as Heads or Polls do."[37] Whatever its merits of design, however, the hearth tax was hated from the start. The month after the first count of hearths was due, Samuel Pepys was telling his diary of how people "clamour against the chimney-money and say they will not pay it without force."[38] What stung was not only (or even mainly) the tax itself, but the power (indeed obligation) of those collecting the tax to enter people's homes to check the accuracy of their claims about the number of hearths. And resistance there was. In 1668, "the collectors of the hearth money at Bridport were followed about the town by men, women and children who threw stones at them. . . . Mr. Knight was hit on the head twice and has since died."[39]

The hearth tax was repealed in 1689,[40] one of the first of William III's actions after the Glorious Revolution of the previous year; doubtless an easy win for quick popularity following what was in effect an unresisted invasion. He had taken care to make known his opposition to the tax,[41] and "along William's whole line of march, from Torbay to London, he had been importuned by the common people to relieve them from the intolerable burden of the hearth money."[42] It had become, as the repealing legislation put it, "a badge of slavery upon the whole people, exposing every man's house to be entered into and searched at pleasure by persons unknown to him."[43] Repeal of the hearth tax was explicitly listed in the Bill of Rights passed by Parliament in 1689. Troubled though this short-lived experience was, the hearth tax provides a way to see the nature and workings of excess burden through the eyes of one taxpayer who went through it.

In 1662, when the hearth tax was introduced, John Windover was living in Holy Rood parish, just outside Southampton, on the south coast.[44] He was doing pretty well: His home had five fireplaces, which was around the average for all those in the parish that were liable to the tax.[45] Eight years later, however, Mr. Windover had only four fireplaces. We do not know if it was the tax that led him to have one less fireplace, but suppose that it was. On his remaining fireplaces, Mr. Windover remitted a total tax of 8 shillings. But the true cost to him of the tax was more than that: In addition to having less to spend on other things, he now lived in a colder and no doubt less welcoming house. That additional cost, over and above the tax he paid—the numb fingers, the nightcap pulled lower to warm his ears—was the excess burden that Mr. Windover suffered from the hearth tax.

This loss is less tangible than the 8s that Mr. Windover handed over to the tax collector, but it was no less real for that. And we can even put a money value on it. The additional loss that he bore was the value to him of the one hearth that he no longer had in 1670. How much was that worth to him (over and above the cost of the fireplace itself)? Certainly less than the extra 2s of tax it would have triggered had it had still been there: If it had been worth more to him than that, he would have kept the fireplace and endured the extra tax liability it caused. And it was also worth to him no less than nothing: otherwise he would not have had it to begin with. So the value to him of the fireplace he no longer had in 1670 was between 2s and nothing. A reasonable guess would be in the middle, at 1s. So the total loss to him from the hearth tax was about 9s. Of that, 8s was in the very obvious form of a tax payment and at least had the merit to wider society of helping to finance government spending. The other 1s, the excess burden, was not just hard to see but benefited no one: It was, for both John Windover in particular and Restoration England in general, pure waste.

The attribute-based taxation and notches looked at earlier in this chapter also give rise to excess burden, of different forms but sometimes easier to see than missing fireplaces. After they had contorted the shape of their vessels, the British shipowners of the nineteenth century found themselves not only paying port and other fees—albeit less than they would have without the contortions—but also with ships that may have cost more to produce and were certainly more likely to capsize. The additional costs they incurred, including perhaps in having to carry more ballast or paying higher insurance premiums, was a form of excess burden. And firms that hover below the VAT threshold, for instance, will remit no VAT but will nonetheless suffer a burden from their hovering, whether though artificially limiting their growth or perhaps going to the trouble of splitting into smaller enterprises that manage to be treated as below the threshold.

The excess burden of taxing hearths is not a pressing policy concern these days, and less dangerous ways have been found to tax ships. But the same concern—a loss of well-being of the taxed (and sometimes the not-taxed), over and above that associated with the payment itself—applies to pretty much all taxes. Excess burden arises from taxes that affect the bigger things on which economic activity and well-being turn: investment and firm growth, labor market participation, savings, occupational choice, and borrowing and lending decisions. Taxes that affect them all potentially generate excess burden. The only taxes that create no excess burden are those that taxpayers cannot avoid or evade: lump-sum taxes of the kind touched on in chapter 4, which we will have more to say about in the next chapter. All other taxes impose a real cost on people in addition to that inherent in taking resources out of their hands and transferring them to the government.

There is a possible exception to this rule: It may be that attribute-based taxation spurs innovation that turns out to be pretty useful. This virtue probably cannot be claimed for the three-wheeled, long-seated Indonesian ~~motorbike~~ car. It could be claimed, however, for the *fluyt*, a type of merchant vessel developed by the Dutch around the end of the sixteenth century. Its origins apparently lay in the taxes levied on vessels passing through the Øresund, the main channel between the North Sea

Tax-efficient ships: A fluyt of fancy.

and the Baltic. These were reportedly based on the size of the deck, prompting the development of ships that had small decks but were wide at the waterline.[46] This design proved just the thing for carrying large cargoes in often shallow water,[47] and the *fluyt* became the mainstay of the Dutch seaborne empire of the seventeenth century. In this case, the excess burden of the deck-based tax may even have been negative. Of course, attributing this innovation entirely to taxation is problematic: The same design improvement might have occurred anyway. But this— and maybe the case of the elegant excise glasses—is as close as we can get to an example in which tax-induced innovation may have proved inherently beneficial. No less likely is that tax-induced innovation actually impedes more useful creativity: Had it not been for their peculiar tonnage rule, for instance, perhaps the British would have been quicker to develop the (shallow-hulled) fast clipper.[48]

And while taxation can spur innovation, innovation can also spur taxation. When the scientist Michael Faraday was asked by William

Gladstone what was the practical value of electricity, he reportedly answered: "Why, sir, there is every probability that you will soon be able to tax it." And so, whether Faraday truly said this or not, it came to be.

The idea of excess burden has long been a staple of economists: John Stuart Mill wrote about it nearly two centuries ago.[49] And the reality goes back as far as taxation itself. Many of those who see heavy taxes as contributing to the decline of the western Roman Empire blame not the overall level of tax but rather the excess burden it created, in the form of untilled fields and fleeing industry.[50]

But it has proved very hard to convey the idea of excess burden into practical policy making and debate. The trouble is that it is very nebulous. It does not show up in anyone's budget. And it usually takes the form of things that are not there (Mr. Windover's missing fireplace, a boyar's absent but much-loved beard, the profits and wages not earned because of an investment that did not happen) or actions that are not taken (the overtime not worked or the entrepreneurial career path not chosen).

Sometimes, too, excess burden takes the shape of things that are there but really ought not to be. This is because taxes, or outright subsidies, can lead to actions being taken that actually cost the rest of us more than they benefit those most immediately affected. If Charles II had instead subsidized fireplaces by enough for Mr. Windover to decide to have a sixth, he would have enjoyed the extra warmth, but we know he valued this at less than it cost to construct: otherwise, he would have paid for it without any subsidy. In the same way, tariffs on cars, for instance, replace low-cost imports with high-cost domestic production: Domestic car manufacturers gain from this, and the government collects some revenue, but the loss to consumers, who now buy fewer and more expensive cars, is even bigger.

The intangibility of the idea of excess burden means that, when it comes to practical policy making, it often gets less attention than things that are much more tangible. The costs to taxpayers and the government of collecting a tax, for example, are often much more obvious and easier to understand. It is easy to please crowds with talk of tax simplification, for instance, but reductions in excess burden rarely bring standing ovations, or votes.

Whether this relative neglect of excess burden in public debate really matters depends, of course, on whether it matters much in itself. So, how big is it? The key issue here is the responsiveness of behavior to taxation. To see this, go back to Holy Rood and meet Cornelius Fox. Like his neighbor John Windover, Mr. Fox had five fireplaces in 1662. But by 1670, he had cut back even more in face of the same 2s tax rate, shedding not just one fireplace but three. So Mr. Fox ended up with a lower tax bill than Mr. Windover—only 4s. But his fingers were, presumably, even more numb and his cold nights even colder, meaning a larger excess burden. With each of the three no-longer-present fireplaces valued, by the same logic as above, at 1s, a reasonable guess at the excess burden suffered by Mr. Fox is 3s. For him, almost half of the total loss (of 7s, made up of 4s of tax remitted plus 3s of excess burden) comes not in the form of tax remitted but excess burden. There is a general truth here. Because Mr. Fox responded more strongly to the tax than did Mr. Windover—his demand elasticity was much higher—he was better able to reduce his tax bill in response to the tax. However, it also meant that Mr. Fox suffered a larger excess burden from doing so, both in money terms and relative to the tax revenue actually collected.

So, a greater responsiveness to tax means not only less revenue for the government but also a bigger excess burden for the taxpayer. Measuring the extent of such behavioral responses is the bread and butter of modern empirical economics. All kinds of fancy statistical techniques and clever research designs using natural and randomized controlled field experiments have been developed to pin down the magnitude of responses to various taxes. The excess burden from taxing the labor income of those already working, for instance, turns out to be pretty low per dollar raised. This is not to say that labor supply is not affected by taxation at all, but only that there is little effect beyond what is an inescapable consequence of extracting revenue from them. The decision of whether or not to work at all, however, proves quite responsive to taxation, over and above this inevitable effect (particularly among women), and so the excess burden per dollar raised from taxes that discourage labor force participation can be pretty large.[51]

When we think of behavioral responses in this context, it is not just a matter of real things, like the number of hearths or hours worked, that matters, but also any cost incurred in somehow avoiding or evading the tax. To see this, suppose that our friend John Windover had not really bricked up or otherwise got rid of that fifth hearth, but had somehow managed to hide it when the "chimney man" called, or had simply bribed him not to count it. Then Mr. Windover's fingers did not become more numb as a consequence of the tax. But he still incurred some cost in escaping the tax on that fireplace, whether in the expense of covering it up or of slipping some cash to the taxman. How big were those costs? The bribe that John would have been willing to pay to avoid tax of 2s (had he been that sort of person) is somewhere between 2s and nothing. So 1s is a decent guess. But that is exactly the same as the excess burden that, we reckoned above, he suffered when the fireplace really did disappear. And the same logic applies to the cost of any other way of avoiding or evading the tax. The lesson here is that the excess burden suffered by the taxpayer[52] is the same whether the response is in terms of real economic activity, such as having fewer fireplaces (or reduced labor supply or investment), or takes the form of evasion and avoidance. It is only quite recently that economists have come to realize this,[53] though the truth was already there in J. B. Handelsman's story cited at the beginning of Part III: whether the dog had really got rid of the fleas, or somehow managed to conceal them, it comes, in terms of excess burden, to the same thing.

This observation has the extremely convenient implication that one can figure out the key drivers of excess burden by looking at how the tax base (the amount of taxable income declared, for instance) responds to taxation without having to know how much of that response is real (lower labor supply, for instance) and how much is avoidance by other means (such as shifting to untaxed fringe benefits) or evasion (like simply not reporting some income). All of these responses reduce the tax base, and it is that overall effect that matters. This realization has created a small industry of economists measuring this tax-base responsiveness, sometimes in very clever ways. For the income tax, reams of articles have tried to estimate the "elasticity of taxable income." One recent survey of this vast literature[54] settles on a typical elasticity of taxable income between 0.2 and 0.3. Here's what that means. Say the income tax rate increases from 30 percent to 37 percent. Then the "net-of-tax rate" (the percentage of a dollar earned that the earner gets to keep) falls from 70 percent to 63 percent, a 10 percent decline. An elasticity of taxable income equal to between 0.2 and 0.3 suggests that reported taxable income would, in response to the tax increase, fall between 2 percent and 3 percent.

A Window on Excess Burden

The English tax on hearths was replaced by the tax on windows, also an indicator of how opulent a house is but one that could be measured in a less intrusive way. We mentioned that one response of English home-owners was to brick up some windows. In 1848, the president of the Carpenters' Society in London testified to Parliament that almost every house on Compton Street in Soho had employed him to reduce the number of windows.[55] One feature of the window tax was that liability jumped once a certain number of windows was reached—what we earlier called "notches." Centuries later, such notches have turned out to provide a clever way of gauging the extent of excess burden.[56]

To see how, go back to 1747. No tax was then paid on properties with fewer than 10 windows, but for those with between 10 and 14, a tax of 6d was payable on each and every window—not just the number exceeding that threshold. So adding one window to go from nine to 10 windows implied a tax liability of 5 shillings (6d times 10). This large jump in tax liability made that tenth window very expensive. If people did not respond at all to the tax, then we would simply expect there to be somewhat fewer houses with 10 windows than with nine (because there are somewhat fewer people who could afford 10 than could afford nine), and somewhat fewer with nine than with eight. In contrast, if people reacted strongly to the tax, we would find an otherwise inexplicably large bunch of houses with nine (reported) windows, just below the notch (perhaps even more houses than had eight) and far fewer with exactly 10 windows. And the more marked is that "bunching," the greater, we can conclude, was responsiveness to the window tax—and the greater, correspondingly, the excess burden it generated.

An inspired study applies this insight to local window tax records for 493 English homes, mostly from the town of Ludlow in Shropshire, between 1747 and 1757.[57] Sure enough, these records show a massive spike in the number of houses having exactly nine windows: more than four times as many as had either eight or 10. And there were similar spikes at 14 and 19 windows, reflecting further notches in tax liability at 15 and 20 windows. There was simply far too much bunching to be attributable to just chance. Given the kind of responsiveness that could explain this pattern, the implied excess burden of the tax is estimated, for the average property, to be about 13 percent of the revenue raised by the tax. However, for those who wound up cutting back to exactly one of the notches—to 14, for example—the excess burden was much larger, at about 62 percent of the tax payable. Among these, for those who cut to nine windows, and so had no liability, the tax was pure excess burden: no revenue was raised from them, but their behavior was distorted.

These kinds of notches in tax systems are generally not a good thing, precisely because of the marked responses they can elicit. But researchers have come to love them, precisely because they make the strength (or weakness) of behavioral responses very clear. The same idea has been applied, for example, to assess the distortionary costs of the income tax in Pakistan (which, unusually these days, once had many such notches) and of distortions created by the threshold of the U.K. VAT.[58]

Even when there is no sudden jump in liability, changes in the marginal tax rate (the tax rate on the last dollar)—"kinks" in the tax schedule—can be similarly exploited. Someone might be willing, for example, to earn an additional dollar if it is taxed at 20 percent, but not if it is taxed at 50 percent. So we might expect a strangely large number of people to be earning an amount at or around[59] the level at which the marginal tax rate rises. The seminal study of taxpayer response to kinks focused on the U.S. Earned Income Tax Credit. This, as we saw in chapter 7, features a subsidy to earnings up to a certain level of income, when the subsidy reaches its maximum value. At a higher level of income, the credit starts to be "clawed back" by reducing the amount of subsidy as more income is earned. The schedule thus has three kinks: from a negative marginal tax rate (subsidy) to a rate of zero, when the amount of the credit is maximized; from a zero tax rate to a positive one, when the clawback begins; and from a positive tax rate to zero, at the income level at which the credit completely disappears. The study found clear evidence of bunching at the first kink only for self-employed people, who have more flexibility over their (reported) earnings, interpreting this behavior to reflect mostly overreporting of true income to get more credit, a form of tax evasion.[60]

Before we move on from the taxation of windows, however, lest you think that the taxation of light is no longer an issue, you may wish to visit the historic town of Conegliano in northeast Italy, known for its prosecco. In Conegliano, a tax is owed by storeowners when their signs placed outside the shop create a shadow on public walkways.[61]

Keeping excess burden as low as possible—in the jargon, making the tax system as "efficient" as it can be, and "distortions" as minimal as possible—is thus a good idea when designing tax systems. So too, of course is making it fair, as we saw in the first part of the book. We have seen too something about what each of these desirable properties requires, with efficiency calling for heavier taxes on things that respond least to taxation and vertical equity requiring that taxes be linked to ability to pay. But we have looked at each element—efficiency and equity—in isolation from the other. What is needed are principles to guide us when we need to worry about both—which is always.

10

How to Pluck a Goose

The art of taxation consists in so plucking the goose as to obtain the largest possible amount of feathers with the smallest amount of hissing.

JEAN-BAPTISTE COLBERT[1]

IF YOU HAPPENED to own a coal mine, or be an arms manufacturer, the outbreak of the First World War was pretty good news—at least for your pocketbook. High prices meant an opportunity to earn profits above the minimum you required to stay in business: to receive, that is, rents (in the Ricardian sense). This did not go unnoticed, either by those whose sons were dying in the trenches or by governments looking for ways to finance their massively increased spending. The response was the adoption, by all the major belligerents (Austro-Hungary, Britain, France, Germany, Italy, Russia, and the United States) and many other countries[2] of "excess profit taxes" targeted on those rents. And they worked well. By war's end, these taxes were raising one-quarter of the federal government's revenue in the United States[3] and more than one-third of central government receipts in the United Kingdom.[4]

What made these taxes so attractive was their combination of two features. The first is that, as taxes on rents, they created (in principle) no distortions: So long as it would have been profitable to produce arms in the absence of the tax, it would be profitable to do so in its presence. They were thus essentially a form of what we called in chapter 4 "lump-sum" taxation, creating no excess burden. The important thing about lump-sum taxes is not that they have no effect on behavior. They do have an effect: Any tax transfers resources out of the private sector, leaving someone financially worse off and, as a result, changing what they do. If you were to wake up tomorrow and find a nice thank-you note from the government saying they had taken tax of $100 out of your wallet or purse, you would have no choice but to spend less, save less, or work more. Beyond that, there is nothing you can do but fume. That is the essence of a lump-sum tax.

The author P. G. Wodehouse, faced with a large tax demand, even managed to find something positive in this: "In many ways," he wrote, "I am not sorry this income tax business has happened. Everything was so easy for me before I was getting a bit bored. I now can spit on my hands and start sweating again, feeling that it really matters when I make a bit of money."[5] The unexpected tax demand that Wodehouse faced captures the defining feature of lump-sum taxation: it was a charge that he could do nothing to change. It of course made him worse off (financially if not in his spirits), and had an "income effect" on his behavior that led him to work more. But that effect is an inescapable consequence of taking resources away from him, which any tax must have. A lump-sum tax is one that has *only* such an income effect. It is any *additional* effects that a tax may have which gives rise to excess burden. Suppose, for instance, that Wodehouse had faced not a demand for past taxes, but a higher tax rate on his future earnings. He might have reflected that he had less to gain by writing—and the excess burden would have arisen in the form of fewer japes and scrapes for Bertie Wooster, Jeeves, and their chums. That would be an excess burden because it is a change in Wodehouse's behavior over and above the income effect inherent in raising revenue from him. It is the presence of "substitution effects" of this kind—reflecting any changes in the prices or after-tax wage rate that the taxpayer faces—that generates excess burden, and makes a tax non-lump sum.

The second attraction of the excess profit taxes is that they met widely held ideas of fairness and ability to pay. Not all lump-sum taxes meet that standard: A poll tax, for example, is also lump-sum, but is notoriously unfair. But what patriot could object to taxing war profits, as long as it did not disrupt production?

Similar aspirations—to being lump-sum and fair—can be seen in the taxes on social rank discussed in chapter 4: little risk of changing behavior, and a reasonable link to likely ability to pay. All these taxes had imperfections, as we saw. There were doubtless some poor(-ish) dukes, and the excess profit taxes were vulnerable to avoidance. But both aspirations give a glimpse of what would be in many respects an ideal tax system: lump-sum taxes attuned to each individual's inherent ability to pay and consistent with wider social notions of fairness. Such a system would provide Colbert his feathers (tax revenue) with as little hissing (in the form of either excess burden or cries of unfairness) as possible.

There is, however, a big obstacle to establishing such a system. It requires that there be some observable indicator of each person's ability to pay that they cannot or will not choose to change in response to the tax: Taxing anything that taxpayers choose to change—by working more or less, emigrating, or (like Mr. Windover from chapter 9) by bricking up their fireplaces—will lead them to change it (or appear to do so) and so generate excess burden. And there is simply no such perfect indicator of inherent ability to pay (not yet at least)—maybe there is no such thing. This chapter looks at how, in such an imperfect world, tax systems nonetheless have been and might be shaped so as to at least approach the Holy Grail of tax analysis: a nondistorting and fair tax system.

We look first at some attempts to find taxes that are both lump-sum and fair—and the political movements and board games they have sometimes inspired. Such levies, though, are unlikely to meet all of governments' revenue needs. Excess burden then becomes unavoidable, so we then look at truth and myth on how this tax-induced waste can be limited, and at the tension between efficiency and fairness that can result.

Searching for the Holy Grail

The search for tax bases that generate minimal excess burden and are at the same time fair has given rise to almost religious fervor, and even to fears of revolution.

War Profiteers and the Corporate Tax Revisited

By 1920, the idea that wars produce tax innovations was already so ingrained that the excess profits tax was hailed as "the only invention of consequence developed during the war in the field of finance."[6] This was wrong (Georgia had a tax of this kind during the Civil War)[7] but prescient, as it is only in the past few years that the full potential of the idea has begun to be fully recognized.

The excess profit taxes of the Great War took somewhat different forms, though even the British came to recognize the technical superiority of an approach adopted by the United States.[8] In this approach, all earnings above an 8 percent return on invested capital were taxed, the idea being that 8 percent represented something like the minimum return that investors could reasonably require. This is what made the base something approaching rents, in the sense of Ricardo and Malthus.

Levied at rates of up to 80 percent in both the United States and the United Kingdom,[9] we have already seen that these taxes raised substantial amounts. So successful were they that there was talk of continuing them after the war. But they were allowed to fade out. They had been explicitly temporary, and business, no doubt, found it easier to resist them in peacetime than they did when "evasion of the tax was considered little short of treason."[10] Excess profit taxes reappeared in France, Germany, and the United Kingdom in the early months of 1939, even before the declarations of war.[11] Having again served their purpose, however, over time the memory of excess profits taxes faded,[12] and the traditional corporate tax became the mainstay of business taxation. However, beginning in the mid-1970s, there was growing awareness of the distortions created by the usual corporation tax. These arise from its taxing not only rents but also the minimum return required by providers of equity finance, giving rise to a hodgepodge of distortions to both financing and investment decisions. The thought began to emerge that perhaps those distortions could be eliminated, and revenue raised in something close to lump-sum fashion, by converting the corporate tax into one on rents (leaving open the possibility of taxing the return to equity, in the form of dividends and capital gains, in the hands of the shareholder).

What is needed for a tax to be on a business's rents is that it allow the deduction of all costs incurred by the business. That is ultimately impossible, because some costs (the unpaid slog of hard-working owner-managers, for instance) are hard to observe and verify. But we know how to get a long way toward it—with the logic of the excess profits tax as a helpful guide.

Indeed, one way to convert the standard corporate tax into a rent tax looks very much like the excess profits tax of the Great War: this is by taking the normal return to equity out of the corporate tax base by allowing companies a deduction for a notional return on the equity invested in the company to go along with the deduction of interest. Taxes of this kind—"Allowance for Corporate Equity" forms of corporate tax—have been tried since the 1990s, with what many see as success, in Belgium, Brazil, Italy, and elsewhere.[13]

An alternative approach is to provide "cash flow" treatment of investment, which simply means allowing all investment costs to be deductible when incurred (instead of written off over time in the form of depreciation allowances), while no longer allowing interest deductibility (because allowing both would amount to allowing two tax deductions for one investment). In this way, the government in effect becomes a silent partner of the investor. Imagine, for instance, that the tax rate is 20 percent. Then under a cash flow tax, the government effectively puts up 20 percent of the cost of investment upfront, through the immediate deduction (which reduces the companies' tax liability);[14] but it then also takes 20 percent of whatever money the investment later brings in. Bearing an equal share of all costs and earnings, the silent partnership of the government does not affect the attractiveness of an investment, and that is true whether the rate is 20 percent, 80 percent, or whatever. The tax rate just determines the government's share of the rents. There is experience with such "cash flow" taxes. Mexico has had one,[15] and the 2017 U.S. tax reform means that investment there now receives something very close to cash flow treatment (although, because interest remains deductible, the system still differs from being a rent tax)—putting pressure on other countries that wanted to provide equally attractive tax treatment of investment to do the same, as Canada did the following year.

Rent taxes of various kinds have long been advocated, and to some degree implemented, in relation to natural resources, especially oil and gas.[16] These are sectors in which substantial rents are evident in times of high commodity prices—and governments have long sought to get a share of them. No doubt it is partly the high profits earned by Facebook, Google, and a few others that accounts for the recent rise of interest in ensuring effective taxation of rents.

But, in one key respect, rents may be easier to tax in relation to oil and gas than in the multinational giants of the digital era. Oil and gas fields are hard to move around, so that the rents they generate are in an important sense specific to a particular location. That makes it harder (though far from impossible) for companies to have those rents appear to arise wherever in the world they will be taxed at the lowest rate. However, such "profit shifting" is far easier to do when those rents are tied not to oil under the ground in a specific location but to, for instance, intellectual property—central to the business models of today's most profitable and powerful multinationals—whose ownership can fairly readily be arranged to be wherever happens to be tax-convenient. The problems that such shifting causes for the taxation of multinationals are taken up in chapter 11. There is, however, one other important case in which location-specific rents may arise: land.

Give Me Land, Lots of Land[17]

Taxes on land, as we saw in our brief gallop through tax history, have been a mainstay of governments' revenue through the ages. But there is more significance to land taxation than that.

Land is in (something like)[18] perfectly inelastic supply and was the prime example used by Ricardo and Malthus to illustrate the prospect of substantial economic rents. After Ricardo, considerable support emerged for taxing "unimproved" land values—meaning the value currently placed on the "original and indestructible powers of the soil."[19]

Being beyond the owner's control, taxing this would generate no excess burden. In addition, because landowners are likely to be among the better off (especially the larger among them), this began to look like a great tax base. John Stuart Mill argued for a tax on the "future unearned increase" in land values, capturing a large part of the increase "which is continually taking place, without any effort or outlay by the proprietors, merely through the growth of population and wealth."[20] Unlike today's property tax, which typically reflects how much a property could be rented or sold for, a tax on the unimproved value of land would not discourage efforts to improve and develop it by adding farmhouses, building a hotel, or whatever. So attractive was the idea that the taxation of unimproved land values—a "land value tax"[21]—found almost evangelical support.

Its prophet was the American economist and activist Henry George (1829–1897), who stressed the moral repugnance of landowners enjoying, through increased land values, the benefits of other people's efforts—in building a nearby railroad, for instance—and also from much government spending. George went further, arguing that a land value tax could remove the need for any other tax, and so launching the "single tax" movement. His 1879 book *Progress and Poverty*, a best seller of its time, combined some shrewd economics with messianic fervor: The single tax was to bring "the culmination of Christianity—the City of God on Earth, with its walls of jasper and its gates of pearl!"[22] George was, in the words of *The Economist*, "perhaps the only tax theorist in history whose beliefs have become the object of almost cult-like devotion."[23]

George's mass appeal, however, never quite turned into electoral success,[24] although it did give him the best-attended funeral procession in New York City since Abraham Lincoln's. And it won him many distinguished supporters, including George Bernard Shaw, Leo Tolstoy, and Sun Yat-sen (who reportedly became a believer after encountering "an American missionary . . . carrying the Bible in one hand and *Progress and Poverty* in the other"[25]). Even Milton Friedman, not known for thinking highly of any tax, was a grudging fan, saying that "the least bad tax is the property tax on the unimproved value of land."[26]

Land taxation brings the City of God to Earth.

A less-well-known devotee, Elizabeth Magie Phillips, may have had even more impact, self-publishing in 1906 a board game intended to illustrate the evils of undeserved profits associated with land ownership. Called *The Landlord's Game*, this became (subject to some dispute)[27] the precursor to *Monopoly*. (Incidentally, board-game lovers will be happy to learn that they can purchase on eBay *Stick the IRS: The Tax Shelter Game*; the winner is the player who pays the least tax.)

Georgism did have some early successes. New Zealand introduced a tax on unimproved land in 1878 (though it lasted only 1 year).[28] Henry George's speaking tour of Australia may have had some effect: Several parts of Australia (later states) had such a tax by the mid-1890s. We have also seen that Lloyd George's budget of 1909–1910 proposed a tax on future unearned increments in land values, though it was not enacted.[29] Several U.S. states introduced "split-rate" systems, which taxed land and buildings at different rates.[30] And Sun Yat-sen proved an influential

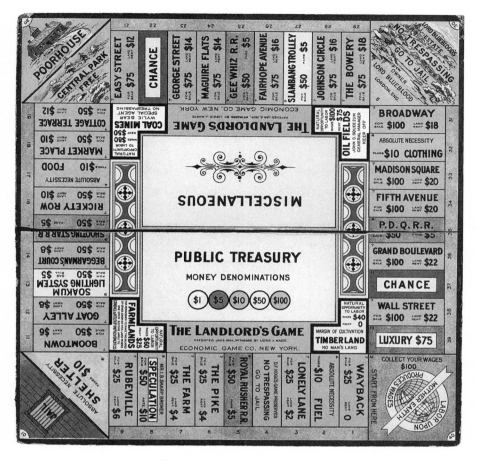

Economic theory as a board game.

advocate, as his successors in Taiwan put into practice his commitment
that "the teachings of [the] single taxer, Henry George, will be the basis
of our program of reform."[31]

Sun Yat-sen even embellished Georgism by proposing a neat idea
for valuing land for tax purposes when land itself was rarely traded, so
that there were few useful market prices to use. His idea—an echo of
the liturgies of the ancient world—was to have landowners declare the
value of their property for tax purposes, but with the wrinkle that the
government would have the option to purchase it at the price declared.[32]

This approach provides an incentive to declare the true market value: Declaring too high means more tax is paid than need be; declaring too low runs the risk of having to sell for less than the property is worth. In fact, such a scheme was already being implemented in New Zealand by 1891, with the Crown empowered to buy any land at 10 percent over its self-declared value.[33] And the Sun Yat-sen scheme has been adopted in some places since. In 1993—and largely to elicit declaration from properties not then on the cadastral register—Bogotá introduced a scheme requiring self-assessment, with the option of compulsory purchase at a price 25 percent above the declared value. The number of declared properties more than doubled between 1993 and 1994.

However, no land tax revolution occurred. By the early 2000s, only about 25 countries had some form of differential tax on land values.[34] Elsewhere it has been in demise. In Hawaii, the split-rate system was ended in 2002, perhaps having been too successful in encouraging the development of hotels and tourist attractions; Joni Mitchell's line "they paved paradise and put up a parking lot" was reputedly written while vacationing in Waikiki.[35]

The idea, nonetheless, has never entirely gone away.[36] A key challenge remains valuation, a very practical problem being that unimproved land (say, in central New York City) is rarely traded, so there is generally no handy market price by which to assess directly the "original and indestructible" value of land. Conceptual issues also arise: Land in its unimproved state may have been observable for the early settlers in New Zealand, but in time it becomes impossible to abstract from basic improvements in clearing, draining, leveling, and the like. But there do seem to be ways in which reasonable valuations of land can be arrived at.[37] Indeed, it seems that virtually all assessing units in the United States at least purport to value land and improvements separately, even where they are taxed at the same rate.[38]

Even Henry George would now be hard-pressed to believe that a tax on land values can replace all taxes. Property tax revenues in the United Kingdom, for instance—the base of which is wider than that of a land value tax, because it includes the value of improvements—would need to be increased almost tenfold to replace all other taxes.[39] But neither is the revenue potential trivial. And there is another attraction. As tax bases become more mobile internationally (a theme of chapter 11), the attractions of taxing location-specific land rents become more obvious. Henry George's ideas may yet acquire new life.

Conscripting Wealth

At the end of the First World War, despite the success of their excess profit taxes, the governments of Europe were buried in debt. The victors had borrowed to win, and the losers were faced with reparations. In Britain, public debt stood in 1922/1923 at 186 percent of national income.[40] One proposal to deal with this "hideous war memorial"[41] was for a capital levy: a one-off tax on existing wealth. This tax would not be confined to rents (as assets can have positive value even if expected to yield no more than the minimum required). But it would in effect be lump-sum,[42] because that capital reflected decisions already made and so could not be altered in response to the tax: Nothing is harder to change than the past. Reducing government debt by a capital levy would thus replace the future (inefficient) taxes needed to pay off that debt by an excess-burden-free lump-sum payment that fell mainly on the better off.

To many, of course, the idea was pure Bolshevism. Nevertheless, the capital levy was serious politics in the 1920s. In Britain, it found support from strange bedfellows: the Labour Party, the Treasury (initially), and even Winston Churchill.[43] Its academic advocates could not have been more distinguished: Pigou (of externality fame), Schumpeter, and (initially) Keynes were all in favor; and they could all cite Ricardo (writing in the context of the debt accumulated during the Napoleonic Wars), who knew a thing or two about tax incidence. But, in the event, there was no capital levy in Britain. Pale versions were adopted, however, in a few other European countries, and after World War Two—with more success—by Japan. These experiences, however, were not wholly happy.[44]

One reason capital levies are rarely imposed and, if adopted, often disappoint is that even discussing the possibility of such a levy puts capital owners on notice, giving them an opportunity to avoid it by shifting their assets abroad, running them down, or taking other steps to protect them. Because it could be avoided, the tax ceased to be lump-sum. Only if announced unexpectedly and with immediate effect—unlikely in anything close to a democracy (which is why it may have worked in postwar Japan)—can a capital levy truly be lump-sum.

There was another reason to worry about the effect of a capital levy, carrying a more general lesson. If a government shows itself willing to impose such a tax now, might it not do so again in the future? "The advocates of a levy insist strongly on its emergency character," as one of its supporters summarized, "and the opponents on the apprehension of its repetition."[45] The problem is that, however much government may promise (and even truly intend) not to give in to them, the attractions of such a backward-looking tax will be there in the future, and it may simply not be credible to promise never to succumb to them. If so, then behavior today will be influenced by the possibility of a levy in the future, and excess burden arises once more. The world might therefore be better off if governments could bind themselves not to implement a future levy. But no government can bind its successors. What governments can do, unfortunately, is undermine promises not to give in to the future temptation to enact a levy by giving in to that temptation today.

This "time consistency" problem—the potential desirability, but inherent difficulty, of committing not to do something in the future that it will in fact then be desirable to do—impacts tax policy more widely. It is the same self-control problem that, at the level of the individual rather than of government, underpins the internality argument for corrective taxation discussed in chapter 8. It is also one reason that taxpayers deeply resent retrospective taxation: Once a government succumbs to levying taxes not anticipated at the time taxpayers make their decisions, might it not do so again? And it is one reason that tax amnesties—sweet deals for regularizing past evasion combined with promises this will be the last-ever such offer—are a risky business. If the government has an amnesty today, it may make sense to keep evading and wait for another one to come along. The only solution, not easy to do, is for government to build up a reputation for sticking to its tax promises.

Limiting the Damage

If governments could raise all the revenue they needed by taxing rents, or through lump-sum taxes more generally, or by taxing bads, all in a way that provided an acceptable degree of progressivity, the history of taxation would be short (and dull). But they cannot. So some degree of excess burden—like Mr. Windover's missing fireplace (discussed in chapter 9)—is inevitable. The question is how to limit it. Even despots should care about this, as excess burden is a form of waste that benefits no one and ultimately makes someone—possibly a dangerously discontented citizenry—worse off. Happily, some simple guidelines are available for limiting the burden on the Mr. Windovers of the world—as are a few mantras to distrust.

The Cleverest Man in England

Frank Ramsey, fellow of King's College, Cambridge, was the archetype of an incandescently brilliant English academic, so clever that it is seriously debated whether he learned German in a week in order to read Kant. Sadly, he did not.[46] (But he did, while still an undergraduate, translate Wittgenstein into English and later earn his thanks for correcting some "grave mistakes.") By the time he died of jaundice, aged 26, in 1930, Ramsey had made lasting contributions to philosophy and mathematical logic—his main interests. Along the way, he wrote two papers in economics that are still part of the profession's everyday apparatus, though he regarded them as a "waste of time." (By his standards, perhaps they were.) One of these, published in 1927,[47] laid the foundations for rigorous thinking about how best to design tax systems.

What Ramsey did was answer a question posed by Pigou, who saw that it required mathematical tools he did not have. Pigou asked: Ignoring practicalities of evasion and administration, how should a government go about raising the revenue it needs by taxing the consumption of different goods and services, perhaps at different rates (and leaving aside the taxation of income for the moment), so as to minimize excess burden?

Seeing further than most: Frank Ramsey in the Lake District, 1925.

The beginnings of the answer can be found in chapter 9. Comparing the excess burdens that Mr. Windover and Mr. Fox suffered from the hearth tax, we saw in that chapter that excess burden was higher, the more responsive to tax is the thing that is being taxed. Frank Ramsey's analysis confirmed the point rigorously, generating what is known as the "inverse elasticity rule": Minimizing excess burden requires taxing at a higher rate those things that are less responsive to the rate at which they are taxed—the closer to zero, more specifically, the elasticity of demand or supply. And we saw too—an insight that came only a half century later[48]—that it is immaterial whether that response is real (fewer fireplaces) or sham (fireplaces covered up when the collector calls). Minimizing excess burden—also known, in the jargon, as pursuing "efficiency" or minimizing "distortions"—requires taxing more heavily tax bases that are less responsive to the rate at which they are taxed. The usual suspects include things like tobacco products, alcoholic drink, and fuels—reinforcing the case for heavy taxes on these items on the breaking bad grounds of chapter 8 (although we have seen that demand elasticities for these things may not be as low as often supposed).

As an implication of this rule, one can be pretty sure that it is likely to be unwise to tax very heavily things for which there are good substitutes (unless those substitutes are similarly taxed), because the presence of these alternatives likely means a high sensitivity to price.[49] That is, people can then easily rearrange their affairs to avoid the tax, so that higher tax rates will be needed to chase the vanishing tax base. Similar things should be taxed at similar rates.

Frank Ramsey's algebra held another lesson: It is a good idea, in general, to tax at relatively low rates things that people tend to consume in larger amounts the more paid work they undertake; and conversely, to tax at relatively high rates what are inelegantly called "complements with leisure."[50] The reason is simply that by making working less rewarding in terms of what it can buy, commodity taxes generally induce people to work less.[51] One way to dampen that effect (in theory) is to cleverly differentiate tax rates across commodities so as to favor things that people value more the harder they work and penalize things they value when not working.[52] This implies, for instance, low tax rates on child care services and high ones on watching sports events.

One thing all this teaches us is that a standard rallying call of tax reformers for a uniform tax on all consumption (and/or on types of income) is almost always not, in principle, the right answer: There may well be good efficiency reasons to single out some commodity for a particularly high (or low) tax rate. The trouble is that figuring out, concretely, precisely which commodities to single out for such treatment turns out to be very hard: It depends on features of demand responses that we still cannot pin down in practice with enough confidence to hang practical recommendations on.[53]

So, at least until our empirical understanding improves, the real question of principle—still leaving practicalities aside—is how to set about taxing goods and services when knowledge of demand responses is imperfect. Suppose, for example, we know nothing about the demand elasticities of the commodities that we need to tax in order to raise revenue. Would it be better to tax them all at a moderately low rate, or to toss a coin and pick a few things for heavy taxation while leaving the rest exempt? There are certainly strong practical reasons for preferring uniform treatment: Multiple tax rates require drawing lines, with all the games we have seen that involves; and once one preferentially reduced tax rate is conceded, policy can get swept away on a slippery slope of self-serving arguments for others. And there is another inherent feature of excess burden which gives good reason to think that uniform tax treatment will often be a sensible benchmark for trying to limit excess burden.

Broaden the Base, Lower the Rate (Maybe)

When, in chapter 9, Mr. Windover responded to a 2s tax on fireplaces by somehow getting rid of one of his, we estimated the excess burden he suffered at 1s. (This was on the grounds that we could be sure he valued that lost fireplace at less than 2s but more than nothing, so 1s seemed a good guess). Suppose now that the tax rate is increased by a further 2s, to 4s per fireplace, and Mr. Windover responds by getting rid of another fireplace. By the same logic, he valued each of the two fireplaces that he has now lost at no more than 4s (the tax rate he now faces), or he would have kept them, but at more than nothing, or he would not have installed them in the first place: 2s seems a good guess. So, with two lost fireplaces, his excess burden is now 4s.

What is striking about this is that doubling the tax rate has led to a more than doubling—in fact a fourfold increase—of excess burden. And that is the important general point: Excess burden increases more than proportionally with the tax rate.[54] The broad implication is that, beyond cases in which we can confidently apply the inverse elasticity or complements-with-leisure rules, the way to keep excess burden low is to tax a lot of things at a low rate rather than a few things at a high rate.

This observation is the origin of a common mantra in tax design, carved in stone—or at least left on the blackboard and covered in wax— by one outgoing U.S. administration for the benefit of the next: "Broaden the base, and lower the rates."[55] There is much truth and use- fulness in that, to be sure. (It is this principle, for instance, that provides the promised explanation for the desirability of smoothing taxes over time that we asserted in chapter 2.) But this tax mantra, like others, can be a bit too glib.

We have already seen one example of a base-narrowing reform that may well be a good idea: converting the standard corporate income tax into a rent tax by allowing a deduction for a notional return on equity. The resulting tax is nondistorting, and so, even though the base is nar- rower, more revenue can be raised by setting the rate high enough (because the higher rate does not discourage the underlying activity). But this is just one of many examples warning us to be (very) skeptical of claims that a particular tax must be efficient because the base is so broad that it enables a very low tax rate.

One could, for instance, raise the same revenue as under a retail sales tax or a VAT that aims to tax only final consumption by instead charging a turnover tax on all sales, including business-to-business sales. But tax- ing business inputs is generally a bad idea, unless there is some partic- ular reason to do so (which might be to deal with externalities, such as the use of fossil fuels). The reason that taxing business inputs is mis- guided is because such taxes not only distort which final goods are con- sumed but also lead to waste in their production: They encourage busi- nesses to produce things in ways that make commercial sense given the taxes on those inputs that they face, but would not have made sense in their absence. Businesses may try to use untaxed inputs instead of taxed ones (decorating walls, for instance, not with taxed printed wallpaper but by painting over untaxed plain wallpaper) or merge to escape a layer of taxation.[56] Such responses by producers imply that, at the end of the day, because they are doing things in ways that would not otherwise be their choice, the value of final output is reduced (fewer nicely decorated walls): what is known as "production inefficiency." And that cannot be wise if anything useful could have been done with that forgone output.

The formal articulation of the undesirability of taxing business purchases did not come until the 1970s,[57] but it has been in sensible policymakers' blood for much longer. The window tax statutes got this right without appealing to optimal tax proofs, by exempting industrial or retail buildings and windows in rooms in which no one lived, such as dairies and pantries. These exemptions created their own difficulties, as rooms were dressed up as empty or for business use when the surveyors came.[58] Applying the principle of not taxing business inputs always runs up against the problem of distinguishing personal from business use. But it remains one of the most powerful tax principles we have.

Sadly, not all policy makers have intuited the point so well. Under the Austrian sales tax of 1923, tax was to be collected only once on each commodity, at a specified stage of production, but at a rate "designed to reflect the typical cumulated tax burden on the commodity to which the latter would be subject if it were actually taxed at each stage." In other words, the tax deliberately tried to mimic the inefficient distortions that would arise from a turnover tax. This led a normally very dry scholar of sales taxes, John F. Due, to reflect that "the basic objection against the system was the complete absurdity of the principle on which it was based" and to nominate the tax as a "leading candidate for the museum of tax curiousae"—which, decades later, we now know to be this very book.[59]

The general inefficiency caused by taxing business inputs also gives reason to suspect that a financial transactions tax—a tax at a very low rate on all financial transactions—may not be so great an idea as it sounds. The scale of such transactions is indeed so vast that, its advocates happily point out, even an extremely low rate could produce a large amount of revenue.[60] But because it is levied on a wide range of intermediate transactions, it could be highly inefficient even at such a low rate: Proposed rates are often not so low, for instance, relative to the very narrow margins associated with some transactions. Practical proposals quickly end up excluding transactions that might be especially sensitive to even a low tax rate, such as repos (the rapid sale and repurchase of securities). This has been the fate, for instance, of proposals in the European Union in recent years. And on top of all that, despite the "Robin Hood" label beloved by its advocates, there is no good reason to suppose that the incidence of a financial transactions tax would be on highly-paid workers in the financial sector rather than, for instance, on people building up and managing assets for their retirement.[61]

Shaping a Tax System

Making good tax policy would be easy if the only thing that mattered was minimizing excess burden. We would not even have to worry about Ramsey's rule: a poll tax, the same for everyone, would do the trick. And it would also be easy if inequality was all that mattered: Edgeworth's solution, encountered in chapter 5, of taxing away everything and then sharing it out equally would give as egalitarian an outcome as one could imagine. But neither efficiency nor fairness can be ignored, which is what makes tax design a puzzle. The need to strike a balance between the two arises as soon as one tries to put the Ramsey rule into practice. Things for which demand is relatively inelastic tend to be things that are basic to a decent existence, such as food and shelter. So while the Ramsey rule of taxing them at a relatively high rate looks good on efficiency grounds, it looks bad on fairness grounds.

But the front line in the debate on balancing fairness and efficiency concerns in tax design is in deciding the shape of the income tax schedule: How progressive should it be? Is it even obvious that it should be progressive? (By "progressive"—and it will turn out to be worth being precise—is meant that the average tax rate always increases as income rises.) Practice has varied widely over time and across countries. Pitt the Younger's income tax had 28 different tax rates, albeit rising to a modest top rate of 10 percent. By the end of the First World War, marginal rates in the United States ranged from 6 percent on the lowest taxable incomes to 77 percent on the highest; in the United Kingdom, the range was from 11.3 percent to 52.5 percent.[62] By 1979, the top marginal rate on earned income in the United Kingdom was 83 percent; now it is

45 percent. And progressivity of the income tax varies hugely around the world.[63] "Flat tax" countries, such as Russia and Romania, have just one (typically quite low) marginal rate of tax, applied to all income above (usually) some exempt amount—which is progressive, in the sense that the average rate of tax increases with income, but not by very much.

This variation in the progressivity of the income tax largely reflects differences and changes in ethical values bearing on the fairness of alternative tax arrangements—and we have seen that economists have no special expertise on the justness of alternative ethical positions. What they can contribute is an understanding of the extent to which increased progressivity will create an excess burden—distortions to decisions as to how much, and whether, to work, earn, and save—against which any distributional gains can be weighed. Over the years, economists have become increasingly good at this, often by making use (in the same way as we saw above of eighteenth-century window taxes) of the kinks and sometimes weird jumps with which policy makers have over the centuries sprinkled their tax systems. And economists have become increasingly good at understanding the implications of these distortions for good tax design.

A first step in this understanding is recognizing that it is not enough to look only at what happens to be called the "personal income" tax. The shaping of tax systems also needs to embrace the design and impact of social security contributions and benefit payments linked to income, such as an earned income tax credit, as well as amounts paid in taxes on consumption (since these vary fairly systematically with income). Taking all these factors into account, the effective marginal tax rates on earnings—the additional tax that results when earnings rise by $1—can be strikingly high. For example, with a marginal personal income tax rate of 30 percent, social security tax at 15 percent, and a VAT at 20 percent, the effective marginal tax rate on someone spending all their earnings is over 50 percent.

Figuring out what sort of shape an income tax schedule (combining these effects) should have when excess burden and fairness are both concerns is a fiendishly hard mathematical problem. Harder even than the problem solved by Frank Ramsey, which looked only at the excess burden aspect, and so could abstract from the complications raised by taxing income. It was only in 1971 that James Mirrlees, another Cambridge (United Kingdom) economist, managed to extend Edgeworth's analysis to recognize the potentially adverse impact of taxation on incentives to earn income. And doing so went a long way towards his winning the Nobel prize for economics 25 years later. Even more fiendishly difficult than working out the solution to the problems, however, is figuring out how to explain it. Here is the best we can do. (But if you want to cut to the chase, skip the next four paragraphs.)

One way to think about the problem of designing an income tax schedule—more precisely, a schedule for relating tax due to the level of earned income[64]—is to compare, for each possible income level, two effects of increasing the marginal tax rate at that point, while holding it constant everywhere else. One (bad) effect of that higher marginal tax rate is that it discourages work effort by those initially earning just that amount of income. The other effect (a good one, because we need to raise some money) is to increase the tax revenue raised from all those earning higher incomes: Although the marginal tax rate they face is unchanged, the increase in the marginal tax rate lower down in the distribution increases the average rate of tax they pay, having only an income effect that gives rise to no excess burden.

This latter benefit of high marginal rates tends to be especially pronounced toward the lower end of the earnings distribution, because there are many people and much potential tax base higher up in the income distribution. So the good effect is very strong. This does not mean that the poorest pay a large amount of tax. To the contrary, they might be receiving a large subsidy, with the high marginal rate meaning that the subsidy is reduced quickly as income rises, so that its benefit is targeted on those with the very lowest incomes.

Things are a bit more complex at the higher end. Suppose first that one person can be identified as the very highest earner of all. Then, as no one is higher in the income distribution to collect more from, there is no good effect from increasing the marginal tax rate there, only a bad one. So the marginal tax rate on that person should be zero. This is a pretty striking result,[65] and has the further remarkable implication that in this case the tax system should not everywhere be progressive (as the term was defined above). But the underlying logic is impeccable. The practical implications of the result are limited, however, because even if we could identify, a priori, a single highest earner and how much they would earn, it tells us nothing about what the rate on the second-highest earner should be. A more practicable approach is to suppose that there is no such highest earner: that there is no limit to how much someone might earn. The good effect of high marginal tax rates then comes into play and with some force. And the bad incentive effect may well be out-weighed by the fairness gained by using the additional revenue that is raised from those even higher in the income distribution to reduce the tax payments of those lower down.

It is in the middle range of incomes, where most earners are to be found, that the adverse incentive effects are likely to be most pervasive (because they affect a large number of taxpayers). So it is in this range that the case for low marginal tax rates can be especially powerful.

Combining these observations, the picture that emerges is of a system that provides a significant basic income to all, but with high marginal tax rates in the lower ranges, partly in the form of withdrawal of benefits, and moderate ones in the middle. How things play out in the upper ranges of income depends on patterns of behavioral response and the shape of the income distribution: Optimal marginal tax rates in this range may increase with income, which we normally taken for granted—but they might not. Probably the most common view is that they should indeed increase.[66] The best pattern of marginal tax rates, if so, is U-shaped. (All this leaves open, by the way, the very real possibility that—common sense in this case not being wholly sensible—that the best possible in-come tax is not everywhere progressive: that is, the average tax rate may, over some range, be lower at higher incomes.)

Quite how all these considerations should be turned into the actual numbers that shape an income tax depends on how responsive people are to tax incentives, the distribution of earning ability, the relative val-ues that society places on income accruing to the poor and the rich, and how much tax revenue the government needs for things other than redistribution. These are things that economists are increasingly able to provide actionable advice on.[67] A full answer to how progressive the tax system should be, however, also needs to recognize a range of considerations about which there is still much to learn. Account also needs to be taken, for instance, of the potential role that commodity taxes can play when combined with an income tax—with the key Ramsey lessons, on for instance, relatively low taxation of substitutes for work, continuing to apply.[68] Other problematic issues include incidence questions as to how the tax system affects pretax incomes (we saw, for example, that the Earned Income Tax Credit [EITC] likely results in some reduction in pretax earnings) and how much of observed earnings actually reflects rents (of highly paid executives, for instance) that can be taxed without creating any excess burden.[69]

The theory of optimal taxation—which is what we have been talking about—does not provide simple answers. But it points to the things that really matter, and protects us against ideas that sound plausible but are actually wrong. And it is becoming increasingly capable of telling us how, in particular circumstances, to achieve whatever the objectives of tax policy makers may be.

How Many Feathers?

One other element of Colbert's metaphor remains to be explored. Ramsey and Mirrlees were both asking how best to raise some given amount of revenue, without considering what that amount ought to be. But how much revenue should a government raise? Just how many feathers, that is, does a goose-plucker need?

For some reason, 10 percent has had a historical ring about it—for tax rates, if not necessarily for the overall share of government in the economy. Confucius set out 10 percent as the appropriate tax rate, in line with which Genghis Khan demanded only a 10 percent tax when he rampaged through Russia.[70] The very word "tithe" means "one-tenth," and there are also the Spanish tenth, the Venetian Decima, Cromwell's decimation tax, and the French *dixième* of the eighteenth century. Pitt's income tax of 1799 had a top rate of 10 percent.

One might, however, expect economists to come up with a somewhat less arbitrary response. Practice varies widely, even among the more advanced economies. Denmark and Sweden have supported tax ratios around or even over 50 percent of GDP; in the United States, such a tax ratio is still widely regarded as essentially equivalent to Bolshevism (though many there would presumably welcome a top income tax rate of 13 percent, as introduced by Stalin in 1943, applied through much of the Soviet era and again now in Russia).[71]

No country taxes for the sheer fun of it. The point—of other than the breaking bad corrective taxes of chapter 8—is to finance public spending. So it is spending needs that drive how much revenue governments must raise (at least in the longer term, and leaving aside the possibility for lower-income countries, of grants from abroad). But things work the other way around, too: What can—and should—be achieved on the spending side is constrained by imperfections of the tax system. The true social cost of raising that 8s of tax revenue from taxing Mr. Windover's fireplaces in chapter 9, for example, was, because of the excess burden, not 8s but 9s. And so the spending that 8s financed would need to have been worth more than 9s in social terms (or at least to Charles I and his government) for the tax to have been truly worthwhile. That may sound weird. But if governments did not value every dollar they raise in taxes more than they value one dollar left in the hands of taxpayers, they would never impose any taxes at all. The more efficient the tax instruments available to governments (and the less harm they do to distributional objectives), the bigger, all else equal, one would expect government to be.

Whether more efficient tax collection actually causes bigger government is tricky to establish empirically. A country that anticipates more spending, such as on military costs for a looming war, may build the capacity to raise revenue in advance: hire more auditors, require more information reporting, acquire faster computers. The ability to tax more efficiently would then precede the higher taxation, but it would be wrong to conclude that the former caused the latter.

Experience with the VAT, however, provides some clues. This is a fundamental tax innovation that has grown over the past half century from a smart idea in theory to a major source of revenue in practice, notably in many of the European countries that have seen a large increase in government size over much the same period. There are two possible interpretations of this correlation. One is that the discovery of the VAT meant access to a more efficient way of raising revenues, and so led to the growth of government in these countries (as many of those who oppose adoption of a VAT in the United States fear would be the case there). If so, we would expect to see the growth of VAT accompanied by reduced reliance on now-inferior alternative taxes. The other interpretation is that the development of the VAT was a consequence of a search for ways to finance a desired increase in spending. In this case, we would expect to see increased revenue from other taxes, too. There turns out be evidence of both effects at work in OECD countries. But support is slightly stronger for the first possibility: that the VAT has been a "money machine" in the sense of actually spurring larger government.[72]

Less subtly, but no less to the point, one might wonder whether there is some link between tax levels and economic growth that could help tie down how big government should be. It turns out, however, that there is no simple or universal relationship between the two things. Long-run growth rates in the richer countries have not changed much since the latter part of the nineteenth century, for example, even though government has become much larger. And long-run growth rates have been much the same in the United States as in countries like Belgium, Denmark, and Finland, which in the early 1960s had about the same income per capita and tax take but have since increased their tax ratio by 10–15 percent of GDP or more. The lack of anything like a mechanical relationship between tax ratio and growth is not very surprising, because while some aspects of the tax system may seem likely to be bad for growth, discouraging private activities of various kinds, some aspects of the public spending they finance—on education, infrastructure and so on—can clearly be good for growth. But some evidence suggests a threshold effect at work, more relevant to today's developing countries, with sustained growth only taking off once a tax ratio of about 15 percent is achieved:[73] the minimum, arguably, needed to finance the basic functions of a tolerably well-run state.

So, some powerful principles of tax design have emerged over many years, partly by instinct and more recently from formal analysis. But they essentially assume away any problems in actually enforcing tax rules: the key business of tax administration through the ages. Those will the focus in the next part of the book. The principles we have looked at also abstract from the distinct problems that arise when tax effects can spill across national borders. These issues—at the heart of many current controversies, and with no shortage of follies—are the subject of the next chapter.

11

Citizens of the World

> The proprietor of a stock is properly a citizen of the world. . . . He would
> be apt to abandon the country in which he was exposed to a vexatious
> inquisition . . . and would remove his stock to some other country, where
> he could either carry on his business or enjoy his fortune more at his ease.
>
> ADAM SMITH[1]

IN OCTOBER 1962, while the world stared into the abyss of nuclear destruction during the Cuban Missile Crisis, another crisis in international relations was unfolding in Europe. Here, too, rising tensions culminated in a blockade. This blockade was not, though, enforced by the might of the U.S. Navy, but by six damp French customs officers, standing in the rain to close the border with the diminutive independent principality of Monaco.[2] What so enraged the French, and President Charles de Gaulle in particular, was not the presence of ballistic missiles hidden among the mansions and glitzy apartment buildings of Monaco, but the absence there of any tax on income.

This lack of an income tax made it attractive for French people and businesses to reside—or appear to reside—in Monaco. With the tiny principality surrounded by France and the Mediterranean, and no border checks in place, that was relatively easy to do. Hard as it is to imagine, the Minister of Finance (and later President) Valerie Giscard d'Estaing spent an evening picking names from the Monaco phone book and

More Clouseau than Maigret.

making calls—three-quarters of those he tried to reach, he said, turned out to be in Paris. And in 1962, the stakes were being raised by the exodus of French colonists, the *pieds noirs*, from newly independent Algeria, the richer among whom were showing a taste for putting their money in Monaco. That was irritating enough to de Gaulle, who was not well disposed to *pieds noirs*, given the attempts of extremists among them to assassinate him. And he was not made happier by the closer relations with the United States that Monaco was developing after the marriage of Grace Kelly to Prince Rainier.

So it was that on October 12, customs officers were sent to impose a blockade on Monaco. It lasted only a few hours, though manufactured delays at the border continued. The point, in any case, was made. Finding a solution took rather longer than resolving the Cuban Missile Crisis, but by May of 1963 an agreement had been reached that French citizens resident in Monaco would be liable for French income tax (unless they had already been there for five years in October 1962), and that all businesses with more than one-quarter of their receipts coming from outside Monaco would also be liable to income tax on their earnings. And so things remain today.

The somewhat ludicrous clash between France and Monaco is just one example—an unusually confrontational one—of the force identified by Adam Smith 250 years ago: When the tax base can move across frontiers, it (in this case, the income of French citizens and businesses) will tend to move to where the tax rate is lowest. Not foreseen by Smith, but made evident in 1962, is that the movement of tax bases creates spillover effects across borders—much like the externalities described in chapter 8—and perceived inequities that can be a source of political tension.

These issues are the stuff of today's headlines, with the ability of the wealthy and large multinational companies to reduce their tax burden— legally or otherwise—by exploiting gaps in the international tax system attracting widespread concern, putting the issue high on the political agenda. It has become hard to keep track of all the tax-related leaks— the Panama Papers, LuxLeaks, and so on—each with unique features, but all bringing international tax arrangements into disrepute. Embarrassed politicians, like the prime minister of Iceland, have resigned. Some companies have attracted special opprobrium (those with household names being perhaps unfairly singled out), as with the protests provoked by disgust that the apparently profitable Starbucks chain had, for more than a decade, somehow managed to claim a loss for U.K. tax purposes. Prompted by both public pressure and their own need for revenue, governments of the advanced economies have in the last few years turned their attention to the problems of international taxation. They may not be setting up blockades, but the G20 members do now routinely speak of taking "defensive measures" against jurisdictions[3] not complying with the new international tax standards being established. Even among themselves, however, the G20 members are at loggerheads on tax issues. This time, as we saw in chapter 1, it is the French (among others) cast as villains of the piece, with the United States threatening retaliatory action in response to a proposed tax on digital services.

This chapter looks at how opportunities for cross-border tax minimization have been, and are, exploited by people and companies, and at how governments react to, exploit, and have recently begun to address them.

Squeezing a Rice Pudding

Topical though it now is, there is nothing new in clever people turning international tax rules to their advantage. Many of the basic techniques still used today were developed a century ago by the founders of a dynasty that came to pride itself on paying little tax: the Vesteys.

By the start of the First World War, William and Edmund Vestey had built up one of the modern era's first major multinational companies. Pioneers in cold storage, with operations in Argentina, China, and Russia, they brought cheap meat to a global mass market. Already multimillionaires by the outbreak of war, by its end they had lucrative contracts to provide the British army with one million pounds of meat a day. The war also launched them on a series of creative tax planning schemes, which bemused and infuriated the Inland Revenue (precursor of today's HMRC) for decades. "Trying to come to grips with the Vesteys over tax," one revenue officer declared, "is like trying to squeeze a rice pudding."[4]

The game began in November 1915. As the war moved into bloody stalemate (and, perhaps not entirely coincidentally, the Excess Profits Duty described in chapter 10 came into effect), the Vesteys moved offshore. They had previously enjoyed the benefits of what is called "deferral": U.K. tax was payable only when profits earned abroad were repatriated to the United Kingdom and so could be avoided indefinitely by simply not bringing the money back. At the start of the war, however, the British government switched to taxing such profits immediately (and also increased rates of income tax and death duty). So—in an early example of "inversion" (the movement of a company's headquarters abroad)—the Vesteys' business and at least one of the brothers moved to Argentina (central to their operations, and then having no income tax), and they arranged for their profits to be earned by a company that they owned in the United States, which did still apply deferral.

After the war, however, the Vestey brothers wanted to return to Britain. A direct appeal for favorable treatment to Prime Minister Lloyd George failed, though he did sell William a peerage—much to the disgust of King George V and others, who felt that "there does not appear to be any good reason why a person who, during the war, removed his business from this country to avoid taxation, should be made a peer."[5]

The Vestey brothers: Keeping meat prices, and their taxes, low.

But the Vesteys were not easily rebuffed and, looking for alternative avoidance devices, hit on the use of trust funds.

Trusts date back to the Crusades, when knights sought ways to make sure they did not come back to find that their assets had vanished. The risk they faced in simply relying on the promises of others to look after their interests was faced centuries later by a P. G. Wodehouse character:

> Some time ago, in order to do down the income tax people, old Pyke had transferred a large mass of wealth to . . . [Roddy's] account, the understanding being that Roddy . . . was to return it in due season. "Be a man," I said [to Roddy], "Collar the cash, send a few wires of farewell and leg it for foreign parts."[6]

Trusts developed to protect people like the crusaders, and Pyke, who gave other people control of their assets. Their essence is that the ownership is passed (by the "settlor") to trustees who are obliged to spend the money in ways specified by the settlor. Under the trust arrangements that they set up in 1921, the Vesteys leased their operations to a British company that then paid a (tax-deductible) fixed amount every year not to the Vesteys themselves, but to a fund whose trustees then advanced money to a holding company owned by the Vesteys. The trustees were empowered to make loans and advances on whatever terms were acceptable to—the Vesteys. If that all sounds complicated, it was.

Not until the Second World War did the Inland Revenue feel it had enough information and legal authority to challenge these arrangements. But it lost in the House of Lords, partly on the argument—which, grudgingly, one can only admire—that the relevant legislation spoke of an "individual" having power, whereas the authorization under the trust had to come from both brothers.

Through all this, the Vesteys were operating a highly integrated business, with companies undertaking a range of closely related activities—owning ranches, packing houses, refrigerated ships, wholesale businesses, and retail butcher shops. And that created one of the core and ongoing problems in the taxation of multinational companies. With the companies that comprise a multinational, such as the Vestey group, taxed separately—as is still the case today—profit can be made to appear within the group wherever taxes are low (and removed from where they are high) by playing around with "transfer prices": the prices, that is, at which these related companies trade with one another. Are the ranchers lightly taxed? Then pay a high price for the meat that another company you own buys from them. The price paid by one part of a company to another part is irrelevant—except for its tax implications.

The response to this problem has been general adoption of the principle of "arm's length pricing." This says that transactions within multinationals should be valued for tax purposes at the prices that unrelated parties doing the same thing would have settled on. Alas, this is easier said than done, as William Vestey patiently explained to a Royal Commission on Income Tax in 1919:

> In a business of this nature, you cannot say how much [profit] is made in one country and how much is made in another. You kill an

animal and the product . . . is sold in fifty different countries. You cannot say how much is made in England and how much abroad.[7]

Transfer pricing certainly has its legal gray areas, but it seems that sometimes the Vesteys strayed outside them. When in 1934 the Argentine authorities (now having an income tax) became curious as to the true costs incurred by the Vesteys' meatpacking operation (which would be a guide to how much profit it had really earned), they discovered documents with payroll, balance sheet and other information in crates marked "corned beef," packed underneath guano, in a boat about to sail for London.

And so were laid the foundations of a lasting family fortune and a lasting saga of tax avoidance. In 1978, the Vestey-owned Dewhurst chain of butchers reportedly remitted just £10 tax on earnings of more than £2.3 million. When it was announced in 1993 that the Queen would pay income tax, the then Lord Vestey is said to have declared, "Well, that makes me the last one."[8]

Havens from the Tax Storm

The long history of the Vesteys and their kind trying to find ways to exploit international tax arrangements has been matched by a long story of countries and jurisdictions devising ways to help them do it. These are the tax havens of the world.

For many, this label conjures up pictures of blue seas, palm-fringed beaches, and martinis at sunset. But there are advanced countries fringed by the not-so-blue North Sea that have also offered some very sweet tax deals. Widely used though it is, there is no agreed definition of what exactly a "tax haven" is,[9] and some find the term derogatory. So there is good reason to be wary of the "haven" label, and we will speak instead of "tax sanctuaries." What we have in mind is a low or zero tax rate, combined perhaps with practices that help avoid or even evade taxes due elsewhere.

Jurisdictions offering tax sanctuary date back to the late nineteenth century.[10] In 1862, the Swiss canton of Vaud introduced special tax deals to encourage wealthy foreigners to retire there. Other early starters were the U.S. states of New Jersey and Delaware, which in the early 1880s originated the technique of "easy incorporation": allowing anyone to form a corporation by simply filing articles of incorporation, without a special act of the state legislature in return for a franchise fee lower than that charged by other states. Sanctuaries spread further after the First World War, with taxes rising to unprecedented levels and the widespread prospect of capital levies discussed in the previous chapter. The Swiss Banking Act of 1934, for example, strengthened bank secrecy by making its violation not just a civil but a criminal offense.[11] On the business tax side, in 1929, Luxembourg introduced a holding company regime[12] that could be much more attractive than, for instance, holding ownership in the United Kingdom or the United States. By 1937, Treasury Secretary Morgenthau was warning President Roosevelt of the use of low-tax jurisdictions and concealed ownership to evade U.S. taxes.[13]

But it is only since the Second World War—and the removal of exchange controls by advanced economies in the late 1970s—that tax sanctuaries have become a major force in the global economy. Each has its own story and its own tax specialty. The Bahamas, for example, reputedly attracted the attention of American tax-planning gangster Meyer Lansky after the Cuban revolution,[14] Mauritius proved attractive for investments into India, as Hong Kong did for investments into China. Switzerland continued to make itself especially attractive to wealthy foreigners through rules known, after Charlie Chaplin moved there in 1953, as the "Lex Chaplin," under which nonworking foreigners are subject to an annual lump-sum levy based on their living expenses (often limited to rent paid) rather than to a standard income tax.

Not all tax sanctuaries offer azure beaches, agreeable après-ski, or scintillating night life. Wyoming, Delaware, and South Dakota, for instance, allow firms to incorporate without revealing who their true owners are: even the federal government cannot find out unless it can prove that the corporations are mere facades or are acting fraudulently. When Barack Obama called Ugland House in the Cayman Islands, the home of more than 12,000 corporations, "either the biggest building or the biggest tax scam,"[15] the chair of the Cayman Islands Financial

There aren't always palm trees: Ugland House in the Caymans and
1209 North Orange Street in Delaware.

Services Authority responded by noting that 1209 North Orange Street in Wilmington, Delaware, housed 285,000 separate businesses.

Equally not-known for being a tropical paradise is the Netherlands, which has long had tax attractions as an intermediary stop in routing investment overseas. Further along the North Sea coast is the small German village with the mellifluous name of Norderfriedrichskoog, which for many years did not levy any local business tax.[16] As a result, Norderfriedrichskoog became a sanctuary for Deutsche Bank, Lufthansa, and others. To enjoy the exemption, companies had to base records, communications, and core business activities in Norderfriedrichskoog. And so farmers cashed in by renting out attics, barns, and cowsheds; locals were hired as office managers, and Deutsche Telekom laid extra telephone cables to cope with the explosion of faxes. All this cost about €300 million in tax revenues over 10 years. But it did not last. From 2004, all German municipalities were required to levy local business tax at a rate of at least 9.1 percent.

What tax sanctuaries do tend to have in common is not palm trees, but scale. They are, in general, very small:[17] Monaco could easily fit into Central Park in New York City. The reason is straightforward. Almost mechanically, small countries have an incentive to set low tax rates on internationally mobile activities: A tax cut loses them little revenue from domestic activities—because there is not much—but can attract a large inflow of tax base from the very large rest of the world. This inflow brings in revenue not only from whatever remains of the corporate tax but also from registration fees and the like. And there are the side benefits of tourism, development of a financial services sector, renting out barns, or whatever. These benefits can be pretty attractive for jurisdictions that may not have a whole lot going for themselves economically, and so they seek sources of income deriving from what they do have: their own identity. Being a tax sanctuary is another example—like the issuance of stamps attractive to collectors—of the "commercialization of state sovereignty"[18] discussed in chapter 3.

But there is more to it than that. Another characteristic of successful tax sanctuaries is that they score well on indicators of good governance.[19] Many, for instance, are part of the "British spiderweb"[20] of crown dependencies and overseas territories that, ultimately, borrow credibility from oversight by the U.K. government. Investors want not just low taxes but also assurance that contracts will be enforced, so that they can get their money back. Providing this requires establishing a reputation for a strong commitment to the rule of law—which is much more challenging, but can be ultimately far more rewarding, than printing a few pretty postage stamps.

Small though they may generally be, tax sanctuaries have left a big mark on the global economy. In 2018, for example, Luxembourg had the world's third highest share of global foreign direct investment, and the Netherlands had the highest.[21] No doubt there is more to this than taxes, but small, low-tax jurisdictions have clearly had an outsized impact. Things, however, are changing. Powerful countries are now leading initiatives that—taken at face value—aim to drive the tax sanctuaries out of business; we look at these efforts later in this chapter.

The Rich Are Different from Us[22]

The story of the Vesteys shows how, with a little creativity and a lot of nerve, taxpayers have long found ways to exploit weaknesses in international tax arrangements. And the rise of the tax sanctuaries shows how some jurisdictions have been more than happy to help them. The outrage they have come to cause is understandable. But more than outrage is needed if the underlying problems are to be addressed, which means understanding exactly what games taxpayers can play across borders. The Vesteys have shown us some, but there are plenty of others.

Indeed the list of cross-border tax tricks is almost endless. Even inanimate objects—aircraft, for instance—tend to move around in search of low taxes. Some U.S. states tax them as personal property, with the tax based on where the plane is hangared as of the assessment date. Sure enough, just before that date there are unusually more departing flights from states that tax aircraft than from those that do not.[23]

But among all the wheezes by which people exploit cross-border tax differences, we focus on two broad strategies at the heart of the matter before looking at the policy responses that could be, or—quite impressively—are being undertaken.

They Don't Live Here Any More

One legal, time-honored way to avoid tax is to live somewhere that taxes are low, preferably with agreeable surroundings. P. G. Wodehouse, dogged by tax problems for much of his life, realized that—or at least his accountant did. "Even now," Wodehouse recalled, "I can't see how he worked the thing. . . . I see him proving us non-residents for years when—I should have said—we were out of England for about three days."[24] By 1934, Wodehouse was (really) living in France, which, unusually, exempted from tax income (like, say, book royalties) arising outside France. In his tax exile, Wodehouse must stand here for all the rich and famous who have done the same.

The fear of inducing emigration is often cited as a reason to limit tax rates on the wealthy. There are certainly plenty of enjoyable anecdotes of tax exile, but sensible policy making requires more systematic evidence on how sensitive to tax the decisions of ordinary rich people (if there is such a thing) are about where to live. A few prominent cases do not necessarily imply a significant issue. Responses to tax differences across the U.S. states, for example, have been found to be noticeable, most clearly for retirees, but not particularly large. For France, too, it has proved hard to find effects that are large in the grand scheme of things (though about one-third of all French billionaires live, or have substantial assets, in Belgium or Switzerland).[25] But some people have more opportunities to move than others. With that in mind, one study looks at the employment decisions of an especially mobile group of workers: European footballers. It turns out that their decisions, especially those of the most highly paid, are very responsive to taxes.[26] What makes this significant is that footballers may be an archetype of the highly able professional whose skills are easily transferred across locations. For these citizens of the world, residence may really be quite tax sensitive.

An alternative to cutting taxes as a way to prevent emigration is to write the rules so that emigration does not remove the liability to taxation at home. So it was that in ancient Greece and Rome, the rich were required to finance liturgies not only of the city in which they lived but also of their native city, too.[27] When the Emperor Diocletian found that, rather than paying taxes, many small farmers holding marginal land were abandoning their plots he made sure that those moving away remained liable for the tax due on their land.[28] Almost uniquely, the United States does much the same by taxing its citizens on all their income, wherever they are resident, though with a credit for taxes paid outside the United States. As people become more mobile, this idea may come to attract more attention: as a way, for instance, to prevent people deducting their pension contributions during their working life where the tax rate is high and then enjoying that pension somewhere else where the tax rate is low. Taxation by citizenship does make it tough for Americans to become tax exiles, but citizenship can be renounced.[29] Among those who have done so is the co-founder of Facebook, Eduardo Saverin, who became a permanent resident in Singapore, which does not tax capital gains. Perhaps not coincidentally, renunciations of U.S. citizenship tripled in the 2 years before 2014—which is when the Foreign Account Tax Compliance Act (FATCA), aimed at uncovering unreported assets held abroad, came into effect.[30]

Don't Tell

One of the simplest (and, for many years, safest) forms of straight-up tax evasion is to hold bank deposits and other financial assets "offshore"—meaning here simply "abroad," though of course typically a foreign jurisdiction with low taxes and easy concealment—and not report any income from these assets to the tax authorities where you live. One widely cited, but contentious, estimate is that about 8 percent of all household wealth (around $6 trillion) is held offshore, with much presumably hidden from the tax authorities.[31] For the Gulf states and some Latin American countries, such holdings may be on the order of 60 percent of GDP; even in Continental Europe, they may amount to 15 percent.[32] And, as one might expect, offshore holdings are mainly for the rich. For Scandinavia, the richest 0.01 percent of households have been estimated to have used offshore accounts to evade about a quarter of the tax they ought to pay, behavior that was not picked up by random audits;[33] and that is for a region known for good tax compliance. Even taken with a whole shaker-full of salt, given the difficulty of getting reliable data about tax evasion, these are big numbers.

The obvious solution is for national tax authorities to obtain information on the foreign income and assets of their residents, returning the favor by providing foreign tax authorities with similar information on their nationals. Just as obviously, however, this has not been in the interests of many influential people and of jurisdictions (and companies) wanting to attract this business. And so, until recently, a tax authority that wanted to track down its residents' offshore income typically found it very hard to do so. It could only ask for such information if an appropriate treaty was in place, and if it had a demonstrably good reason to suspect evasion. And the foreign tax authority being asked, even if it wanted to comply, might be stymied by bank secrecy rules.

Since the Global Financial Crisis, however, this state of affairs has been changing fast. The link between offshore tax evasion and the crisis was, to put it mildly, unclear. But governments found themselves in need of revenue, and offshore evasion proved a politically attractive target, with the G20 becoming highly active in aiming to curb it. Now the international standard is "automatic exchange of information" (AEOI): the routine, spontaneous passing on of information on nonresidents' bank deposits, mutual fund holdings and the like—their value and the income they generate—to the tax authorities of the country in which they are resident. The idea is to leave no hiding place for assets and income.

The U.S. FATCA mentioned earlier led the way.[34] It induces most non-U.S. banks and other financial institutions to provide the IRS with details of any account belonging to a U.S. taxpayer with a value exceeding $50,000. Under a parallel G20-led process, organized under the grandly named "Global Forum,"[35] the expectation is that all member jurisdictions—now numbering more than 150—commit to adopting AEOI.[36] Over 100 countries have begun such automatic exchanges.[37] As one might expect, this has not been achieved without an element of compulsion.[38] Under FATCA, noncompliance risks the imposition by the United States of a 30 percent withholding tax on all payments made by U.S. financial institutions. And failure to meet the standards of the Global Forum can result in a jurisdiction being subject to those "defensive measures" (whose precise nature has yet to be specified).[39]

These initiatives seem to be having an effect, with bank deposits falling in jurisdictions that have committed to exchange information. Also clear, however, is that these deposits have largely shifted to jurisdictions that have not committed.[40] The difficulty here is that persuading some jurisdictions to provide information makes it more attractive for others not to.[41] Nor is the process wholly seamless. It is one thing to receive gigabytes of information from a tax authority abroad, another to usefully match it to domestic taxpayers.[42] And some developing countries may find themselves providing information to others but, unable to provide adequate assurances that confidentiality will be preserved, receiving none in return. It is too soon to tell whether these initiatives will lead to a sustained increase in tax revenue,[43] and there is little sign that governments have felt more confident (or inclined) to raise tax rates on capital income without fear of driving financial wealth offshore. But these are early days, and the progress made was unthinkable—politically and technically—just a decade ago.

False Profits

The transfer pricing shenanigans of the Vesteys were a pale foretaste of the tax avoidance by multinationals that has come to so infuriate at least some vociferous British Starbucks drinkers, and many others besides. Whistleblowing on what multinationals had been getting up to has fed this discontent and raised the pressure on politicians to act, with LuxLeaks in 2014 for instance, leading to the characterization of the professional services firm PwC as "promot[ing] tax avoidance on an industrial scale."[44] Multinationals exposed to public obloquy have felt the need to react. Starbucks, to general contempt, announced that it would voluntarily remit £20 million in tax to the U.K. government over the 2 years following the boycotts. Policy makers have also felt the need to do something. The international corporate tax system is now widely recognized to be broken.

If I Were You, I Wouldn't Start from Here

The first step to understanding the current international corporate tax system—and so how it might be fixed—is to recognize that there is no such thing as "the international corporate tax system." Instead there are national laws that address international tax issues and 3,000 or so bilateral tax treaties that have tried to align national tax systems in a reasonably sensible way (and, in particular, avoid the same thing being fully taxed by two different jurisdictions). Underlying all these treaties and laws are norms that are the product of a long historical process, although not going back quite so far as the Sumerians.

Landmarks along the way include the first international tax treaty[45] in 1872 (between Great Britain and the canton of Vaud in Switzerland, dealing with any luckless Briton who dropped off the perch in Vaud, only to have both jurisdictions levy death duties on the entire estate);[46] the first tax treaty relating to income tax matters in 1899, between Germany and Austro-Hungary; and the work of the League of Nations in the 1920s, building on a report of four eminent economists to establish norms built on these experiences.[47] Since then, the guardians of standards in international taxation have been the United Nations and, especially, the OECD. But there is not very much in today's practices, embodied in all those tax treaties, that would surprise the architects of the agreement between Imperial Germany and the Austro-Hungarian Empire.

Cutting an extremely long story short, there are two norms at the heart of current arrangements. One is the principle of "arm's length pricing," which we saw the Vesteys running rings around: Multinationals are taxed by attributing their income to each distinct entity in the group, as if they were independent operators, and then taxing them separately. Each jurisdiction then gets first crack at taxing the "active" (that is, business-related) income of the entities there, and the jurisdiction of the parent company which owns that entity may or may not then impose tax too, but if so, then giving some credit for the tax already paid.

The second norm is that jurisdictions can only tax the income of entities that, roughly, are either incorporated in, managed from, or have some physical presence there. Simply exporting from the United States to Germany, for instance, without having some brick-and-mortar presence in Germany, does not allow Germany to tax the profit associated with the sales there.

These norms might have worked well in the days of Kaiser Wilhelm I and the Emperor Franz Joseph, or even those of the League of Nations. The arm's length principle makes sense, for instance, as a way to try to ensure that independent companies are not at a tax advantage or disadvantage relative to multinationals doing the same things—a form of production efficiency, which we saw in chapter 10 to be generally desirable. And requiring physical presence may have been the obvious thing to do when not very much foreign investment was happening, and what there was took the form of things like a British company's ownership of railways in Nigeria. But these norms work a lot less well now.

Beginning with the first norm—arm's length pricing—we have seen how the Vesteys spotted the possibility of manipulating transfer prices to shift profits within the group from entities that were taxed at a high rate to other entities that were taxed at a low rate. And what can be done by changing the price of beef within the group can be done in many other ways. One favorite is artificial borrowing. This is done by putting equity finance into an entity in a low-tax jurisdiction (maybe a "cash cow" created solely for this purpose) and having it lend to one of your other entities in a high-tax jurisdiction. The former has to pay tax on the interest it receives, but at a low tax rate; the latter gets a deduction, at a high rate: So overall, the multinational reduces its worldwide tax liability and increases its after-tax profits.[48] If you get bored doing these tricks with debt, well, you can do the same thing with management fees, or—increasingly important in a world in which intangible assets are central to business activity (and easy to relocate)—royalty payments for the use of patents, trademarks, trade names, goodwill, and the like. That is how Starbucks, for instance—just one example of many—ended up paying little tax on its U.K. operations: By paying royalties for the use of its trademark and so on to an affiliate in the Netherlands, paying other Starbucks subsidiaries in the Netherlands and Switzerland to acquire and roast its beans, and financing itself by borrowing.[49]

Allocating profits within a multinational can get horrendously hard. Just imagine having to work out where the income arises for a new drug developed in an R&D lab in one country, with the resulting patent held in another, finance coming from yet another, and the drug itself then produced and sold all over the world. To some, applying arm's length pricing even in these circumstances is just a matter of careful analysis and a little ingenuity. To others, arm's length pricing is inherently non-sensical: Multinationals, they argue, exist precisely because they can do things better and differently than could unrelated companies. So searching for the prices that unrelated companies would agree on is not just fiction, it's fantasy.

The problems with the second norm—the need for physical or some other real presence to be taxable somewhere—have become more prominent in recent years, and more contentious. They arise from the increased possibility of doing business in a country without much (if any) of a physical presence there. The archetypal examples are Google and Facebook: Even if they charged for their search services or access to social media, their profits would not be taxable in jurisdictions where they had no physical presence. For many nontax people, for whom these companies are a familiar part of their daily lives, this seems to be a case of "hang on, that can't be right." Under current rules, however, it is; whether that should remain the case is taken up in a moment. For now, the point is that avoiding physical presence in a country is one way to avoid owing taxes there—and technological change means that this is much easier to do, and a much bigger deal, than it used to be.

All this is Multinational Tax Avoidance 101. There are many other ways in which multinationals can exploit the two norms, and take other opportunities, so as to reduce their tax liability. Vestey-like deferral remained a possibility for U.S. multinationals until the 2017 tax reform, by when they were retaining in entities abroad more than $2.8 trillion. Apple alone avoided—at least delayed—tax on more than $280 billion. Another trick is to use that web of tax treaties to route payments within the group artificially so as to minimize taxes charged along the way ("treaty shopping"). And some companies exploited mismatches in national rules so as to be tax resident nowhere.[50] It all gets extraordinarily complicated. The

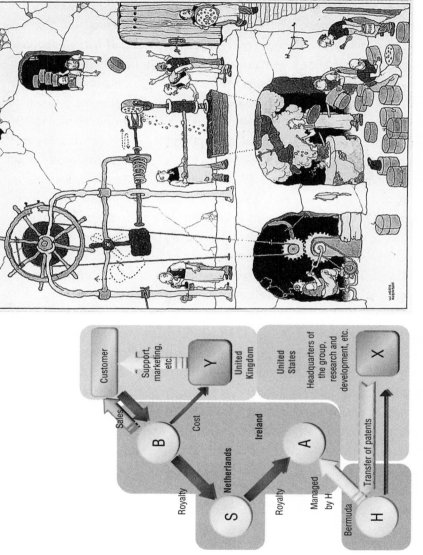

Which is the "Double Irish with a Dutch Sandwich," and which is the "Doubling Gloucester Cheese by the Gruyère Method"?

(in)famous "Double Irish with a Dutch Sandwich" scheme[51]—particularly associated with Google—shown in the picture looks, and is, no less ludicrous than the accompanying Heath Robinson contraption.[52]

How big a deal are all these machinations? There are plenty of signs of extensive shifting of profits to low-tax jurisdictions. It has been claimed that in 2012 U.S. companies reported more profit in low-tax Bermuda than in China, France, Germany, and Japan combined.[53] Single tax cases can involve huge sums: in India the tax amount at issue in one was $2.6 billion.[54] Over the past few years, a small industry has emerged to quantify the revenue losses from multinational tax avoidance more systematically. One study puts the global loss at about 4–10 percent of corporate tax revenue, or between $100 and $240 billion per year, for a group of 50 or so advanced and emerging countries.[55] Another study, looking at more countries, comes up with revenue losses of about $400 billion per year for OECD countries and $200 billion for the others.[56] Such estimates are contentious, and putting numbers on the impact for specific countries is even harder, but for the United States—the most studied case, and likely one with a relatively high loss—they might be on the order of 15–25 percent of the corporate tax revenue actually collected.[57]

For the advanced countries, views might differ as to how consequential these numbers are: the higher of those figures for the United States amounts to only about 0.6 percent of GDP. But they do seem to be large for developing countries, perhaps over one percent of GDP. That is a lot for countries that often collect less than 15 percent of GDP in tax revenue, have critical revenue needs, tend to be more reliant on corporate tax revenues than advanced economies,[58] and have few unexploited sources of additional revenue.

A Farewell to Arms (Length Pricing)?

In 1961, President Kennedy was already bemoaning that

> more and more enterprises organized abroad by American firms have arranged their corporate structures—aided by artificial arrangements between parent and subsidiary regarding intercompany

pricing, the transfer of patent licensing rights, the shifting of management fees, and similar practices which maximize the accumulation
of profits in the tax haven [so as to] reduce sharply or eliminate completely their tax liabilities both at home and abroad.[59]

It took another half century, however, for any significant action on tax
avoidance by multinationals to be taken. The centerpiece of recent policy activity has been a G20/OECD-led project on Base Erosion and
Profit Shifting, lovingly known as BEPS. This resulted, in 2015, in the
endorsement of a mixture of agreed-on standards and shared aspirations intended, for instance, to address treaty shopping and encourage
countries to do things like imposing tight limits on interest deductions.
The BEPS outcome does not, and was emphatically never intended to,
change the norms of international taxation set out above. Even its most
ardent advocates saw BEPS as no more than a fire-fighting exercise.
How much has really been achieved—the figures discussed above are
pre-BEPS—is not yet known. But, in any case, the fire is still not out,
and real changes to those norms are now (at long last, many would say)
receiving serious attention.

The mantra of the BEPS project was the objective of taxing "where
value is created." It is hard to disagree with that as a glorious principle;
and it may be easy enough to agree where value is not created. But the
four economists reporting to the League of Nations in 1923 saw that
parceling out value creation is not easy:

> The oranges upon the trees in California are not acquired wealth until
> they are picked, and not even at that stage until they are packed, and
> not even at that stage until they are transported to the place where
> demand exists and until they are put where the consumer can use
> them.[60]

In cases like this, with each stage in the process, from picking to munch-
ing, an essential element in the chain, there is simply no uniquely correct way to allocate parts of the overall value creation to each stage. And
when it comes to real money, practical policy makers, while nodding in
sage agreement with the principle itself, could hardly disagree more as

to where exactly value is created. The mantra, sadly, is essentially vacuous.

This became painfully clear when thinking about taxing the likes of Facebook or Google, the classic examples of firms that can do lots of business in countries where they have little physical presence. Some see no need on this account to jettison the second of the norms above: To them, the value these companies create is provided by whoever it is that puts together the underlying algorithms that make the services they provide possible. Others, however, see a sensible point of principle behind the "that can't be right" reaction mentioned above. For them, when you search on Google or post on Facebook, you are not just a consumer: You are also making a "user contribution," creating value by providing information that these companies suck up and use to target advertising. And so the country in which you are doing the clicking should have a right to tax the associated earnings of these companies just as if they had set up there an information-extracting factory. Another argument leads to a similar conclusion. When *The Economist* rates information as the world's most valuable resource, replacing oil,[61] this suggests that we might think of it as akin to oil in tax terms too, as simply another potential source of rents that could be taxed with minimal efficiency loss.[62]

How exactly this right to tax would best be exercised, and the amount of earnings to be taxed calculated, is not yet fully worked out. But for the short term, the European Commission and the United Kingdom propose—and France aims to be among the first to implement—a "digital services tax" that would apply primarily to the advertising revenues of these companies. In the information-as-oil analogy, these taxes could be thought of as analogous to the royalties that are now often charged on the sales of many natural resources. Most commonly, however, digital services taxes are thought of as steps toward some as-yet undefined profit-based tax. From a U.S. perspective, all this looks like an invention of principle to cover a naked revenue grab: A very large proportion of the companies likely to be taxed under the EU's proposal are headquartered in the United States.[63] Hence the current tensions in international tax relations, and the U.S. threat of retaliation mentioned in chapter 1.

But, prominent though they are, the tax concerns around the digital giants are really just emblematic of the wider problems with the current system set out above, not the essence of the problem itself. Almost all activities and products are acquiring some digital component: refrigerators, for instance, sending back to the manufacturer information on your eating and cooking habits—which looks a lot like a user contribution. And the core issues (related for instance to figuring out an appropriate royalty payment for the use of some intangible asset) apply at least as much to companies doing highly nondigital things—like, for instance, selling coffee. So, some more fundamental solution is needed to the problems that remain post-BEPS, with the G20 and OECD having set themselves the task of coming up with a better way ahead by mid-2021. And several ideas for changing the system quite profoundly are now, at last, receiving serious attention.[64]

Some of these ideas are broadly consistent with current norms. One such is for others to follow the route set by the United States in the Tax Cuts and Jobs Act of 2017. Its headline corporate tax measure was a dramatic cut in the federal rate, from 35 to 21 percent, but it also changed the U.S. international tax provisions in ways that may well prove at least as important. And it had good acronyms. Through the neatly named "GILTI" provisions,[65] profits earned abroad in excess of a benchmark return are now taxed in the United States, without deferral, at half the rate applied to domestic earnings. For a U.S. parent company, this makes shifting high profits being earned abroad to a low or zero tax jurisdiction much less attractive, because they are in any case going to end up being taxed at least 10.5 percent. Working in parallel, on income earned in the United States, the "BEAT"[66] provisions limit the ability of companies there to deduct some types of payments often used to shift profits out of the United States.[67] Having figured out how clever both measures are, other countries have shown interest in emulating them.

Other proposals, however, drive a stake through the two norms described above. One would entirely abandon the idea of taxing the component entities of a multinational group separately and instead simply allocate its total global profit across jurisdictions by some mechanical formula, depending for instance on the shares of its total worldwide sales, assets, payroll, and/or employment in each: this is known as "formula apportionment." There would then simply be no gain to the multinational from shifting profits around within the group, because for tax purposes it is only its total profit that ever matters. This is how the corporate tax works at state and provincial levels in the United States and Canada, for instance: Applying arm's length pricing in highly integrated economies is simply impracticable. And so, as the world becomes ever more integrated, its supporters argue that formula apportionment is evidently the way to go.[68] Something of this kind has indeed been formally proposed in the European Union.[69] A variant, residual profit allocation, would share out by some such mechanical rule only the multinational's profit in excess of some minimum return on its assets and activities—these residual profits being, to a rough approximation, much the same thing as rents in the Ricardian sense of the term.[70]

Other schemes would do away with the second norm—the requirement of physical presence—by allocating some taxing rights to the jurisdiction in which some user contribution is made, or in which its customers are located. The latter approach, introducing an element of taxation in the "destination" or "market" country, would be an even more profound divergence from current norms: Simply selling into a jurisdiction would create a liability to tax even if the multinational had no physical presence there. But the idea is gathering momentum. One argument made by its proponents is that the idea of user contribution is so hard to measure that basing taxation in the place of final sale helps limit avoidance insofar as the location of final consumers is harder to change than, say, the country in which the rights to some patent are held. This reasoning leads some to argue for movement to—the ugliest of all acronyms and, we promise, the last—a DBCFT: a "destination-based cash flow tax."

The essence of the DBCFT, which briefly became a real contender in the early days of the Trump administration, is that exports would not be taxed, imports would be taxed (but deductible for businesses), and all investment would be immediately deducted. This approach can be thought of as simply combining a VAT (which also excludes exports from the tax base and includes imports) with a deduction for wage costs. Adopted universally, the DBCFT has many attractions. Like the VAT, it is immune to profit shifting: In both cases, for example, exports are untaxed, and the prices that businesses pay for their imports are immaterial for tax purposes,[71] so there is simply no point in playing around with transfer prices. Similarly, the DBCFT gives no tax advantage to producing in one country rather than another.[72] And, the final ingredient, in giving an immediate deduction for all costs—the cash flow treatment described in chapter 10—the DBCFT acts as a rent tax.[73] Although many economists like the DBCFT, its time has not yet come.

None of these ideas is without problems, both technical and political. Sharing profits across countries by formula, for example, would require unprecedented cross-country agreement on the sharing rule—which even the European Union has not managed to obtain. Moving away from a test of physical presence will require changes to all those tax treaties. But the fact that we could describe each of these schemes in a paragraph suggests that systems could be devised that would function better than what we have now.

And there are, perhaps, hopeful signs. In 2019, after a century of glacial movement in international tax rules, discussions in the OECD-led Inclusive Framework—bringing together more than 135 countries—suddenly started with unprecedented speed and openness to break down the norms. The OECD secretariat itself proposed general application of something like a residual profit allocation scheme, as just described, to some part of the earnings of the largest multinationals, and with some of that residual allocated to market countries.[74] As proposed, this may not be a big deal in terms of the money involved.[75] And it is not instead of current arrangements, but an addition to them—the opposite of a simplification. Moreover, it may not happen—the COVID-19 pandemic has made already difficult negotiations logistically harder. What is remarkable and encouraging, however, is that the OECD, long the sometimes-abrasive defender of both of the two core norms of international taxation, has effectively conceded that both may have outlived their time.

Tumbling Taxes

The governments of countries that are not tax sanctuaries have, to a large degree, brought their problems on themselves—or are at least deeply complicit. Outrage at the little tax paid by some multinationals has been directed mainly at the companies themselves, but they may reasonably believe they are doing no more than their duty in enriching their shareholders to the maximum legal extent, just as Lord Clyde encouraged them to do. It is, after all, governments that set the tax rules, and they have long competed with each other—with the encouragement, of course, of those who will benefit—to make their jurisdiction more attractive in tax terms than others. Such "tax competition" not only leads to generally low tax rates on things that can move across borders; it has created many of the opportunities for profit shifting just discussed.

Tax sanctuaries are just the extreme example. This game has been going on for centuries. Catherine the Great, anxious to build up Russian industry, in 1763 offered to "foreigners that have settled themselves in Russia [to] erect Fabricks or Works, and manufacture there such Merchandizes as have not been made yet in Russia" the right to "sell and export the said Merchandizes out of our Empire for ten Years, without paying any inland Tolls, Port duties or Customs on the Borders."[76] James Watt, of steam engine fame, is reported to have been seriously tempted.[77] Alexander Hamilton, seeking to establish his Society for Establishing Useful Manufactures in 1791, intended to impose a 10-year tax exemption in the belief that manufacturers, to escape "the burthens and restraints, which they endure in the old world . . . would probably flock from Europe to the United States."[78] And many governments since have done much the same. Some go beyond tax breaks to offering outright subsidies: Free looms were provided for immigrants into the Silesian linen industry in Prussia during the 1750s.[79] And there are plenty of even earlier precedents. In medieval Venice, foreign craftsmen, glass and lacemakers, and the like, were given a 2-year tax exemption.[80]

The game continues. It is most obvious in the massive reduction in headline rates of corporation tax around the world since the mid-1980s. The median rate in the advanced economies has fallen from about

38 percent in 1990 to less than 20 percent. Already seeing the problem, in 1992, a report for the European Commission recommended a minimum rate in the European Union of 30 percent[81]—which now looks laughably anachronistic. The dramatic reduction in the U.S. federal corporate tax rate as a centerpiece of the 2017 tax reform was an arguably belated recognition of the reality of competing tax rate cuts. Tax competition is not, however, simply a matter of headline tax rates. All kinds of special attractions can be offered. Tellingly, the LuxLeaks revelation was not about low headline rates of tax, but of generous tax rulings being provided by Belgium, Luxembourg, and the Netherlands, on such matters as transfer pricing arrangements.

These downward pressures on corporate taxation are a real issue. In terms of the direct impact on revenue, the loss from a general reduction in corporate tax rates of just a few points swamps those from multinational tax avoidance. Some, it is true, would welcome this withering away of the corporate tax: They would see it as a way to "starve the beast"—that is, deprive government of resources that it will only waste—and might point to (disputed) evidence that the corporate tax is more damaging to growth and investment than are other taxes.[82] Quite why the vagaries of tax competition should be better at constraining government spending than are fiscal rules that do so explicitly, however, is unclear. And we saw in chapter 10 that a well-designed corporate tax can actually come close to the ideal of a nondistorting revenue-raiser. Added to that, reduced corporate tax rates also create pressure to reduce top rates of personal tax, given the ability of many businesses to organize themselves not as corporations but rather as, for example, partnerships, and so be taxed as individuals. None of this plays well at a time of political tensions about inequality and the imperfect sharing of the benefits of globalization.

At its core, tax competition is an externality issue, much like the ones we looked at in chapter 8: When trying to attract investment or tax base by offering more generous tax treatment, each country ignores any loss of investment or tax base it may be imposing on others. As a result, all countries end up worse off than they need be. Something, it is reasonable to believe, should be done. The question is: what?

An obvious solution—as proposed for Europe all those years ago—
is for all countries to agree, if not on a common rate of corporate tax, at
least on some minimum level below which none will go. Importantly,
even countries required to raise their tax rate could benefit from doing
so. This is because the other countries, already above the minimum, will
now have less competition to worry about and so tend to raise their
rates—which may offset the reduction in investment and tax base that
those obliged to raise their rate would otherwise suffer. A couple of regional blocs in Africa have indeed agreed to set corporate tax rates of at
least 25 percent.[83] But, for years, the idea seemed to be going no further.
Now it may have acquired some legs, with the Inclusive Framework
mentioned above now also considering the adoption of a minimum
effective tax rate.[84] This could be achieved either by having the country
in which the multinational is resident top up whatever taxes are paid
abroad to ensure that the minimum total amount is paid (a bit like the
U.S. GILTI) or by having the country in which the income arises do so
(a bit like the U.S. BEAT). The two approaches differ, of course, in
which country gets the money—a recipe for disagreement. And there
are also real technical difficulties. The key question of what the minimum rate would be remains open: It seems likely to be somewhere
around 12 percent, which will strike many people as low. Quite where
these proposals will lead is, in any event, unclear: Perhaps the enhanced
need for revenue in the wake of the COVID-19 crisis will help lend it
momentum. But, again, it is a brave new world in which even countries
traditionally opposed to any meaningful international cooperation on
tax rates are now willing to talk about establishing a global minimum.

In any event, there are alternatives to minimum taxation as a way
to start putting the brakes on corporate tax competition—and perhaps better ones. One of these is by incorporating elements of destination taxation, most clearly with the DBCFT. After all, little tax
competition takes place under the VAT (because the location of final
consumers is largely fixed) and most labor—subsidizing which is the
other part of the DBCFT—is also largely immobile. And, for the
same reason, there would be no need for a minimum: Countries

could effectively ignore what other countries do and set their tax rates as high as they like.

Tax competition concerns are especially evident in relation to corporate taxation, but they go far beyond that. One reason countries are reluctant to address climate change by adopting strong carbon pricing, for example, is fear that doing so will disadvantage them unless other countries do the same. Experience with fuels used in international shipping[85] illustrates the point in the extreme. These fuels account for 3 percent of global CO_2 emissions (and rising). Yet, not only are they excluded from climate agreements, they also do not bear the usual fuel taxes. Why? Because, as California found out when in 1991 it imposed a sales tax on maritime fuel, if one port tries to tax the fuel they take up, large ships can and will easily reroute to take it up elsewhere. And so the tax has been competed all the way to zero. One idea for overcoming countries' general reluctance to adopt aggressive measures to cut emissions on their own—especially stark in the maritime sector, but much more general—is to seek agreement on a minimum carbon price.[86]

Mobility across national borders—of people, goods, and money—now preoccupies policy makers more than ever. Countries are jealously protective of their tax powers. For Prince Rainier of Monaco, the adoption of an income tax would be "a direct attack at the very roots of our national sovereignty."[87] But real tax sovereignty is a thing of the past—a distant memory, and largely a false one. The real question is how countries will choose to pool and exercise the collective sovereignty that they still possess.

———

This part of the book has looked mainly at tax design and at taxpayers: How they are affected by, and respond to, the rules they face, and how those responses shape what those rules might sensibly be. But even the most cleverly designed tax rules need to be enforced. So in part IV we put the focus squarely on tax administration.

PART IV

Taxes Don't Collect Themselves

I told the Inland Revenue I didn't owe them a penny because I lived near the seaside.

KEN DODD[1]

12

Vlad the Impaler and the Gentle Art of Tax Collection

I went down to the revenue office . . . I stood up and swore to lie after lie, fraud after fraud, villainy after villainy, till my soul was coated inches and inches thick with perjury, and my self-respect was gone for ever and ever. But what of it? It is nothing more than thousands of the highest, and richest and proudest, and most respected, honored, and courted men in America do every year.

MARK TWAIN[1]

IN 1459, the merchants of Brasov (now in Romania) refused to hand over the taxes they owed to the Prince of Wallachia. This, it turned out, was a bad decision, as the prince was to become known to history as Vlad the Impaler.[2] Sure enough, Vlad attacked and torched the town, impaling many of its inhabitants.[3] Ensuring that taxes due are collected is indeed largely a matter of sticks and carrots. Sometimes, however, the stick part is taken a bit too far.

The basic problem for tax administrators is, of course, that people dislike paying taxes. Sometimes they will change their behavior to reduce the amount due while staying within the letter of the law: that is tax avoidance, which we looked at in chapter 9. And sometimes they will simply not remit the tax legally due: that is tax evasion. The line

Whipping up money for the Pharaoh.

between avoidance and evasion is not always clear: Plenty of well-heeled tax advisors live pampered lives by testing exactly where it is. But if the line between them is thin, it is also important—it has "the thickness of a prison wall."[4] Some nonetheless see a moral equivalence between avoidance and evasion, using terms like "tax dodging" or "illicit flows" to elide the two—an approach that blurs the important distinction of legality. In any case, this chapter simply focuses on evasion and the strategies that governments use to deal with it.

Evasion is the oldest tax challenge that governments face. A nineteenth-century BCE Sumerian cuneiform tablet reports that an unhappy trader called Pushuken was imprisoned for receiving smuggled goods. And a papyrus from Egypt of the seventh-century BCE tells of an old man transferring his property to his sons at an understated value, with the aim of evading inheritance tax,[5] while a later tomb painting of tax evaders being whipped shows what the consequence may have been. How a government enforces its taxes has been, and always will be critical not only to how taxation affects the economy and society, but to its own success and even survival.

The sticks-and-carrots metaphor is helpful in thinking about tax evasion: as a gamble much like any other, such as investing in risky assets or (not) buying flood insurance.[6] In this view, taxpayers decide whether and how much to evade in much the same way that they approach any other risky decision: by considering whether the expected gain (escaping a liability) outweighs the expected loss (being punished if caught.[7] Enforcement is then a matter of making tax evasion a bad bet, using sticks and, less commonly, carrots. We will see in this chapter that, while the ways in which governments have done this over the millennia sometimes seem ludicrous (even lunatic), the underlying logic has not greatly changed. To see what is at stake, we begin with a parade of prominent tax rascals and the basic question of how big a deal tax evasion really is. We then look at ways in which governments through the ages have tried to counter it.

Mind the Gap

Some tax evaders get caught. The hard part is finding out about those who do not.

A Gallery of Tax Rascals

History is enlivened by an apparently inexhaustible supply of high-profile tax evaders. The American gangster Al Capone famously ended up in Alcatraz not for organizing the Valentine's Day massacre or the like, but for evading income tax on his ill-gotten earnings—smart drafters of laws always making sure that illegal income is just as taxable as legal income. The gangsters' lawyers were also clever, but not quite clever enough. The case against Capone was made possible by the Supreme Court's earlier rejection of their argument that requiring someone to report illegal income violated the constitutional protection from self-incrimination. In response to their further argument that if illegal receipts were taxable, then surely illegal expenses should be deductible, Justice Holmes took the view that "it will be time enough to consider the question when a taxpayer has the temerity to raise it."[8]

Tax evasion is a way of life for gangsters, but others have been notable dabblers. Politicians have a long tradition of happily evading the taxes they legislate and oversee. Robert Walpole conspired with his Secretary of the Admiralty to smuggle goods from Holland.[9] Richard Nixon's vice president Spiro Agnew resigned in 1973 after pleading no contest to a charge of income tax evasion. Nixon had his own tax troubles too, one of his aides receiving a four-month jail sentence for his role in claiming for Nixon a fraudulent $576,000 tax deduction.[10] Former Italian Prime Minister Silvio Berlusconi was sentenced to four years in prison for tax fraud in 2012.[11]

For business people, evasion can be a useful source of funds, especially when times are hard. A young Richard Branson, the British entrepreneur and head of the Virgin group of companies, went to jail briefly for falsely claiming that he had exported 30,000 records (so that no purchase tax was due on their sales).[12] More generally, tax compliance tends to decline in recessions (which may actually serve some positive role in mitigating the impact of the downturn). But hard times are not always the reason for business people's evasion. It was New York real-estate tycoon Leona Helmsley, convicted of tax fraud in 1992 for claiming $2.6 million in ineligible business expenses, who (reportedly) expressed the notorious view that "only little people pay taxes."[13]

Sportspeople have played the tax-evasion game with enthusiasm. Losers include Pete Rose, the legendary Major League Baseball player and manager, who struck out for a $50,000 fine and 1,000 hours of community service for failing to report income from special appearances and autographs. Boris Becker, formerly the world's number 1 male professional tennis player, suffered a double (or multiple) fault, costing $3 million in back taxes and interest, for having claimed to be living in low-tax Monaco when actually at home in Munich. Lester Piggott, the Queen's favorite horse jockey and nine-time Derby winner, was given a 3-year prison term in 1987 for tax fraud of more than £3 million, following an investigation code-named Operation Centaur. And many of the great footballers of our time—Lionel Messi, Cristiano Ronaldo, and Neymar among them—have had run-ins with the tax authorities. Even English cricketers have been ungentlemanly enough to invest in partnerships challenged by HMRC as abusive tax-avoidance schemes.[14]

And then there are the artists. William Shakespeare apparently ran into trouble for tax evasion connected to his dealings as a grain merchant and property owner in Stratford-upon-Avon.[15] Rock stars have been noted more for moaning about their tax bills and going into tax exile, and for avoidance more generally, than for outright evasion: David Bowie even had a tax avoidance scheme named after him.[16] On the other side of the legality line, however, Willie Nelson doubtless had a touch of the blues when most of his assets were seized in 1990, after he was charged $16 million in back taxes and fines for his involvement with a bogus tax shelter. Judy Garland was unable to click the heels of her ruby slippers and escape a $4 million tax bill from New York State in 1964. China's most famous actress, Fan Bingbing, was fined nearly $70 million in 2018 for unpaid taxes and penalties—having the good grace to be "shamed and guilty for what I have done."[17]

The unfamous have also created some ingenious tax-evasion schemes. When Jeanne Calment died in Arles in 1997, she was widely reported to be the world's oldest-ever person. But, in 2018, two researchers claimed that the woman who died in 1997 was in fact Jeanne's daughter, who had pretended to be Jeanne since 1934 to avoid inheritance tax.[18] If that sounds a tad extreme, one of the authors of this book won an Ig Nobel Prize for showing that when estate tax rates are known to be about to go up (or down), the reported deaths of some people are accelerated (or postponed).[19] Taking us from the creepy to the merely cheeky is the man from Rostock, Germany, who tried to evade the German dog tax by claiming his Spanish water dog was in fact a (tax-exempt) sheep. A veterinarian confirmed the species, and the owner was disciplined with a fine and perhaps a lawsuit.[20]

These stories show us that the powerful, rich, and famous—and sometimes the ingenious unfamous—occasionally lie and cheat (no surprise there), and that the rest of us take a righteous pleasure when they are caught. What they do not tell us is how extensive tax evasion really is.

Known Unknowns

That is a tough question. If evasion were easy to measure, then it would be easy to detect and punish, and so would not happen.

Most countries have a surprisingly vague idea of how much tax evasion goes on. The United States probably has the best handle on its extent and composition, having put substantial resources into measuring the "tax gap": the amount of tax that should be paid but in fact is not paid voluntarily in a timely way.[21] The IRS's latest estimate, for 2011–2013, suggests that about one-sixth of the federal taxes that should have been collected were not[22]—which is a lot. More countries are now making serious efforts to assess their tax gaps. The personal income tax gap in the United Kingdom, for example, was a bit over 4 percent in 2016–2017,[23] and that in Denmark is around 3 percent.[24] Tax gaps in developing countries, not surprisingly, are much larger than is common in most advanced economies. The median VAT gap in the European Union, for example, is around 10 percent, while in Uganda it is about 50 percent.[25]

These studies can also cast light on a form of noncompliance that is one step beyond simply failing to remit tax due: outright fraud, by obtaining tax credits or refunds to which the taxpayer is not entitled. Smart criminals (even, on some rumors, intelligence agencies short of cash) have devised extraordinarily clever schemes to generate refunds of tax that had never been remitted. In the European Union, one such wheeze—"missing trader intracommunity" (MTIC) fraud[26]—has been estimated to cost member states about €60 billion every year.[27] At its peak, MTIC fraud may have accounted for about one-quarter of the U.K. VAT gap. While that is a lot, it also means that there were more important sources of the VAT gap. Large-scale criminal frauds make better headlines than small-scale daily dishonesty, but at least in terms of revenue, they are not necessarily the bigger problem.

Beyond revenue, tax evasion also matters for fairness and for trust in the integrity of the tax system. If people think others are evading, they may be more inclined to evade themselves, both because it is then apparently some kind of social norm to do so, and, moreover, because the existence of widespread evasion suggests that the chance of getting caught is low. But even in simple revenue terms (leaving aside the damage it can do to the perceived fairness of the tax system) evasion is almost everywhere a real issue. The idea of evasion as a calculated gamble suggests how to limit it: Increase the odds of getting caught and increase the penalty when caught (the sticks) and provide some incentive (the carrot) for good tax behavior.

Many Sticks—and a Carrot or Two

Vlad the Impaler is not alone in having used extreme violence to encourage tax payment. In ancien régime France, punishments for salt smuggling included breaking on the wheel. In 1898, the German authorities near Kilimanjaro were accused of executing 2,000 tax refusers.[28] China did not eliminate the death penalty for tax fraud until 2011.[29] Punishments have plunged into the bizarre. In Mughal India, the governor of Bengal forced those coming up short on their tax payments "to wear long leather drawers, filled with live cats."[30] No less peculiar, although quite possibly mythical,[31] was the treatment of the tax-resisting William Tell. When, in 1273, the Austrian Habsburg family refused to acknowledge the independence of the communities of Schwyz and Uri, the locals, Tell among them, refused to pay Habsburg taxes. It was in punishment for this that Tell was forced to shoot an apple off his son's head.

These days, recalcitrant taxpayers are less likely to be called on to display remarkable feats of archery than to cough up some cash, in the form of payment, penalties, and interest. But there can be non-monetary penalties too. Excommunication was the ultimate punishment for failing to remit medieval papal taxes,[32] the modern variant being the use of such "collateral tax sanctions" as revoking drivers' licenses or even passports, as has been possible in the United States since 2015 for people with "seriously delinquent" tax debt. The ultimate punishment for tax crimes these days is prison, although fewer people end up there than you might think: about 2,000 each year in the United States and 200 in the United Kingdom.[33] The occasional inclusion in their number of the rich and famous has the merit of sending a clear message that the tax authorities are neither asleep nor powerless.[34]

Tax carrots—rewards for good compliance—are much rarer than sticks. Suggestions include providing good compliers with faster access to phone lines, reduced public transport fares, free admission to museums and/or cultural events, awarding tax-compliant businesses a special certificate,[35] and even giving lower tax rates as a reward for exemplary tax compliance.[36] Some governments have put such ideas into practice. Pakistan awards a "Taxpayers Privileges and Honour Card" to those who remitted the most in each of four categories of taxpayer. Holders are invited to a ceremony hosted by the prime minister, to the State Dinner on the Pakistan and Republic Day, and they receive other benefits, such as a free passport. One problem with this way of rewarding taxpayers, however, is that a scheme based on the size of tax payments would likely end up honoring the country's richest people, even if their tax compliance was not great. Better to reward taxpayers who have complied most fully, even if that does not mean paying much tax. In this spirit, a municipality in Argentina randomly selected 400 individuals who had complied with payment of their property taxes, publicly recognized them, and provided each of them with a spanking new sidewalk. In the 1950s, the Japanese government reportedly recognized municipalities whose residents remitted their taxes correctly and on time. Town officials were invited to a commendation ceremony sometimes attended by, and with a chance to meet, the emperor himself.

Between impaling and rewarding, tax agencies have over the centuries developed a powerful array of principles for effective administration and enforcement.

Get to the Money First

Henry VIII's tax of 1512 on social class, which we came across in chapter 4, was not a new idea. It did, however, contain one novelty that was to prove a landmark. Among those liable for tax were household servants, even the lowest paid. They were not, however, to remit the tax themselves. Instead, their master was to do so, and deduct the corresponding amount from their wages.[37] This is the oldest known instance of one bedrock principle of tax administration: If possible, get the money from a relatively reliable source before the ultimate recipient has a chance to hide, spend, or otherwise blow it. Such "withholding" is a basic element of any effective tax system, and is now applied in many contexts.

The most familiar application of withholding is to income tax on labor earnings. While people casually refer to income tax as being levied "on" employees, they know full well that it is the employer who remits the money. That has two advantages. It is much more efficient to collect the money from employers or other enterprises making payments, as they can handle remittance as part for their payment process. And it is easier for the tax administration to pursue a relatively small number of recalcitrant employers than to go after each evading employee.

Withholding was crucial to the rise of the personal income tax. We saw in chapter 5 that what made the British income tax of 1803 so much more successful than Pitt's 1799 version was the introduction of withholding on dividends, rent, and income from government securities (in 1806). Systematic withholding by employers came much later, during the Second World War. Before 1939, U.K. employees remitted tax directly every 6 months. Wartime revenue needs put this arrangement under pressure, and in 1944, the government enacted what became today's Pay As You Earn system. This proved a magnificent success. Sadly, however, one of its main proponents—Churchill's Chancellor of the Exchequer, Kingsley Wood—did not live to see it: He died the day that the proposal came to Parliament.

In the United States, withholding began with the first income tax; by 1865, it accounted for almost 40 percent of receipts.[38] The reborn income tax of 1913 contained broad withholding provisions, but these proved widely unpopular and were eliminated in 1917. Uncle Sam was not, though, to be foiled forever. The Social Security System introduced in the 1930s rested on the withholding of payroll taxes at source. As in the United Kingdom, employer withholding for income tax on wages and salaries came during the Second World War, in 1943, replacing a system in which payment was not due until March 15 (yes, not April)[39]

A thinner wage packet.

of the following year.[40] (The date at which taxes are due, by the way, is not entirely innocuous: In the United States, the income tax filing deadline is associated with an increase in the risk of a fatal automobile crash similar in scale to the increase in crashes on Super Bowl Sunday, possibly due to the stressful deadline.)[41]

Withholding made the mass income tax possible. That proved to be a source of regret for one of its main architects in the United States, who did live to see his handwork in action: Milton Friedman, the Nobel-prize winning advocate of small government. "It never occurred to me," he later bemoaned, "that I was helping to develop machinery that would make possible a government that I would come to criticize severely as too large, too intrusive, too destructive of freedom."[42]

The rise to prominence of withholding—and so of the mass income tax—was made possible by the emergence of large modern enter-prises. After all, what prevents an employer and employee from agree-ing to keep the payment between them quiet, and split the tax saving? The danger is that a tax inspector will come calling. Large businesses are hard to hide, not only physically but in terms of, for instance, marketing material. And when there are many employees, there is greater risk of informing about noncompliance either by scrupulously honest employ-ees or those seeking a reward from the authorities.[43]

Employer withholding of income tax on labor earnings is now the norm, though in ways that differ substantially across countries. Among OECD countries, only Switzerland does not withhold (though France has done so only since 2019).[44] About half of all OECD countries have a system like that of the United Kingdom, with liability recalculated throughout the year to ensure that at year's end, the exact amount has been withheld, removing any need for most workers to file a return. Not so in the United States, where the withholding rules result in most workers receiving a refund upon filing. This provides an incentive to file, which helps the IRS keep track of potential taxpayers (and perhaps bur-nishes its otherwise less-than-favorable public image). Overwithholding amounts to the taxpayer giving the government an interest-free loan. But many Americans apparently like the idea of receiving a payment come May, perhaps because they otherwise find it difficult to accumu-late a large sum of money, making this an attractive form of (self-imposed) forced saving.[45]

The principle of withholding can also be powerfully applied to the taxation of commodities (goods and services). It is at the heart of the VAT, the defining feature of which is that every business owes tax on all its sales, for which the buyer—if also a business—can obtain a credit or refund. It is as if each seller withheld and remitted to the tax authority part of the tax that its customers would otherwise remit on its subsequent sales. In a perfect world, the outcome would be exactly the same as under a retail sales tax: After all the crediting and refunding has played out, the only tax remaining would be that on sales to final consumers. But things generally do not work perfectly, and it is its "fractional" nature—being collected in stages—that gives the VAT a key practical advantage over a retail sales tax. Suppose that, for some reason, the final retailer fails to remit tax due. Under a retail sales tax, that means the government collects no tax revenue in relation to that sale—and experience has been that at rates above 10 percent or so, evasion becomes a real problem. Under a VAT, however, tax is at least collected, one can hope, on the retailer's purchases; or, if not, on the purchases of the retailer's suppliers, and so on. Revenue under a VAT is thus protected against a break in compliance somewhere in the commercial chain. When a break does occur, there will be some taxation of inputs. That violates the principle of production efficiency set out in chapter 10, but the need for revenue may make that a price worth paying. And the evidence is that—albeit less clearly in sub-Saharan Africa than elsewhere—the VAT has proved a highly effective tax;[46] too much so for some tastes, as we will see.

So great is the apparent ease of collection brought by withholding that tax administrations have proved wondrously creative in extending its scope beyond wages. It is now also pervasive on interest payments (to residents at least) and dividends, and in some cases is applied to capital gains on shareholdings.[47] Administrations often use special withholding schemes to reach those that cannot safely be trusted to remit tax themselves. Many developing countries, for instance, levy withholding taxes on imports, and even on things like mobile phones.[48]

But the question remains as to whether withholding really works, in the sense of generating, for given policy choices, additional revenue. Tax administrators have believed so for centuries. So have politicians. Echoing Milton Friedman, conservative legislators in the United States have repeatedly proposed eliminating withholding and instead requiring individuals to remit income taxes every month. "Only by taking people's money before they ever see it," said Republican Dick Armey, "has the government been able to raise taxes to their current height without sparking a revolt."[49] Academic economists, however, are generally not content to simply place their trust in centuries of experience and wisdom, and so they look for direct evidence of an impact from withholding. After all, a belief that who remits matters runs counter to one of the basic tenets of incidence analysis discussed in chapter 7: that the final outcome of imposing a tax does not depend on who is formally responsible for remitting it.

It is hard to assess the revenue impact of income tax withholding, because it was introduced in the United Kingdom and (at the federal level) the United States in wartime, making it well-nigh impossible to disentangle its effects from those of everything else that was going on at the same time. The U.S. states, however, adopted withholding for their income taxes at different times. On average, one study estimates, adoption was accompanied by about a 25 percent increase in revenue. But did withholding actually cause these higher revenues, or was it simply one effect of governments wanting to raise more revenue finding new ways to do so? It turns out that the revenue from other taxes also increased when withholding was adopted—which is a clue that the states introducing withholding were looking for revenue wherever they could find it, suggesting that adoption of withholding was motivated by higher demand for government spending. Allowing for this, it seems that withholding as such accounted for about 10–12 percent of the growth of state income taxes during the period in question. That is still pretty sizable.[50]

Whatever its real effects, withholding can certainly affect how people feel about being taxed. In early nineteenth-century Ireland, many Catholic tenant farmers refused to remit tithes to the Protestant church. Things turned violent in the Tithe War of 1831–1836, with 200 deaths in 1831 alone.[51] The solution came with the Tithe Commutation Act of 1838, which made landlords, rather than tenants, responsible for remittance. This made little difference for who ended up bearing the burden of the tax, as rents were increased to offset landlords' responsibility to remit.[52] But it settled things down in Ireland (for a time, at least).

Religion makes remittance relevant.

Big Businesses Are the Tax Administrator's Friend...

The crucial role of withholding has put businesses at the center of tax collection. In advanced economies, they remit (including as withholding) about 85 percent of all tax revenue. The same is true in the one developing country for which comparable data have been closely studied: India.[53] That businesses, especially large ones, can be a blessing for tax collectors is a lesson our ancestors learned centuries ago.

In England, the drinking of cheap distilled spirits, especially gin and especially in London, had emerged in the 1720s as a serious social and, increasingly, political problem. Average weekly consumption in London had ballooned to around 2 pints per person. Horror stories abounded, casting gin as the Georgian version of crack cocaine. In one sad tale, Judith Dufour reclaimed her two-year-old daughter from the workhouse, where she had been given a new petticoat and suit—and then strangled her, left the body in a ditch, sold the new clothes for 1 shilling and 4 pence and spent the money on gin.[54] Gin came to be seen as the "principall cause of the increase of our poor and of all the vices and debauchery among the inferior sort of people, as well as of the felonies and other disorders committed in and about this town."[55] The streets were generally unpleasant, presumably much like Saturday night in many an English town these days.

The British government decided that it needed to do something about the gin binge, and the route it chose was taxation. But how to do it? There were relatively few producers of raw spirits, just "a couple of dozen" in London, this being an expensive business to enter.[56] And there were hundreds of "compound distillers," turning raw spirits into gin, and even more outlets for selling it, often with the addition of fruits and spices.

The government's first attempt was the 1729 Gin Act, which imposed a stringent per-gallon tax on gin retailers and required them to purchase an annual license. But with 6,187 gin sellers in Middlesex County alone, this quickly proved impossible to administer.[57] Then came the 1743 Gin Act, which at least put a stop to the remorseless increase in gin consumption. And, after the quaintly named Tipple Act of 1751, consumption went into marked decline.[58] No doubt many factors contributed to this. But one big difference was that the 1743 and subsequent acts targeted not the hundreds of small retailers, but rather the few easily monitored, large wholesale distillers. Tax was charged at a rate lower than the combined rates of wholesale and retail taxes in 1729 but was more effectively enforced. Taxing the big players was cost-effective and reduced evasion. And the English sobered up (kind of).

Underpinning this more successful approach to tax collection was a logic similar to that behind withholding: imposing the obligation to remit on relatively organized businesses. But there is another lesson. Not only can a large part of potential tax revenue be collected directly from businesses: Among those businesses, a few of the very largest commonly account for a very large share of that potential.

The realization that large amounts of revenue could be raised by concentrating collection on a few very large firms was not new even in Georgian England. As we saw in chapter 3, the Tudors and Stuarts deliberately created monopolies that were an easy source of ready cash. And today, a centerpiece of any modern tax administration is the "large taxpayer unit" focused on monitoring the very largest enterprises. Nearly 90 percent of all tax administrations have a large taxpayer unit (or something similar), often collecting just under half of all revenue from the major taxes from perhaps only 2 percent of all corporations.[59]

Thus, while businesses as a whole account for an impressive 85 percent or so of all tax revenue, the proportion of that collected from the largest among them can be staggering. In the United States, for instance, in 2013 the largest 0.055 percent of active corporations remitted 70 percent of all corporate tax revenue.[60] In developing countries, the concentration of tax payments is no less and may even be greater: The largest 1 percent of businesses (often banks, telecoms, and any natural resource companies) may account for 70 percent of all (not just corporate) tax revenue. The remarkable concentration of the potential tax base among a relatively small number of businesses is an inestimable gift of nature to tax administrators.[61] It means that close monitoring of a few firms—often just a handful in developing countries—is critical to building an effective tax administration. This is not just a matter of ensuring that these large firms do not evade tax. Ensuring that a giant multinational is not late with its tax payment may dwarf the revenue gain from catching a stadium-full of waiters who fail to declare their tips.

. . . And Small Businesses Are Their Nightmare

If large businesses are the tax administration's friend—at least, setting aside the issues of avoidance addressed in chapter 11—small businesses are their nightmare.

A recurring finding of the tax gap studies mentioned above is that noncompliance is especially rampant among this group. In the United States, for instance, more than half of the income of small businesses (which includes the self-employed) is evaded—compared to only 1 percent of wages and salaries. And this adds up to a large amount: Nearly half of the total income tax gap in the United States is attributable to the underreporting of business income.[62] In Japan, the phenomenon of the self-employed (and farmers) being able to evade tax more successfully than employees even has its own name: *Ku-ro-yon*, a portmanteau of *ku* (9), *ro* (6), and *yon* (4), conveying the belief that on average, 90 percent of the income of salaried workers is identified by the tax authorities, but only 60 percent of the income of the self-employed, and just 40 percent of farmers' income.[63] The situation does not seem quite as dire elsewhere, but is still grim: In the United Kingdom, evasion among small businesses accounts for more than 40 percent of the total tax gap.[64] The issue is not simply about the local handyperson failing to remit VAT, or even about small service or manufacturing businesses. It is largely about lawyers, accountants, architects, and the like lying about their earnings and/or expenses. In Greece, self-employed professionals were recently found to be declaring income below even the interest they were paying on consumer loans.[65]

The high rate of noncompliance with their tax obligations among small businesses is easily explained. The preconditions for effective withholding by the business on the payments it makes, discussed above, are not met; third-party information is largely absent; the dividing line between business purchases and personal consumption can be hard to monitor; and record-keeping may be (perhaps willfully) poor. One way governments have responded is by the kind of presumptive taxation of small businesses discussed in chapter 4. Another is by establishing withholding on payments to small businesses.[66] In Sweden, for example, buyers of home renovation and domestic services can pay the supplier for materials but for only half of the labor cost, with the rest going to the government. The company then applies to the tax authority for that other half, thereby revealing to the tax authority its existence and some of its taxable income and VAT base.

There is nothing new in the problems posed by small businesses. In the late Roman Empire, it was largely to avoid taxation that all but a few merchants stopped keeping accounts.[67] In 1870, the U.K. Board of Inland Revenue claimed that 40 percent of assessments from unincorporated businesses were understated.[68] The problems of taxing small businesses might though be increasing in importance, as new business models built around digital platforms—Uber is the classic example—are making self-employment even more prevalent, an issue encountered in chapter 9. Much depends on whether the digital methods that are driving this fragmentation of industrial structures can themselves be used to provide the tax authorities with the information on the earnings of small businesses and the self-employed that they have had such trouble obtaining.

Information Rules

Vlad the Impaler, bane of the merchants of Brasov, married Ilona Szilágyi. Five centuries later, in the early 1980s, John Szilagyi—who, if there is any poetry in life, is surely related—was a research officer in the IRS. He strongly suspected that some taxpayers were fraudulently claiming dependents—such as, perhaps, one called "Fluffy"—to garner extra exemptions. Szilagyi suggested addressing this problem by requiring taxpayers to provide Social Security numbers for the dependents claimed, which could be checked. His suggestion was enacted in 1986; and 7 million dependents promptly vanished. By way of reward—on some estimates, his idea had generated about $14 billion in additional revenue—John Szilagyi received a check for $25,000.[69] Sometimes, it seems, there are fairly easy ways to make tax evasion harder. But don't expect everyone to thank you if you find one.

There is another and more uplifting lesson from Szilagyi's story: that independently verifiable information can be used to make evasion harder. Wise administrations find all kinds of ways to gather it. Frederick the Great used sniffers to wander around town finding where the taxable coffee he so much hated was being roasted.[70] There are, however, more systematic approaches.

WHEN ALL ELSE FAILS, TELL THE TRUTH

The basic problem, of course, is that taxpayers have no inherent incentive to tell the truth about things they have done that create a tax liability.[71] Governments have tried many ways to tease out the truth from them, ranging from extravagant punishment to the gentler subtleties of the liturgy self-assessment scheme. Today's variant is the use of new(-ish) technologies to elicit truthful information from taxpayers themselves. Making electronic invoicing mandatory is one way to generate verifiable trails of transactions for enforcement of the VAT, and this does seem to be effective.[72] However, requiring the use of electronic cash registers—in the hope that they will provide verifiable information on the sales of small retailers—has been undermined by the development of "zappers": software that randomly and untraceably deletes sales from a cash register.[73] They were found, for instance, in Céline Dion's restaurant chain Nickels.[74] To counter zappers, several European countries require retailers to use certified cash registers that include a black box that can be accessed only by the tax authority.[75] And now the trend, pioneered in Russia, is to mandate online cash registers that upload sales data to the tax authorities instantly.[76] But all this still leaves the unsubtle method of simply not putting sales through the register. Just because people are told to record things electronically does not mean they will. And just because information is stored electronically does not mean it is right.

A different but complementary strategy is to make use of information from "third parties" of various kinds[77]—businesses, most often—that know what has happened and, ideally, have no incentive to lie about it. Sometimes this third party is also in a position to withhold and remit tax, the most powerful possibility; sometimes they simply pass on the information, with likely a lesser but still potentially strong impact on compliance.[78]

The leading example is the typical requirement that employers tell the tax authority what they have paid their workers, which can then be checked against the workers' own reports. These arrangements are not foolproof: A collusive agreement between the employer and employee to understate wages might benefit both sides. But, as with withholding, when employers are large and easily identified, the risk is unlikely to be worth taking.

Information reporting requirements extend far beyond employers and are on the rise around the world. More than two-thirds of all OECD countries require information from the payers of interest, dividends, some types of business income, and rent; nearly as many require it for sales of stock shares, real estate sales, or rent—items on which there is generally no withholding.[79] And the trend toward greater use of third-party information continues, with the movement to cross-border automatic information exchange encountered in chapter 11 being only the most prominent example.

Experience does call for some caveats. Since 2011, the United States has required that credit card companies (such as Visa) and payment settlement entities (like PayPal) report to the IRS the gross value of companies' receipts. The idea is that the IRS can then see whether a business reported revenues less than, or suspiciously close to, the amount they are known to have received via payment cards. (The presumption is that for credit card companies, the risks from collusion with merchants are off-puttingly large.) Some evidence suggests that many businesses did increase their declared sales to at least the level independently reported. But there was a catch: Many businesses that reported more revenue also reported more hard-to-check expenses, which reduced the extra tax liability they might otherwise incur.[80] Something similar has been seen in Ecuador: After the introduction of third-party information on sales, some firms did indeed report increased revenues—but they also increased their reported deductions, not subject to information reporting, by almost as much.[81] Partial truths can always be misleading.

DETHRONING CASH

For tax evaders, cash has for centuries been king, providing a way to avoid leaving an information trail that the tax authorities (and others) could sniff along. Some countries provide tax carrots to encourage non-cash payments. South Korea allows a deduction from taxable income of 15 percent of credit card charges (up to about $2,600) for those whose income does not exceed about $60,000.[82] Whether the revenue gain from any increased compliance this induces more than offsets the loss from the lower tax rate, however, remains unclear.

The most direct approach is to legislate against the use of cash, particularly high-denomination notes—and not just for tax reasons. Some countries simply ban the use of cash for transactions above some limit:

€1,000 in Italy, for example. Most dramatically, in 2016, India announced that 500 and 1,000 rupee notes, making up 86 percent of currency in circulation, would cease to be legal tender, giving people less than 2 months to deposit or change a limited amount of their old notes at banks for new ones.[83] The rationale is simply that big bills facilitate tax evasion and money laundering, it being ten times as cumbersome to carry or conceal 10,000 hundred-dollar bills as it is 1,000 thousand-dollar bills. But not everyone feels the same about the use of cash. In 2019, Switzerland issued a new series of one-thousand franc (about $1,000) notes, with the vice chair of the Swiss National Bank seeing no indication that this bill "is more risk prone to use for criminal purposes."[84] And in 2018 Philadelphia banned cashless stores on the grounds that they discriminate against people who do not have credit or debit cards.[85] Nevertheless, the aura of inevitability around the demise of cash, already evident before the COVID-19 pandemic, shines even brighter now.

GRASSES, FERRETS, AND WHISTLEBLOWERS

In the depths of the gin craze, the Excise Board was given the power to use informers, with a £5 payoff for each conviction.[86] Unsurprisingly, several of these grasses[87] were murdered, and the courts were overwhelmed with a surge of petty cases.[88] But the practice has continued. Since the early nineteenth century, many local U.S. jurisdictions have occasionally contracted with private contractors—"ferrets"—to identify unreported or undervalued properties, in return for a percentage of the additional property tax revenue recovered.[89] At the height of its financial crisis, in April 2015, the Greek government proposed enlisting tourists, students, and others to check up on retailers' tax compliance by "posing as . . . customers . . . [while] wired for sound and video."[90] This proposal came to nothing, but elsewhere the use of informers proceeds discreetly. The Australian Taxation Office, for instance, provides an online form for reporting suspected tax evasion.[91] It apparently does not offer any rewards to informers, but the United States does: up to 30 percent of the additional tax, penalty, and other amounts that the information they provide generates.

Bradley Birkenfeld, a happy whistleblower.

The most spectacular beneficiary of this policy (publicly known, at least) is Bradley Birkenfeld, who, soon after leaving his job with the Swiss-based financial services company UBS, turned over to the IRS details of its facilitation of tax evasion by U.S. citizens. UBS eventually settled with the U.S. government in 2009 for $780 million (with an additional $200 million to the Securities and Exchange Commission) and handed over information on more than 4,000 U.S. clients. The revenue ultimately recovered by the United States has been put at around $4 billion.[92] For his own role in aiding evasion, Mr. Birkenfeld got 3 years of jail time—not in Switzerland (whose clutches he kept out of), but in the United States, for his role in facilitating evasion. But there was a sweetener: Mr. Birkenfeld was due a $104 million reward from the IRS.[93]

And then there are the whistleblowers who have made information public rather than reporting directly to the authorities: the Panama Papers, LuxLeaks, Appleby (Paradise Papers), and all that. The Panama Papers, leaking the activities of the Panamanian law firm Mossack Fonseca, made the biggest splash, with details on 214,000 offshore entities linked to more than 100 politicians, as well as to Lionel Messi, Jackie

Chan, Simon Cowell, and other celebrities.[94] Much of what was revealed was probably avoidance rather than outright evasion. But that
was embarrassing enough, and these leaks played a big role in driving
the reforms to international tax rules that we looked at in chapter 11.
They are also proving a goldmine for academics: It was leaks from the
British bank HSBC and the Panama Papers that were used to infer the
unexpectedly high rates of evasion among the wealthiest Scandinavians
mentioned in chapter 11. All this comes with the bonus for conspiracy
theorists that the source of the Panama Papers leaks has remained unclear, with—given a notable absence of prominent American names—
the CIA at the top of some people's lists.[95]

SHINING A LIGHT

Under the first U.S. income tax, of 1861, tax returns were made public.[96]
So it was that the narrator of Mark Twain's story cited above could say:
"I am acquainted with a very opulent man, whose house is a palace,
whose table is regal, whose outlays are enormous, yet . . . who has no
income, as I have often noticed, by the revenue returns."[97] (It was the
generous advice of this same friend that led him to the moral vacuum
described in the passage that opened this chapter.) But the publication
of tax returns proved highly unpopular, and the practice ended in 1870.[98]
In Italy, public disclosure of tax liabilities lasted all of one day.[99]

Publishing information from tax returns can serve as a lead for
would-be informers, and perhaps also shame (or scare) those who are
evading. In classical Athens, individuals' tax payments were carved
in stone and made public.[100] Whatever the reason, there is evidence
that publication does increase individual tax payments. Norway, for
instance, has published this information since 1863,[101] but if you
wanted to find out the taxable income of Liv Ullmann or your friend
the Sami reindeer herder, you had to visit an office. When this information was posted online in 2001, however, there was about a 3 percent
average increase in reported income among small business owners.[102]
Similarly, Pakistan's public disclosure program (begun in 2012) seems
to have increased reported tax payments of the self-employed by nearly

10 percent.[103] Publication can also lead to improved accountability: It was, for instance, probably informative for the people of Pakistan to learn a few years ago that only about 30 percent of their representatives in the national assembly and 40 percent of all cabinet members had filed tax returns.[104]

There have also been initiatives aimed at publishing tax payments by corporations—whose payments are much harder to find out than you might think[105]—the main motivation being concern with the apparently small amounts of tax that many multinationals remit. In the natural resource sector, publication is encouraged by the Extractive Industries Transparency Initiative, and required by the European Union, as a way of keeping track of all payments made to and received by government, the idea being to make bribery harder.[106] More generally, one outcome of the G20/OECD BEPS project discussed in chapter 11 is "country-by-country" reporting on the tax affairs of large multinationals. The company-specific information that this is now collecting, however, is available only to tax administrations, not the public. Business has generally been strongly opposed to publication, partly on grounds of commercial secrecy but also in the fear that low tax payments (maybe reflecting past losses) will be misinterpreted; but some do now voluntarily publish how much tax they pay and where. And in 2015, Australia began publishing the taxable income and tax payments of large public and private companies. This disclosure, heavily covered by the media, caused Australian private companies to remit more tax, on average, although some—as with a similar scheme in Japan[107]—seem to have taken action to avoid disclosure by holding reported income below the threshold at which reporting was required.[108]

Trust but Verify

No mass tax can work by having each taxpayer meet with an assessor to check in detail what tax is due. Apart from the opportunities for bribery and extortion this would create, it is simply too costly. As a consequence, the essence of modern tax administration—"the very base of the democratic way of life," according to a former IRS commissioner[109]—is self-assessment: Taxpayers declare and remit how much tax they believe they owe—knowing, however, that their declaration is subject to the possibility of check and audit. More generally, modern tax administration is an exercise in risk management: using scarce resources most efficiently by identifying taxpayers, or transactions, that look potentially dodgy and significant, and taking appropriately measured actions to do something about it.

At the heart of risk management is selective audit, choosing for the closest scrutiny just some subset of all declarations—not only to detect and correct any "error" made by that particular taxpayer, but also to send a message to all taxpayers that deceit puts them in jeopardy. For this purpose, declarations could be picked at random. That would be the best way of getting an overall picture of taxpayer compliance. But a more immediate impact on collection comes from selecting audit cases by looking for signs that something fishy is going on. This assessment can rest on the experience and intuition of the tax audit officials, though that carries obvious risks of corruption. Increasingly, use is being made of formal algorithms that parse the evidence from prior audit activities, and other sources of intelligence, to "score" returns for their audit potential. The IRS, for instance, uses an algorithm-generated score as the principal criterion, though not the only one, for selecting returns (and particular items) for audit. This systematic approach remains less common than you might guess: Only half of all tax administrations in high-income countries use techniques of this kind.[110] And those that do keep their formula secret. Quite why is not entirely obvious. Admittedly, public knowledge of the formula would help people reduce their odds of audit by, for example, claiming fewer deductions of a kind known to raise red flags. But that is what we want them to do.

Governments are also cagey about the likelihood of being audited, perhaps because it is often lower than many might imagine. Across the OECD, only about 0.7 percent of all individual tax returns are audited.[111] The U.S. audit rate has declined strikingly over the 2010s, falling from above 1 percent in 2010 to 0.45 percent in 2019, driven primarily by steep budget cuts that resulted in a 39 percent decline in the number of revenue agents. For those with total positive income above $10 million, the audit coverage fell by more than two-thirds.[112] Compliance might be lower if people were to realize how slim their chances of being audited really are.

There can be an element of carrot in effective audit and risk-management strategies. Taxpayers with a history of good compliance are sometimes given "gold card" treatment that allows them faster clear times at customs, for instance, or to receive their VAT refunds quicker. That can carry its own risks. Chichikov, the central figure of Gogol's *Dead Souls*, was a customs official at one point in his creatively scheming career, in which role he carefully built up a reputation for integrity and honesty—all, however, as the preliminary to an enormous scam.[113] When it comes to taxation, trust can never be absolute.

Taxpayers Are People Too

The suite of instruments described so far have a "gotcha" flavor: They aim to make it harder to get away with the gamble of trying to hide a tax liability. But taxpayers have more complex motives than simply minimizing their expected payments. Sometimes they refuse to pay out of principle. And sometimes it's just too hard to be honest.

Principled (and Singing) Evaders

People do seem more likely to remit the tax they owe—even when their short-term self-interest makes evasion a good bet—if they believe the government acts fairly and in their interests.[114] The Mayor of Tirana (later Prime Minister of Albania), Edi Rama, oversaw a program that repainted gray Communist-era buildings in kaleidoscopic colors: "When we started painting . . . [people] started paying taxes."[115] Conversely, compliance can collapse when trust in government, or support for the uses to which revenue raised is put, breaks down. Just ask Wat Tyler or John Hancock.

Sometimes noncompliance is a matter of heartfelt principle. Since at least the Reformation, some religious groups have struggled between their pacifism and their tax obligations. In revolutionary Philadelphia of 1776, a Quaker meeting resolved that "a tax levied for the purchasing of drums, colors, or for other warlike use, cannot be paid consistently with our Christian testimony."[116] Henry David Thoreau refused to remit tax in protest against the Mexican-American War of 1846 and the expansion of slavery into the Southwest, leading to a night in a jail (his aunt Maria, it is said, having paid the tax by morning). In 1968, nearly 500 writers and editors refused to pay a proposed 10 percent tax surcharge to help fund the Vietnam War.[117] And there are still passionate advocates for the right to redirect tax payments into a "peace tax fund" that could not be used for military spending.[118] Such earmarking would have no real impact so long as there was enough non-peace fund revenue to cover military spending. But it would send a message.

Tax protests have even inspired poetry and song. In England, the *Song against the King's Taxes*, of 1338–1339, voiced dissatisfaction with taxes levied to pay for another war with France. In 1626, protesting Austrian peasants often broke into song, their go-to tune being a 55-stanza (14 lines per stanza) number, the *Baurenlied* or *Fadinglerlied*, which laid out their demands. And in the Swiss Peasant War of 1653, the resistance leaders composed a protest marching song that invoked the folk memory of William Tell.[119]

The weirdest example of nonviolent tax resistance, however, must be the "Johnson cult" protest in an island of Papua New Guinea, circa 1964. The locals wanted to buy (sic) President Lyndon B. Johnson and appoint him as their political leader, financing this by refusing to remit the £2 Papuan poll tax and instead setting the money aside in anticipation of their unusual purchase.[120]

Making Honesty the Easiest Policy

At least some of us seem to have a preference for being honest.[121] If so, then it makes sense to try to make complying with our tax obligations easy. That will never be enough to combat determined tax evaders, but modern tax administrators commonly presume that the vast bulk of taxpayers have a strong "intrinsic" motivation to comply with the tax rules (as opposed to an "extrinsic" motivation from the fear of punishment).

A minimal requirement for people to be expected to meet their legal obligations—and for accountability and democracy—is that the tax law be clear. Or at least reasonably so: No decent modern tax system is ever likely to be truly simple. It should, though, be possible to do better than the Emperor Caligula, who once promulgated new tax laws only by word of mouth. Responding with characteristic charm to the discontented mutterings that followed, he "acceded to the urgent popular demand, by posting the regulations up, but in an awkwardly cramped spot and written so small that no one could take a copy."[122]

Even knowing the rules, however, being fully honest on tax matters is often hard. It takes time and trouble to understand and fill in forms, keep the necessary records, hire specialist advice, and all that. These compliance costs incurred by the taxpayer are hard to measure, and not much is known, for instance, about how they vary with aspects of tax design. But we do know two things about them. One is that compliance costs can be large, often much larger than the (easier to measure) costs incurred by the tax administration itself: For the U.S. income tax, compliance costs are perhaps 10 percent of revenue collected, making them about 20 times higher than administrative costs. The other thing we know is that compliance costs are particularly problematic for small businesses, because many of these costs—like that of completing a VAT return—increase only fairly modestly with the scale of the enterprise.[123] These costs represent a real expenditure of talent and resources that could be put to better use. Keeping them low is partly a matter of tax design, but tax administrations are also increasingly focused on providing services—electronic filing, call-in centers, and the like—that reduce the costs of being compliant.

In their observation and manipulation of human nature, governments have, without knowing it, long been practitioners of now-fashionable behavioral economics. They have sought not only to threaten and facilitate, but also to play on emotions underpinning an inclination to honesty: conscience and fear of shame. "Why have you not yet sent to Babylon the 30 lambs as your tax?" thundered King Hammurabi of ancient Babylon, "Are you not ashamed of such behavior?"[124] Four millennia later, shame is still used to encourage compliance. In one small Pacific island, for instance, the answer given to an advisor who asked how the tax administration pursues those who fail to file or remit—the expected answer being that some sort of formal enforcement action was taken—was simply "I call their father." Publishing the names of those with unpaid tax debts or convictions for evasion is routine in many countries. In New Zealand, many readers will have been disappointed to find that the *Tax Evaders' Gazette*[125] was not a how-to guide, but rather a listing of tax miscreants. More out of the box is the occasional use by the tax authorities in Pakistan of *hijras*, members of the transgender community, to go to tax delinquents' residences or offices, "clapping, shouting, and generally making a scene" until the tax bill is paid. This reportedly raised collection rates by 15 percent.

Governments have also been adept at leveraging patriotism, especially though not only in wartime.[126] Even Donald Duck did his bit during World War Two, taking time out from a busy schedule to urge Americans to "gladly and proudly" meet their tax obligations. And in the past few years, more systematic thought has been given to ways of exploiting human nature to encourage compliance (or avoid inadvertently discouraging it).

One idea is that "nudges"—messaging of the Hammurabi type, or more subtle—can significantly impact how people behave. With just a few exceptions, however, randomized field experiments find that appealing to taxpayers' consciences, stressing the beneficial effects of tax-funded projects, asserting that most other taxpayers are compliant, or highlighting the civic responsibility to comply, all do little to improve tax compliance.[127] Another idea is that punitive enforcement policies might backfire, crowding out an intrinsic motivation to comply by making people feel they pay taxes because they have to, not because they want to.[128] There is evidence of this phenomenon outside of the tax world,[129] but one study that looked for such an effect in the context of a local church tax in Germany—for which there is literally no enforcement and yet some people nevertheless comply—found no such evidence. Church-going German Protestants not being your typical taxpayer, however, the generality of this finding may be limited.[130]

Not too much faith should be put in taxpayers' intrinsic honesty. The community charge debacle in the United Kingdom showed the potential fragility of tax compliance even in a society with a reputation for being broadly law-abiding. The rapid breakdown of traditions and norms seemed to hinge largely on interdependencies in individual decisions about whether to remit taxes due. Noncompliance with the community charge was greater, all else equal, the higher it was in neighboring localities.[131] Maybe that is because the poor compliance of others reduces the guilt people feel in not complying themselves. Or maybe, more mechanically, they interpret the noncompliance of others as indicating that the risks of being detected and punished are low. In either case, such interdependencies create the possibility of two very different possible outcomes for tax compliance: a "good equilibrium," in which (mostly) everyone complies because everyone else complies, and a "bad equilibrium," in which hardly anyone complies. Many societies, especially in the developing world, still struggle to break out of a bad-compliance equilibrium.

Compulsion thus remains key to tax enforcement, and the core job of the tax administration remains that of shaping taxpayers' incentives by using the kinds of gotcha tools discussed in this chapter. How good a job they do depends also on the incentives faced by tax administrators and tax administrations themselves, and on the technology available to them—which are the subject of the next chapter.

13

Someone Has to Do It

I say to you, tax collectors and prostitutes are entering the kingdom of
God before you.

MATTHEW 21:31[1]

ONE DAY IN 88 BCE, the subjects of Mithridates VI ("the Great," 120–63
BCE), the rising power in Asia Minor, slaughtered, at his order, every
Roman they could find. They seem to have needed little urging. Prominent among the victims were the tax collectors, anti-Roman feeling having been aroused by their "usurious and extortive" behavior.[2] Tax collectors have certainly dished out violence over the ages. But they have
also been its victims. As a relatively pedestrian example, in 1916, the Salt
Tax Bureau at Ba Maoqi was burned to the ground and the bureau's
director killed.[3] Among the most gruesome fates was that of customs
officer William Galley and suspected informant Daniel Chater at the
hands of smugglers in eighteenth-century England. This included the
cutting off of genitals, hanging, being thrown down a well, and being
buried alive. In many countries, the life of a tax administrator is still
shaded by overtones of violence. Elsewhere, they are at best treated with
caution at dinner parties.

By the same token, one of the ways in which Jesus showed the uni-
versality of his love and forgiveness was precisely in his embrace of tax
collectors (who at the time incurred special contempt for their

collaboration with Rome). In the Gospel of Luke, his sympathetic treatment of the tax collector Zacchaeus causes outrage. Most telling of all, however, was his choice of a tax collector from Galilee, Matthew, to become one of his disciples.[4]

Our concern here, however, is not with tax collectors' prospects in the next life but their behavior in this one. In chapter 12, we looked at taxpayers' potentially evading ways. Now we turn to the tax collectors themselves.

The Tax Collectors' Gallery

Few people become famous as tax administrators, but quite a few involved in tax administration have become famous for other reasons. And so, to complement the rogues' gallery of tax evaders in chapter 12, we present here a gallery of tax collectors.

It opens with two heroes of the American Revolution who served as tax collectors—both with less than stellar performance assessments. One was Sam Adams of Boston Tea Party fame (though now even more famous for giving his name to a brand of craft beers).[5] Elected in 1756 to serve as tax collector for Boston, opinions of his performance vary. To some, Adams was simply lax in collection, to the extent of about £4,000 (gaining popularity on that account). He was, however, "legally, if not morally, an embezzler,"[6] being ordered in 1766 to repay £1,463—which, in the excitement of the times, he never completely did.[7] The other was Tom Paine, author of *Common Sense* and *The American Crisis*. Working as an excise collector in Lincolnshire, he was sacked in 1765 for claiming to have inspected goods that he had not, but was rehired.[8] Showing early his powers of radical advocacy, in 1772, Paine published a pamphlet arguing for higher wages for excise officers, and he became a full-time lobbyist on their behalf.

Several writers spent time administering taxes (or not). Geoffrey Chaucer managed to work on the *Canterbury Tales* while serving, between 1374 and 1386, as Comptroller of Customs in the Port of London. Miguel de Cervantes served prison time for embezzling money as a tax collector. Herman Melville was more upright. After his masterwork

Moby Dick sank without a trace, he worked as a customs inspector in New York City,[9] winning a reputation as the only honest employee in a notoriously corrupt department. Whether his curious short story of office life, *Barnaby*, was built on his time there seems to be unknown. Robert Burns, the iconic eighteenth-century Scottish poet, also worked as a customs official. Having, however, penned the immortal but incomprehensible lines:

> mony braw thanks to the meikel black deil
> That danc's away wi' th' Exciseman,[10]

he found himself in trouble with his employer and was obliged to apologize "grovelingly" to avoid being fired. At least Burns found some inspiration in his work. So, too, did David Foster Wallace, who based his (unfinished) novel *The Pale King*—"the first great literary work about taxation"[11]—on his experiences working in 1985–1986 for the regional IRS center in Peoria, Illinois. "I learned, in my time with the Service," wrote Wallace, "something about dullness, information, and irrelevant complexity. About negotiating boredom as one would a terrain, its levels and forests and endless wastes."[12]

Philosophers also make a decent showing in the parade of history's tax collectors. John Locke served as Commissioner of Appeals in Excise from 1689 until 1704, when he was succeeded by Joseph Addison, the essayist and cofounder of *The Spectator*. As we will see, despite being outraged by the behavior of tax collectors in ancien régime France, Voltaire reportedly became a tax commissioner.[13] And, with presumably unintended irony, Adam Smith, the apostle of free trade, became Commissioner of Customs and Salt Duties soon after publishing *The Wealth of Nations*.[14]

Politicians, in contrast, seem to have been less attracted to collecting taxes than to evading them. One of America's least-known presidents, Chester Arthur, was a notable and, by the standards of the time, reasonably honorable exception. Before unexpectedly becoming the twenty-first President of the United States (1881–1885) after the assassination of James Garfield, Arthur was Collector of the Customs House in the Port of New York (overlapping with Melville)—which collected more than one-third of all the government's revenue at the time.[15] Although his salary was $12,000, his total income in the job exceeded $50,000[16] due to the "moiety" system that awarded him, perfectly legally, a percentage of the cargoes seized and fines levied on importers who were deemed to have evaded the tariffs.[17] Perhaps also squeezing in under this category is Madame de Pompadour, Mistress of Louis XV. She was the daughter of an employee of the *fermiers généraux* (tax farmers, of whom more soon), the wife of a tax farmer, the protégée of another, and indirectly, a tax farmer herself.

Then there are the miscellaneous. Antony von Leeuwenhoek, the "father of microbiology" and a prominent figure in the golden age of Dutch science and technology, joined the Delft tax farming operation in 1679 as a wine gauger, his job being to determine the volume of wine in a barrel of given dimensions so that the correct amount of tax could be assessed.[18] Inevitably, dogs also enter the story. In the 1800s, it is said, a German tax collector grew tired of the disrespect and attacks he encountered in his tax-collecting duties and set out to develop a breed of dog that was a fighter and whose mere appearance would intimidate potential attackers.[19] The collector was Karl Friedrich Louis Dobermann, and the dog took his name (losing one "n" somewhere along the way): the Doberman Pinscher. In terms of parental influence, Hitler's brutal and unloved father, Alois, stands out. He rose through the Austrian civil service to become a full inspector of customs at Braunau am Inn, on the border with Germany. It is probably no coincidence that Hitler tended to see tax collectors—along with judges, clergymen, and prostitutes—as the dregs of society.[20] Happier to relate is the story of the post-Impressionist painter Henri Rousseau. When young, he collected the *octroi* on goods entering Paris. His friends called him "Douanier" (customs officer), and the poet Guillaume Apollinaire continued the joke in his epitaph for Rousseau: "Let our luggage pass duty free through the gates of heaven. We will bring you brushes, paints, and canvas."[21]

None of these people became famous because they were tax collectors. Few tax administrators get their five minutes of fame, or even much respect. There is, however, one magnificent exception.

Robert Hart, a serious and devout young man from Portadown in Northern Ireland, with a talent for languages, arrived in China in 1854.[22] The previous year, the seizure of Shanghai by organized crime syndicates had caused such chaos that the Western powers (who had appointed themselves to collect tariff revenue on behalf of the Imperial government) forced the creation of the Imperial Maritime Customs Service[23]—answerable to the Chinese government in principle, run by foreigners in practice. In 1863, Hart became its head, and remained so for the next 46 years, earning a proud reputation for honesty. Along the way, he became a key figure in supporting wider efforts at modernization, promoting China's reputation abroad, and, among other things, founding the post office, building lighthouses, and establishing a meteorological service.[24] "The Service which I direct is called the Chinese Customs Service," he told the British prime minister in 1885, "but its scope is wide and its aim is to do good work for China in every possible direction."[25]

The Chinese showered honors on Hart. His titles included Red Button of the Highest Rank, Order of the Double Dragon, and Senior Guardian of the Heir Apparent. The reforming Prince Kung called him "our Hart." In 1889, when the Empress Dowager nominally retired on the coming of age of her adopted son, she honored 100 officials, living and dead. Hart was number 2. He was awarded "Ancestral Rank of the First Class of the First Order for Three Generations," a mark of respect so high that it conferred honor on three generations of his ancestors.[26] The British, on their side, made him a baronet. Few tax administrators get their own statue. Hart did, on the Bund in Shanghai. Vilified under Mao as an archetypal colonialist, his reputation is now being reassessed even in China.[27]

Hart is a glorious exception, as it is the fate of the typical tax administrator to remain unknown to history. Sometimes, as for David Foster Wallace, the job is boring. For many it has been fatal. After Virginia introduced a state income tax in 1909, some of the revenue agents sent off to collect it were never heard from again.[28] Around the world today, there are dedicated men and women trying to do good by making the tax system work efficiently and fairly, often in inconceivably trying

Robert Hart: A "True Friend of the Chinese People."

circumstances. It is people like them that we have to thank for today's tax systems, and so, to a large degree, such civilization as we now enjoy.

Who Collects?

We are used to the idea that government entrusts tax collection to a tax administration—the IRS in the United States, HMRC in the United Kingdom, the Australian Tax Office, the State Tax Administration in China—that is just another part of the civil service. The government gives it a budget, its employees get paid wages, and everyone gets on with their job.

But there are many ways in which tax collection can be organized, and how we do things now is the historical exception, not the rule.

Collectors getting a fixed salary and the government keeping whatever remains after expenses is just one extreme possibility. Things could be the other way around: The government might receive some fixed amount in return for selling the right to collect taxes, with collections over and above that amount going to those who purchased those rights. This kind of arrangement—"tax farming"—is how taxes have been collected throughout much of the world's history.

The Rise and Demise of Tax Farming (and Tax Farmers)

May 8, 1794, was a bad day in the history of tax administrators. Antoine-Laurent de Lavoisier—the "father of modern chemistry"—along with his father and 24 others, went to the guillotine. Their exact crime was not very clear, but in Robespierre's Paris, it did not need to be. Enough that tax farmers, the *fermiers généraux*, had been excoriated for decades, the vituperative Marat warning them to "Tremble, you who have sucked out the blood of unhappy wretches."[29] Among the first targets of the Parisian mob in July 1789, as we saw in chapter 4, was the wall that the *fermiers* were then building around Paris to help them collect taxes on goods entering the city.

The *fermiers généraux* have come to epitomize tax farming, representing in many respects its highest form.[30] But they were following in a long tradition. Tax farming was the practice in ancient Mesopotamia, introduced in Egypt by Ptolemy II in 282 BCE, practiced in ancient Greece, and adopted in republican Rome in 123 BCE. It was prevalent in Judea at the time of Jesus. The "rendering unto Caesar" was really rendering unto those who had rendered unto Caesar for the right to be rendered unto. The Mughal Empire (1526–1857) and the Qing dynasty (1644–1911) also made extensive use of tax farming, as did Safavid Persia (1502–1736). The practice came to Western Europe from around the mid-sixteenth century, when monarchs accustomed to renting out their personal lands started to apply the same principle to tax collection: hence, at least on one theory, the "farming" label.[31]

For the British, tax farming became a cornerstone of their empire. The truly pivotal moment in the British rise to ascendancy in India was

Lavoisier: Tax-collecting (and doomed) scientist.

not their victory over the Nawab of Bengal and his French allies in the Battle of Plassey in 1757, but the landmark event of 1765 that we came across in chapter 1: the grant by the Mughal Emperor to the East India Company of the *diwani*. For an annual payment of £350,000, the Company took over the entire tax farming machinery of the Mughals. Robert Clive—"Clive of India" and the victor at Plassey—was alarmingly frank about the attractions of the deal, which he saw as "obtaining the absolute possession of these rich kingdoms; and that with the Moghul's own consent, on condition of paying him less than a fifth of the revenues thereof."[32] All seemed set for the Company (and the British government) to make some easy money. But, as we have seen, things did not turn out as the British had hoped.

The tax farmers often also became in effect lenders to the crown. They advanced money secured by future revenues and were either paid explicit interest for doing so or adjusted the terms of the lease contract to the same effect. The monarch, however, always had the option of defaulting, either canceling the contract or reneging on the debt. And this they often did. Between 1598 and 1655, only a third of leases in France went to their specified length.[33] The farmers also occasionally took on significant spending responsibilities on behalf of the crown—paving the streets of Paris, for instance[34]—subtracting what they spent from payments to the government, and so avoiding the shipping of specie or complex banking arrangements. The *fermiers généraux* in particular thus came close to being an agency for the implementation of all aspects of fiscal policy. The monarch, of course, could have cut out these middlemen, taken control of revenue collection, and borrowed elsewhere. But there was a catch. Building an effective revenue system required investment, financing that investment required borrowing, and—given the inadequacy of other regal collateral—borrowing required having an effective revenue collection system. In effect, the monarch's hands were tied.

Tax farmers have been almost universally reviled, from the collaborators with Rome to the *fermiers généraux*. Even the mild-mannered Dutch rose up against their tax farmers, the 1748 *pachter* riots being "the most significant . . . in the Republic's history."[35] Homes in Amsterdam were ransacked, and the politicians dragged from their beds to end tax farming there and then. As late as 1874–1875, the Christians of Bosnia revolted against Ottoman tax farmers, leading to the effective takeover of Bosnia by the Habsburgs.[36]

The demise of farming was not always violent, however, and it came at very different times—some surprisingly recent. In Britain, it ended in the early 1680s. But in Russia, farming of the tax on vodka by hundreds of regional syndicates—accounting for something like a third of all Imperial revenues—lasted until 1863. In the Ottoman Empire, "tax farming . . . dominated the Islamic world from the Mediterranean to the Indian Ocean, from the earliest days to the early modern period."[37] And the Dutch, though no longer tax farming at home, farmed out the taxes in Java until 1925. There are reports of *octroi*—taxes on entry into some local area—being farmed in Pakistan until very recently.[38]

What are we to make of the long and not wholly glorious history of tax farming? Compared to the use of salaried public officials as tax collectors, tax farming offers three potential advantages.

The first is efficiency. A private enterprise will seek to maximize profits, which requires that it minimize the costs of doing whatever it chooses to do: a core argument in favor of privatization generally. And in efficiency terms, the *fermiers généraux* at least are generally reckoned to have done a reasonable job. Some were notably diligent and serious. One reason we know so much about them is because Lavoisier was extraordinarily scrupulous and analytical in his record-keeping. Another farmer used his profits to build the Canal du Midi in southern France. The returns that the *fermiers* earned on the money they put into farming seem to have been high, but not outrageously so.[39] And when their accounts finally came to be closed in 1806, it turned out that the *fermiers*, alleged by the Jacobins to have defrauded the king of 130 million livres, were in fact owed more than 70 million.[40] Arguably, they were victims of their own success. Had the *fermiers* not collected indirect taxes so effectively, pressures to address the weakness of the exemption-riddled *taille*—administered in essence by a salaried bureaucracy—would likely have been still greater, and the chances of building a more equitable tax system correspondingly higher. And had that happened, the farmers might have survived rather longer.

The second advantage of farming is that, because the right to collect is sold for a fixed fee, it provides government with certainty as to its receipts. If revenue potential turns out to be lower than expected, perhaps because of hard times or an outbreak of war, it is not the government that suffers but the farmers—who correspondingly gain, of course, if things turn out better than expected. In practice, however, farmers often managed to renegotiate terms if things turned out badly: In 1744, for instance, the *fermiers généraux* negotiated a deal with reduced payments in the event of war, so leaving some risk with the Crown. The third advantage of farming is that it provides strong incentives for tax collection, because the collector gets to keep each additional dollar or livre they collect.

Against these advantages are two main downsides. One is that farmers may have only limited incentives to undertake investments that will enhance the long-run capacity to collect revenue: The lease having a fixed term, they may not be sure they will recoup the full value of such investments. One response to this problem was the emergence of "cabal" tax farming: restricting farming to a small and long-lived group. The *fermiers généraux* were an evolving partnership with just 60 members, and they did create an effective organizational, human, and physical infrastructure for collection. They were capable (at Lavoisier's suggestion) of building that wall around Paris, later staffed by Rousseau and others, to ease the collection of taxes on goods entering the city, with its ownership being vested in the crown.[41] From 1695, the Ottomans gave some tax farms for life (*malikâne*), which should have helped address the underinvestment problem—but then they found it difficult to retake the rights upon the death of the farmer.[42]

The second disadvantage, and the most fundamental, is the dark side of the strong incentive to collect: Farming creates a strong temptation to extortion and falsehood when assessing liabilities. While the farmer has little incentive to collude with the taxpayer to understate tax due, since that reduces their profit, they may be able to extract a bribe in order not to overstate a taxpayer's liability. More generally, farming implies an incentive to squeeze every last drop out of the taxpayer without regard to the damage it does to the taxpayers or to the future tax base. Adam Smith saw the risks:

Even a bad sovereign feels more compassion for his people than can ever be expected from the farmers of his revenue. He knows that the permanent grandeur of his family depends upon the prosperity of his people, and he will never knowingly ruin that prosperity for the sake of any momentary interest of his own. It is otherwise with the farmers of his revenue, whose grandeur may frequently be the effect of the ruin, and not of the prosperity of his people.[43]

Nor were governments, or even the tax farmers themselves, always oblivious to these concerns and the need to monitor collection activities. John the Baptist urged repentant tax collectors to "collect no more than what is appointed for you" (Luke 3:13). Imperial Rome had provisions for the crucifixion or burning of oppressive agents;[44] and the *fermiers* undertook demanding provincial tours to look into abuses.

The extent of abuse associated with farming is hard to judge. The question is not whether abuses took place or if farmers were hated; they clearly did, and were. In India, for instance, there were frequent reports of tax farmers torturing taxpayers and the desertion of tax-farmed villages.[45] Certainly the farmers' powers of entry and search were deeply resented. Voltaire, for instance, speaks of one episode in which the guards "stopped all the vehicles, searched all the pockets, forced their way into all the houses and made every kind of damage there in the name of the king, and made the peasants buy them off. . . . I cannot conceive why the people did not ring the tocsin against them . . . and why they were not exterminated."[46] The real question, however, is whether abuses were greater than they would have been under a tax bureaucracy of the time—opportunities for abuse and corruption arise under any system.

What was clearly different and objectionable about farming compared to a tax bureaucracy, however, was the perception that tax collection was directly serving to enrich the few, often including a direct cut for the monarch and his friends. Charles I, always anxious for money other than through parliament, received not only the annual rents paid by the farmers of the Irish customs but also half or more of their profits.[47] And in ancien régime France, there was outrage on learning that those sharing the farming profits included the royal mistresses, Mesdames de Pompadour and du Barry. Farming came to be seen as just one more element in, and symbol of, a massively unfair tax system.

Kickbacks—Legal and Otherwise

Today's tax administrations, as public bodies, look very different from tax farmers. But while the form has changed, the underlying challenges faced in the days of tax farming largely remain. The core problem of collecting the tax due is unchanged. The short-lease issue does go away in the presumptively infinitely lived public sector, but a choice still has to be made in allocating resources between current operations and building capacity for the longer term. Tax officials' private interests may still conflict with those of the public. The basic incentive problems are thus still there, arising at both the level of the individual employee and of the organization as a whole. Governments have tried to address them in a variety of ways, some of which, while short of farming, do—and, perhaps, will increasingly—use market-like incentives. After all, a whole spectrum of possibilities lies between full-blown tax farming, remunerating collectors only in relation to what they collect, and fixed-wage systems in which they receive the same remuneration however little or much revenue they bring in.

Rewarding tax administrators partly by allowing them to keep a share of the revenue they collect, for example, has been even more common than tax farming itself. The collectors of Cromwell's decimation tax kept 3 percent of the proceeds as a commission, and under the hearth tax of 1662, of each £1 collected, the constables took 2d, the high constables 1d, the Sheriff 4d, and the Clerk of the Peace 1d.[48] In the late seventeenth and eighteenth centuries, British excise officers kept about half of the amounts they seized,[49] were paid something like £50 (about a year's salary) for the detection and capture of smugglers,[50] and took a slice of the money they collected. "Poundage"—the retention by officers of part of what they collected—lasted in Britain until 1872. And we have seen how Chester Arthur profited from the moiety system.

Studies of modern versions of such schemes leave little doubt that they can be effective in raising revenue. A bonus program to reward Brazilian tax officials for collecting overdue taxes in 1989, for instance, resulted in fines (per inspection) increasing 75 percent faster than before the program was implemented.[51] Even more compelling evidence comes from a field experiment in the Punjab, Pakistan, exploring the impact of various incentive schemes for tax officials. This study found that a scheme awarding a bonus of up to 40 percent of additional amounts collected increased revenue growth by about 65 percent.[52]

As with tax farming, the primary risk of such schemes is extortion. The Punjab study did indeed find an increase in average bribes—although, somewhat strangely, no reduction in taxpayers' reported "satisfaction."

But corruption also arises, in the form of collusively understated liabilities, when officials are simply paid fixed wages. There is no easy way to address corruption so long as wages are independent of performance.[53] One possibility is to set the wage equal to what the official could earn if fired; but then, without stiff penalties, being corrupt is a one-way bet. Another is to set the wage below that alternative level, in the knowledge that the difference will be made up by corrupt means—which basically means giving up. A third method is to set the wage so high that the official's best choice is to be honest and not risk dismissal. That also provides a good incentive for efficiency in collection, and is presumably why the shrewd Frederick II of Prussia made systematic use of wounded war veterans as tax collectors: The job provided them support, and with some assurance of decent conduct, because they knew that they had few alternatives if dismissed for bad behavior. The trouble with this approach more generally is that the required wage would in many cases be huge: It is hard to match the potential return to corruptly waving through a truck full of cigarettes on which the tax due is in the hundreds of thousands of dollars.

So it is perhaps not surprising that commission payments to officials do not seem to have entirely gone away. Internal performance assessment these days does usually relate to nonrevenue criteria—the percentage of returns filed electronically, number of audits completed, and so on.[54] (That Punjab study, by the way, found this approach to have no effect on anything.) But there are signs that revenue-based incentive schemes have not vanished. One study of 12 tax administrations found that five of them used revenue collected as one criterion for bonus payments—the rationale in some cases being precisely to combat corruption in the form of collusive underreporting.[55] In Romania, for instance, the bonus was based on revenue in excess of agreed targets and the number of detected frauds, with the amount paid being up to three times the salary. The same study cites the Philippines, where up to 20 percent of the value of contraband could be paid to officers instrumental in its detection and seizure.

Certainly tax administrations themselves seem to recognize the power of revenue-based incentives in their relations with one another.

In the European Union, for instance, all tariff revenue ultimately goes not to the governments of the member states but to finance the operations of the Union itself. That revenue must be collected, however, by national customs agencies. This is not simply left to the good will of each of them, and nor are they recompensed by reimbursement of their costs: they get to keep 10 percent of whatever they collect.

Tax administrations have long used other measures to combat corruption. Promotion and seniority systems may perhaps help by deferring significantly increased wages until honesty is proven. The *fermiers généraux* tried something of this kind, introducing in 1768 the first pension system in the French civil service.[56] Some ways of trying to counter corruption are even simpler. One of the most basic is limiting one-on-one personal contact between taxpayers and those assessing them. The excise officers of eighteenth-century England, for instance, worked in pairs, which Robert Walpole believed meant "they chequed one another, which made them not liable to be bribed."[57] They were also periodically relocated around the country, and the routine but unpredictable relocation of customs officers practiced by Robert Hart—"to counteract a tendency to local entanglements"—was already long-established practice in the Chinese civil service.[58] Another method is to create tamper-proof trails of information on officers' actions. Sometimes this has been as simple a matter as ensuring that their ledger books had numbered and irremovable pages, and looking for unexplained changes. One eighteenth-century British exciseman recorded his panicked horror that in covering up a blemish in his ledger he made a hole in the page, knowing that "scratching erasing or altering any figure" was "almost unpardonable."[59]

While quite a lot is known about how to address corruption in tax administration, it continues to be a major concern and a reality of daily life in many countries. In 2015, Brazilian prosecutors launched an investigation into allegations that tax officials solicited bribes to reduce major companies' tax liabilities, with the estimated losses to the treasury put at $6.1 billion over 15 years.[60] That same year, Guatemala's current and former tax chiefs were detained in a crackdown on a ring, led by a top aide to the vice president, that defrauded the state through bribery and theft.[61] All this, of course, can not only damage the tax system but also undermine the perceived legitimacy of the state more widely.

Political interference poses yet another risk to honest tax administration. Martin Luther King, Jr., was repeatedly investigated by the IRS, and in 1960 was the first person ever criminally charged for tax fraud by the state of Alabama. Tried by an all-white jury, he was, amazingly enough, acquitted.[62] Richard Nixon saw political interference as part of the job description for the IRS commissioner, telling his aides John Ehrlichman and Bob Haldeman in May 1971:

> I want to be sure he is a ruthless son of a bitch, that he will do what he's told, that every income tax I want to see I see, that he will go after our enemies and not go after our friends. Now it's as simple as that. If he isn't, he doesn't get the job.[63]

In this spirit, Nixon allegedly encouraged an IRS program called the Special Service Staff to investigate his political opponents and harass them with audits.[64] Forty years later, in 2013, controversy erupted over allegations that the IRS had targeted conservative nonprofit groups for special scrutiny.

Plenty of others seem to have had the same idea of using the tax administration for political purposes. According to *The Economist*, in 2017, the Rwandan government detained an opposition candidate for president, as well as her mother and sister, for alleged tax evasion, while the Zambian Revenue Authority shut down a dissenting tabloid for unpaid taxes. And in Kenya, two NGOs that had challenged an election result were at least temporarily shut down for alleged tax improprieties.[65]

Tax Independence

One innovative (and fashionable) approach to improving the performance of tax administrations—not least by removing political interference—has been to transform them into "semi-autonomous revenue agencies" (SARAs). Developed first in South America—the recovery of revenue in Peru between 1992 and 1997 is the shining example[66]—this approach continues to spread in Africa, and it has been adopted in Canada and some other advanced countries, too.

SARAs remain in the public service and vary greatly among themselves. But they generally differ from the rest of the bureaucracy in two respects. One is in detaching the hiring and remuneration policies of the tax administration from usual civil service rules. This means moving, in effect, closer to the model described above in which the wage is set sufficiently high to attract the specialist skills that the job requires, providing some protection against corruption and encouraging sufficient diligence. The second difference comes from giving the tax administration enough independence to protect tax collection from political interference. And one aspect of the resultant autonomy is, in many cases, retention by the SARA of some proportion of the revenue it collects: tax farming on a modest scale. Such arrangements are generally rationalized in terms of protecting the revenue agency from the vagaries of budget allocations while also reducing the ability of the powerful to discipline it. But one would expect it also to have some impact on the enthusiasm with which the agency goes about collecting revenue.

Many practitioners remain guarded about the benefits of transforming traditional tax administrations into SARAs. Adoption can be highly disruptive: In some cases, the effort to sift out the corrupt requires all employees of the tax administration to reapply for their jobs. In at least one case, tax officials' reaction to a proposed shift to a SARA was to go on strike. While this disruption may ultimately be to the benefit of the administration and wider public, it can come at a stiff price in terms of damage to current operations. Many practitioners also argue that progress can be made along both of the lines above without creating a new agency. Such evidence as there is does, nonetheless, suggest that movement toward the SARAs has been associated with increased revenue.[67]

Privatizing Tax Collection

Although tax farming now seems archaic, the essential idea of farming—harnessing private incentives to public purposes—has a modern feel. In some cases, it came close to the model of a revenue-maximizing auction now much recommended for allocating rights to extract oil or to use parts of the radio spectrum. Around 120 BCE, for example, provincial tax farms were put up for bidding in Rome,[68] and the Dutch East

India Company auctioned the customs farm from 1744 to 1795. Back in Europe, the tax farms in France around the mid-sixteenth century were also allocated primarily by open, public competitive bidding. Elizabeth I of England followed suit, seeking "to grant our customs to farm so as there be sufficient persons that have offered to take them."[69]

Over the past decades, moreover, an increasingly wide range of activities once thought of as the exclusive preserve of the public sector—railways, air traffic control, airlines, energy supply—have in many places been transferred to the private sector. In Bangladesh and India, for example, tolls on bridges and roads and dues from public properties (such as lakes and forests) are often leased to private persons or firms. In 2006, the state of Indiana received $3.8 billion from an Australian-Spanish business consortium in exchange for ceding toll proceeds of the 157-mile Indiana Toll Road for the subsequent 75 years. That is not a million miles away from tax farming.

And indeed, privatization has also come to tax administration, although on a modest scale, through the outsourcing of some tax-collection tasks. This is not just a matter of contracting a few basic functions to private companies, which is now commonplace. About 67 percent of all tax administrations outsource something; nearly half of those, for instance, outsource their IT services.[70] In some countries, privatization has also reached one of the core functions of any tax administration: collecting unpaid taxes.

In the United Kingdom, beginning in July 2010, some tax collection of "lower-value debts" has been outsourced by HM Revenue & Customs to debt-collection agencies. Worldwide, as of 2013, 15 percent of revenue administrations outsourced debt collection, and 8 percent outsourced auditing—with both proportions on the rise.[71] More than 40 U.S. states have used private debt collectors to assist in collecting unpaid tax debt. In 2017, the IRS announced that it would begin using four private debt-collection companies to help collect overdue tax payments. Under this scheme, the companies keep up to 25 percent of the delinquent debt they collect. Although the Joint Committee on Taxation estimated that this outsourcing could bring in $2.4 billion of revenue over a decade, not everyone was thrilled. The head of the U.S. Office of the Taxpayer Advocate, Nina Olson, worried that when this approach had been tried in the past the outside collectors used "psychological tricks" to coerce tax debtors into making payments they could not afford. Although earlier programs were discontinued because costs outstripped collections, the latest program raised $213 million in fiscal year 2019 at a cost of $65 million.[72]

Full-blown tax farming is not coming back any time soon. Nonetheless, tax administrations can be expected to continue experimenting with ways of harnessing private incentives, at both institutional and personal levels, to overcome the millennia-old problems of balancing the need to collect revenue against the risks of corruption and abuse that are inherent in the power to tax. As has been discovered in other areas of economic life, so in tax collection there may be more scope for the operation of market-type incentives than often thought.

How Big Should Tax Administrations Be?

Tax administration is big business, and has been for a long time. The syndicate holding contracts in Bithnia (northwest Anatolia) in the first century BCE reportedly employed tens of thousands,[73] and the tax farms of Augustan Rome employed about 20,000 people.[74] Lavoisier estimated the number of full-time employees of the *fermiers généraux* at around 24,000 in 1774; only the army and navy had more. In England, there were already 2,500 revenue officials by 1690.

But their size does vary quite widely. The IRS, by international standards, is actually relatively small. As of 2013, its administrative costs came to 0.47 percent of revenue collected, the fifth lowest of 28 OECD countries with comparable data; much lower than, for instance, the 0.73 percent of HM Revenue & Customs in the United Kingdom.[75] There may be very good reasons for the low figure in the United States: Unlike other administrations, the IRS does not collect any VAT or sales tax. Opinion in the United States nonetheless varies from those who see the IRS as horribly bloated to those who see it as desperately under-resourced. Who is right? How, that is, can one decide whether a tax administration ought to be bigger or smaller?

One simple answer is that—taking the tax rules themselves as given—a tax administration should be expanded as long as an additional dollar spent on it brings in more than one dollar of tax revenue. Following this rule would maximize revenue collected net of the costs of collecting it. Tempting though it is, this is the wrong answer.

An immediate problem is that this rule ignores the additional compliance costs incurred by taxpayers when enforcement expands. These costs are borne not only by evaders but also by those who would never contemplate evasion but incur time and trouble because of the additional information they are required to keep and the occasional audit they must endure. As we saw earlier, these compliance costs can be much larger than the costs incurred by the administration itself.

But there is another problem with the net-revenue-maximizing rule.[76] Take, just to illustrate, the numbers from the IRS outsourcing of some debt-collection services mentioned above: the $213 million that the program brought in and the $65 million that it cost to administer. Now suppose (we do not know the truth) that it also gave rise to $40 million of compliance costs. The $213 million extra revenue exceeds $65 million, and even $65 million plus $40 million. The problem with this comparison is that it compares apples and oranges. The $65 million of administrative costs and the $40 million of compliance costs are real resource costs, in terms of people's time, computers, and such. The revenue collected, in contrast, turns into spending by the government. And what makes collecting tax revenue worthwhile, as we saw earlier, is that the government believes the spending it finances is socially more valuable than whatever use the private sector would have done with that money: That $1 transferred from the private sector enables spending that is really worth, in social terms, say, $1.20; so it is worth 20 cents more to society than whatever would have happened if the resources had not been transferred to the government. So the true social value of the $148 million net receipts under the debt collection program is just 20 percent of that amount, which is $29.6 million. That it is much smaller than the resource costs of collecting it, $105 million.

The key points here are that resources are used up in enforcing and complying with tax rules, and that taxation does not create additional resources but simply transfers them to the government. Thus, expanding tax administrations whenever doing so raises more in additional revenue than it costs will result in tax administrations that are too large.

Tax Tech

Technology has always been important for tax administration. Perhaps the most exquisite example is to be found in the Beijing tax museum. (Yes, there are such things.) These are the *jie*, cast in 323 BCE to enforce a tax exemption granted by King Chu Huai for the river transportation of specified goods. They consist of two halves, each with gold and silver inlaid in bronze: one half was carried with the ships, the other held by the customs authorities. Only if the two matched, and the very precise conditions of cargo and route engraved on the *jie* were met, could the ships pass untaxed. Their shape speaks to a still older practice of matching parts of a split piece of bamboo. At around the same time, Ptolemaic Egypt was equipped with technology tracking the height of the Nile in flood, which determined how good the harvest would be—which could then be used, in presumptive fashion, to set tax rates.[77]

Over the centuries, tax administrations have taken advantage of the tools becoming available to them. But much of what they were doing—weighing, counting, searching, watching—remained largely unchanged. Their work benefited from technological advances— uniformity of weight and measures, von Leeuwenhoek's work on estimating the volume of liquid in a barrel—but was hardly transformed by them. The coming of the steam engine made little difference to the work of the tax inspector standing in the rain and counting windows. What has made a big difference to tax collection, and now more than ever, is the enhanced ability to collect, analyze, and act on large amounts of data.

The tools for effectively implementing mass taxation described in chapter 12—withholding, self-assessment, informed audit, and the use of third-party information—would simply not be feasible without the

Beauty in tax administration: The *Jie* of ancient China.

capacity to deal with massive amounts of information. The ideas of cross-checking millions of VAT invoices, or of routinely sharing information about thousands of taxpayers between tax administrations, were unthinkable even 20 years ago. Electronic filing of tax returns is now the norm in many advanced countries. And several have moved even further, using the third-party and other information they receive to issue "pre-filled" (also called "pre-populated") income tax returns. Come tax time, taxpayers are presented, often by e-mail, with a tax return that is largely filled out. They just need to click if it is okay as is, or correct it if it is not.

Creative applications of new (or new-ish) technologies now abound. In 2014, the Buenos Aires provincial tax agency used drones to identify some 200 mansions and about 100 swimming pools that had not been declared by their owners, who were then subject to fines summing to about $2 million: a good return on drones that cost about $10,000 each, even by the standard we set just above. The Indonesian tax authority uses drones to catch tax evaders who underreport the size of their plantations or the value of their mineral extractions.[78] In a similar spirit, the Italian government launched in 2007 a Ghost Buildings program, which aimed to unearth properties not included in the land registry, and so hidden from tax authorities, by overlaying aerial photographs and digital land registry maps. The program uncovered more than 2 million parcels with ghost buildings.[79] And in 2010, the Greek government used police helicopters to film homes owned by affluent families; they discovered 16,974 swimming pools, quite a bit more than the 324 that had been self-reported.[80]

The temptation is to think that technology is a solution in itself, offering at least the prospect that developing countries, less encumbered with legacy technologies, could even leapfrog over the administrations of some advanced countries. For instance, among developed countries, Estonia, perhaps most notably, has achieved remarkable things by using technology to improve tax collection; and so has Kenya.[81] But we should not get too carried away. Just because governments acquire massive amounts of information about, say, their residents' assets abroad does not mean that they can absorb and make good use of it. And governments are not always good (putting it mildly) at large projects to upgrade their information systems. The experience of the United Kingdom in trying, from 2003, to introduce a system of tax credits to be administered by the revenue agency, not the benefit office, is not atypical. The policy and its design were inherently complex, and paying benefits proved to require skills and work practices quite different from those needed to collect taxes. In the event, the system itself fell way short. It sometimes confused people with similar names. This was not all the fault of the IT system, but one way or another—including through organized criminal fraud—the government ended up overpaying more than a billion pounds of tax credits. The next government returned the responsibility for making payments, under a reformed credit system, back to the benefits agency.

But taxpayers, and especially those looking to evade their liability or even obtain fraudulent payments, can also exploit technology. Take, for instance, an idea for using technology to strengthen tax enforcement that seemed to be to dye for. We mentioned in chapter 9 that in the United States, the tax on diesel fuel depends on its final use: lower if for off-road use (such as farm tractors or for residential heating) and higher for use in on-road motor vehicles. Because the tax is collected prior to the final use, how can the differential rate system be enforced? Starting in 1993, the U.S. government instituted a dyed-fuel program as an easy way to tell whether untaxed fuel was being used in on-road vehicles. When the nontaxable fuel is dyed red, pulling over a truck and finding dyed fuel in the tank is pretty good evidence of tax evasion. This idea sounds great, and has been copied around the world. The only problem is that the dye can be removed. In 2010, authorities discovered in County Armagh in Ireland an illegal diesel plant capable of removing the dye from 8.5 million liters of fuel per year—costing taxpayers around £5.5 million.[82]

Examples abound of taxpayers finding ways to outmaneuver the tax authorities. We have seen how zappers can undermine electronic cash registers. Fraudsters have even proved adept at turning new technologies to their advantage. In 2015, for example, criminals used stolen data to gain access to past tax returns of more than 100,000 people through an app on the IRS's website, and then used the stolen information to file fraudulent tax returns, receiving $50 million in refunds before the IRS detected the scheme.[83] In Eastern Europe, they found ways, by making very large numbers of small refund claims, of exploiting a (sophisticated) system that followed the standard "good practice" of focusing control on larger refund claims. Digitalization may become an arms race between administrators and imaginative dishonest taxpayers. And a centuries-long track record of tax administrations playing catch up with tax avoidance schemes—the private sector finds a scheme, the administration closes it down, the private sector finds another one, and so on—does not inspire full confidence that the administrations will win.

So far, most applications of technology to tax administration have been trying to do what is done already, just better. The task of a drone looking for swimming pools is not that different, after all, from that of an inspector looking for chimneys. And customs officials from centuries back would understand what the non-invasive scanning of cargo containers is trying to do. Electronic VAT invoices provide an easier way of tracking and checking than paper ones do, but the information they contain is much the same. And electronic filing involves much the same forms as does manual filing. But we will see in chapter 15, when we come to look the future in the face, that the opportunities created by digitalization are likely to prove much more fundamental—as are the new problems.

———

"The whole subject of tax policy and administration," says David Foster Wallace in *The Pale King* "is dull. Massively, spectacularly dull."[84] Having persevered with the book this far, we hope you disagree. And by now, we have some fairly clear ideas of what makes a tax system well designed and effectively enforced. The hard part is putting that wisdom into practice. That is the subject of the final part of this book, which starts by looking at the reality—usually ugly, often dispiriting, but also chalking up some surprising successes—of creating tax systems.

PART V

Making Taxes

The Nation should have a tax system which looks like someone designed it on purpose.

WILLIAM E. SIMON[1]

14

Taxing and Pleasing

To tax and to please, no more than to love and to be wise, is not given to men.

EDMUND BURKE[1]

IN THE Soviet Union of the early 1920s, the Politburo deliberated the future of agricultural taxation:

RYKOV: "Each peasant raises the question whether, if he doesn't join the collective farm, he will have to pay a tax and bear all kinds of burdens. . . . it will be a coercive system."
TROTSKY: "Not coercive but stimulative."[2]

The making of tax rules is not always quite so cynical, but it is rarely pretty. "Laws," said Jon Godfrey Saxe (or Bismarck),[3] "like sausages, cease to inspire respect in proportion as we know how they are made." This chapter looks at how tax rules get made in practice, and how this process, always unlovely, sometimes somehow produces a palatable outcome.

The Finance Minister's Dream

Smuggling was big business in eighteenth-century England. And a violent one. Behind the portly vicar enjoying a surreptitious brandy, or the genteel shopkeeper taking tea with his friends, were highly organized

Smugglers make sure that the English can have a nice cup of tea.

and often vicious criminal enterprises. There was fighting on the beaches, and on the landing grounds. There was fighting on the sea, where the customs boats were often outgunned. And there was fighting inland. Between 1723 and 1736, 250 customs officers were beaten and six murdered.[4]

Prominent among the smuggled goods was tea. In just one east coast county, Suffolk, a Parliamentary Committee was told in 1745 that 1,835 cartloads of tea had been brought ashore untaxed, with armed guards of up to 70 men taking them inland. Organized gangs had 20,000 members.[5] And while the taste for tea was growing, revenue from duties on tea—a significant source of revenue—was actually falling.[6] In 1745, Prime Minister Henry Pelham took an axe to this social and fiscal problem. He halved the duties on tea—from something more than 100 percent to around 50 percent.[7] This led to a large fall in price to the tea drinker. Purchases of legal, taxed tea tripled. This expansion of the quantity taxed was more than enough to outweigh the lower rate, so that the revenue from duties on tea actually went up. Comparing the 5 years before and after the reduction, they nearly doubled.

This, of course, is any finance minister's dream: cut taxes and yet still collect more revenue. Everyone is happy (or at least the losers are not well-placed to complain). The idea that behavioral responses—less smuggling, in the eighteenth-century case of tea in England—might lead to such a large expansion of the tax base that revenue increases when tax rates are cut—was not new even in Pelham's day. It dates back at least to the Muslim philosopher Ibn Khaldûn, who wrote in 1377: "At the beginning of a dynasty, taxation yields a large revenue from small assessments. At the end of the dynasty, taxation yields a small revenue from large assessments."[8]

Others who have made the same point over the years include[9] Jonathan Swift, Adam Smith, David Hume, Jean-Baptiste Say, James Madison, and Alexander Hamilton. Nowadays, the idea has come to be associated with the Laffer curve, scribbled (according to legend) by Arthur Laffer—who had served on President Ronald Reagan's Economic Policy Advisory Board—on a napkin in a Washington, DC, restaurant in 1974. The logic underlying the curve is straightforward. A tax on some endeavor at a rate of 100 percent[10] will raise no revenue, because if people get no return from doing something, they will not do it. So long as a lower tax rate would raise positive revenue, there must be some rate less than 100 percent at which revenue reaches its highest possible level. And then it must be the case that increasing the rate beyond that level will actually reduce revenue. Fair enough. Of course, the trouble is that this tells us nothing about what that critical revenue-maximizing tax rate actually is. The policy implications are profoundly different if revenue is maximized at 10 percent or at 90 percent. Pelham took a guess, and the initial tax on tea was indeed above the revenue-maximizing tax rate. But where we are on the Laffer curve in any context these days is rarely obvious.

In fact, beyond a few examples like Pelham's cut in the tea duty—or a cut in the coffee excise a few years before[11]—it is hard to find examples of major tax reforms that led to lasting revenue gains by reducing the tax rate. The main candidate for a Laffer-curve effect of recent years was the Russian "flat tax" reform of 2001, mentioned in chapter 5. This involved slashing higher rates of 20 and 30 percent to establish a single rate of 13 percent[12] and scaling back some exemptions. In the year after, revenue from the personal income tax increased by about 23 percent. This seemed like a Laffer/Pelham-curve phenomenon and attracted great attention—and much emulation: Over the next few years, a dozen or so countries adopted some form of flat tax.[13] But the consensus now is that the reform in Russia did not do much to increase labor supply or investment. Tax compliance did improve substantially, partly because of a simultaneous enforcement crackdown that tended to increase revenues, but not by enough to outweigh the reduced rate.[14]

In the United States, revenue increases did not follow, as some claimed they would, when the Reagan administration sharply cut income tax rates in 1981. Nor did revenues grow in Kansas, when a new governor slashed tax rates in 2012: After the tax cut, the state's economic record badly lagged its neighbors and it collected less revenue, forcing it to cut spending on roads and schools.[15]

Pelham's triumph has become a fool's errand, an undertaking almost certain to fail: There is little evidence that major taxes around the world

Art Laffer's napkin.

are often above levels at which revenue would be increased by cutting rates.

The important truth remains, nonetheless, that behavioral responses tend to reduce the revenue loss from cutting tax rates even if they do not reverse it. "Static" revenue estimates that ignore responses to changed incentives and human ingenuity in avoidance and evasion will always overestimate both the revenue loss from tax cuts and the revenue gain from tax increases. Quantifying the revenue effects of responses to tax changes—known as "dynamic scoring"—is not easy. And it can be contentious. In the United States, the estimated static revenue loss over

10 years from President Trump's 2017 Tax Cuts and Jobs Act was about
$1.5 trillion dollars. Advocates of the reform commonly claimed that its
effects on behavior would be so strong as to recoup this revenue loss. The
nonpartisan Joint Committee on Taxation, however, estimated that only
about $0.5 trillion would be made up in this way. This is, of course, just
an informed guess. But precision is not the point of dynamic scoring. Its
purpose is to provide a broad reality check on the revenue impact of tax
reform—which, given politicians' tendency to want to please by cutting
taxes while vaguely invoking behavioral responses to wave away charges
of fiscal irresponsibility, is often much needed.

Starving the Beast

The finance minister's dream is of cutting taxes and yet increasing tax
revenue. Other dreamers like cutting tax rates precisely because they
will lose revenue, and so constrain governments that they see as being
bloated by the pursuit of their own interests or those of some narrow
clique. It was on these grounds, we saw in chapter 11, that some see the
downward pressure on corporate tax revenues from international tax
competition as a good thing.

This view was articulated most forcefully by Geoffrey Brennan and
the 1986 Nobel Laureate James Buchanan, who thought of government
as a "leviathan" (a biblical sea monster) concerned not with citizens'
welfare but only with maximizing its own size and, hence, inclined to
massive overtaxation. The view one takes of this depends, of course, on
what one thinks of the public spending that tax revenue finances. Certainly, tax dollars have often been frittered away on pointless projects,
benefiting only a powerful few, or simply pilfered. Everyone has their
favorite "bridge to nowhere,"[16] and another book could be written
about governments' spending follies over the millennia. Ultimately,
however, what one person sees as a valuable use of public resources—
perhaps for redistribution—another sees as waste; and meaningful dialogue sometimes goes little further.

This leviathan view of government turns much standard thinking
about taxes on its head. It means, most curiously, that good taxes are

bad: Improvements in the tax technology that make it less costly for government to raise revenue are actually undesirable, as they enable already-bloated government to get even bigger.[17] The curious implication is that governments should be constrained to use only tax instruments with very high excess burden.

An alternative way to limit government size, without wasting resources through inefficient tax policies, is through constitutional restrictions. About half of all U.S. states' constitutions restrict the level or growth of government revenue or spending to a fixed numerical target or else to increases in population, inflation, or personal income. Others require a supermajority of each chamber of the state's congress or voter approval of amendments for passage of new taxes. At the federal level, the idea of a balanced-budget amendment to the Constitution, stipulating that federal spending not exceed federal receipts, has been volleyed back and forth over the years. One notch down from constitutional limits are legislative fiscal rules of various kinds. These have spread rapidly since the Global Financial Crisis: by 2015, more than 90 countries had some such rule in place.[18] They are often aimed more at correcting deficit bias—the tendency for governments to pile up excessive debt—than at limiting the size of government. But rules limiting deficits or debt can be met not only by limiting spending but also by increasing revenues. Rules setting some explicit upper limit to total tax revenue are in fact rare, although there may be indirect limits. About 20 countries set upper limits on spending,[19] which are more directly aimed at curtailing the growth of government: Sweden, for instance, sets a 3-year rolling limit on government spending. Combined (one hopes) with overall fiscal responsibility, and these rules often operate together with debt/deficit rules, these spending limits set an implicit upper limit on revenue.

And then there is the strategy of deliberately "starving the beast": pursuing tax cuts expressly to create deficits that will induce deficit-fearing legislators to cut back on spending.[20] The problem with this approach is that the evidence suggests it does not work, and it may even backfire:[21] Financing by increased deficits rather than increased taxes might lead voters to perceive the provision of government services not manifestly accompanied by taxes as being cheaper than it really is, and so support more government activity, not less.[22]

From Coventry to K Street

People and businesses are constantly trying to shape tax policy to suit themselves. And when big money is involved in pending legislation, big lobbying money follows. So it was, for example, leading up to the 2017 Tax Cuts and Jobs Act. According to Public Citizen, a nonpartisan watchdog organization, more than 4,600 lobbyists were engaged in lobbying specifically on the tax reform. And just in the last quarter of that year, the National Association of Realtors spent $22.2 million on lobbying, the Business Roundtable laid out $17.3 million, and the U.S. Chamber of Commerce spent $16.8 million.[23]

The Naked Truth about Lobbying

As so often in tax matters, however, there is little inherently new in this. Daniel Defoe, author of *Robinson Crusoe*, wrote powerfully in support of the distillers in the early part of the Gin Craze, before switching sides to become an equally powerful advocate for their opponents. Tom Paine spent 2 years in London lobbying for higher pay for excisemen. The most romantic of all tax lobbyists, however, is Lady Godiva, known for her golden locks rather than her gold-filled PACs.[24]

The story goes that, in the early eleventh century, Lady Godiva pleaded with her husband, Leofric, the Earl of Mercer and Lord of Coventry, to lighten taxes on the people of Coventry. Leofric, doubting the strength of her commitment, agreed to do so if she were to ride naked on a horse through the town. She called his bluff, but ordered the people of Coventry to remain indoors with their windows and doors barred. Loosening her long hair to cover her as a cloak, she rode through the silent streets unseen. Except, that is, for one man, Tom, who was unable to resist looking (hence the term, "Peeping Tom"). He unbarred his window but, before he could satisfy his gaze, was struck blind. Less remembered, but more to the point of the exercise, Leofric, true to his word, freed the town from all tolls[25]—except those on horses.[26]

Lady Godiva, famous tax protestor.

Lady Godiva was apparently not in the pocket of any special interest. But most lobbyists are and always have been. During their campaign in the late seventeenth century to repeal leather duties in
England, the leather trades presented more than 150 petitions from 100
locations to Parliament.[27] In 1694, playing-card manufacturers levied
a subscription fee to cover their expenses in seeking repeal of the excise tax on cards.[28]

By the early eighteenth century, lobbyists had developed five main
types of argument against proposed tax increases, which still remain
their stock in trade. The first is that the trade or occupation in question
would suffer decreases in production, increased unemployment, and
other dire consequences. The authors of the classic account of the run
up to Tax Reform Act of 1986 could scarcely contain their incredulity at
the claims then made:

According to various studies circulated on Capitol Hill, the bill [which contained provisions to scale back investment incentives] would force "a dose of Jonestown-type cyanide" on the construction industry, raise apartment rents by 20 to 40 percent, destroy old urban neighborhoods, and jeopardize "the oral health of the American people." Horse breeding would fall 18 percent, American Samoa would be devastated, and canned tuna would become obsolete.[29]

The second tack is that the proposal is unworkable: It would incur so much administrative cost as to make the tax more trouble and expensive than it is worth. A third, as circumstances allow, is that it would violate the constitution. The fourth is macroeconomic: that it would, for example, adversely affect the balance of trade.[30]

Finally, advocates often display an apparently selfless concern that the questioned legislation would harm the well-being of others. Opponents of Britain's proposed excise taxes in 1733, for example, argued that they were not merely defending the economic interests of the tobacco and wine business but also protecting the political interests of every British subject, because the excise-tax proposal deprived Englishmen of their liberties.[31] This form of argument is common these days, with the representatives of special interests selflessly focusing on the impact not on them but on the innocent, vulnerable, average Joes and Janes. In 2017, in response to the proposal for a "border-adjusted" form of business tax (along the lines of the destination-based cash flow tax (DBCFT) discussed in chapter 11)—which would tax imports and exempt exports—a lobbying group supported by the Koch brothers (who have extensive oil interests), launched a television ad saying the scheme would "harm hard-working families that deserve relief from the tax code, not a new consumer tax that would drive up the cost of everyday items."[32] The ad did not point out that the tax would in effect be accompanied by an offsetting subsidy to wages, nor did it address the impact on the profits of oil-import-related industries. As Huey Long put it succinctly: "You have to convince them it's for them even if it isn't."[33]

Even proposed tax changes that sound innocuous threaten some interest. It would be hard to object, one might think, to return-free tax filing, as in the "Tax Filing Simplification Act of 2016." But the private tax software industry, led by the maker of industry-leading TurboTax, found that it would be surprisingly harmful for the rest of us. Not only would it

> create a tremendous and potentially harmful conflict of interest for the American people by enshrining roles of tax preparer, tax collector, tax auditor and tax enforcer together in one entity, the IRS, but the system's very creation would also be a huge burden for taxpayers. . . . The proposal would make the essential tax administration work of the IRS impossible, while disadvantaging the taxpayer.[34]

No, we don't quite understand that either.

I Can't Believe It's Not (Taxed Like) Butter

Sometimes tax lobbying is about killing off your competitors.

In the 1860s, the price of butter in France was soaring, and the anticipated war with Prussia threatened to worsen the looming shortage. In response, Napoleon III offered a prize at the Paris World Exhibition in 1866 to anyone who could create a cheap, plentiful butter substitute. The French chemist Hippolyte Mège-Mouriès hit on the idea that pure oil resembling butterfat could be extracted from beef fat. This could be combined with milk to form an inexpensive butter-like substitute, which he called "oleomargarine." The U.S. Dairy Company bought Mège-Mouriès's American patent in 1874 and subsequently introduced margarine to consumers in the United States. (And, yes, Mège-Mouriès did win a prize.)

The U.S. dairy industry, however, soon took notice of this low-cost alternative to real butter, and urged legislators to limit (preferably eliminate) the competition it posed. In 1877, two states introduced labeling laws, ostensibly to prevent consumers from being fooled into thinking they were purchasing butter. In 1882, local dairy associations united to form the National Association for the Prevention of Adulteration of Butter, to combat the "adulteration and risk to health" supposedly posed by margarine. Lurid anti-margarine propaganda featured horrific tales of repulsive ingredients used to make "bogus butter." By 1886, 22 states had some form of anti-margarine legislation, with 7 simply prohibiting its manufacture and sale.[35] By 1900, 30 states had laws regulating the color of margarine, to ensure that it did not look too butter-like; five states required it to be dyed pink.

Taxes were soon added to the arsenal of butter protection. In 1886, the Federal Margarine Act slathered a special 2 cents per pound tax on margarine and imposed annual license fees on margarine producers of $600 a year; wholesalers owed $480 annually, and retailers had to remit $48 for the right to sell margarine. Supporters of the taxes hardly disguised their real intent. One congressman from cow-intensive Wisconsin was keen to prove the accuracy of Daniel Webster's view of the power of taxation: "I fly the flag of an intent to destroy the manufacture [of margarine] by taxing it out of existence."[36] By 1937, 31 states taxed oleomargarine.

And thus the U.S. dairy industry succeeded in winning over tax policy to its side. After all, for a business, owing no tax is better than owing some, but better still is a tax only on one's competitors.[37]

The Taxes Chain Store Massacre

In the 1920s, chain stores around the United States experienced explosive growth. J.C. Penney operated 312 stores in 1920; by 1930, it had 1,452. Walgreens grew to 440 outlets from 23 over the same decade, while A&P ballooned to 15,737 stores from 4,621.[38] The competition took note.

Small merchants, who were often politically powerful locally, started to organize "buy-at-home" campaigns. And state legislatures began to consider tax measures to contain the rise of chain stores.[39] The first of these were struck down in the courts, but in 1929, North Carolina and Indiana legislated chain-store taxes that survived court challenges. Louisiana passed a graduated chain-store tax based on the nationwide total of outlets, although only on Louisiana-based stores. Ultimately, 28 states, plus some municipalities, passed some kind of chain-store tax. The tide turned, however, in 1936, when a referendum in California rejected a new chain-store tax that featured—literally—an exponentially increasing marginal tax rate: $1 on the first store, $2 on the second store,

$4 on the third store, . . . $256 on the ninth store, and then $500 per store for the tenth store and additional outlets after that.

Meanwhile, and not for the first time, the use of taxation to achieve some intended outcome—in this case, to discourage big stores—was turning out to backfire. The chain stores "discovered that one of the best methods of minimizing the effects of the tax is to combine individual units into superstores, having a total business volume in excess of the combined sales of the formerly individual outlets."[40] No states passed similar chain-store taxes after the early 1940s, and by 1980, only six states still had chain-store tax laws on the books, none of them very harsh.[41]

The tension between small businesses and big corporate enterprises persists, as do the tax and regulatory responses. In 2004, San Francisco began requiring chain stores to obtain additional approvals to open out-lets in certain parts of the city and provided other retailers and city residents with opportunities to object. Walmart has become emblematic of the mom-and-pop-store-killing mammoth corporation, with critics charging that the Walton family owners benefit from a number of federal tax provisions as well as economic development subsidies from state and local governments that amount to $70 million per year.[42]

Small businesses also resent, with some reason, the ability of large multinationals to use clever schemes of the type we saw in chapter 11 to reduce their tax liability in ways that smaller businesses cannot: Not the least of those upset by Starbucks were the small local coffee shops. But it is the Internet that has revived the concerns of the 1930s in many countries. Huge remote sellers such as Amazon threaten not only the mom-and-pop stores but also brick-and-mortar chain stores and even behemoths like Walmart. And taxes may be one reason for their ascendancy.

Until very recently, U.S. law had held that states could not collect retail sales tax on sales by vendors in other states (including but not limited to those operating through the Internet) to customers within their borders, even though the same purchase would be taxed if made from a local storefront. The mom-and-pop stores argued, with some justification, that this practice provides a competitive advantage to the remote sellers. But this is changing. In 2018, the U.S. Supreme Court ruled that South Dakota could require out-of-state sellers (above a certain size) to remit sales tax on sales to its residents.[43] Many states are expected to adopt such rules in short order.

Similar issues arise at the international level, too, particularly in relation to "intangible services": things like professional services or downloadable software, which, unlike physical goods, cannot be intercepted and taxed at the border. VAT rules increasingly provide for the taxation of such services by the country of the purchaser, the difficulty being to ensure that sellers—who may have no physical presence in the buyer's country—are identified and registered. There are issues for goods, too, as low-value imports are often exempt from VAT; as the sales of such goods have expanded in volume, so the trend now is to lower the threshold at which VAT on personal imports becomes payable.

Emerging from COVID-19, many retail businesses face, at best, uncertain futures. Removing the tax biases that favor remote sellers is likely to become still more of a focus for policy makers—and for lobbyists.

One Man's Exemption

From seventeenth-century makers of playing cards to the expensively dressed executives in the elegant atriums along K Street in Washington, DC, what underlies lobbying is the asymmetry between the concentration of the benefits of particular tax measures on a small number and the dissipation of their costs among many others. "The exemption of one man," Gladstone reminds us, "means the extra taxation of another"[44]—or more likely, the taxation, in small amounts, of many others. Corralling many small losers is more costly than corralling a few winners.

Lobbying creates no resources but just diverts their use, in ways driven—despite the lobbyist's pretended concern with the ordinary Joe and Jane—more by private than by public interests. The vulnerability to special pleading it creates is one reason why economists are reluctant to recommend in practice the kind of excess burden-minimizing variation of tax rates across commodities that Frank Ramsey came up with in chapter 10: better to stick with uniform treatment, or what economists often call "neutrality."

But, experience suggests that sensible advice from economists is unlikely to prove an effective way to limit lobbying. More promising are rules designed to limit it. Moving between politics and lobbying could be limited. Constitutional rules may help: In Germany, for instance, tax measures that benefit particular groups are prohibited. Later in this chapter we will see some other tactics governments have used to defeat lobbies. But the fundamental asymmetry retains its force, making it hard for governments—often not as well informed about the impact of their measures as are those most directly affected—to take a firm Gladstonian line of equal treatment. In the past few years, civil society organizations have come to provide an important and increasingly effective check on some special pleading, and in protecting the general interest as they see it. But the distortion of tax systems through special pleading will remain one of the less savory ingredients in the sausage-making of tax policy.

You Just Don't Do That: Four Centuries of Not Taxing Food in Britain

Tax policy has its taboos: things that, even without much lobbying from special interests, wise governments find it better not to do. Many are specific to particular countries and cultures. It is a foolhardy policy maker who argues against tax exemptions for sales of the Bible or Koran.[45] In the United Kingdom, the taboo is the taxation of food.

Food sales are not taxed in the United Kingdom.[46] The standard rationale is that this is helpful to the poor, who spend a larger proportion of their income on food than do the rich. However, everyone who has looked seriously at the issue knows that this argument is at best incomplete and at worst is simply nonsense. Taxing food and using part of the revenue raised to increase existing social welfare payments could leave the poor better off, while leaving some money left over for cutting taxes or increasing public spending.[47] This is because the benefit of a zero tax rate goes overwhelmingly to the rich: They may spend a smaller proportion of their income on food, but they spend absolutely more on it and so derive a larger money benefit from its non-taxation. Policy makers understand that zero rating food makes little sense as a way of helping the least well-off, but nothing happens. Why? Maybe precisely because the rich and powerful understand all too well that they are the ones who truly benefit. But, whether that is true or not, Britain's failure to tax food emerges from a long tradition that is littered with political casualties.

Troubles with taxing food in England go back to the civil war of the 1640s. Before that, excises—taxes on domestically produced items (as opposed to tariffs, which are taxes only on imports)—were very modest.[48] On the continent, in contrast, they were already part of life—including excises on food. The Dutch had introduced what was effectively a tax on bread in 1574,[49] and many cities had long found taxing agricultural produce (among other things) coming in through their gates a handy source of revenue.[50] On the outbreak of war in 1642, English royalists and parliamentarians both looked to excises to finance their cause. For parliament, as we saw in chapter 2, it was John Pym who pioneered them. It began with excises on beer and some other drinks in 1643. (Consistent with wider traditions in tax policy making, the excises were imposed a few months after members of parliament had indignantly denied rumors that they planned to introduce them;[51] and the excises, when they came, were announced to be temporary.) But soon excises also appeared on meat, fish, and other food items, and the mood became foul. By 1647, there were riots in Smithfield Market,[52] and the army, increasingly powerful and radical, was demanding that the "excise . . . be taken off from such Commodities, whereon the poor People of the Land do ordinarily live."[53] The excises on meat, bread, and vegetables were removed;[54] others, notably that on beer, became an accepted part of everyday life.

A marker had been put down. Taxing things important to the poor could be politically problematic, and the excises in general remained deeply unpopular. Dr. Johnson caught the mood in later defining an excise as "a hateful tax levied upon commodities."[55] Things got so heated that officials once nailed a woman to a tree by her tongue simply for speaking badly of the tax.[56] Excises on some things important to the poor—beer, soap, salt, candles—did, nonetheless, prove more or less politically sustainable. Try to tax food itself, however, and the English could turn nasty.

They next showed this trait during the Excise Crisis of 1733–1734, which brought "one of the most shattering defeats ever suffered by a minister of the crown at the bar of public opinion."[57] A tax on food was not even being proposed: The idea was to introduce excises on tobacco and wine and reduce the land tax to 1 shilling on the pound.[58] But those who had had enough of Prime Minister Robert Walpole were able to provoke widespread fears that a much more broadly based excise tax was coming next: "There was hardly a town in England, great or small," reported Lord Hervey, "where nine part in ten of the inhabitants did not believe that this project was to establish a general Excise, and that everything they eat or wore was to be taxed."[59] The result was a political storm that even the most adept of prime ministers barely managed to survive. A hundred years later, the fight over the Corn Laws—a protective tariff on food imports—became, as seen in chapter 7, the defining political struggle of its day, with the upshot that the Tory party, seen as supporting a measure that raised the price of food, lost power for a generation.

Apparently not having learned their lesson, 50 years later, the Conservative Party again tore itself apart on the taxation of food. In 1903, the monocled, orchid-wearing high priest of British imperialism, Joseph Chamberlain, launched a campaign for "Imperial Preference." That meant preferentially low tariff rates for trade within the British Empire and protective tariffs against everyone else. Because much of Britain's food imports came from outside the Empire, the specter this created was of higher food prices.[60] Arthur Balfour, the Tory prime minister at the time—brilliant enough to be a Fellow of All Souls College at Oxford—had learned the lessons of British history: "The prejudice against a small tax on food," he said, "is a deep-rooted prejudice affecting the large mass of voters."[61] Despite his own doubts, however, Balfour did not manage to dispel the perception of his party as wanting to tax food. Electoral

Trader Joe Chamberlain puts a tax on food.

disaster followed, in 1906, with the Conservatives out of power until after the First World War.[62]

In former times, governments did not have the policy instruments that are now available, such as social assistance payments, to mitigate the impact of taxing food on the less well off. (Joseph Chamberlain did though have something of that sort in mind, seeing tariffs on imports from outside the Empire as one way to finance expanded old-age pensions.)[63] But it is not surprising that, however well they understand its inferiority as public policy, no British politician with a smattering of history dares suggest taxing food. If they had forgotten, the vehement reaction to a proposed (but quickly dropped) "pasty tax" in 2012 was a painful reminder.[64]

Games Governments Play

Policy makers can be as sneaky as lobbyists. They know that how voters react to and exert political pressure on tax policy depends on what the voters know about taxes and how they perceive them—and are often quite adept in manipulating both.

Vanishing Acts

"When a tax is blended with the Price of the Commodity," wrote an English pamphleteer in 1756, "the tax is forgot, or its Remembrance makes little Impression," whereas if a tax is assessed directly on the consumer, "it will be very disgustful."[65] Politicians have long had the same thought, having an obvious incentive, and often the ability, to hide taxes as one way to take advantage of taxpayers' behavioral quirks and cognitive limitations, or just plain ignorance.

They have developed many tricks to deliver "stealth taxes." Taxes can be presented as fees, when they actually cover more than the cost of any service being provided. Tax brackets and thresholds can be set in nominal amounts and unindexed, so that inflation quietly draws people into income ranges subject to higher rates. Income tax design, according to some social scientists, includes many features that exploit cognitive biases to reduce the tax burden perceived by taxpayers. This is accomplished through something marketing-science gurus call "price presentation," such as using discounts (as in deductions from a broad measure of income) and frequent but small disbursements (as in employer withholding).[66] Laboratory findings suggest such a strategy can work: People tend to underestimate a given total tax burden when it is spread among multiple taxes and broken into small pieces.[67] In practice, too, evidence suggests that what matters is not only how much we pay but how we pay it. Switching from manual, per-trip remittance of traffic tolls to automatic electronic charging has been found to make raising tolls easier politically, because the act of remittance is then less salient to drivers and voters.[68]

To some, the apparent painlessness of invisible taxes means that there will ultimately be too many of them, serving only to finance unworthy government spending. Many conservatives in the United States, for example, oppose the VAT precisely because they see it as both hidden from voters and as such an efficient "money machine" that it inevitably leads to big government[69]—in their minds, too big. To many Europeans, however, this visibility argument seems more than a little odd, as the receipts that consumers receive there typically show the precise amount of VAT due (at the retail level). Those same Europeans may also be irritated to find, when they arrive at a cash register in the United States, carefully counted payment in hand, that the prices posted on the shelf commonly do not include sales tax. Neither approach seems to leave the tax very hidden, though struggling for change may be a more effective reminder of the tax being charged than glancing at a receipt. What does seem to be the case, however, is that—whether or not it reflects some difference as to how the tax itself is perceived—these two approaches do have different behavioral effects: There is evidence that people buy less when posted prices on the shelf include the tax than when they do not.[70]

So are stealth taxes good or bad? They may have some advantages. After all, if people think the income tax is less disincentivizing than it really is, then the socially costly behavioral responses they would make, such as working less, will probably be smaller than otherwise. For instance, many people apparently act as if their marginal tax rate (the tax on earning another dollar) is actually their average tax rate (total tax divided by income), which, at least when there is not just a single rate applying to most people, is easier to compute and almost always less than their marginal tax rate. And so, when deciding whether to earn more money, they underestimate the tax penalty from so doing.[71]

But what incumbent politicians like about stealth taxes, of course, is an erosion of their accountability—which the rest of us should worry about. Awareness of the resources they are transferring to government is a pretty sure way to encourage people to take notice of what is done with their money. For this reason, some observers now emphasize the conscious payment of taxes as important for building responsible and responsive states. There are also signs that, in some sub-Saharan African countries, awareness of the VAT is associated with a more positive attitude to paying income tax.[72] The potential role of taxation in encouraging citizens to hold their governments accountable favors direct remittance of tax, evidently the most salient way to tax people. For this reason, it may even be desirable to have all but the very poorest remit some small amount of tax, even if the revenue this generates is less than the costs of collecting it. (The Incas had a strangely similar idea: When a province claimed to be unable to afford the standard tribute, each inhabitant would have to periodically remit a large quill of live lice, as a way of "teaching and accustoming them to pay tribute."[73] In this case, though, it was not the government being held accountable to its citizens but subjects being made accountable to their rulers.) Because inefficient and unfair taxes get more attention than efficient and fair ones, there is even a somewhat mad logic in this view of the world, suggesting that the worse a tax is in itself, the better it is for accountability. One does not have to go quite that far, however, to believe that salience in taxation is a lot better for the public at large than it is for politicians in office.

What's in a Name?

Competitive naming is another front in tax policy battles. When Prime Minister Addington reintroduced William Pitt's unloved income tax in 1803, one problem was what to call it. "Ministers have shewn a very unworthy desire," one critic complained, "that this tax should not be [called a tax upon income], but they have not yet hit upon any other name which can be properly applied to it."[74]

Opponents can be skillful at attaching distasteful names to whatever it is they oppose. Rarely more so than when, in the late 1990s, Republican opponents resolved to always refer to the U.S. estate tax (a name conjuring a levy based on wealth and privilege) as the "death tax" (conjuring two of life's more unpleasant aspects).[75] Jack Faris, president and chief executive officer of the National Federation of Independent Business, required everyone in his office to use the label; those who forgot paid $1 into a pizza fund. The label made its way to Capitol Hill in the late 1990s, where Newt Gingrich, Speaker of the House of Representatives, and others adopted it. In 2002, the estate tax rate was reduced and the exemption level increased.[76] How big a role the clever naming played in this is unclear—but it surely did not hurt.

Others have played the same game. In the United Kingdom, a 2016 Conservative Party proposal to reduce benefits if a single parent moved in with a partner or married was dubbed the "Love Tax" by the Liberal Democrats. And a Tory proposal to require elderly people to pay for care in their own home unless they have less than £100,000 in assets was gleefully christened the "dementia tax" by the Labour Party, so pinning the burden of the tax to about as vulnerable a group as one can imagine.[77] A 1971 New York law extending the retail sales tax to restaurant meals costing less than a dollar was christened the "hot dog tax" and inspired a petition for repeal signed by more than a million people.[78] Finally, the efforts to extend VAT to food served hot but designed to cool down became the doomed "pasty tax" mentioned above.[79]

Tax advocates can be no less imaginative, or misleading. By labeling a small tax on all financial transactions as a "Robin Hood" tax, the implication was sent that its real burden would somehow fall on rich bankers. But there is at least as much reason to suppose that it would largely fall on savers—and not necessarily well-off ones—because the tax would be triggered every time they bought or sold financial assets (directly, or indirectly through, for instance, pension funds).

Sometimes the name of a tax reflects an earmarking, strong or weak, of the proceeds. Many states of India, for example, levy what is known as a "cow cess,"[80] revenue from which is used to take care of stray cows, by constructing cow shelters and buying fodder.

Some tax names seem simply to be chosen by bored drafters in search of entertainment. Case in point: the Leaky Underground Storage Tank (LUST) fund. The acronym for the 2010 U.S. Foreign Account Tax Compliance Act, FATCA, is one letter short of its presumably intended fat cat target, and it is hard not to believe that the GILTI and BEAT acronyms of the 2017 Tax Cuts and Jobs Act reflect the mood of the tax code writers as they tried to counter multinationals' tax avoidance. And the true purpose of the ponderously titled House bill H.R.6690 in 2020—Bring Entrepreneurial Advancements to Consumers Here in North America— was eloquently revealed by its acronym: BEAT CHINA.

While the names of taxes sometimes clearly matter, tax has sometimes mattered for names. In Eastern Europe, most Jews, other than the wealthiest, did not get surnames until the Napoleonic years. Jews from Russia, Poland, Germany, and other countries taken by Napoleon were ordered to assume surnames, primarily for tax and conscription purposes. Some bureaucrats, it turned out, welcomed an occasion to supplement their income with a new kind of blackmail. Jews with means could buy surnames containing such pleasing attractive bits as *Gold, Fein* ("fine"), or *-blum* ("flower"). Those without were often stuck with such identities as *Schmalz* ("grease"), *Ochsenschwanz* ("oxtail"), or *Eselkopf* ("donkey's head").[81]

Oops

And sometimes, governments simply mess up.

In 1872, the U.S. government released its thirteenth Tariff Act, which reduced rates on many imported manufactured goods. Prior acts had specified that "fruit plants, tropical and semi-tropical for the purpose of propagation or cultivation" were exempt from import tariffs. Fruits themselves, however, were subject to quite substantial tariffs. In the 1872 act, however, a crucial comma (intended to be a hyphen) found its way between the words "fruit" and "plants," giving fruit importers a tariff exemption: a windfall worth millions of dollars. At first, the secretary of the treasury tossed out exemption claims on the grounds that the text was "clearly intended to read otherwise." However, 2 years later, the government capitulated: fruit imports were indeed free from tariff liability. Duties were subsequently refunded to the tune of $2 million, about 1 percent of the government's total tariff income in 1875.[82]

There is a suitably bizarre coda to this story. In the 1883 tariff act, fruits were exempt but vegetables were not. That led tomato producers to point out that, botanically speaking, tomatoes are fruit, and so should be exempt. The Supreme Court, however, was persuaded[83] that people really thought of tomatoes as vegetables (who would eat one for dessert?) and therefore, for the purpose of the customs tariff, tomatoes were, legally speaking, a vegetable. Shades of Jaffa Cakes, indeed.

Some Triumphs of Pretty Good Tax Policy

Governments tinker with their tax systems all the time. A rate change here, an exemption added (or rarer, removed) there. Much tax policy making remains as described by the playwright and politician Richard Brinsley Sheridan[84] in the eighteenth century:

256   TARIFF ACT OF JUNE 6, 1872.   [42D CONG.,

Diamonds, rough or uncut, including glazier's diamonds;
Dried bugs;
Dried blood;
Dried and prepared flowers;
Elecampane root;
Ergot;
Fans, common palm-leaf;
Farina;
Flowers, leaves, plants, roots, barks, and seeds, for medicinal pur-
poses, in a crude state, not otherwise provided for;
Firewood;
Flint, flints, and ground flint-stones;
Articles exempt   Fossels;
from duty on and after   Fruit, plants tropical and semi-tropical for the purpose of propaga-
August 1, 1872.   tion or cultivation;
Galanga, or galangal;
Garancine;
Gentian-root;
Ginger-root;
Ginseng-root;
Goldbeaters' molds and goldbeaters' skins;

A two-million-dollar comma.

First there comes the act imposing the tax; next comes an act to amend the act for imposing the tax; then comes an act to explain the act that amended the act, and next an act to remedy the defects of the act for explaining the act that amended the act.

A tax bill is like a ship . . . which put to sea on the first voyage before it was discovered that they had forgotten the rudder. After every voyage, it revealed some new defect . . . it had to be caulked, then to be new-planked, then to be new-rigged, then to be careened, and after all these expensive alterations, the vessel was obliged to be broken up and rebuilt.[85]

Sometimes, in this unending process of tax change, governments mess things up even more scandalously than by mistakenly inserting a comma. Sometimes, however, they make substantive structural changes—fundamental enough to be called "reform"—that work out pretty well. We have seen that the staggering costs of war have played an important role in spurring many such reforms. But there have been remarkable peacetime reforms, too, and here we look at some of these; "remarkable" meaning not that their merits are uncontested, but rather that even their opponents would recognize that the changes were more than tinkering.

It would be nice if these experiences gave clear guidance as to what makes good tax reform happen. Every tax reform, however, has its own peculiarities of constitution, procedure, electoral rules and cycles, its own personalities—and its own economic, social, and political contexts. In the United Kingdom, for instance, tax changes generally undergo little modification after being pulled from the chancellor's red case (handed down from Gladstone): Rejection of any substantive element would be taken as a vote of no confidence in the government. In the United States, in contrast, tax legislation generally goes through substantial changes in the House, Senate, and in subsequent reconciliation between the two.[86] The circumstances in which tax reforms happen are as remarkable in how they differ as in any similarities. Some degree of dissatisfaction with the prior system is a prerequisite (even if this is sometimes no more than a desire to undo the work of predecessors). Beyond that, we can detect only two clear essentials, both almost tautologically inherent in the idea of successful reform.[87] One is a clear vision of what a better system might be. This is not to say that reform needs to be guided by some explicit articulation of the fine ideas of vertical equity, excess burden, and the like (though many of those ideas have quietly, over many years, shaped the broad vision that reformers have in mind). Trite but true, the other necessary condition is leadership, from the very top of government. Reform creates winners and losers, and the losers will shout their discontent more loudly than the winners celebrate their gain. Conflict is inherent, and victory requires the successful exercise of power, including sheer political skill. Beyond these two commonalities, the characteristics of successful tax reforms have varied widely.

Lessons from Gucci Gulch and Elsewhere

Now and then, albeit not very often, peacetime tax reform emerges from a political consensus.[88] The classic modern example is the U.S. Tax Reform Act of 1986 (TRA86).[89] At the time, it was recognized as the most significant change in the U.S. income tax since World War Two. Now people are astonished that such a comprehensive tax overhaul could be achieved with wide bipartisan support. Most observers, though certainly not all, hailed it as a successful attempt to intelligently broaden the tax base while lowering tax rates, and doing so in a way that both protected tax revenue and was generally accepted as fair.

Even those most closely involved in the politics of TRA86 were surprised by its success. Certainly everyone recognized that the income tax was in a mess. Discontent had been simmering for a while. Inflation was pushing families into higher tax brackets, and there was a sense that tax loopholes had made the system highly dysfunctional and unfair. But there was no groundswell movement for major change. And power was split: The Republicans had both the White House and the Senate, while the Democrats controlled the House of Representatives. Stalemate would have been a reasonable expectation.

Two things broke the logjam. One was a realization by those pressing for reform that rate reduction combined with base broadening held elements of a historic deal: rate reductions to please the Republicans, closing loopholes for the wealthy to please the Democrats. Both sides could claim victory. The other was the leadership of President Reagan, then hugely popular (the Iran-Contra scandal did not break until 2 weeks after the bill was passed). Although not involved in the details, he intervened to keep reform alive at key moments, insisted on revenue neutrality (which helped keep special interests at bay), and was willing to swallow a good deal that was anathema to some Republicans in order to bring about a massive reduction in the top rate of personal tax. Without his support, TRA86 would not have happened.

But such consensus on tax reform is the exception. President Trump's Tax Cuts and Jobs Act of 2017 passed without a single Democratic vote.[90] That is closer to the norm, fundamental tax reform being vehemently opposed by some and forced through by a government that has the ability, will, and sheer power to override that resistance.

Sometimes that opposition is pro forma. Opposition parties are there, after all, to oppose. Many parties have resisted the introduction of a VAT, for instance, but almost none have repealed it when their turn in office arrived.[91] But opposition can be deep and visceral, especially when the reform has an overtone of class antagonism. So it was in the United Kingdom in 1979, when the newly elected government of Margaret Thatcher launched a fundamental overhaul of the tax system. This in some ways anticipated elements of TRA86, addressing the same combination of high tax rates, base narrowing, and inflation-induced problems, the ludicrous symbol of which was a top marginal rate on unearned income of 98 percent. The Thatcher government cut the top rate of personal income tax on earned income from 83 percent to 60 percent, and the basic rate by a much more modest three points to 30 percent.[92] The VAT rate was raised from 12.5 percent on luxuries and 8 percent on most other goods to a single rate of 15 percent. However, in one key respect this reform differed from TRA86: It was not distributionally neutral, but instead brought a large shift in the likely burden of the taxation away from the better-off. Many economists would likely regard this rebalancing of the tax system as improving efficiency, but the redistribution inherent in the reform was marked and was strongly resisted by the losers—but to no effect, given a new government with a comfortable majority.

Sometimes, as with TRA86, successful tax reform is a lengthy process carried out with glaring publicity. But sometimes it happens quickly and largely in the dark. Behind the Russian flat tax reform of 2001, for instance, was a new president, Vladimir Putin, bringing to power with him "an odd combination of FSB officers and liberal economists."[93] Determined to put order into a dysfunctional system, he quickly signaled that tax enforcement was going to get tough, not least for the oligarchs.[94] From announcement of the flat tax to legislation took about 6 months. This speed reflected President Putin's power but was also seen as important in ensuring that the opposing special interests did not have time to mobilize themselves.

Such speed may not always be possible in mature democracies and goes against the more conventional wisdom that wide consultation and careful analysis are important prerequisites for sensible, lasting reform. But other ways can be used to limit the reach of special interests. Some of the key discussions in the run-up to the Tax Reform Act of 1986, for instance, were held behind closed doors: "When we're in the back room," said the Chair of the Senate Finance Committee, Bob Packwood, "the senators can vote their conscience. . . . Then they can go out to the lobbyists and say: 'God, I fought for you. . . . But Packwood just wouldn't give in, you know. It's so damn horrible.'"[95] Later, lawmakers rushed to reach a deal before the summer recess in the fear that postponing would give special interests time to regroup.

When concessions to lobbyists are irresistible, there may be ways of at least limiting their revenue cost, perhaps by a strategy of dividing and conquering them. This, presumably, lies behind the striking (even shocking) provisions in the U.S. known as "rifle shots," drafted so that only one specific taxpayer could benefit but without actually naming them. The 1986 U.S. tax act, for instance, contained a provision beneficial to "an automobile manufacturer that was incorporated in Delaware on October 13, 1916"—which was none other than General Motors.

Sometimes tax reform happens because it has to. Fiscal crises can create, if not consensus, at least a grudging recognition that things have to change. But tax reform may not happen even when it must: ancien régime France never found either the vision or the leadership to escape its fiscal ills.

The Rise (and Rise) of the VAT

Necessity also lies to a large degree behind the most remarkable fiscal success story of the last half century: the rise of the VAT. Barely heard of 60 years ago, it is now in use in over 160 countries and raises about 30 percent of the world's tax revenue. The rise of the VAT began in 1967, when the European Economic Community adopted it as the common form of consumption tax, largely because (not being levied on exports and treating imports just like domestic sales) it would not interfere with the free flow of goods and services even if countries levied it at different rates. But the VAT now extends far beyond Europe, and indeed, most of its spread since 1985 has been to low- and middle-income countries outside Europe and the Americas. This ascendancy has, for the most part, been applauded by tax experts, especially to the extent that a broad-based VAT has replaced tariffs or cascading turn-over taxes.

Necessity has played a role in the rise of the VAT. It was obligatory for late-coming members of the European Union, membership of which requires adoption of the VAT. For developing countries, there was encouragement from external advisors: Adopting a VAT is positively correlated with participation in an IMF-supported program.[96] But it has been the necessity for greater revenue, raised in relatively less distorting ways, that has been key. While each VAT adoption has its own story, when the history of the VAT comes to be written, there will be much to say about leadership.

Few instances are more dramatic than that of Brian Mulroney, the prime minister of Canada responsible for introducing a federal VAT (known as the General Sales Tax, or GST) in 1991. This tax was hugely unpopular, required desperate measures—having the Queen appoint additional senators—to pass, and was a leading cause of both Mulroney's resignation and a subsequent electoral bloodbath. Notably, however, no subsequent Canadian government removed the GST. Indeed, the political heirs of the deposed Brian Mulroney have extended it, in various forms, to most of the provinces, too.

The VAT experience also carries lessons about where the vision for tax reform comes from. Often, it comes from next door. Countries have looked at their neighbors to see a demonstrably effective revenue-raiser in action: the spread of the VAT has come in regional bursts.[97] Similarly, the Russian flat tax experience attracted much emulation in Central and Eastern Europe, governments there being attracted by the observation that revenues actually increased after the rate cut[98] (shaky though we have seen the evidence for that to be). Again, nothing new here: Governments have always been happy to import tax ideas from abroad. In the 1620s, to acquire more money to fund a war with Spain, Holland offered a considerable reward to anyone who could devise the best new tax. The stamp duty won and was introduced in 1624. Sure enough, the British were happy to borrow the idea of the stamp tax from the Dutch, as the French were to borrow the window tax from the

British. "There is no art which one government sooner learns of another," Adam Smith recognized, "than that of draining money from the pockets of people."[99]

The global tax success story of the past half-century has not, though, reached the shores of the United States, which levies no VAT. Some blame this on the fate of Al Ullman, Chair of the House Ways and Means Committee, from whence all U.S. tax legislation must originate, which in 1979 proposed a 10 percent VAT. Having served 12 terms in Congress, Ullman then proceeded to lose his seat.[100] The idea that a VAT is the tax taboo of the United States has stuck. A simpler explanation is that Americans tend to be tax-phobic, and the thought of a big new tax—especially with European origins—is immediately suspect. And state governments fear that a federal VAT would undermine their reliance on retail sales taxation. A more succinct explanation is given by former Secretary of the Treasury and President of Harvard University, Larry Summers: Republicans oppose a VAT because it is a money machine, and Democrats oppose it because it is regressive—and the United States will get a VAT once each side of the political divide realizes the other is right.[101]

But the tide may be turning. In the 2016 Republican presidential campaign, two candidates (Ted Cruz and Rand Paul) proposed a VAT, although both, knowing the importance of naming, called it something else. Even renamed, this did not go unnoticed by their opponents. Most vivid was a TV ad put on by a political action committee aligned with candidate Marco Rubio: "Cruz wants a value-added tax," it said, adding scarily, "like they have in Canada, and European socialist economies," while across the screen crawled country names, such as Italy, France, and (in especially bold font) Sweden. The voice-over continued: "Conservatives call the Cruz scheme a liberal's dream, because it makes it so easy to raise taxes."[102] In the event, neither Cruz nor Paul (nor Rubio) was nominated, and the incoming Trump administration made clear that a VAT was not under consideration. Perhaps the need to pay for the extraordinary spending during the COVID-19 pandemic will bring forward its adoption in the United States. If it does, we can be sure it will not be called a VAT.

The VAT has certainly provided many countries with a clear vision of what a better tax system might look like. The other essential for reform, leadership, is of course not an unqualified virtue. Even well-intentioned leadership can become hubris: The Thatcher fiscal project imploded with the poll tax experience described in chapter 4. But leadership and political skill remain essential even for more modest improvements in the tax system, the kind of leadership shown by Robert Hart in building the Imperial Chinese Customs Service, for instance, and shown today by many commissioners working to build effective tax administrations in Africa. Sometimes people with power, even politicians, have an odd compulsion to do the right thing. And from Robert Peel to Brian Mulroney, they have often paid a price for doing so.

By now, however, we have spent long enough in the past. Time to take stock and look to the future of taxation.

15

The Shape of Things to Come

The past is a foreign country: they do things differently there.

L. P. HARTLEY[1]

TRUE ENOUGH. But the fundamentals of life have not really changed that much, whether it is conducting doomed love affairs, as in Hartley's novel *The Go-Between*, or raising tax revenue. What changes are the circumstances and characters. Just as Marian Maudley, the novel's heroine, loves but unwisely, so governments try to tax without incurring too much displeasure. That the core problems they face in doing so have not greatly changed throughout history is a central message of this book.

In this final chapter, we try to draw out some of the lessons of the past several millennia of taxation to peer into what may lie ahead. One disadvantage of turning our attention to the future is that it gives us no stories to tell—no tales of impalements or cat-filled trousers. Maybe, however, those whose job it is to imagine the future have already divined the shape of future tax systems for us.

Taxes in Naboo and Utopia

At the start of *Star Wars 1: The Phantom Menace*, the Galactic Republic is in turmoil:[2]

The taxation of trade routes to outlying star systems is in dispute. Hoping to resolve the matter with a blockade of deadly battleships, the greedy Trade Federation has stopped all shipping to the small planet of Naboo. While the Congress of the Republic endlessly debates this alarming chain of events, the Supreme Chancellor has secretly dispatched two Jedi Knights.

That sounds familiar. Science fiction writers envisioned voyages to the moon, submarines, and laws for robots long before they became reality. They do not, however, seem to have brought similar ingenuity to taxation.[3] Insofar as taxes feature in the science fiction literature (which is hardly at all), they seem to do little more than trigger old-fashioned revolts. Sometimes science fiction writers have been all too happy to stir up such rebellions in their minds. In *The Moon Is a Harsh Mistress*, the great Robert Heinlein imagines a revolutionary movement for lunar independence that is largely focused on achieving a tax-free moon.[4] Its theoretician, Professor Bernardo de la Paz, knows his Daniel Webster: "The power to tax, once conceded, has no limits; it contains until it destroys. . . . It may not be possible to do away with government . . . but it may be possible to keep it small and starved and inoffensive."[5]

A more laid-back view is taken by Hotblack Desiato, the fabulously wealthy rock star in Douglas Adams's *The Restaurant at the End of the Universe*: He is spending a year dead "for tax reasons."[6]

And yes, the business of science fiction itself—literature, toys, the lot—has been proposed as something to tax, in order to . . . fund NASA. The idea is that people who like science fiction would be happy to pay for NASA so that it can fool around with more cool stuff. The originator of this flash of tax genius, who was then running for Congress, "conceded that he hadn't done any calculations on the matter"[7]—as is of course the time-honored practice of politicians running for office. Inexplicably, he was not elected, and returned to his day job as a supermarket bagger.

So, disappointingly, there are few insights about the future of taxation to be gleaned from science fiction. But as we will see later in this chapter, much of what once seemed science fiction is now becoming tax reality.

Looking in another direction for insights as to where taxation might be heading, one might also wonder—in an optimistic mood—what the deep thinkers of the past two millennia on utopias have come up with.

Literary utopias, however, go light on the tax details. In Thomas More's 1516 book that coined the term, all households are required to bring their produce to a central store, from which people take what they need.[8] Not everyone contributes, however. The elderly, infirm, administrators, and, happily, professional scholars, do not. On average, then, everyone else contributes more than they receive. That sounds like taxation, without being labeled as such. The same is true in Edward Bellamy's 1888 novel *Looking Backward*. "We have no army or navy, and no military organization. We have no departments of state or treasury, no excise or revenue services, no taxes or tax collectors."[9] There is no formal taxation, but there is "surplus product which, not being returned to the citizens individually, can be regarded as a form of taxation."[10] These are socialist, or communitarian, utopias, where resources are meant to be shared equally or according to need.

Right-wing and libertarian utopias are less well-known, but they do exist. In the society of August Schwan's *Towards a New Social Order*, published in 1922, there is almost no taxation, and to fund the very limited government needed (to protect everyone's liberty, provide roads, sewage service, fire service, and so on), citizens voluntarily remit "certain dues"—a touch vague. The only tax is one on land, on the Henry Georgian grounds that landowners exclude others from the use of their land and thereby infringe on their liberty. In the libertarian ideal society of Ayn Rand, author of *Atlas Shrugged*, taxes are voluntary and remitted only to obtain wanted services. She mentions government lotteries but does not take on the issue of the implicit tax determined by the improbability of winning that we discussed in chapter 3.

What these communitarian and libertarian utopias share is minimal taxes—they are utopias, after all. How they differ is that in the former, the contribution to society is required, albeit done with a smile. In the latter, the contributions are made voluntarily, without much detail given on the repercussions if they are not sufficient to provide for whatever government is wanted.

Dystopian novels, perhaps, can at least tell us what we need to avoid. But there, too, lotteries are prominent. In *Nineteen Eighty-Four*, George Orwell,[11] conscious no doubt of its widespread use in the Soviet Union during the 1930s, wrote of the lottery as:

> the one public event to which the proles paid serious attention. It was probable that there were some millions of proles for whom the Lottery was the principal if not the only reason for remaining alive. . . . Winston . . . was aware (indeed everyone in the party was aware) that the prizes were largely imaginary. Only small sums were actually paid out, the winners of the big prizes being non-existent persons.

With almost nothing to draw on from the visionaries, in looking to the future of taxation, we are left only with lessons from the past.

Pillars of Tax Wisdom

Here then are eleven[12] lessons that millennia of enduring, arguing, and thinking about taxation teach us.

Tax Revolts Are Rarely Just about Tax

When tax blazes across history, it is usually because of some kind of rebellion or resistance. But there is almost always more to these episodes than tax. Tax measures are more often a tipping point, sparking conflict whose deeper source lies in more fundamental disputes over the ways in which a wider range of sovereign powers are allocated or being exercised—the coercive power to tax being almost the definition, and certainly one of the most salient manifestations, of state sovereignty.

The ultimate aim, and sometimes outcome, of the most tumultuous tax revolts is to reallocate power, not just to change the tax system. This is so whether the dispute is between countries (actual or would-be), as with the misremembered Boston Tea Party or the Ten Cents War of nineteenth-century South America, or within them, as with both the English Civil War and the French Revolution. Wat Tyler's rebellious peasants did not even mention the poll tax in their demands when they controlled London. Their deeper distress lay in the obstacles being placed to prevent them from realizing their strengthened economic hand after the Black Death. And the despised *gabelle* of the ancien régime, removed in 1790, was quietly reintroduced by Napoleon in 1806.

Especially likely to provoke tax resistance is manifest unfairness—not only regarding the level and structure of taxation, but also, as the tax collectors of Shimabara and untold instances of petty corruption through the ages remind us, how it is enforced. But governments seen as unfair are likely to be seen as unfair in much more than just taxation. The British poll tax of 1990 came after bruising battles with the trade unions. And the *gilets jaunes* movement in France, prompted by a fuel tax increase, is generally seen as reflecting a wider "anger at the perception that Mr. Macron governs for the better-off, Paris-based elite."[13] Tax resistance and boycotts are a natural focal point for expressing discontent with government, because they simultaneously deny both the legitimacy and the practical possibility of exercising the most basic coercive power of the state.

Be Careful with Words

Governments can obtain resources from the private sector in many ways not called "taxes." Nonetheless, their ability to obtain significant resources ultimately rests on the power to do so compulsorily: that is, to tax. Government can only borrow, for instance, to the extent that lenders believe they will be repaid, the ultimate guarantee of which is the capacity of the government to find the resources necessary to do so by, if need be, taxing its own people. And seigniorage—acquiring resources by creating money—is simply another way in which coercive powers of taxation can be exercised, through the ability to dictate what constitutes legal tender. Ultimately, if the government somehow gets hold of resources, someone in the private sector has less, whatever name is attached to the process of obtaining those resources.

The one name that governments like to avoid, of course, is the very word "tax." They often reach instead for terms like "fee," "charge," or "levy"—which suggest that taxpayers receive something in return for the taxes they remit (which is, of course, in some broad sense true, even if they do not like what they get). And governments spin taxes by giving them misleading names. Mrs. Thatcher's community charge was really a poll tax (while the 1381 poll tax was really a community charge). But while the label may affect political perceptions and support, and may matter for the governments' bookkeeping, it is unlikely to make a major difference to who bears the real burden that is imposed, or the behavioral responses it induces.

Language does, however, matter. It matters for the political economy of taxation, as politicians and lobbyists routinely try to change the terms of policy debate, whether it is Dickens lambasting the window tax as a charge on light and air or today's Republicans attaching the "death tax" label to the estate tax. And it matters for the legal framing of taxation, in ways large and small. Constitutional peculiarities continue to constrain tax policy in odd ways—the obstacles to wealth taxation in the United States posed by references in the Constitution to "direct taxation" being one example, another being the difficulties that both India and Pakistan have faced in adopting a national VAT as a consequence of the 1935 Government of India Act.[14] Constitutional provisions which, echoing the Virginia tax law of 1634, aim to legislate that taxation be fair—such as those in Italy requiring "The taxation system shall be based on criteria of progression"[15]—sound wonderful but defy simple or even meaningful application. And the legal fine print matters. A misplaced comma in the tariff law can cost the government dear, and the precise formula used to tax ships can cost lives.

You May Be the One Paying for Lunch

One of the hardest questions to answer about any tax is the question of who really bears it, in the sense of suffering a loss of purchasing power as a consequence. Public debate rarely even stops to think about this. But just because something is called a tax (or levy, or whatever) "on" some person or activity does not mean that it actually imposes a real burden on those people or on those who engage in that activity. The point is that the tax burden can and generally will be shifted as prices adjust to reflect the impact of the tax on supply and demand. This is especially true when "on" refers to who, for a given tax base and rate, must remit the money to the government. The tax on female servants in Georgian England was remitted by the employer but may have driven many female servants into alternative employment, and subsidizing low-income workers' earnings can benefit employers by pushing down pre-subsidy wages. Governments may not have intended these outcomes, and they may have had a clear view of where they wanted the real burden to fall. But the true incidence of any tax is shaped not by their wishes but by the playing out of behavioral responses to taxation.

Pinning down exactly who does bear the burden of a tax can be hard. Even such a basic question as who it is that ends up bearing the corporate income tax—workers, shareholders, or consumers—remains opaque and spiritedly controversial. Empirical understanding of tax incidence, while developing fairly rapidly, remains limited. And while modern techniques have proved well suited to analyzing the incidence of fairly narrowly defined taxes in very specific circumstances—such as a reduction in the tax on haircuts in some part of the European Union—policy makers still have relatively little guidance on when, for instance, an increase in the standard rate of VAT will be fully passed onto consumer prices, or partly borne by workers and business owners.

Economists thus know embarrassingly little about the real incidence of many taxes and can say even less about the incidence of the tax system as a whole. But there is a straightforward principle—which began to emerge in the Corn Law debates of Victorian Britain—that points to where the burden is likely to reside: The burden will tend to stick on those who have the fewest alternatives to whatever item or activity is being taxed. At one extreme are rents—receipts in excess of the minimum required by the owner—which reflect some underlying asset in fixed supply: Taxes on these will stick with the owner. At the other end are things that have very close substitutes: A tax on red wine but not on white would be unlikely to fall wholly on red-wine connoisseurs.

It is impossible to be perfectly sure where the burden of some tax will ultimately fall. But the real point of these simple ideas is that they can focus debate squarely on the real issues instead of simply taking labels and policy makers' intentions at face value.

Fair Taxation, Whatever That Is, Is Hard to Achieve

Views on what makes an acceptable basis for different tax treatments of different people, beyond differences in their ability to pay—that is, on horizontal equity—change over time. These days, taxes that explicitly discriminate by religion, race, gender, or facial hair are rare. The issue now is more often implicit differentiation, which does not name any groups of people, but instead reflects, for example, the systematically different tastes and needs of men and women, or of different racial groups. Completely eliminating such discrimination is probably impossible and may even conflict with other reasonable objectives. For instance, it is mathematically impossible to combine equal treatment of single and married households with a progressive income tax. And personal characteristics may be associated with a lack of responsiveness of behavior that, on grounds of minimizing excess burden, point to relatively high tax rates. The question is when implicit discrimination becomes sufficiently offensive to require action.

The second, "vertical," dimension of fairness raises even more profound issues. Quite how the tax burden should be shared between the better off and the less-well off has been a central issue since at least the liturgies of classical Athens, and was at the heart of nineteenth-century tax debates when revenue was needed only for basic functions of defense and the like. It has become still more central since, with the rise of the welfare state meaning that a central purpose of both tax and spending policies is now to redistribute resources from richer people to poorer ones. Quite how far the tax burden should be tilted toward the richer, however, is in part a matter of personal judgment: of philosophy more than economics. What economists can do, however, is point to and, ideally, quantify the wider social costs that such tilting may impose. The difficulty—in the absence of lump-sum taxes tied to ability to pay—is that, whatever proxy for well-being is used, it is impossible to tax more those who are better off without reducing the incentive for others to become equally well off. There are some ways in which revenue can likely be raised from the more affluent without causing much or any excess burden. This was how Henry George's land tax was to bring the City of God to earth, and can, for many, lend great appeal to the idea of restructuring the corporate tax so that it falls on rents, and hence mainly on shareholders. But identifying rents is not always easy, and taxes of this kind cannot plausibly meet all of governments' revenue needs. Some trade-off between progressivity and efficiency is, ultimately, inevitable. That difficult choice remains a—perhaps the— central problem of tax system design.

But it is important to remember that taxes, even including negative ones in the form of cash benefits, are only one weapon in the policy arsenal for addressing vertical equity, and may not even be the most effective of them. One of the most powerful ways in which governments support the poor—especially in low-income countries—is by providing basic education and health care. By enabling such spending, a not-very-progressive tax that raises a lot of revenue, such as the VAT, can do more for the poor than a very progressive one that raises little.

Taxation Is About Finding Good Proxies

For a tax system to be anything other than capricious, it has to be based on things that can be measured and, ideally, verified in a court of law. Over the centuries, these powers of observation have increased massively. In Georgian England, for Lord North the taxes on coaches and servants were "proper and eligible, as they were visible signs of ability to pay them."[16] Now we look primarily to income as a better indicator. Instead of counting the windows on a house, we can now often get a pretty good idea of its market value. And as economies moved away from being dominated by small agricultural enterprises, it became feasible to rely heavily on employers to report on, withhold, and remit tax based on their employees' earnings. This has made tax systems enormously more powerful. But it remains the case that we are often taxing not the thing of most interest in itself but some proxy for that thing.

Sometimes the proxying is relatively straightforward. For taxes on commodities, it manifests itself in the need to define the essence of the thing to be taxed: What exactly, for example, is a cigarette? How the tax rules choose to answer that question can give rise to oddities but is broadly manageable. And there is little need for proxying in externality contexts where it is clear exactly what causes damage, and so should be taxed, such as the carbon content of fuels. But in some cases, especially when it comes to trying to make the tax system fair, the search for a good proxy is a continuing process and one that goes to the heart of what the tax system is trying to do.

The value of a property, for example, is not a wholly accurate or complete indicator of the well-being of the person who owns it, nor of their total wealth. Even for large corporations, our measures of their earnings rest on presumptions about the value of their assets, including intangible ones, that may be far from reality. And for smaller businesses, we are often forced to rely on still cruder proxies of their income, such as their turnover. Policy debates still revolve around how best to measure income to ensure a fair tax base—what deductions to allow for health expenses and the like—and on what to include in the base of new or revamped annual taxes on wealth. But the problem is not simply one of measuring and taxing income or wealth accurately, critical though that evidently is. Much more fundamentally, while it is widely agreed that tax liability should be tailored to ability to pay, we have no firm way of measuring that ability in its most meaningful sense—which, ultimately, is not in terms of how much income or wealth someone actually has, but of how much they could have. Taxes may, for instance, induce the secondary earner in some households not to take a job: Their observed ability to pay—as measured by income—is then much lower than their potential. A more efficient tax system would recognize that potential, imposing some associated liability that does not depend on whether the job was taken and so does not provide a disincentive to work—but which does reflect an equity judgment as to the appropriate rate at which to tax those potential earnings.

That would be the ideal of a lump-sum tax: One, that is, which is independent of anything the taxpayer does and, when fairness concerns are taken into account, is tailored to potential ability to pay. The trouble is that taxpayers, even if they know it, have an incentive to disguise that potential: People and companies would be unlikely to respond truthfully if we were to simply ask how much they *could* earn. And, failing largely untried schemes like the self-assessment scheme of the Athenian liturgies and Sun Yat-sen, there seems to be no clever way of inducing them to reveal the truth. We are thus left only with proxies for that unknown ability to pay, and ones that taxpayers can manipulate to their advantage by changing the ways in which they behave—one source of the excess burden that will soon merit a lesson itself.

Tax Avoiders and Evaders Are Wonderfully Creative

History shows that people's ingenuity in trying to escape taxation has few limits. If that means having only 9 windows when 10 or more would attract tax liability, someone is sure to do it. Living in skinny houses when street frontage triggers tax; replacing walls with movable partitions when the latter, but not the former, qualify for an investment tax credit; dogs without tails (if only that story was true)—all of these are examples of behavior that cannot be explained absent tax-minimizing behavior. And those tricks were all legal. On the other side of a fuzzy gray line is evasion, which, being essentially a matter of lying, tends to be less creative. One can only be impressed, however, by the cheek of the taxpayer claiming an allowance for a child called Fluffy and the cleverness of those who design carousel and even more mind-boggling forms of VAT fraud.

At one level, this tax creativity is simply a nuisance. Governments have to find some way to stop giving tax breaks for imaginary children and to close down the other loopholes that taxpayers will keep finding. And of course, taxpayers' innovativeness either reduces tax revenue or requires the more honest or less creative among them to pay more. Most fundamentally, however, these reactions, both avoidance and evasion, imply inefficient use of resources: They happen only because of the tax rules, and so, however privately remunerative they may be, are in a social sense wasteful.

The Biggest Costs of Taxation May Be the Ones You Can't See

However much revenue a tax raises, that number will underestimate the true cost to society that the tax has imposed.[17] This is because taxes generate an additional social cost—an "excess burden"—that arises when they alter the decisions that people and businesses would otherwise make.

These distortions are rarely as easy to see as ridiculously long cigarettes, or buildings shaped like rockets. They do not require creative schemes of avoidance or evasion of the kind just warned about: They may simply mean buying less of something (or supplying less of something, such as labor) because it is more heavily taxed. These reactions are pervasive. They involve big decisions as to how much and how hard to work, and in what occupations (it is easier to evade tax if self-employed, for instance), about how much to save and invest and in what forms (in housing, say, or a bank account in a low-tax jurisdiction), and about whether or not to take the risks inherent in innovating. Through such routes, tax distortions can profoundly affect economic performance. The trouble is, that while blocked-up windows make the point obvious, the losses that really matter are almost always manifest in things that cannot be seen, because they are not there: investments not undertaken, for example, or workers not in the workforce. Because they are hard to see and understand, but may well be large, these real costs get too far little attention in tax policy debates.

But we do have a pretty good idea of what taxes perform badly in terms of the excess burden they create, and of how to measure that burden. The key lesson is that excess burden is greater the more responsive to taxation is the tax base. The changes in behavior that cause the tax base to change could be real, like blocking up a chimney or deciding not to take on a part-time job, or they could simply be avoidance or evasion, like financing a firm by borrowing rather than injecting new equity, or not declaring the income from a part-time job. In either case, the more responsive the tax base is to the tax rate, the larger is the excess burden per dollar of revenue raised.

Recognizing this relation helps give us a pretty good idea of how to design taxes so as to limit excess burden. In the extreme, we know how to design taxes that provide no incentives to change behavior, and so generate no excess burden. The clearest example is a lump-sum tax: a fixed amount, unaffected by any choices made by the taxpayer. Ricardo and Malthus showed the way to a wider set of instruments that also leave behavior unaffected, by explaining how land could earn "rents"—payment in excess of the minimum that the landowner required. Such rents can arise from other sources too: from having a unique skill, say, or from having developed a uniquely valued product. And when they do arise, rents, precisely because they are an excess of what is needed to ensure supply, can be taxed without causing any change in behavior. Both world wars produced excess profit taxes intended to do exactly that, and today's corporate taxes could be reconfigured to have similar properties by ensuring full deduction of all costs.

Beyond this, the basic prescription for limiting excess burden (but not wholly eliminating it) is to interfere as little as possible with the choices that businesses and people make as to how to go about doing the things they do—unless there is good reason to do so. The reasons are somewhat different in the two cases. Interfering with businesses' input decisions tends to reduce the total output produced from available resources, which is very unlikely to be a good thing. Some distortion of consumers' choices is inevitable, however, if we are to raise any revenue at all. Tilting their choices between different commodities can in principle make sense as a way to reduce excess burden. But beyond a few broad ideas—notably the implication of the principle that goods with especially inelastic demand are attractive targets for high taxation on efficiency grounds—we know little about how best to do this in practice. All kinds of differentiation, in any case, open the door to lobbies and special pleading.

Only if there is a clear reason to do so—most obviously, to address externalities or because fairness objectives are so manifestly served as to outweigh the excess burden—should tax design depart from a basic principle of neutrality: refraining from trying to fine-tune consumers' or businesses' decisions.

Taxes Are Not Just for Raising Money

Targeting particular behaviors for taxation can be a good thing in itself if directed toward societal "bads," such as pollution or road congestion. By charging people for the harm they cause others—negative "externalities"—such Pigovian taxes can make people better off even if the benefits of cleaner air and water, or uncongested streets, are not reflected in how we measure GDP. These taxes need to be carefully targeted to the bad activity: It is better, for instance, to tax cars on congested streets rather than all cars. And for what is arguably "the mother of all externalities," economists are almost unanimous in advocating carbon pricing as a primary means to address global warming. Taxes can also be used to address problems of self-control—"internalities"—by inducing people not to take up habits they will later regret but will then be unable to quit. This is probably the strongest argument for today's heavy taxes on cigarettes and is now being applied more widely, with soft drinks and fatty foods now at the frontier, and e-cigarettes posing new questions.

But taxation is not always the answer to undesirable behavior; at least, not the whole answer. Regulatory responses may also have a complementary role: Drunk driving may be better addressed by penalizing offenses rather than taxing alcohol even when used in moderation. Or regulations may simply be an intrinsically better response, as with the social distancing rules imposed during the COVID-19 pandemic.

There is, though, a dark side to taxes motivated by other than a need for money. From the medieval taxes on Jews, through Cromwell's decimation tax and the 1930s taxes on chain stores, and up to the whiff of revenge in calls for taxation of bankers' bonuses following the Global Financial Crisis, taxes have been used to punish enemies and reward friends. But, leaving aside whether it can be defensible in practice, taxation for retribution is often simply ineffective, as the villains of the piece, like expatriated Royalists, have often vanished before they can be taxed.

And favoring cronies, by the use of exemptions and special deals for the favored—meaning specially unfavorable deals for the unfavored—is not only odious but also a source of excess burden.

People Pay Taxes Because They Are Scared

That many people hand over significant amounts of tax with relatively little fuss reflects a range of considerations and motives. Some degree of trust in government and officialdom, and a sense that the proceeds will not be wasted, likely play some role[18] and help establish a social norm that supports and reinforces what seems in many people to be an intrinsic preference for being honest. And trust in the opposite direction matters, too, enabling tax administrations to treat taxpayers as something more than latent criminals. A strong tax system is built on mutual and reinforcing trust.

But while wise tax administrations try to make it easy for people to comply with their obligations, and try to trust where trust is due, they do not simply sit back and wait for the money to roll in. Behind all their nice words about voluntary compliance, or of taxpayers as customers, they know that, ultimately, it is the fear of being caught and penalized that constrains evasion. Although it is hard to get a good handle on how much evasion there actually is, one thing we do know is that those whose evasion runs the least risk of detection and penalty—like the self-employed or small businesses—have always done more of it. So tax laws have to be enforced. Celebrated evaders who get caught make headlines, but those who get away with it increase the tax burden on the dutiful chumps who remit all that they owe. Evasion is not a victimless crime, even though its dispersed victims are not identified.

Tax enforcement has often been chillingly heavy-handed. The peasants burned alive in Shimabara and the merchants impaled by Vlad are not alone at the horrendous end of the spectrum. Over the centuries, however, tax administrations have developed increasingly effective—and mostly humane—ways to root out and deter evasion. Targeted audits provide a relatively cheap way of instilling generalized anxiety at the thought of evasion, and epitomize the public image of enforcement. The rise of large-scale businesses, hard to hide, has enabled widespread use of withholding, eliminating the opportunity to blow or hide the payments workers receive before they are taxed—a technique so effective that tax administrations are still finding ways to extend its use. And an increasingly crucial role is played by the information reports provided to the tax authority by employers, financial institutions, and other entities.

None of this makes tax officials popular. Not many people pretend at parties to be a tax officer. But without competent, dedicated tax administrators, no tax system can be even tolerably fair or efficient. Finding ways to encourage them to do their jobs effectively, honestly, and without political interference is a challenge everywhere, as it always has been. But concerns about corruption should not blind us to there having been, over the millennia, countless dutiful and even courageous tax officials, underpaid and unrecognized.

Tax Sovereignty Is Becoming a Thing of the Past

Adam Smith saw early that one of the ways in which tax bases can respond to taxation is by moving somewhere else, and globalization has placed his citizen of the world firmly at the center of the tax stage. This mobility means that the excess burden of taxing can be high from the perspective of any national government even if from a global perspective—*Star Wars* aside, the tax base being rather immobile between this planet and others—it would be low if the tax were applied collectively. It also means that national sovereignty in setting tax rates and base can be illusory: A country may have the power to levy tax on domestic profits at some very high rate, but that does not mean much if no profits will then remain for it to tax. And, just as Catherine the Great nearly attracted James Watt to Russia by offering tax exemptions, so now—maybe more than ever—governments compete among themselves with the aggressive intent of stealing others' tax base, or at least with the defensive intent of protecting their own. Much though they may wish to deny it, their sovereignty in tax matters is largely notional rather than real. And, in exercising what remains of it, they indulge in tax competition that, quite possibly, ends up making many of their citizens worse off.

Since the late nineteenth century, governments have gone some way toward pooling their sovereignty in tax matters, notably by signing tax treaties to establish who can tax what. But, for decades, the Vesteys and others of the well-heeled and well-advised set, have managed to exploit the lack of coordination in international tax policies—to the disgust of many. Since the Global Financial Crisis, and largely reflecting public pressures stoked by the Panama Papers and other leaks, along with the manifest ability of multinationals to end up with remarkably low tax bills, progress has been made in exercising a collective sovereignty by adopting measures aimed at ending some of the most egregious abuses. It is now notably harder to conceal income by locating assets in low-tax jurisdictions, and the norms underlying the international corporate tax system are now widely recognized to be untenable, opening the way to serious reform, including some limitation of tax competition. But the coordination achieved is still far from matching the scale of the challenge, and simmering disputes over digital services taxes show just how hard it will be to reform the international tax system by truly collective action.

Beware of Mantras

In tax as in other areas, slogans are rarely a good basis for making policy. Sometimes they are completely vacuous. The idea that "business should pay its fair share of taxes," for example, falls into the trap of supposing that the real burden of taxation does not ultimately fall on real people (even leaving aside what is meant by "fair"). Sometimes mantras are merely vacuous. The idea, for instance, that we should "tax where value is created"—the slogan of the G20-OECD project on Base Erosion and Profit Shifting—sounds great. But, since no one can agree where that is, that mantra does not take us very far.

Mantras can even be dangerous, having a kernel of truth that can be taken too far. Take the slogan that we should aim to "broaden the base and lower the rate." It is indeed generally true that taxing on a broad base at a uniform rate causes less economic damage than does raising the same amount by taxing on a narrow base at a high rate. The problem is that some apparently broad bases are also bad bases, and that good taxes can have relatively narrow bases.

A tax on financial transactions, for instance, would have an enormous base. However, it would also be highly distortionary, because even a small tax rate can cumulate to a large amount on successive transactions and so end up discouraging socially worthwhile financial activity. The same is true of a turnover tax applied to all business sales, and in this case, the distortionary effect—incentives to artificial mergers being just one—is a key reason the world has for the most part opted instead for the VAT. The VAT inherently has a much narrower base, because, if done well, it does not tax business inputs. But, for precisely that reason, it is potentially far less distorting to economic activity. A similar point applies to corporate taxation. Narrowing the base of the standard corporate tax by allowing a deduction not just for interest but also for a notional return on equity, for instance, would convert it into a tax on rents, reducing the distortions that now arise, not least from an unwarranted tax preference for debt over equity finance that, by encouraging firms to be more highly leveraged than they otherwise would be, can pose risks to financial stability.

The cases for the VAT and for turning the corporate tax into something like a tax on rents both illustrate the general principle of tax design set out in this book: Avoid distorting the decisions of people and firms unless there is a very good reason for doing so, perhaps because some externality is at work or because fairness objectives are so manifestly served as to outweigh the excess burden. That, if a mantra is really needed, would be high on our list. We wish it were snappier.

The only exceptions to this last lesson are, of course, the eleven mantras we have now set out.

The Future and Beyond

The point of lessons is to help us cope with whatever lies ahead. Forecasting the future by extrapolating current trends, as the COVID-19 pandemic has reminded us, is far from foolproof. In the wake of the unprecedented measures to address it, in 2020 many speculated that the role of government would change forever. But we cannot be sure that the broad consensus in favor of massive fiscal intervention, not to mention unprecedented monitoring of people's movements and associations, will survive once the pandemic fades.

What we can be sure of is that the world's tax systems will have much to do in the coming decades. They will be called on to play a central role in addressing many of the most pressing global challenges—high levels of public debt, development needs, aging of the population, growing inequality, globalization, and climate change—with implications that interconnect in ways that are complex and often compounding. And overlaying all these are the potentials and perils of massively rapid technological change.

Hard Times

Almost all countries will emerge from the COVID-19 crisis with massive increases in levels of public debt, from what were already extremely high levels by peacetime standards: Between 2019 and 2020, global levels of public debt are projected to rise by around 15 percent of GDP, to nearly 100 percent—in the advanced economies, to over 125 percent, levels not seen since the end of the Second World War.[19] The problems this poses can be addressed in many ways: by strong growth, ideally (especially powerful in reducing debt levels when interest rates are low); by default or debt relief in some cases; and by monetary financing or spending cuts in others. But in all cases there is likely to be a need to increase tax revenue substantially.

The nature of the revenue challenge takes different forms in different countries. For many developing countries, about half of which now collect less than 15 percent of their GDP in tax revenue, it is a matter of securing a decent life for their people. For many of them, meeting the 2030 Sustainable Development Goals requires somehow financing spending amounting to another 15 percent of GDP.[20] A large chunk of that will doubtless have to come from building up their own tax systems. That is a daunting task, requiring these countries to do in a few years what it took today's advanced economies decades to achieve. All the lessons above will apply. But none among them guarantees that progress on such a scale is easy or quick.

For almost all countries, real pressures to raise more revenue are coming from the substantial aging of their population that is now hardwired into their futures. Over the next 40 years or so, the fraction of the world's population that is over 65 is expected to double, and the proportion of the "oldest old" (aged 80 or over) to triple.[21] The impact is especially marked, and especially problematic, in advanced economies, where by 2060, there are expected to be as many people over 65 as there are of working age—as is already the case in Japan.[22] (Developing countries, generally having young populations, are spared quite such intense pressures.) The fraction of the population working and paying income-related taxes will thus fall, and because most governments shoulder a high proportion of health care costs, public health and long-term care expenditures will soar. One estimate has them roughly double in OECD countries by 2060, requiring an additional 8 percent of GDP in tax revenue.[23] Pressures are also building for additional pension financing, though these are likely to be more modest. Some of this additional revenue might come from the older generations themselves, by, for instance, extending retirement ages for social security benefits or, more subtly, through higher rates of VAT and other consumption taxes (which bear more heavily on the elderly, because they tend to be running down rather than accumulating savings). But the expectation of the young supporting the elderly while also providing for their own retirement may raise difficult issues of horizontal equity between the generations.

More generally, we have seen that tax systems become seriously compromised unless they are perceived as reasonably fair. Further challenges thus come from increasing inequality, which has been called "the defining challenge of our time"[24] (though there are plenty of contenders for that title)—not least through its links with the rise of populism. Globally, around one percent of the world's population now owns about half of its total wealth.[25] In many advanced countries, though not all, income inequality has been growing rapidly since the 1980s. In the United States, for example, the share of pretax income going to the richest 1 percent has more than doubled, reaching 20 percent by 2012. It has also been on the rise in most other countries—from 7 to 12 percent in the United Kingdom, for example, and from 8 to 11 percent in France—but at a slower pace, and the rate of increase seems to have leveled off since the Global Financial Crisis and the subsequent recession.[26]

Public spending—on income transfers, health, education, and the like—has in the past done at least as much to reduce inequality of real incomes as has taxation.[27] That, of course, reinforces the need for more revenue to finance such spending. On the tax side itself, calls for increasing tax progressivity are becoming louder, and will be amplified if the COVID-19 pandemic leads to a sense that, the most vulnerable having suffered most in the response to the common challenge, the more affluent need and wish to show solidarity in sharing the burden.[28]

All these trends point to a future of increased pressures on tax systems, with a need to raise more revenue and to do so in ways that match evolving views of fairness. These pressures will vary in force across countries, and countries will react in different ways. But the lessons above can help navigate these challenges. The search for ways to limit their economic cost—excess burden—will intensify. This may mean, for instance, more reliance on taxes on economic rent of various kinds, though these alone will surely not be enough to meet revenue needs. Improving compliance can help raise revenue in ways perceived as fair. Incidence considerations, meanwhile, should warn us of the distinction between appearance and reality in trying to tax the better off. But ultimately, the lesson above applies: If tax systems are well designed, there must be a tradeoff between fairness and efficiency that only politics, broadly interpreted, can resolve.

One other existential issue provides some opportunity to square the need for revenue and the desire to promote efficient resource allocation: climate change. What this should mean for tax systems is obvious. The world needs carbon taxation, or some similar way of pricing carbon. Even a quite modest charge could raise about 1 percent of GDP in many countries,[29] far from enough to meet the needs for revenue discussed here but a significant contribution nonetheless.

There is, however, a fundamental problem to be faced in addressing all these challenges: the increased mobility of tax bases. This may abate somewhat as countries seek to identify and protect national interests more firmly in the wake of the pandemic, but the essence seems sure to remain. And that makes it more difficult for countries to do all the things they are likely to be called on to do—raise more money, increase the relative burden on the more affluent, and impose increasingly aggressive carbon pricing—without considerably closer international cooperation than now. It forces government to rely more heavily on tax bases that do not readily move across national borders, such as the consumption by ordinary and relatively immobile people, bases not suitable for addressing inequality. Taxes on land, and other sources of location-specific economic rent, may also come to play an increased role and are more likely to bear on the better-off. But these sources are unlikely to raise enough to dispense with taxes falling substantially on immobile consumers.

The only way to address these challenges is through deeper international cooperation. Without it, the mobile wealthy will remain hard to tax, the international tax system will fall further into disrepute, and effective carbon pricing will remain stymied. On the optimistic side, one can see signs of such cooperation emerging, in the multilateral discussions on corporate tax reform and the Paris climate agreement. But these are small steps. More innovative approaches will surely be needed, perhaps in the use of revenue-sharing arrangements across countries of a kind that are now commonplace within federal countries but almost unknown across countries. Perhaps, in a day far away, there will even be a World Tax Organization, setting and enforcing some aspects of tax rules in the way that the World Trade Organization has done for trade.

Brave New Worlds

Deep though they are, the broad nature of these problems would have been understood very easily by policy makers 20 years or even a century ago. What would have stunned them, however, are the advances in technology—whose implications for tax matters are still largely imponderable.

We saw in chapter 13 how these changes are allowing tax administration to do what they already do in a whole host of more effective ways: by combining information from multiple sources, moving toward pre-population of tax returns, using mobile technology for tax payments and salient messaging to taxpayers, developing and applying the capacity to collect and match information on taxpayers across jurisdictions, and using drones to identify undeclared real estate. And there is much more. Tax agencies are now beginning to harness the predictive power of "big data" to improve their ability to detect reporting anomalies. In Australia and New Zealand, voice recognition systems are already being used to securely identify taxpayers calling for customer support. Nothing could have brought out the strengths of digital methods more spectacularly than the shock of the COVID-19 pandemic. Administrations making fuller use of them coped better with the disruption of methods based on physical interactions and paper—and the rest realized the importance of catching up.

There are problems. Fraudsters also make use of digital technologies. There are real issues of security and privacy. In 2007, HMRC lost data discs with information about 25 million taxpayers.[30] And for the moment at least, many people seem quite willing to let Google, Amazon, and the like profit from what they learn about their buying habits while hating the idea of government—with its greater powers of coercion— knowing too much about them.

Digitalization is also stretching current ways of doing tax business. Take the platform revolution, exemplified by business models like those of Airbnb, Uber, and eBay. Are Uber drivers employees, so that Uber must withhold income taxes on their behalf? Or are they independent contractors, potentially subject to all the problems now associated with taxing the self-employed? We have seen too that increased ability to do business in countries without having a physical presence there is undermining support for a core norm of the international corporate tax system.

But we can be pretty sure that all these issues are just the start. Beyond pre-population, for instance, some have proposed a data retrieval platform that would allow taxpayers and tax professionals to access and download tax information from a secure database maintained by the government.[31] Rather than having to gather this information themselves from employers, financial institutions, and third parties, taxpayers and their advisors could rely on this centralized clearinghouse of information. Such a database promises a substantial saving in compliance costs, but potentially amplifies worries about privacy and security.

There is though an even more fundamental point. Digitalization is not simply a matter of doing what we do now in different (hopefully better) ways. It will let us do things that were previously unthinkable.[32]

We do not expect to see the taxation of robots, which has been suggested as a way to blunt the impact of automation on employment.[33] That risks stifling innovation. A better response is likely to be action to ensure that the gains from technological advances are shared reasonably evenly and do not accrue overwhelmingly to a few superstar innovators.[34] Perhaps more promising as a tax base is the value associated with the "new oil": information itself.

But there are even more fundamental changes that, ultimately, can be envisaged. Blockchain, for example, is presented as enabling tamper-proof and entirely complete records of all transactions—a distinctly updated version of the exciseman's ledger—and some have suggested embedding within such systems "smart contracts" by which VAT would be remitted automatically. But if all transactions are perfectly recorded in this way, including sales to final consumers (some means, imagine, having been found to ensure this), there is no real need for a VAT—the merit of which, after all, is ensuring that at least some tax is remitted even on unrecorded transactions. A retail sales tax would then work just as well.

Another core element of today's tax systems, the corporation tax, may ultimately also be in for fundamental change. Indeed, it may vanish. What we have in mind is not unintended erosion through international tax competition, or even the changes by which outdated norms of arm's length pricing and tests of physical presence can be set aside. It is rather that the increased ability to acquire and manipulate large amounts of information may at some point enable us to get away from taxing earnings at the corporate level and instead attribute them to underlying shareholders, and better pursue vertical equity by taxing that income in their hands. That is far from a practical possibility today—but so, until recently, was the kind of automatic information exchange on interest payments and assets that is now on the way to becoming routine.

It may also become possible to move away from the quaint habit of taxing, for the most part, on the basis of a single year, linking information over time to tax people on something like a lifetime basis—and so on an assessment of ability to pay that abstracts from the ups and downs that we all experience over our lives. And it may become possible, at the same time, for governments to react more rapidly and fully to those high and lows by getting support to people when they need it—which may be by the end of today, not in a few weeks' time or at the end of the tax year. That means tying together more closely the tax and benefit sides of the public finances, which have traditionally been distinct arms of the bureaucracy. After all, much the same information on material and personal circumstances is required for both tax and benefit purposes, and as that information becomes richer, more timely, and easier to manage, so a more holistic approach will enable interventions to be more effective and more coherently designed. This system would be capable of taking both a long- and a short-term view, with tax liability determined (and perhaps remitted) and cash benefits received continuously, in light of life's unfolding surprises.

But perhaps the most dramatic possibilities may arise from the stunning technological developments in the knowledge of the human genome. As we discover genetic markers that are statistically correlated with lifetime income or other measures of well-being or potential ability to pay, these could be used in a tax-and-transfer regime as an input to determine an individual's (possibly negative) tax liability, in the way that disability, age, and marital status are often used now.[35] It may seem that we are here veering back to science fiction, but some reports claim that researchers have already uncovered evidence of a gene that seems to influence some aspects of intelligence, and they have certainly identified genes that affect the propensity to acquire debilitating diseases. Using such information can lead to more efficient tax design: If genetic information is immutable[36] and related to ability to earn, it could in principle be used to impose idealized lump-sum taxation. But that would raise an awkward question of horizontal equity, giving a new twist to the age-old problem of deciding what are, and are not, acceptable differences on which to base differential treatment. Should the knowledge that I am more likely to acquire some horrid disease than you be a legitimate basis for treating us differently under the tax-benefit system?

Realizing any of this technological potential, however, will require no less fundamental changes in institutions and attitudes. Some are deeply philosophical. Some are more prosaic. Tax administrations, for example, are already increasingly called on to deliver some benefit payments. But collecting taxes and paying benefits turns out to require quite different approaches. When HMRC moved to administering EITC-type benefits in the United Kingdom, even the waiting rooms proved problematic, not having enough toilets for expectant mothers.[37] But there, for sure, we already have the technology.

What Will They Think of Us?

The future will doubtless find plenty of folly in how we set about taxing today. The corporate income tax in its current form, with the angels-dancing-on-pinheads logic of "arm's-length pricing," is likely to look as bizarre to our successors as medieval theological disputes do to us. Other sources of jollity will include the tax return, surely destined to go the way of the rotary phone, and the curious habit of basing tax liability on how long it takes the earth to go around the sun. Even the most successful tax development of our times—the VAT—may also raise a tolerant smile.

Doubtless the future will also see plenty of folly in the things we do not do. It is likely to shake its head in disbelief at our not already fully integrating taxation with the benefit side of public spending, and may be surprised by how little use we make of private companies in collecting taxes, and at the crudeness of performance reward systems in our tax agencies. Perhaps they will also have a good laugh at how we have let special interests shape our tax systems to suit them rather than any notion of a wider good. That, however, may be too much to hope.

And what wisdom will they see in us? It would be nice to think they will admire us for our stern action in introducing effective carbon taxation in time (just) to avert calamitous damage from climate change, and for developing institutions for effective collaboration in international tax matters. Maybe, when things get bad enough, we will actually do these things.

But the wisdom that future governments will build on was not produced by our generation, but by the generations of tax designers and collectors before us: The importance of using judgement and information on taxpayers' behavior and characteristics to establish tax systems that are sensitive to both the risks of collateral damage to economic activity and prevailing standards of fairness. This has been a common thread of tax design and collection, all the way from the advice of the sages of ancient China to lay out rice fields in squares of nine to the decision of the G20 that automatic exchange of information on taxpayers' interest income should be the international norm. Now, as the information potentially available about any individual becomes fantastically rich, the possibilities begin to stretch the imagination.

How future governments use the unimaginably abundant information available to them in shaping their tax systems will say a lot about how they will use their powers of coercion more generally. In navigating the opportunities and sensitivities in this new era, there will be plenty of scope for future follies, and much need for wisdom.

NOTES

Preface

1. Mencken (1922, p. 279).
2. Matthews (1958, p. viii).

Part I

1. Paine ([1792] 1894, p. 412).
2. Schumpeter ([1918] 1991, p. 101).

Chapter 1

1. Burke ([1790] 1935, p. 223).
2. University of Pennsylvania (2002).
3. OECD (n.d.a)
4. de Tocqueville (1866, p. 152): "Il n'y a presque pas d'affaires publiques qui ne naissent d'une taxe ou qui n'aboutissent à une taxe . . ." Authors' translation.
5. For kings and the like, the dates we give in this book are those of their rule.
6. Strictly, he did not sign it, but affixed his seal. But he was, in any case, soon reneging on it.
7. Bank of England (n.d., table A29).
8. Quoted in Brogan (1985, p. 116).
9. Johnson (1998, p. 132). There were 20 shillings (s) to the pound (£), and 12 pennies (d) to the shilling.
10. Cited in Robins (2012, p. 17).
11. Davidson (2011, p. 25).
12. Cited in Burke (1774, p. 9).
13. Quoted in Hibbert (1990, p. 18).
14. Bowen (1991, Table 2, p. 104).
15. Quoted in Dalrymple (2015). A jaghire was a landed estate.
16. Robins (2012, p. 114).
17. Bowen (1991) provides an account of the 1772 crisis of the East India Company.
18. Bowen (1991, p. 122).
19. Bowen (1991, p. 126).
20. Dalrymple (2015) reports that a quarter of all MPs then held shares in the Company.

21. Burke (1774, p. 12).

22. Bowen (1991, p. 27). Frederick North, 2nd Earl of Guilford (1732–1792), was prime minister from 1770 to 1782, spanning the American Revolutionary War. Appointed chancellor of the exchequer in 1767, he combined this office with the premiership.

23. Labaree (1966, p. 7). This estimate is for the 1760s prior to the Townshend Duties.

24. Burke (1774, p. 13).

25. Bohea tea, the cheapest, was then selling at auction in London for around 2s per pound (Labaree 1966, p. 76). The impact in 1773 would have been less than this suggests, as 60 percent of the import duty had been removed in 1772. In this respect, the 1773 Tea Act is best seen as a further tightening of the screws on the smugglers.

26. Here "publican" refers to a pub owner, not, in its now archaic sense, to a tax collector. Both words derive from the Latin *publicus*, meaning "public," referring to keeping a public house in the former case and public revenue in the latter.

27. Johnson (1998, pp. 141–142).

28. Adams (2001, p. 313).

29. Brogan (1985, p. 159).

30. Shays' Rebellion of 1786–1787, an armed uprising in Massachusetts, broke out even before the U.S. Constitution was completed; but tax was just one area in which the rebels, weighed down by hard times, sought relief.

31. It applied to all distilled spirits, but whiskey was the big-ticket item.

32. The tax due was either 9 cents per gallon or a flat fee per barrel: By choosing the latter, the large distillers could reduce the cost to something like 6 cents per gallon.

33. The tax itself remained largely ineffective and was repealed when the anti-Federalist President Jefferson came to power in 1801. But this was not quite the last armed tax revolt in the United States. That was Fries's Rebellion of 1799–1800.

34. Roberts (2014, p. 48).

35. Hernon (2003, p. 714).

36. As argued by Abraham (1974).

37. Hernon (2003, p. 728).

38. Military aspects of the conflict are described in Hernon (2003).

39. Hernon (2003, p. 717).

40. Kup (1975, p. 187).

41. *New African* (2011).

42. Quoted in Kup (1975, p. 181).

43. Hernon (2003, p. 731).

44. Ochiai (2017, p. 72).

45. Kup (1975, p. 181).

46. Hernon (2003, p. 709).

47. Ochiai (2017, p. 75).

48. Hernon (2003, p. 730).

49. See Ballara (1993). His prediction had already come true: New Zealand had had an income tax (on people) since 1819, but it was unlikely to be owed by Maori.

50. A full account of the revolt is in Lewis (1977).

51. Crawford (2002, p. 276).

52. The issue then was that France claimed a right to tax American companies operating in France on their profits all over the world. This led to the adoption by the United States of provisions allowing massive retaliation against such measures. They did not in the event need to be used then—but it has not gone unnoticed that they are still on the books (Thorndike, 2016).

53. Also known as the "Pacific War" or "Saltpeter War."

54. de la Riva-Agüero ([1874–1875] 1929, p. 62).

55. A quintal is about 100 pounds (mass). The tax was imposed to help address damage caused by an earthquake and tsunami in 1877 (Farcau, 2000).

56. Pictured is the death of the Peruvian commander in the Battle of Arica in 1880.

57. International Court of Justice (n.d.).

58. *BBC News* (2018a) and C. Mann (2011, p. 255).

59. The window tax never took hold in North America. In Charles Dickens's *Martin Chuzzlewit*, set in 1840s America, a local boasts to Martin and the companionable Brit Mark Tapley: "No window dues here, sir." "And no windows to put 'em on," Mark replies. The tax applied in Scotland only from 1748, and in Ireland only from 1799.

60. Hughes and White (1991). The term is dismissive. But over time, improvements in the administration of the window tax, including the assertion of central control over the exercise of discretion (legal or not) by local elites ultimately responsible for assessment and appeals, were key to the emergence of a disinterested and professional tax administration capable of implementing the income tax; see Ward (1952).

61. See, for instance, Eckert (2008).

62. Smith ([1776] 1868, p. 357). From 1808, some adjustment was made for this problem by charging a higher amount, for any given number of windows, on properties with a higher rental value. Those who think tax complexity is something new might look at that rule, set out in Glantz (2008, p. 21).

63. This story is recounted in Ydema and Vording (2014, p. 514). Excess burden is also known as "deadweight loss."

64. Stebbings (2011, p. 61).

65. Glantz (2008, pp. 32–35).

66. Franklin (1931, p. 20).

67. Dickens (1850), cited in Oates and Schwab (2015, p. 163).

68. Hugo ([1862] 1982, p. 29).

69. Austen (1906, p. 244). The lasting architectural consequences of the window tax are described in Glantz (2008), including current examples of using false bricked-up windows to liven up bare exterior walls.

70. Braddick (1996, p. 159).

71. From a 1747 report of the Commissioner for Taxes, cited in Glantz (2008, p. 25).

72. Dowell (1884c, p. 201).

73. Ward (1952, p. 536).

74. Thornton and Ekelund (2004).

75. As suggested, for instance, by Wood (1934, p. 88). Some recent analyses of the Reformation come to much the same conclusion. In this view, the medieval Catholic Church

earned immense profits from its monopoly over salvation and the endorsement of princes' temporal authority. But it became an inefficient and disreputable monopolist, opening the way to competition from Protestant churches that could offer the same services without extracting such large profits from, in particular, the princes (Ekelund, Hébert, and Tollison, 2002).

76. In 1532, the year before his marriage to Anne Boleyn and the decisive break, Henry allowed only 5 percent of the revenues from the papal taxes to go to Rome, and threatened to take them all. Which, in 1534, he did. The dissolution of the monasteries began in 1536.

77. Cunich (1999, p. 129). This revenue was, moreover, just his recurrent receipts—that is, leaving aside one-offs.

78. Cunich (1999, p. 135).

79. See Spartacus Educational (n.d.).

Chapter 2

1. Schumpeter ([1918] 1991, p. 100). In this same piece, Joseph Schumpeter (1883–1950—briefly minister of finance of Austria in 1919, and one of the most influential economists of the twentieth century) goes on to argue the need for "a special field: fiscal sociology" (p. 101). This thought was not really picked up until the end of the century, but as noted shortly, is now a very active area of inquiry.

2. Waugh ([1938] 2012, p. 95).

3. The phrase comes from Belsey (1985, p. 2).

4. There are strong echoes in the account we now give of the ideas coming out of the new "fiscal history" that is emerging from Schumpeter's challenge above. Focusing on the links between developments in fiscal systems and of the state, one influential approach distinguishes four stages in fiscal and state systems. The "tribute state" (what we call "plunder"); the "domain state" (with the ruler financing him or herself, except in special circumstances—usually war); the "tax state" (raising revenue by well-defined rules), and the "fiscal state" (capable of managing and financing large debt). Things get complex, however, since progression between these stages is not always in one direction, some stages can be jumped over, societies can at any moment have characteristics of more than one stage, and people can reasonably disagree (for instance, as to whether Anglo-Saxon England was a tribute state or a tax state). To keep up the gallop, however, we jump over this conceptual apparatus (on which, see in particular Ormrod, Bonney, and Bonney 1999).

5. Beard (2015, pp. 214, 483).

6. Hurstfield (1955, p. 57).

7. *The Magnificent Seven* (1960).

8. Strassler (2009, p. 12). The Emperor Tiberius (14–37) also saw the point: When it was suggested that he increase provincial taxes, he responded that "It is the duty of a good shepherd to shear his flock; he does not flay them" (Suetonius [121] 1957, p. 126). To which Eli Wallach's character in *The Magnificent Seven* added the thought: "If God didn't want them sheared, he would not have made them sheep."

9. Goldsmith (1987, p. 33).

10. Dietz (1921, p. 184).

11. Machiavelli ([1515] 1908, p. 125).

12. This was known as the "well-field" system, the character for "well," 井, conveying its essence visually. See Huang (2016) and Theobald (2016).

13. *Beijing Tax Museum* (2019, p. 1).

14. The term "land tax" is often used as a convenient catchall term for taxes aimed in one way or another at agricultural activities. Such taxes have often been imposed indirectly by taxing agricultural products.

15. Lactantius, advisor to Roman emperor Constantine I, cited in Bartlett (1994, p. 298).

16. Gilmour (2006, p. 111).

17. Chen (1911, p. 669).

18. On the liturgies of ancient Greece and Rome, see Webber and Wildavsky (1986, pp. 102–107).

19. Bernardi (1970, p. 75).

20. Goldsmith (1987, p. 32).

21. This was the English term. The French and Spanish had similar terms: *vivre du sien, conformare con lo suyo* (Ferguson 2001, p. 53).

22. Stressed by Schumpeter ([1918] 1991, p. 105).

23. On the links between changes in military technology and developments in state structures, see, for instance, Bobbitt (2003). Ferguson (2001) charts the course and "bangs-for-buck" cost of military technology over the past few centuries.

24. Ferguson (2001, p. 57).

25. Grapperhaus (1998, p. 17). This refers to Roxanne, but we believe the correct reference to be to today's Roanne.

26. Tarver and Slape (2016).

27. Goldsmith (1987, p. 165).

28. *Merriam-Webster's Collegiate Dictionary* (2005).

29. A leader of the resistance to Charles I, John Pym (1584–1643) was one of five MPs that Charles I tried to arrest in the chamber of the House of Commons, only to find "the birds have flown"—and himself soon at war.

30. Webber and Wildavsky (1986, pp. 102–105).

31. Dietz (1921, pp. 386–387).

32. J. Marshall (1836, p. 37).

33. Robert Walpole, first Earl of Orford, (1676–1745); generally regarded as the first prime minister of Great Britain.

34. This decline partly also reflected the seemingly universal political difficulty of revaluing taxable assets. The British Land Tax, for instance, was based on 1692 values throughout its life, which was one reason for its falling contribution to revenues over the eighteenth-century (Mathias 2013, p. 462). The decline of revenue from the land tax in nineteenth century British India largely reflected the Permanent Settlement of land revenues in Bengal in 1793, which fixed the nominal amount due in perpetuity (Richards 2012, pp. 420–421). And, as we will see in chapter 4, it was the U.K. government's desire to avoid a revaluation that prompted the (second) poll tax disaster in the United Kingdom.

35. Cited in Dowell (1884b, p. 99).

36. Clark (2006, p. 88).

37. Grapperhaus (1998, p. 63) refers, though, to an income tax in the Batavian Republic in 1797.

38. David Lloyd George (1863–1945) was a radical Liberal chancellor of the exchequer from 1908 to 1915 and prime minister from 1916 to 1922.

39. There is some dispute about who actually invented the modern VAT. Another leading contender is the American economist Thomas S. Adams, who may have been close to the idea as early as 1911. See James (2015).

40. HM Revenue & Customs (2018, charts 8 and 9). Admittedly, this is unusually high, because the U.K. "zero rates"—meaning that it levies no tax on sales and provides businesses with a full refund of the VAT remitted by suppliers—not only exports (as is standard) but also food, a large part of consumers' expenditures.

41. The rise of the VAT is analyzed in Ebrill et al. (2001), Keen and Lockwood (2010), and James (2015).

42. Goode (1993, p. 37).

43. Meade (1977, p. 320).

44. Jones (2014, p. 120).

45. Goldsmith (1987, p. 32); this excludes receipts from other states allied under Athens in the Delian League.

46. Goldsmith (1987, p. 78).

47. Goldsmith (1987, p. 92).

48. Nakabayashi (2012, pp. 395–396).

49. Goldsmith (1987, p. 122).

50. Goldsmith (1987, p. 226).

51. Ferguson (2001, p. 94); see also Hellie (1999, pp. 496–497) and Gerschenkron (1970).

52. Goldsmith (1987, p. 226).

53. Williams (2017).

54. Stubbs ([1870] 1936, p. 189).

55. North and Weingast (1989, p. 809); figures are for 1617. The calculation here excludes revenue from crown lands and makes some allowance for purveyance (on which, see chapter 3).

56. Denmark, where the state church is regarded as part of "general government," is an exception.

57. Huey Long (1893–1935) was governor of Louisiana from 1928 to 1932, and then senator from 1932 until his assassination in 1935. By both fair means and extremely foul ones, he "seized more control over an American state than any politician before or since" (White 2006, p. ix).

58. White (2006, p. 91).

59. The figures for Britain in this paragraph are from Bank of England (n.d.). They are for the central government alone and include national insurance contributions. Local taxes for Britain during the Industrial Revolution were about 10–17 percent of the central government number given in the text; Hartwell (1981, pp. 137–138).

60. Hungerford (2006) and Office of Management and Budget (n.d.).

61. Bank of England (n.d., table A27).

62. Office of Management and Budget (n.d., table 14.1).

63. OECD (2019c, table 3.1).

64. OECD (2019c, table 3.1).

65. Even the astute comedian Jon Stewart missed the point of tax expenditures. After President Obama called for a reduction in tax expenditures in 2011, Stewart attacked: "What? The tax code isn't where we spend. It's where we collect. . . . You managed to talk about a tax hike as a spending reduction. Can we afford that and the royalty checks you'll have to send to George Orwell?" An exasperated public finance economist took Mr. Stewart to task, noting there are a multitude of spending programs masquerading as tax cuts: "You don't believe there's spending in the tax code??? Here's a real life example: the chicken-s**t tax credit." (Strange but true: chicken farmers get a tax credit for spending on environmentally sound ways to dispose of, well, chicken s**t.) See Burman (2011).

66. Gaspar et al. (2019).

67. Bean (1973, p. 212).

68. Brewer (1988) provides a magisterial account.

69. Clark (2006, p. 88).

70. Peacock and Wiseman (1961).

71. It had also been repealed briefly in 1802–1803, during the Peace of Amiens.

72. But this number varies quite widely, from 11 percent of GDP in the Republic of Korea to 32 percent in France.

73. Handcock (1996, p. 127).

74. Goldsmith (1987, pp. 55–57).

75. Thane (2000, p. 108).

76. Tanzi and Schuknecht (2000) elaborate on this.

77. Schumpeter ([1918] 1991, p. 131).

78. A huge empirical literature explores the determinants of the size of government, recent and representative examples being Le, Moreno-Dodson, and Bayraktar (2012) and Bird, Martinez-Vazquez and Torgler (2008). This literature—which has not always found that high income per capita is associated with bigger government (see Rodrik 1998, for example)—has pointed to a wide range of other characteristics as being associated with high tax ratios: greater openness to trade, a lesser population, a proportional rather than majoritarian electoral system, a higher dependency ratio (old and young as a percentage of the population), a smaller agricultural sector, lower corruption, wider participation in the political process, and freer media, to name a few.

79. Genovese, Scheve, and Stasavage (2016).

80. Scheve and Stasavage (2016, p. 80).

81. Ferguson (2001).

82. Guicciardini ([1534] 1994, p. 49).

83. Ireton, Cromwell's son-in-law, was a leading officer in the Parliamentary army during the English Civil War.

84. Kekewich (1994, p. 45).

85. Babbage (1851, p. 22).

86. The Liberal William Ewart Gladstone (1809–1898), the Grand Old Man of nineteenth-century British politics, was four times Chancellor of the Exchequer (1852–1855, 1859–1866, 1873–1874, and 1880–1882) and four times Prime Minister (1868–1874, 1880–1885, 1886, and 1892–1894).

87. Cited in Matthew (1979, p. 630).

88. Ferguson (2001, p. 86).

89. Scheve and Stasavage (2016, p. 64). This result is for a sample of 15 countries.

90. That is, from 7d to 1s per pound. (For the latter figure, see Daunton, 2001, p. 361).

91. That is, 1s 8d per pound (Daunton 2001, p. 361).

92. The phrase is that of Lord Derby, prime minister at the time.

93. Disraeli also considered making voting rights conditional on liability to the income tax (Ferguson, 2001, p. 84) and may not have had as much confidence that this leap would work as he later claimed (Blake, 1969).

94. Unless, of course, they saw benefit in enfeebling the rich even if that did not directly enrich themselves.

95. Kagan (2003, p. 452).

96. *Hansard's Parliamentary Debates* (1854, p. 376).

97. Goldsmith (1987, p. 214).

98. Ferguson (2001, p. 121).

99. Belasco (2014).

100. It is not quite as easy as it may sound to figure out how wars (or any other particular item of spending) are financed; for example, without the post–9/11 engagements perhaps taxes would have been cut. Bank, Stark, and Thorndike (2008) present a comprehensive history of the U.S. experience of taxation during wartime, focusing on the role in the fiscal debates of the notion of sacrifice.

101. R. Barro (1987, p. 239).

102. Adding the squares of 2 and 4, for instance, gives $4 + 16 = 20$; which is more than twice the square of the average of 2 and 4, which is $2 \times 3^2 = 18$. Moreover—another rationale for tax smoothing—changing tax rates over time can give rise to distorted incentives in itself, as we will see in chapter 9.

103. Gaspar (2015).

104. By reneging on a promise to redeem 1918 Liberty Bonds in gold; see Bott (2013). The Supreme Court did, however, hold that, viewed together with related measures adopted, this was not unconstitutional.

105. Reinhart and Rogoff (2009, figure 5.7, p. 80).

106. Koyama (2010, p. 397).

107. Katznelson (2005, p. 119).

108. Ferguson (2001, p. 172).

109. We are here thinking of the central bank, which actually does the creating, as part of "government."

110. Hopkins (1980, p. 123).

111. Board of Governors of the Federal Reserve System (2017).

112. A possible exception is the issuance of large-denomination bills, whose main users may well be particularly unpleasant criminals. Rogoff (2016, p. 4) calls the creation of such bills "reverse money laundering." The perils of cash are discussed in chapter 12.

113. Keynes (1919, p. 220).

114. These figures are taken from Bernholz (2003, pp. 48, 107).

115. This definition of hyperinflation dates back to Cagan (1956).

116. Spang (2015, p. 63).

117. Cited in Sargent and Velde (1995, p. 502).

118. Seigniorage from issuing assignats paid for about 80 percent of all government spending from 1792 to 1795 (Sargent and Velde 1995, p. 507).

119. By the standard definition, France was in hyperinflation from May to December 1795 (Sargent and Velde 1995, fn. 37, p. 500).

120. Levasseur (1894, p. 191).

121. The government formally repudiated the assignat in 1797 (Levasseur 1894, p. 195).

122. Burke ([1790] 1935, p. 233).

123. Quoted in Spieth (2006, p. 22).

124. Spang (2015, p. 216).

125. Cited in Cooper ([1932] 2001, p. 39).

126. Levasseur (1894, fn. 1, p. 189).

127. Levasseur (1894, p. 187).

128. Taylor (2013, p. 269).

129. Keynes (1923, p. 46).

130. Hanke and Kwok (2009, p. 355).

131. Click (1998).

132. Rogoff (2016, figure 6.1, p. 84).

133. Spicer (2015).

134. See, for instance, Blanchard and Pisani-Ferry (2020).

Chapter 3

1. Hicks (1969, p. 81).

2. Gibbon ([1776] 1946, p. 100).

3. The word "salad" also originated from "salt," dating back to the early Romans salting their leafy greens and vegetables.

4. Viard (2014).

5. The monopoly is being relaxed. As of 2017, salt producers other than the national corporation can set prices and sell directly to the market (Hancock, 2017).

6. Webber and Wildavsky (1986, p. 170).

7. Newman (1985, pp. 90–91).

8. Dowell (1884a, p. 206).

9. Lockyer (1964, p. 209).

10. Monopolies raised around £100,000 (Loades 1974, p. 385), when total revenue was around £900,000 annually (Bank of England n.d., table A26).

11. Rapport (2009, p. 43); Beales and Biagini (2013, p. 88); Smith (2000, p. 62).

12. Dupuit ([1844] 1969).

13. Such sales are often represented as a source of revenue, and they do indeed produce cash receipts today, but there is also a loss of future revenue from the asset being sold. Accounting

standards have now caught up with this trick, and government sales of financial assets are best treated as simply swapping one asset for another, with no impact on either the deficit or the government's net debt. Plenty of other possible tricks remain, however; see, for instance, Irwin (2012).

14. Cramton (2010, p. 301).

15. Binmore and Klemperer (2002) and Klemperer (2004); the per capita calculation is from p. 152 of the latter, using the exchange rate that Klemperer appears to be using to translate £22.5 billion to €39 billion.

16. Roller (2001, p. 204).

17. Palan (2002).

18. Steinberg and McDowell (2003, p. 49).

19. Slemrod (2008) provides evidence that commercialization of state sovereignty is more likely in countries where it is more difficult to raise revenue in alternative ways.

20. Beech (2016).

21. International Monetary Fund (2017b, p. 8).

22. Henley & Partners (n.d.).

23. BBC (2014).

24. Webber and Wildavsky (1986, p. 68). More recent archaeological research suggests that the number was more likely 20,000–25,000, and that some of the workers may have toiled voluntarily.

25. Carpenter (2003, p. 84).

26. Judson (2016, p. 194).

27. Rwanda Governance Board (n.d.).

28. Olken and Singhal (2011).

29. Grapperhaus (1998, p. 43).

30. Levi (1997, p. 89).

31. Meier (1994).

32. Levi (1997, p. 97) and Meier (1994).

33. Edsel, remembered for a wildly unsuccessful line of cars named after himself.

34. *BBC News* (2014).

35. Scheve and Stasavage (2016).

36. Chambers (1987, p. 213).

37. Chambers (1987, p. 185).

38. *New York Times* (1863).

39. Ellis and Noyes (1990, p. 190).

40. Levi (1997, p. 111). One infamous example was that of Seaman George Samson, who was presented with a white feather on his way in civilian clothes to a public reception in his honor. He had been awarded the Victoria Cross for gallantry in the Gallipoli campaign.

41. MacFarlane (1844–1845, vol. 1, p. 130).

42. "The meanness which shrunk from fair and equal contribution," Pitt reflected, "has been compensated . . . by the voluntary exertions of patriotism" (Seligman 1914, p. 71).

43. Marshall (1912, p. 30).

44. This was ironic, as the Baldwin family fortune came from an iron- and steel-making business.

45. Brunner and Sonstelie (2003, p. 2180).

46. The contribution is tax deductible—which is somewhat bizarre, as that deduction reduces tax revenue and so to that extent increases the national debt.

47. Weir (1998, p. 265).

48. Dowell (1884a, p. 243).

49. As numbered by convention, clause (12): Bagley and Rowley (1968, p. 103).

50. Hurstfield (1955, p. 53).

51. Kenyon (1990, p. 118).

52. Powicke (1950).

53. Quintrell (2014). This amount was comparable to that from one of his early ship writs, discussed next.

54. By then generally commuted to money, although not always in London (Gill 1990, p. 347).

55. Dowell (1884a, p. 228).

56. Nonetheless, the writs of 1636–1637 each raised nearly £200,000 (Kenyon 1990, p. 119).

57. Gill (1990, p. 357).

58. Dowell (1884a, pp. 240–241).

59. Constitution Society (n.d.).

60. Johnson, Coleman-Norton, and Bourne (1961, p. 120).

61. Aftalion (1990, p. 160).

62. Cunich (1999, p. 126). The last installment was forgiven in 1534, when Henry took over the papal taxes.

63. City of Doraville (2013).

64. Simmons (2014).

65. Seidl (2015).

66. Philip Morris Inc., R. J. Reynolds, Brown & Williamson, and Lorillard.

67. Plus the District of Columbia, Puerto Rico, and the Virgin Islands. The four other states had settled with the major companies the year before.

68. So long, that is, as other companies do not cut their sales to more than offset that increase.

69. Bulow and Klemperer (1998, p. 340). It is, in theory, even possible that the deal *increased* companies' profits: When just a few firms compete with one another, a tax increase can in effect allow them to tacitly agree (explicit agreement being illegal) to reduce output and raise prices by even more than the tax, possibly to such an extent that after-tax profits actually increase. See, for instance, Delipalla and Keen (1992) and Weyl and Fabinger (2013). Few ideas ever being really new, the basic observation goes back to one of the earliest (and greatest) mathematical economists, Augustin Cournot [1838] (1897).

70. In *The Republic* and *Politics*, respectively.

71. Brewer (1988) attributes the lesser hold of venality in Britain to the relative modesty of military spending needs.

72. Brewer (1988, p. 15).

73. Doyle (1996, p. 9).

74. It did, nonetheless, finance a handy 5 percent or so of the Seven Years' War (Doyle 1996, p. 99).

75. Doyle (1996, p. 60).

76. Doyle (1996, p. 77).

77. Doyle (1996, p. 12).

78. Not de jure, as he was Protestant.

79. Doyle (1996, p. 266).

80. Doyle (1996, p. 11). One of the few people to have a good word for venality was Montesquieu, who himself inherited a venal position as a president of the Bordeaux parlement (Doyle 1996, pp. 76–77). His argument was that allocating positions by the king's will would likely be even more corrupt and inefficient. Voltaire was against venality, though that did not stop him from benefiting by selling a position as gentleman of the bedchamber given to him by Madame de Pompadour (Doyle 1996, p. 250).

81. Doyle (1996, pp. 275–276).

82. Indeed, the first large expansion of issuance of assignats, in September 1790, was to pay off officeholders.

83. A curious instance of venality in Britain was the survival of the purchase of army offices until 1871, much later than elsewhere. Ludicrous though this may seem, it may have had desirable incentive effects. Cowardice was discouraged, as commissions were then forfeit; so was foolhardiness, as they were also forfeit if killed in action (throwing widows and orphans on the doubtful charity of the army). While the system produced Lord Cardigan, who led the ill-fated Charge of the Light Brigade in 1854, it also produced the Duke of Wellington, who bought his way to the rank of colonel without doing any fighting at all (Allen 1998, p. 45).

84. One reported beneficiary being William Vestey, who will have a starring role in chapter 11.

85. North and Weingast (1989, p. 811).

86. Even when participants are well aware of the low odds of winning, many still find lottery tickets attractive; see Clotfelter and Cook (1991).

87. Pearson (2016).

88. For example, a study of the New York State lottery found that lottery purchases in 2009 accounted for approximately 3 percent of total household income for wage earners making $20,000 per year, but just 1 percent for those with annual income of between $60,000 and $80,000. The average losses would be similarly regressive. See Kramer (2010).

89. Ezell (1960).

90. Statista (2017a, 2017b). The six states without a state lottery are Alabama, Alaska, Hawaii, Mississippi, Nevada(!), and Utah.

Part II

1. Gibbon ([1746] 1946, p. 488).

Chapter 4

1. From *De Cive* (Hobbes 1651, p. 199).

2. The quotations of Cassius Dio are taken from Dio ([61] 1925, pp. 85, 87).

3. Cassius Dio even gives her a nice line on inheritance tax: "Even dying is not free of cost with them . . . Among the rest of mankind death frees even those who are in slavery to others; only in the case of the Romans do the very dead remain alive for their profit" (Dio [61] 1925, p. 87).

4. Speaking simply of "rich" and "poor," as we shall, is a horrible simplification, gliding over issues that can be of considerable importance when thinking about taxation. Those with low incomes this year, for instance, may have high incomes in the future. Some people may have high incomes but few assets. And a different view may be taken of affluence, depending on whether it comes from inheritance or successful innovation. That said, the simplification does help keep things tolerably short.

5. Marx (1852, p. 1).

6. Quoted in Oman (1906, p. 9).

7. Among the irritations these included were *heriot*, the payment to the lord of the best chattel (usually an animal) on the death of a tenant; and *merchet*, payment for permission to marry off a daughter or, less often, a son (Hilton 1969, p. 66).

8. This tax began with the "Saladin tithe" mentioned in chapter 2, a charge on movables of 10 percent, to finance the third crusade in 1188 (Dowell 1884a, p. 44).

9. The poorest areas (and, for some reason, Chester and Durham) were exempt.

10. Dowell (1884a, p. 97). A fifteenth and tenth had thus come to mean simply raising an amount of about £39,000, and the practice became to grant whatever multiple of that was needed to raise the revenue desired.

11. The issue—as more generally with outdated property valuations—was not so much the overall level of prosperity: that could be taken care of by adjusting the tax rate (how many multiples of the fifteenth and tenth to raise). The real issue was the changes in relative prosperity of different regions.

12. Quoted in Dowell (1884a, p. 102).

13. Only beggars were exempt, and married couples were subject to a single charge (Oman 1906, p. 25).

14. Oman (1906, p. 27).

15. Oman (1906, p. 24).

16. Oman (1906, p. 25).

17. But the point should not be overstated. Some regressivity seems to have been intended as another way to tame the uppity lower orders, "all the wealth of England [having] gone into the hands of the labourers and workmen" (quoted in Oman 1906, p. 24). And not every place was like Brockley. In neighboring Chevington, with just one wealthy landowner, the poorest had to cough up the full 1s (Oman 1906, p. 27).

18. McLean and Smith (1994, p. 132).

19. Dickens (1914, p. 134).

20. Oman (1906, p. 76).

21. Troubles did continue for a while outside London.

22. Oman (1906, p. 84).

23. Quoted in Dowell (1884a, p. 116).

24. Chapter 7 looks more closely at the issue of who really bears the tax burden.

25. Except that students and welfare recipients owed only 20 percent of the full charge.

26. Thatcher (1993, p. 648).

27. Smith (1991, p. 429).

28. See, for instance, Keen (2013) and the references there.

29. The community charge was first introduced in Scotland in 1989, where it quickly encountered strong resistance (Bagguley 1995, p. 699). Cynics suggested that the Conservative government felt free to experiment in Scotland at little cost, as their electoral position there was in any case extraordinarily poor. The tax was never tried in troubled Northern Ireland.

30. Smith (1991, p. 429).

31. Figures by borough are from Bowles and Jones (1993, p. 446).

32. Quoted in Bagguley (1995, p. 713).

33. Smith (1991, p. 432).

34. See Bowles and Jones (1993) and Besley, Preston, and Ridge (1997).

35. Bagguley (1995).

36. Council tax is charged on the basis of capital (not rental) values, grouped in (currently) eight bands, and with single occupants owing only 75 percent of the basic charge.

37. Liability was not based on the electoral register, but the authorities had access to it when implementing the tax.

38. Oliver Letwin, cited in McLean and Smith (1994, p. 128).

39. McLean and Smith (1994, pp. 141–142). And thus the community charge came to resemble rather too closely the poll tax of the southern U.S. states, discussed in chapter 6.

40. Scutage may even date back to the Anglo-Saxons (Hollister, 1960).

41. Bagley and Rowley (1968, p. 103).

42. Clark (2006, pp. 91, 94).

43. Judson (2016, p. 46).

44. Dewald (1996, p. 32).

45. Cobban (1963, p. 58).

46. Vauban, the great military engineer, proposed in 1707 to replace the *taille* and all other taxes by what was in effect a 10 percent income tax, with no exemptions. On this proposal and evolving thinking on income taxation in France more generally, see Chambas and Combes (2001).

47. Quoted in Schama (1989, p. 86).

48. The *vingtième*, for example, which applied from 1749 to 1790 (replacing the *dixième*) was a tax of 6 percent on income from land, offices, and industry (Kwass 1999, p. 359).

49. Quoted in Jeanneney (1982, p. 29; authors' translation). The du Pont family reappears later in the history of American taxation. Pierre Samuel du Pont, then among the wealthiest people in the world as chair of his family's vast chemical business as well as the du Pont–controlled General Motors Corporation, lobbied vigorously for the end of Prohibition. He hoped that the revenues from taxing newly legal beer would make unnecessary the income tax, which he detested.

50. Davies (2009, p. 20).

51. Schama (1989, p. 386).

52. Three times unsuccessful Democrat Candidate for President (in 1896, 1900 and 1908), spellbinding orator, Secretary of State under President Wilson (resigning on principle as he saw policy drifting to war), and unhappily now perhaps best known for defending creationism in the Scopes Monkey Trial of 1925.

53. Bryan and Bryan (1900, p. 243).

54. Dissenting opinion in *Compañía General de Tabacos de Filipinas v. Collector of Internal Revenue*, 275 U.S. 87 (1927).

55. Babbage (1851, p. 15).

56. Also known as "hypothecation." This usage differs from the common use in the United States of "earmark" to refer to the insertion in legislation of spending measures in ways that avoid normal allocation processes.

57. Daunton (2001, p. 68).

58. Bird and Jun (2005, p. 27).

59. Pérez (2008).

60. Daunton (2002, p. 130).

61. Institute for Fiscal Studies (1993, pp. 64–65).

62. Seligman (1914, p. 368).

63. All kinds of questions arise on the extent to which one can, and needs to, measure and compare across individuals the quantitative indicators of well-being that this approach presumes to exist. And there are alternatives to this "welfarist" approach of focusing on notions of individual well-being, perhaps emphasizing instead people's capacity to fully participate in wider society (as set out by Sen 2009).

64. Rawls (1971).

65. Cited in Lockyer (1964, p. 33).

66. Dowell (1884a, pp. 170–171).

67. Dowell (1884a, pp. 105–107). There were differences between the 1379 and 1513 versions. The charges on dukes, earls, and barons were unchanged, but the 1513 version used a less fine-grained categorization and had some relation to earnings.

68. Including one on birth, death, and marriage that differentiated between dukes, earls, viscounts, etc.

69. North (2012, p. 161).

70. Hill (1892).

71. Latham (1985, pp. 102–103). It has also been noticed that Pepys is curiously absent from the 1666 hearth tax returns (Wareham 2017, p. 472).

72. Hill (1892, p. 211).

73. Liability under the French *capitation*, for instance, soon began to vary within social class: Seligman (1914, p. 50) asserts that by 1705, the *capitation* had virtually become an income tax in three-fourths of France. And liability never depended solely on social class under the *Klassensteuer*. This is made explicit in the ministerial instructions accompanying the 1821 *Klassensteuer*: "The class tax is intended to occupy a middle position between a uniform poll tax . . . and an income tax, which cannot be enforced without a searching investigation of the affairs . . . of the tax-payer, and is therefore always obnoxious." Cited in Hill (1892, p. 210).

74. Babylon and Assyria also had to produce 500 eunuch boys: Strassler (2009, pp. 250–255).

75. Dowell (1884a, p. 98).

76. In its design, this tax was a rudimentary income tax—salaries were taxable, for instance (except for serving officers in the army and navy)—but it quickly became overwhelmingly a tax

on land. Civil servants, for instance, had their tax refunded. The land tax was also the start of direct taxation as a regular, essentially annual, matter rather than a sporadic event (Ward 1953, pp. 7, 28, 16).

77. Ward (1953, p. 20).

78. Ward (1953, p. 3).

79. Pezzolo (2012, p. 274).

80. Nakabayashi (2012, p. 384).

81. Gatrell (2012, p. 197).

82. Goldsmith (1987, p. 73).

83. Scott (1998, fn. 69, p. 38).

84. Ward (1953, p. 37). The quote is from Plumb (1967, p. 148), citing a piece in *The Spectator*.

85. Goldsmith (1987, p. 226).

86. For possession of a forged printing plate: see Rickards (2000).

87. Previously, a tax on hats was imposed by France in 1690 (Dowell, 1884d, p. 401).

88. Uglow (2014, p. 149). The hat tax lasted until 1811, that on wigs until 1869.

89. Quoted in Ward (1953, p. 123).

90. Simons (1938, p. 40).

91. *Robertson's British Tax Tables* (Robertson 1792, p. 58). Tallow candles—made from animal fat—did not last as long as those made from wax (or sperm oil) and were foul smelling; rush lighting was made by soaking the dried pith of rush plants in fat or grease. For recognition of the tax on candles as aimed at the better off, see, for instance, Plumb (1960, pp. 241–242).

92. Brown (2007, pp. 12–13).

93. Cited in Dillon (2002, p. 136).

94. Smith (1820, p. 78).

95. The story is told in *This Way Caribbean Islands* (2001, p. 167).

96. The tax lasted until 1792. Cited in Brown (2007, p. 19).

97. Ward (1953, p. 123).

98. Smith ([1776] 1868, Book V, chapter II, para v. 2.155.)

99. For example, see Tax Research Foundation (1938, pp. 29–30).

100. The others were taxes on windows and doors in the taxpayer's principal residence, on the rental value of real estate, and on personal property.

101. See Rajaraman (1995) and Yitzhaki (2007). As with the *tachshiv*, these presumptive assessments might be "rebuttable": If the restaurant owner could prove that their income was less than the *tachshiv* formula indicated, that lesser amount would be accepted.

102. Paine ([1792] 1894, p. 496).

Chapter 5

1. Seligman (1914, p. 672). Edwin R. A. Seligman (1861–1939) was an American economist who taught at Columbia University from 1885 until 1931. He did seminal work in taxation and public finance, and he was the most distinguished scholar of the income tax, exemplified by his magisterial book *The Income Tax: A Study of the History, Theory and Practice of Income Taxation*

at Home and Abroad, first published in 1911. Seligman was also a founder of the American Economic Association. He is one of the authors' academic heroes.

2. Mitchell (1988, p. 580).

3. Details of the Triple Assessment are in Dowell (1884b, pp. 221–222) and Seligman (1914, pp. 65–66).

4. A tax on the rental value of inhabited housing, introduced by Lord North in 1778 (Shehab 1953, p. 35), was payable in addition to the window tax.

5. The hair powder tax of 1795, for instance, was not a charge on its purchase but an annual license for its use. It was levied in addition (until 1800) to what was in effect a tax on its purchase (Jeffrey-Cook 2010, p. 384).

6. Kennedy (1913, p. 169).

7. Quoted in Seligman (1914, p. 71).

8. The income tax did not replace the assessed taxes, several of which survived for many years: The window tax was repealed only in 1851, and the land tax survived until 1963.

9. As usual, this was not as silly as it may seem. The idea was that the highest incomes should pay 10 percent on all their incomes, not just (as we are used to these days) that part above £60. But then if the 10 percent rate were to be applied at the £60 threshold, by receiving just £1 more, the taxpayer could end up paying £6 more in tax. The multiple rates served to smooth such jumps in liability, but it did not eliminate them. Just above £60, for example, the rate was 1/120th; so the additional tax was only 10s. Such jumps ("notches") remained an issue in the United Kingdom until after the First World War.

10. These labels had impressive longevity: Labor income in the United Kingdom was taxed under Schedule E until 2003.

11. Jeffrey-Cook (2010, p. 389).

12. Daunton (2001, table 2.1, p. 35).

13. The story is told by Shehab (1953, p. 60), who argues that the demise had more to do with politicking than objections to the tax itself.

14. Robert Peel (1788–1850), twice Prime Minister (1834–1835, 1841–1846), is now among the most admired to have held the office and has been claimed as the founder of the Conservative Party. The quote is from Gladstone (1863, p. 18).

15. Seligman (1914, pp. 128–129).

16. Gladstone (1863, p. 48).

17. Seligman (1914, p. 153).

18. Seligman (1914, pp. 172–173).

19. Technically, the U.K. income tax remains a temporary tax that expires on April 5 each year and has to be renewed as a provision in the annual Finance Bill.

20. Heilbroner (1999, p. 173).

21. The genial but unfortunate Harcourt twice became a source of general amusement. First, when an unknown compositor inserted into *The Times*' (1882) account of one his speeches the surprising remark that "The speaker then said he felt inclined for a bit of f**king." Second, when late in life, he unexpectedly inherited an estate that was subject to the very death duties he had instituted—only to himself die soon thereafter, triggering yet more duties for his successor.

22. The objection was that if withholding were to be relied on to collect tax at this higher rate, the number of taxpayers entitled to a refund would become unmanageable.

23. Chaired by the gifted radical Sir Charles Dilke, whose career had been ruined by a "three-in-a-bed" scandal. Victorian politics was not dull.

24. To preserve withholding arrangements, the super-tax was structured as a distinct tax. Those with reason to think they were liable were required to submit a return—the first time total incomes had been required to be revealed to the government since Pitt the Younger.

25. Mallet (1913), summarized in Daunton (2001, p. 361).

26. *The Public* (1909).

27. *Hansard's Parliamentary Debates* (1909, p. 1959).

28. A "deduction" is a subtraction from taxable income (or some other tax base), which reduces tax by an amount depending on the taxpayer's marginal tax rate; in contrast, a "credit" is an amount subtracted directly from tax liability.

29. Quoted in Seligman (1914, p. 203).

30. Disraeli attempted to introduce differentiation in his 1852 budget, but the minority government of which he was part was defeated. Accounts of this at times quite sophisticated debate are in Daunton (2001) and Shehab (1953).

31. Respectively, 9d (on income up to £2,000) and 1s on the pound (Daunton 2001, p. 361).

32. Seligman (1914, p. 430).

33. The South did introduce an income tax in 1863, and Seligman (1914, p. 492) for one thought it better designed than the North's.

34. Weisman (2002, p. 34).

35. Seligman (1914, p. 439).

36. Weisman (2002, p. 102).

37. Seligman (1914, p. 472).

38. In 1880, customs duties made up 56 percent of the federal government's tax receipts while alcohol and tobacco excise taxes accounted for 34 percent, with a variety of other levies making up the rest (Mehrotra 2013, table 1.1, p. 7).

39. State and local governments relied for financing on property taxes, whose collection by part-time assessors was rife with evasion. Although, in principle, the property tax extended to all property, critics contended that in practice it discriminated against farmers, whose holdings of land, livestock, and machinery were easily observable, while urban wealth owners held financial assets, which often escaped assessment (Mehrotra 2013, p. 44).

40. *New York Times* (1891).

41. Congressman David A. De Armond, quoted in Seligman (1914, p. 502).

42. Article 1, Section 9, Clause 4.

43. Even this interpretation is confusing, as the French *capitation* mentioned in chapter 4 was certainly not a poll tax.

44. Jensen (2016, p. 10).

45. Seligman (1914, p. 568).

46. Seligman (1914) goes so far as to say of the debates leading to the Civil War income tax that everyone agreed on this interpretation.

47. Seligman (1914, p. 435).

48. One possible source of this now weird-seeming interpretation is the view of the physiocrats of the eighteenth century, touched on in chapter 7, that the burden of all taxes ultimately falls on land (read "landowners"): so the distinction is between taxes that do so directly and the rest. This argument was indeed cited during the *Pollock* case (discussed later in this section). But with scholarship of which we stand in awe, Seligman (1914, pp. 562–564) shows that the references to the great physiocrat Anne Robert Jacques Turgot (1727–1781) used to support the argument that the income tax is "indirect" were wholly misleading; that the memorandum referred to was never published in France (let alone translated into English); and that in other writings, Turgot explicitly categorizes the income tax as "indirect." (Now you can see why Seligman is our hero.) Quite where slaves fitted into this logic, in any case, is unclear.

49. Article 1, Section 2, Clause 3.

50. Weisman (2002, p. 33). And there was reason not to be too concerned. In 1795, the Supreme Court held (in *Hylton v. United States*) that a tax on carriages was not a direct tax, because if it were, it would have to be apportioned, and the consequences of that—higher tax rates in poorer states with fewer carriages—would have been so ludicrous that it could not possibly be consistent with the purposes of the Constitution.

51. Strong (1917, p. 225).

52. *Pollock v. Farmers' Loan & Trust Company* 158 U.S. 601.

53. The comparison with this 1857 decision of the Supreme Court—holding that those of African descent could not be U.S. citizens—is cited by Seligman (1914, p. 589) as a common response to the decision in *Pollock v. Farmers' Loan & Trust Company*. Unusually, Seligman, who thought it an appallingly bad decision, does not give a source, but Jones (1895) comes close.

54. Blakey and Blakey (1940, p. 20).

55. Roosevelt (1919).

56. Just before the expansion of income taxation during the First World War, alcohol taxes overtook tariffs as the biggest source of federal tax revenue.

57. Okrent (2010, p. 54).

58. Weisman (2002, pp. 210–211).

59. Weisman (2002, p. 102).

60. When, as Governor General of the Philippines, Taft reported to Secretary of State Elihu Root that he had been riding horseback in the mountains, Root cabled back: "How is the horse?" (Zimmerman, 2002, p. 392).

61. The constitutionality of this bill was challenged—opponents arguing that the privilege of incorporation is a state function, and thus only the states could tax corporations—but it was upheld by the Supreme Court in *Flint v. Stone Tracy Co.* 220 U.S. 107 (1911).

62. Quoted in Blakey and Blakey (1940, p. 62).

63. Hormats (2007, p. 103).

64. Paris and Hilgert (1983).

65. Cited in Mehrotra (2004, p. 188).

66. See Internal Revenue Service (1918, 1919).

67. Mellon (1924, pp. 56–58).

68. This is explicit in the Scandinavian dual income tax systems: see Sørensen (2010).

69. This account of the Caillaux affair draws on Le Naour (2007).

70. The discussion that follows draws particularly from Seligman (1914), Jeanneney (1982), and Didier (2014).

71. Institut des Politiques Publiques (2014, p. 2).

72. Seligman (1914, p. 281).

73. Quoted in Seligman (1914, p. 318).

74. Things did not end so well for Joseph Caillaux, who was jailed for treason in 1917. In one respect, however, he had a lucky escape. On July 31, the nationalist Raoul Villain went looking for victims with two initials carved on his pistol. One was "J," for Jean Jaurès—an iconic leader for the French left, and resolutely antiwar; Villain found him at a café in Montmartre and shot him dead. The other was "C," for Caillaux.

75. The share in France is 18.6 percent, compared to an average of 23.9 percent in the OECD, even though France's overall tax ratio is the highest among member countries (OECD 2019c, table 1.1).

76. About three-fifths of the total revenue classified as personal income taxation (the 18.6 percent of total revenue in the preceding note) is from the *Contribution Sociale Généralisée* and closely related taxes (from OECD 2019c, table 5.10).

77. Chambas and Combes (2001).

78. Chambas (2005, pp. 82–86).

79. Ironically, we struggled to name a founding father for the United States. Other candidates would be Edwin Seligman, who did much to foster understanding of the income tax in the United States, and Alexander Dallas, who as Secretary of the Treasury was behind the 1815 proposal mentioned earlier.

80. Cited in Matthew (1979, p. 627).

81. OECD (n.d.b, table I.7).

82. We look at this experience in chapter 14.

83. An incoherent idea, because corporations are not (except in a legal sense) persons.

84. Daunton (2001, p. 95).

85. A difference between the two approaches is that under the second, but not the first, the government becomes a partner in sharing, for better or worse, the return realized on savings. U.S. readers may recognize that the first type of treatment is that under a Roth IRA, the latter that under a 401(k).

86. We have in mind Thomas Piketty (2013) as well as Emmanuel Saez and Gabriel Zucman (2019b), who have argued for substantial new taxes on wealth.

87. Seligman (1914, p. 89).

88. United Kingdom of Great Britain and Ireland (1920).

89. See, for example, Gordon (1992), Mintz (1994), and Sørensen (2007).

Chapter 6

1. *Congressional Globe* (1870, p. 4038). Roots was a one-term Congressman from Arkansas.

2. Thornton (1983, p. 24).

3. Dowell (1884a, p. 28).

4. Holloway and Wilson (2017, p. 180).

5. The sentiment is attributed to Russell Long, Democratic Senator for Louisiana, chair of the Senate Finance Committee from 1966 to 1981, and son of Huey Long (Pine, 1978).

6. This incident is discussed by Sadasivan (2000, p. 394), Radhakrishnan (2009), and Surendranath (2013). As to its historical veracity, Arya (2016) calls this "a village tale that is not officially recognised in any of India's historical accounts." Accounts of the date also differ, some putting it in 1803.

7. Tutt (2010).

8. Crawford (2003, pp. 293–294).

9. This story is in Frances (2004).

10. As of 2018; see U.S. Agency for International Development (2018, p. 28).

11. The distinction between explicit and implicit gender bias is developed in Stotsky (1997). Discrimination against women, dubbed a "pink tax" or "woman tax," has been alleged in pretax prices as well. For example, in 2010, *Consumer Reports* found that drugstores set higher prices for identical products marketed to women (*New York Times*, 2014).

12. See Larimer (2016), Leskin (2016), and Geiger and Garcia (2016).

13. An efficiency argument can also be made for taxing secondary earners, most often women, at lower marginal tax rates than primary earners. Most research concludes that, on average, women's labor-market decisions, especially about whether to be in the labor force at all, are more responsive to the after-tax return than are men's. As we discuss in chapter 10, this means that taxing women creates more excess burden, because a given tax reduces labor supply more than for men. Reducing the tax on women and increasing it on men would increase total labor supply. See Boskin and Sheshinski (1983).

14. Hitchman and Fong (2011).

15. See Thomas (1990, 1993) and Lundberg, Pollak, and Wales (1997). This is probably why a striking feature of spending-side responses to COVID-19 has been that several countries—including, for example, India and Togo—have deliberately treated women more generously than men.

16. Ogden (1958, p. 6).

17. Our description of poll taxes in the South relies on Ogden (1958, pp. 59–66). The quotation is from page 59.

18. Quoted in White (2006, p. 160).

19. Johnson (2010, p. 93).

20. The 24th Amendment referred only to federal elections, but a series of federal court decisions in 1966 extended abolition to state elections.

21. The Sentencing Project (2016).

22. Sheets (2017).

23. This account draws on Clements (2016).

24. This meant, in effect, Catholics. The Protestant Dutch provided help, albeit reluctantly, in suppressing the Shimabara rebellion. Some apparently had no difficulty walking on an image of Christ, known as *fumi-e*, which was the test used to identify Christians.

25. Clements (2016, p. 65); the following two quotes are from pages 79 and 54, respectively.

26. Also known as Amakusa Shirō or Amakusa Shirō Tokisada. Since the 1960s, a character with that name has featured in popular Japanese culture in numerous manga, anime, and video games.

27. Clements (2016, p. 200).

28. Heemstra (2010).

29. Koyama (2010).

30. Katznelson (2005, p. 108).

31. Dowell (1884b, pp. 62–63).

32. Jewish Virtual Library (n.d.).

33. Jewish Virtual Library (n.d.). It was not always as harsh as one might think. In Austria as of 1244, corpses were exempted.

34. Gelber (1967).

35. Under the Act of Uniformity 1558.

36. The act was repealed during the Interregnum, but all laws of that period were negated at the restoration. Little noticed, it remained on the statutes until 1888.

37. Weir (1998, p. 63).

38. Ward (1953, p. 69).

39. Sometimes subsidies emerged. Under the Sun King Louis XIV of France (1643–1715), Huguenots (French Protestants) were offered cash payments to convert back to Catholicism.

40. Ansary (2009, p. 47).

41. Cited in the *Oxford Dictionary of Islam* (n.d.).

42. In Saudi Arabia, for instance, the *zakat* is collected by the tax administration and the funds passed to the Ministry of Social Affairs for spending in accordance with *sharia*.

43. Eraly (1997, p. 405).

44. Eraly (1997, p. 401).

45. Montefiore (2011, pp. 198, 343–344).

46. Hanioğlu (2008, p. 90).

47. Ibrahim (2013).

48. Ibrahim (2015).

49. Dennett (1950, p. 74).

50. Saleh (2018).

51. Bowman (2000, p. 86).

52. Gernet (1995, pp. 37, 57).

53. Abbott and Johnson (1926, p. 225).

54. Martinez (2011).

55. Williams (1981).

56. As an aside, in *Bray v. Alexandria Women's Health Clinic* 506 U.S. 263 (1993), the Supreme Court argued that if adverse treatment is given to some activities that "happen to be engaged in exclusively or predominantly by a particular class of people, an intent to disfavor that class can readily be presumed." The (hypothetical, as far as we know) example mentioned was that "A tax on wearing yarmulkes is a tax on Jews."

57. Kraal and Kasipillai (2014, p. 277).

58. See Stiem (2016) and Kassam (2016).

59. U.S. Constitution art. IV, cl. 1.

60. Harington, an English courtier and author (1561–1612), made an even greater contribution to humankind by inventing the flush toilet.

61. Hyden (2015).

62. Formally known as the "Extraordinary Tax," the popular name recalled the ancient Roman practice of executing one in ten of those troops showing cowardice or mutiny. The account here draws on Durston (2001),

63. Those with no estate but property worth £1,500 were to pay £100 for every £1,500.

64. Vaughan (1840, p. 523).

65. Hazlitt ([1744] 1875, p. 355).

66. Letter from William Goffe to John Thurloe, secretary of state during Oliver Cromwell's Protectorate, in Birch (1742, p. 344).

67. A married couple can file separate returns, but it is almost always tax minimizing to file jointly.

Chapter 7

1. Evidence to the Colwyn Committee (1927, p. 65).

2. By 1280, customs (mainly from wool) made up around 40 percent of the king's regular revenue (Barratt, 1999, table 3.6.2, p. 77).

3. Quoted in Power (1941, p. 42).

4. Dowell (1884a, pp. 135–136).

5. Salpukas (1992).

6. Sun-Sentinel (1993).

7. So said the executive director of the Tax Foundation of Hawaii: Kalapa (2012).

8. There is a twist here, in that a 25 percent (or any) rate means something different for an income versus a consumption tax. To see this, consider what a 100 percent tax rate entails. For an income tax, a 100 percent rate means the taxpayer ends up with nothing after tax. Not so for a consumption tax, as a 100 percent retail sales tax or VAT, if fully passed though, (merely) doubles the price of all goods and services, halving—not wiping out—what can be consumed. So a 100 percent consumption tax is actually equivalent to a 50 percent income tax, and a 25 percent consumption tax is equivalent to a 20 percent tax on income.

9. The story is told by McCulloch ([1845] 1975, p. 156), whose translation this is.

10. Aguado (2018).

11. Kopczuk et al. (2016).

12. Rucker (2011).

13. The most vivid description of the immortality doctrine comes from the British jurist Sir William Blackstone, who, in his Commentaries, said that although the shareholders and managers of a corporation may change, it is still the same corporation, just "as the river Thames is still the same river, though the parts which compose it are changing every instant." Blackstone (1794, p. 495).

14. Haig (1934, pp. 31–32).

15. Haig (1934, p. 30).

16. Kornhauser (2010, p. 334).

17. Colorado, Connecticut, Kentucky, and Nebraska.

18. Cole (2014).

19. *BBC News* (2009).

20. And so not just corn as Americans know it.

21. The mark of the East India Company runs throughout this book. Malthus was a professor at the Company's training college at Haileybury. John Stuart Mill, who will appear in a moment, was also an employee of the East India Company—as was his father, the philosopher James Mill (Robins 2012, p. 187).

22. The Malthus-Ricardo debate of 1814–1815 continues to generate an impressively large scholarly literature, especially given that, analytically, they basically agreed. See, for instance, Dorfman (1989), who considers their relationship more generally, and Salvadori and Signorino (2015).

23. Quite how protective the Corn Laws actually were remains a matter of dispute; see, for instance, Sharp (2010).

24. Dorfman (1989, fn. 12, p. 158) mentions James Anderson as anticipating their ideas, in 1777.

25. Ricardo and Malthus agreed on this analysis but disagreed on the policy implications. Ricardo argued that the additional wealth of the landowners would simply be spent on consumption and therefore contributed nothing to growth. Malthus saw nothing wrong with that; moreover, he contended that even an artificial expansion of agriculture was good for national security. Ricardo's counterargument was that cutting off food supplies to Britain would be so damaging to foreign suppliers that they would not in fact do so. Even Napoleon's France, after all, had sold food to the British.

26. *The Economist* (2018a).

27. Irwin (1989, p. 54).

28. The money wage, that is, adjusted for prices so as to measure what that wage could actually buy.

29. Keynes (1923, p. 80).

30. This was Thomas Thompson, as described in the *Evening Sun* (cited in Turner 1998, p. 1011).

31. Peel (1853, p. 601).

32. Peel (1853, p. 591).

33. Peel (1853, p. 651).

34. Quoted in Blake (1969, p. 236). Later in life, Disraeli changed his opinion of Peel (or at least how he spoke of him): "What posterity will acknowledge him to have been, is the greatest member of Parliament that ever lived" (Lexden, 2011).

35. Hurd (2007, pp. 368–370).

36. Seligman (1899).

37. Locke (1691, vol. 2, p. 36).

38. Rothstein (2008).

39. The phenomenon of benefit shifting is not limited to the EITC. One study found that between 73 and 90 cents of every dollar of the U.S. Child and Dependent Care Credit is passed through to care providers in the form of higher prices and wages, rather than in a lower price for child care. Another concluded that the benefit to students and their families from federal

student aid to higher education is substantially offset by price increases by colleges and universities. See Rodgers (2018) and Turner (2012).

40. Churchill (1909).

41. Constitutional considerations lie behind this, too. The 1895 *Pollock* case that ruled an income tax unconstitutional also held that levying tax on state and local bond interest would be unconstitutional, on the grounds that it would violate the doctrine of intergovernmental tax immunity. Although the 16th Amendment that allowed a federal income tax did not address the issue, the Revenue Act of 1913 that introduced an income tax specifically excluded municipal bond interest from federal taxation, and this has remained in effect. Whether a constitutional issue would arise if the exemption were to be abolished is controversial.

42. This story assumes that the risk of holding the two types of bonds is comparable. In the wake of COVID-19, at the time of writing the yield on municipal bonds was actually higher than the yield on Treasury bonds, largely because the perceived risk of municipal bond default had risen relative to that of treasuries.

43. Because $(1-0.233) \times 2.02 = 1.55$.

44. *Congressional Record* (1909, p. 3989).

45. It may be that consumer prices will rise, too, although the scope for that may be limited by the possibility of importing consumer goods from abroad.

46. See, for instance, the review of evidence in de Mooij (2011).

47. Furman (2017).

48. Summers (2017).

49. Gravelle (2017, p. 33).

50. They say that "[t]hese distributions between capital and labor reflect the middle of the range of estimates for distributing business taxes in the economic literature." (Joint Committee on Taxation 2013, p. 30).

51. Yglesias (2013).

52. A major objective was to advise on whether to adopt capital levy; in the event, the majority report concluded against.

53. Colwyn Committee (1927, par. 845, p. 66).

54. Office for National Statistics (2020). These studies have been somewhat out of fashion for many years, doubtless in part reflecting the concerns we now describe. But a notable exception is the series of analyses for middle- and low-income countries produced by the Commitment to Equity Institute, whose handbook gives a clear account of its methods (Lustig, 2018).

55. Compare Saez and Zucman (2019a) to Splinter (2020).

56. Some studies try to take account not only of transfers in the form of negative taxes, but also of public services provided largely for free, such as basic education and healthcare. That is good—delivering these, after all, is one of the main reasons for taxing in the first place—but they are often valued in these studies at the cost of producing them, which may be far from the money equivalent of the value that recipients place on them.

57. One way of thinking about a tariff, as the Corn Law story suggests, is as a tax on consumption combined with a subsidy to domestic production. But that is not how tariffs are generally treated in incidence studies.

58. As, for instance, in the Commitment to Equity Institute studies: Lustig (2018, p. lxv).

59. In particular, such studies routinely assume that taxes on consumption (such as the VAT) are fully passed on to consumers, while taxes on wage income are fully passed on to labor. The equivalence between the two taxes, noted earlier in the chapter, suggests some inconsistency in this. Applying the general principles discussed there, for the tax on consumption to fall wholly on labor it must be the case that the demand for consumption goods is perfectly inelastic. But then, as consumption prices go up (because of the tax), labor supplied must also go up in order to pay for the increased cost of the (unchanging) consumption. So labor supply has some elasticity. But then labor supply is not completely inelastic, in which case it cannot bear all the burden of a tax on wage income.

60. Whalley (1984).

61. This interpretation of the kind of study produced by the Office for National Statistics is set out in Dilnot, Kay, and Keen (1990).

62. The analysis in Benedek et al. (2020) tends to support this presumption—but the issue is far from resolved.

Part III

1. From "The Dog and the Accountant," quoted in Barzel (1976, p. 1177), and found on page 40 of the September 17, 1973, issue of the *New Yorker*.

Chapter 8

1. From Webster's argument in the Supreme Court case, *McCulloch v. Maryland,* 1819. 17 US 36.

2. Peasants were subject to a modified version of the tax, only being required to shave or pay a tax of one kopeck (one-hundredth of a ruble) when entering a city. To put the beard tax liability in context, the average wage of unskilled workers under Peter the Great was 5–8 kopecks per day (Sudakov, 2013). For a noble or merchant, the charge could be up to 100 rubles every year (Eschner, 2017). The beard tax survived until 1772.

3. Dating back to 403 BCE in Rome (Peck, 1898).

4. Compare this to the current U.K. "wealthy bachelor" discount for local property tax. This provides a 25 percent reduction in council tax on properties for which only one taxpayer is liable. Not to be outdone in tax branding, the Local Government Minister Brandon Lewis called the proposal to revoke this discount the "Bridget Jones tax" (Eleftheriou-Smith, 2014).

5. Cited in Redman (1959, p. 33).

6. Forcucci (2010) and Mann (1943).

7. Kornhauser (2013).

8. Matthews et al. (1919, p. 133). Barnett (2013, pp. 18–19) alludes to the racial motive.

9. This is the premise of a historical romance novel, *The Bachelor Tax*, by Carolyn Davidson (2000).

10. *Los Angeles Herald* (1903).

11. The surcharge lasted until 1992.

12. All childless men and women older than 25, married or unmarried, were subject to a tax that could reach 30 dollars a month, apparently more than 10 percent of a typical salary at the time. Details are in Vâlsan (2014).

13. The government collected a "social fostering" or "maintenance fee" in the year of the second child's birth, calculated as a percentage of the annual disposable income of city dwellers or the cash income of peasants. The parents were fined, and had to foot the bill for both the first and second children to go to school, as well as the entire family's health care.

14. *BBC News* (2019).

15. Gans and Leigh (2009, p. 246).

16. History House (n.d.).

17. Oats and Sadler (2007, p. 358).

18. Oats and Sadler (2007, pp. 367–368).

19. Jenkins (2002, pp. 226–227).

20. Musson (1958, p. 411).

21. *Printers' Ink* (1897).

22. Kolbert (2006).

23. Waterson (2020).

24. If the initial allocation of property rights were the other way around, so that the polluter had no inherent right to pollute, the bribe would also switch from polluter to polluted.

25. Due to Coase (1960).

26. Pigou (1920).

27. Externalities are an example of "market failure," because in their presence, free markets will fail to achieve an efficient allocation of resources—there will be too much pollution, for example, or too little beautifying of house fronts or fundamental research.

28. Pigovian taxation is not about punishment but about efficiency in the use of resources—too many used in activities generating negative externalities and too few used in activities generating positive ones. An essential part of the logic of Pigovian taxation is that not only the pollutee but also the polluter can be made better off if the tax is combined with an appropriate transfer between the two (mimicking the payment that bargaining between them would have produced). This point is generally forgotten for "sin" taxes, but provides some rationale for the fairly widespread earmarking of the proceeds of environmental taxes to ease businesses' cost of moving to cleaner technologies.

29. A more vivid example is the U.S. National Firearms Act of 1934 (endorsed by the National Rifle Association!), which levied a federal tax on manufacturing most firearms and on transferring them. The tax is still in place, at the same nominal amount. We leave aside the issue of whether the possession (or transfer) of firearms generates negative externalities, but note that since 2012 at least 12 U.S. states have increased fees on guns and ammunition.

30. One estimate is that, without action to reduce carbon emissions, output per capita in a typical low-income country will be nearly 10 percent lower at the end of the century than it otherwise would have been (International Monetary Fund, 2017c, p. 119).

31. Tol (2009, p. 29).

32. Relative to the energy generated, coal has the highest CO_2 emission of any fossil fuel; gasoline has about two-thirds as much as coal, and natural gas only about half as much.

33. See, for instance, International Monetary Fund (2019a).

34. There is another incidence point here, applying the same lesson from Ricardo and Malthus. Part of the burden of a tax on fossil fuel emissions may fall on the rents earned by owners of deposits that are cheaper to exploit, and so have little if any effect on supply. This point may have some relevance to oil, but seems unlikely to matter for coal, given that the world has several hundred years' worth of usable deposits and rents are, as a result, likely to be small.

35. Carbon Tax Center (n.d.).

36. The U.S. Environmental Protection Agency (2016), for instance, arrives at a central estimate of $36 per ton in 2015, while Nordhaus (2017)—reflecting his Nobel-prize winning work in the area—estimates $31 per ton for 2015.

37. Dale (1922) and Archer (2016). Obelisks marking the boundaries of the coal tax catchment area can still be found in London.

38. This assumes global application, and needed accompanying nontax measures. See International Monetary Fund (2019a, p. 7).

39. There are nonetheless important differences between the two approaches. The carbon price under a cap and trade system will vary according to the demand for emissions, for instance, but will not under a carbon tax. For a comparison of the two, see Goulder and Parry (2008).

40. These are far from enough to limit global average temperature increases to 1.5–2 °C above preindustrial levels, which is the aim of the Agreement. But a start.

41. For example, "gas guzzler" taxes on low-fuel-efficiency vehicles combined with subsidies for high-fuel-efficiency vehicles can also discourage emissions. But these methods achieve less than does carbon pricing because they do not discourage driving as such.

42. The greenhouse gas figures are from Gerber et al. (2013) and Ritchie (2020). While more immediately damaging, methane lingers in the atmosphere for a shorter time than does carbon dioxide.

43. We feel obliged to mention the Florida rent-a-cow kerfuffle. The state of Florida has a greenbelt law designed to preserve farmland by offering it a preferential low property tax rate. To qualify for the low rate, the land must be used for a "bona fide" agricultural purpose. It turns out that renting a few cows to ruminate on your land can be enough. This law and the creative avoidance it spurred are documented in Weissmann (2012).

44. Erb (2013b).

45. George Best, first rock-star footballer and noted roué of the 1960s–1980s (*BBC News*, 2005).

46. King James I (1604).

47. King James I (1604).

48. Smith (2008) and Crawford, Keen, and Smith (2010).

49. Shiono and Behrman (1995).

50. Some reputable studies, such as Viscusi (1995), have argued that the net externalities are indeed most likely to be negative, but this conclusion remains highly contentious.

51. A 2008 Gallup poll documents that poorer people in the United States are more likely to smoke; see Goszkowski (2008).

52. Gruber and Kőszegi (2004) and Allcott, Lockwood and Taubinsky (2019).

53. Gruber and Kőszegi (2002).

54. The state tax information is from Boonn (2020).

55. Statista (2019a, 2019b).

56. Bouw (2017), Statista (2018), and OECD (2018).

57. The gentlemanly and multiply-escaped American bank robber of the 1930s to 1950s, who reportedly responded when asked why he robbed banks: "Because that's where the money is."

58. Chaloupka, Powell, and Warner (2019, p. 189).

59. Foster (2009).

60. Matthews (1958, pp. 95–98).

61. In Canada, they are subject to the federal cigarette excise but not the Goods and Services Tax (Lickers and Griffin, 2015).

62. In both Canada and the United States, a variety of measures are used to bolster enforcement of tax on sales to nonmembers of the tribe, such as the allocation to the tribe of some quota of tax-free cigarettes: see DeLong et al. (2016) and Lickers and Griffin (2015).

63. In the United States, for instance, tribes cannot be forced to remit the tobacco tax that federal law obliges them to charge on sales to nonmembers of the tribe.

64. DeLong et al. (2016, p. i32).

65. Marsden (2009) and Dowd (2010).

66. Petit and Nagy (2016, p. 11).

67. Sen and Fatima (2011).

68. Marsden (2009).

69. National Coalition Against Contraband Tobacco (2017).

70. HM Revenue & Customs (2018, table 1.2). There appears to be no more recent official estimate.

71. See Petit and Nagy (2016, p. 9) and the studies cited there.

72. Or, more generally, electronic nicotine delivery systems (ENDS).

73. As cited, for instance, in Fruits (2018). Products that heat tobacco but do not burn it lie somewhere between cigarettes and ENDS in harmfulness.

74. To be fair, this tendency may not be too surprising, given the long-established idea, endorsed by the World Health Organization, that all tobacco products should be taxed equivalently.

75. As of September 2019 (Dadayan, 2019).

76. Fruits (2018).

77. Some tax vapor products by millimeter of liquid or nicotine, which would be consistent with aiming to deter addiction (an objective that has its own limitations, as noted earlier in the chapter); others tax in proportion to price. See Fruits (2018) and Dadayan (2019).

78. For more on this argument, see Chaloupka, Sweanor, and Warner (2015), especially p. 595.

79. Several U.S. states, for instance, issued "tobacco bonds" secured by expected receipts from the Tobacco Master Settlement Agreement described in chapter 3. But these receipts depend on cigarette sales. As e-cigarettes make large and unanticipated inroads into this market, it would be a virtuous policymaker indeed who did not feel inclined to tax them similarly.

80. O'Brien (2007, table 1).

81. Vaisey (1985, p. 159).

82. Cnossen (2008, p. 514).

83. This is from Cnossen (2008, p. 518), who reviews evidence in this area, as do Crawford, Keen, and Smith (2010).

84. Oliver (2011, p. 48).

85. "... work is the curse of the drinking classes of this country" (Harris, 1918, p. 166).

86. See Dorn (1983) and Harrison (1994).

87. Dingle (1972, p. 611). The figure is for 1850–1900 and includes license duties.

88. Marks (2017).

89. Sunley (2008) discusses the taxation of *bidis*. In 2017, as part of the new Goods and Services Tax, a central tax on *tendu* leaf was imposed for the first time. See Kukreti (2017).

90. Johari (2015) and Nair (2015).

91. *Monty Python* (1969). One of them responds that such a levy would make chartered accountancy a much more interesting job.

92. The tax was finally abolished in the year 498 (Kornhauser, 2013).

93. Ditmore (2009). The same article reports that the main source of revenue in some Nevada counties is the property tax remitted by brothels.

94. Sahadi and Lobb (2004).

95. Tax issues have arisen in relation to conception even when no actual sex takes place. A 2015 U.S. Tax Court case focused on whether a woman who underwent fertility treatment and subsequently sold her eggs could exclude her compensation from taxation due to the pain and suffering she endured during the procedure. The Tax Court said no (Wood, 2015).

96. Quoted in Jenkins (2002, p. 60).

97. Feige and Miron (2008).

98. Peters (2006, p. 4).

99. Grund and Breeksema (2013).

100. Tax revenue from marijuana sales was nearly $70 million, compared to $42 million from alcohol sales (Basu, 2015).

101. Staggs (2020).

102. Bishop-Henchman (2014).

103. In "Success Story," recorded in 1975.

104. *The Economist* (2012).

105. Asen (2019). A summary and account of experience is in Petit, Mansour, and Wingender (forthcoming).

106. Watson and Treanor (2016).

107. Cited in Gallucci (2015).

108. University of Oxford (2018).

109. Hamermesh and Slemrod (2008).

110. Regulation is also better suited to dealing with certain problems of imperfect information: Taxation can do little, for instance, to deal with the ignorance of consumers as to the side effects of particular drugs, which is better dealt with by providing such drugs only by prescription.

111. Lovenheim and Slemrod (2010).

112. Wilson (2016).

113. That reduction could be substantial. For both the United Kingdom and the United States, Parry and Small (2005) find the Pigovian tax needed to address congestion externalities as part of a fuel tax to be at least as large as that needed to address climate change.

Chapter 9

1. Opinion in *Ayrshire Pullman Motor Services and D.M. Ritchie v. The Commissioners of Inland Revenue*, 14 TC 754, 1929.

2. Graham (1956, p. 78).

3. It seems that customs officials found it hard to measure the depth of a laden ship (Lane 1964, p. 228), so it was simply assumed that a ship's depth was half its length. Further details, including the somewhat weird formula used, are in French (1973). The system lasted until 1836, but the replacement was not fully applied for another 20 years (Graham 1956, p. 78).

4. Cited in Graham (1956, fn. 2, p. 78).

5. Cited in Mackay (1991) and elsewhere, but original source unknown.

6. On tax-driven product innovation, see Gillitzer, Kleven, and Slemrod (2017).

7. Nakamura and Maeguchi (2013).

8. Sauvegrain (2001).

9. See, for example, *Beautiful Puglia* (n.d.).

10. Laffer (2014).

11. This saga is discussed in McCulloch ([1845] 1975, pp. 159–160).

12. Johnson (1787, p. 417).

13. The vehicle examples are taken from Harberger (1995).

14. Atiyeh (2013). This tariff was known as the "chicken tax," as it was levied in retaliation for French and German tariffs on exports of American chicken.

15. Lasting until 1836.

16. Lasting until 1845.

17. *The Lancet* (1845, p. 214).

18. Vose (1980).

19. There is a curiously large literature on the brick tax. See, for instance, Exwood (1981) and, in particular, Lucas (1997), who vehemently disputes the importance of the brick-size tax avoidance phenomenon.

20. See Festa (2009) and Tague (2008).

21. The classic exposition of this point is Barzel (1976).

22. However, even ad valorem taxation can affect the nature of the things sold. Compared to "specific" taxation (levied per unit of the commodity, and so independent of the selling price), it favors lower-quality products. This is because covering $1 spent on improving quality requires increasing the price to the consumer by more than $1 under ad valorem taxation (because the government will tax away some of that higher price), whereas a $1 increase is enough under specific taxation. Technical though it sounds (and is), this difference can be a big deal. In Europe, for example, tobacco companies realize that lobbying over tax level is a lost cause, and so focus instead on lobbying, with their positions depending on

whether they aim for higher or lower ends of the market, over the balance between specific and ad valorem components. See Keen (1998).

23. State of Wisconsin (2010).

24. *CBC News* (2014).

25. Hays (2013).

26. *The Economist* (2018b, p. 48).

27. McHugh (2016).

28. Greene (2016, pp. 23–24).

29. Burman, Clausing, and O'Hare (1994).

30. Gans and Leigh (2009).

31. The bonus depreciation provision allowed half of the value of most assets (other than real estate) acquired by year-end 2008 to be written off in the year of purchase (with the other half subject to normal depreciation rules); it was subsequently extended.

32. Tax Advisory Partnership (n.d.). The explanation of that one-day shift (something to do with leap years) is at taxback.com (n.d.).

33. Soled (1997).

34. Until the Middle Kingdom: Webber and Wildavsky (1986, p. 71).

35. See, for example, Liu et al. (2019).

36. More precisely, England, Wales, and the disputed (between England and Scotland) town of Berwick-upon-Tweed. Scotland levied a hearth tax from 1691 to 1695, as did Ireland from about 1663 to 1795.

37. Petty (1662, p. 74).

38. In his observations for June 1662 (Latham 1985, p. 210).

39. Hervey (1905, p. xxi).

40. Except in Ireland, where it lasted until the early nineteenth century.

41. Douglas (1999, p. 13).

42. Macaulay (1855, p. 11).

43. *Hansard's Parliamentary Debates* (1818, p. 243).

44. The information on Holy Rood used here is from Hughes and White (1991).

45. This was after the introduction of the tax, but it seems unlikely that Mr. Windover had already reacted to the tax: It was then very new (the tax became law in March, and first payment was due in September) and it takes some time to brick up or otherwise change the number of fireplaces one has. Moreover, the tax was widely expected to be temporary, so why bother?

46. See, for example, Misa (2011, p. 41). Although this claim is often made, we have not been able to find precise corroboration. Other accounts highlight instead that the tax was levied by the same trick as seen earlier for the liturgies (and later for property values): The taxable value of cargo was self-declared, but the King of Denmark had the right to buy it at that price (Haan et al., 2012).

47. For the British approach described at the start of this chapter, breadth was instead measured at the waterline.

48. This is suggested by Graham (1956, p. 78).

49. In his seminal *Principles of Political Economy*, first published in 1848, when discussing discriminating taxes Mill ([1848] 2009, p. 654) wrote: "[the tax] creates an artificial motive for

preferring the untaxed process, though the inferior of the two. If, therefore, it has any effect at all, it causes the commodity to be produced of worse quality, or at a greater expense of labour; it causes so much of the labour of the community to be wasted, and the capital employed in supporting and remunerating the labour to be expended as uselessly as if it were spent in hiring men to dig holes and fill them up again."

50. Bartlett (1994).

51. Keane (2011) provides a survey of the recent econometric literature on this subject.

52. When one person's response to taxation affects other people too, the loss to society can be either less or more than the excess burden suffered by the taxpayer herself. It will be less, for instance, if that excess burden reflects the payment of a bribe, as the recipient presumably derives some benefit from it—unless one thinks that such ill-gotten gains should not be counted as a gain to society.

53. The point was first made formally by Feldstein (1999).

54. Saez, Slemrod, and Giertz (2012).

55. See Oates and Schwab (2015), on which this section draws. A present-day Google Maps stroll down Old Compton Street in Soho shows signs of this a century and a half later.

56. For more on the joys of notches, see Slemrod (2013), which bears the proud title of "Buenas Notches."

57. Oates and Schwab (2015).

58. The Pakistan study is Kleven and Waseem (2013) and the VAT study is Liu et al. (2019).

59. The "around" qualifier matters. With the kink, having income a few dollars into the 50 percent bracket is no big deal. But being on the wrong side of a notch—having 10 windows instead of nine—is.

60. Saez (2010).

61. See Kirchgaessner (2017).

Chapter 10

1. Attributed to Colbert, minister of finance under Louis XIV of France from 1665 to 1683.

2. The others included Australia, Canada, Holland, New Zealand, Spain, and Switzerland. Denmark and Sweden, though neutral, were early adopters: Their companies stood to make big profits from the war, prompting the labeling of this as the "German stew" tax (Stamp, 1917; *Encyclopedia Britannica*, 1922).

3. *Encyclopedia Britannica* (1922).

4. Daunton (2002, p. 83).

5. McCrum (2004, p. 216).

6. Haig (1920, p. 1).

7. *Encyclopedia Britannica* (1922).

8. Haig (1920, p. 4).

9. Buehler (1940, p. 292) and *Encyclopedia Britannica* (1922).

10. Haig (1920, p. 9).

11. Buehler (1940).

12. The coronavirus crisis has rekindled some interest; see Avi-Yonah (2020).

13. Experience with and the design of these taxes is reviewed in International Monetary Fund (2016) and de Mooij (2012).

14. If the company has no other tax liability, the government needs instead to provide either cash or an equivalent reduction in future liability.

15. The Impuesto Empresarial a Tasa Única (IETU) was a minimum tax: Companies paid the larger of their liabilities under the normal corporate tax and under the IETU. This proved awkward, and the IETU was abolished in 2013.

16. On the use and design of rent taxes for the extractive industries, see Boadway and Keen (2010), Land (2010), and International Monetary Fund (2012).

17. From Cole Porter's "Don't Fence Me In" (Porter, 1944).

18. Useful land in aggregate is in practice clearly not completely fixed in supply: Reclaimed land accounts for a substantial fraction of all land in Hong Kong, the Netherlands, and Singapore. What is in inelastic supply (when the minimum required return is earned) is land of a particular quality.

19. Ricardo ([1817] 2004).

20. Mill (1875, p. 225).

21. Sometimes also called a "location value" or "site value" tax.

22. George ([1879] 2005, p. 392).

23. The Economist (2015).

24. George ran in 1886 for the mayoralty of New York City. He lost, but he did manage to outpoll Theodore Roosevelt.

25. New York Times (1912, p. 12).

26. Friedman (1978, p. 14).

27. Pilon (2015).

28. McCluskey, Grimes, and Timmins (2002).

29. Douglas (1999, 2011–2012).

30. A land tax has also survived in Australia, where all the states and territories have some variant. On experience with land value taxes worldwide, see Franzsen (2009).

31. As reported in The Public (1912, p. 349). See also Kaizen Certified Public Accountants Limited (n.d.).

32. A variant, proposed by Harberger (1965), would enable anyone to purchase at some premium above the self-assessed price. This idea has recently been further extended by Posner and Weyl (2018), who propose a high tax on wealth with the feature that owners would themselves set the value of their assets but must then be willing to sell those assets at the price they set.

33. Legal complications arose, however, and the provision in any case seems not to have been much used. It was removed in 1900.

34. Dye and England (2009, p. 5).

35. Bourassa (2009, p. 17).

36. Economists have even come up with a "Henry George Theorem": Under certain assumptions (of course), a 100 percent tax on land rents would yield exactly enough revenue to finance all public spending (Stiglitz, 1977).

37. One longstanding method is to subtract from the value of a parcel, complete with human-made improvements (like buildings), the cost of those improvements. More recent approaches

involve statistical modeling: explaining properties' observed market prices (or expert valuations) in terms of a variety of characteristics, including location, and estimating from this a value implicitly associated with plots of land. Bell, Bowman, and German (2009) provide a detailed account of the methods available and used in the United States; see also chapter 16 of Mirrlees et al. (2011).

38. Brunori and Carr (2002).

39. Calculated from revenue data in OECD (2013).

40. Bank of England (n.d.).

41. Hugh Dalton, cited in Daunton (2002, p. 60). Chancellor of the Exchequer from 1945 to 1947, Dalton resigned over the scandal caused by his revealing to a journalist, on his way to deliver his budget speech, some of the tax changes in it. Economists remember Dalton for his pathbreaking work on inequality.

42. We say "in effect," because by "lump-sum," we mean that the amount of tax payable is unchanged by any behavioral response. With a tax on rents, whose extent depends, say, on how much oil is extracted, tax due does depend on behavior. The point, however, is that this behavior will be the same when rents are taxed as when they are not.

43. Daunton (2002, pp. 66, 69, 80).

44. These events are reviewed in Eichengreen (1990).

45. John A. Hobson, cited in Eichengreen (1990, p. 200).

46. Duarte (2009, pp. 450–451).

47. Ramsey (1927). For Keynes (1933, p. 295), Ramsey "lived without effort in a rarer atmosphere than most economists care to breathe, and handled the technical apparatus of our science with the easy grace of one accustomed to something far more difficult."

48. Feldstein (1999).

49. Indeed, the inverse elasticity rule as stated above is exactly true only when there is no substitution at all between the commodities being taxed.

50. This insight was formalized by Corlett and Hague (1953).

51. More precisely, it is the substitution effect of generally higher commodity taxes—the one that matters for excess burden—that discourages work.

52. This argument points to the link with the inverse elasticity rule: If a good is in highly elastic demand, an increase in its price will lead to a relatively large fall in spending on it, which can be accommodated by a relatively large reduction in earnings and hence in work effort—which, in terms of excess burden, is bad.

53. For a flavor of the difficulties, see Crawford, Keen, and Smith (2010).

54. Suspicious readers may think we have fixed the numbers to reach this conclusion. Not so. Suppose, for instance, that Mr. Windover had reacted to the increase of the tax to 4s by losing only an additional half fireplace (this is, after all, only an example). Then, given the same 2s average value that he placed on each of these, excess burden would be 3s (1.5 times 2s), which is still more than a doubling.

55. The message was left by R. Glenn Hubbard, deputy assistant treasury secretary for tax policy during the administration of George H. W. Bush (Hubbard, 2010).

56. Turnover taxes have a long history, but were mostly eliminated as the VAT rose to ascendancy. They have, however, been revived in recent years in several U.S. states (including

Delaware, Illinois, New Mexico, and Ohio) under the name "gross receipts taxes." As we noted in chapter 4, turnover taxes are also used in many developing countries as a simple presumptive way to tax small businesses.

57. Diamond and Mirrlees (1971).

58. Glantz (2008).

59. Due (1957).

60. A 2011 proposal by the European Commission to levy a 0.1 percent tax rate on the exchange of shares and bonds and a 0.01 percent rate on derivative contracts was estimated to raise €57 billion per year. Matheson (2011) provides a level-headed discussion of the pros and cons of a financial transactions tax.

61. Matheson (2011).

62. The U.K. figures, which related to earned income, are from Daunton (2002, table 2.5).

63. Peter, Buttrick, and Duncan (2010).

64. We ignore here the taxation of savings and capital income, which was discussed in chapter 5.

65. Due to Phelps (1973), Sadka (1976), and Seade (1977).

66. See, for example, Dahan and Strawczynski (2000).

67. See, for instance, Brewer, Saez, and Shephard (2010).

68. One of the authors helped discover the striking result that in this case, the marginal income tax rate on the highest earner should actually be negative (because it is the overall additional tax payment that matters for the logic of the "zero rate at the top" result, and consumption tax payments will rise with income) (Edwards, Keen, and Tuomala, 1994). The other author reminds him of Edgeworth's remark, in another context, that "only a very clever man would discover that exceptional case; only a very foolish man would take it as the basis of a rule for general practice." (Edgeworth 1915, p. 9).

69. Piketty, Saez, and Stantcheva (2014).

70. Adams (2001, p. 46).

71. Holzman (1955, pp. 178–180). But it is misleading to compare explicit tax rates in a communist economy: Where everyone ostensibly works for the state, what we call "taxes" might simply be reflected in reduced compensation.

72. Keen and Lockwood (2006).

73. Gaspar, Jaramillo, and Wingender (2016).

Chapter 11

1. Smith ([1776] 1868, Book 5 Ch. 2 pt. 2).

2. This account draws on Bezias (2007), Hassan (2015), and Askolovitch (2017).

3. We often talk about "jurisdictions" rather than "countries" in this chapter, so as to recognize that the effects at issue may involve dependent territories, crown colonies and the like, and can also operate at the subnational level.

4. *The Guardian* (1999).

5. Sir Frederick Banbury MP, writing to the *Morning Post*, quoted in Knightley (1993, p. 47).

6. McCrum (2004, p. 207).

7. Quoted in Knightley (1993, p. 35).

8. Knightley (1993, p. 8). Technically, the Queen voluntarily pays a sum equivalent to the income tax that would be due.

9. The OECD (1998, p. 20) defined a tax haven as a jurisdiction that imposes no or only nominal income taxes and offers itself as a place to be used by nonresidents to escape tax in their country of residence—but it no longer uses the term, and nor does the International Monetary Fund.

10. This discussion draws on Palan (2002) and Shaxson (2011).

11. Some have explained this restriction as a benevolent effort to protect from the Nazis the assets of Jews placed in Switzerland—and indeed it had some such effect. Others note that this measure came 2 years after the Basler Handelsbank had been found to have facilitated the evasion of French tax by two bishops, several generals, and the owners of both *Le Figaro* and *Le Matin* (Shaxson 2011, p. 157).

12. These were arrangements under which holding companies—companies, that is, which own other companies—were exempted from corporate taxation in return for some more modest payment, even though they might be in receipt of significant dividend income from those companies. With no restriction on the nationality of owners, and secrecy provisions impeding the revelation of their incomes to their country of residence, this arrangement could be a nice deal.

13. Higham, Hudson, and Guevara (2013).

14. Shaxson (2011, p. 89).

15. Halperin and Palan (2015, p. 52).

16. The hamlet was even founded on a tax exemption. Around 300 years ago, a local duke issued a decree freeing locals from "tithes and other tributes" in return for building a dyke to keep the sea out (Larner and Collinson, 2004).

17. Lists of "tax havens" can be misleading, for the reasons given, but, for what it's worth, those listed by Gravelle (2015) have an average population of 1.26 million, and 37 of the 50 are islands.

18. Palan (2002).

19. Dharmapala and Hines (2009).

20. Shaxson (2011, p. 19).

21. This ranking is based on the sum of inward and outward foreign direct investment, as reported in International Monetary Fund (2020b).

22. F. Scott Fitzgerald is reported to have remarked to Ernest Hemingway, "You know, the rich are different from you and me," to which Hemingway replied, "Yes. They've got more money."

23. Strumpf (2017).

24. McCrum (2004, p. 221).

25. Trannoy (2015, p. 35).

26. Kleven, Landais, and Saez (2013). The president of Spain's top soccer league speculated that Spain's high tax rate contributed to Cristiano Ronaldo's departure to Juventus, an Italian team (Garcia, 2018).

27. Abbott, Frost, and Johnson (1926, pp. 96–97).

28. Webber and Wildavsky (1986, p. 141). In much the same spirit, when rich Florentine merchants in the fourteenth century established residences outside the city to escape taxation, the communal government reacted by extending the city boundaries into the countryside (Webber and Wildavsky, 1986, pp. 201–202).

29. An "exit tax" may be due, calculated as the capital gains tax that would have been due if the expatriate had sold all her assets just before expatriation.

30. Organ (2020).

31. Zucman (2013).

32. Alstadsæter, Johannesen, and Zucman (2018).

33. Alstadsæter, Johannesen, and Zucman (2019).

34. There was a precursor in the European Union, with a 2003 Directive requiring member states to either provide information automatically or impose a withholding tax on payments to nonresidents in other member states, with 75 percent of the proceeds going to the country of residence. (Details are in Keen and Ligthart, 2006a.)

35. More precisely, the Global Forum on Transparency and Exchange of Information for Tax Purposes.

36. Except developing countries that do not host a financial center.

37. See the statement of commitments at OECD (2018).

38. It could have been otherwise: Countries might be given some incentive to provide information by receiving some share in the revenue that the information generates (Keen and Ligthart, 2006b).

39. The European Union also operates a "blacklist" of jurisdictions deemed non-cooperative on tax matters, exclusion from which requires, among other things, adherence to standards on the exchange of information standards.

40. Johannesen and Zucman (2014) and Beer, Coelho, and Leduc (2019).

41. And the gains from holding out can be considerable (Elsayyad and Konrad, 2012).

42. European Commission (2018, p. 10) reports matching rates (between information received and domestic taxpayers) varying from only 37 to 80 percent.

43. Many countries have offered "voluntary disclosure" schemes prior to strengthening exchange of information (generally offering reduced penalties or interest charges for those revealing offshore holdings). These have raised significant amounts—around €95 billion (Kerfs, 2019)—but are not ongoing additions to revenue.

44. U.K. Parliament (2015).

45. On policy issues at least. The first international agreement on tax matters dates from 1843, when France and Belgium agreed to aspects of administrative cooperation (Jogarajan, 2011, p. 687).

46. Jogarajan (2011, p. 684).

47. These economists included our hero, Edwin Seligman. Another member was the British tax expert, Sir Josiah Stamp, who, sadly, suffered a fate similar to that of William Harcourt described in chapter 5. Killed by a bomb, along with his son, in the Second World War, the law at the time deemed that he had died first, and two layers of estate tax duty applied.

48. In case this sounds too much like magic, here is an example. Suppose that a multinational has a subsidiary in country A where the tax rate is 50 percent and another in country B where

the rate is 10 percent. Now lend $10 million from the subsidiary in B to that in A, at an interest rate of 5 percent. The interest payments of $500,000 will be taxable in B, resulting in a tax bill there of $50,000. But that interest will be a deductible expense in country A, so the tax bill there goes down by 50 percent of $500,000, that is by $250,000. Overall, the multinational is $200,000 ahead.

49. As reported in Bergin (2012). This operation is just part of a much more complex structure, the rest of the trick being to ensure that the deductions taken in the United Kingdom did not create any tax liability elsewhere. Starbucks has since restructured its U.K. and European operations.

50. Here's how. If one country regards a company as resident if it is incorporated there, while another treats it as resident where it is effectively managed from, then incorporate in the latter and manage from the former.

51. The workings of this are explained in International Monetary Fund (2013).

52. Heath Robinson (1872–1944) was the English counterpart of the American cartoonist Rube Goldberg (1883–1970).

53. Tax Justice Network et al. (2015).

54. This case related to the sale of an asset there by Vodafone. On this, and the wider avoidance issues it raises, see Platform for Collaboration on Tax (2020).

55. OECD (2015a, p. 15).

56. Crivelli, de Mooij, and Keen (2016, figure 3).

57. See, for instance, the country-specific results in table 1 of International Monetary Fund (2019c). The results cited for the United States predate the 2017 Tax Cuts and Jobs Act, since when profit shifting is likely to have decreased.

58. See, for instance, figure 4 of International Monetary Fund (2019c).

59. Kennedy (1961).

60. League of Nations (1923, p. 23).

61. *The Economist* (2017b).

62. Once revealed, a fact is in fixed supply, just as, once discovered, is a deposit of oil. The analogy between information and natural resources, and its tax implications, are explored in Cui (2019), International Monetary Fund (2019c) and Aslam and Shah (2020).

63. Hufbauer and Lu (2018).

64. International Monetary Fund (2019c) provides about as clear a guide to these schemes as there is.

65. More precisely, the Global Intangible Low-Taxed Income provision brings into the U.S. tax base, without deferral, at half the usual rate, earnings abroad in excess of a 10 percent return on tangible assets; it has a partial (80 percent) credit for taxes paid abroad.

66. The Base Erosion Anti-Abuse Tax.

67. For a tour around the novel international provisions of the Tax Cuts and Jobs Act, see Chalk, Keen, and Perry (2018) and Dharmapala (2018).

68. Some civil society organizations, such as the Independent Commission for the Reform of International Corporate Taxation (2018), have long advocated global formula apportionment.

69. The Common Consolidated Corporate Tax Base: see European Commission (2016).

70. Devereux et al. (2019).

71. Imports are taxable under the VAT, but for business purchases, this tax is fully creditable against tax on sales: the effects cancel out.

72. But you might wonder: Wouldn't there be an incentive to incur wage costs in high-tax countries, as that would generate a larger tax deduction? Any such increased demand for labor, however, would lead to an increase in wage rates or a currency appreciation (making that labor more expensive in foreign currency)—tending to offset the effect. More generally, exchange rates and/or domestic prices will in principle adjust to offset any cross-country differences in rates at which countries apply a DBCFT. On this, and more on the design and impact of the DBCFT, see Auerbach et al. (2017).

73. These nice properties only apply if all countries adopt the DBCFT. If some do not, then, for example, there will be an incentive to overprice exports from a DBCFT country to a non-DBCFT one, because that has no impact on tax liability in the DBCFT country but, through the deduction of import costs, will reduce it in the non-DBCFT one.

74. The reference is to Part A of the "Pillar One" proposal in OECD (2019d).

75. See OECD (2020).

76. Weightman (2007, p. 31).

77. Weightman (2007, p. 32).

78. Hamilton (1791, p. 13).

79. Clark (2006, p. 176).

80. Norwich (2003, p. 273).

81. Ruding (1992).

82. See Djankov et al. (2010).

83. The West African Economic and Monetary Union and Communauté Economique et Monétaire de l'Afrique Centrale.

84. This is the "Pillar Two" proposal in OECD (2019b).

85. Keen, Parry, and Strand (2013).

86. International Monetary Fund (2019a, 2019b).

87. Mourlane (2005); our translation.

Part IV

1. English comedian (1927–2018). *BBC News* (2018b).

Chapter 12

1. Twain (1870, p. 2).

2. He was also known by his patronymic as Dracula, but was not the Bram Stoker/Boris Karloff one.

3. Tibballs (2017).

4. Denis Healey, Labour Chancellor of the Exchequer from 1974 to 1979 (quoted in *The Economist*, 2006).

5. West (1908, pp. 11–12).

6. This approach was first formalized by Allingham and Sandmo (1972), who adapted to tax evasion the seminal treatment of the economics of crime by Nobel Laureate Gary Becker (1968).

7. As with any other bet, the taxpayer should consider not only the expected net gain but also the risk it implies.

8. *United States v. Sullivan* 274 U.S. 259. Potential gangsters may be pleasantly surprised to learn that now necessary expenses incurred in conducting illegal activities generally are deductible unless—as with bribes and prohibited drugs—they are specifically disallowed.

9. Plumb (1960, pp. 121–122) and Pearce (2011, p. 36).

10. Samson (2005).

11. In view of his advanced age, in the event he served just one year of community service.

12. Nelson (2014).

13. Wood (2015).

14. Conn (2015).

15. Lawless (2013).

16. Known as the "Bowie bond," the idea is to issue a bond secured by future royalties on past works. Carefully structured, this bond can give immediate untaxed access to future income, and the interest paid on the loan can be offset against those royalties. The scheme has potential nontax benefits, too: The risk of lower-than-expected royalties is passed on to the creditors— which, given the emergence of streaming and the like, is what happened (Gupta, 2016).

17. Myers (2018, p. A12).

18. Collins (2020) discusses the controversy.

19. On the former, see Rowland (2019). On the latter, see Kopczuk and Slemrod (2003). Some of this shift was probably due to changes in the time of death, but some of it was probably illegal misreporting of the date of death. The former is creepier, but the latter is tax evasion.

20. *DW News* (2017).

21. This category is a bit broader than willful intent not to pay, also including, for example, honest mistakes (though for these, the understatements of tax liability should be roughly offset by overstatements). The IRS comes up with these estimates by combining information obtained from a special program of intensive random audits with information from its ongoing enforcement activities and special studies about particular sources of income that even audits are likely to miss (such as the tips and cash earnings of nannies and house painters). Even this most thorough of approaches, however, may miss income from assets concealed abroad.

22. Internal Revenue Service (2019a).

23. Including also National Insurance Contributions (HM Revenue & Customs, 2018, table 1.2). The United Kingdom is unusual in including some avoidance activities in the reported gap.

24. Kleven et al. (2011, p. 668). Some of the reported variation across countries is likely due to different definitions and methods.

25. The EU number is from Poniatowski et al. (2019). That for Uganda is from Hutton, Thackray, and Wingender (2014).

26. One variant of MTIC fraud that has found its way into the headlines is "carousel fraud." Here's how it works. Goods are imported into one member state VAT-free from another, the

criminal importer then sells them on without remitting VAT; the chain continues until reaching a firm that exports, reclaiming VAT that has in effect never been paid—and then (hence the name) the goods go round again. This may seem complex, but it is VAT Fraud 101: There are much more complicated schemes than this. For more on VAT fraud, see Keen and Smith (2006).

27. Europol (n.d.).

28. Mwakikagile (2000, p. 66).

29. Hogg (2011).

30. Dalrymple (2019, p. 34).

31. It is not certain whether Tell was arrested for failing to pay homage to the Austrian governor or for resisting taxation—or that he ever existed.

32. Lunt (1909, p. 268).

33. The U.S. numbers are from Internal Revenue Service (2020, table 24). The U.K. numbers are from Houlder (2015).

34. In the early 2000s, the U.S. Department of Justice seems to have made a habit of issuing a large number of press releases about successful tax enforcement cases in the run-up to Tax Day, when taxpayers contemplating evasion might be paying especially close attention: Blank and Levin (2010).

35. Kornhauser (2007).

36. Rosenberg (1996, p. 221).

37. Soos (1997, pp. 36–37).

38. Soos (1990, p. 124).

39. When the 16th Amendment was passed in 1913, Congress chose March 1 as the deadline for filing returns. In 1918, Congress moved the date forward to March 15. The next change came in 1955, when it was set to April 15.

40. Moving from a system with remittance after the tax year to concurrent employer withholding raises the problem that, in the transition period, tax is owed on the income of 2 years. For example, in the United States during 1943, taxes were in principle due on both 1942 and 1943 incomes. Although the United States was in dire need of revenue for the war, owing 2 years of tax liability in 1943 was too much to stomach. So, in the Current Tax Payment Act of 1943, Congress largely forgave 1942 taxes in the transition. France did much the same when moving to withholding in 2019.

41. See Redelmeier and Yarnell (2012).

42. Friedman and Friedman (1998, p. 123). A U.S. champion of tax withholding was the director of the New York Federal Reserve Bank, Beardsley Ruml, who, as an executive of R. H. Macy & Company, had apparently learned of the attractiveness to consumers of purchasing goods on an installment plan, not unlike owing tax in small increments rather than in one big sum.

43. This argument is formalized in Kleven, Kreiner, and Saez (2016). The incentive to collude is also blunted by the deductibility of wage payments under the taxation of profits: If that is levied at a rate above the personal tax on wages, it may be cheaper for the employer to deduct and withhold than to conceal a wage payment.

44. OECD (2019e).

45. Taxpayers can file a form to reduce the amount of withholding so that they do not receive a refund, but most do not do so. See Fennell (2006).

46. See Keen and Lockwood (2010) and, for contrasting results on sub-Saharan Africa, Alavuotunki, Haapanen, and Pirttila (2019) and Ebeke, Mansour, and Rota-Graziosi (2016).

47. See, for instance, OECD (2015b, table 9.6).

48. The prevalence and potential usefulness of such taxes in low-income countries is discussed in Keen (2008).

49. Armey (1996, p. 99).

50. Dušek and Bagchi (2018, p. 5). Analytically, this question is similar to that addressed earlier of whether the VAT was a cause or a consequence of government growth.

51. Maseko (2008, p. 164).

52. Douglas (1999).

53. OECD (2017a) and Slemrod and Velayudhan (2018).

54. The full story is in Dillon (2002).

55. George (1965, p. 44).

56. Dillon (2002, p. 75).

57. As, quite possibly, the powerful big distillers and the landed elite of large corn growers fully expected. Prime Minister Walpole himself clearly anticipated the problem.

58. There are no data on consumption itself; the figures here are for all home-produced spirits subjected to tax, from Mitchell (1988, p. 407).

59. Crandall, Gavin, and Masters (2019, table 34).

60. Internal Revenue Service (2018, table 2.1).

61. Some governments in low-income countries may deliberately amplify this gift by using regulatory and other restrictions to favor easy-to-tax large firms (Auriol and Warlters, 2005).

62. Internal Revenue Service (2019a, table 2). The total individual income tax gap due to underreporting was $245 billion, of which $110 billion was business income; the tax gap for corporate income tax was an additional $38 billion, of which $11 billion was attributed to corporations with assets of less than $10 million.

63. Ishi (1993, p. 68).

64. HM Revenue & Customs (2020, figure 1.5).

65. Artavanis, Morse, and Tsoutsora (2016).

66. Some emerging market and developing economies do this even within the VAT, requiring large and/or public companies to remit some tax in relation to their purchases, for which the seller is entitled to claim credit.

67. Webber and Wildavsky (1986, p. 141).

68. Daunton (2001, p. 197).

69. This account of Szilagyi's sad tale is based on Dubner and Levitt (2006).

70. Weinberg and Bealer (2002, pp. 86–87).

71. The title of this subsection is attributed to Donald Regan, U.S. Secretary of the Treasury from 1981 to 1985, who was a major player in developing the 1986 Tax Reform Act.

72. Bellon et al. (2019), for instance, find that e-invoicing significantly increased the sales and purchases reported by small businesses in Peru.

73. See OECD (2013).

74. One of the most famous U.S. zapper cases, the Middle Eastern restaurant chain La Shish, had an outlet just down the street from one of this book's authors (Ellison, 2012).

75. These policies are discussed in Williams (2014, pp. 102–103); on zappers and alternative policy responses, see Ainsworth (2010).

76. On this innovation and the varieties of electronic cash registers, see OECD (2019a).

77. Meaning someone other than the taxpayer or the government itself.

78. For instance, Internal Revenue Service (2019a, figure 3) reports compliance gaps for 2011–2013 of 1 percent for income subject to both substantial information reporting and withholding (wages and salaries), 5 percent for amounts subject only to substantial information reporting, and 55 percent for amounts subject to neither withholding nor information reporting.

79. OECD (2015b, table 9.6).

80. Slemrod et al. (2017).

81. Carrillo, Pomeranz, and Singhal (2017).

82. Sung, Awasthi, and Lee (2017).

83. Rowlatt (2016).

84. Blackstone (2019).

85. Calvert (2019).

86. Clark (1988, p. 80).

87. Note to speakers of American English: "grasses" = "informers."

88. Warner and Ivis (1999, p. 309).

89. Carver (1898, p. 426), discussed in Mehrotra (2013, pp. 202–203).

90. Letter from the then-Greek finance minister, Yanis Varoufakis, to the head of the Eurozone finance ministers, cited in Traynor and Smith (2015).

91. Australian Taxation Office (n.d.).

92. UBS's tax troubles did not end there: In February 2019, a French court fined the bank €3.7 billion for helping its clients to evade taxes (Bisserbe and Blackstone, 2019).

93. Kocieniewski (2012). And, in case you're wondering: Yes, a whistleblower award is taxable (Saunders, 2015).

94. Kroll (2016) and Watt et al. (2016).

95. Addady (2016).

96. Under the initial U.S. corporate tax of 1909, corporate tax returns were considered to be public records "and open to inspection as such." But the funds for this were not appropriated, so the public disclosure was not implemented.

97. Twain (1870, p. 2).

98. Weisman (2002, p. 99).

99. Italy's data-protection agency ordered the information taken down after a day, stating that its publication was an illegal violation of privacy (Coronel, 2013).

100. There is a nice picture of this in Webber and Wildavsky (1986, p. 298).

101. Disclosure does seem to be something of a Nordic thing. In Sweden, for instance, tax returns have been made public since 1903. See Coronel (2013).

102. This increase is for places where posting online made searching easier, relative to elsewhere (Bø, Slemrod, and Thoresen 2015).

103. Slemrod, Ur Rehman, and Waseem (forthcoming). To distinguish the impact of disclosure from the many other changes that happened in 2012, the authors compare the change in reported income of those with common names, who were effectively not disclosed because only

the taxpayer's name and tax liability was released, to those with unique names, whose tax information was effectively disclosed.

104. Boone (2012).

105. Public corporations must reveal much information about their operations, but in most countries the definition of income used for tax purposes is different enough from income reported on a financial statement that tax liability and tax payments cannot be readily discerned. And they generally do not need to report tax actually remitted. Lenter, Shackelford, and Slemrod (2003) review the arguments for and against public disclosure of corporations' tax return information.

106. In April 2016, the EU Commission proposed to require all multinational groups to publish a yearly report on profits and tax paid in each country where they are active. The European Parliament approved a version of the proposal in 2017, but as of this writing, it has not been implemented.

107. See Hasegawa et al. (2013).

108. Hoopes, Robinson, and Slemrod (2018).

109. Johnnie Walters, quoted in Langer (2014).

110. Crandall, Gavin, and Masters (2019, table 40).

111. OECD (2017b, p. 99). The odds of being audited rise with income, being nearly 20 percent for those reporting more than $10,000,000; and, in the United States and elsewhere, the audit process is essentially continuous for the largest corporations.

112. Internal Revenue Service (2020).

113. Taxes play another and better-known part in *Dead Souls*, which revolves around Chichikov's attempt to create collateral for a loan by acquiring serfs—dead ones, not yet removed from the tax rolls and so a burden that their owners are (mostly) happy to sell him cheaply.

114. Levi (1989).

115. Crevar (2015, p. 8, travel section).

116. Gross (2016).

117. Including James Baldwin, Noam Chomsky, Lawrence Ferlinghetti, Betty Friedan, Allen Ginsberg, Norman Mailer, Thomas Pynchon, Susan Sontag, Benjamin Spock, Gloria Steinem, Hunter Thompson, and Kurt Vonnegut.

118. See, for instance, the legislative proposal in U.S. Congress House Committee on Ways and Means (2017).

119. Burg (2004, pp. 108–109, 193, 219).

120. Billings (1969). Not to be outdone, the people of the Yaohnanen area of the Pacific island of Vanuatu believed that Prince Philip, Duke of Edinburgh and consort to Queen Elizabeth, is a divine being (Shears, 2006). Disappointingly, however, there is no apparent tax angle to the Prince Philip cult.

121. Indeed, in surveys worldwide, most people claim to believe that tax evasion is not justifiable. But talk is cheap.

122. Suetonius [121] (1957). Taxation went on to play a bit part in Caligula's assassination. Suetonius ascribes the motive to Caligula's charging the leader of the conspiracy (and assassin), Cassius Chaerea, with effeminacy, because he had a weak voice and was not firm in collecting taxes (Barrett, 1990, p. 161).

123. Marcuss et al. (2013).

124. Webber and Wildavsky (1986, p. 58).

125. Now discontinued.

126. There is indeed evidence of a link between patriotism and tax compliance: see Konrad and Qari (2012).

127. The first field experiment on taxation was Blumenthal, Christian, and Slemrod (2001), and there have been plenty more since, surveyed in Slemrod (2019).

128. See Frey (1997).

129. In a study of an Israeli daycare center at which parents routinely arrived late to pick up their children, when a monetary fine was introduced for late-arriving parents the number of late parents went up. Introducing a penalty may have changed the parents' perspective on coming late from an obligation that they sometimes failed to meet to a commodity they could purchase as much or as little of as they wanted (Gneezy and Rustichini, 2000).

130. Dwenger et al. (2016).

131. Besley, Preston, and Ridge (1997) and Besley, Jensen, and Persson (2015).

Chapter 13

1. United States Conference of Catholic Bishops (2019).

2. Doran and Tucker (2019, p. 828).

3. Burg (2004).

4. A recent, admittedly idiosyncratic, account of early Christianity gives a sense of the low regard in which tax collectors were held by including them in a list of those for whom Jesus showed love, along with "psychopaths, pedophiles, hit-and-run drivers, people who talk to themselves in the street . . . skinheads capable of setting vagrants on fire, child abusers . . ." (Carrère 2017, p. 261).

5. This is ironic, given that his contribution was to drive the family brewing business into bankruptcy.

6. Brogan (1985, p. 141).

7. Unger (2011, pp. 100, 106).

8. Conway ([1909] 1970, pp. 7–8).

9. U.S. Customs and Border Protection (n.d.).

10. ". . . many loud thanks to the big black devil/That danced away with the Exciseman." The story (and translation) is from Ferguson (2001, pp. 76, 444).

11. Salih (2011). There is not, it has to be said, much competition for this honor. But we would rate Mark Twain's little-known short story, *Mysterious Visit*, quoted at the start of chapter 12, as an easy winner.

12. Wallace (2012, p. 87). Beware, though, that not all the "facts" in *The Pale King* are true—though some of the weirdest ones are, such as the existence of plans for tax collection in the event of a nuclear attack (*New York Times*, 1989).

13. Davidson (2010, p. 429).

14. The post was no sinecure. "There were eight hundred separate acts of parliament affecting customs duties to superintend [and] endless adjudications to attend to" (Phillipson 2010, p. 257).

15. Karabell (2004, p. 4).

16. Karabell (2004, p. 25).

17. In 1874, Congress repealed the moiety system, reducing Arthur's income back to $12,000 (Reeves, 1975).

18. Lens on Leeuwenhoek (n.d.).

19. Pet Health Network (2014).

20. Waite (1993, pp. 133, 221).

21. Eisinger (2013).

22. This account draws particularly on Bickers (2011) and—less fulsome in praise—Spence (1969). A radio series, *Our Man in China: The Diaries* (BBC Radio, 2016), draws on Hart's largely unpublished diaries.

23. Hall (1977, pp. 8–12).

24. He also found time to organize his own private band and to enjoy, with ample guilt, the sexual opportunities open to a foreigner in China as well as to take, with great affection, a Chinese partner, Ayaou, with whom he had three children. Hart's eventful life has even inspired a novel, *My Splendid Concubine* (Lofthouse, 2013), not entirely about tax administration.

25. Hall (1977, p. 35).

26. Chang (2013, p. 140).

27. Hart left China in 1908, retaining the title of Inspector General until his death in 1911, 3 weeks before the fall of the dynasty (Spence 1969, p. 128). The Customs Service lasted until 1950.

28. Weisman (2002, p. 253).

29. Matthews (1958, p. 279).

30. Some of their contracts, for example, were highly sophisticated. Jacques Necker structured the lease of 1774 so that the farmers retained 50 percent of the first 4 million livres above the lease price, and then 80 percent of anything more than 12 million livres above the lease price—an interesting echo of the prescription in chapter 10 that the marginal tax rate on the highest earner should, in some circumstances, be zero.

31. Farming was not universal. It was not used in Tokugawa Japan, for instance, and in China—with its large, complex bureaucracy—it was utilized only when the dynasty was weak.

32. Forrest (1918, p. 413).

33. Johnson and Koyama (2014, p. 11).

34. Matthews (1958, pp. 224–225).

35. de Vries (1976, p. 202).

36. McCarthy (2005, p. 640).

37. Pamuk (2012, p. 317).

38. Pakistan had private contractors collecting *octroi* in the mid-1990s (Zaidi 1996, pp. 2950–2951).

39. White (2004).

40. Matthews (1958, p. 283).

41. Lavoisier's body was reportedly dumped, along with other victims of the Terror, in catacombs underneath part of the wall still visible in the Place de la Bataille de Stalingrad.

42. Salzmann (1993).

43. Smith ([1776] 1868, p. 46).

44. Adams (2001, p. 104).

45. Copland and Godley (1993, p. 64).

46. Davidson (2010, p. 429).

47. Wedgwood (1961, pp. 196, 212).

48. Hervey (1905, p. xxii).

49. Plumb (1967, p. 123).

50. Brewer (1988, p. 108).

51. Kahn, Silva, and Ziliak (2001).

52. Khan, Khwaja, and Olken (2016).

53. Besley and McLaren (1993).

54. Crandall (2010) discusses the state of performance assessment in tax administrations.

55. World Bank (2001).

56. Matthews (1958, p. 216).

57. Brewer (1988, p. 102).

58. Spence (1969, p. 113).

59. Thanks to a trusting supervisor, he did, however, survive (Brewer 1988, p. 109).

60. Trevisani (2015).

61. Perez (2015).

62. Galloway (2017).

63. In the event, the man he chose for the job, Johnnie Walters, refused (with the support of Treasury Secretary George Schultz) to go after those on Nixon's enemies list. There may be more to the story. Nixon can be heard on the White House tapes complaining about his own audit under the previous administration, and Walters recognized that "during the Kennedy years, things were done that shouldn't have been done" (Langer, 2014).

64. The history of the Special Service Staff is extensively discussed in Andrew (2002).

65. *The Economist* (2017a).

66. Mann (2004).

67. Ebeke, Mansour, and Rota-Graziosi (2016).

68. Beard (2015, p. 263).

69. Quoted in Johnson and Koyama (2014, p. 10).

70. Cleary, Crandall, and Masters (2017, table 5).

71. Calculated from table 5 of Cleary, Crandall, and Masters (2017).

72. Internal Revenue Service (2019b).

73. Webber and Wildavsky (1986, p. 116).

74. Goldsmith (1987, p. 50).

75. OECD (2015b).

76. The argument that follows draws on Keen and Slemrod (2017).

77. Romeo (2016).

78. Brummitt and Purnomo (2015).

79. Casaburi and Troiano (2016).

80. Daley (2010).

81. On the experience of both countries, see annex 2.1 of International Monetary Fund (2018); on Kenya, see also Ndung'u (2017).

82. *BBC News* (2010).

83. Smith (2015).

84. Wallace (2012, p. 85).

Part V

1. U.S. Secretary of the Treasury, 1974–1977; cited at U.S. Department of the Treasury (1977, p. 1).

Chapter 14

1. Burke (1774). The speech was delivered on April 19, 1774.

2. Service (2009, p. 350).

3. As quoted in the *University Chronicle* of the University of Michigan (1869, p. 4). Saxe (1816–1887) was an American poet. Similar remarks are often attributed to Otto von Bismarck, but this attribution has not been confirmed. We cannot explain why a poet rather than a statesman first made the law-as-sausage analogy,

4. Jarvis (1987, p. 20).

5. Jarvis (1987, p. 21).

6. McCulloch ([1845] 1975, p. 344).

7. Figures in this paragraph are taken, or calculated, from McCulloch ([1845] 1975, p. 332). Strictly, we cannot be completely sure that the tax cut *caused* the increased volume of legal purchases. Many other things may have changed at the same time, and indeed, the cut was accompanied by intensified enforcement measures: The death penalty, for instance, was extended to those merely harboring a smuggler; Jarvis (1987, pp. 25–27) lists this and other measures. But it is hard to believe that the tax cut was not a dominant factor.

8. Ibn Khaldûn ([1377] 1967, p. 89).

9. As noted by Bartlett (2012, pp. 1207–1208).

10. Here the 100 percent figure refers to an income tax, such that earning more income provides no increase in after-tax income. Note the difference with a 100 percent tariff in the Pelham example, which (merely) doubles the price.

11. McCulloch ([1845] 1975, p. 340).

12. It also involved raising the lowest rate slightly, from 12 percent.

13. Keen, Kim, and Varsano (2008).

14. The impact of the Russian flat tax is analyzed in Ivanova, Keen, and Klemm (2005) and Gorodnichenko, Martinez-Vazquez, and Peter (2009).

15. On the 1981 tax cut, see Slemrod and Bakija (2017, p. 224). On Kansas, see Ritholtz (2017).

16. The emblematic example in the United States is the proposed bridge in Alaska between Ketchikan (population 8,900) and its airport on Gravina Island (population 50), estimated to cost as much as $320 million. It was not built (Utt, 2005).

17. Becker and Mulligan (2003).

18. Lledó et al. (2017).

19. Cordes et al. (2015, p. 4).

20. Activist Grover Norquist, a prominent American proponent of the strategy, once described his ambition to cut the size of government in half within 25 years as an effort to "reduce it to the size where I could drag it into the bathroom and drown it in the bathtub." From an interview by Liasson (2001).

21. Romer and Romer (2009).

22. This explanation was suggested by the prominent libertarian William Niskanen (2006).

23. These figures are all from *CBS News* (2018).

24. PAC stands for political action committee, a U.S. organization that raises money from its members and donates the money to campaigns for or against specific candidates or legislation.

25. According to Ranulf Higden's *Polychronicon* (circa 1342).

26. An inquiry made in the reign of Edward I shows that, indeed, at that time no tolls were levied in Coventry except on horses (Barber, 1855; Harris, 1909).

27. Brewer (1988, p. 233).

28. Brewer (1988, p. 237).

29. Birnbaum and Murray (1988, p. 111).

30. Brewer (1988, pp. 243–244).

31. Brewer (1988, p. 247).

32. Jagoda (2017).

33. White (2006, p. 253).

34. Free File Alliance (2016).

35. Sundelson (1941, p. 86).

36. Sundelson (1941, p. 87).

37. Times have changed. In the United Kingdom and the United States, for health reasons, spreads that are not butter have gained a commercial advantage. Hence, the brand-name product, *I Can't Believe It's Not Butter!®*, which is made with a blend of oils, has become a popular choice for some diet-conscious shoppers.

38. Numbers are from Lebhar (1959, pp. 16, 20, and 29).

39. Mom-and-pop retailers also sought, often successfully, regulations and taxes (generally in the form of vendor fees) to protect them from smaller, less organized, itinerant vendors. The proud city of Ann Arbor, Michigan, at one time imposed a license fee of $150 per year for each vehicle used by a "hawker" or "peddler." This was upheld in *People v. Riksen*, 284 Mich. 284, 279 N.W. 513 (1938), which noted that peddling, although a lawful pursuit, is liable to become a great nuisance. See Arlt (1941, p. 180).

40. Lee (1941, p. 158).

41. Ross (1986). Louisiana authorizes its parishes and incorporated municipalities to levy an annual chain-store tax, and counties in Maryland levy a chain-store license fee that can amount to $300 per store for chains of 20 or more stores in the state.

42. Americans for Tax Fairness (2014).

43. *South Dakota v. Wayfair, Inc., et al.*

44. Quoted in Seligman (1914, p. 154).

45. Another example of how a tax can become tainted because of historical associations is the South African VAT, brought in at the end of the apartheid era and now difficult to raise in part because of this association. See Naidoo (2012).

46. Food is zero-rated under the VAT in the United Kingdom, meaning that no tax is charged on sales, while tax on inputs can be refunded.

47. As shown, for instance, by Crawford, Keen, and Smith (2010).

48. "Largely," because the monopolies discussed in chapter 3 had similar economic effects, and there were taxes on some domestic production of natural resources, such as coal. But only a few explicit taxes were imposed on things of daily use. (O'Brien and Hunt 1999, pp. 204–205). The absence of excises in England was weird enough for foreigners to note: The Venetian ambassador to Queen Mary in the 1550s found it "singular and wonderful" (Dowell, 1884b, p. 8).

49. de Vries (2012).

50. Grapperhaus (1998, p. 24).

51. Kennedy (1913, pp. 51–52).

52. Kennedy (1913, p. 53).

53. In their proposed constitutional settlement, the "Heads of Proposal" (Hughes 1934, pp. 122–123).

54. O'Brien and Hunt (1999, p. 210).

55. Webber and Wildavsky (1986, p. 390). Samuel Johnson's definition continues: "and adjudged not by the common judges of property, but wretches hired by those to whom excise is paid."

56. O'Brien and Hunt (1999, p. 211).

57. Langford (1975, p. 1).

58. Plumb (1960, p. 241).

59. Hervey (1848, p. 179).

60. The left panel of the poster shown in the text depicts women eagerly waiting in line at a shop featuring abundant and low-priced fare in a world of free trade. The shop under protectionism, pictured at the right, has cobwebs in its window, a sparse selection, higher prices, and no female customers in sight—just a male tax collection officer and a shopkeeper who bears a striking resemblance to Joseph Chamberlain.

61. Crosby (2011, p. 176).

62. A weak form of Imperial Preference was applied from 1932 to 1937, by which time there was plenty else to complain about.

63. Crosby (2011, p. 164).

64. Pasties are a kind of English empanada. The proposal, more exactly, was to bring into VAT at the standard rate food freshly produced for consuming while hot. The kind of thing, that is, you might want to eat between the pub and the last train home.

65. Quoted in Seligman (1899, p. 87). He cites Anonymous (1756, p. 28).

66. See McCaffery (1994) and Krishna and Slemrod (2003).

67. McCaffery and Baron (2003).

68. Finkelstein (2009).

69. The evidence in Keen and Lockwood (2006) mentioned earlier suggests there is some truth to this suspicion.

70. Chetty, Looney, and Kroft (2009).

71. Rees-Jones and Taubinsky (2020).

72. Ali, Fjeldstad, and Sjursen (2014).

73. de León (2005, p. 71).

74. Courtenay (1803).

75. The label is clever but misleading. As noted by our esteemed colleague, James Hines, Jr., the estate tax could with equal accuracy be described as a "life subsidy." Moreover, as Slemrod and Gale (2001) point out, death is neither necessary nor sufficient to trigger the U.S. estate and gift tax. It is unnecessary, because transfers between living persons can trigger gift taxes. It is insufficient, because 99.8 percent of people who die owe no estate tax due to the high exemption level.

76. See Alvarez (2001).

77. Mason and Campbell (2017).

78. Erb (2013a).

79. Quinn (2012).

80. The base of the cow cess varies by state, from the transfer of property to the purchase of four-wheelers or liquor.

81. Petersen (1997, p. 232).

82. Crockett (2014).

83. In *Nix v. Hedden* 149 U.S. 304 (1893).

84. Best known as author of *The Rivals* and *The School for Scandal*.

85. Quoted in Rhodes (1933, pp. 94–95).

86. This difference in procedure is discussed in Daunton (2002, pp. 18–20) and Keen (2005).

87. There is a large literature on this topic. IMF (2013) and the references therein offer a good start for the interested reader.

88. Gucci Gulch is the name given to the hallway outside the U.S. congressional tax–writing committee meeting rooms, where well-dressed lobbyists congregate.

89. A summary of the substance of TRA86 is in Slemrod and Bakija (2017, pp. 392–395).

90. See Slemrod (2018) for a review of the Tax Cuts and Jobs Act and a comparison to TRA86.

91. Six countries have removed a VAT. But all—except Malaysia, which removed its VAT in 2018—have subsequently reinstated it.

92. Adam and Shaw (2003, p. 24). More cuts followed: The 15 percent surcharge on unearned income was removed in 1984, and in 1988 the top rate was cut to 40 percent and the basic rate to 25 percent. The rate of corporation tax, initially left at 40 percent, was down to 30 percent by 1984 (Corporation Tax Rates, n.d.).

93. Treisman (2002, p. 60). The FSB is the Federal Security Service, successor to the KGB.

94. Gaddy and Gale (2005, p. 985).

95. Birnbaum and Murray (1988, p. 260).

96. Keen and Lockwood (2010).

97. Keen and Lockwood (2010).

98. The spread of the flat tax, in varying forms, is discussed in Keen, Kim, and Varsano (2008).

99. Smith ([1776] 1868, pp. 392–393).

100. See Thorndike (2013). Whether it was really the VAT proposal that sealed his fate is disputed.

101. This is recounted in Barro (2015).

102. Neff (2016).

Chapter 15

1. Opening line of *The Go-Between* (Hartley 1953, p. 17).

2. *Star Wars* (1999).

3. This discussion draws on the review of the fairly sparse literature about taxation in science fiction in Anders and Jackson (2011).

4. Heinlein (2008, pp. 256–257).

5. Heinlein (2008, pp. 308–309).

6. Adams (1980, p. 115). This book is part of the larger Adams series, *The Hitchhiker's Guide to the Galaxy*. The *Hitchhiker* series originated in 1978 as a BBC radio show, the same year that the members of the British rock band Pink Floyd spent exactly 1 year outside the United Kingdom, also for tax reasons. Adams is reputed to have once gone on stage to play with Pink Floyd; see Sale (2012).

7. Manjoo (2002).

8. This discussion of tax in utopias draws heavily on Goodwin (2008).

9. Bellamy (1888, p. 134).

10. Goodwin (2008, pp. 316–317).

11. Orwell (1949, p. 85).

12. Why eleven? This, the number of players on a side, is the only element common to football (known as "soccer" in the United States) in the United Kingdom and the rest of the world and American football (barely known elsewhere).

13. *The Economist* (2018c).

14. This act split the power to tax services and goods between different levels of government (central and provincial/state, respectively)—an unworkable distinction for a VAT. India was able to adopt a federal VAT only after amending its constitution in 2016. In Pakistan, the issue still lingers.

15. Article 53 of the Italian Constitution.

16. Shehab (1953, p. 35).

17. Here leaving Pigovian taxes aside.

18. Things like trust in government, satisfaction with public services, absence of corruption, and even degree of patriotism tend to be positively associated with an inclination to comply with tax obligations, although results vary widely and characteristics such as age and religious inclination are also important; see, for instance, Ali, Fjeldstad, and Sjursen (2014), Konrad and Qari (2012), and OECD (2019f). But correlation does not imply causation: It may be, for instance, that those who are intrinsically more inclined to be compliant tend also to be more satisfied with whatever services they receive.

19. IMF (2020a, table 1.2). Figures are for general government gross debt.

20. Gaspar et al. (2019).

21. He, Goodkind, and Kowal (2016).

22. United Nations (n.d.). In low-income countries, the ratio of those over 65 to those age 15–64 is projected to nearly double, but to only around 11 percent.

23. This figure assumes that policies are not adopted to rein in some of this spending growth.

24. Thus said Barack Obama: White House, Office of the Press Secretary (2013).

25. Credit Suisse Research Institute (2017).

26. World Inequality Database. https://wid.world/world/#sptinc_p99p100_z /US;FR;DE;CN;ZA;GB;WO/last/eu/k/p/yearly/s/false/5.11/30/curve/false/country.

27. Around three-quarters of the redistribution achieved in advanced economies, for instance, is achieved on the spending side (including through monetary transfers): See, for example, International Monetary Fund (2017a, p. ix).

28. For the United Kingdom, for instance, Blundell et al. (2020) show how, through the lockdown phase, the pandemic amplified preexisting inequalities not only in income but also along gender, age, and geographical lines as well.

29. This figure is for a carbon tax at what many would regard as the modest level of $35 per ton (International Monetary Fund, 2019a, p. 28).

30. Wintour (2007).

31. Ventry (2011).

32. For more on the kinds of speculation mentioned here, see Gupta et al. (2017) and Jacobs (2017).

33. Seamans (2017).

34. See Scheuer and Slemrod (2020) for a review of the issues that arise in taxing the superrich.

35. The promise of and problems with using genetic information in the tax system are discussed in Logue and Slemrod (2008).

36. The "if" is because there may come a day in which the genetic code itself becomes manipulable, a point stressed by Chen, Grimshaw, and Myles (2017).

37. King and Crewe (2013, p. 154).

REFERENCES

Abbott, Frank Frost, and Allan Chester Johnson. 1926. *Municipal Administration in the Roman Empire.* Princeton, NJ: Princeton University Press.

Abraham, Arthur. 1974. "Bai Bureh, the British, and the Hut Tax War." *International Journal of African Historical Studies* 7 (1): 99–106.

Act of Uniformity 1559. Public Act, 1 Elizabeth I, c. 2.

Adam, Stuart, and Jonathan Shaw. 2003. *A Survey of the U.K. Tax System.* Institute for Fiscal Studies Briefing Note 9, London.

Adams, Charles. 2001. *For Good and Evil: The Impact of Taxes on the Course of Civilization,* 2nd ed. Lanham, MD: Madison Books.

Adams, Douglas. 1980. *The Restaurant at the End of the Galaxy.* New York: Harmony Books.

Addady, Michal. 2016. "Bank Whistleblower Believes CIA Is Behind the Panama Papers Leak." *Fortune,* April 13.

Aftalion, Florin. 1990. *The French Revolution: An Economic Interpretation,* translated by Martin Thom. Cambridge: Cambridge University Press.

Aguado, Jesús. 2018. "Spain to Change Law to Force Banks to Pay Mortgage Stamp Duty." *Reuters,* November 7.

Ainsworth, Richard Thomas. 2010. "Zappers—Retail VAT Fraud." Boston University School of Law Working Paper No. 10-04, Boston, MA.

Alavuotunki, Kaisa, Mika Haapanen, and Jukka Pirttila. 2019. "The Effects of the Value Added Tax on Revenue and Inequality." *Journal of Development Studies* 55 (4): 490–508.

Ali, Merima, Odd-Helge Fjeldstad, and Ingrid Hoem Sjursen. 2014. "To Pay or Not to Pay? Citizens' Attitudes toward Taxation in Kenya, Tanzania, Uganda, and South Africa." *World Development* 64: 828–842.

Allcott, Hunt, Benjamin B. Lockwood, and Dmitry Taubinsky. 2019. "Regressive Sin Taxes, with an Application to the Optimal Soda Tax." *Quarterly Journal of Economics* 134 (3): 1557–1626.

Allen, Douglas W. 1998. "Compatible Incentives and the Purchase of Military Commissions." *Journal of Legal Studies* 27 (1): 45–66.

Allingham, Michael, and Agnar Sandmo. 1972. "Income Tax Evasion: A Theoretical Analysis." *Journal of Public Economics* 1 (3–4): 323–338.

Alstadsæter, Annette, Niels Johannesen, and Gabriel Zucman. 2018. "Who Owns the Wealth in Tax Havens? Macro Evidence and Implications for Global Inequality." *Journal of Public Economics* 162: 89–100.

Alstadsæter, Annette, Niels Johannesen, and Gabriel Zucman. 2019. "Tax Evasion and In-equality." *American Economic Review* 109 (6): 2073–2103.

Alvarez, Lizette. 2001. "Capitol Hill Memo—In 2 Parties' War of Words, Shibboleths Emerge as Clear Winner." *New York Times*, April 27.

Americans for Tax Fairness. 2014. "Walmart on Tax Day: How Taxpayers Subsidize America's Biggest Employer and Richest Family." Americans for Tax Fairness, Washington, DC.

Anders, Charlie Jane, and Gordon Jackson. 2011. "Nobody Pays Taxes Today: Tax Revolts from Science Fiction and Fantasy." *Gizmodo*, April 14.

Andrew, John A. 2002. *Power to Destroy: The Political Uses of the IRS from Kennedy to Nixon.* Chicago: Ivan R. Dee.

Anonymous. 1756. *A Letter from a Member of Parliament, on the Plate-Tax.* London: Printed for J. Scott at the Black Swan.

Ansary, Tamim. 2009. *Destiny Disrupted: A History of the World through Islamic Eyes.* New York: Public Affairs.

Archer, Ian. 2016. "Facing Up to Catastrophe: The Great Fire of London." *The Oxford Historian.* Michaelmas Term. Faculty of History, University of Oxford.

Arlt, Carl T. 1941. "Discriminatory Vendor Licensing and Taxing of Out-of-State Corporations." In *Tax Barriers to Trade*, by Mark Eisner, Robert L. Cochran, Edgar L. Burtis et al., 176–186. Philadelphia: University of Pennsylvania Tax Institute.

Armey, Dick. 1996. "Why America Needs the Flat Tax." In *Fairness and Efficiency in the Flat Tax*, by Robert E. Hall, Alvin Rabushka, Dick Armey, Robert Eisner, and Herbert Stein, 96–101. Washington, DC: AEI Press.

Artavanis, Nikolaos, Adair Morse, and Margarita Tsoutsoura. 2016. "Measuring Income Tax Evasion Using Bank Credit: Evidence from Greece." *Quarterly Journal of Economics* 131 (2): 739–798.

Arya, Divya. 2016. "The Woman Who Cut Off Her Breasts to Protest a Tax." *BBC News*, July 26.

Asen, Elke. 2019. "Soda Taxes in Europe." Tax Foundation online, September 5.

Askolovitch, Claude, 2017. "En 1962, le Général de Gaulle Lance La Guerre Fiscale contre Monaco." *France Inter*, March 19.

Aslam, Aqib, and Alpa Shah. 2020. "Tec(h)tonic Shifts: Taxing the 'Digital Economy.'" International Monetary Fund Working Paper No. 20/76, Washington, DC.

Atiyeh, Clifford. 2013. "Feds Watching: Ford's Run Around on 'Chicken Tax' Riles U.S. Customs Officials." *Car and Driver* online, September 26.

Auerbach, Alan J., Michael P. Devereux, Michael Keen, and John Vella. 2017. "Destination-Based Cash Flow Taxation." Saïd Business School Research Paper 2017–09, University of Oxford, Oxford, UK.

Auriol, Emmanuelle, and Michael Warlters. 2005. "Taxation Base in Developing Countries." *Journal of Public Economics* 89 (4): 625–646.

Austen, Jane. 1906. *Pride and Prejudice.* In *The Novels of Jane Austen*, edited by R. Brimley Johnson. New York: Frank S. Holby.

Australian Taxation Office. n.d. *ATO Tip Off Form.* Sydney.

Avi-Yonah, Reuven. 2020. "It's Time to Revive the Excess Profits Tax." *The American Prospect*, March 27.

Babbage, Charles. 1851. *Thoughts on the Principles of Taxation, with Reference to a Property Tax, and Its Exceptions*, 2nd ed. London: John Murray.

Bagguley, Paul. 1995. "Protest, Poverty and Power: A Case Study of the Anti-Poll Tax Movement." *The Sociological Review* 43 (4): 693–719.

Bagley, J. J., and P. B. Rowley. 1968. *A Documentary History of England: Vol. 1 (1066–1540)*. Harmondsworth, U.K.: Penguin.

Ballara, Angela. 1993. "Tōia, Hōne Riiwi." In *Dictionary of New Zealand Biography, Te Ara—The Encyclopedia of New Zealand*. Wellington, New Zealand.

Bank, Steven A., Kirk J. Stark, and Joseph J. Thorndike. 2008. *War and Taxes*. Washington, DC: Urban Institute Press.

Bank of England. n.d. *A Millennium of Macroeconomic Data*. https://www.bankofengland.co.uk/statistics/research-datasets.

Barber, John W. 1855. *European Historical Collections; Comprising England, Scotland, with Holland, Belgium, and Part of France*. New Haven, CT: John W. Barber.

Barnett, Le Roy. 2013. "The Attempts to Tax Bachelors in Michigan." *HSM Chronicle* 4 (35): 18–19.

Barratt, Nick. 1999. "English Royal Revenue in the Early Thirteenth Century and Its Wider Context, 1130–1330." In *Crises, Revolutions and Self-Sustained Growth: Essays in European Fiscal History, 1130–1830*, edited by William Mark Ormrod, Margaret Bonney, and Richard Bonney, 58–96. Stamford, U.K.: Shaun Tyas.

Barrett, Anthony A. 1990. *Caligula: The Corruption of Power*. New Haven, CT: Yale University Press.

Barro, Josh. 2015. "Rand Paul and the VAT That Dare Not Speak Its Name." *New York Times*, June 18.

Barro, Robert J. 1987. "Government Spending, Interest Rates, Prices, and Budget Deficits in the United Kingdom, 1701–1918." *Journal of Monetary Economics* 20 (2): 221–247.

Bartlett, Bruce. 1994. "How Excessive Government Killed Ancient Rome." *Cato Institute Journal* 14 (2): 297–299.

Bartlett, Bruce. 2012. "The Laffer Curve, Part 2." *Tax Notes* 136 (10): 1207–1209.

Barzel, Yoram. 1976. "An Alternative Approach to the Analysis of Taxation." *Journal of Political Economy* 84 (6): 1177–1197.

Basu, Tanya. 2015. "Colorado Raised More Tax Revenue from Marijuana Than from Alcohol." *Time*, September 16.

BBC. 2014. "Seven Man Made Wonders: Silbury Hill." September 24.

BBC News. 2005. "Best: Decline of the Golden Boy." June 4.

BBC News. 2009. "VAT Cut Boosts French Restaurants." July 1.

BBC News. 2010. "Customs Raid the Largest Illegal Fuel Plant Found in NI." February 5.

BBC News. 2014. "10 Big Myths about World War I Debunked." February 25.

BBC News. 2018a. "Bolivia Sea Dispute: UN Rules in Chile's Favour." October 1.

BBC News. 2018b. "Ken Dodd: 17 of His Funniest One-Liners." March 12.

BBC News. 2019. "Hungary Tries for Baby Boom with Tax Breaks and Loan Forgiveness." February 11.

BBC Radio. 2016. "Our Man in China: The Diaries." November 7.

Beales, Derek, and Eugenio F. Biagini. 2013. *The Risorgimento and the Unification of Italy*, 2nd ed. London: Routledge.

Bean, Richard. 1973. "War and the Birth of the Nation State." *Journal of Economic History* 33 (1): 203–221.

Beard, Mary. 2015. *SPQR: A History of Ancient Rome.* New York: Liveright.

Beatles, The. 1966. *Taxman.* Studio 2, EMI Studios, Abbey Road. Recorded April 20–22 as the first song on the *Revolver* album.

Beautiful Puglia. n.d. "Alberobello." Italy.

Becker, Gary S. 1968. "Crime and Punishment: An Economic Approach." *Journal of Political Economy* 76 (2): 169–217.

Becker, Gary S., and Casey B. Mulligan. 2003. "Deadweight Costs and the Size of Government." *Journal of Law & Economics* 46 (2): 293–340.

Beech, Samantha. 2016. "The Island Nation of Tuvalu Is Being Kept Afloat by Its Domain Name." *News Corp Australia Network*, March 7.

Beer, Sebastian, Maria Coelho, and Sebastien Leduc. 2019. "Hidden Treasure: The Impact of Automatic Exchange of Information on Cross-Border Tax Evasion." International Monetary Fund Working Paper No. 19/286, Washington, DC.

Beijing Tax Museum. 2019. *Introduction to Beijing Tax Museum.* Beijing.

Belasco, Amy. 2014. "The Cost of Iraq, Afghanistan, and Other Global War on Terror Operations since 9/11." Working paper, Congressional Research Service, Washington, DC.

Bell, Michael E., John H. Bowman, and Jerome C. German. 2009. "The Assessment Requirements for a Separate Tax on Land." In *Land Value Taxation: Theory, Evidence and Practice,* edited by Richard F. Dye and Richard W. England, 171–194. Cambridge, MA: Lincoln Institute of Land Policy.

Bellamy, Edward. 1888. *Looking Backward.* Boston: Ticknor and Co.

Bellon, Matthieu, Jillie Chang, Era Dabla-Norris, Salma Khalid, Frederico Lima, Enrique Rojas, and Pilar Villena. 2019. "Digitalization to Improve Tax Compliance: Evidence from VAT e-Invoicing in Peru." International Monetary Fund Working Paper No. 19/231, Washington, DC.

Belsey, Catherine. 1985. *The Subject of Tragedy: Identity and Difference in Renaissance Drama.* London: Methuen.

Benedek, Dora, Ruud de Mooij, Michael Keen, and Philippe Wingender. 2020. "Varieties of VAT Pass Through." *International Tax and Public Finance* 27 (4): 890–930.

Bergin, Tom. 2012. "Special Report—How Starbucks Avoids UK Taxes." *Reuters*, October 15.

Bernardi, Aurelio. 1970. "The Economic Problems of the Roman Empire at the Time of Its Decline." In *The Economic Decline of Empires,* edited by Carlo M. Cipolla, 16–83. London: Methuen.

Bernholz, Peter. 2003. *Monetary Regimes and Inflation: History, Economic and Political Relationships.* Northampton, MA: Edward Elgar.

Besley, Timothy, Anders Jensen, and Torsten Persson. 2015. "Norms, Enforcement, and Tax Evasion." Centre for Economic Policy Research Discussion Paper DP10372, London.

Besley, Timothy, and John McLaren. 1993. "Taxes and Bribery: The Role of Wage Incentives." *Economic Journal* 103 (416): 119–141.

Besley, Timothy, Ian Preston, and Michael Ridge. 1997. "Fiscal Anarchy in the UK: Modeling Poll Tax Noncompliance." *Journal of Public Economics* 64 (2): 137–152.

Bezias, Jean-Rémy. 2007. "Les Alpes-Maritimes et la Crise Franco-Monégasque de1962." *Cahiers de la Méditerranée* 74: 321–336.

Bickers, Robert. 2011. *The Scramble for China: Foreign Devils in the Qing Empire, 1832–1914*. London: Penguin Global.

Billings, Dorothy K. 1969. "The Johnson Cult of New Hanover." *Oceania* 40 (1): 13–19.

Binmore, Kenneth, and Paul Klemperer. 2002. "The Biggest Auction Ever: The Sale of the British 3G Telecom Licenses." *Economic Journal* 112 (478): C74–C96.

Birch, Thomas, ed. 1742. *A Collection of the State Papers of John Thurloe*. London: Fletcher Gyles.

Bird, Richard M., and Joosung Jun. 2005. "Earmarking in Theory and Korean Practice." International Tax Program Paper 0153, University of Toronto.

Bird, Richard M., Jorge Martinez-Vazquez, and Benno Torgler. 2008. "Tax Effort in Developing Countries and High Income Countries: The Impact of Corruption, Voice and Accountability." *Economic Analysis and Policy* 38 (1): 55–71.

Birnbaum, Jeffrey H., and Alan S. Murray. 1988. *Showdown at Gucci Gulch: Lawmakers, Lobbyists, and the Unlikely Triumph of Tax Reform*. New York: Vintage Books.

Bishop-Henchman, Joseph. 2014. "Tax Code Disallows Business Deductions for Marijuana Sales." Tax Foundation online, February 6.

Bisserbe, Noemie, and Brian Blackstone. 2019. "UBS Is Fined $4.2 Billion in French Tax-Evasion Case." *Wall Street Journal*, February 20.

Blackstone, Brian. 2019. "Big-Money Bills Get Little Love—Except in Switzerland." *Wall Street Journal*, March 5.

Blackstone, William. 1794. *Commentaries on the Laws of England*, 12th ed. Dublin: L. White, William Jones, and John Rice.

Blake, Robert. 1969. *Disraeli*. London: Methuen.

Blakey, Roy G., and Gladys C. Blakey. 1940. *The Federal Income Tax*. New York: Longmans, Green and Co.

Blanchard, Olivier, and Jean Pisani-Ferry. 2020. "Monetisation: Do Not Panic." *VoxEU*, April 10.

Blank, Joshua D., and Daniel Z. Levin. 2010. "When Is Tax Enforcement Publicized?" *Virginia Tax Review* 30 (1): 1–38.

Blumenthal, Marsha, Charles Christian, and Joel Slemrod. 2001. "Do Normative Appeals Affect Tax Compliance? Evidence from a Controlled Experiment in Minnesota." *National Tax Journal* 54 (1): 125–138.

Blundell, Richard, Monica Costa Dias, Robert Joyce, and Xiaowei Xu. 2020. "COVID-19 and Inequalities." *Fiscal Studies* 41 (2): 291–319.

Bø, Erlend E., Joel Slemrod, and Thor O. Thoresen. 2015. "Taxes on the Internet: Deterrence Effects of Public Disclosure." *American Economic Journal: Economic Policy* 7 (1): 36–62.

Boadway, Robin, and Michael Keen. 2010. "Theoretical Perspectives on Resource Tax Design." In *The Taxation of Petroleum and Minerals: Principles, Practices and Problems*, edited by Philip Daniel, Michael Keen, and Charles McPherson, 14–74. London: Routledge.

Board of Governors of the Federal Reserve System. 2017. "How Much Does It Cost to Produce Currency and Coin?" Washington, DC.

Bobbitt, Philip. 2003. *The Shield of Achilles: War, Peace, and the Course of History*. New York: Anchor Books.

Boone, Jon. 2012. "Pakistan Politicians Engulfed by Tax Evasion Storm." *The Guardian,* December 12.

Boonn, Ann. 2020. *Cigarette Tax Increases by State per Year 2000–2018.* Washington, DC: Campaign for Tobacco-Free Kids.

Boskin, Michael J., and Eytan Sheshinski. 1983. "Optimal Tax Treatment of the Family: Married Couples." *Journal of Public Economics* 20 (3): 281–297.

Bott, Uwe. 2013. "A Brief History of U.S. Defaults." *The Globalist,* January 16.

Bourassa, Steven. 2009. "The U.S. Experience." In *Land Value Taxation: Theory, Evidence, and Practice,* edited by Richard F. Dye and Richard W. England, 11–26. Cambridge, MA: Lincoln Institute of Land Policy.

Bouw, Annerie. 2017. "Tobacco Taxation in the European Union: An Overview." World Bank Group. Brussels, Belgium.

Bowen, H. V. 1991. *Revenue and Reform: The Indian Problem in British Politics, 1757–1773.* Cambridge: Cambridge University Press.

Bowles, Roger, and Philip Jones. 1993. "Nonpayment of Poll Tax: An Exploratory Analysis of Tax Resistance." *International Review of Law and Economics* 13 (4): 445–455.

Bowman, John. 2000. *Columbia Chronologies of Asia History and Culture.* New York: Columbia University Press.

Braddick. Michael J. 1996. *The Nerves of State: Taxation and the Financing of the English State, 1558–1714.* Manchester, U.K.: Manchester University Press.

Brewer, John. 1988. *The Sinews of Power: War, Money and the English State, 1688–1783.* New York: Alfred A. Knopf.

Brewer, Michael, Emmanuel Saez, and Andrew Shephard. 2010. "Means Testing and Tax Rates on Earnings." In *Dimensions of Tax Design: The Mirrlees Review,* edited by Stuart Adam, Tim Besley, Richard Blundell, Stephen Bond, Robert Chote et al., 90–173. Oxford: Oxford University Press.

Brogan, Hugh. 1985. *The Longman History of the United States of America.* New York: William Morrow.

Brown, Susan E. 2007. "Assessing Men and Maids: The Female Servant Tax and Meanings of Productive Labour in Late-Eighteenth-Century Britain." *Left History: An Interdisciplinary Journal of Historical Inquiry and Debate* 12 (2): 11–32.

Brummitt, Chris, and Herdaru Purnomo. 2015. "Indonesia Is Using Drones to Catch Tax Cheats." *Bloomberg* online, June 3.

Brunner, Eric, and Jon Sonstelie. 2003. "School Finance Reform and Voluntary Fiscal Federalism." *Journal of Public Economics* 87 (9–10): 2157–2185.

Brunori, David, and Jennifer Carr. 2002. "Valuing Land and Improvements: State Laws and Local Government Practices." *State Tax Notes* 25: 1023–1033.

Bryan, William Jennings, and Mary Baird Bryan. 1900. *The Life and Speeches of Hon. Wm. Jennings Bryan.* Baltimore, MD: R. H. Woodward Company.

Buehler, Alfred G. 1940. "The Taxation of Corporate Excess Profits in Peace and War Times." *Law and Contemporary Problems* 7 (Spring): 291–300.

Bulow, Jeremy, and Paul Klemperer. 1998. "The Tobacco Deal." *Brookings Papers on Economic Activity: Microeconomics:* 323–394.

Burg, David F. 2004. *A World History of Tax Rebellions: An Encyclopedia of Tax Rebels, Revolts, and Riots from Antiquity to the Present*. New York: Routledge.

Burke, Edmund. 1774. *Speech of Edmund Burke, Esq., on American Taxation, April 19, 1774*, 4th ed. London: J. Dodsley.

Burke, Edmund. [1790] 1935. *Reflections on the French Revolution*. Introduction by A. J. Grieve. London: J. M. Dent & Sons.

Burman, Leonard E. 2011. "Jon Stewart's Fake News on Tax Expenditures." *Forbes*, May 10.

Burman, Leonard E., Kimberly A. Clausing, and John O'Hare. 1994. "Tax Reform and Realizations of Capital Gains in 1986." *National Tax Journal* 47 (1): 1–18.

Cagan, Phillip. 1956. "The Monetary Dynamics of Hyperinflation." In *Studies in the Quantity Theory of Money*, edited by Milton Friedman, 25–117. Chicago: University of Chicago Press.

Calvert, Scott. 2019. "Philadelphia Is the First City to Ban Cashless Stores." *Wall Street Journal*, March 7.

Carbon Tax Center. n.d. *Carbon Tax FAQs*. New York.

Carpenter, David. 2003. *The Struggle for Mastery: The Penguin History of Britain 1066–1284*. London: Penguin.

Carrère, Emmanuel. 2017. *The Kingdom: A Novel*, translated by John Lambert. New York: Farrar, Straus, and Giroux.

Carrillo, Paul, Dina Pomeranz, and Monica Singhal. 2017. "Dodging the Taxman: Firm Misreporting and Limits to Tax Enforcement." *American Economic Journal: Applied Economics* 9 (2): 144–164.

Carver, Thomas Nixon. 1898. *The Ohio Tax Inquisitor Law*. New York: Macmillan.

Casaburi, Lorenzo, and Ugo Troiano. 2016. "Ghost-House Busters: The Electoral Response to a Large Anti-Tax Evasion Program." *Quarterly Journal of Economics* 131 (1): 273–314.

CBC News. 2014. "Twinkies, Pop Tarts among Tax-Exempt Foods." January 22.

CBS News. 2018. "Money Spent on Lobbying Skyrocketed During Tax Overhaul." February 2.

Chalk, Nigel A., Michael Keen, and Victoria J. Perry. 2018. "The Tax Cuts and Jobs Act: An Appraisal." International Monetary Fund Working Paper No. 18/185, Washington, DC.

Chaloupka, Frank J., Lisa W. Powell, and Kenneth E. Warner. 2019. "The Use of Excise Taxes to Reduce Tobacco, Alcohol, and Sugary Beverage Consumption." *Annual Review of Public Health* 40: 187–201.

Chaloupka, Frank J., David Sweanor, and Kenneth E. Warner. 2015. "Differential Taxes for Differential Risks—Toward Reduced Harm from Nicotine-Yielding Products." *New England Journal of Medicine* 373 (7): 594–597.

Chambas, Gérard. 2005. *Afrique au Sud du Sahara: Mobiliser des Ressources Fiscales pour le Développement*. Paris: Economica.

Chambas, Gérard, and Jean-Louis Combes. 2001. "L'impôt Progressif sur le Revenu: Deux siècles de débat sur la progressivité de l'impôt en France 1700–1917." *Revue Française de Finances Publiques* 74: 197–213.

Chambers, John Whiteclay II. 1987. *To Raise an Army: The Draft Comes to Modern America*. New York: Free Press.

Chang, Jung. 2013. *Empress Dowager Cixi*. New York: Alfred A. Knopf.

Chen, Huan-Chang. 1911. *The Economic Principles of Confucius and His School*, vol. 45, Studies in History, Economics and Public Law. New York: Columbia University.

Chen, Jignan (Cecilia), Shaun Grimshaw, and Gareth D. Myles. 2017. "Testing and Implementing Digital Tax Administration." In *Digital Revolutions in Public Finance*, edited by Sanjeev Gupta, Michael Keen, Alpa Shah, and Geneviève Verdier, 113–145. Washington, DC: International Monetary Fund.

Chetty, Raj, Adam Looney, and Kory Kroft. 2009. "Salience and Taxation: Theory and Evidence." *American Economic Review* 99 (4): 1145–1177.

Churchill, Winston. 1909. "On Land Monopoly." Speech in the House of Commons, May 4. London.

City of Doraville, GA. 2013. *Annual Financial Report.*

Clark, Christopher. 2006. *Iron Kingdom: The Rise and Downfall of Prussia.* Cambridge, MA: Harvard University Press.

Clark, Peter. 1988. "The 'Mother Gin' Controversy in the Early Eighteenth Century." *Transactions of the Royal Historical Society* 38: 63–84.

Cleary, Duncan, William Crandall, and Andrew Masters. 2017. "Understanding Revenue Administration: Results from the Second Survey of the Revenue Administration-Fiscal Information Tool." International Monetary Fund, Washington, DC.

Clements, Jonathan. 2016. *Christ's Samurai: The True Story of the Shimabara Rebellion.* London: Robinson.

Click, Reid W. 1998. "Seigniorage in a Cross-Section of Countries." *Journal of Money, Credit and Banking* 30 (2): 154–171.

Clotfelter, Charles T., and Philip J. Cook. 1991. *Selling Hope: State Lotteries in America.* Cambridge, MA: Harvard University Press.

Cnossen, Sijbren. 2008. "Do Drinkers Pay Their Way in the European Union?" *Finanzarchiv* 64 (4): 508–539.

Coase, Ronald H. 1960. "The Problem of Social Cost." *Journal of Law and Economics* 3: 1–44.

Cobban, Alfred. 1963. *A History of Modern France, Vol. 1: 1715–1799*, 3rd ed. Harmondsworth, U.K.: Penguin.

Cole, Gail. 2014. "It's Against the Law to Advertise No Sales Tax." *Sales Tax News*, March 14.

Collins, Lauren. 2020. "Was Jeanne Calment the Oldest Person Who Ever Lived—Or a Fraud?" *New Yorker*, February 10.

Colwyn Committee. 1927. *Minutes of Evidence Taken before the Committee on National Debt and Taxation*, vol. 1. London: His Majesty's Stationery Office.

Compañía General de Tabacos de Filipinas v. Collector of Internal Revenue, 275 U.S. 87 (1927).

Congressional Globe. 1870. 2nd sess. 41st Cong. *The Debates and Proceedings of the Second Session Forty-First Congress together with An Appendix, Embracing the Laws Passed at That Session.* Washington, DC.

Congressional Record 44. 1909. 3989. Statement of Senator William Borah.

Conn, David. 2015. "England Ashes Heroes among Cricketers Facing Large Bills for Tax Avoidance Schemes." *The Guardian*, March 15.

Constitution Society. n.d. "The Code of Hammurabi." San Antonio, TX.

Conway, Moncure Daniel. [1909] 1970. *The Life of Thomas Paine.* New York: Benjamin Blom.

Cooper, Duff. [1932] 2001. *Talleyrand.* London: Jonathan Cape.

Copland, Ian, and Michael R. Godley. 1993. "Revenue Farming in Comparative Perspective: Reflections on Taxation, Social Structure and Development in the Early-Modern Period." In *The Rise and Fall of Revenue Farming*, edited by John G. Butcher and Howard W. Dick, 45–68. London: Palgrave Macmillan.

Cordes, Till, Tidiane Kinda, Priscilla Muthoora, and Anke Weber. 2015. "Expenditure Rules: Effective Tools for Sound Fiscal Policy?" International Monetary Fund Working Paper No. 15/29, Washington, DC.

Corlett, Wilfred J., and Douglas C. Hague. 1953. "Complementarity and the Excess Burden of Taxation." *Review of Economic Studies* 21 (1): 21–30.

Coronel, Sheila. 2013. "Time for Public Officials to Disclose Their Tax Payments?" International Consortium of Investigative Journalists, Washington, DC.

Corporation Tax Rates. n.d. https://www.figurewizard.com/list-uk-corporation-tax-rates .html.

Cournot, Antoine Augustin. [1838] 1897. *Researches into the Mathematical Principles of the Theory of Wealth*, translated by Nathaniel T. Bacon. New York: Macmillan.

Courtenay, Thomas Peregrine. 1803. *Observations upon the Present State of the Finances of Great Britain; Suggested by Mr. Morgan's Supplement to His "Comparative View," and by Mr. Addington's Financial Measures.* London: J. Budd.

Cramton, Peter. 2010. "How Best to Auction Natural Resources." In *The Taxation of Petroleum and Minerals: Principles, Practices and Problems*, edited by Philip Daniel, Michael Keen, and Charles McPherson, 289–316. Abingdon, U.K.: Routledge.

Crandall, William. 2010. "Revenue Administration: Performance Measurement in Tax Administration." International Monetary Fund, Fiscal Affairs Department, Technical Notes and Manuals 10/11, Washington, DC.

Crandall, William, Elizabeth Gavin, and Andrew Masters. 2019. "ISORA 2016: Understanding Revenue Administration." International Monetary Fund, Fiscal Affairs Department, Paper 19/05, Washington, DC.

Crawford, Elizabeth. 2003. *The Women's Suffrage Movement: A Reference Guide 1866–1928.* London: UCL Press.

Crawford, Ian, Michael Keen, and Stephen Smith. 2010. "Value Added Tax and Excises." In *Dimensions of Tax Design: The Mirrlees Review*, edited by James Mirrlees, Stuart Adam, Timothy Besley, Richard Blundell, Stephen Bond et al., 275–362. Oxford: Oxford University Press.

Crawford, Neta C. 2002. *Argument and Change in World Politics: Ethics, Decolonization, and Humanitarian Intervention.* Cambridge: Cambridge University Press.

Credit Suisse Research Institute. 2017. *Global Wealth Report 2017: Where Are We Ten Years after the Crisis?* Online, November 14.

Crevar, Alex. 2015. "In the Heart of the Balkans, a City Transformed." *New York Times*, August 30.

Crivelli, Ernesto, Ruud de Mooij, and Michael Keen. 2016. "Base Erosion, Profit Shifting and Developing Countries." *Finanzarchiv* 72 (3): 268–301.

Crockett, Zachary. 2014. "The Most Expensive Typo in Legislative History." *Priceonomics Blog*, October 9.

Crosby, Travis L. 2011. *Joseph Chamberlain: A Most Radical Imperialist.* London: I. B. Tauris.

Cui, Wei. 2019. "The Digital Services Tax: A Conceptual Defense." *Tax Law Review* 73 (1): 69–111.

Cunich, Peter. 1999. "Revolution and Crisis in English State Finance, 1534–47." In *Crises, Revolutions and Self-Sustained Growth: Essays in European Fiscal History, 1130–1830*, edited by William Mark Ormrod, Margaret Bonney, and Richard Bonney, 110–137. Stamford, U.K.: Shaun Tyas.

Dadayan, Lucy. 2019. "Are States Betting on Sin? The Murky Future of State Taxation." Tax Policy Center Research Report, October. Washington, DC.

Dahan, Momi, and Michel Strawczynski. 2000. "Optimal Income Taxation: An Example with a U-Shaped Pattern of Optimal Marginal Tax Rates: Comment." *American Economic Review* 90 (3): 681–686.

Dale, Hylton B. 1922. "The Worshipful Company of the Woodmongers and The Coal Trade of London." *Journal of the Royal Society of Arts* 70: 816–823.

Daley, Suzanne. 2010. "Greek Wealth Is Everywhere but Tax Forms." *New York Times*, May 1.

Dalrymple, William. 2015. "The East India Company: The Original Corporate Raiders." *The Guardian*, March 4.

Dalrymple, William. 2019. *The Anarchy: The Relentless Rise of the East India Company*. London: Bloomsbury Publishing.

Daunton, Martin. 2001. *Trusting Leviathan: The Politics of Taxation in Britain, 1799–1914*. Cambridge: Cambridge University Press.

Daunton, Martin. 2002. *Just Taxes: The Politics of Taxation in Britain, 1914–1979*. Cambridge: Cambridge University Press.

Davidson, Carolyn. 2000. *The Bachelor Tax*. Toronto: Harlequin.

Davidson, Ian. 2010. *Voltaire: A Life*. New York: Pegasus Books.

Davidson, Jonathan. 2011. *Downing Street Blues: A History of Depression and Other Mental Afflictions in British Prime Ministers*. Jefferson, NC: McFarland and Company.

Davies, Peter. 2009. *The French Revolution: A Beginner's Guide*. Oxford: Oneworld.

de la Riva-Agüero, J. [1874–1875] 1929. "No. 25. The Treaty of Sucre or the Martinez-Baptista Agreement." In *University of Iowa Studies in the Social Sciences*, vol. 8, no. 3, edited by William Jefferson Dennis, 61–63. Iowa City, IA: University of Iowa.

de León, Pedro de Cieza. 2005. "Taxation and the Incas." In *The Peru Reader: History, Culture, Politics*, edited by Orin Starn, Robin Kirk, and Carlos Iván Degregori, 70–74. Durham, NC: Duke University Press.

Delipalla, Sofia, and Michael Keen. 1992. "The Comparison between Ad Valorem and Specific Taxation under Imperfect Competition." *Journal of Public Economics* 49 (3): 351–367.

DeLong, Hillary, Jamie Chriqui, Julien Leider, and Frank J. Chaloupka. 2016. "Common State Mechanisms Regulating Tribal Tobacco Taxation and Sales, the USA, 2015." *Tobacco Control* 25 (Suppl. 1): 132–137.

de Mooij, Ruud. 2011. "The Tax Elasticity of Corporate Debt: A Synthesis of Size and Variations." International Monetary Fund Working Paper No. 11/95, Washington, DC.

de Mooij, Ruud. 2012. "Tax Biases to Debt Finance: Assessing the Problem, Finding Solutions." *Fiscal Studies* 33 (4): 489–512.

Dennett, Daniel C. 1950. *Conversion and the Poll Tax in Early Islam*. Cambridge, MA: Harvard University Press.

de Tocqueville, Alexis. 1866. *L'Ancien Régime et la Révolution*, 7th ed. Paris: Michel Lévy Frères.

Devereux, Michael P., Alan J. Auerbach, Michael Keen, Paul Oosterhuis, Wolfgang Schön, and John Vella. 2019. "Residual Profit Allocation by Income." Said Business School Working Paper No. 19/01, University of Oxford, Oxford, U.K.

de Vries, Jan. 1976. *The Economy of Europe in an Age of Crisis, 1600–1750*. Cambridge: Cambridge University Press.

de Vries, Jan. 2012. "Taxing the Staff of Life: The Dutch Bread Tax, 1574–1855." Paper for presentation to the Yale Economic History Seminar, April 23.

Dewald, Jonathan. 1996. *The European Nobility, 1400–1800*. Cambridge: Cambridge University Press.

Dharmapala, Dhammika. 2018. "International Spillovers from Proposed US Tax Reforms." *Australian Tax Forum* 33: 79–100.

Dharmapala, Dhammika, and James R. Hines Jr. 2009. "Which Countries Become Tax Havens?" *Journal of Public Economics* 93 (9–10): 1058–1068.

Diamond, Peter A., and James A. Mirrlees. 1971. "Optimal Taxation and Public Production I: Production Efficiency." *American Economic Review* 61 (1): 8–27.

Dickens, Charles. 1850. *Household Words*, vol. 1. London: Bradbury and Evans.

Dickens, Charles. 1914. *The Works of Charles Dickens*, vol. 4. London: Chapman & Hall.

Didier, Anne-Céline. 2014. "Impôt sur le Revenu, Contribution Sociale Généralisée (CSG): Quelles Réformes?" Conseil des Prélèvements Obligatoires, online.

Dietz, Frederick C. 1921. *English Government Finance, 1485–1558*. Urbana, IL: University of Illinois.

Dillon, Patrick. 2002. *Gin: The Much Lamented Death of Madam Geneva*. London: Review.

Dilnot, Andrew, John Kay, and Michael Keen. 1990. "Allocating Taxes to Households: A Methodology." *Oxford Economic Papers* 42: 210–230.

Dingle, Anthony E. 1972. "Drink and Working-Class Living Standards in Britain, 1870–1914." *Economic History Review* 25 (4): 608–622.

Dio, Cassius. [61] 1925. *Roman History*, vol. VIII. Cambridge, MA: Loeb Classical Library.

Ditmore, Melissa. 2009. "Sex and Taxes." *The Guardian*, April 16.

Djankov, Simeon, Tim Ganser, Caralee McLiesh, Rita Ramalho, and Andrei Shleifer. 2010. "The Effect of Corporate Taxes on Investment and Entrepreneurship." *American Economic Journal: Macroeconomics* 2 (3): 31–64.

Doran, Timothy, and Spencer C. Tucker. 2019. "Mithridates VI Eupator Dionysius (ca. 134–63 BCE)." In *Middle East Conflicts from Ancient Egypt to the 21st Century*, edited by Spencer C. Tucker, 827–828. Santa Barbara, CA: ABC-CLIO.

Dorfman, Robert. 1989. "Thomas Robert Malthus and David Ricardo." *Journal of Economic Perspectives* 3 (3): 153–164.

Dorn, Nicholas. 1983. *Alcohol, Youth, and the State*. London: Croom Helm.

Douglas, Roy. 1999. *Taxation in Britain since 1660*. Basingstoke, Hampshire, U.K.: Macmillan.

Douglas, Roy. 2011–2012. "The Lloyd George Land Taxes." *Journal of Liberal History* 73: 4–13.

Dowd, Allan. 2010. "Reynolds, JTI Settle Cigarette Smuggling Case." *The Globe and Mail*, April 13.

Dowell, Stephen. 1884a. *A History of Taxation and Taxes in England from the Earliest Times to the Present Day*, vol. 1. London: Routledge. First published by Longmans Green.

Dowell, Stephen. 1884b. *A History of Taxation and Taxes in England from the Earliest Times to the Present Day*, vol. 2. London: Routledge. First published by Longmans Green.

Dowell, Stephen. 1884c. *A History of Taxation and Taxes in England from the Earliest Times to the Present Day*, vol. 3. London: Routledge. First published by Longmans Green.

Dowell, Stephen. 1884d. *A History of Taxation and Taxes in England from the Earliest Times to the Present Day*, vol. 4. London: Routledge. First published by Longmans Green.

Doyle, William. 1996. *Venality: The Sale of Offices in Eighteenth-Century France*. Oxford: Clarendon Press.

Duarte, Pedro Garcia. 2009. "Frank P. Ramsey: A Cambridge Economist." *History of Political Economy* 41 (3): 445–470.

Dubner, Stephen J., and Steven J. Levitt. 2006. "Filling in the Tax Gap." *New York Times*, April 2.

Due, John F. 1957. *Sales Taxation*. Urbana, IL: University of Illinois Press.

Dupuit, Jules. [1844] 1969. "De la Mesure de l'Utilité des Travaux Publics." Reprinted in *Readings in Welfare Economics*, edited by Kenneth J. Arrow and Tibor Scitovsky, 255–283. Homewood, IL: Richard D. Irwin.

Durston, Christopher. 2001. *Cromwell's Major-Generals: Godly Government during the English Revolution*. Manchester, U.K.: Manchester University Press.

Dušek, Libor, and Sutirtha Bagchi. 2018. "Are Efficient Taxes Responsible for Big Government? Evidence from Tax Withholding." Working Paper, Villanova University, Villanova, PA.

DW News. 2017. "German Man Pretends His Dog Is a Sheep to Save Taxes." January 27.

Dwenger, Nadja, Henrik Kleven, Imran Rasul, and Johannes Rincke. 2016. "Extrinsic and Intrinsic Motivations for Tax Compliance: Evidence from a Field Experiment in Germany." *American Economic Journal: Economic Policy* 8 (3): 203–232.

Dye, Richard, and Richard England. 2009. "The Principles and Promises of Land Value Taxation." In *Land Value Taxation: Theory, Evidence, and Practice*, edited by Richard F. Dye and Richard W. England, 3–10. Cambridge, MA: Lincoln Institute of Land Policy.

Ebeke, Christian, Mario Mansour, and Grégoire Rota-Graziosi. 2016. "The Power to Tax in Sub-Saharan Africa: LTUs, VATs, and SARAs." Working Paper No. 201611, CERDI, Clermont-Ferrand, France.

Ebrill, Liam, Michael Keen, Jean-Paul Bodin, and Victoria Summers. 2001. *The Modern VAT*. Washington, DC: International Monetary Fund.

Eckert, Joseph. 2008. "Computer-Assisted Mass Appraisal Options for Transitional and Developing Countries." In *Making the Property Tax Work: Experiences in Developing and Transitional Countries*, edited by Roy Bahl, Jorge Martinez-Vazquez, and Joan Youngman. Cambridge, MA: Lincoln Institute of Land Policy.

Economist, The. 2006. "Holes in the Net." May 4.

Economist, The. 2012. "Denmark's Food Taxes: A Fat Chance." November 17.

Economist, The. 2015. "Why Henry George Had a Point." April 2.

Economist, The. 2017a. "Tax Authorities Are the Latest Tools of Repression in Africa." September 30.

Economist, The. 2017b. "The World's Most Valuable Resource Is No Longer Oil but Data." May 6.

Economist, The. 2018a. "A Manifesto for Renewing Liberalism." September 13.

Economist, The. 2018b. "Ditch Sugar or Raise Prices? Drinks-Makers Face a New Tax." April 5.

Economist, The. 2018c. "What, and Who, Are France's 'Gilets Jaunes'?" November 17.

Edgeworth, Francis Y. 1915. *On the Relations of Political Economy to War.* London: Oxford University Press.

Edwards, Jeremy, Michael Keen, and Matti Tuomala. 1994. "Income Tax, Commodity Taxes and Public Good Provision: A Brief Guide." *Finanzarchiv/Public Finance Analysis* 51 (4): 472–487.

Eichengreen, Barry. 1990. "The Capital Levy in Theory and Practice." In *Public Debt Management: Theory and History,* edited by Rudiger Dornbusch and Mario Draghi, 191–220. Cambridge: Cambridge University Press.

Eisinger, Dale. 2013. "Where the Graves of Famous Artists Are Located." *Complex* online. September 1.

Ekelund, Robert B., Robert F. Hébert, and Robert D. Tollison. 2002. "An Economic Analysis of the Protestant Reformation." *Journal of Political Economy* 110 (3): 646–671.

Eleftheriou-Smith, Loulla-Mae. 2014. "'Bridget Jones Tax': LGA Wants to Claw Back £200m Lost in 'Wealthy Bachelor' Council Tax Discounts to Rich Singletons Living Alone." *The Independent,* March 15.

Ellis, Susan J., and Katherine H. Noyes. 1990. *By the People: A History of Americans as Volunteers.* San Francisco: Jossey-Bass.

Ellison, Garrett. 2012. "New Michigan Law Cracks Down on Cheating 'Zapper' Technology." *MLive.* August 31.

Elsayyad, May, and Kai A. Konrad. 2012. "Fighting Multiple Tax Havens." *Journal of International Economics* 86 (2): 295–305.

Encyclopedia Britannica. 1922. "Excess Profits Duty and Tax." 31: 36–40.

Eraly, Abraham. 1997. *Emperors of the Peacock Throne.* New Delhi: Penguin.

Erb, Kelly Phillips. 2013a. "Remembering the 'Hot Dog Tax' on National Hot Dog Day." *Forbes,* July 23.

Erb, Kelly Phillips. 2013b. "Scientist Pitches Proposal to Curb Bird Deaths: A Tax on Cats." *Forbes,* May 14.

Eschner, Kat. 2017. "Why Peter the Great Established a Beard Tax." *Smithsonian Magazine* online, September 5.

European Commission. 2016. *Proposal for a Council Directive on a Common Corporate Tax Base and a Common Consolidated Corporate Tax Base.* COM No. 683, Brussels, Belgium.

European Commission. 2018. *Report from the Commission to the European Parliament and the Council on Overview and Assessment of the Statistics and Information on the Automatic Exchanges in the Field of Direct Taxation.* COM No. 844, Brussels, Belgium.

Europol. n.d. "MTIC (Missing Trader Intra Community) Fraud." The Netherlands.

Exwood, Maurice. 1981. "The Brick Tax and Large Bricks." *British Brick Society Information* 24: 5–7.

Ezell, John Samuel. 1960. *Fortune's Merry Wheel: The Lottery in America.* Cambridge, MA: Harvard University Press.

Farcau, Bruce W. 2000. *The Ten Cents War: Chile, Peru, and Bolivia in the War of the Pacific, 1879–1884.* Westport, CT: Praeger.

Feige, Chris, and Jeffrey Miron. 2008. "The Opium Wars, Opium Legalization and Opium Consumption in China." *Applied Economics Letters* 15 (12): 911–913.

Feldstein, Martin S. 1999. "Tax Avoidance and the Deadweight Loss of the Income Tax." *Review of Economics and Statistics* 81 (4): 674–680.

Fennell, Lee Anne. 2006. "Hyperopia in Public Finance." In *Behavioral Public Finance*, edited by Edward J. McCaffery and Joel Slemrod, 141–171. New York: Russell Sage Foundation.

Ferguson, Niall. 2001. *The Cash Nexus: Money and Power in the Modern World, 1700–2000*. New York: Basic Books.

Festa, Lynn. 2009. "Person, Animal, Thing: The 1796 Dog Tax and the Right to Superfluous Things." *Eighteenth-Century Life* 33 (2): 1–44.

Finkelstein, Amy. 2009. "E-ztax: Tax Salience and Tax Rates." *Quarterly Journal of Economics* 124 (3): 969–1010.

Forcucci, Lauren E. 2010. "Battle for Births: The Fascist Pronatalist Campaign in Italy 1925 to 1938." *Journal of the Society for the Anthropology of Europe* 10 (1): 4–13.

Forrest, George. 1918. *The Life of Lord Clive*, vol. 2. London: Cassell.

Foster, Peter. 2009. "Chinese Ordered to Smoke More to Boost Economy." *The Telegraph*, May 4.

Frances, Hilary. 2004. "Wilks [*née* Bennett], Elizabeth." *Oxford Dictionary of National Biography*. Oxford: Oxford University Press.

Franklin, Benjamin. 1931. "Daylight Saving: To the Authors of *The Journal of Paris, 1784*." In *The Ingenious Dr. Franklin: Selected Scientific Letters of Benjamin Franklin*, edited by Nathan G. Goodman, 17–22. Philadelphia: University of Pennsylvania Press.

Franzsen, Riël. 2009. "International Experience." In *Land Value Taxation: Theory, Evidence, and Practice*, edited by Richard F. Dye and Richard W. England, 27–50. Cambridge, MA: Lincoln Institute of Land Policy.

Free File Alliance. 2016. "Free File Program: 'Tax Filing Simplification Act' Would Create a Conflict of Interest & End a Free Program that's Working for Taxpayers." Centreville, VA, April 14.

French, Christopher J. 1973. "Eighteenth-Century Shipping Tonnage Measurements." *Journal of Economic History* 33 (2): 434–443.

Frey, Bruno S. 1997. "A Constitution of Knaves Crowds Out Civic Virtues." *Economic Journal* 107 (443): 1043–1053.

Friedman, Milton. 1978. "An Interview with Dr. Milton Friedman." *Human Events* 38 (46): 14.

Friedman, Milton, and Rose D. Friedman. 1998. *Two Lucky People: Memoirs*. Chicago: University of Chicago Press.

Fruits, Eric. 2018. "Vapor Products, Harm Reduction, and Taxation." International Center for Law and Economics, Portland, Oregon.

Furman, Jason. 2017. "No, the GOP Tax Plan Won't Give You a $9,000 Raise: The White House's Wild Claims about the Wage Effects of Corporate Rate Cuts Don't Add Up." *Wall Street Journal*, October 22.

Gaddy, Clifford G., and William G. Gale. 2005. "Demythologizing the Russian Flat Tax." *Tax Notes International* (March): 983–988.

Galloway, Jim. 2017. "That Time an Alabama Jury of 12 White Men Declared MLK 'Not Guilty.'" *Political Insider*, February 5.

Gallucci, Maria. 2015. "As Mexico's Sugary Drink Tax Turns 1 Year Old, US Health Proponents Hope It Can Sway American Voters." *International Business Times*, January 11.

Gans, Joshua S., and Andrew Leigh. 2009. "Born on the First of July: An (Un)natural Experiment in Birth Timing." *Journal of Public Economics* 93 (1–2): 246–263.

Garcia, Adriana. 2018. "Cristiano Ronaldo Move to Juventus Influenced by Spain Tax Rate—La Liga Chief." *ESPN*, July 19.

Gaspar, Vitor. 2015. "A Prudent Man's Curse." *Finance and Development* 52 (1): 50–51.

Gaspar, Vitor, David Amaglobeli, Mercedes Garcia-Escribano, Delphine Prady, and Mauricio Soto. 2019. "Fiscal Policy and Development: Human, Social, and Physical Investments for the SDGs." International Monetary Fund Staff Discussion Notes 19/03, Washington, DC.

Gaspar, Vitor, Laura Jaramillo, and Philippe Wingender. 2016. "Political Institutions, State Building, and Tax Capacity: Crossing the Tipping Point." International Monetary Fund Working Paper No. 16/233, Washington, DC.

Gatrell, Peter. 2012. "The Russian Fiscal State, 1600–1914." In *The Rise of Fiscal States: A Global History, 1500–1914*, edited by Yun-Casalilla Bartolomé and Patrick K. O'Brien, with Francisco Comín Comín, 191–212. Cambridge: Cambridge University Press.

Geiger, Kim, and Monique Garcia. 2016. "Rauner Approves Repeal of Sales Tax on Tampons." *Chicago Tribune*, August 19.

Gelber, Nathan M. 1967. "The Period of Austrian Rule, 1772–1848." In *The History of the Jews of Rzeszow*, translated by Jerrold Landau, 47–55. New York.

Genovese, Federica, Kenneth Scheve, and David Stasavage. 2016. *Comparative Income Taxation Database*. http://data.stanford.edu/citd.

George, Henry. [1879] 2005. *Progress and Poverty*. New York: Cosimo.

George, Mary Dorothy. 1965. *London Life in the 18th Century*. New York: Harper & Row.

Gerber, Pierre J., Henning Steinfeld, Benjamin Henderson, Anne Mottet, Carolyn Opio, Jeroen Dijkman, Alessandra Falcucci, and Giuseppe Tempio. 2013. *Tackling Climate Change through Livestock – A Global Assessment of Emissions and Mitigation Opportunities*. Rome: Food and Agriculture Organization of the United Nations.

Gernet, Jacques. 1995. *Buddhism in Chinese Society: An Economic History from the Fifth to the Tenth Centuries*, translated by Franciscus Verellen. New York: Columbia University Press.

Gerschenkron, Alexander. 1970. *Europe in the Russian Mirror: Four Lectures in Economic History*. Cambridge: Cambridge University Press.

Gibbon, Edward. [1776] 1946. *The Decline and Fall of the Roman Empire*, vol. 1, edited by J. B. Bury. New York: Heritage Press.

Gill, Alison Ann McKay 1990. "Ship Money during the Personal Rule of Charles I: Politics, Ideology and the Law 1643 to 1640." Ph.D. thesis, University of Sheffield.

Gillitzer, Christian, Henrik Jacobsen Kleven, and Joel Slemrod. 2017. "A Characteristics Approach to Optimal Taxation: Line Drawing and Tax-Driven Product Innovation." *Scandinavian Journal of Economics* 119 (2): 240–267.

Gilmour, David. 2006. *The Ruling Caste: Imperial Lives in the Victorian Raj*. New York: Farrar, Straus and Giroux.

Gladstone, William E. 1863. *The Financial Statements of 1853, 1860–1863: To Which Are Added, a Speech on Tax-Bills, 1861, and on Charities*. London: J. Murray.

Glantz, Andrew E. 2008. "A Tax on Light and Air: Impact of the Window Duty on Tax Administration and Architecture, 1696–1851." *Penn History Review* 15 (2): 18–40.

Gneezy, Uri, and Aldo Rustichini. 2000. "A Fine Is a Price." *Journal of Legal Studies* 29 (1): 1–17.

Goldsmith, Raymond W. 1987. *Premodern Financial Systems: A Historical Comparative Study*. Cambridge: Cambridge University Press.

Goode, Richard. 1993. "Tax Advice to Developing Countries: An Historical Survey." *World Development* 21 (1): 37–53.

Goodwin, Barbara. 2008. "Taxation in Utopia." *Utopian Studies* 19 (2): 313–332.

Gordon, Roger H. 1992. "Can Capital Income Taxes Survive in Open Economies?" *Journal of Finance* 47 (3): 1159–1180.

Gorodnichenko, Yuriy, Jorge Martinez-Vazquez, and Klara Sabirianova Peter. 2009. "Myth and Reality of Flat Tax Reform: Micro Estimates of Tax Evasion Response and Welfare Effects in Russia." *Journal of Political Economy* 117 (3): 504–554.

Goszkowski, Rob. 2008. "Among Americans, Smoking Decreases as Income Increases." *Gallup News*, March 21.

Goulder, Lawrence H., and Ian W. H. Parry. 2008. "Instrument Choice in Environmental Policy." *Review of Environmental Economics and Policy* 2: 152–174.

Graham, Gerald S. 1956. "The Ascendancy of the Sailing Ship 1850–85." *Economic History Review* 9 (1): 74–88.

Grapperhaus, Ferdinand H. M. 1998. *Tax Tales from the Second Millennium: Taxation in Europe (1000 to 2000), the United States of America (1765 to 1801) and India (1526 to 1709)*. Amsterdam: International Bureau of Fiscal Documentation.

Gravelle, Jane G. 2015. "Tax Havens: International Tax Avoidance and Evasion." Congressional Research Service Report, Washington, DC, January 15.

Gravelle, Jane G. 2017. "Corporate Tax Reform: Issues for Congress." Congressional Research Service Report, Washington, DC, September 22.

Greene, Robert W. 2016. "Understanding Cocos: What Operational Concerns & Global Trends Mean for U.S. Policymakers." Harvard Kennedy School, M-RCBG Associate Working Paper Series No. 62, Cambridge, MA.

Gross, David M. 2016. "How Quaker War Tax Resistance Came and Went, Twice." *Friends Journal*, February 1.

Gruber, Jonathan, and Botond Kőszegi. 2002. "A Theory of Government Regulation of Addictive Bads: Optimal Tax Levels and Tax Incidence for Cigarette Excise Taxation." NBER Working Paper No. 8777, Cambridge, MA.

Gruber, Jonathan, and Botond Kőszegi. 2004. "Tax Incidence When Individuals Are Time-Inconsistent: The Case of Cigarette Excise Taxes." *Journal of Public Economics* 88 (9–10): 1959–1987.

Grund, Jean-Paul, and Joost Breeksema. 2013. "Coffee Shops and Compromise: Separated Illicit Drug Markets in the Netherlands." Open Society Foundation, New York.

Guardian, The. 1999. "Heirs and Disgraces." August 10.

Guicciardini, Francesco. [1534] 1994. *Dialogue on the Government of Florence*, edited and translated by Alison Brown. Cambridge: Cambridge University Press.

Gupta, Ajay. 2016. "David Bowie: Rock Star of Tax Planning." *Tax Notes*, January 28.

Gupta, Sanjeev, Michael Keen, Alpa Shah, and Geneviève Verdier. 2017. "Introduction." In *Digital Revolutions in Public Finance*, by Sanjeev Gupta, Michael Keen, Alpa Shah, and Geneviève Verdier, 1–21. Washington, DC: International Monetary Fund.

Haan, Marco A., Pim Heijnen, Lambert Schoonbeek, and Linda A. Toolsma. 2012. "Sound Taxation? On the Use of Self-Declared Value." *European Economic Review* 56 (2): 205–215.

Haig, Robert Murray. 1920. "British Experience with Excess Profits Taxation." *American Economic Review* 10 (Supplement): 1–14.

Haig, Robert Murray. 1934. *The Sales Tax in the American States*. A study made under the direction of Robert Murray Haig by Carl Shoup with the assistance of Reavis Cox, Louis Shere, Edwin H. Spengler, and staff members. New York: Columbia University Press.

Hall, Basil E. Foster. 1977. "The Chinese Maritime Customs: An International Service, 1854–1950." Edited and updated by Robert Bickers. University of Bristol Occasional Papers No. 5, Bristol, U.K.

Halperin, Sandra, and Ronen Palan, eds. 2015. *Legacies of Empire: Imperial Roots of the Contemporary Global Order*. Cambridge: Cambridge University Press.

Hamermesh, Daniel, and Joel Slemrod. 2008. "The Economics of Workaholism: We Should Not Have Worked on This Paper." *BE Journal of Economic Analysis & Policy* 8 (1): 1–29.

Hamilton, Alexander. 1791. *Final Version of the Report on the Subject of Manufactures*. Philadelphia, December 5.

Hancock, Tom. 2017. "China Shakes up 2,000-Year-Old Salt Monopoly." *Financial Times*, January 2.

Handcock, W. D. 1996. *English Historical Documents*, vol. X. c. 1874–1914. Abingdon, U.K.: Routledge.

Hanioğlu, M. Sükrü. 2008. *A Brief History of the Late Ottoman Empire*. Princeton, N.J.: Princeton University Press.

Hanke, Steven H., and Alex K. F. Kwok. 2009. "On the Measurement of Zimbabwe's Hyperinflation." *Cato Journal* 29 (2): 353–364.

Hansard's Parliamentary Debates. 1818. From the Year 1803 to the Present Time, vol. 38. Comprising the Period from the Thirteenth Day of April to the Tenth Day of June. London: T. C. Hansard.

Hansard's Parliamentary Debates. 1854. Third Series, Second Volume of the Session. Commencing with the Accession of William IV, vol. 131. Comprising the Period from the Twenty-Eighth Day of February 1854 and the Twenty-Eighth Day of March 1854. London: T. C. Hansard.

Hansard's Parliamentary Debates. 1909. Income Tax, vol. 4, May 12. London: T. C. Hansard.

Harberger, Arnold C. 1965. "Issues of Tax Reform for Latin America." In *Fiscal Policy for Economic Growth in Latin America*. Conference on Fiscal Policy for Economic Growth in Latin America, 110–121. Baltimore, MD: Johns Hopkins Press.

Harberger, Arnold. 1995. "Tax Lore for Budding Reformers." In *Reform, Recovery, and Growth: Latin America and the Middle East*, edited by Rudiger Dornbusch and Sebastian Edwards, 291–310. Chicago: University of Chicago Press and NBER.

Harris, Frank. 1918. *Oscar Wilde: His Life and Confessions*, vol. 1. New York: Frank Harris.

Harris, Mary Dormer, trans. and ed. 1909. *The Coventry Leet Book: Or Manor's Register*. London: Early English Text Society.

Harrison, Brian Howard. 1994. *Drink and the Victorians: The Temperance Question in England 1815–1872*. Staffordshire, U.K.: Keele University Press.

Hartley, L. P. 1953. *The Go-Between*. New York: New York Review Books.

Hartwell, Ronald Max. 1981. "Taxation in England during the Industrial Revolution." *Cato Journal* 1 (1): 129–153.

Hasegawa, Makoto, Jeffrey L. Hoopes, Ryo Ishida, and Joel Slemrod. 2013. "The Effect of Public Disclosure on Reported Taxable Income: Evidence from Individuals and Corporations in Japan." *National Tax Journal* 66 (3): 571–608.

Hassan, Fabien. 2015. "Lessons from History #11—The Monaco Crisis from 1962–1963 and the Emancipation of Tax Havens." *Finance Watch*, April 27.

Hays, Jeffrey. 2013. "Beer in Japan: Asahi, Kirin, Sapporo, Suntory, Low Malt and Third Category Beers." Facts and Details online, January.

Hazlitt, William Carew. [1744] 1875. *A Select Collection of Old English Plays*, vol. 14. London: Robert Dodsley.

He, Wan, Daniel Goodkind, and Paul Kowal. 2016. "An Aging World: 2015." U.S. Census Bureau, International Population Reports, P95/16-1, Washington, DC.

Heemstra, Marius. 2010. *The Fiscus Judaicus and the Parting of the Ways*. Tübingen, Germany: Mohr Siebeck.

Heilbroner, Robert. 1999. *The Worldly Philosophers: The Lives, Times, and Ideas of the Great Economic Thinkers*, 7th ed. New York: Touchstone.

Heinlein, Robert A. 2008. *The Moon Is a Harsh Mistress*. London: Victor Gollancz.

Hellie, Richard. 1999. "Russia, 1200–1815." In *The Rise of the Fiscal State in Europe c.1200–1815*, edited by Richard Bonney, 496–497. Oxford: Oxford University Press.

Henley & Partners. n.d. *A Selection of Prime Citizenship Programs*. Malta.

Hernon, Ian. 2003. *Britain's Forgotten Wars: Colonial Campaigns of the 19th Century*. Stroud, U.K.: Sutton Publishing.

Hervey, Ian. 1848. *Memories of the Reign of George the Second from His Accession to the Death of Queen Caroline*, vol. 1. Philadelphia: Lea and Blanchard.

Hervey, Sydenham Henry Augustus. 1905. *Suffolk in 1674, Being the Hearth Tax Returns*, XI ed., vol. 13. Woodbridge, U.K.: George Booth.

Hibbert, Christopher. 1990. *Redcoats and Rebels: The American Revolution through British Eyes*. New York: W. W. Norton.

Hicks, John. 1969. *A Theory of Economic History*. Oxford: Oxford University Press.

Higham, Scott, Michael Hudson, and Marina Walker Guevara. 2013. "Piercing the Secrecy of Offshore Tax Havens." *Washington Post*, April 6.

Hill, Joseph A. 1892. "The Prussian Income Tax." *Quarterly Journal of Economics* 6 (2): 207–226.

Hilton, Rodney H. 1969. *The Decline of Serfdom in Medieval England*. London: Palgrave Macmillan.

History House. n.d. "What Was Known as a 'Tax on Knowledge'? Campaign against a Tax on Newspapers." https://historyhouse.co.uk/articles/tax_on_knowledge.html.

Hitchman, Sara C., and Geoffrey T. Fong. 2011. "Gender Empowerment and Female-to-Male Smoking Prevalence Ratios." *Bulletin of the World Health Organization* 89: 195–202.

HM Revenue & Customs. 2018. *Annual VAT Statistics. Commentary and Tables, 2017–2018.* https://assets.publishing.service.gov.uk/government/uploads/system/uploads/attachment_data/file/763555/Annual_VAT_Statistics_-_Commentary.pdf. London.

HM Revenue & Customs. 2020. *Measuring Tax Gaps 2020 Edition: Tax Gap Estimates for 2018–19.* London, July 9.

Hobbes, Thomas. 1651. *De Cive.* Translated as *Philosophical Rudiments Concerning Government and Society.* London: R. Royston.

Hogg, Chris. 2011. "China Ends Death Penalty for 13 Economic Crimes." *BBC News,* February 25.

Hollister, C. Warren. 1960. "The Significance of Scutage Rates in Eleventh- and Twelfth-Century England." *English Historical Review* 75 (297): 577–588.

Holloway, Carson, and Bradford P. Wilson, eds. 2017. *The Political Writings of Alexander Hamilton, Vol. 1: 1767–1789.* Cambridge: Cambridge University Press.

Holzman, Franklyn D. 1955. *Soviet Taxation: The Fiscal and Monetary Problems of a Planned Economy.* Cambridge, MA: Harvard University Press.

Hoopes, Jeffrey L., Leslie Robinson, and Joel Slemrod. 2018. "Public Tax-Return Disclosure." *Journal of Accounting and Economics* 66 (1): 142–162.

Hopkins, Keith. 1980. "Taxes and Trade in the Roman Empire (200 B.C.–A.D. 400)." *Journal of Roman Studies* 70: 101–125.

Hormats, Robert D. 2007. *The Price of Liberty: Paying for America's Wars.* New York: Macmillan.

Houlder, Vanessa. 2015. "More UK Tax Evaders Going to Jail but Prison Terms Are Falling." *Financial Times,* May 31.

Huang, Grace. 2016. "Well-Field System." In *Encyclopedia of Chinese History,* edited by Michael Dillon. Abingdon, U.K.: Routledge.

Hubbard, R. Glenn. 2010. "Left, Right and Wrong on Taxes." *New York Times,* November 15.

Hufbauer, Gary C., and Zhiyao (Lucy) Lu. 2018. "The European Union's Proposed Digital Services Tax: A De Facto Tariff." Petersen Institute for International Economics Policy Brief 18-15, Washington, DC.

Hughes, Edward. 1934. *Studies in Administration and Finance, 1558–1825: With Special Reference to the History of Salt Taxation in England.* Manchester, U.K.: Manchester University Press.

Hughes, Elizabeth, and Philippa White, eds. 1991. *The Hampshire Hearth Tax Assessment 1665 with the Southampton Assessments for 1662 and 1670.* Winchester, U.K.: Hampshire County Council.

Hugo, Victor. [1862] 1982. *Les Misérables.* Harmondsworth, U.K.: Penguin.

Hungerford, Thomas L. 2006. "U.S. Government Revenues: 1790 to the Present." Congressional Research Service Report, Washington, DC.

Hurd, Douglas. 2007. *Robert Peel: A Biography*. London: Weidenfeld & Nicolson.

Hurstfield, J. 1955. "The Profits of Fiscal Feudalism, 1541–1602." *Economic History Review* 8 (1): 53–61.

Hutton, Eric, Mick Thackray, and Philippe Wingender. 2014. "Uganda, Revenue Administration Gap Analysis Program—The Value-Added Tax Gap." International Monetary Fund, Fiscal Affairs Department, Washington, DC.

Hyden, Marc. 2015. "Lucius Cornelius Sulla: Guardian or Enemy of the Roman Republic." *Ancient History Encyclopedia* online. https://www.ancient.eu/article/818/lucius-cornelius-sulla -guardian-or-enemy-of-the-ro/.

Ibn Khaldûn. [1377] 1967. *The Muqaddimah: An Introduction to History*, vol. 2, 2nd ed., translated by Franz Rosenthal. Princeton, NJ: Princeton University Press.

Ibrahim, Raymond. 2013. "Brotherhood Imposes Jizya Tribute on Egypt's Christians." *Human Events*, September 10.

Ibrahim, Raymond. 2015. "Islamic Jizya: Fact and Fiction." *FrontPage*, May 28.

Independent Commission for the Reform of International Corporate Taxation. 2018. "A Roadmap to Improve Rules for Taxing Multinationals: A Fairer Future for Global Taxation." Online.

Institut des Politiques Publiques. 2014. "1914–2014: Cent Ans d'Impôt sur le Revenu." Les Notes de l'IPP No. 12, Paris.

Institute for Fiscal Studies. 1993. *Options for 1994: The Green Budget*. London: Institute for Fiscal Studies.

Internal Revenue Service. 1918. *Statistics of Income*. Washington, DC. U.S. Government Printing Office.

Internal Revenue Service. 1919. *Statistics of Income*. Washington, DC. U.S. Government Printing Office.

Internal Revenue Service. 2018. *SOI Tax Stats–Corporation Complete Report*. Washington, DC.

Internal Revenue Service. 2019a. *Federal Tax Compliance Research: Tax Gap Estimates for Tax Years 2011–2013*. Publication 1415 (Rev. 9-2019), Washington, DC.

Internal Revenue Service. 2019b. *Private Debt Collection Program 4th Quarter Update FY 2019*. Washington, DC.

Internal Revenue Service. 2020. *Data Book, 2019*. Publication 55-B. Washington, DC.

International Court of Justice. n.d. *Obligation to Negotiate Access to the Pacific Ocean (Bolivia v. Chile)*. The Hague, Netherlands.

International Monetary Fund. 2012. *Fiscal Regimes for Extractive Industries—Design and Implementation*. Washington, DC.

International Monetary Fund. 2013. *Fiscal Monitor: Taxing Times*. Washington, DC.

International Monetary Fund. 2016. *Tax Policy, Leverage and Macroeconomic Stability*. Washington, DC.

International Monetary Fund. 2017a. *Fiscal Monitor: Tackling Inequality*. Washington, DC.

International Monetary Fund. 2017b. *St. Kitts and Nevis*. IMF Country Report No. 17/186. Washington, DC.

International Monetary Fund. 2017c. *World Economic Outlook: Seeking Sustainable Growth: Short-Term Recovery, Long-Term Challenges*. Washington, DC.

International Monetary Fund. 2018. *Fiscal Monitor: Capitalizing on Good Times*. Washington, DC.

International Monetary Fund. 2019a. *Fiscal Monitor: How to Mitigate Climate Change*. Washington, DC.

International Monetary Fund. 2019b. *Fiscal Policies for Paris Climate Strategies—From Principle to Practice*. Washington, DC.

International Monetary Fund. 2019c. *Corporate Taxation in the Global Economy*. Washington, DC.

International Monetary Fund. 2020a. *Fiscal Monitor: Policies for the Recovery*. Washington, DC.

International Monetary Fund. 2020b. *Coordinated Direct Investment Survey*. https://data.imf.org/?sk=40313609-F037-48C1-84B1-E1F1CE54D6D5.

Irwin, Douglas A. 1989. "Political Economy and Peel's Repeal of the Corn Laws." *Economics and Politics* 1 (1): 41–59.

Irwin, Timothy C. 2012. "Accounting Devices and Fiscal Illusions." IMF Staff Discussion Note 12/02. Washington, DC.

Ishi, Hiromitsu. 1993. *The Japanese Tax System*, 2nd ed. Oxford: Clarendon Press.

Ivanova, Anna, Michael Keen, and Alexander Klemm. 2005. "The Russian 'Flat Tax' Reform." *Economic Policy* 20 (43): 398–444.

Jacobs, Bas. 2017. "Digitalization and Taxation." In *Digital Revolutions in Public Finance*, edited by Sanjeev Gupta, Michael Keen, Alpa Shah, and Geneviève Verdier, 25–55. Washington, DC: International Monetary Fund.

Jagoda, Naomi. 2017. "Koch-Backed Group Unveils TV Ad against Border Tax." *The Hill*, April 10.

James, Kathryn. 2015. *The Rise of the Value-Added Tax*. Cambridge: Cambridge University Press.

Jarvis, Stan. 1987. *Smuggling in East Anglia 1700–1840*. Newbury, U.K.: Countryside Books.

Jeanneney, Jean-Noël. 1982. "La Bataille de la Progressivité sous la IIIᵉ République." *Pouvoirs* 23: 21–31.

Jeffrey-Cook, John. 2010. "William Pitt and His Taxes." *British Tax Review* (4): 376–391.

Jenkins, Roy. 2002. *Gladstone*. New York: Random House.

Jensen, Erik M. 2016. "The Power to Tax." In *The Powers of the U.S. Congress: Where Constitutional Authority Begins and Ends*, edited by Brien Hallett, 1–14. Santa Barbara, CA: ABC-CLIO.

Jewish Virtual Library. n.d. "Louis XII." Online.

Jogarajan, Sunita. 2011. "Prelude to the International Tax Treaty Network: 1815–1914; Early Tax Treaties and the Conditions for Action." *Oxford Journal of Legal Studies* 31 (4): 679–707.

Johannesen, Niels, and Gabriel Zucman. 2014. "The End of Bank Secrecy? An Evaluation of the G20 Tax Crackdown." *American Economic Journal: Economic Policy* 6 (1): 65–91.

Johari, Aarefa. 2015. "Why Do Poor Indians Continue to Drink Deadly Moonshine?" *Quartz*, June 22.

Johnson, Allan Chester, Paul Robinson Coleman-Norton, and Frank Card Bourne. 1961. *Ancient Roman Statutes*. Clark, NJ: The Lawbook Exchange.

Johnson, Kimberley. 2010. *Reforming Jim Crow: Southern Politics and State in the Age before Brown*. Oxford: Oxford University Press.

Johnson, Noel D., and Mark Koyama. 2014. "Tax Farming and the Origins of State Capacity in England and France." *Explorations in Economic History* 51 (1): 1–20.

Johnson, Paul. 1998. *A History of the American People.* New York: Harper Collins.

Johnson, Samuel. 1787. *Debates in Parliament*, vol. 2. London: John Stockdale.

Joint Committee on Taxation. 2013. *Modeling the Distribution of Taxes on Business Income.* JCX-14-13. Washington, DC.

Jones, Dan. 2014. *The Plantagenets: The Warrior Kings and Queens Who Made England*, rev. ed. New York: Penguin.

Jones, Francis R. 1895. "Pollock v. Farmers' Loan and Trust Company." *Harvard Law Review* 9 (3): 198–211.

Judson, Pieter M. 2016. *The Habsburg Empire: A New History.* Cambridge, MA: Harvard University Press.

Kagan, Donald. 2003. *The Peloponnesian War.* London: Penguin Books.

Kahn, Charles M., Emilson C. D. Silva, and James P. Ziliak. 2001. "Performance-Based Wages in Tax Collection: The Brazilian Tax Collection Reform and Its Effects." *Economic Journal* 111 (468): 188–205.

Kaizen Certified Public Accountants Limited. n.d. "Guide to Taiwan Land Value Increment Tax." Hong Kong.

Kalapa, Lowell. 2012. "Unintended Consequences of Tapping the 'Rich.'" Foundation of Hawaii, Honolulu.

Karabell, Zachary. 2004. *Chester Alan Arthur.* New York: Time Books.

Kassam, Ashifa. 2016. "Vancouver Slaps 15% Tax on Foreign House Buyers in Effort to Cool Market." *The Guardian*, August 2.

Katznelson, Ira. 2005. "To Give Counsel and to Consent: Why the King (Edward I) Expelled the Jews (in 1290)." In *Preferences and Situations*, edited by Ira Katznelson and Barry Weingast, 88–126. New York: Russell Sage Foundation.

Keane, Michael P. 2011. "Labor Supply and Taxes: A Survey." *Journal of Economic Literature* 49 (4): 961–1075.

Keen, Michael. 1998. "The Balance between Specific and *Ad Valorem* Taxation." *Fiscal Studies* 19 (1): 1–37.

Keen, Michael. 2005. "Peculiar Institutions: A British Perspective on Tax Policy in the United States." *National Tax Journal* 18 (4): 371–400.

Keen, Michael. 2008. "VAT, Tariffs, and Withholding: Border Taxes and Informality in Developing Countries." *Journal of Public Economics* 92 (10–11): 1892–1906.

Keen, Michael. 2013. "Taxation and Development—Again." In *Studies of Critical Issues in Taxation and Development*, edited by Clemens Fuest and George Zodrow, 13–41. Cambridge, MA: MIT Press.

Keen, Michael, Yitae Kim, and Ricardo Varsano. 2008. "The Flat Tax(es): Principles and Experience." *International Tax and Public Finance* 15 (16): 712–751.

Keen, Michael, and Jenny E. Ligthart. 2006a. "Information Sharing and International Taxation: A Primer." *International Tax and Public Finance* 13 (1): 81–110.

Keen, Michael, and Jenny E. Ligthart. 2006b. "Incentives and Information Exchange in International Taxation." *International Tax and Public Finance* 13 (2): 163–180.

Keen, Michael, and Ben Lockwood. 2006. "Is the VAT a Money Machine?" *National Tax Journal* 59 (4): 905–928.

Keen, Michael, and Ben Lockwood. 2010. "The Value Added Tax: Its Causes and Consequences." *Journal of Development Economics* 92 (2): 138–151.

Keen, Michael, Ian Parry, and Jon Strand. 2013. "Planes, Ships, and Taxes: Charging for International Aviation and Maritime Emissions." *Economic Policy* 28 (76): 701–749.

Keen, Michael, and Joel Slemrod. 2017. "Optimal Tax Administration." *Journal of Public Economics* 152: 133–142.

Keen, Michael, and Stephen Smith. 2006. "VAT Fraud and Evasion: What Do We Know and What Can Be Done?" *National Tax Journal* 59 (4): 861–887.

Kekewich, Margaret Lucille, ed. 1994. *Princes and Peoples: France and the British Isles, 1620–1714.* Manchester, U.K.: Manchester University Press.

Kennedy, John F. 1961. "Special Message to the Congress on Taxation, April 20." Washington, DC.

Kennedy, William. 1913. *English Taxation 1640–1799: An Essay on Policy and Opinion.* London: G. Bell & Sons.

Kenyon, J. P. 1990. *Stuart England*, 2nd ed. London: Penguin.

Kerfs, Phillip. 2019. "Effective Use of CRS Data." Presentation, Tenth IMF-Japan High-Level Tax Conference for Asian Countries, Tokyo.

Keynes, John Maynard. 1919. *The Economic Consequences of the Peace.* New York: Harcourt, Brace and Howe.

Keynes, John Maynard. 1923. *A Tract on Monetary Reform.* London: Macmillan.

Keynes, John Maynard. 1933. *Essays in Biography.* New York: Harcourt, Brace.

Khan, Adnan Q., Asim I. Khwaja, and Benjamin Olken. 2016. "Tax Farming Redux: Experimental Evidence on Performance Pay for Tax Collectors." *Quarterly Journal of Economics* 131 (1): 219–271.

King, Antony, and Ivor Crewe. 2013. *The Blunders of Our Governments.* London: Oneworld Publications.

King James I. [1604] 2008. *A Counterblaste to Tobacco.* https://www.amazon.com/Counter-Blaste-Tobacco-King-James-I/dp/1438504829.

Kirchgaessner, Stephanie. 2017. "Shady Deal: Italian Shop Owners in Conegliano Fight Tax on Shadows." *The Guardian*, January 17.

Klemperer, Paul. 2004. *Auctions: Theory and Practice.* Princeton, NJ: Princeton University Press.

Kleven, Henrik, Martin Knudsen, Claus Kreiner, Søren Pedersen, and Emmanuel Saez. 2011. "Unwilling or Unable to Cheat? Evidence from a Randomized Tax Audit Experiment in Denmark." *Econometrica* 79 (3): 651–692.

Kleven, Henrik, Claus Kreiner, and Emmanuel Saez. 2016. "Why Can Modern Governments Tax So Much? An Agency Model of Firms as Fiscal Intermediaries." *Economica* 83 (330): 219–246.

Kleven, Henrik, Camille Landais, and Emmanuel Saez. 2013. "Taxation and International Migration of Superstars: Evidence from the European Football Market." *American Economic Review* 103 (5): 1892–1924.

Kleven, Henrik, and Mazhar Waseem. 2013. "Using Notches to Uncover Optimization Frictions and Structural Elasticities: Theory and Evidence from Pakistan." *Quarterly Journal of Economics* 128 (2): 669–723.

Knightley, Philip. 1993. *The Rise and Fall of the House of Vestey*, 2nd ed. London: Warner.

Kocieniewski, David. 2012. "Whistle-Blower Awarded $104 Million by I.R.S." *New York Times*, September 11.

Kolbert, Elizabeth. 2006. "The Big Sleazy." *The New Yorker*, June 12.

Konrad, Kai A., and Salmai Qari. 2012. "The Last Refuge of a Scoundrel? Patriotism and Tax Compliance." *Economica* 79 (315): 516–533.

Kopczuk, Wojciech, Justin Marion, Eric Muehlegger, and Joel Slemrod. 2016. "Does Tax-Collection Invariance Hold? Evasion and the Pass-Through of State Diesel Taxes." *American Economic Journal: Economic Policy* 8 (2): 251–286.

Kopczuk, Wojciech, and Joel Slemrod. 2003. "Dying to Save Taxes: Evidence from Estate Tax Returns on the Death Elasticity." *Review of Economics and Statistics* 85 (2): 256–265.

Kornhauser, Marjorie E. 2007. "Tax Morale Approach to Compliance: Recommendations for the IRS." *Florida Tax Review* 8 (6): 599–640.

Kornhauser, Marjorie E. 2010. "Remembering the 'Forgotten Man' (and Woman): Hidden Taxes and the 1936 Election." In *Studies in the History of Tax Law*, vol. 4, edited by John Tiley, 327–340. Oxford: Hart Publishing.

Kornhauser, Marjorie E. 2013. "Taxing Bachelors in America, 1895–1939." In *Studies in the History of Tax Law*, vol. 6, edited by John Tiley, 467–488. Oxford: Hart Publishing.

Koyama, Mark. 2010. "The Political Economy of Expulsion: The Regulation of Jewish Money-lending in Medieval England." *Constitutional Political Economy* 21 (4): 374–406.

Kraal, Diane, and Jeyapalan Kasipillai. 2014. "The Dutch East India Company's Tax Farming in 18th Century Malacca." *eJournal of Tax Research* 12 (1): 253–281.

Kramer, Brent. 2010. "The New York State Lottery: A Regressive Tax." *State Tax Notes* (March 29): 961–966.

Krishna, Aradhna, and Joel Slemrod. 2003. "Behavioral Public Finance: Tax Design as Price Presentation." *International Tax and Public Finance* 10 (2): 189–203.

Kroll, Luisa. 2016. "Billionaires, Former Billionaires Outed for Offshore Wealth by the Panama Papers." *Forbes*, April 3.

Kukreti, Ishan. 2017. "GST of 18% on Tendu Leaves: How It Will Impact Tribals." *DownToEarth*, July 17.

Kup, Alexander P. 1975. *Sierra Leone: A Concise History*. Vancouver, BC: Douglas Davis & Charles.

Kwass, Michael. 1999. "A Welfare State for the Privileged? Direct Taxation and the Changing Face of Absolutism from Louis XIV to the French Revolution." In *Crises, Revolutions and Self-Sustained Growth: Essays in European Fiscal History, 1130–1830*, edited by William Mark Ormrod, Margaret Bonney, and Richard Bonney, 344–376. Stamford, U.K.: Shaun Tyas.

Labaree, Benjamin Woods. 1966. *The Boston Tea Party*. Oxford: Oxford University Press.

Laffer, Arthur B. 2014. *Handbook of Tobacco Taxation: Theory and Practice*. San Francisco: The Laffer Center at the Pacific Research Institute.

Lancet, The. 1845. "The Duty on Glass," February 22.

Land, Bryan C. 2010. "Resource Rent Taxes: A Re-appraisal." In *The Taxation of Petroleum and Minerals: Principles, Practices and Problems*, edited by Philip Daniel, Michael Keen, and Charles McPherson, 241–262. London: Routledge.

Lane, Frederic C. 1964. "Tonnages, Medieval and Modern." *Economic History Review* 17 (2): 213–233.

Langer, Emily. 2014. "Johnnie Walters, IRS Commissioner under President Richard M. Nixon, Dies at 94." *Washington Post*, June 26.

Langford, Paul. 1975. *The Excise Crisis: Society and Politics in the Age of Walpole*. Oxford: Oxford University Press.

Larimer, Sarah. 2016. "The 'Tampon Tax' Explained." *Washington Post*, January 8.

Larner, Judith, and Patrick Collinson. 2004. "A Haven Right Here on Earth." *The Guardian*, February 21.

Latham, Robert, ed. 1985. *The Shorter Pepys*. London: Bell and Hyman.

Lawless, Jill. 2013. "William Shakespeare: Tax Dodger, Shady Businessman?" *Christian Science Monitor*, April 1.

Le, Tuan Minh, Blanca Moreno-Dodson, and Nihal Bayraktar. 2012. "Tax Capacity and Tax Effort: Extended Cross-Country Analysis from 1994 to 2009." Policy Research Working Paper No. 6252, World Bank, Washington, DC.

League of Nations. 1923. *Report on Double Taxation Submitted to the Financial Committee*. Economic and Financial Commission Report by the Experts on Double Taxation. Geneva.

Lebhar, Godfrey M. 1959. *Chain Stores in America, 1859–1959*. New York: Chain Store Publishing Company.

Lee, Maurice W. 1941. "Protectionism and Chain Store Taxes." In *Tax Barriers to Trade*, edited by Mark Eisner, Robert L. Cochran, Edgar L. Burtis et al., 151–164. Philadelphia: University of Pennsylvania Tax Institute.

Le Naour, Jean-Yves. 2007. *Meurtre au Figaro*. Paris: Larousse.

Lens on Leeuwenhoek. n.d. "Antony van Leeuwenhoek." https://lensonleeuwenhoek.net/.

Lenter, David, Douglas Shackelford, and Joel Slemrod. 2003. "Public Disclosure of Corporate Tax Return Information: Accounting, Economics, and Legal Perspectives." *National Tax Journal* 56 (4): 803–830.

Leskin, Paige. 2016. "'Tampon Tax' Officially Eliminated in New York." *PIX11News*, July 21.

Levasseur, E. 1894. "The Assignats: A Study in the Finances of the French Revolution." *Journal of Political Economy* 2 (2): 179–202.

Levi, Margaret. 1989. *Of Rule and Revenue*. Berkeley: University of California Press.

Levi, Margaret. 1997. *Consent, Dissent, and Patriotism*. Cambridge: Cambridge University Press.

Lewis, Gavin Llewellyn MacKenzie. 1977. *The Bondelswarts Rebellion of 1922*. Master of Arts thesis, Rhodes University, Grahamstown, South Africa.

Lexden, Lord Alistair. 2011. "Peel and Disraeli." https://www.alistairlexden.org.uk/news/peel-and-disraeli.

Liasson, Mara. 2001. "Conservative Advocate." Interview with Grover Norquist on National Public Radio, May 25.

Lickers, Kathleen, and Peter Griffin. 2015. *Review of the First Nations Cigarette Allocation System in Ontario*. Discussion Paper 2.0. Ontario, Canada.

Liu, Li, Ben Lockwood, Miguel Almunia, and Eddy H. F. Tam. 2019. "VAT Notches, Voluntary Registration, and Bunching: Theory and UK Evidence." *Review of Economics and Statistics*: 1–45.

Lledó, Victor, Sungwook Yoon, Xiangming Fang, Samba Mbaye, and Young Kim. 2017. *Fiscal Rules at a Glance*. International Monetary Fund. Washington, DC.

Loades, David M. 1974. *Politics and the Nation, 1450–1660: Obedience, Resistance, and Public Order*. London: William Collins, Sons.

Locke, John. 1691. *Some Considerations of the Consequences of the Lowering of Interest and Raising the Value of Money*. London: Printed for Awnsham and John Churchill.

Lockyer, Roger. 1964. *Tudor and Stuart Britain: 1471–1714*. London: Longman, Green.

Lofthouse, Lloyd F. 2013. *My Splendid Concubine*. San Diego: Three Clover Press.

Logue, Kyle, and Joel Slemrod. 2008. "Genes as Tags: The Tax Implications of Widely Available Genetic Information." *National Tax Journal* 61 (4, Part 2): 843–863.

Los Angeles Herald. 1903. "Hire Girls to Say 'No': Young Argentines Escape the Celibacy Tax." July 7. California Digital Newspaper Collection.

Lovenheim, Michael F., and Joel Slemrod. 2010. "The Fatal Toll of Driving to Drink: The Effect of Minimum Legal Drinking Age Evasion on Traffic Fatalities." *Journal of Health Economics* 29 (1): 62–77.

Lucas, Robin. 1997. "The Tax on Bricks and Tiles, 1784–1850: Its Application to the Country at Large and, in Particular, to the County of Norfolk." *Construction History* 13: 29–55.

Lundberg, Shelly J., Robert A. Pollak, and Terence J. Wales. 1997. "Do Husbands and Wives Pool Their Resources? Evidence from the United Kingdom Child Benefit." *Journal of Human Resources* 32 (3): 463–480.

Lunt, W. E. 1909. "The Financial System of the Medieval Papacy in Light of Recent Literature." *Quarterly Journal of Economics* 23 (2): 251–295.

Lustig, Nora, ed. 2018. *Commitment to Equity Handbook: Estimating the Impact of Fiscal Policy on Inequality and Poverty*. Washington, DC: Brookings Institution.

Macaulay, Thomas Babbington. 1855. *The History of England: From the Accession of James the Second*, vol. 3. London: Longman, Brown, Green, and Longmans.

MacFarlane, Charles. 1844–1845. *The French Revolution*, 4 vols. London: Charles Knight.

Machiavelli, Niccolò. [1515] 1908. *The Prince*. Translated with an introduction by W. K. Marriott. London: J. M. Dent & Sons.

Mackay, Alan. 1991. *A Dictionary of Scientific Quotations*. London: Institute of Physics Publishing.

Magnificent Seven, The. 1960. Directed by John Sturges. Beverly Hills, CA: United Artists and Mirish Company.

Mallet, Bernard. 1913. *British Budgets, 1887–88 to 1912–13*. London: Macmillan.

Manjoo, Farhad. 2002. "A Tax Plan to (and from) Space." *Wired.com*, April 26.

Mann, Arthur J. 2004. "Are Semi-Autonomous Revenue Authorities the Answer to Tax Administration Problems in Developing Countries? A Practical Guide." Research paper for the project titled Fiscal Reform in Support of Trade Liberalization.

Mann, Charles C. 2011. *1491: New Revelations of the Americas before Columbus*, 2nd ed. New York: Vintage Books.

Mann, Fritz Karl. 1943. "The Sociology of Taxation." *Review of Politics* 5 (2): 225–235.

Marcuss, Rosemary, George Contos, John Guyton, Patrick Langetieg, Allen Lerman, Susan Nelson, Brenda Schafer, and Melissa Vigil. 2013. "Income Taxes and Compliance Costs: How They Are Related?" *National Tax Journal* 66 (4): 833–854.

Marks, Steven G. 2017. "War Finance (Russian Empire)." *International Encyclopedia of the First World War*. Online.

Marsden, William. 2009, updated 2014. *Canada's Boom in Smuggled Cigarettes: Indian Tobacco Factories, Organized Crime Control a Billion-Dollar Black Market*. Center for Public Integrity, Washington, DC.

Marshall, Henrietta Elizabeth. 1912. *Through Great Britain and Ireland with Cromwell*. London: T. C. and E. C. Jack.

Marshall, John. 1836. *The Life of George Washington: Commander in Chief of the American Forces, during the War Which Established the Independence of His Country, and First President of the United States*, vol. 1. Philadelphia: James Crissy.

Martinez, Michael. 2011. "Arizona Church Is a House of Prostitution, Police Say." *CNN*, September 10.

Marx, Karl. 1852. "The Eighteenth Brumaire of Louis Bonaparte." *Die Revolution* 1.

Maseko, Achim Nkosi. 2008. *Church Schisms & Corruption: Tithes*. Book 5. Durban, South Africa.

Mason, Rowena, and Denis Campbell. 2017. "Theresa May under Pressure over 'Dementia Tax' Social Care Shakeup." *The Guardian*, May 21.

Matheson, Thornton. 2011. *Taxing Financial Transactions: Issues and Evidence*. International Monetary Fund Working Paper No. 11/54, Washington, DC.

Mathias, Peter. 2013. *The Transformation of England: Essays in the Economic and Social History of England in the Eighteenth Century*. London: Routledge.

Matthew, H. C. G. 1979. "Disraeli, Gladstone, and the Politics of Mid-Victorian Budgets." *Historical Journal* 22 (3): 615–643.

Matthews, E. L., G. M. Swift, G. Hartog, and Cecil Bayley. 1919. "South Africa." *Journal of Comparative Legislation and International Law* 1 (2): 103–136.

Matthews, George T. 1958. *The Royal General Farms in Eighteenth-Century France*. New York: Columbia University Press.

McCaffery, Edward J. 1994. "Cognitive Theory and Tax." *UCLA Law Review* 41 (7): 1861–1948.

McCaffery, Edward J., and Jonathan Baron. 2003. "The Humpty Dumpty Blues: Disaggregation Bias in the Evaluation of Tax Systems." *Organizational Behavior and Human Decision Processes* 91 (2): 230–242.

McCarthy, Katherine. 2005. "Bosnia-Hercegovina." In *Eastern Europe: An Introduction to the People, Lands, and Culture*, vol. 3 (Southeastern Europe), edited by Richard Frucht, 621–694. Santa Barbara, CA: ABC-CLIO.

McCluskey, William, with Arthur Grimes and Jason Timmins. 2002. "Property Taxation in New Zealand." Lincoln Institute of Land Policy Working Paper WP02WM1, Cambridge, MA.

McCrum, Robert. 2004. *Wodehouse: A Life*. New York: W. W. Norton.

McCulloch, John Ramsay. [1845] 1975. *A Treatise on the Principles and Practical Influence of Taxation and the Funding System*. Edited and with an Introduction by D. P. O'Brien. Edinburgh: Scottish Academic Press.

McHugh, Erin. 2016. "Understanding Contingent Convertible Securers: A Primer." NERA Economic Consulting, New York.

McLean, Iain, and Jeremy Smith. 1994. "The Poll Tax, the Electoral Register, and the 1991 Census: An Update." *British Elections and Parties Yearbook* 4 (1): 128–147.

Meade, Marion. 1977. *Eleanor of Aquitaine: A Biography*. New York: Penguin.

Mehrotra, Ajay K. 2004. "'More Mighty Than the Waves of the Sea': Toilers, Tariffs, and the Income Tax Movement, 1880–1913." *Labor History* 45 (2): 165–198.

Mehrotra, Ajay K. 2013. *Making the Modern American Fiscal State: Law, Politics, and the Rise of Progressive Taxation, 1877–1929*. Cambridge: Cambridge University Press.

Meier, Michael T. 1994. "Civil War Draft Records: Exemptions and Enrollments." *Prologue* 26 (4).

Mellon, Andrew M. 1924. *Taxation: The People's Business*. New York: Macmillan.

Mencken, Henry L. 1922. "The Dismal Science." In *Prejudices: Third Series*, Chapter 15. New York: Alfred A. Knopf.

Merriam-Webster's Collegiate Dictionary. 2005. 11th ed. s.v. "excise." Springfield, IL: Merriam-Webster.

Mill, John Stuart. [1848] 2009. *Principles of Political Economy*. Project Gutenberg Ebook.

Mill, John Stuart. 1875. "Papers on Land Tenure." In *Dissertations and Discussions: Political, Philosophical, and Historical*, vol. 5, 224–294. New York: Henry Holt and Co.

Miller, John C. 1943. *Origins of the American Revolution*. Boston: Little, Brown.

Mintz, Jack M. 1994. "Is There a Future for Capital Income Taxation?" *Canadian Tax Journal* 42 (6): 1469–1503.

Mirrlees, James, Stuart Adam, Tim Besley, Richard Blundell, Stephen Bond, Robert Chote, Malcom Gammie, Paul Johnson, Gareth Myles, and James M. Poterba. 2011. *Tax by Design*. Oxford: Oxford University Press.

Misa, Thomas J. 2011. *Leonardo to the Internet: Technology and Culture from the Renaissance to the Present*. Baltimore: The Johns Hopkins University Press.

Mitchell, Brian R. 1988. *British Historical Statistics*. Cambridge: Cambridge University Press.

Montefiore, Simon Sebag. 2011. *Jerusalem: The Biography*. New York: Vintage.

Monty Python. 1969. Television show featuring Graham Chapman, Eric Idle, Terry Gilliam, Terry Jones, John Cleese, and Michael Palin. BBC.

Mourlane, Stéphane. 2005. "La Crise Franco-monégasque de 1962–1963." *Recherches Régionales Côte d'Azur et Contrées Limitrophes* 46: 109–116.

Musson, Alfred Edward. 1958. "Newspaper Printing in the Industrial Revolution." *Economic History Review* 10 (3): 411–426.

Mwakikagile, Godfrey. 2000. *Africa and the West*. Hauppauge, NY: Nova Publishers.

Myers, Steven Lee. 2018. "Fan Bingbing, China's Most Famous Actress, Faces Huge Fines in Tax Evasion." *New York Times*, October 2.

Naidoo, Jay. 2012. "South Africa: Marikana Signals Our Second Chance." *Equal Times*, Opinions, September 1.

Nair, Smitha. 2015. "Mumbai Hooch Tragedy Claims Over 100 Lives, Main Supplier Arrested in Delhi." *News18*, June 23.

Nakabayashi, Masaki. 2012. "The Rise of a Japanese Fiscal State." In *The Rise of Fiscal States: A Global History, 1500–1914*, edited by Bartolomé Yun-Casalilla and Patrick K. O'Brien, with Francisco Comín Comín, 378–409. Cambridge: Cambridge University Press.

Nakamura, Yuko, and Aina Maeguchi. 2013. "Kyoto Machiya and Their Renovation." *The Kyoto Project*. Kyoto University of Foreign Studies, May 27.

National Coalition Against Contraband Tobacco. 2017. "1 in 3 Cigarettes Sold in Ontario Are Contraband." Ottawa, Canada.

Ndung'u, Njuguna. 2017. "Digitalization in Kenya: Revolutionizing Tax Design and Revenue Administration." In *Digital Revolutions in Public Finance*, edited by Sanjeev Gupta, Michael Keen, Alpa Shah, and Geneviève Verdier, 241–257. Washington, DC: International Monetary Fund.

Neff, Blake. 2016. "Rubio-Aligned PAC Hits Cruz for 'Canadian' Tax Plan." *Daily Caller*, January 19.

Nelson, Jerry. 2014. "Richard Branson: From Tax Fraud to Billionaire." *Liberty Voice*, May 29.

New African. 2011. "Sierra Leone: How Independence Was Won." August 9.

Newman, Peter C. 1985. *Company of Adventurers*, vol. 1. New York: Viking Press.

New Yorker. 1973. "FABLES: The Dog and the Accountant." September 17.

New York Times. 1863. "The Diseases and Infirmities Exempting from the Draft." November 15.

New York Times. 1891. "Taxing Food." June 1.

New York Times. 1912. "Single Tax Attracts Orient: Dr. Sen's Advocacy Due to Missionaries, Says Henry George, Jr." April 6.

New York Times. 1989. "Nuclear War Plan by I.R.S." March 28.

New York Times. 2014. "The Pink Tax." Editorial. November 12.

Niskanen, William A. 2006. "Limiting Government: The Failure of Starve the Beast." *Cato Journal* 26 (3): 553–558.

Nordhaus, William. 2017. "Revisiting the Social Cost of Carbon." *Proceedings of the National Academy of Sciences* 114 (7): 1518–1523.

North, Douglass C., and Barry R. Weingast. 1989. "Constitution and Commitment: The Evolution of Institutions Governing Public Choice in Seventeenth-Century England." *Journal of Economic History* 49 (4): 803–832.

North, Michael. 2012. "Finances and Power in the German State System." In *The Rise of Fiscal States: A Global History, 1500–1914*, edited by Yun-Casalilla Bartolomé and Patrick K. O'Brien, with Francisco Comín Comín, 145–163. Cambridge: Cambridge University Press.

Norwich, John Julius. 2003. *A History of Venice*, 2nd ed. London: Penguin.

Oates, Wallace, and Robert Schwab. 2015. "The Window Tax: A Case Study in Excess Burden." *Journal of Economic Perspectives* 29 (1): 163–180.

Oats, Lynne, and Pauline Sadler. 2007. "Securing the Repeal of a Tax on the 'Raw Material of Thought.'" *Accounting, Business & Financial History* 17 (3): 355–373.

O'Brien, Patrick K. 2007. "The Triumph and Denouement of the British Fiscal State: Taxation for the Wars against Revolutionary and Napoleonic France, 1793–1815." LSE Department of Economic History Working Paper No. 99/07, London.

O'Brien, Patrick K., and Philip A. Hunt. 1999. "Excises and the Rise of a Fiscal State in England, 1586–1688." In *Crises, Revolutions and Self-Sustained Growth: Essays in European Fiscal History, 1130–1830*, edited by William Mark Ormrod, Margaret Bonney, and Richard Bonney, 198–224. Stamford, U.K.: Shaun Tyas.

Ochiai, Takehiko. 2017. "In a Grove? Sierra Leone's 1898 Hut Tax War Reconsidered." *Asia Journal of African Studies* 41: 55–86.

OECD. 1998. *Harmful Tax Competition. An Emerging Global Issue*. Paris.

OECD. 2013. *Electronic Sales Suppression: A Threat to Tax Revenues.* Paris.

OECD. 2015a. *Measuring and Monitoring BEPS, Action 11-2015 Final Report.* Paris.

OECD. 2015b. *Tax Administration 2015: Comparative Information on OECD and Other Advanced and Emerging Economies.* Paris.

OECD. 2017a. "Legal Tax Liability, Legal Remittance Responsibility & Tax Incidence: Three Dimensions of Business Taxation." OECD Taxation Working Paper Series, Paris.

OECD. 2017b. *Tax Administration 2017: Comparative Information on OECD and Other Advanced and Emerging Economies.* Paris.

OECD. 2018. *Automatic Exchange of Information: Implementation Report 2018.* Paris.

OECD. 2019a. *Implementing Online Cash Registers: Benefits, Considerations and Guidance.* Paris.

OECD. 2019b. *Public Consultation Document: Global Anti-Base Erosion Proposal ("GloBE")—Pillar Two.* Paris.

OECD. 2019c. *Revenue Statistics 2019: Tax Revenue Trends in the OECD.* Paris.

OECD. 2019d. *Secretariat Proposal for a "Unified Approach" under Pillar One.* Paris.

OECD. 2019e. *Tax Administration 2019: Comparative Information on OECD and Other Advanced and Emerging Economies.* Paris.

OECD. 2019f. *Tax Morale: What Drives People and Businesses to Pay Tax?* Paris.

OECD. 2020. *Tax Challenges Arising from Digitalisation—Economic Impact Assessment.* Paris.

OECD. n.d.a. OECD Library. Definition of the Word "Tax."

OECD. n.d.b. Top Statutory Personal Income Tax Rates and Top Marginal Tax Rates for Employees. OECD.Stat. https://stats.oecd.org/index.aspx?DataSetCode=TABLE_I7.

Office for National Statistics. 2020. *Effects of Taxes and Benefits on UK Household Income: Financial Year Ending 2019.* London.

Office of Management and Budget. n.d. *Historical Tables.* Washington, DC. https://www.whitehouse.gov/omb/historical-tables/.

Ogden, Frederic D. 1958. *The Poll Tax in the South.* Tuscaloosa: University of Alabama Press.

Okrent, Daniel. 2010. *Last Call: The Rise and Fall of Prohibition.* New York: Scribner.

Oliver, Garrett, ed. 2011. *The Oxford Companion to Beer.* Oxford: Oxford University Press.

Olken, Ben, and Monica Singhal. 2011. "Informal Taxation." *American Economic Journal: Applied Economics* 3 (4): 1–28.

Oman, Charles. 1906. *The Great Revolt of 1381.* Oxford: Clarendon Press.

Organ, Paul. 2020. "U.S. Citizenship Renunciation and the Tax System." University of Michigan Working Paper, Ann Arbor, MI.

Ormrod, William Mark, Margaret Bonney, and Richard Bonney, eds. 1999. *Crises, Revolutions and Self-Sustained Growth: Essays in European Fiscal History, 1130–1830.* Stamford, U.K.: Shaun Tyas.

Orwell, George. 1949. *Nineteen Eighty-Four.* New York: Harcourt, Brace.

Oxford Dictionary of Islam. n.d. "Jizyah." Oxford Islamic Studies Online. http://www.oxfordislamicstudies.com/article/opr/t125/e1206.

Paine, Thomas. [1792] 1894. "Rights of Man." In *The Writings of Thomas Paine,* vol. 2, collected and edited by Moncure Daniel Conway, 398–523. New York: The Knickerbocker Press. First published by G. P. Putnam's Sons in London.

Palan, Ronen. 2002. "Tax Havens and the Commercialization of State Sovereignty." *International Organization* 56 (1): 151–176.

Pamuk, Şevket. 2012. "The Evolution of Fiscal Institutions in the Ottoman Empire, 1500–1914." In *The Rise of Fiscal States: A Global History, 1500–1914*, edited by Yun-Casalilla Bartolomé and Patrick K. O'Brien, with Francisco Comín Comín, 304–331. Cambridge: Cambridge University Press.

Paris, David, and Cecelia Hilgert. 1983. "70th Year of Individual Income and Tax Statistics, 1913–1982." *Statistics of Income Bulletin.* Internal Revenue Service, Winter 84: 1–10.

Parry, Ian W. H., and Kenneth A. Small. 2005. "Does Britain or the United States Have the Right Gasoline Tax?" *American Economic Review* 95 (4): 1276–1289.

Peacock, Alan T., and Jack Wiseman. 1961. *The Growth of Public Expenditure in the United Kingdom.* Princeton, NJ: Princeton University Press.

Pearce, Edward. 2011. *The Great Man. Sir Robert Walpole: Scoundrel, Genius and Britain's First Prime Minister.* London: Random House.

Pearson, Roger. 2016. "Voltaire's Luck." *Lapham's Quarterly* IX (3).

Peck, Harry Thurston, ed. 1898. *Harper's Dictionary of Classical Antiquities.* New York: Harper and Brothers.

Peel, Robert. 1853. *The Speeches of the Late Right Honourable Sir Robert Peel, Bart.,* vol. 3. Delivered in the House of Commons. London: Routledge.

Pérez, Arturo. 2008. "Earmarking State Taxes." National Conference of State Legislatures, Washington, DC.

Perez, Sonia. 2015. "Guatemala Arrests Current, Former Tax Chiefs, Over a Dozen Others, in Corruption Case." *Associated Press*, April 16.

Peter, Klara Sabirianova, Steve Buttrick, and Denvil Duncan. 2010. "Global Reform of Personal Income Taxation, 1981–2005: Evidence from 189 Countries." *National Tax Journal* 63 (3): 447–478.

Peters, Gretchen. 2006. "Taliban Drug Trade: Echoes of Colombia." *Christian Science Monitor*, November 21.

Petersen, William. 1997. *Ethnicity Counts.* New Brunswick, NJ: Transaction Publishers.

Pet Health Network. 2014. "The Doberman Pinscher." IDEXX Laboratories, Westbrook, ME.

Petit, Patrick, Mario Mansour, and Philippe Wingender. Forthcoming. *Excise Taxes and Obesity: A How to Note.* Washington, DC: International Monetary Fund.

Petit, Patrick, and Janos Nagy. 2016. *How to Design and Enforce Tobacco Excises?* Washington, DC: International Monetary Fund.

Petty, William. 1662. *A Treatise of Taxes & Contributions.* London: Cornhill.

Pezzolo, Luciano. 2012. "Republics and Principalities in Italy." In *The Rise of Fiscal States: A Global History, 1500–1914*, edited by Yun-Casalilla Bartolomé and Patrick K. O'Brien, with Francisco Comín Comín, 267–284. Cambridge: Cambridge University Press.

Phelps, Edmund S. 1973. "Taxation of Wage Income for Economic Justice." *Quarterly Journal of Economics* 87 (3): 331–354.

Phillipson, Nicholas. 2010. *Adam Smith: An Enlightened Life.* New Haven, CT: Yale University Press.

Pigou, Arthur Cecil. 1920. *The Economics of Welfare.* London: Macmillan & Co.

Piketty, Thomas. 2013. *Capital in the Twenty-first Century.* Cambridge, MA: Belknap Press.

Piketty, Thomas, Emmanuel Saez, and Stefanie Stantcheva. 2014. "Optimal Taxation of Top Labor Incomes: A Tale of Three Elasticities." *American Economic Journal: Economic Policy* 6 (1): 230–271.

Pilon, Mary. 2015. *The Monopolists: Obsession, Fury, and the Scandal behind the World's Favorite Board Game*. New York: Bloomsbury.

Pine, Art. 1978. "Thoughts of Chairman Long." *Washington Post*, February 26.

Platform for Collaboration on Tax. 2020. *The Taxation of Offshore Indirect Transfers—A Toolkit*. Washington, DC.

Plumb, John Harold. 1960. *Sir Robert Walpole: The King's Minister*, vol. 2. London: Cresset Press.

Plumb, John Harold. 1967. *The Growth of Political Stability in England, 1675–1725*. London: Macmillan.

Poniatowski, Grzegorz, Mikhail Bonch-Osmolovskiy, José María Durán-Cabré, Alejandro Esteller-Moré, and Adam Śmietanka. 2019. "Study and Reports on the VAT Gap in the EU-28 Member States: 2019 Final Report." Center for Social and Economic Research Paper No. 500, Warsaw.

Porter, Cole. 1944. "Don't Fence Me In." Original lyrics written by Bob Fletcher. Published by Warner Bros.

Posner, Eric A., and E. Glen Weyl. 2018. *Radical Markets: Uprooting Capitalism and Democracy for a Just Society*. Princeton, NJ: Princeton University Press.

Power, Eileen. 1941. *The Wool Trade in English Medieval History*. London: Oxford University Press.

Powicke, Michael R. 1950. "Distraint of Knighthood and Military Obligation under Henry III." *Speculum* 25 (4): 457–470.

Printer's Ink. 1897. "The Austrian Press." 19 (10): 28.

Public, The. 1909. "Portions of a Speech Made at Newcastle by Lloyd George, the British Chancellor." October 29.

Public, The. 1912. "Sun Yat Sen's Economic Program for China," April 12.

Quinn, Ben. 2012. "A Brief History of the Pasty Tax." *The Guardian*, May 29.

Quintrell, Brian. 2014. *Charles I 1625–1640*. Oxford: Routledge.

Radhakrishnan, C. 2009. "The Unforgettable Contributions of Nangeli, Kerala". *DeviantArt*, September 30. Online.

Rajaraman, Indira. 1995. "Presumptive Direct Taxation: Lessons from Experience in Developing Countries." *Economic and Political Weekly* 30 (18–19): 1103–1124.

Ramsey, Frank P. 1927. "A Contribution to the Theory of Taxation." *Economic Journal* 37 (145): 47–61.

Rapport, Mike. 2009. *1848: Year of Revolution*. New York: Basic Books.

Rawls, John. 1971. *A Theory of Justice*. Cambridge, MA: Harvard University Press.

Redelmeier, Donald A., and Christopher J. Yarnell. 2012. "Road Crash Fatalities on US Income Tax Days." *Journal of the American Medical Association* 307 (14): 1486–1488.

Redman, Alvin, ed. 1959. *The Wit and Humor of Oscar Wilde*. New York: Dover.

Rees-Jones, Alex, and Dmitry Taubinsky. 2020. "Measuring 'Schmeduling.'" *Review of Economic Studies* 87 (5): 2399–2438.

Reeves, Thomas C. 1975. *Gentleman Boss: The Life of Chester Alan Arthur*. New York: Alfred A. Knopf.

Reinhart, Carmen M., and Kenneth S. Rogoff. 2009. *This Time Is Different: Eight Centuries of Financial Folly*. Princeton, NJ: Princeton University Press.

Rhodes, Raymond Crompton. 1933. *Harlequin Sheridan: The Man and the Legends*. Oxford: Basil Blackwell.

Ricardo, David. [1817] 2004. *The Principles of Political Economy and Taxation*. London and New York: J. M. Dent & Sons and Dover.

Richards, John F. 2012. "Fiscal States in Mughal and British India." In *The Rise of Fiscal States: A Global History, 1500–1914*, edited by Bartolomé Yun-Castalilla and Patrick K. O'Brien, with Francisco Comín Comín, 410–441. Cambridge: Cambridge University Press.

Rickards, Maurice. 2000. *The Encyclopedia of Ephemera: A Guide to the Fragmentary Documents of Everyday Life for the Collector, Curator, and Historian*, edited by Michael Twyman, with the assistance of Sally De Beaumont and Amoret Tanner. New York: Routledge.

Ritchie, Hannah. 2020. "Sector by Sector: Where Do Global Greenhouse Gas Emissions Come From?" *Our World in Data*. https://ourworldindata.org/ghg-emissions-by-sector.

Ritholtz, Barry. 2017. "Lessons from Kansas Tax-Cutting Experiment." *The Big Picture*, June 19.

Roberts, Andrew. 2014. *The Holy Fox: The Life of Lord Halifax*. London: Head of Zeus.

Robertson. 1792. *Robertson's British Tax-Tables, on an Improved Plan; Containing All the Taxes Which Affect Every Description of Men, Both in England and Scotland. Together with Useful Regulations for the Cities of London and Edinburgh*. London: Printed for and Sold by All the Booksellers.

Robins, Nick. 2012. *The Corporation That Changed the World: How the East India Company Shaped the Modern Multinational*, 2nd ed. New York: Pluto Press.

Rodgers, Luke. 2018. "Give Credit Where? The Incidence of Child Care Tax Credits." *Journal of Urban Economics* 108: 51–71.

Rodrik, Dani. 1998. "Why Do More Open Economies Have Bigger Governments?" *Journal of Political Economy* 106 (5): 997–1032.

Rogoff, Kenneth S. 2016. *The Curse of Cash*. Princeton, NJ: Princeton University Press.

Roller, Matthew B. 2001. *Constructing Autocracy: Aristocrats and Emperors in Julio-Claudian Rome*. Princeton, NJ: Princeton University Press.

Romeo, Nick. 2016. "Ancient Device for Determining Taxes Discovered in Egypt." *National Geographic* online. May 16.

Romer, Christina D., and David H. Romer. 2009. "Do Tax Cuts Starve the Beast: The Effect of Tax Changes on Government Spending." *Brookings Papers on Economic Activity* 40 (1): 139–214.

Roosevelt, Theodore. 1919. *The Roosevelt Policy*, vol. 2, edited by William Griffith. New York: Current Literature Publishing Company.

Rosenberg, Joshua D. 1996. "The Psychology of Taxes: Why They Drive Us Crazy and How We Can Make Them Sane." *Virginia Tax Review* 16 (2): 155–236.

Ross, Thomas W. 1986. "Store Wars: The Chain Tax Movement." *Journal of Law and Economics* 29 (1): 125–137.

Rothstein, Jesse. 2008. "The Unintended Consequences of Encouraging Work: Tax Incidence and the EITC." Center for Economic Policy Studies, Princeton University.

Rowland, Oliver. 2019. "Oldest Ever Woman Accused of Having Faked Age." *The Connection*, January 2.

Rowlatt, Justin. 2016. "Why India Wiped Out 86% of Its Cash Overnight." *BBC News*, November 14.

Rucker, Philip. 2011. "Mitt Romney Says 'Corporations Are People.'" *Washington Post*, August 11.

Ruding, Onno. 1992. *Report of the Committee of Independent Experts on Company Taxation*. Executive Summary, European Commission, Brussels.

Rwanda Governance Board. n.d. "Umuganda." Kigali.

Sadasivan, S. N. 2000. *A Social History of India*. New Delhi: APH Publishing.

Sadka, Efraim. 1976. "On Income Distribution, Incentive Effects and Optimal Income Taxation." *Review of Economic Studies* 43 (2): 261–267.

Saez, Emmanuel. 2010. "Do Taxpayers Bunch at Kink Points?" *American Economic Journal: Economic Policy* 2 (3): 180–212.

Saez, Emmanuel, and Gabriel Zucman. 2019a. *The Triumphs of Injustice: How the Rich Dodge Taxes and How to Make Them Pay*. New York: Academic Press.

Saez, Emmanuel, and Gabriel Zucman. 2019b. "Progressive Wealth Taxation," *Brookings Papers on Economic Activity* Fall: 437–511.

Saez, Emmanuel, Joel Slemrod, and Seth H. Giertz. 2012. "The Elasticity of Taxable Income with Respect to Marginal Tax Rates: A Critical Review." *Journal of Economic Literature* 50 (1): 3–50.

Sahadi, Jeanne, and Annelena Lobb. 2004. "Strangest Taxes: You Might Pay Taxes on Illegal Drugs, Pepsi, Playing Cards and Being a Star. And That's Not All." *CNN/Money*, April 9.

Sale, Jonathan. 2012. "Douglas Adams's 60th Birthday Marked with Liff, the Universe and Pink Floyd." *The Guardian*, March 6.

Saleh, Mohamed. 2018. "On the Road to Heaven: Taxation, Conversions, and the Coptic-Muslim Socioeconomic Gap in Medieval Egypt." *Journal of Economic History* 78 (2): 394–434.

Salih, Zak M. 2011. "Fiction Review: The Pale King." *Richmond Times–Dispatch*, July 31.

Salpukas, Agis. 1992. "Falling Tax Would Lift All Yachts." *New York Times*, February 7.

Salvadori, Neri, and Rodolfo Signorino. 2015. "Defense versus Opulence? An Appraisal of the Malthus-Ricardo 1815 Controversy on the Corn Laws." *History of Political Economy* 47 (1): 151–184.

Salzmann, Ariel. 1993. "An Ancien Régime Revisited: 'Privatization' and Political Economy in the Eighteenth-Century Ottoman Empire." *Politics & Society* 21 (4): 393–423.

Samson, William D. 2005. "President Nixon's Troublesome Tax Returns." *Tax Notes*, April 11.

Sargent, Thomas, and Francois Velde. 1995. "Macroeconomic Features of the French Revolution." *Journal of Political Economy* 103 (3): 474–518.

Saunders, Laura. 2015. "Blowing the Whistle on Tax Cheats." *Wall Street Journal*, September 4.

Sauvegrain, Alexandra. 2001. "Dialogues of Architectural Preservation in Modern Vietnam: The 36 Streets Commercial Quarter of Hanoi." *Traditional Dwellings and Settlements Review* 13 (1): 23–32.

Schama, Simon. 1989. *Citizens: A Chronicle of the French Revolution*. New York: Alfred A. Knopf.

Scheuer, Florian, and Joel Slemrod. 2020. "Taxation and the Superrich." *Annual Review of Economics* 12: 189–211.

Scheve, Kenneth, and David Stasavage. 2016. *Taxing the Rich: A History of Fiscal Fairness in the United States and Europe*. Princeton, NJ: Princeton University Press.

Schumpeter, Joseph A. [1918] 1991. "The Crisis of the Tax State." In *Joseph A. Schumpeter: The Economics and Sociology of Capitalism*, edited by Richard Swedberg, 99–140. Princeton, NJ: Princeton University Press.

Scott, James C. 1998. *Seeing Like a State: How Certain Schemes to Improve the Human Condition Have Failed*. New Haven, CT: Yale University Press.

Seade, Jesus K. 1977. "On the Shape of Optimal Tax Schedules." *Journal of Public Economics* 7 (2): 203–235.

Seamans, Robert. 2017. "No, Robots Should Not Be Taxed." *Forbes*, March 3.

Seidl, Jonathon M. 2015. "There's Something Odd about Some Tickets in Texas—and a Judge Has Resigned Over It." *The Blaze*, June 4.

Seligman, Edwin R. A. 1899. *The Shifting and Incidence of Taxation*, 2nd ed. New York: Macmillan.

Seligman, Edwin R. A. 1914. *The Income Tax: A Study of the History, Theory and Practice of Income Taxation at Home and Abroad*, 2nd ed. New York: Macmillan.

Sen, Amartya. 2009. *The Idea of Justice*. Cambridge, MA: Belknap Press.

Sen, Anindya, and Nafeez Fatima. 2011. "Do Lower Taxes Increase Smoking? Evidence from the Canadian National Experiment." *Canadian Tax Journal* 59 (2): 221–238.

Sentencing Project, The. 2016. *6 Million Lost Voters: State-Level Estimates of Felony Disenfranchisement, 2016*. Washington, DC.

Service, Robert. 2009. *Trotsky: A Biography*. Cambridge, MA: Belknap Press.

Sharp, Paul. 2010. "1846 and All That: The Rise and Fall of British Wheat Protection in the Nineteenth Century." *Agricultural History Review* 58 (1): 76–94.

Shaxson, Nicholas. 2011. *Treasure Islands: Uncovering the Damage of Offshore Banking and Tax Havens*. New York: St. Martin's Griffin.

Shears, Richard. 2006. "Is Prince Philip a God?" *Daily Mail*, June 3.

Sheets, Connor. 2017. "Too Poor to Vote: How Alabama's 'New Poll Tax' Bars Thousands of People from Voting." *The Guardian*, October 4.

Shehab, Fakhri. 1953. *Progressive Taxation: A Study in the Development of the Progressive Principle in the British Income Tax*. Oxford: Clarendon Press.

Shiono, Patricia H., and Richard E. Behrman. 1995. "Low Birth Weight: Analysis and Recommendations." *Future of Children* 5 (1): 4–18.

Simmons, Andria. 2014. "Georgia Towns Are Getting Rich Off Speeding Tickets." *Governing*, October 23.

Simons, Henry. 1938. *Personal Income Taxation: The Definition of Income as a Problem of Fiscal Policy*. Chicago: University of Chicago Press.

Slemrod, Joel. 2008. "Why Is Elvis on Burkina Faso Postage Stamps? Cross-Country Evidence on the Commercialization of State Sovereignty." *Journal of Empirical Legal Studies* 5 (4): 683–712.

Slemrod, Joel. 2013. "Buenas Notches: Lines and Notches in Tax System Design." *eJournal of Tax Research* 11 (3): 259–283.

Slemrod, Joel. 2018. "Is This Tax Reform, or Just Confusion?" *Journal of Economic Perspectives* 32 (4): 73–96.

Slemrod, Joel. 2019. "Tax Compliance and Enforcement." *Journal of Economic Literature* 57 (4): 904–954.

Slemrod, Joel, and Jon Bakija. 2017. *Taxing Ourselves: A Citizen's Guide to the Debate over Taxes*, 5th ed. Cambridge, MA: MIT Press.

Slemrod, Joel, Brett Collins, Jeffrey L. Hoopes, Daniel Reck, and Michael Sebastiani. 2017. "Does Credit-Card Information Reporting Improve Small-Business Tax Compliance?" *Journal of Public Economics* 149: 1–19.

Slemrod, Joel, and William G. Gale. 2001. "Rethinking the Estate and Gift Tax," Conference Report, The Brookings Institution, Washington, DC.

Slemrod, Joel, Obeid Ur Rehman, and Mazhar Waseem. Forthcoming. "Pecuniary and Non-pecuniary Motivations for Tax Compliance: Evidence from Pakistan." *Review of Economics and Statistics.*

Slemrod, Joel, and Tejaswi Velayudhan. 2018. "Do Firms Remit at Least 85 Percent of Tax Everywhere? New Evidence from India." *Journal of Tax Administration* 4 (1): 24–37.

Smith, Adam. [1776] 1868. *An Inquiry into the Nature and Causes of The Wealth of Nations*, edited by Edwin Cannan. Chicago: University of Chicago Press.

Smith, Denis Mack. 2000. "The Revolutions of 1848–1849 in Italy." In *The Revolutions in Europe, 1848–1849: From Reform to Reaction*, edited by R. J. W. Evans and Hartmut Pogge von Strandmann, 55–82. Oxford: Oxford University Press.

Smith, Jada F. 2015. "Cyberattack Exposes I.R.S. Tax Returns." *New York Times*, May 26.

Smith, Peter. 1991. "Lessons from the British Poll Tax Disaster." *National Tax Journal* 44 (4, Part 2): 421–436.

Smith, Stephen. 2008. "Restraining the Golden Weed: Taxation and Regulation of Tobacco." *FinanzArchiv/Public Finance Analysis* 64 (4): 476–507.

Smith, Sydney. 1820. "Review of Seybert's Annals of the United States." *Edinburgh Review* 33.

Soled, Jay A. 1997. "A Proposal to Lengthen the Tax Accounting Period." *American Journal of Tax Policy* 14 (1): 35–68.

Soos, Piroska E. 1990. "Self-Employed Evasion and Tax Withholding: A Comparative Study and Analysis of the Issues." *University of California Davis Law Review* 24 (1): 107–193.

Soos, Piroska E. 1997. *The Origins of Taxation at Source in England*. Amsterdam: International Bureau of Fiscal Documentation.

Sørensen, Peter Birch. 2007. "Can Capital Income Taxes Survive? And Should They?" *CESifo Economic Studies* 53 (2): 172–228.

Sørensen, Peter Birch. 2010. "Dual Income Taxes: A Nordic Tax System." In *Tax Reform in Open Economies: International and Country Perspectives*, edited by Iris Claus, Norman Gemmell, Michelle Harding, and David White, 78–108. Cheltenham, U.K.: Edward Elgar.

Spang, Rebecca L. 2015. *Stuff and Money in the Time of the French Revolution*. Cambridge, MA: Harvard University Press.

Spartacus Educational. n.d. *JFK Theory: Texas Oil Men*. Online.

Spence, Jonathan. 1969. *To Change China: Western Advisors in China*. Boston, MA: Little, Brown.

Spicer, Jonathan. 2015. "Fed Handed Record $96.9 Bln Profit to Government Last Year." *Reuters Bond News*, March 20.

Spieth, Darius A. 2006. "The Corsets Assignat in David's *Death of Marat*." *Notes in the History of Art* 25 (3): 22–28.

Splinter, David. 2020. "U.S. Tax Progressivity and Redistribution." *National Tax Journal,* forthcoming.

Staggs, Brooke. 2020. "California Passes $1 Billion in Cannabis Tax Revenue Two Years after Launching Legal Market." *The Mercury News,* March 11.

Stamp, Josiah. 1917. "The Taxation of Excess Profits Abroad." *Economic Journal* 27: 26–37.

Star Wars. 1999. "Opening Scene from *The Phantom Menace: Episode 1.*" Written and directed by George Lucas. San Francisco, CA: Lucasfilm.

State of Wisconsin. Department of Revenue. 2010. "Sales of Ice Cream Cakes and Similar Items." November 8.

Statista. 2017a. "Profits of State Lotteries in the United States from 2009 to 2016 (in billion U.S. dollars)."

Statista. 2017b. "Sales of State Lotteries in the United States from 2009 to 2016 (in billion U.S. dollars)."

Statista. 2018. "Tobacco Tax Revenue and Forecast in the United States from 2000 to 2023."

Statista. 2019a. "Annual Average Price of a Pack of the Most Sold Brand of Cigarettes in France from 2000 to 2015 (in euros)."

Statista. 2019b. "Recommended Retail Price of a Typical Pack of 20 Cigarettes in the United Kingdom (UK) from 2005 to 2017 (in GBP)."

Stebbings, Chantal. 2011. "Public Health Imperatives and Taxation Policy: The Window Tax as an Early Paradigm in English Law." In *Studies in the History of Tax Law,* vol. 5, edited by John Tiley, 43–72. Oxford: Hart Publishing.

Steinberg, Philip E., and Stephen D. McDowell. 2003. "Mutiny on the Bandwidth: The Semiotics of Statehood in the Internet Domain Name Registries of Pitcairn Island and Niue." *New Media & Society* 5 (1): 47–67.

Stiem, Tyler. 2016. "Race and Real Estate: How Hot Chinese Money Is Making Vancouver Unlivable." *The Guardian,* July 7.

Stiglitz, Joseph E. 1977. "The Theory of Local Public Goods." In *The Economics of Public Services,* edited by Martin S. Feldstein and Robert P. Inman, 274–333. London: Macmillan.

Stotsky, Janet G. 1997. "Gender Bias in Tax Systems." *Tax Notes International* (June 9): 1913–1923.

Strassler, Robert B., ed. 2009. *The Landmark Herodotus: The Histories.* New York: Anchor Books.

Strong, Theron George. 1917. *Joseph H. Choate: New Englander, New Yorker, Lawyer, Ambassador.* New York: Dodd, Mead.

Strumpf, Koleman. 2017. "Tax Flights." Wake Forest University Working Paper, Winston-Salem, NC.

Stubbs, William, ed. [1870] 1936. *Select Charters and Other Illustrations of English Constitutional History from the Earliest Times to the Reign of Edward the First.* Oxford: Clarendon Press.

Sudakov, Dmitry. 2013. "Russian Kopeck Goes Down in History Yet Again." *Pravda,* January 29.

Suetonius. [121] 1957. *The Twelve Caesars,* edited by E. V. Kieu, 150–179. Durham, NC: Duke University.

Summers, Lawrence H. 2017. "Trump's Top Economist's Tax Analysis Isn't Just Wrong, It's Dishonest." *Washington Post,* October 17.

Sundelson, J. Wilner. 1941. "Banning the Use of Margarine through Taxation." In *Tax Barriers to Trade* by Mark Eisner, Robert L. Cochran, Edgar L. Burtis et al., 85–104. Philadelphia: University of Pennsylvania Tax Institute.

Sung, Myung Jae, Rajul Awasthi, and Hyung Chul Lee. 2017. "Can Tax Incentives for Electronic Payments Reduce the Shadow Economy? Korea's Attempt to Reduce Underreporting in Retail Businesses." World Bank, Washington, DC.

Sunley, Emil. 2008. "India: The Tax Treatment of Bidis." Presentation given at the World Bank, Washington, DC, April 8.

Sun-Sentinel. 1993. "Boat Builders Scuttled by Yacht Tax." August 16.

Surendranath, Nidhi. 2013. "200 Years On, Nangeli's Sacrifice Only a Fading Memory." *The Hindu*, October 21.

Tague, Ingrid H. 2008. "Eighteenth-Century English Debates on a Dog Tax." *Historical Journal* 51 (4): 901–920.

Tanzi, Vito, and Ludger Schuknecht. 2000. *Public Spending in the 20th Century: A Global Perspective*. Cambridge: Cambridge University Press.

Tarver, H. Micheal, and Emily Slape, eds. 2016. *The Spanish Empire: A Historical Encyclopedia*, vol. 1. Santa Barbara, CA: ABC-CLIO.

Tax Advisory Partnership. n.d. "Why Does the UK Tax Year Start on April 6 Each Year?" London.

Taxback.com. n.d. "UK Tax History Lesson—How Come the UK Tax Year Ends on April 5th?" Online.

Tax Justice Network, Global Alliance for Tax Justice, PSI, and Oxfam. 2015. *Still Broken: Governments Must Do More to Fix the International Corporate Tax System*. Joint Agency Briefing Note 15, November 10. Oxford, U.K.

Tax Research Foundation. 1938. *Tax Systems of the World*, 7th ed. Chicago: Commerce Clearing House.

Taylor, Frederick. 2013. *The Downfall of Money: Germany's Hyperinflation and the Destruction of the Middle Class*. London: Bloomsbury Publishing.

Thane, Pat. 2000. *Old Age in English History: Past Experiences, Present Issues*. Oxford: Oxford University Press.

Thatcher, Margaret. 1993. *The Downing Street Years*. New York: HarperCollins.

Theobald, Ulrich, 2016. "*jingtian zhi* 井田制, The Well-Field System." http://www.chinaknowledge.de/History/Terms/jingtian.html.

This Way Caribbean Islands. 2001. Winston-Salem, NC: Hunter Publishing.

Thomas, Duncan. 1990. "Intra-household Resource Allocation: An Inferential Approach." *Journal of Human Resources* 25 (4): 635–664.

Thomas, Duncan. 1993. "The Distribution of Income and Expenditure within the Household." *Annales d'Economie et de Statistique* 29: 109–135.

Thorndike, Joseph J. 2013. "Tax History: Is the VAT a Career Killer for Politicians?" *Tax Analysts*, Tax History Project, December 12.

Thorndike, Joseph J. 2016. "Threats, Leverage, and the Early Success of Reprisal Taxes." *Tax Analysts*, Tax History Project, March 17.

Thornton, John. 1983. *The Kingdom of Kongo: Civil War and Transition, 1641–1718*. Madison: University of Wisconsin Press.

Thornton, Mark, and Robert Burton Ekelund Jr. 2004. *Tariffs, Blockades, and Inflation: The Economics of the Civil War.* Wilmington, DE: Scholarly Resources.

Tibballs, Geoff. 2017. *Royalty's Strangest Tales.* London: Pavilion Books.

Times, The. 1882. Speech made by Home Secretary Sir William Harcourt at Burton upon Trent, January 23.

Tol, Richard S. J. 2009. "The Economic Effects of Climate Change." *Journal of Economic Perspectives* 23 (2): 29–51.

Trannoy, Alain. 2015. "Much Ado about Nothing: The Solidarity Tax on Wealth (ISF) in France." In *Taxing Wealth: Past, Present and Future,* edited by Caterina Astarita, 32–37. European Commission Discussion Paper 003.

Traynor, Ian, and Helena Smith. 2015. "Wired-up Tax Snoopers Could Be Unleashed in Greece." *The Guardian,* March 6.

Treisman, Daniel. 2002. "Russia Renewed." *Foreign Affairs* 81 (6): 58–72.

Trevisani, Paulo. 2015. "Brazil Probes Alleged Corruption among Tax Officials." *Wall Street Journal,* April 7.

Turner, Michael J. 1998. "The 'Bonaparte of Free Trade' and the Anti-Corn Law League." *Historical Journal* 41 (4): 1011–1034.

Turner, Nicholas. 2012. "Who Benefits from Student Aid? The Economic Incidence of Tax-Based Federal Student Aid." *Economics of Education Review* 31 (4): 463–481.

Tutt, Juliana. 2010. "'No Taxation without Representation' in the American Woman Suffrage Movement." *Stanford Law Review* 62 (5): 1473–1512.

Twain, Mark. 1870. "A Mysterious Visit." *Buffalo Express,* March 19.

Uglow, Jenny. 2014. *In These Times: Living in Britain through Napoleon's Wars, 1793–1815.* London: Faber & Faber.

U.K. Parliament. Public Accounts Committee. 2015. *Tax Avoidance: The Role of Large Accountancy Firms.* London.

Unger, Harlow Giles. 2011. *American Tempest: How the Boston Tea Party Sparked a Revolution.* Boston: Da Capo.

United Kingdom of Great Britain and Ireland. 1920. *Report of the Royal Commission on the Income Tax.* London: His Majesty's Stationery Office.

United Nations. n.d. *World Population Prospects 2019,* File POP/13-A (median estimates). https://population.un.org/wpp/Download/Standard/Population/.

United States Conference of Catholic Bishops. 2019. "Matthew, Chapter 21, Verse 31." *Bible.*

University Chronicle. 1869. "An Impeachment Trial." University of Michigan, March 27.

University of Oxford. 2018. "Tax on Meat Could Offset Health Costs." Press Release, November 6.

University of Pennsylvania. 2002. "Taxes in the Ancient World." *Almanac* 48 (28).

U.S. Agency for International Development. 2018. *Morocco Gender Analysis (Final).* Washington, DC: Banyan Global.

U.S. Congress. House Committee on Ways and Means. 2017. H.R.1947—Religious Freedom Peace Tax Fund Act of 2017, 115th Cong.

U.S. Customs and Border Protection. n.d. "Did You Know . . . Thomas Melvill, Herman Melville and Nathaniel Hawthorne All Are Part of CBP History?" Washington, DC.

U.S. Department of the Treasury. 1977. *Blueprints for Basic Tax Reform.* Washington, DC.

U.S. Environmental Protection Agency. 2016. *Social Cost of Carbon*. Washington, DC.

Utt, Robert. 2005. "The Bridge to Nowhere: A National Embarrassment." The Heritage Foundation, Washington, DC.

Vaisey, David, ed. 1985. *The Diary of Thomas Turner, 1754–1765*. Oxford: Oxford University Press.

Vâlsan, Lucian. 2014. "A Bachelor's Tax—Not So Unlikely." *A Voice for Men Blog*.

Vaughan, Robert. 1840. *The History of England under the House of Stuart, including the Commonwealth, Part II*. London: Baldwin and Cradock.

Ventry, Dennis J. Jr. 2011. "Americans Don't Hate Taxes, They Hate Paying Taxes." *UBC Law Review* 44 (3): 835–890.

Viard, Brian. 2014. "China's Salt Monopoly: Cracking Down on Illegal Contraband." *Forbes*, August 4.

Viscusi, W. Kip. 1995. "Cigarette Taxation and the Social Consequences of Smoking." In *Tax Policy and the Economy*, vol. 9, edited by James Poterba, 51–102. Cambridge, MA: MIT Press.

Vose, Ruth Hurst. 1980. *Glass*. London: HarperCollins Distribution Services.

Waite, Robert G. L. 1993. *The Psychopathic God: Adolf Hitler*. New York: Da Capo.

Wallace, David Foster. 2012. *The Pale King*. New York: Little, Brown.

Ward, William R. 1952. "The Administration of the Window and Assessed Taxes, 1696–1798." *English Historical Review* 67 (265): 522–542.

Ward, William R. 1953. *The English Land Tax in the Eighteenth Century*. Oxford: Oxford University Press.

Wareham, Andrew. 2017. "The Unpopularity of the Hearth Tax and the Social Geography of London in 1666." *Economic History Review* 70 (2): 452–482.

Warner, Jessica, and Frank Ivis. 1999. "'Damn You, You Informing Bitch.' Vox Populi and the Unmaking of the Gin Act of 1736." *Journal of Social History* 33 (2): 299–330.

Waterson, Jim. 2020. "Government Will Abolish the 20% 'Reading Tax.'" *The Guardian*, March 11.

Watson, Katy, and Sarah Treanor. 2016. "The Mexicans Dying for a Fizzy Drink." *BBC News*, Mexico, February 2.

Watt, Holly, David Pegg, Juliette Garside, and Helena Bengtsson. 2016. "From Kubrick to Cowell: Panama Papers Expose Offshore Dealings of the Stars." *The Guardian*, April 6.

Waugh, Evelyn. [1938] 2012. *Scoop*. New York: Little, Brown.

Webber, Carolyn, and Aaron Wildavsky. 1986. *A History of Taxation and Expenditure in the Western World*. New York: Simon & Schuster.

Wedgwood, Cicely Veronica. 1961. *Thomas Wentworth, First Earl of Strafford, 1593–1641*. London: Phoenix Press.

Weightman, Gavin, 2007. *The Industrial Revolutionaries: The Making of the Modern World, 1776–1914*. New York: Grove Press.

Weinberg, Bennett Alan, and Bonnie K. Bealer. 2002. *The World of Caffeine: The Science and Culture of the World's Most Popular Drug*. New York: Routledge.

Weir, Alison. 1998. *The Life of Elizabeth I*. New York: Ballantine Books.

Weisman, Steven R. 2002. *The Great Tax Wars*. New York: Simon & Schuster.

Weissmann, Jordan. 2012. "America's Dumbest Tax Loophole: The Florida Rent-a-Cow Scam." *The Atlantic*, April 17.

West, Max. 1908. *The Inheritance Tax*. New York: Columbia University Press.

Weyl, E. Glen, and Michael Fabinger. 2013. "Pass-Through as an Economic Tool: Principles of Incidence under Imperfect Competition." *Journal of Political Economy* 121 (3): 528–583.

Whalley, John. 1984. "Regression or Progression: The Taxing Question of Incidence Analysis." *Canadian Journal of Economics* 17 (4): 654–682.

White, Eugene N. 2004. "From Privatized to Government-Administered Tax Collection: Tax Farming in Eighteenth-Century France." *Economic History Review* 57 (4): 636–663.

White, Richard D. Jr. 2006. *Kingfish: The Reign of Huey P. Long*. New York: Random House.

White House. Office of the Press Secretary. 2013. "Remarks by the President on Economic Mobility." December 4.

Williams, Colin C. 2014. *Confronting the Shadow Economy: Evaluating Tax Compliance and Behaviour Policies*. Cheltenham, U.K.: Edward Elgar.

Williams, Judith. 2017. *Little History of Essex*. Gloucestershire: History Press.

Williams, Lena. 1981. "Town of Ministers Still Battling Taxes: The Talk of Hardenburgh." *New York Times*, May 4.

Wilson, Scott. 2016. "Singapore Will Have World's First GNSS Urban Congestion Pricing Scheme by 2020." *D'Artagnan Consulting Blog*, March 18.

Wintour, Patrick. 2007. "Lost in the Post—25 Million at Risk after Data Discs Go Missing." *The Guardian*, November 21.

Wood, Robert W. 2015. "10 Notorious Tax Cheats: Queen of Mean Leona Helmsley Proved Little People Can Put You in Jail." *Forbes*, April 17.

Wood, Samuel. 1934. *Tithes*. Fresno, CA: Crown Printing and Engraving.

World Bank. 2001. *Salary Supplements and Bonuses in Revenue Departments: Final Report*. Washington, DC: World Bank.

Ydema, Onno, and Henk Vording. 2014. "Dutch Tax Reforms in the Napoleonic Era." In *Studies in the History of Tax Law*, vol. 6, edited by John Tiley, 489–522. Oxford: Hart Publishing.

Yglesias, Matthew. 2013. "Scrap the Corporate Income Tax." *Slate.com*, April 9.

Yitzhaki, Shlomo. 2007. "Cost-Benefit Analysis of Presumptive Taxation." *FinanzArchiv: Public Finance Analysis* 63 (3): 311–326.

Zaidi, S. Akbar. 1996. "Urban Local Government in Pakistan: Expecting Too Much from Too Little?" *Economic and Political Weekly* 31 (44): 2948–2953.

Zimmermann, Warren. 2002. *First Great Triumph: How Five Americans Made their Country a World Power*. New York: Farrar, Straus and Giroux.

Zucman, Gabriel. 2013. "The Missing Wealth of Nations: Are Europe and the U.S. Net Debtors or Net Creditors?" *Quarterly Journal of Economics* 128 (3): 1321–1364.

ILLUSTRATION CREDITS

206   *Eighteenth Century English Drinking Glasses: An Illustrated Guide* by
       L.M Bickerton (Barrie & Jenkins 1971). Page 148, Plate 385.

207   Courtesy of JRPG. CC BY-SA 3.0.

208   Arterra Picture Library / Alamy Stock Photo.

209   Kevin Wheal / Alamy Stock Photo.

218   Courtesy of Vladimir Sitnik.

233   Courtesy Thomas Forsyth, LandlordsGame.

238   Photo courtesy of Stephen Burch.

252   Georges Lukomski—Archives du Palais de Monaco /Institut audiovisuel.

255   Source: Unknown.

259   (bottom) Photo: DAVIDT8. Public Domain.

269   (right) William Heath Robinson, "Doubling Gloucester cheeses by the Gruyere
       method in an old Gloucester cheese works when cheese is scarce," *The Sketch*,
       15 May 1940. Pen and wash, 390 x 295mm. With kind permission of the Heath
       Robinson Museum.

292   Mary Evans Picture Library Ltd.

296   Alamy Stock Photo / Image ID: ERGGN3.

304   Photographer: Bradley C. Bower / Bloomberg via Getty Images. Reprinted by
       permission.

320   Geraldine Simonnet.

342   *Smugglers* by John Augustus Atkinson, 1808.

345   Division of Work and Industry, National Museum of American History, Smithsonian
       Institution.

349   *Lady Godiva* by John Collier (1897).

358   "Free Trade and Protections," London School of Economics.

INDEX

Figures are indicated by page numbers in italics. Taxes specific to a country appear under that country.

Abbasid caliphate, 35, 100

Adams, Douglas, 373, 451n6

Adams, Samuel, 9, 314, 444n5

Adams, Thomas S., 404n39

Addington, Henry, 111, 127, 130, 361

Addison, Joseph, 315

ad valorem taxation, 207, 429n22

Africa, colonial taxes, 13–15

Agnew, Spiro, 286

agriculture, taxation of, 26, 401n60

alcoholic drink. *See* food and drink taxes

Algeria, 252

Alyattes (King of Lydia), 25, 43

Amakusa, Jerome, 139, 419n26

Anne (Queen of England), 78

Anthony, Susan B., 134

Apollinaire, Guillaume, 316

Apple, 268

Argentina, 46, 175, 254, 257, 290, 335

arm's length pricing and principle, 256, 266–68, 270, 274, 395

Arthur, Chester, 315, 325, 445n17

Asquith, Herbert, 115

Athens, 35, 38, 144, 191, 305, 404n45; liturgies, 27, 30, 69, 262, 379

Atlas Shrugged (Rand), 374

attribute-based taxation, 207, 214, 217

Austen, Jane, 20

Australia, 176, 232, 303, 306, 394, 431n2, 432n30

Austria, 51, 60, 64, 109, 178, 242, 402n1, 420n33; tax refusers, 309

automatic exchange of information, 264, 436n43

Babbage, Charles, 42–43, 94

The Bachelor Tax (Davidson), 424n9

The Bahamas, 258

Baldwin, Stanley, 69, 408n44

Balfour, Arthur, 357

Bangladesh, 330

Barry, Madame du, 324

Base Erosion and Profit Shifting (BEPS), 271, 273, 306, 388

Battle of Arica, 17, 401n56

Becker, Boris, 286

Belgium, 229, 249, 262, 277, 436n45

Bellamy, Edward, 374

Berlusconi, Silvio, 286, 439n11

Bermuda, 270

Berthold, Peter, 184

Best, George, 184, 426n45

biennial tax cycle, 213

Birkenfeld, Bradley, 304, *304*, 442n92

birth rate, 157, 174–77

Blackstone, William, 421n13

Blair, Tony, 77

blockchain, 395

Bolivia: fiscal stability clause, 16; "Ten Cents War," 15–17, 401n53

Bonaparte, Napoleon, 3, 68, 112, 376

Borah, William, 164

border taxes, 28

Boston Tea Party: Bohea tea, 400n25; British tax oppression, 5–6, 9–10; smuggling, 8–9, 11, 23, 400nn25–26; Townshend Duties, 7–8, 11, 375, 400n23

Boudicca, 83–84

Bowie, David, 287

Branson, Richard, 286

Bray v. Alexandria Women's Health Clinic, 420n56

Brazil, 229, 325, 327

Brennan, Geoffrey, 346

Britain: alcoholic drink and taxes, 189, 204, 348, 428n87, 441nn57–58; bachelor taxes, 175, 424n4; benevolences, 70–71; Beveridge Report (1942), 41, 128; brick tax, 205, 429n19; calendar year, 213; capital levy on war debt, 235; Church of England and, 22, 28, 73, 401n75, 401nn75–77, 402n77, 409n62; class-based tax, 98, 413nn67–68; coal tax, 181, 426n37; community charge, 85, 87, 89–91, 312, 377, 411n17, 411n25, 412n29, 412n39; conscription system, 66, 68, 408n40; council tax, 91, 412nn36–37; *danegeld*, 35; decimation tax, 145–46, 247, 325, 385, 421n62; dementia tax, 361–62; Excise Crisis of 1733–1734, 357; excise taxes, 103, 107, 177, 350, 356–57, 449n48; expulsion of Jews, 46; feudal dues, 36, 71–72, 85, 404n55, 409nn53–54, 411nn7–11; gifts, government requests, 68–69, 408n42; grasses (informers), 303, 442n87; hair powder tax, 415n5; hat and wig tax, 102, 414n86, 414n88; hearth tax, 215–17, 219, 430n36, 430n40, 430n45; income tax, 32, 42, 109–15, 406nn90–91, 415nn8–10, 416n23, 416n28, 416n31; lottery, Jamestown funding, 78; Land Tax (1697), 31; Love Tax, 361; luxury taxes, 102–4, 414n91; merchant marine ships, 199–200, 217, 429n3, 430n47; natural monopolies and privatization, 60–61; newspaper taxes, 177–78; opium wars, 192; pasty tax, 362, 449n64; "People's Budget" (1909), 32, 39–40, 42, 114; poll taxes, 85–91, 376, 411n13; pounds and shillings, 399n9; Putney Debates of 1647, 42; quota arrangements, 99–101, 413n76; scutage, 91–92, 412n40; ship money, 72, 409nn53–54, 409n56; smuggling, tea, 341–43, 447n7; social security, 95; state monopolies, 58–60, 407n10; sugar tax, 211; tax collectors, 325, 327; tax evasion informants, 303; tax farming, 319–21, 330; tax refusers, 309; Triple Assessment of 1798, 110, 415nn4–5; trust funds, 255–56; unearned income tax rate, 123; venality, sale of public positions, 77, 409n71; venality of army offices, 410n83; voting rights, 42, 406n89, 406nn89–93; war financing, 6–7, 12–13, 28, 31, 38–40, 403n21, 403n23, 405n71; welfare funding, 41, 128; window tax, 369; withholding, 112, 415n13, 416nn22–23; women and taxation, 134; wool export tax, 149, 421n2. *See also* Boston Tea Party; HMRC; United Kingdom

Britain, statutes: Corn Laws, 112, 155–59, 357, 378, 421n20, 421n23; Gin Act, 204, 297, 441n57; Stamp Act (1765), 178, 369; Tea Act, 400n25; Tipple Act, 297

Bryan, William Jennings, 94, 119, 121, 412n52

Buchanan, James, 346

burden of taxation. *See* fairness; incidence of taxation

Bureh, Bai, 12–13, 14

Burke, Edmund, 3, 8, 50, 447n1

Burns, Robert, 315, 444n10

Cahiers de doléances, 93

Caillaux, Henriette, 123–26

Caillaux, Joseph, 125–26, 418n74

Caligula, 61, 191, 310, 443n122

Calment, Jeanne, 287

Calmette, Gaston, 123–24

Canada: childbirth incentive, 187; cigarette taxes, 187–88, 427nn61–63; excess profit taxes, 431n2; feminine products and VAT, 135; foreigners, taxes on, 144; multinational corporations, 274; state monopolies, 61; VAT in, 369–70

Cannan, Edwin, 149, 167–68

capital income and gains, 123, 129–30, 211–12, 229, 263, 294, 418n85, 418n86, 436n29

Capone, Al, 285

Cardew, Frederick, 12

Carlyle, Thomas, 155

Casanova, Giacomo, 78

cash flow taxes, 229–30, 432nn14–15. *See also* destination-based cash flow tax

Cassius Dio, 83, 411n3

Catherine II (Empress of Russia), 276

Cayman Islands Financial Services Authority, 258–60

Cervantes, Miguel de, 314

Chamberlain, Joseph, 12, 357, 449n60

Chan, Jackie, 304–5

Chaplin, Charlie, 258

Charles I (King of England), 5, 42, 46, 59, 71–72, 324, 324403n29

Charles II (King of England), 58, 215, 219

Chater, Daniel, 313

Chaucer, Geoffrey, 314

Chile, 15–17, 204

China: agriculture, taxation of, 26, 403n12, 445n31; Beijing tax museum, 333–34; birth rate, 176, 425n13; Imperial Maritime Customs Service, 317, 327, 446n59; labor, taxation of, 27, 64; luxury taxes, 103; opium tax, 192; opium wars, 192; Qing dynasty and hair, 195; salt monopoly, 56–57, 407n5; smoking quota, 187; tax avoidance, 143, 287; tax collection, 318, 398; tax fraud, 289

China National Salt Industry Corporation, 56

Churchill, Winston, 41, 95, 163, 235

Cicero, 38

cigarette taxes, 184–88, 427n77; e-cigarettes, 188–89, 427nn72–74; smuggling and illegal sales, 187–88, 427nn61–63

Civil War, American, 22, 39, 49, 65–67, 116–17; Civil War income tax, 416n33, 416n46, 417n48

Civil War, English, 30, 68, 72, 375

Cleopatra, 189

Cleveland, Grover, 65, 117

climate change and taxation: cap and trade, 182; carbon pricing and taxing, 385, 392, 425n30, 425n32, 426n34, 426n36, 426n39, 452n29; gas guzzler taxes, 426n41; greenhouse gas emissions, 180–83; Paris climate agreement, 393; ruminants and methane, 426n42, 426n43; taxation or regulation, 196, 279

Clive, Robert, 320

commodity taxes, 29, 43, 135, 205, 239, 247, 433n51, 434n68

Compagnie des Indes Orientales, 58

Confucius, 247

Congressional Budget Office, 166

Constantine I, 143

Contingent Convertible Security (CoCo), 211–12

Copley, Ira C., 122

Corn Laws, repeal of, 155–59, 168, 357

coronavirus (COVID-19). *See* COVID-19

corporate taxes: allowance for corporate equity, 432n13; 423n51; future of, 395; incidence of, 164–67; public disclosure of payments, 306, 443n105; rent taxes and, 228–29. *See also* multinational corporations

Council of Economic Advisers (CEA), 165–66

A Counterblaste to Tobacco (James I), 184

COVID-19, 44, 54, 197, 390, 419n15, 431n12, 452n28

Cowell, Simon, 305

Cromwell, Oliver, 42, 145–46, 247, 325, 385

Cruz, Ted, 370

Curaçao, 104, 201, 414n96

Dallas, Alexander, 418n79

Dalton, Hugh, 433n41

Danton, Georges, 50
Darius, the Great, 99
Dead Souls (Gogol), 308, 443n113
de Pompadour, Madame, 316, 324, 410n80
deadweight loss. *See* excess burden
Defoe, Daniel, 348
de Gaulle, Charles, 251–52
Denmark, 35, 40, 194, 205, 248–49, 288,
    404n56, 431n2
destination-based cash flow tax, 274–75,
    278, 350, 438nn72–73
Diceto, Ralph de, 34
Dickens, Charles, 19, 377, 401n59
diesel fuel, dyeing of, 336
digital services tax, 15, 253, 272, 388
Dilke, Charles, 416n23
Diocletian, 27, 219, 263
Dion, Céline, 301
dismal science, 155, 157
Disraeli, Benjamin, 43, 158, 406n93, 416n30,
    422n34
Dobermann, Karl Friedrich Louis, 316
Dodd, Ken, 281
Doing Business reports, 151
Douglas, Scott, 138
Drake, Francis, 25
drugs and drug abuse, 192–93
Due, John F., 242
du Pont, Samuel, 93, 412n49
Dutch East India Company, 144, 330
dynamic scoring, 345–46

earmarking, 95–96, 413n56
Earned Income Tax Credit (EITC), 128, 162,
    223, 244, 422n37, 422n40
East India Company, 6–9, 58, 320, 399n17,
    399n20, 422n21
The Economist, 157, 231, 272, 328
Ecuador, 302
Edgeworth, Francis Ysidro, 113–14, 128, 243,
    245, 434n68
Edward I (King of England), 46, 141
Egypt, 3, 35, 64, 142–43, 284, 319, 333
Ehrlichman, John, 328

elasticity, of demand 159; of supply, 156; of
    taxable income, 221–22
Eleanor of Aquitaine, 35
Elizabeth I (Queen of England), 25, 30, 59,
    70, 72, 330
Elizabeth II (Queen of England), 59
Estonia, 335
European Commission, 272, 277, 434n60,
    436n42
European Union (EU): "blacklist" of
    non-cooperative jurisdictions, 436n39; cigar
    and cigarette taxes, 201–2; corporate taxes
    in, 277; Extractive Industries Transparency
    Initiative, 306; financial transactions tax,
    243; formula apportionment proposed,
    274; missing trader intracommunity
    fraud (MTIC), 288; nonresident tax
    information, 436n34; public disclosure,
    306, 443n106; quota arrangements, 101;
    revenue-based incentives, 327. *See also*
    value-added tax (VAT)
excess burden: avoidance of, 221, 227, 384;
    defined, 29, 45; distortions, 214, 389;
    Dutch ship design improvement, 218,
    430n46, 430n49; efficiency and, 224,
    419n13; explanation of, 219, 430n49,
    431n52; gauging through notches, 222–23;
    gender bias, 135–36, 419n13; globalization
    and, 387; goal of low excess burden,
    240–43; government size and, 347;
    hearth tax and, 216–17, 219; implicit
    discrimination and, 148, 386; innovation
    and, 219; intangibility of, 219–21;
    jouissance de moins (enjoyment of less),
    19; lobbying and, 354; lump-sum taxation
    and, 226; mathematical problem of
    minimizing, 245; progressivity and, 244,
    379–80; social cost of, 248, 383–84,
    431n52; synonymous with deadweight
    loss, 401n63; uniform tax treatment and,
    237–40, 433n54; unimproved land and,
    231. *See also* notches
excess profit taxes, 38, 225–26, 228, 431n2
excise glasses, 205, 218

excise taxes, 29–31, 59, 141, 190

externality: cigarette taxes, 185–86, 426n51; congestion and automobile fuel tax, 198; definition of, 179; distortions, 389; market failure, 425n27; pollution and, 179, 425n24, 425n28, 426n42; taxation or regulation, 195–98, 385, 428n110; tax competition and, 277; tax design and, 384–85. *See also* cigarette taxes; climate change and taxation; drugs and drug abuse; food and drink taxes; Pigovian taxation

Facebook, 164, 230, 268, 272

fairness: ability-to-pay principle, 96–99, 413n63; benefit principle, 94; consumption or income tax, 129–30; earmarking taxes, 95–96, 413n56; efficiency and, 243, 381; enforcement and, 376; horizontal equity, 84, 132, 136, 147–48, 163, 379, 391, 397; inequality and, 391–92, 452n27; luxury taxes, 102–4; meaning of, 93; measure of earnings and, 381; occupational taxes, 106; presumptive taxes, 106; quota arrangements, 30–31, 99–102, 413n74; vertical equity, 84, 106, 108, 136, 224, 360, 379, 396, 411n4. *See also* income tax

Fan Bingbing, 287

Faraday, Michael, 218–19

Faris, Jack, 361

Fessenden, William Pitt, 116

feudal dues, 36, 71–72. *See also* medieval Europe

financial transactions tax, 242, 434n60

Fitzgerald, F. Scott, 435n22

food and drink taxes, 209–11; alcoholic drink and, 204; avoidance of, 202; damage or benefit, 179, 189–91; definition of fruits, 363; health effects, 193–95; hot dog tax, 362; public health, 197–98; soda tax, 194; taboos on, 355. forced labor, 63–64, 408n24

Ford, Henry, 66, 205, 408n33

foreigners, taxes on, 144–45

formula apportionment, 274, 437n68

France, 36; assignats, 49–51, 77, 407n118, 407n121, 410n82; *capitation*, 92, 98, 109, 413n73, 416n43; church property, 50; class-based tax, 98; conflict with Monaco, 251–53; conscription system, 65; *Contribution Sociale Généralisée*, 126; *dixième*, 92, 257, 412n48; *fermiers généraux* (tax farmers), 319, 321–24, 327, 330–31, 445n30; fuel taxes, 376; *gabelle*, tax on salt, 29, 376; gifts, government requests, 68–69; hat tax, 414n87; hyperinflation, 49–50, 407n119; income tax, 32, 125–27, 418nn75–76; *le projet Caillaux*, 125, 127; *les quatre vieilles*, 106; *levée en masse*, 65; lotteries in, 77–78; National Assembly funding, 49–50, 407n118; oleomargarine, 351; *patente*, tax on professions, 106, 414n100; patriotic gifts, 68–69; salt smuggling, 289; *taille* and direct taxes, 92–93, 100, 322, 412n46; tariffs within, 15, 401n52; venality in, 76–77, 409n74, 410n80, 410n84; *vingtième*, 92, 412n48. *See also* French Revolution

Franklin, Benjamin, 19

Frederick II (King of Prussia), 300, 326

Frederick William I (King of Prussia), 31

Frederick William III (King of Prussia), 68

French Revolution, 125, 375; hyperinflation, 49; property confiscation, 73, 145; tax aspects, 30, 90–93. *See also* France.

Friedman, Milton, 128, 231, 293–94

Furman, Jason, 166

Galley, William, 313

Gandhi, Mahatma, 11

Garcia, Cristina, 135

Garcia, Jerry, 62

Garland, Judy, 287

Gates, William, Sr., 94

gender, 132–36, 419n11, 419n13, 419n15

Genghis Khan, 247

Gentleman's Magazine, 6

George, Henry and Georgism, 231–35, 380, 432n24, 432n32, 432n36

George V (King of England), 254

German East Africa, 13

German Southwest Africa, Bondelswarts dog tax, 14–15, 400n49

Germany: bachelor taxes, 175; COVID-19 recovery and VAT, 212–13; hyperinflation, 51; lobbying in, 355; Norderfriedrichskoog, 260, 435n16; stew tax, 431n2; tax compliance, 311; tax sanctuaries in, 260; tax on dogs (*Hundesteuer*), 183; tax refusers, 289; welfare expenditures, 40

Ghana, 95–96

Gingrich, Newt, 361

Giscard d'Estaing, Valerie, 251

Gladstone, William, 42–43, 112, 127, 178, 219, 354, 406n86

Global Financial Crisis, 44, 53, 146, 212–13, 347, 385, 388, 392, 430n31

Global Forum on Transparency and Exchange of Information for Tax Purposes, 264, 436nn35–39, 436n41

The Go-Between (Hartley), 371

Google, 15, 230, 268, 270, 272, 394

government, powers of: natural monopolies, 60; sovereignty and taxes, 388; state auctions, 61, 408n15; state monopolies, 56, 58, 61, 407n13

governments, non-tax financing of: creating money, 48–51; defaults, 46–47; fines and penalties, 73–75; future of, 390, 392; gifts to government, 68, 70; inflation tax, 48–49; lotteries, 77, 410n86; low inflation, 54; nontax taxes, 78–79; "quantitative easing," 53–54; reasons for, 40–41; taxes, reform of, 363–64; taxing vs. borrowing, 44–45, 406n94. *See also* seigniorage

Greece, 201, 299, 303, 335

Greece, ancient, 175, 262, 319

Grenville, George, 6

Guatemala, 327

Haldeman, Bob, 328

Hamilton, Alexander, 11, 117, 131, 276, 343

Hammurabi (King of Babylon), 73, 310

Hampden, John, 5, 72

Hancock, John, 9, 308

Hancock, Tony, 5

Handelsman, John Bernard, 221

Harberger, Arnold, 432n32

Harcourt, William, 114, 436n47; income tax, 415n21

Harington, John, 145, 420n60

Hart, Robert, 317–18, 327, 371, 445n22, 445n24, 445n27

Hartley, Leslie P., 372

Hassett, Kevin, 165–66

Hegel, Georg, 85

Heinlein, Robert, 373

Helmsley, Leona, 286

Henry II (King of England), 35, 141

Henry VI (Holy Roman Emperor), 34–35

Henry VIII (King of England), 22, 28, 73, 98, 125, 290, 401n76–2n76, 409n65

Herodotus, 25, 99

Hines, James R. Jr., 450n75

The Hitchhiker's Guide to the Galaxy, 451n6

Hitler, Alois, 316

HMRC (Her Majesty's Revenue and Customs), 188, 287, 394, 397. *See also* Inland Revenue

Hobbes, Thomas, 129

Holmes, Oliver Wendell, 94, 285

Hong Kong, 258

Housman, Clemence, 134–35

Hudson's Bay Company, 58

Hull, Cordell, 121

Hume, David, 343

Hungary, 51, 92, 141, 176

hut tax revolts: in German East Africa, 14–15; in Sierra Leone, 13–14

hyperinflation, 50–53

Ibn Khaldûn, 343

Ig Nobel Prize, 52, 287

Impuesto Empresarial a Tasa Única (IETU), 432n15

incidence of taxation, 149–50, 153–55, 158, 163, 377–78, 422n37; studies of, 167–69, 423n53, 423n55, 423n57, 423n60; tariffs, 423n58

income tax: capital income, 129–30, 265, 434n64; differentiation, 115–16; graduation, 113, 127–28; history of, 108–13, 404n37; marginal tax rates, 113, 127, 164, 223–24, 244–46; negative income tax, 128; progressive tax rates, 32, 41, 94–95, 125, 127, 243–45, 247; public disclosure, 305–6; women's rights and, 133–34. *See also* Britain; Earned Income Tax Credit (EITC); France; United States

India: agriculture, taxation of, 27; *bidis*, taxation of, 189; Bohea tea, 400n25; breast tax (*mulakkaram*), 132–33, 419n6; British rule, 11; British tax revenues in, 6–8; cow cess, 362, 450n80; *diwani*, 6–7, 320, 324; Government of India Act, 377, 451n14; *jizya* in, 141–43; Mughal Empire, 6, 27, 35, 289, 319–20; noncash payments, 303; taxation and caste, 132; tax fraud, 289; tax privatization, 330; tobacco taxes, 190, 428n89; treatment of individuals and married couples, 147–48; *Vodafone* case, 437n54

Indonesia, 204, 217, 335

information reporting. *See* automatic exchange of information, third party information

inheritance and estate taxes, 72, 108, 119, 284, 287, 361, 377, 411n3, 436n47, 450n75

Inland Revenue, 199, 254, 256, 281, 299, 429n1. *See also* HMRC

internality, 185–86, 195, 236

Internal Revenue Service (IRS): form numbers, 122; headquarters, 94; political harassment, 328, 446n63; selective audits, 307–8; tax gap, 288, 439n21; tax return hack, 336–37; voluntary contributions, 70

International Agency for Research on Cancer, 195

International Monetary Fund (IMF), 34, 47, 369, 437n57, 437n64

international tax rules, 254, 261; cooperation and, 393; history of, 266; international tax treaties, 266, 436n45, 436n47; national laws, and 266;. *See also* multinational corporations; Vestey, William and Edmund

inverse elasticity rule, 238–40, 433n49, 433n52

Ireton, Henry, 42, 405n83

Israel, 106, 414n101, 444n129

Italy: bachelor taxes, 175; data protection, 305, 442n99; Florentine sales taxes, 29; Ghost Buildings program, 335; gifts, government requests, 68–69; noncash payments, 303; shadow tax, 224; tobacco riots, 60; *trulli* houses, 201, 204. *See also* Rome

Jackson, Howell Edmunds, 119

Jaffa Cake, 209

James I (King of England), 28, 59, 77–78, 184–85

Japan: agriculture, taxation of, 27; alcoholic drink and taxes, 210–11; low inflation, 54; Shimabara revolt, 139–40, 419n26; tax compliance, 290; Tokugawa period, 35, 100, 139–40, 201, 445n31

Jean Le Bon (King of France), 71, 85

Jesus, 313–14

Jewish lenders, 46

Jews, tax treatment of, 140–42, 362–63, 385, 420n56

jie, 333, 334

John (King of England), 5, 28

Johnson, Lyndon B., cult protest, 309, 443n120

Johnson, Samuel, 204, 356, 449n55

John the Baptist, 324

Julianus, Didius, 55

Kennedy, John Fitzgerald, 22

Kenya, 328, 335

Keynes, John Maynard, 48, 157, 200, 235, 433n47

Khufu, 64
King, Martin Luther, Jr., 328
King, Rufus, 117
King of Kongo, 131
The Kinks, 193
kinks, 223–24, 244, 431n59

labor, taxation of, 26–27
Lady Godiva, 348–49, 448n26
Laffer, Arthur, his curve and precursors,
    343–44, 447n10; his napkin, 345
The Lancet, 205
The Landlord's Game (Phillips), 232–33
land taxes, 230–34, 380, 432n30
Lansky, Meyer, 258
Lavoisier, Antoine-Laurent, 319–20, 322, 331,
    445n41
League of Nations, 266–67, 271, 436n47
Leeuwenhoek, Antony von, 316, 333
Le Figaro, 123–25
Les Misérables, 19
liturgies, in Athens and Rome, 27, 30. 69,
    262–63. See also self-assessment, for
    valuation
Lloyd George, David, 32, 39–40, 77, 114,
    196–97, 232, 254, 404n38
lobbying, 348–52, 354–55, 358, 368, 429n22;
    Gucci Gulch, 450n88; Lady Godiva and,
    348; PAC, 448n24
Locke, John, 159, 315
Long, Huey, 36, 138, 178, 350, 404n57
Long, Russell, 419n5
Looking Backward (Bellamy), 373
Louis XII (King of France), 141
Louis XIV (King of France), 92, 420n39
lump-sum taxation: ability-to-pay, 147, 382;
    capital levy, war debt, 235–36, 433n42;
    class-based tax, 98; create no distortions,
    225–26; defined, 98–99; design of, 384;
    fairness of, 228; on foreigners, 258; poll tax,
    99; on social rank, 227; on war profits, 227
Luxembourg, 258, 261, 277, 435n12
LuxLeaks, 265, 277, 304

Machiavelli, Niccoló, 26, 144
Macron, Emmanuel, 376
Maddox, Lester, 74
Madison, James, 117, 343
Magna Carta, 5, 71, 92, 399n6
The Magnificent Seven, 25, 402n8
Malthus, Thomas, 155–60, 228, 230, 384,
    422nn21–22, 422n25, 426n34
Marat, Jean-Paul, 50
marriage and childbirth, tax policies and,
    67, 141, 148, 174–77, 421n67
Martin Chuzzlewit (Dickens), 401n59
Marx, Groucho, 62
Marx, Karl, 85
Matsukura (daimyo), 139
Mauritius, 258
medieval Europe, 27–28; forced labor in, 64;
    funding defaults, 46; ransom and feudal
    dues, 92
Mège-Mouriès, Hippolyte, 351
Mellon, Andrew, 123
Melville, Herman, 314
Mencius, 26
Messi, Lionel, 286, 304
Mexico, 37, 194, 229
military conscription, 65–67
Mill, John Stuart, 129, 219, 231, 422n21, 430n49
mineral resources, 16–17, 25
minimum tax proposals, 277, 438n84
Mirabeau, Honoré Gabriel Riquetti,
    Comte de, 50
Mirrlees, James, 245, 247
Mitchell, Joni, 234
Mithridates VI, 313
Monaco, 251–53, 260, 279, 286
Monopoly (the game), 232
Monroe, Marilyn, 62
Montesquieu, Charles de Secondat, 410n80
Monty Python, 190, 428n91
The Moon Is a Harsh Mistress (Heinlein), 373
More, Thomas, 374
Morgenthau, Henry, 258
Morocco, 134

Mulroney, Brian, 369, 371

multinational corporations, 26, 253; current rules for the taxation of, 266–68; information use by, 272, 437n62; proposed reforms to the taxation of, 273–75, 277, 438n74 438n84; small business and, 352–54; tax avoidance by, 265, 267–68, 436n48, 437n50. *See also* arm's length pricing; destination based cash flow tax; formula apportionment; minimum tax proposals; residual profit allocation; tax treaties; transfer pricing; Vestey, William and Edmund

Mussolini, Benito, 68

Mysterious Visit (Twain), 444n11

Nangeli, 133

Napoleon III (Emperor of France), 351

Nation, 178

National Association for the Prevention of Adulteration of Butter, 351

National Woman's Rights Convention, 133–34

Native Americans, cigarettes and, 187–88

Nelson, Willie, 287

Nero, 83, 152

The Netherlands: bread tax, 356; differentiation of VAT rates, 208; Dutch revolt of 1568–1648, 29; *fluyt* merchant vessel, 217–18, 430n46; *pachter* riots, 321; property taxes, 201; reclaimed land in, 432n18; reward for best tax, 369; tax farming in, 316, 321–22; tax sanctuaries, 260–61; tax on marijuana, 192; tax ratio in United Provinces, 35

neutrality, 355, 383

newspaper taxes, 177–78

New York Times, 117, 150

New York World, 119

New Zealand: farm animals, proposed tax on, 183; Hokianga Maori dog tax, 14–15, 400n49; market value of land, 432n33; pension rights, 40; tax administration in,

128; tax evasion in, 311; technology and, 394; unimproved land and, 232, 234

Neymar, 286

Nicholas II (Czar of Russia), 195

Nineteen Eighty-Four (Orwell), 275

Nixon, Richard, 286, 328, 446n63

Nobel prize, 245, 426n36

Norquist, Grover, 448n20

North, Frederick (Lord North), 8, 102, 104, 380, 400n22, 415n4

Norway, 61, 194, 305

notches, 146, 210, 217, 222–23, 415n9

Obama, Barack, 258, 405n65

Office for National Statistics (Britain), 167, 423n55

Olson, Nina, 331

Organisation for Economic Co-operation and Development (OECD): Inclusive Framework, 275, 278; international tax standards, 266; marginal tax rates in, 127; multinational tax avoidance, 270–71, 273; reforms to taxation of multinationals proposed by, 275, 278, 438n74, 438n84; revenue pressures in, 391, 452n23; social spending in, 39, 405n72; tax audits in, 307, 443n111; tax ratios in, 37; VAT in, 249; withholding taxes in, 293. *See also* Base Erosion and Profit Shifting (BEPS)

Orwell, George, 275

Ottoman empire, 33, 35, 142, 175, 321, 323

Packwood, Bob, 368

Paine, Thomas, 107, 113, 314, 348

Pakistan, 223, 290, 305, 311, 325; *octroi*, 322, 445n38; VAT in, 377, 451n14

The Pale King (Wallace), 315, 337, 444n12

Palmerston, Lord, 178

Panama Papers, 304–5, 388

Papua New Guinea, 309, 443n120

Paradise Papers (Appleby), 304

Paris agreement of 2015, 182, 426n38, 426n40

Payne, Sereno, 121

Peasants' Revolt (1381), 85–89

Peel, Robert, 112, 157–58, 371, 415n14, 422n34

Pelham, Henry, 343–44, 447n10

People v. Riksen, 448n39

Pepys, Samuel, 99, 215, 413n71

Pertinax, Publius Helvius, 55

Peru, 15–16, 328, 401n56, 441n72

Peter the Great (Tsar of Russia), 173, 177, 195

Philip II (King of Spain), 30, 45

Philippines, 326

Phillips, Elizabeth Magie, 232

Piers Plowman, 85

Piggott, Lester, 286

Pigou, Arthur Cecil, 179, 235, 237

Pigovian taxation, 180–81, 183, 184, 197, 385, 425n28, 429n113

Piketty, Thomas, 418n86

Pitt, William (Elder), 6

Pitt, William (Younger), 31, 38, 68, 100, 105, 109–10, 243, 247, 361, 408n42

Poland, 51, 200, 202

Pollock, Charles, 118

Pollock v. Farmers' Loan & Trust Company, 119, 417n53, 423n42

poll taxes, in Athens and China, 26–27; defined, 27; in England, 84–85, 99, on Jews, 140; race and 137–38

Pompadour, Madame de, 316, 324

pornography, taxes on, 192

postage stamps, 62–63

Presley, Elvis, 62–63

presumptive taxes, 105–106, 206, 299, 333

Pride and Prejudice (Austen), 20

production efficiency, meaning and desirability of, 241–42

professional tax refusers, 175

Progress and Poverty (George), 231

property taxes, 26–27, 31, 38, 234, 403n14, 432n37

prostitutes, 68, 105, 335, 428n93; taxes on 68, 190–91

proxies, taxation of, 105, 380–82

Prussia, 31, 68, 92, 98–99, 125, 276, 326

Putin, Vladimir, 367

Pym, John, 198, 356, 403n29

Queen Emma Bridge, 104

Raleigh, Walter, 30, 59

Ramsey, Frank, 237–39, 245, 247, 354, 433n47

Ramsey rule, 243, 247

Rand, Ayn, 374

Reagan, Ronald, 344, 366

Regan, Donald, 441n71

religion and religious taxes: in Britain, 141; on Catholics, 141, 419n24, 419n26, 420n36; in China, 143; conversions and, 143, 420n39; discrimination and, 420n56; on Jews, 140–41, 420n33; *jizya*, 141–43; tax collectors, 444n4; tax dodges and, 143–44; tithes and *zakat*, 36, 404n56, 420n42. *See also* Japan

rents (Ricardian), defined, 155

rent taxes, 229–30, 241, 275, 432n16, 432n18; efficiency of, 225–26

The Restaurant at the End of the Universe (Adams), 373

residual profit allocation, 274

retail sales tax. *See* sales tax.

Ricardian equivalence, 45

Ricardo, David, 155–56, 158–59, 228, 230, 235, 384, 422n22, 422n25, 426n34

Richard I (King of England), 34–35, 71

Richard II (King of England), 86–88

Rights of Man (Paine), 113

Robinson, Heath, 270, 437n52

Rockefeller, John D., 65

Romania, 176, 244, 326, 425n12

Rome: coins, silver content, 48; decline of, 219; gifts to King, 70; homosexuality and taxation, 190, 428n91; liturgies, 262; property confiscation, 145; salt monopoly, 56, 407n3; taxation in, 26–27; unmarried men, tax on, 175, 424n3; welfare expenditures, 40

Romney, Mitt, 153

Ronaldo, Cristiano, 286, 435n26
Roosevelt, Franklin Delano, 153, 161, 258
Roosevelt, Theodore, 119, 432n24
Rose, Pete, 286
Rosetta Stone, 3
Rousseau, Henri, 316, 323
Royal Commission on Income Tax, 256
Rubio, Marco, 370
Ruml, Beardsley, 440n42
Russia: flat tax reform, 344, 367, 369, 447n12; high tax take, 35; income tax, 32; quota arrangements, 100; tax farming, 321; tax on beards, 173–74, 424n2; vodka tax, 189–90, 195. *See also* Soviet Union
Rwanda, 64, 328

Saladin (Sultan of Egypt and Syria), 142, 411n8
Saladin tithe, 35
sales taxes, 29, 242; compared with VAT, 294
salt taxes and monopoly, 11, 29, 56–57, 59, 187, 289, 407n3
Saxe, Jon Godfrey, 341, 447n3
Say, Jean-Baptiste, 19, 343
Schumpeter, Joseph, 40, 235, 402n1, 402n4, 403n22
Schwan, August, 374
science fiction, 373–75
Scoop (Waugh), 24
Scotland, 202, 401n59, 412n29, 430n36
Scripps, E. W., 66
seigniorage, 47–49, 53–54, 376, 406n109, 406n112, 407n118
Sierra Leone, 12–13
Seligman, Edwin R. A., 158, 413n73, 414n1, 416n33, 416n46, 417n48, 417n53, 418n79, 436n47
self-assessment, as tool for tax administration, 306–7; for valuation, 233–34, 382, 432n32. *See also* liturgies
semi-autonomous revenue agencies, 329
sex and taxes, 190–92
Shakespeare, William, 287
Shays' Rebellion, 400n30

Sheridan, Richard Brinsley, 363, 450n84
Shimabara revolt, 139–*40*
Siemens, Wilhelm von, 33
Sierra Leone, Hut Tax War, 12–13, 15
Simons, Henry, 102
Singapore, 176, 198, 263, 432n18
slogans, 388–89
Smith, Adam, 18, 196, 253, 315, 323, 343, 370, 387, 444n14
Smith, Sydney, 103
smuggling. *See* Boston Tea Party; cigarette taxes; salt taxes and tea taxes
social engineering, 11, 173–74
social security, 151, 244, 291, 300
Song against the King's Taxes, 309
South Africa, 14, 175, 449n45
South Korea, 95, 302
sovereignty, 5, 10, 387–88; commercialization of, 62–63, 408n19
Soviet Union, 176, 424n11; agriculture, taxation of, 341
Spain, 431n2; *alcabala* excise tax, 29; debt defaults, 45; *servicios*, 28; "tenth penny," 29
Stamp, Josiah, 436n47
Stanton, Elizabeth Cady, 134
Starbucks, 253, 265, 267, 353, 437n49
Star Wars I, 372–73
starve the beast, 277
state monopolies, 56–61; auctioned, 61; privatized, 60–61; trading companies, 58–59
stealth taxes, 359–61
Stewart, Jon, 405n65
Sudbury, Simon, 85, 87–88
Sumer, 3–4, 25, 284
Summers, Lawrence, 106, 166, 370
Sun-Sentinel, 150
Sun Yat-sen, 232–34
Sustainable Development Goals, 38, 390
Sutton, Willie, 186, 427n57
Sweden, 53, 61, 194, 248, 299, 347, 431n2, 442n101
Swift, Jonathan, 343
Swiss Banking Act (1934), 258, 435n11

Swiss Peasant War, 309

Switzerland, 157, 257–58, 262, 293–94, 303, 431n2, 435n11

Szilagyi, John, 300

Tacitus, 152

Taft, William Howard, 121, 127, 417n60

Taizong (Emperor of China), 143

Talleyrand, Charles-Maurice de, 50

tariffs (taxes on trade), 11, 15, 28–29, 32, 116–18, 157, 168, 219, 357–58, 363, 369, 417n56, 423n57. *See also* Corn Laws

tax administration: appropriate size of a, 331–33; drones and, 335; future of, 394–98; genetic information and, 396–97, 452n36; public disclosure, 305–6; technology and, 333, 335–37, 394–96, 441n72, 441n74, 442nn102–103; trust and enforcement, 386–87. *See also* self-assessment, as tool for tax administration; third party information; withholding

taxation: definition of, 3

tax audits, 264, 307–8, 326, 328, 386, 439n21, 443n111

tax avoidance, 277; alcoholic drink, 202; commodity taxes, 205; creativity of, 382; debt vs. equity finance, 211–12; dog tails, 205–6, *208*; motor vehicles, 204–5; offshore deposits, 263, 265, 387; product differentiation, 206–10; property taxes, 201, *203*; tax rules and timing, 212; tobacco products, 201–2. *See also* multinational corporations

tax base mobility, 392–93

tax collection and collectors: animosity toward, 313, 317, 444n4; corruption and, 325–27; honesty and, 312; incentives to, 325–27; Matthew, 314; methods of, 309–11; moiety system, 316, 325, 445n17; notable people, 313–17; semi-autonomous revenue agencies (SARAs), 328–29; privatization of tax agency functions, 330; withholding, 290–91

tax competition, 276–79, 388, 394

tax compliance, 290, 311

Tax Evaders' Gazette, 311, 444n125

tax evasion, 283–85; artists, 287; business people, 286; enforcement and, 386–87, 451n18; excommunication as punishment, 289; gamble of, 439nn6–7; missing trader intracommunity fraud (MTIC), 288, 439n26; misreporting sales, 300; politicians, 286; principled evaders, 308–9; schemers, 287, 439n19; self-incrimination defense fails, 285; sportspeople, 286; tax evasion informants, 303–4; third party information, 301–2, 442nn77–78

tax farming, 319–24, 329–31, 445nn30–31, 445n38

Taxman (Beatles), 115

tax ratios, 36–38, 248–49, 405n78, 418n75, 434n71

tax havens, 257, 271, 435n9, 435n17

tax sanctuaries, 257–61, 435n9, 435n17, 435n21

tax smoothing, 406n102;

tax treaties, 264, 266–68; treaty shopping 268, 271

taxes, naming of, 361–63, 376–77

Tea party, 10. *See also* Boston tea party

tea taxes, smuggling, 9–10, 341–43

Tell, William, 289, 440n31

"Ten Cents War," 15–17, 375

Thatcher, Margaret, 60, 87, 89–91, 367, 371, 377

Thiers, Adolphe, 125

third party information, 301–2, 335, 442n78

Thompson, Thomas, 422n30

Thoreau, Henry David, 309

Tiberius (Emperor of Rome), 73, 402n8

time consistency, 236

tobacco taxes, 186, 190, 428n89

Tocqueville, Alexis de, 4, 22, 399n4

Toia, Hone, 14

Towards a New Social Order (Schwan), 374

trade taxes, 28–29

transfer pricing, 257, 265

Trump, Donald and Trump Administration, 15, 274, 346, 366, 370

tumulus, 63–64

Turgot, Anne Robert Jacques, 92, 417n48

Turner, Thomas, 189

turnover taxes, compared to VAT, 241–42, 369, 389, 433n56

Twain, Mark, 305, 444n11

Tyler, Wat, 87–88, 308, 375

Uganda, 288

Ullman, Al, 370, 451n100

United Kingdom: Board of Inland Revenue, 299; community charge, 85, 89–91, 312, 377, 412n29, 412n39; dependencies, 260; deferral of tax, 254; food taxes, resistance to 355–58, 449nn45–46, 449n48, 449n60, 449n62; income tax, 415n19; inequality effects of pandemic lockdown, 452n28; Land Tax (1697), 403n34; Office for National Statistics, 423n55, 424n61; Queen's taxes, 257, 435n8; reading tax, 178; Starbucks' tax position in, 253, 265, 267, 437n49; tax audits, 330; 1979 tax reform, 367; tax gap, 288, 439n23; outsourcing of debt collection, 330; reform of tax credits, 336–37; wealthy bachelor discount, 424n4; withholding, 291; zero rating, 404n40. *See also* Britain; HMRC (Her Majesty's Revenue and Customs); Inland Revenue

United States: agricultural industry, 351–52; alcohol and Prohibition, 190–91, 412n49, 417n56; bachelor taxes, 175; Base Erosion Anti-Abuse Tax (BEAT), 273, 437n66; bonus depreciation provision, 213, 430n31; "capitation clause," 116–18, 123, 416n43, 417n50; chain store taxes, 352–53, 448n39, 448n41; chicken tax, 429n14; cigarette taxes, 187, 427nn62–63, 427n79; conscription system, 65, 122–23; default (1933), 46, 406n104; drug taxation, 192–93; earmarking taxes, 95, 413n56; estate tax or death tax, 361, 377, 450n75; excise taxes, 95, 121, 154, 193, 421n17; food taxes, 210; fuel taxes, 152–53, 210, 336; gender bias, 136; gifts to government, 69–70, 409n70; Global Intangible Low-Taxed Income (GILTI), 273, 437n65; income tax, 32, 116, 118–23, 305, 417n60, 418n79; income tax, corporate, 128, 164–67, 417n61, 418n83; income tax and slavery, 118, 417n48, 417n53; inflation, 49; lotteries in, 78, 410n88, 410n90; luxury taxes, 150; marijuana taxation, 193, 428n100; motor vehicle taxes, 205; municipal bonds, 163–64, 423n43; outsourcing of debt collection, 330; political donations, 36; poll tax and voting rights, 117–19, 137–38; property taxes, 416n39; rifle shot tax provision, 368; sales taxes, 153–54, 353–54; speed traps and traffic fines, 73–74; state government limits, 347; state tax sanctuaries, 257–58; taxes, reform of, 365, 450n88; tax ratios, 36, 39, 405n65; tax revenue, 416n38; tax tokens, 160–61; third party information, 302, 442n78; Tobacco Master Settlement Agreement, 74–75, 186, 409nn67–69; U.S. Child and Dependent Care Credit, 422n40; war financing, 43–44; withholding taxes, 291–92, 440nn39–40, 440n42, 440n43, 440n45, 441n50; women and taxation, 134. *See also* Civil War, American; corporate taxes; Earned Income Tax Credit (EITC); Internal Revenue Service (IRS)

United States, Constitution: balanced-budget amendment, 347; Capitation Clause, 116–118, 123; Comity Clause, 145; income tax constitutionality, 423n42; 16th Amendment, 121–22, 440n39; 24th Amendment, 138, 419n20

United States, statutes: Affordable Care Act (2010), 195; Coronavirus Aid, Relief, and Economic Security (CARES) Act, 54; Current Tax Payment Act (1943), 440n40; Federal Margarine Act, 352, 448n37; Foreign Account Tax Compliance Act

United States, statutes (*continued*)
(FATCA), 263–64, 362; Harrison Narcotics Tax Act (1914), 193; independent contractors vs. employees, 211; National Firearms Act (1934), 425n29; Revenue Act investment credit, 201; Tariff Acts, 363–64; Tax Cuts and Jobs Act (2017), 273, 346, 348, 362, 366, 437n57; Tax Filing Simplification Act (2016), 351; U.S. Tax Reform Act of 1969, 123; U.S. Tax Reform Act of 1986 (TRA86), 212, 349–50, 365–68, 441n71, 450n90, 450n92; War Revenue Act (1917), 122

United States v. Sullivan, 439n8

Uruguay, 106

U.S. Department of Justice, 440n34

U.S. Environmental Protection Agency, 426n36

U.S. Joint Committee on Taxation, 166, 330, 346, 423n50

U.S. Office of the Taxpayer Advocate, 331

Utopia (More), 373

value-added tax (VAT): comparison to retail sales tax, 294; comparison to turnover tax, 241–42; COVID-19 recovery and, 212–13, 370; defining features, 33; efficiency and, 248–49, 371; equivalence to wage tax, 151–52, 421n8; exclusion of food in U.K., 208–9, 355–56; fraud, 382; history of, 368–69; imports, 275, 438n71; intangible services, 354; inventor of, 404n39; opposition to, 359–60, 366–67, 449n69, 450n91; printed books, 178; spread and revenue yield, 33, 369–70; threshold, 214, 217; transparency and, 154; U.S. resistance to, 369–70; zero rating, 404n40

Vauban, Sébastien, 412n46

venality, 75–77

Venezuela, 46–47

Verenigde Oost-Indische Compagnie (VOC), 58

Vespasian (Emperor of Rome), 27, 140

Vestey, William and Edmund, 254–57, 261, 265–67, 388, 410n84

Victoria (Queen of Great Britain), 178

Vietnam, 100, 201

Vlad the Impaler, 283, 289, 300, 438n2

Voltaire, 77, 315, 324, 410n80

voting rights, universal suffrage, 41–43

Wagner, Adolph, 40

Wallace, David Foster, 315, 317, 337, 444n12, 447n84

Wallach, Eli, 25, 402n8

Wall Street Journal, 163

Walmart, 353

Walpole, Robert, 31, 141, 286, 327, 357, 403n33, 441n57

wars and taxes: bangs-for-buck, 403n23; "Battle of the Spurs," 98; capital levy to address war debt, 235; Crimean War, 112; crusade financing, 411n8; dog tax wars, 14–15; financing of, 31, 406n100; Hut Tax War, 12–13, 15; Prussia, superministry 31; Quaker tax refusal, 309; "Ten Cents War," 15–17, 375; Vietnam War, 309, 443n117; world wars, 32, 39, 122, 126, 229

Washington, George, 11, 31, 38

Watt, James, 276, 387

Waugh, Evelyn, 24

Webster, Daniel, 352, 373

welfare state and taxes, 32, 39–41, 402n1, 405n78

Wesley, John, 21

Whiskey Rebellion, 11, 400nn31–33

whistleblowers, 265, 303–4, 442n93

The Who, 193

Wilde, Oscar, 175

Wilks, Elizabeth, 134

Wilks, Mark, 134

William I (King of England), 64

William III (King of England), 78, 215

Wilson, Woodrow, 122, 194

Windover, John, 216, 219–21, 237–38, 240, 248, 430n45, 433n54

window tax: avoidance of, 21, 222–23, 240, 401n69; fairness of, 17–18, 21–22, 401n62; in France, 19; health effects, 19; not in United States, 401n59; wealth and, 20, 30; "window peepers," 18, 21, 401n60

withholding, 32–33, 112, 126–27, 128, 211, 264, 290–95, 299, 359, 416n22. 416n24, 436n34, 440n40, 440n42, 440n45, 442n78

Wodehouse, P. G., 226, 255, 262

Women's Tax Resistance League, 134

Wood, Kingsley, 291

World Bank, 151

Zambia, 328

zappers, 301, 337, 441n74

A NOTE ON THE TYPE

This book has been composed in Arno, an Old-style serif typeface in the classic Venetian tradition, designed by Robert Slimbach at Adobe.